# OECD Employment Outlook 2019

## THE FUTURE OF WORK

This work is published under the responsibility of the Secretary-General of the OECD. The opinions expressed and arguments employed herein do not necessarily reflect the official views of OECD member countries.

This document, as well as any data and any map included herein, are without prejudice to the status of or sovereignty over any territory, to the delimitation of international frontiers and boundaries and to the name of any territory, city or area.

**Please cite this publication as:**
OECD (2019), *OECD Employment Outlook 2019: The Future of Work*, OECD Publishing, Paris.
*https://doi.org/10.1787/9ee00155-en*

ISBN 978-92-64-72715-1 (print)
ISBN 978-92-64-49700-9 (pdf)

OECD Employment Outlook
ISSN 1013-0241 (print)
ISSN 1999-1266 (online)

The statistical data for Israel are supplied by and under the responsibility of the relevant Israeli authorities. The use of such data by the OECD is without prejudice to the status of the Golan Heights, East Jerusalem and Israeli settlements in the West Bank under the terms of international law.

**Photo credits:** Cover © Jacob Lund, Dragon Images, PaO_STUDIO, Daisy Daisy /Shutterstock.com.

Corrigenda to OECD publications may be found on line at: *www.oecd.org/about/publishing/corrigenda.htm*.

# Foreword

The world is changing at lightning speed. Digitalisation, globalisation and demographic changes are having a profound impact on our lives, on our cultures, on our societies. These and other megatrends are constantly (and rapidly) transforming the way we interact with our friends and families; how and where businesses operate; what goods and services we consume; what dreams we dream. Our education and health, the distribution of income and wealth, the jobs we have and how we work are all particularly sensitive to these changes. It is a transformational era. Disruption is the new normal.

As any revolution, this one is charged with opportunities. Multilateral co-operation, regional integration and the complex global interdependence that have developed over the past decades, have multiplied these opportunities. The new technologies are game-changers, but now they are also part of our daily lives. More and more people and devices are connecting to the internet, while artificial intelligence is silently spreading. Blockchain and other technologies are also becoming more prevalent across economies and societies. This is amplifying our capacity to promote higher productivity growth, better services, improved well-being; it also allows for new business models and innovative ways of working to emerge, providing more flexibility to both employers and workers.

But there are also challenges, especially for labour. Middle-skilled jobs are increasingly exposed to this profound transformation. We estimate that 14% of existing jobs could disappear as a result of automation in the next 15-20 years, and another 32% are likely to change radically as individual tasks are automated. Many people and communities have been left behind by globalisation and a digital divide persists in access to new technologies – resulting in inequalities along age, gender, and socio-economic lines. Not everyone has been able to benefit from the better jobs that have emerged, and many are stuck in precarious working arrangements with little pay and limited or no access to social protection, lifelong learning and collective bargaining. Moreover, there is a very real concern of a "hollowing out" of the middle-class as technological advancements have been accompanied by the emergence of many lower-quality and precarious jobs. In some countries, for example, non-standard workers are 40-50% less likely than standard employees to receive any form of income support when they are out-of-work. And low-skilled adults across OECD countries, on average, are 40 percentage points less likely than high-skilled adults to participate in training.

Unsurprisingly, these changes result in anxiety about the future. The growth of inequalities of income and opportunities, distortions in cross-border competition, the perception of fiscal unfairness, the risk of climate change and the slowdown of the global economy, are all cause for concern. Disruption also elicits growing discontent about the effectiveness of our systems. A recent OECD survey (Risks that Matter, 2019) shows that many people believe public services and social benefits are inadequate and hard to reach. More than half say they do not receive their fair share of benefits given the taxes they pay, and two-thirds believe others get more than they deserve. Nearly three out of four people say they want their government to do more to protect their social and economic security.

In this challenging context, it is crucial to refocus our attention towards people and well-being. In the digital era, it is important that people feel that they will be supported if they lose out, and helped in their search for new and better opportunities. The pace and speed of this change requires swift and decisive policy action inspired by a new type of growth, one that is more inclusive and more sustainable.

To help governments deliver on this objective, the OECD launched the Inclusive Growth initiative and developed a *Framework for Policy Action on Inclusive Growth*. This not only helps us to get answers to many of these questions but it crucially offers governments concrete guidance on how to design and implement policies that will give all people, firms and regions the opportunity to thrive – particularly those who are struggling or have been left behind. Strong labour market performance is crucial in this goal to achieve inclusive growth.

We also launched the OECD's Future of Work Initiative which, over the past few years, has been looking at how globalisation, technological progress and demographic change are impacting OECD labour markets, and what this means for skills and social policies. The present volume is a key milestone in this effort, and provides policy makers with a thorough diagnosis of the challenges, as well as a detailed set of policy directions for maximising opportunities to create better jobs for all.

The key message of this *OECD Employment Outlook* is that the future of work is in our hands and will largely depend on the policy decisions countries make. It will be the nature of such policies, our ability to harness the potential of the unprecedented digital and technological change while coping with the challenges it poses, which will determine whether we succeed or fail.

In some policy areas, however, changes at the margin will not be sufficient and an overhaul of current policies might be necessary. Shaping the future of work calls for a Transition Agenda for a Future that Works for All. In this respect, the report highlights the need to help workers in their job transitions through effective and timely employment services as well as prevention and early intervention measures. Looking ahead, countries should focus on putting in place comprehensive adult learning strategies – in particular for low-skilled adults – to prevent skills depreciation and obsolescence, and facilitate transitions across jobs. Adult learning systems will also need to be strengthened and adapted to provide all workers with adequate opportunities for retraining throughout their careers.

We also argue that social protection provisions should be reshaped to ensure better coverage of workers in non-standard forms of employment and to take into account a reality where jobs are evolving and long-term employment is disappearing. In this context, policy makers can focus on boosting the portability of entitlements, making means-testing more responsive to people's needs and changing situations, and complementing targeted measures with more universal support. Greater focus must also be placed on collective bargaining and social dialogue, both of which can complement government efforts to make labour markets more adaptable, secure and inclusive. In this respect, the Global Deal is helping us to carry the message that social dialogue has a critical role to play in reducing inequalities and in shaping the Future of Work.

With the right policies and institutions in place and with a whole-of-government approach – as highlighted by the OECD's Going Digital project, the OECD Jobs Strategy and the OECD Skills Strategy – the opportunities that digitalisation, globalisation and longer lives will bring can be seized, and the risks can be mitigated. Together, we can design, develop and deliver better employment policies for better lives.

Angel Gurría
OECD Secretary-General

# Acknowledgements

The *OECD Employment Outlook* provides an annual assessment of key labour market developments and prospects in OECD member countries. Each edition also contains several chapters focusing on specific aspects of how labour markets function and the implications for policy in order to promote more and better jobs. The 2019 edition is devoted to the *future of work*. The chapters cover: how technology, globalisation, population ageing, and other megatrends are transforming the labour market of OECD countries; new evidence on recent changes in job stability, underemployment and the share of well-paid jobs; and the implications of these developments for: labour market regulation; collective bargaining and social dialogue; lifelong learning policies; and social protection. The first chapter provides an overview of the main messages.

The *OECD Employment Outlook 2019* is the joint work of staff of the Directorate for Employment, Labour and Social Affairs. The whole *Outlook* has also greatly benefited from comments from other OECD directorates and contributions from national government delegates. However, its assessments of each country's labour market prospects do not necessarily correspond to those made by the national authorities concerned.

This report was edited by Andrea Bassanini and Stijn Broecke, and is based on contributions from Andrea Bassanini, Stijn Broecke and Paolo Falco (Chapter 1), Paolo Falco (Chapter 2), Paolo Falco, Andrew Green, Duncan MacDonald and Andrea Salvatori (Chapter 3), Andrea Bassanini and Stijn Broecke (Chapter 4), Sandrine Cazes, Andrea Garnero and Chloé Touzet (Chapter 5), Alessia Forti and Glenda Quintini (Chapter 6), and Rodrigo Fernandez, Raphaela Hyee, Herwig Immervoll and Daniele Pacifico (Chapter 7). Daniel Alonso Soto provided specific contributions on emerging economies in Chapter 2 and Maciej Lis and Marius Luske provided specific contributions on pension issues in Chapter 7. Research assistance was provided by Sébastien Martin and Agnès Puymoyen. Editorial assistance was provided by Natalie Corry, Lucy Hulett, Anna Irvin Sigal and Katerina Kodlova.

This edition of the *OECD Employment Outlook* is dedicated to the memory of Alan Krueger, a friend and a lasting source of inspiration for all of us.

# Table of contents

Foreword 3

Acknowledgements 5

Editorial: A transition agenda for a *Future that Works* for all 14

Executive summary 19

1 Overview: The future of work is in our hands 23
    Should we brace for a jobless future? 24
    Is the end nigh for the standard employment relationship? 27
    Has the balance of power between bosses and workers tipped too far? 29
    A Future that Works for All – can we afford it? 30

2 The future of work: What do we know? 37
    In Brief 38
    Introduction 38
    2.1. An overview of the megatrends transforming labour markets 40
    2.2. Job quantity: The ongoing transformations are unlikely to result in *fewer* jobs 44
    2.3. Job quality: A future of better opportunities or increased risks for workers? 52
    2.4. Inclusiveness: Preventing a more unequal future of work 62
    2.5. Concluding remarks 73
    References 74
    Notes 85

3 The future of work: New evidence on job stability, under-employment and access to good jobs 91
    In Brief 92
    Introduction 93
    3.1. Are jobs becoming less stable? 94
    3.2. Not unemployed, but under-employed? 100
    3.3. Job polarisation and access to good jobs 105
    3.4. Concluding remarks 115
    References 117
    Annex 3.A. Additional results 119
    Notes 126

4 Labour market regulation 4.0: Protecting workers in a changing world of work    131
　In Brief    132
　Introduction    133
　4.1. Employment status: A gateway to workers' rights and protections    135
　4.2. Extending rights and protections beyond standard employees    146
　4.3. Monopsony power, labour market efficiency and worker vulnerability    151
　4.4. International competition    155
　4.5. Concluding remarks    157
　References    159
　Annex 4.A. Labour market monopsony: Evidence and regulation    173
　Notes    182

5 Facing the future of work: How to make the most of collective bargaining    189
　In Brief    190
　Introduction    191
　5.1. Collective bargaining in a changing world of work    192
　5.2. Adapting regulations to more diverse forms of employment    204
　5.3. How can social partners enhance collective bargaining and social dialogue in non-standard and new forms of work?    206
　5.4. Increased pressure and new challenges have led to the emergence of non-traditional initiatives    212
　5.5. Concluding remarks    215
　References    217
　Annex 5.A. Union density and forms of employment: Sources and additional material    223
　Annex 5.B. Additional material on youth and collective actions    227
　Notes    230

6 Making adult learning systems future-ready for all    235
　In Brief    236
　Introduction    237
　6.1. How megatrends are influencing the demand and supply for skills    239
　6.2. Some groups are more affected than others    243
　6.3. Encouraging participation in adult learning by under-represented groups    250
　6.4. Can individual learning accounts make adult learning accessible to a broader group of adults?    274
　6.5. Building adequate financing, governance, and quality assessment mechanisms    277
　6.6. Concluding remarks    279
　References    282
　Notes    289

7 Left on your own? Social protection when labour markets are in flux    293
　In Brief    294
　Introduction    296
　7.1. Prevention, protection, promotion: Social protection and the future of work    297
　7.2. Social protection for alternative forms of employment: What are the gaps?    299
　7.3. Addressing social protection gaps: Key policy issues    311
　7.4. Concluding remarks    324
　References    326
　Notes    333

FIGURES

Figure 2.1. The rapid spread of information and communication technologies in the workplace  41
Figure 2.2. The march of the robots  41
Figure 2.3. International trade keeps rising  42
Figure 2.4. Many countries are ageing rapidly  43
Figure 2.5. Employment rates have been rising in recent decades  45
Figure 2.6. Jobs at risk of automation in OECD countries  49
Figure 2.7. The potential cost savings from using robots are significant in some emerging economies  50
Figure 2.8. The rapid growth of online work has recently slowed down  57
Figure 2.9. Temporary employment has risen in one half of OECD countries  58
Figure 2.10. Part-time employment has generally increased  59
Figure 2.11. Short part-time is on the rise in many countries  60
Figure 2.12. Self-employment is on a long-term downward trajectory  61
Figure 2.13. The decline of the manufacturing sector  63
Figure 2.14. The labour market is polarising  64
Figure 2.15. Real median wages have decoupled from labour productivity  67
Figure 2.16. Income inequality is growing rapidly  70
Figure 2.17. Labour markets are polarising in many emerging economies too  72
Figure 3.1. Job stability has decreased in the majority of countries after accounting for population ageing  95
Figure 3.2. The largest declines in job stability have occurred for low-educated workers  96
Figure 3.3. Job-to-job flows and transitions out of work differ significantly across the OECD  97
Figure 3.4. Involuntary separations show very different trends across countries  98
Figure 3.5. Men saw the largest increase in the risk of involuntary entry into unemployment  99
Figure 3.6. The majority of countries have seen increases in under-employment, but particularly those hit hardest by the crisis  101
Figure 3.7. Under-employment exhibits an increasing trend even after adjusting for the cycle  102
Figure 3.8. Under-employment is more common in service sectors  103
Figure 3.9. The young and those with low education have seen the largest increases in under-employment  104
Figure 3.10. Job polarisation explains a small part of the change in the share of middle-paid jobs  107
Figure 3.11. The probability of being in a high-paid job has declined across demographic groups  109
Figure 3.12. Young workers with middle education have seen a shift towards low-paid employment in many countries  111
Figure 3.13. Changes in the education wage premium across countries  113
Figure 3.14. The young with low and medium education suffered the largest increases in the probability of non-employment  114
Figure 4.1. Worker classification and coverage of labour law protection  135
Figure 4.2. The incidence of own-account workers who generally have one dominant client  144
Figure 5.1. Non-standard workers are underrepresented by trade unions  196
Figure 5.2. Trend in union density among youth aged 20-34 in selected OECD countries  198
Figure 5.3. Individual values and support for collective action among young people  199
Figure 5.4. Trust and perceived necessity of trade unions among young people aged 20-34  200
Figure 5.5. Access to collective bargaining for different forms of employment, current situation  202
Figure 6.1. Risk of automation and skill content of jobs, OECD average  240
Figure 6.2. Trends in skill shortages and surpluses, OECD unweighted average, 2004-17  240
Figure 6.3. Share of workers in changing workplaces, 2015  241
Figure 6.4. Organisational change and changing skill needs, EU countries  242
Figure 6.5. Participation in job-related training by group, OECD average  244
Figure 6.6. Willingness to train by group, OECD average  246
Figure 6.7. Reasons for not training by group, OECD average  247
Figure 6.8. Training provision by firm size, EU28, 2005-15  248
Figure 6.9. Reasons for not providing training or limiting training provision, by firm size, EU 28  249
Figure 6.10. Adults' participation in training, by industry  249
Figure 6.11. Differences in training participation and willingness to train between low and high-skilled adults, by country, 2012, 2015  251
Figure 6.12. Reasons why the low-skilled do not train, by country  254
Figure 6.13. Differences in training participation and willingness to train between temporary and full-time permanent workers, by country, 2012, 2015  259
Figure 6.14. Reasons why temporary workers do not train, by country  260

Figure 6.15. Differences in training participation and willingness to train between own-account workers and full-time permanent employees, by country, 2012, 2015                                263
Figure 6.16. Reasons why own-account workers do not participate in training, by country                264
Figure 6.17. Differences in training participation and willingness to train between young and older adults, by country, 2012, 2015                                271
Figure 6.18. Reasons why older adults do not participate in training, by country                272
Figure 7.1. Employment requirements for unemployment benefits range from 3 to 24 months                300
Figure 7.2. Statutory access for independent workers is often limited                303
Figure 7.3. Pension provisions for workers with unstable careers vary widely across countries                305
Figure 7.4. Only a minority of jobseekers receive unemployment benefits                307
Figure 7.5. Non-standard workers receive little support in some countries                308
Figure 7.6. Support gaps can be sizeable for the self-employed                311
Figure 7.7. In some countries, only a minority of jobseekers are in regular contact with the public employment service                317
Figure 7.8. Unstable work is common, but it may be outside the scope of activation measures                319
Figure 7.9. Very high marginal effective tax rates can discourage people from working longer hours                321
Figure 7.10. Non-wage labour costs vary substantially across contractual arrangements                323

Annex Figure 3.A.1. Change in adjusted tenure by country and level of education                119
Annex Figure 3.A.2. Young workers are more likely to be under-employed                120
Annex Figure 3.A.3. Change in under-employment by country and gender                121
Annex Figure 3.A.4. Jobs by occupation have continued to polarise between 2006 and 2016                122
Annex Figure 3.A.5. The risk of low pay has increased for employees with low and medium education in a number of countries                123
Annex Figure 3.A.6. Young workers have shifted more towards low pay than older ones in some countries                124
Annex Figure 3.A.7. The risk of being out of employment has risen most for youth who have left education                125
Annex Figure 5.A.1. Estimated trade union density for standard workers                225
Annex Figure 5.A.2. Non-standard workers in the private sector are also underrepresented by trade unions                226
Annex Figure 5.B.1. Trend in union density among youth aged 20-34 in selected OECD countries                227
Annex Figure 5.B.2. Trust in trade unions                229
Annex Figure 5.B.3. Perceived necessity and trust in trade unions                229

## INFOGRAPHICS

Infographic 1. The future of work in figures                17

## TABLES

Table 5.1. How much are social partners' involved in training programmes in OECD countries?                195
Table 5.2. Collective agreements for temporary work agency workers                211
Table 6.1. Incidence of training and willingness to participate, by socio-demographic characteristics                245
Table 6.2. Individual Learning Accounts coverage                276

Annex Table 5.A.1. Non-standard forms of employment included in Figure 5.1.                224
Annex Table 5.B.1. Trust in trade unions: Sources and definitions                228

# Follow OECD Publications on:

 *http://twitter.com/OECD_Pubs*

 *http://www.facebook.com/OECDPublications*

 *http://www.linkedin.com/groups/OECD-Publications-4645871*

 *http://www.youtube.com/oecdilibrary*

 *http://www.oecd.org/oecddirect/*

# This book has...

**StatLinks**

A service that delivers Excel® files from the printed page!

Look for the *StatLinks*  at the bottom of the tables or graphs in this book. To download the matching Excel® spreadsheet, just type the link into your Internet browser, starting with the *http://dx.doi.org* prefix, or click on the link from the e-book edition.

# Editorial: A transition agenda for a *Future that Works* for all

***The times they are a-changin'.*** Labour markets are under pressure from the combined effects of several megatrends. Technological progress and greater integration of our economies along global supply chains have been a bonus for many workers equipped with high skills and in expanding occupations, but a challenge for others with low or outdated skills in declining areas of employment. Digitalised business models often employ workers as self-employed rather than as standard employees. People are living and working longer but facing more frequent job changes and the risk of skills obsolescence. Inequalities in earnings and job quality have been widening in many countries. The global financial crisis of 2008-09 led to serious job losses, leaving deep wounds that have not fully healed even a decade after its onset. Turning to the future, the projected slowdown in the global economy over the next two years casts a shadow over short-term job prospects. Beyond that, it is clear that deep and rapid structural changes are on the horizon, bringing with them major new opportunities but also greater uncertainty among those who are not well equipped to grasp them. The pace and depth of the digital transformation is likely to be startling. Orders of industrial robots have increased threefold in just over a decade and are projected to double by 2020, while the amount of private equity invested in artificial intelligence has doubled over the past year. Connecting those at risk of being left behind with better job prospects should be the policy compass to a more inclusive, fairer and sustainable economy and society.

***More people of working age are at work than in past decades.*** The good news is that so far the megatrends have not led to structural unemployment – quite the contrary. The overall employment rate has been rising in most OECD countries, driven by a substantial rise in the share of women at work. The employment rate of older men and women has also increased, partly reflecting a rise in effective retirement ages. The quality of jobs has also improved in some aspects. The share of high-skilled jobs has grown by 25% in OECD countries over the past two decades. And several emerging economies have made some progress in reducing informal employment.

***Technological change and globalisation hold great promise for further improvements in labour market performance.*** Looking ahead, new technologies can give people greater freedom to decide where, when and how they work, which can improve work-life balance and create new opportunities for previously under-represented groups to participate in the labour market. Tedious and dangerous tasks can be automated, health and safety can be improved, and productivity boosted. Further globalisation can also have beneficial effects: it has spurred technological adoption and innovation, and contributed to productivity growth. Greater integration along global supply chains can also boost employment overall by expanding consumer demand. In short, these megatrends could contribute to more and better jobs in the future.

***But people should brace for change.*** A process of creative destruction is under way, whereby certain tasks are either taken over by robots or offshored, and other, new ones, are created. Employment in the manufacturing sector has declined by 20% over the past two decades, while employment in services grew by 27%. This has contributed to labour market polarisation: the shares of low-skilled and (particularly) high-skilled jobs have increased, while there has been a hollowing out of middle-skilled jobs. This trend has also been driven by skill-biased technological change, a process in which technological change mainly benefits workers with higher skills. At the same time, we are observing a widening divide between "super star firms" innovating and adopting digital technologies and those, more numerous, that struggle to keep at pace with digitalisation. This is creating a large divide between those working for super star firms and the others, in terms of employment quality and wages. All this has been a source of widening earnings inequality and put the middle class under pressure. Looking ahead, 14% of existing jobs could disappear as a result of automation in the next 15-20 years, but another 32% are likely to change radically as individual tasks are automated. Together with changes in preferences, business models and contract types, this means that individuals will face deep and rapid changes: many will have to change not only their job but even their occupation, and most will have to modernise their skills and working practices. These transitions towards new jobs and occupations might be difficult and costly for a number of workers. Yet, participation in training by low-skilled adults – those most likely to be affected by the changes ahead – is 40 percentage points below that of high-skilled adults on average across OECD countries. But even for those who do have access to training, the learning options are often closely linked with their current job and may not prepare them for the transition to a new job, let alone a new career.

***A better world of work is not guaranteed – much will depend on having the right policies and institutions in place.*** Some groups are already falling behind and labour market disparities are increasing in many countries. This has been especially marked for many young people and, particularly, the low-skilled in many countries. They face an increased risk of low-paid employment when in work, and have experienced a rise in underemployment. Their risk of being neither in employment nor in education or training has also risen or remains high. Many of these changes appear structural and go beyond the effects of the recent crisis. And they may well exacerbate already high levels of labour market inequality, fostering further social and economic tensions. They also indicate that existing policies and institutions have been inadequate and need to be overhauled.

***One thing is clear: action on the margin will not do.*** Change is required in the well-ingrained behaviour of individual workers, companies, social partners and, above all, in policies. In line with the recommendations of the new OECD Jobs Strategy and Skills Strategy, we should move away from a model of front-loaded education – whereby recognised skills are mainly developed in schools and universities and subsequently used at work – to a system in which skills are continuously updated during the working life to match changing skills needs. We should revise labour market and social protection systems so that they focus on risk prevention as much as on helping people cope with problems when they materialise. And we need to anticipate changes and adapt policies accordingly, in order to better target disadvantaged groups.

***Countries should assess how well current policies match priorities and prevent the most vulnerable workers from being left behind.*** The labour market risks faced by different workers – job loss, accidents at work, skills obsolescence etc. – are evolving and so should policies to help prevent and address them. The risks faced by some workers and the lack of support for them are at least partly related to the misclassification of some employment relationships. Some workers who should be entitled to employee rights and protections are falsely labelled as self-employed in an attempt to avoid taxes and regulations. But there is an urgent need to close the significant gaps in social and labour protections more generally, as well as in access to employment services. For example, due to statutory and practical barriers limiting access to social protection, non-standard workers are, in some countries, 40-50% less likely to receive any form of income support during an out-of-work spell than standard employees. Both access to collective bargaining and coverage of many labour law protections are often limited to employees, so they do not cover the self-employed and those in the "grey zone" between dependent and self-employment, who have much less power in the working relationship than their employer. Similarly, training guarantees often apply only to employees and rights depend on job tenure, and therefore exclude many non-standard workers.

***Shaping a future of work that is more inclusive and rewarding calls for a Transition Agenda for a Future that Works for All – a whole-of-government approach that targets interventions on those who need it most.*** Such an agenda would need to adopt a life course approach, covering education and skills, public employment services and social protection, but also labour market regulation, taxation and even housing, transport, competition law and industrial policy. This approach would combine coping mechanisms, on the one hand, with preventive measures on the other. This holistic approach has been the objective of the OECD "Going Digital" project.

***A Transition Agenda for a Future that Works for All requires adequate funding.*** Scaling up adult learning and extending and improving social protection can be costly, but public budgets in many countries are already under pressure. Countries should start by assessing how well current policies match priorities and whether the most vulnerable are being left behind. Much can be done to enhance the effectiveness and targeting of key policies – e.g. education, adult learning and social protection – by undertaking a comprehensive spending review and deepening the whole-of-government approach to public policy objectives and solutions. But there may also be a need to improve revenue sources. In the area of taxation, we have seen a number of recent initiatives, such as the adoption of the automatic exchange of taxpayer financial account information (AEOI) to reduce tax evasion; and the OECD/G20 Base Erosion and Profit Shifting (BEPS) project to address the tax avoidance of multinational enterprises. Both of these initiatives have provided governments with the tools necessary to broaden their tax bases and strengthen their tax systems against abuse. In the case of other non-tax revenues, the issuing of permits or certificates for automated production or operations, such as driverless trucks, may open the possibility of creating new sources of government revenue. Additional revenues raised from these initiatives would increase the capacity of governments to support the Transition Agenda for a Future that Works for All and help reconnect the many who feel left behind by the digital transformation and globalisation. But governments' interventions, while essential, will likely not be enough by themselves. All stakeholders should participate, including businesses who badly need workers with the appropriate skills and a conducive social and economic environment, ushering in the creation of new public-private partnerships to help achieve this goal.

Stefano Scarpetta
OECD Director for Employment, Labour and Social Affairs

## Infographic 1. The future of work in figures

### Risk of job automation is real but varies greatly across countries

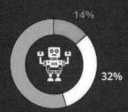

14%

32%

14% of jobs are at high risk of automation
32% of jobs could be radically transformed

### Populations are ageing fast in OECD countries

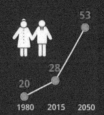

53
28
20

1980    2015    2050

Number of 65+ year-olds per 100 people
of working age in 1980, 2015 and 2050

### Many adults do not have the right skills for the new jobs

6 out of 10 adults lack basic ICT skills
or have no computer experience
(Survey of Adult Skills in 29 OECD countries, 2012/15)

### Adult training should better target the disadvantaged

80%
60%
40%
20%
0%

high skilled    full-time permanent    low automation
low skilled    self employed    high automation

Adults participation in training
by skill level, employment status and risk of automation

### Non-standard work is not a marginal phenomenon

1 in 7 workers is self-employed
and
1 in 9 employees is on a temporary contract

### Social protection needs to be adapted to the future of work

Non-standard workers
(self-employed, temporary, part-time and platform workers)

are 50% less likely to be unionised
and are, in some countries,
40-50% less likely to receive income support
when out of work

# Executive summary

## Digitalisation, globalisation and ageing bring new opportunities but also risks widening disparities among workers

The world of work is changing in response to technological progress, globalisation and ageing populations. In addition, new organisational business models and evolving worker preferences are contributing to the emergence of new forms of work. Despite widespread anxiety about potential job destruction driven by technological change and globalisation, a sharp decline in overall employment seems unlikely. While certain jobs and tasks are disappearing, others are emerging and employment has been growing. As these transformations occur, a key challenge lies in managing the transition of workers in declining industries and regions towards new job opportunities. There are also concerns about job quality. While diversity in employment contracts can provide welcome flexibility for many firms and workers, important challenges remain in ensuring the quality of non-standard work. Moreover, labour market disparities could increase further unless determined policy action is taken to ensure a more equal sharing of the costs of structural adjustment in the world of work. While there are risks, there are also many opportunities – and the future of work is not set in stone. With the right policies and institutions, the future of work can be one of more and better jobs for all.

## The labour market outcomes of young people without tertiary education have worsened in most countries

Over the past decade, labour market conditions have deteriorated for young people with less than tertiary education in many countries, with a rising proportion out of work or, under-employed or low-paid if in work. These changes are unlikely to be the short-lived product of the economic downturn, which raises significant policy challenges for the years to come. From a gender perspective, in a number of countries, men have seen an increase in joblessness and under-employment. Nevertheless, the latter remain more widespread among women, who are also more likely to be in low-paid jobs.

## All workers, regardless of their employment status, should have access to an adequate set of employment protections

The emergence of new, non-standard forms of work poses challenges to employment regulations largely designed for permanent employees working for a single employer. Employment status acts as a gateway to various rights and protections. Ensuring the correct classification of workers (and tackling misclassification) is therefore a key step to ensure that those in non-standard forms of work have access to labour and social protection, collective bargaining and lifelong learning. For some workers, however, there is genuine ambiguity about employment status as they find themselves in a "grey zone" between dependent and self-employment. While the size of this grey zone should be kept as small as possible, labour market regulations need to be extended and adapted to adequately protect workers, and to ensure that firms that respect these regulations are not disadvantaged. Tackling power imbalances between employers/clients and workers also involves addressing abuses of employers' market power, e.g. by fighting labour market collusion by employers, limiting the scope of non-compete covenants and redressing inequalities in the information available to employers and workers.

## Collective bargaining can be a complementary and flexible tool to shape the future of work

Collective bargaining can help workers and companies adapt to the opportunities and challenges of a changing world of work. As an instrument to reach flexible and consensual solutions, it can contribute to shape new rights, regulate the use of new technologies, or foster labour market security and adaptability. However, low levels of organisation among workers, in particular non-standard workers, pose a serious challenge to collective bargaining. This partly reflects legal obstacles for workers classified as self-employed, for whom the right to bargain collectively may be seen as infringing competition law. In this context, some OECD countries have made tailored extensions of collective bargaining rights to some non-standard workers. However, practical difficulties remain. Employers' organisations are being put to the test by the emergence of new forms of business. Established trade unions are developing strategies to reach non-standard workers, while new vehicles of workers' representation are also emerging.

## Strengthening adult learning is crucial to help workers successfully navigate a changing labour market

Effective adult learning can help prevent skills depreciation and facilitate transitions from declining jobs and sectors to those that are expanding. A major overhaul of adult learning programmes to increase their coverage and promote quality is essential to harness the benefits of the changing world of work. In all OECD countries, training participation is lowest among those who need training the most, including the low-skilled, older adults, job losers as well as non-standard workers. These groups face several barriers to training participation, such as poor training choices, and a lack of motivation, time, money or employer support. Policy options revolve around building a learning culture among firms and individuals, removing time and financial constraints to training participation, tackling unequal access to training based on employment status, encouraging firms to train groups at risk, and making training rights portable between jobs. Training also needs to be of good quality and aligned to labour market needs in order to be effective. This requires adequate and sustainable funding, shared by stakeholders in line with the benefits that are received, as well as governance arrangements that can help countries make different parts of adult learning systems work well together.

## Social protection reforms must ensure that support remains accessible for disadvantaged groups

Social protection systems play a key stabilising role in the current context of heightened uncertainties about the pace and extent of labour market changes. But accessing social protection can be especially difficult for workers in less secure forms of employment. More volatile career patterns or a growing diversity of employment forms pose potential challenges for support provisions that link benefit entitlements or financing burdens to past or present employment. Existing social protection systems have many strengths and will remain viable. But they will need to adapt to changing risks. Key priorities include making protection sufficiently agile to respond to changes in people's need for support, ensuring that entitlements are portable across jobs, and adapting the scope of activation and employment support to evolving work patterns.

Keeping funding levels in line with evolving demands on social protection also requires a proactive policy debate on how new or expanded initiatives can be paid for.

## It is time for a transition agenda for a future that works for all

Shaping a future of work that is more inclusive and rewarding calls for a Transition Agenda for a Future that Works for All – a whole-of-government approach that targets interventions on those who need them most. Some policy options involve negligible costs for public finances and may even increase tax revenues. However, many others, and in particular strengthening social protection and adult learning, will require significant additional resources. Much can be done to enhance the effectiveness and targeting of key policies by undertaking a comprehensive spending review and deepening the whole-of-government approach to public policy objectives and solutions. But there may also be a need to improve revenue sources and this requires a profound reflection on tax systems.

# 1 Overview: The future of work is in our hands

"The best way to predict the future is to create it"

— *Alan Kay, 2003 Turing Prize winner*

Despite the many opportunities, much anxiety surrounds the future of work. Doomsday scenarios are unlikely to materialise, but there are some real risks. Many are worried that the world of work is heading for a dystopian future of massive technological unemployment, precarious work, workers with little or no bargaining power, and important skills gaps as populations age rapidly. But the future of work will largely depend on the policy decisions countries make. With the right policies and institutions in place, the opportunities that digitalisation, globalisation and longer lives will bring can be seized, and the risks mitigated.

**New technologies and a more integrated, globalised world offer many opportunities for creating new jobs, improving the quality of existing jobs, and bringing previously underrepresented groups into the labour market.** Both technological change and globalisation create jobs by lowering the price of goods and services, increasing their quality and, hence, boosting consumer demand. They also create entirely new jobs, like big data managers, robot engineers, social media managers and drone operators – all occupations that did not exist a generation ago. The quality of jobs can be improved: dangerous or boring tasks can be automated; people can choose where and when to work more freely, resulting in a better work-life balance; work environments can be made safer and healthier; and informality could be reduced. By breaking down traditional barriers to labour market participation, previously underrepresented groups can increasingly participate in the labour market, resulting in greater inclusiveness. In a world of **rapid population ageing** and longer lives, better working conditions will in turn contribute to more opportunities to continue working at an older age.

---

The future of work will largely depend on the policy decisions countries make

---

**Despite the many opportunities, much anxiety surrounds the future of work. Doomsday scenarios are unlikely to materialise, but there are some real risks.** Many are worried that the world of work is heading for a dystopian future of massive technological unemployment, precarious work, workers with little or no bargaining power, and important skills gaps as populations age rapidly. The key message of the *OECD Employment Outlook 2019* is that **the future of work will largely depend on the policy decisions countries make.** While it is true that the future is already here and labour markets are already changing, with the right policies and institutions in place, the opportunities that digitalisation, globalisation and longer lives will bring can be seized, and the risks mitigated. The remainder of this chapter provides an overview of the *OECD Employment Outlook 2019.* It unpacks some of the key anxieties surrounding the future of work, dispelling myths where necessary, and calling for action where real risks exist.

## Should we brace for a jobless future?

*Despite significant uncertainty, we are not heading for a jobless future anytime soon. However, we do need to prepare for deep structural changes that appear inevitable. Managing transitions well and avoiding growing disparities can be achieved if effective and adequately resourced policies are put in place.*

**As robots, artificial intelligence and the digital transformation increasingly permeate the world of work, and economies across the globe become more integrated, many people are worried about the impact of these mega-trends on the number of jobs.** Some paint a particularly bleak picture of the future, arguing that automation could destroy nearly half of jobs over the next couple of decades.

**However, employment rates in most OECD countries have been on an upward trend.** This is because jobs are being created at a faster rate than they are being destroyed and greater opportunities are opening up to participate in the labour market for many people who were formerly excluded. Technological change and globalisation contribute to this – by lowering the costs of production, boosting the quality of products, and opening up new markets – all of which lead to additional demand and boost productivity and, therefore, further job creation.

**While the future may be uncertain, massive technological unemployment seems unlikely.** The OECD estimates that 14% of jobs are at high risk of automation – significantly fewer than some researchers have argued. Moreover, the fact that a job could potentially be automated does not mean that this will actually happen: automation may not always be cost-effective or desirable, it may raise legal and ethical concerns, and it will be affected by people's preferences and policy decisions.

**Nevertheless, even those who remain in their current job will experience significant change.** In addition to the 14% of jobs at high risk of automation, the tasks performed and how they are carried out may change substantially in another third of existing jobs. The manufacturing sector is at high risk, but so are many service sectors. And, even though the risk of automation is low in health, education and the public sector – many people will be affected because those sectors employ a large share of the workforce. These changes are therefore likely to affect many workers, regardless of where they work.

---

OECD estimates that 14% of jobs are at high risk of automation – significantly fewer than some researchers have argued

---

**There will be further churning of jobs – with new, different jobs replacing those that are destroyed – and this will result in structural change and new skills needs**. Labour markets in most OECD countries have been polarising with substantial growth in the share of high-skilled occupations and some growth in low-skilled jobs, but a fall in the share of middle-skilled ones. Employment in the manufacturing sector in particular has been on a long-term path of decline (shrinking by 20% over the period 1995-2015), while the share of jobs in the service sector has been steadily rising (growing by 27% over the same period). In emerging economies, there has been a substantial decline in the share of agricultural employment.

**A key challenge is to manage successfully the transition towards new opportunities for workers, industries and regions affected by the megatrends of technological change and globalisation**. It will also require employers and workers to make on-the-job adjustments, adopting and learning new technologies and ways of working.

**These transitions will be difficult for many, and will hit some workers more than others.** The labour market experiences of many young people, and in particular those with less than tertiary education, have already worsened in several respects. The risk of non-employment and underemployment has increased over the past decade more for men than for women in most countries but still remains much higher for women. Women are also still more likely than men to be working in low-paid jobs and less likely to be working in high-paid ones. Failing to address these disparities is likely to result in a future of work with deeper social divisions, which could have negative ramifications for productivity, growth, well-being and social cohesion.

**Rapid population ageing in many countries will further compound these challenges.** In 2015, there were 28 people aged 65 and over for every 100 people of working age. By 2050, this ratio is projected to double. In countries with rapidly ageing populations, shortages of qualified labour may arise as the number of older workers retiring rises relative to the number of young people entering the labour market. These shortages may in turn lead to faster automation or stronger pressures to attract immigrant workers. Ageing will also have a direct impact on skills demands and the types of jobs available as consumption shifts from durable goods (such as cars) towards services (such as health care). In some emerging economies, the challenge is to integrate large numbers of young people into the workforce. They will need to take advantage of this demographic dividend to boost growth and prepare for the transition to a much older population.

**Workers who lose their jobs because of technology and globalisation need to be helped to move quickly to new jobs through effective and timely employment services, as well as prevention and early intervention measures.** Adequate income support tied to incentives and support for active job search will be critical in reducing the individual and social costs of these adjustment processes, and can play a key stabilising role in the current context of heightened uncertainties about the future of work. Yet, in many countries, unemployment benefits systems fail to reach a significant share of the unemployed and coverage may shrink further if non-standard work expands.

**Collective bargaining and social dialogue can complement government efforts to make labour markets more adaptable and secure.** In some OECD countries, social partners play a significant role in providing active support to workers who have lost their jobs and in anticipating skills needs. Collective bargaining and social dialogue can be useful institutions to help companies respond to demographic and technological changes by allowing them to adjust wages, working time, work organisation as well as tasks to new needs in a more flexible and pragmatic manner than through labour regulation (while remaining fair). Yet collective bargaining has been on a declining trend for decades and, in the context of a rapidly evolving world of work, this poses serious challenges for workers' rights, benefits and protections and may sometimes leave employers and employers organisations without a clear counterpart.

**Effective skills policies will also be essential if individuals are to minimise the risks and maximise the benefits of changes in the labour market.** In a context of changing skills needs, adult learning can help prevent skills depreciation and obsolescence, and facilitate transitions from declining jobs and sectors to expanding ones.

> Across OECD countries, participation in training by low-skilled adults is 40 percentage points below that of high-skilled adults

**However, skills policies often fail to reach those adults who are more at risk from the changes that lie ahead.** On average across OECD countries, participation in training by low-skilled adults – those who potentially need it the most as their jobs are at highest risk of being automated – is 40 percentage points below that of high-skilled adults. Similarly, workers whose jobs are at high risk of automation are 30 percentage points less likely to engage in adult learning than their peers in jobs with a lower risk. Even when the low-skilled and those in jobs at risk of automation participate in training, its low quality and limited relevance may be letting them down.

**Disadvantaged workers face multiple barriers to training.** Low-skilled workers, those in jobs at high risk of automation and workers who lose their jobs are often reluctant to train or unable to identify relevant learning activities. Even when they are well informed and motivated, some workers face other barriers, such as a lack of time or money to train. Meanwhile, employers are more likely to invest in training higher-skilled workers where the return to such investment is expected to be higher.

**Adult learning systems will need to be strengthened and adapted to provide all workers, and in particular those most vulnerable to the changes that lie ahead, with adequate opportunities for retraining throughout their careers.** Awareness of the benefits of training could be raised through information campaigns and career guidance. However, training formats also need to become more modular and flexible to fit around busy work schedules and family responsibilities. Skills acquired through experience should be recognised, and better financial incentives should be designed to reduce the cost of training borne by the most vulnerable groups. Moreover, it is critical to improve the quality of programmes and their alignment with current and future labour market needs, and to evaluate their effectiveness on a regular basis. Employers can and should play an important role in delivering on this agenda and, with the help of governments, they should be encouraged to train groups at risk.

## Is the end nigh for the standard employment relationship?

*Many countries have seen growth in "new", non-standard forms of employment, but full-time, permanent employment is still (and is likely to remain) the most prevalent form of employment across advanced OECD countries. In many cases, these "new" forms of employment are merely shedding new light on old challenges. However, the rights and protections of vulnerable workers falling outside the traditional remit of labour law and social protection should be strengthened.*

**Standard, full-time, open-ended employment still accounts for the majority of employment across the OECD.** There are several reasons for the continuing appeal of more stable, permanent employment arrangements. From the point of view of workers, such contracts provide more certainty and allow them to plan ahead in both their private and professional lives. From the perspective of employers, permanent contracts allow them to attract and retain talent (which reduces hiring and training costs) and increases the pay-off from investing in staff (which raises productivity).

**New forms of work have emerged due to changes in preferences, innovations in business models and work organisation, as well as technological developments (and policy choices).** These include the platform economy, in which workers provide services through online platforms. Many countries have also experienced an expansion of other non-standard forms of work, such as on-call or zero-hours contracts, as well as various forms of own-account work. These more flexible working arrangements have often emerged in response to the real needs of both employers and workers. Companies need some leeway to adjust workforces and working hours to take account of fluctuating and unpredictable demand. Workers may be seeking greater freedom to fit work around caring responsibilities or leisure in order to achieve a better work-life balance. More flexible forms of employment can also offer new opportunities and a stepping-stone to full-time, open-ended employment for some, including young people and many low-skilled workers.

**However, false self-employment needs to be tackled**. False self-employment refers to situations where working arrangements are essentially the same as those of employees but individuals are hired as self-employed workers in order to avoid regulations, taxes and unionisation. False self-employment not only hurts workers, but also other firms that do comply with regulations. Existing regulations should be clarified and enforced better. It should be made easier for individuals to challenge their employment status. In addition, the penalties for non-compliance should be strengthened. Governments should also ensure that differences in the tax and regulatory treatment of different forms of employment do not further encourage the misclassification of workers. Indeed, in several countries, rapid growth in non-standard forms of work has been driven primarily by fiscal and regulatory differences between employment forms, which have created opportunities for arbitrage.

**Some workers will be genuinely difficult to classify and find themselves in the "grey zone" between dependent employment and self-employment.** While formally classified as self-employed, some workers share some characteristics of employees (e.g. they cannot set their own rates of pay, have to wear a uniform or cannot send a replacement to execute their tasks). This means that they experience some elements of dependence and/or subordination in their working relationship, and have less bargaining power. Yet, because they are classified as self-employed, they will generally not benefit from the same labour law protections, collective bargaining rights, social protection, and equal access to training as employees.

**In a first instance, the size of the grey zone should be managed and kept to a minimum.** In some cases, regulations or guidelines for determining employment status may need to be clarified, revised and/or harmonised, and consistently enforced. This would help reduce uncertainty for both workers and employers, and reduce litigation.

**For those workers who remain in the grey zone, policy-makers should consider strengthening their rights and benefits** by: i) identifying and targeting specific groups of self-employed workers in need of protection (e.g. the financially dependent self-employed or specific occupations); ii) deciding which rights and protections to extend to such workers (e.g. unemployment insurance, holiday pay, collective bargaining rights) and how; and iii) where necessary, clarifying and assigning employer duties and responsibilities in the case of triangular employment relationships, such as those in the platform economy (e.g. by holding platforms and clients jointly liable, or by imposing liability on platforms and only subsidiary liability clients).

**Access to social protection can be difficult for all workers in non-standard employment.** The self-employed are usually less well covered by statutory social protection provisions. This is particularly a problem for the self-employed with little control over their remuneration and working conditions and for risks which cannot be deemed to be entrepreneurial in nature. Other forms of non-standard employment (e.g. part-time and temporary work) are in theory well covered, but in practice many workers on such contracts still struggle to gain access, because they fail to meet minimum contribution periods or earnings thresholds. In some countries, non-standard workers are 40-50% less likely to receive any form of income support during an out-of-work spell than standard employees. For those receiving support, out-of-work income assistance is often significantly less generous than for standard employees.

> In some countries, non-standard workers are 40-50% less likely to receive any form of income support during an out-of-work spell than standard employees

**Social protection provisions should be reshaped to ensure better coverage of workers in non-standard forms of employment.** Reform options include: *i)* ensuring a more neutral treatment of different forms of work to prevent arbitrage between them; *ii)* extending the reach of existing social protection systems to new forms of work; *iii)* boosting the portability of entitlements between social insurance programmes that are intended for different labour market groups; *iv)* making means-tests more responsive to people's needs by changing the reference periods for the needs assessment and putting appropriate weight on recent or current incomes of all family members; and *v)* complementing targeted social protection measures with more universal and unconditional support. However, more radical reforms to replace large parts of traditional social protection with a universal basic income would be either very expensive or have unfavourable distributional outcomes at the expense of the most vulnerable groups.

**Measures to help and encourage jobseekers find work will need to be adapted.** Activation measures, which seek to maximise unemployed people's chances of re-employment and minimise disincentives to work, need to be revised. They have traditionally been set up to help workers in a standard employment relationship who are facing job loss. Consequently, if they lose their job, many non-standard workers have limited access to vocational training, counselling and other employment-oriented programmes for the unemployed. This raises questions as to how activation and employment-oriented social programs can be adapted to meet the needs of non-standard workers.

**Training policies will also need to be modified for workers in non-standard forms of employment.** Workers in non-standard forms of employment also have more difficulties accessing job-related training. This is the case for temporary, part-time and, in particular, own-account workers (i.e. self-employed without employees). Even though equal rights clauses have been introduced in most OECD countries, training rights often accrue with job tenure and depend on the numbers of hours worked. So, in practice, temporary and part-time workers may not acquire the right to train. Own-account workers are still very rarely covered in training rights legislation. Options for governments include extending training rights beyond standard employees, target certain adult learning policies to non-standard workers, and making training rights portable between employment statuses, through individual learning accounts – although none of these will, by themselves, offer a panacea.

**In emerging economies, new forms of work in the platform economy may offer opportunities for formalisation.** In countries with a large incidence of informality, platform work can represent a route to formalisation, since it can reduce its costs and improve monitoring of economic activity through the digitalisation of transactions. However, to capitalise on these opportunities, emerging economies will need to ensure that adequate tax and social protection mechanisms are put in place.

## Has the balance of power between bosses and workers tipped too far?

*Many workers have few alternative employment options and low bargaining power, particularly non-standard workers. Collective bargaining and trade union coverage has declined in most OECD countries, further weakening workers' bargaining power. Strong power imbalances favouring employers over workers tend to put downward pressure on labour demand and wages, but policies can help restore the balance and improve both equity and efficiency.*

**Membership of unions and overall coverage of collective agreements have declined in many countries, weakening workers' bargaining power.** The proportion of workers in the OECD who are covered by collective agreements has steadily declined over the last three decades, falling from 45% in 1985 to 32% in 2016. This has weakened workers' bargaining power in many countries and contributed a decline in the share of national income that goes to workers.

**Union membership and collective bargaining coverage is even lower among non-standard workers.** Non-standard workers are 50% less likely to be unionised, on average, than standard workers. Lower unionisation among non-standard workers reflects the practical and legal difficulties of organising them. It may also be the result of unions historically focusing on standard workers' needs, rather than those of non-standard ones.

> Non-standard workers are 50% less likely to be unionised, on average, than standard workers

**Many workers in the grey zone between dependent and self-employment have little scope to organise and bargain collectively.** Traditionally, only workers in a subordinate employment relationship (i.e. salaried employment) have had an undisputed legal right to collective bargaining. Workers usually classified as self-employed are generally excluded due to competition laws prohibiting cartels, which tend to regard them as business undertakings. This may be fine for many self-employed workers who earn good incomes or are in a position to bargain with their clients over their rates. However, it poses efficiency and fairness problems in the case of self-employed workers who share some characteristics and vulnerabilities with dependent employees and therefore face a power imbalance vis-à-vis their employer or client.

**There is a strong argument for extending collective bargaining rights to workers in the grey zone between dependent employment and self-employment, and some countries have already done so – but the challenge is to ensure that labour market and competition policy remain aligned.** Enforcing the correct classification of workers and fighting misclassification should be the first step in extending collective bargaining rights to as many workers as possible. In addition, some countries have already extended collective bargaining rights to (or sought explicit exemptions to the cartel prohibition for) some workers in the grey zone or specific groups of self-employed – e.g. the dependent self-employed or workers in certain sectors or occupations (such as voice-over actors, session musicians and freelance journalists) where they are most likely to be exposed to strong power imbalances.

**Countries should also consider facilitating the emergence of new forms of social dialogue and accompanying the efforts of unions and employer organisations to expand their membership to non-standard forms of work and business.** The contribution of social dialogue and collective bargaining to shaping the future of work crucially depends on workers and firms being able and willing to associate and negotiate mutually satisfying and binding agreements. The examples of successful collective agreements in the temporary work agency sector and the cultural and creative industries, even in countries where unions are weak, show that collective bargaining, if sufficiently flexible, can adjust to different and new types of employment relationships.

**An absence of collective bargaining rights can accentuate power imbalances that are inherent in the employment relationship, and could lead to a degree of monopsony in the labour market.** Employers (or clients in the case of certain self-employed people) often have a higher degree of control over the relationship than workers, who may have few or no outside options. This can lead to an unbalanced power relationship between the parties, with stronger bargaining power in the hands of employers, which may imply that they can impose lower wages by inefficiently reducing labour demand – a situation usually referred to as labour market monopsony. The consequences of these imbalances on pay and employment tend to be stronger when workers are unable to organise and bargain collectively. When workers negotiate pay and working conditions individually, employers' buyer power is usually not compensated by sufficient bargaining power on the side of workers.

**Labour market monopsony also has negative consequences for businesses.** Abuses of monopsony power in the labour market can be a source of concern for companies too. On the one hand, lack of competition in the labour market – for example because certain companies collude among themselves or resort to restrictive covenants to reduce workers' mobility and bargaining power – may mean that innovative companies are prevented from exploiting new opportunities and recruiting the best people. On the other hand, insufficient enforcement of competition law disadvantages firms that abide by the rules.

**Beyond extending collective bargaining coverage, the sources of monopsony power and its abuse can also be addressed by better regulation and more effective enforcement.** Regulatory actions to tackle labour market monopsony include: *i)* more aggressively enforcing rules against employers colluding in the labour market; *ii)* limiting the scope of restrictive covenants such as non-compete clauses; *iii)* extending coverage of labour market regulations to address the effects of monopsony on workers' well-being (for example by enhancing occupational health and safety standards); and *iv)* amending existing labour market regulations to redress inequalities of information available to employers and workers (e.g. by ensuring that contract obligations are drafted in simple, understandable language). A balanced approach is, however, necessary to avoid that excessively burdensome regulations end up unduly curbing entrepreneurial activity and innovation. In addition, a comprehensive policy strategy to reduce labour market frictions and enhance job mobility would also help address monopsony power.

## A Future that Works for All – can we afford it?

*Policies to build a more rewarding and inclusive world of work will require adequate financial resources – in particular for strengthening adult learning and social protection. Given the constraints on public finances, new thinking is needed on how to find the necessary resources. At the same time, some policy options involve barely any costs for the public finances and may even increase tax revenues.*

**A number of policy interventions under consideration entail little or no cost to the public purse.** Reforms such as improving and enforcing labour market regulations, strengthening collective bargaining, and making training provision more flexible do not have to be costly for the public finances. Similarly, stepping up antitrust action to curb monopsony power would require limited additional resources.

**Some policies may even lead to lower public spending and higher tax revenues.** For instance, well-functioning public employment services and effective and timely activation policies that help workers return quickly to work reduce costs for unemployment benefit systems and can improve productivity by raising the quality of job matches. Some reforms can also directly increase tax revenues by widening the tax base (e.g. by bringing the platform economy into the tax system). Removing unintended fiscal incentives for self-employment and combating false self-employment would also boost revenues.

**However, strengthening social protection and adult learning will require significant additional resources, especially to close existing coverage gaps – and this calls for a review by countries of their spending priorities as well as a reflection on their tax systems**. Although some policy actions pay for themselves, many of the suggested interventions, and notably in the areas of social protection and adult learning, require more resources. In many OECD and emerging economies, the lack of training opportunities and adequate social protection systems will require significant investments. Some of the required resources may be found by increasing the efficiency of current spending and undertaking a spending review to decide – through a whole-of-government approach – where spending priorities lie. But increasing the efficiency of current spending may not suffice. Governments should expect to confront decisions about how new or expanded initiatives will be paid for and who should pay. This is likely to include political discussion about what is fair, what is cost effective, and a variety of views on how the allocation of costs and access to the expanded programmes will affect the performance of the broader economy, including outcomes for business, workers, consumers, and citizens more generally. Finally, finding the right financing solutions is also likely to require some global thinking and action.

> Some policy actions pay for themselves, but some of the suggested interventions, notably in the areas of social protection and adult learning, require more resources

**Countries should continue to assess the labour market impact of technological progress, globalisation and population ageing and to explore how to facilitate positive change with respect to the adaptation of labour market, social and training policies.** Government interventions, while essential, will likely not be enough by themselves. All stakeholders should participate, including businesses who badly need workers with the appropriate skills and a conducive social and economic environment. New public-private partnerships will need to be created to provide adequate responses to the changing world of work. The OECD will continue to support countries by acting as a forum in which governments and other stakeholders can work together to share experiences and seek solutions. It will continue to assess the impact of the mega-trends on job quantity, quality and inclusiveness, and what countries should do to strengthen the resilience and adaptability of labour markets so that workers and businesses can manage the transition with the least possible disruption, while maximising the potential benefits.

Policy Directions

Making the most of the opportunities that lie ahead and ensuring that they lead to better jobs for all will require concerted policy efforts across a number of areas. This will require future proofing across the spectrum of labour market policies and institutions, covering social protection, skills and collective bargaining, as well as appropriate regulation of the labour market. While the precise action required will depend on each country's specific characteristics in terms of its institutional set-up, social preferences, administrative capacity and social capital, policy makers should consider the following policy directions:

**Regulation of the labour market**

Governments should ensure that all workers in the labour market have access to an adequate set of rights and protections, regardless of their employment status or contract type, and guarantee a level playing field among firms by preventing some from gaining a competitive advantage by avoiding their obligations and responsibilities.

In the area of labour market regulation, countries should:

- Tackle false self-employment by:
  - Ensuring that employers and workers are aware of, and understand, existing regulations;
  - Making it easier and less costly for workers to challenge their employment status;
  - Strengthening the penalties for firms misclassifying workers;
  - Strengthening the capacity of labour inspectorates to monitor and detect breaches;
  - Reducing incentives for firms and workers to misclassify employment relationships as self-employment in order to avoid/reduce taxes and regulations.
- Reduce the size of the "grey zone" between self- and dependent employment by revising, updating and/or harmonising definitions of what it means to be an employee and/or a self-employed person – in order to make these definitions as clear as possible and reduce uncertainty for both workers and employers.
- Extend rights and protections to those workers left in the "grey zone" (i.e. where genuine ambiguity in employment status exists) by a combination of:
  - Identifying and targeting specific groups of workers to which certain labour rights and protections could be extended;
  - Deciding which labour rights and protections to (at least partially) extend (e.g.: fair pay, working time protections, occupational health and safety, anti-discrimination and employment protection) and whether and how they should be adapted;
  - Where necessary, clarifying and/or assigning employer duties and responsibilities in the case of triangular employment relationships (including platform work), which may require spreading such responsibilities across multiple legal entities.
- At the international level, build on the recent G20 commitment to promote decent work in the platform economy and consider ways of improving the working conditions of workers with little say over their remuneration and working conditions who provide services globally – including best practice principles or guidelines, which countries and/or platforms could sign up to.

Addressing power imbalances between employers/clients and workers also requires enhancing collective bargaining and social dialogue (see below) and tackling labour market monopsony. Options to fight against abuses of monopsony power include:

- Fighting labour market collusion, for example by providing explicit guidance on illicit behaviours, setting priorities for enforcement agencies and ensuring adequate whistle-blower protection;

- Limiting the scope of non-compete covenants, including in contracts for services – particularly for certain types of jobs, pay levels or skill requirements, where they are most likely to be used to reduce competition in the labour market;

- Reducing the incentives for broad or unlawful non-compete agreements, by banning court redrafting of unreasonable covenants to make them enforceable, and by appropriately sanctioning the abuse of illicit clauses;

- Favouring the development of new tools and instruments to better analyse the effects of mergers and anti-competitive conduct in the labour market;

- Redressing inequalities in the information available to employers and workers by ensuring that workers are fully aware of their rights and responsibilities, improving pay transparency in the labour market and enhancing symmetry of treatment of workers and requesters on online platforms, including as regards mutual evaluations;

## Labour relations, social dialogue and collective bargaining

While each country's situation and traditions are different, a well-functioning system of labour relations can contribute to shaping a more rewarding and inclusive future of work. Depending on the national context, policy makers should consider:

- Promoting national consultations and discussions on the future of work with both social partners and other organisations representing workers and employers to establish a joint diagnosis about challenges, and share practices among actors on new initiatives and technological innovation through common knowledge platforms.

- Leaving scope for collective bargaining and incentivising self-regulation among actors on these issues by making a limited but strategic use of legislative interventions (as exemplified in the case of the temporary work agencies sector in several countries).

- Ensuring broad-based access to training and lifelong learning by promoting collective bargaining over these issues.

- Accompanying the efforts of unions and employers organisations to expand their membership to non-standard forms of work and new forms of business without discouraging the emergence of other forms of organisation.

Enforcing the correct classification of workers' employment status and fighting misclassification is the first step in ensuring that workers have access to collective bargaining. Yet, there would still be scope for potential adaptation of existing regulations to allow collective bargaining for workers in the grey zone and for the self-employed who have little influence on the content of their contractual conditions. Options to be considered include:

- Enlarging the definition of "employee" in labour law, as far as labour relations legislation is concerned, to specific groups of workers in the grey zone; and

- Introducing exemptions to the prohibition of bargaining collectively for specific groups of workers or occupations, in case where power imbalances are likely to be more important.

## Adult learning

A comprehensive adult learning strategy is needed to face the challenges of a changing world of work and to ensure that all workers, particularly the most vulnerable, have adequate opportunities for retraining throughout their careers. As part of this strategy, countries should consider the following policy directions:

- Foster a mind-set for learning among both firms and individuals. This could be done by strengthening career guidance for all adults; putting in place public information campaigns to raise awareness of the benefits of learning; and ensuring that wages reflect more closely the productivity gains resulting from training participation.
- Lower barriers to training by:
  - Tackling time constraints through modular training options, training delivered outside of working hours or online courses, as well as by providing workers with education and training leave.
  - Lowering the cost of training by providing financial incentives for the most vulnerable groups in the labour market.
  - Reducing entry barriers to training courses for workers with low qualifications by strengthening the recognition of skills acquired through experience.
- Encourage employers to train groups at risk. This could be achieved by lowering the cost to employers of training at-risk workers, for example by means of targeted financial incentives.
- Target adult learning policies such as financial subsidies, and career guidance services on the groups that need them most, including non-standard workers.
- Tackle unequal access to training based on employment status. Equal rights clauses have been introduced in most countries to ensure access to training for employees in some non-standard contracts, such as part-time, fixed-term, and temporary agency workers. In practice, however, these workers may not acquire rights to training, which often accrue with job tenure and depend on the numbers of hours worked. Moreover, self-employed workers are still very rarely covered by training rights legislation.
- Make training rights portable between employment statuses. Individual learning accounts have been proposed and implemented in a few countries as one way for workers to acquire and accumulate training rights irrespective of their employer or whether they change jobs or employment status. However, if vulnerable workers are to benefit fully, such schemes need to be complemented by more personal, face-to-face support delivered by specialised career guidance officers and informed by quality information on labour market needs.
- Ensure that training is of good quality and aligned to labour market needs through: the collection and use of high-quality information on skill needs; accreditation and certification of training providers; and a strong culture of evaluation of the effectiveness of policies and programmes.
- Strengthen the governance of adult learning systems, involving all relevant stakeholders, to ensure coherence and co-ordination of adult learning policies. Adult learning is a shared responsibility that calls for the active involvement of all stakeholders, including all levels of government, the social partners, training providers and adults themselves.
- Share the financial burden of scaling up adult learning systems. Significant financial resources will be required to scale up existing adult learning systems, broaden coverage and increase training quality. This calls for a healthy mix of co-financing by government, employers and individuals that takes account of ability to pay and the benefits obtained.

## Social protection

Governments should conduct a thorough review of their social protection systems to examine whether they provide reliable coverage against evolving labour-market and social risks. Most countries mix different social protection design principles, such as means-testing or social insurance, and these provisions shape the ways in which rising non-standard work translates into specific social protection access barriers. Social protection provisions themselves can drive trends towards non-standard employment. Where needed, social protection provisions should be reinforced to ensure effective income and employment support for workers who are ill-equipped to benefit from the opportunities of technological advances and dynamic labour markets.

Preparing social protection for future labour markets requires a pro-active but iterative approach that addresses existing challenges while monitoring and adapting policy approaches as labour markets continue to evolve. Some challenges represent long-standing issues, but they can become more pressing as new technologies provide opportunities for alternative work arrangements. The correct classification of workers' employment status is a pre-requisite for ensuring that they receive protection and support that is appropriate for their circumstances and risks (see above).

However, even with well-defined legal categories and suitable enforcement in place, social protection provisions can lead to significant support gaps for standard and, in particular, non-standard workers. In order to ease access barriers to social protection for both standard and non-standard workers policy makers should consider:

- Reviewing social protection entitlement criteria, such as employment requirements, waiting periods and rules for combining or alternating benefit receipt with intermittent and other non-standard forms of work;

- Enabling workers in independent forms of employment to build up rights to out-of-work support;

- Making social protection provisions less rigid by ensuring that built-up entitlements are portable across jobs and forms of employment;

- Maintaining or strengthening risk sharing across all labour market and income groups by tackling financial incentives that favour non-standard work, such as reduced tax/contribution burdens or voluntary membership;

- Making means tests more responsive to people's needs by shortening the reference periods for needs assessments and by putting appropriate weight on recent or current incomes of all family members;

- Subject to budgetary space, strengthening universal and unconditional forms of support, such as universal child benefits, as complements to existing targeted or insurance-based support measures.

Automation will lead to job displacement for many workers, while novel forms of employment are blurring the distinction between in-work and out-of-work categories. This raises new questions about the scope and ambition of activation and employment-oriented social protection. Policy options and priorities include:

- Tackling gaps in income support, which typically serves as the main gateway to labour market reintegration measures. This may require extending support for "part-time unemployed" and other jobseekers with intermittent or low-paid employment;

- Re-assessing the scope of claimants' responsibilities, such as active job search, as a counter-weight to extending benefit rights. Such a review should ensure that the balance between supporting and demanding provisions remains in line with policy objectives regarding job quantity and quality. For instance, governments should consider if and when employment services should actively connect people to potentially precarious forms of work;

- Ensuring that the content of active labour market programmes is well adapted to the needs and circumstances of an evolving client base. A growing share of part-time unemployed may call for shifting resources from work experience programmes or direct job creation towards tailored training and career counselling (see also above).

Adapting social protection to the future of work will create additional financing pressures at a time when social protection budgets are already under pressure in many countries:

- Keeping funding levels in line with evolving needs for support requires a determined and coordinated approach, including cost-effective social protection delivery, better revenue-collection technologies and enforcement and a suitable balance of revenues from labour and non-labour tax bases.

- Ensuring that social protection systems remain fiscally sustainable also calls for tackling unintended incentives that distort employment or hiring decisions or encourage "gaming" of support systems by workers or employers.

- In particular, the rationale for voluntary social protection membership should be reassessed in light of labour-market developments. If new and emerging work patterns widen the scope for opting out of social protection provisions, such opportunities could compromise the risk-sharing function of social protection and erode its resource base.

- Governments should also assess whether existing social protection financing mechanisms achieve a fair balance of burdens between different employers, e.g. between those making little use of automation and those substituting large shares of their workforce with robots or artificial intelligence.

# 2 The future of work: What do we know?

This chapter discusses the key megatrends that are transforming the labour market and analyses their implications for job quantity, job quality, and inclusiveness, the three key dimensions of the OECD Jobs Strategy framework. Despite growing anxiety about potential job destruction driven by technological change and globalisation, a sharp decline in overall employment seems unlikely. There are, however, increasing concerns about the quality of some new jobs. This may increase disparities among workers if large segments of the workforce are unable to benefit from the good opportunities the economy generates. The most important challenge for policy makers is to prevent such growing disparities. Failing to do so will result in a future of work with deeper social cleavages and increasing discontent, which could have negative ramifications for productivity, growth, well-being, and social cohesion.

The statistical data for Israel are supplied by and under the responsibility of the relevant Israeli authorities. The use of such data by the OECD is without prejudice to the status of the Golan Heights, East Jerusalem and Israeli settlements in the West Bank under the terms of international law.

# In Brief

## Key findings

The world of work is changing. Technological progress, globalisation and ageing populations are re-shaping the labour market. At the same time, new organisational business models and evolving worker preferences are contributing to the emergence of new forms of work. This chapter provides an overview of these changes and highlights the key challenges for policy makers.

- Despite widespread anxiety about potential job destruction driven by technological change and globalisation, a sharp decline in overall employment seems unlikely. While certain jobs and tasks are disappearing, others are emerging, and overall employment has been growing.

- As these transformations occur, a key challenge lies in managing the transition of workers in the different industries and regions that are hard hit by the megatrends towards the new opportunities that are opening up.

- There are growing concerns about the quality of jobs. The purchasing power of wages has been stagnating for many workers and job stability has been declining. Moreover, different forms of non-standard employment have risen in a number of countries. While diversity in employment contracts can provide welcome flexibility for firms and some workers, important policy challenges remain in providing high-quality jobs to non-standard workers.

- Most importantly, without immediate policy action, labour market disparities are set to increase further, as the costs of the structural adjustments occurring in the world of work are not shared equally. Job losses are concentrated among certain groups of workers and in some regions, and some workers suffer disproportionately from poorer job quality than others. Failing to address such growing disparities will result in deeper social divisions, with adverse implications for growth, productivity, well-being, and social cohesion.

- These challenges do not lie on a distant horizon. The future is now as the transformations documented in this chapter are already taking place. In fact, some of them have been occurring for a few decades already. Some of the challenges they entail have therefore been in need of policy action for quite some time, but many countries have been slow to respond. Other challenges, however, are gaining strength now or remain difficult to foresee given the uncertainty about future changes in the world of work. In this context, responsible policy making should aim to enhance the resilience of the labour market, effectively preparing for a range of potential futures.

- The adverse effects on the labour market associated with these deep and rapid structural changes are not inevitable, and policy can and should play an important role in shaping the future of work. Steering these changes will require a whole-of-government approach, engaging with the social partners, and civil society.

## Introduction

The world of work is undergoing significant changes. Technological progress, globalisation and ageing populations are some of the most cited trends shaping the labour market along with efforts to mitigate the effects of climate change. At the same time, new organisational business models and evolving worker preferences are contributing to the emergence of new forms of work that depart from the traditional norm of permanent full-time dependent employment.

Many of these changes are seen as potentially very disruptive. However, concerns about disruptive global trends are not new. Ever since the Industrial Revolution, fears of technology-induced job losses have been common in the public debate. In the 1930s, John Maynard Keynes warned of "a new disease... namely, technological unemployment" (Keynes, 1931[1]). Two years before, the U.S. Republican Party pledged to fortify "certain industries which cannot now successfully compete with foreign producers because of lower foreign wages and a lower cost of living abroad" (Republican Party, 1928[2]). A few decades later, concern about automation was so great that in 1961 US President Kennedy created an Office of Automation and Manpower in the Department of Labor, identifying "the major domestic challenge of the sixties: to maintain full employment at a time when automation, of course, is replacing men." And governments in many countries have been increasingly concerned about rapid population ageing, especially (though, not exclusively) in light of the risks it poses for the sustainability of their social security systems and for economic growth.

Despite such fears, employment in OECD countries has grown steadily over the past decades. Labour markets have evolved to include social groups that were previously left out, most notably many women. Undoubtedly, many workers have been adversely affected by the decline of certain industries – and much of the focus of this chapter is precisely on those who have suffered most from the changing economy – but the fear that the future may hold *fewer* job opportunities than the past has so far not materialised.

Is this time different however? A number of authors have argued that the speed and intensity of technological progress is increasing and that the new wave of transformation may have more disruptive consequences for workers (Brynjolfsson and McAfee, 2011[3]; Mokyr, Vickers and Ziebarth, 2015[4]). Such worries are increasingly widespread and a large share of the population in a number of countries is concerned about the negative impacts of automation on jobs (Pew Research Center, 2018[5]).[1] Moreover, public concerns have been heightened as recent trends threaten to affect people who have been historically sheltered from economic changes, including white-collar workers with relatively high levels of education and secure jobs.

In response to these concerns, this chapter offers an extensive analysis of how labour markets are changing and, in particular, a deeper investigation of the risks of job automation. On the positive side, it finds that technological progress offers new employment opportunities and that a significant risk of high technological unemployment is unlikely. However, without immediate policy action, disparities among workers may rise and social cleavages may deepen between those who gain and those who lose from the ongoing changes in the world of work. In a number of areas, the key policy challenges are well-established, though many countries have been slow to respond. Recent labour market developments, such as transformations linked to automation, the decline in unionisation, and the rise of new forms of work, are exacerbating these challenges and emphasise the need for timely, deliberate, and decisive responses to shape a better future of work for all.

The analysis focuses on three key *megatrends* affecting the labour market today and in the years to come: *technological progress and the digital transformation, globalisation,* and *demographic changes.* Some account is also taken of the role of other trends, such as climate change and new forms of work organisation.

This chapter provides a brief discussion of the main stylised facts that emerge from the OECD's analysis of how the world of work is changing and identifies the key policy challenges addressed in the next chapters.[2] It begins with an overview of the megatrends affecting labour markets. The discussion is then structured around the three pillars of the *OECD Jobs Strategy* for assessing labour market performance – *job quantity, job quality,* and *inclusiveness* – to identify key outcomes of interest (OECD, 2018[6]). The fourth pillar of the Jobs Strategy, labour market resilience and adaptability, is mainstreamed in the policy recommendations by promoting greater flexibility to respond to future changes in the world of work.

## 2.1. An overview of the megatrends transforming labour markets

### 2.1.1. New technologies are rapidly permeating the world of work

Over the past two to three decades, the pace of technological progress and the speed of its diffusion across countries have been startling. For instance, while it took over seven decades for phone penetration to go from 10% to 90% in US households, it took only about fifteen years for mobile phones and just over 8 years for smartphones.[3] Such technological leaps have had major impacts on the way people work and live.

The growth in information and communication technologies (ICT) use in the workplace provides a clear indication of how quickly new technologies permeate the workplace. From 1995 to 2007, the level of ICT capital services per hour worked more than doubled in every country analysed before growing at a slower pace (Figure 2.1). There are, however, substantial country differences in the pace of technology adoption. While in Hungary, Japan, and Slovenia, ICT levels increased by just over 150% over the period, the increase was as much as 300% in the Netherlands, the Czech Republic, Ireland, and Germany and above 350% in the United States, Belgium and the United Kingdom.

The diffusion of industrial robots perhaps best epitomises technological penetration and fears of job automation in the workplace. While robots have been on factory floors for decades, their diffusion has recently accelerated and spread beyond manufacturing. As one example, supermarkets have started to employ robots as shop assistants, and a number of companies are piloting cashier-less stores – e.g. Browne (2018[7]). The capabilities of robots are also expanding within the manufacturing sector. For example, certain robots are now able to move by themselves around the factory floor (Brynjolfsson and McAfee, 2014[8]). Data from the International Federation of Robotics show that orders of industrial robots have increased fivefold between 2001 and 2017, and such a trend is projected to accelerate further (Figure 2.2).[4] Coupled with the increasing share of national income going to capital (as opposed to labour, as discussed below), such a trend directly fuels an important policy debate on the concentration of capital ownership.

These are only some examples of new technologies that have emerged and had an impact on the world of work. Going forward, further leaps in the development of artificial intelligence (AI) are likely to have applications in a broad range of domains, encroaching upon many more tasks that previously could only be performed by humans, with the potential to drive as-yet unforeseen changes in the world of work.

### 2.1.2. The world has become an increasingly integrated place

In conjunction with the diffusion of new technologies, the world economy has become increasingly integrated through international trade. As a share of GDP, international trade has risen across the OECD area in recent decades (Figure 2.3), and many emerging economies have become major players in the world market, both as exporters and importers. Industrial production has become increasingly integrated at the international level, with the world economy organised in global value chains (GVCs) whereby the different stages of the production process are distributed across countries and regions.

The integration of product, service, financial and technology markets fundamentally impacts labour markets around the world. It allows for and encourages greater specialisation in what gets produced and how it is produced with consequences for the skills workers require and the types of jobs that are created. Overall, more jobs are created through trade than are lost. For example, it has been estimated that, on average, 42% of business sector jobs in OECD countries were sustained by consumers in foreign markets in 2014 (OECD, 2017[9]). Yet the actual and potential negative effects of trade on certain occupations and local markets deserve careful scrutiny by policy makers as this constitutes the main cause of a growing discontent with globalisation worldwide.[5] Such discontent is often intertwined with the fear of automation. Since technological progress and globalisation have historically progressed hand in hand and reinforced each other, it is difficult to isolate their individual effects (OECD, 2017[10]).

## Figure 2.1. The rapid spread of information and communication technologies in the workplace

ICT capital services per hour worked, index (1995 = 100), 1995 to 2015

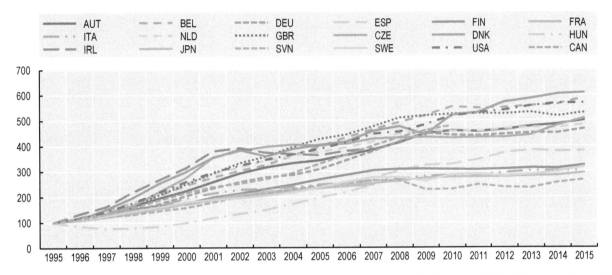

Note: ICT: information and communication technologies. ICT capital intensity per hours worked refer to the CAPIT_QPH variable in the EU KLEMS database. Data for Canada are taken from the World KLEMS database. Data series were extended using growth of the numerator and denominator of the ICT intensity ratio using the various releases of the EU KLEMS database (2009, 2013, and 2016). The 2009 EU KLEMS release covers the largest number of countries, covering the period from 1995 to 2007. Additional data were taken from later releases of EU KLEMS for the following countries: Austria, Belgium, the Czech Republic, Denmark, Finland, France, Germany, Italy, the Netherlands, Slovenia, Spain, Sweden, the United Kingdom and the United States. Values for Denmark have been adjusted to account for abnormally large increases in ICT intensity within the mining industry.
Source: EU KLEMS growth and productivity accounts, World KLEMS.

*StatLink* 🔗 http://dx.doi.org/10.1787/888933965951

## Figure 2.2. The march of the robots

Estimated worldwide annual supply of industrial robots, thousands of units

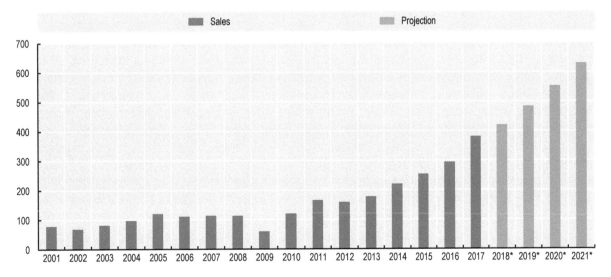

*: forecast
Source: International Federation of Robotics (IFR), https://ifr.org/.

*StatLink* 🔗 http://dx.doi.org/10.1787/888933965970

Figure 2.3. International trade keeps rising

Figure 2.3. International trade keeps rising

Trade in goods and services in selected OECD countries, 1975-2017

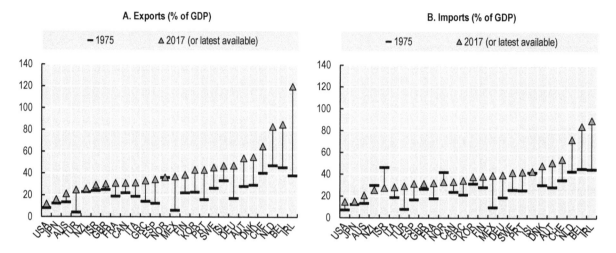

Source: OECD (2019[11]), Trade in goods and services (indicator), https://doi.org/10.1787/0fe445d9-en.

*StatLink* 🔍 http://dx.doi.org/10.1787/888933965989

### 2.1.3. OECD countries are ageing

The transformation of the labour market is occurring against the backdrop of rapid population ageing in both advanced and some emerging economies. In 1980, there were 20 persons aged 65 and over for every 100 people of working age (20-64) on average across the OECD (Figure 2.4); by 2015 this number had risen to 28 and it is projected to almost double between 2015 and 2050 (OECD, 2017[12]). The challenge of rapid population ageing is particularly acute in Greece, Italy, Japan, Korea, Portugal and Spain, as well as in China. In contrast, emerging economies such as Indonesia, South Africa, and India will continue to face the demographic challenge of integrating large numbers of young people into the workforce. They will need to take advantage of the demographic dividend of a relatively young population to boost growth and prepare for the transition to a much older population.

The effects of technological progress and its global diffusion will further contribute to population ageing. Largely as a result of technological advances that increased productivity and living standards, as well as raising the quality and availability of health care, average life expectancy at birth increased across the OECD from 69 years in 1965 to 80 years half a century later.[6] Going forward, scientists anticipate that new gene-editing technologies could lead to further improvements in the diagnosis and treatment of diseases, leading to longer life expectancies (Broad Institute, 2018[13]; Sanders, 2016[14]). Stronger research networks on a global scale and, more generally, the diffusion of knowledge across the world will allow these advances to reach an ever greater share of the global population, as incomes and access to health care increase in emerging economies.[7] But such improvements are not inevitable, as some changes in lifestyle resulting in a rising incidence of obesity and overuse of opioids have slowed or even halted the rise in life expectancy in a few advanced economies (OECD, 2018[15]).[8]

These demographic trends affect the labour market in terms of technology adoption and consumption patterns. In countries with ageing populations, shortages of qualified labour may arise as the number of older workers retiring rises relative to the number of young people entering the labour market. These shortages may in turn lead to faster automation or stronger pressures to attract immigrant workers. Acemoglu and Restrepo (2017[16]) show that countries with the most rapidly ageing populations have also been among the fastest to adopt industrial robots (and consequently they suggest that an ageing population may not necessarily be a harbinger of slower economic growth). Ageing will also have a direct impact on consumption: demand is likely to shift from durable goods (such as cars) towards services (such as health care). As preferences adjust, so too will trade and the relative importance of different industries.[9] All of these factors will have an impact on skill demands and the types of jobs that will be created.

**Figure 2.4. Many countries are ageing rapidly**

Projected change in the old-age dependency ratio, 1980-2050

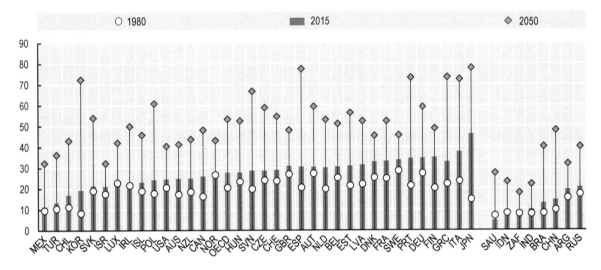

Note: The old-age dependency ratio is defined as the number of people aged 65 and over per 100 people of working-age (20-64).
Source: United Nations World Population Prospects: The 2017 Revision, https://population.un.org/wpp/.

StatLink 🔍 http://dx.doi.org/10.1787/888933966008

### 2.1.4. The global population will increase and migration pressures are likely to grow

As people live longer across the world while fertility rates remain high in a number of developing countries, the global population is expected to increase further. According to the United Nations' *2017 World Population Prospects*, the expected global population will be 9.7 billion in 2050, a 30% increase from 7.5 billion today.[10] Whereas developing countries will account for the bulk of this increase, the population of OECD countries is expected to increase by less than 10%, from 1.3 billion to 1.4 billion people.

Thus, depending on infrastructure, economic opportunity, and policy choices, migration flows may radically change the makeup of the population in advanced economies. As one example, over half of workers in the Silicon Valley with a degree in science, technology, engineering or mathematics (STEM) are foreign born (Melville, Kaiser and Brown, 2017[17]). In 2017, about 258 million people around the world were living outside their country of birth, and about half of all these migrants were living in OECD countries (OECD, 2018[14]). In 2017, more than 5 million people settled permanently in the OECD. In addition, more than 4 million temporary foreign workers were recorded in OECD countries in 2016 in order to fill skills shortages, and more than 3 million international students are enrolled in a higher education establishment in an OECD country. Given the widening demographic imbalances described above, migration flows may further intensify in the coming decades and pose fundamental policy challenges.

With respect to the issues addressed in this chapter, while migrants may help countries with ageing societies to overcome skill shortages, they are also heavily exposed to some key risks. First, in the majority of OECD countries migrants are more concentrated than natives in jobs at high risk of automation. In European OECD countries, for instance, 47% of foreign-born workers are in occupations that primarily involve routine tasks and most exposed to automation (OECD, 2017[18]). Second, migrants are more likely to be in low-skilled jobs, which are frequently of low-quality, despite their relatively high educational level (OECD, 2018[19]).

## 2.2. Job quantity: The ongoing transformations are unlikely to result in *fewer* jobs

Are we headed towards a jobless future? In advanced economies, where the impacts of automation and globalisation have been felt most strongly, this question has generated the most anxiety in the debate on the future of work. Rapid progress in the ability of machines and artificial intelligence (AI) to automate an ever-widening number of job tasks performed by humans has the potential to accelerate the substitution of labour with capital and to induce significant productivity gains, requiring less labour input into the production process. At the same time, rapid globalisation has moved many jobs from advanced economies to countries with lower labour costs. Rapid population ageing could give rise to labour shortages and spur the adoption of new technologies and job automation. Together with digitalisation and globalisation, it could result in a larger number of older workers being displaced from their jobs because of skills obsolescence. For these reasons, some have come to fear that advanced economies may be headed towards a future with fewer jobs (e.g. Frey & Osborne (2017[20]); Brynjolfsson & McAfee (2011[3])).

While it is impossible to know exactly what the future will hold, the OECD's analysis suggests that a substantial contraction of employment is unlikely as a result of digitalisation and globalisation. The forces at play do not just destroy jobs, they also create and transform them. Historically, the net effects of major technological revolutions on employment have been positive, and there are few signs of this trend changing radically in the years to come. Indeed, recent OECD estimates find that only 14% of existing jobs are at risk of complete automation (Nedelkoska and Quintini, 2018[21]) rather than close to 50% as some other research has suggested (Frey and Osborne, 2017[20]).

However, since experts are not in agreement on the speed at which technology may be replacing work in the coming decades, responsible policy making should aim to enhance the resilience of the labour market, effectively preparing for a range of potential futures. Moreover, regardless of how overall job quantity will evolve, significant risks of decreasing job quality and increasing disparities among workers loom large and should be the key focus of policy makers. Finally, while the risk of an overall drop in employment is limited at the aggregate level, certain industries and regions may see net declines in the number of jobs available and policies are required to facilitate labour mobility and respond to regional disparities. These challenges will be the focus of the next two sections.

### 2.2.1. In spite of the continuous transformation of the labour markets, employment has historically been growing

Despite periodic waves of anxiety regarding labour displacement due to technological progress and globalisation, most OECD countries have seen their employment rates – the share of people of working age in employment – on an upward trajectory over past decades with the notable exception of the United States (OECD, 2018[22]) (Figure 2.5). In fact, labour demand rose strongly in line with the increase in labour supply as a result of a greater participation of women and older people. In the United States, the participation rate of women increased from 42% in 1960 to 68% in 2017. Across the OECD, female labour force participation grew by 10 percentage points since the early 1980s (from 54% in 1983 to to 64% in 2017). Countries such Spain and Ireland, where female labour force participation grew from less than 40% to more than 65% over this period, experienced the most striking results in this respect. On the other hand, a number of OECD countries there is still ample scope for further rise in women's participation (in Turkey, for example, fewer than 4 in 10 women participate in the labour market, relative to about 8 in 10 men).

**Figure 2.5. Employment rates have been rising in recent decades**

Employment-to-population ratio, age 15/16-64

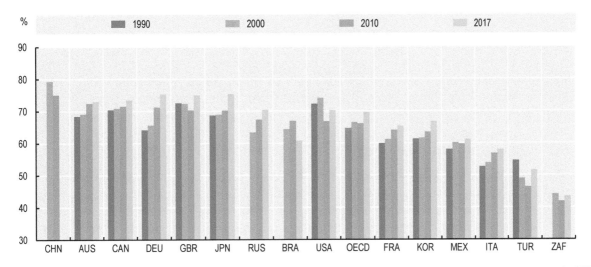

Note: Brazil data for 2000 and 2010 are from 2001 and 2011 respectively. Mexico data for 1990 are from 1991. South Africa data for 2000 are from 2001. The OECD average in the unweighted average of OECD member countries in the year indicated.
Source: OECD Employment Database, www.oecd.org/employment/database.

StatLink 🔗 http://dx.doi.org/10.1787/888933966027

The increase in overall employment has occurred in parallel with rapid technological progress. The previous section offered an overview of the significant rise in ICT, in the use of robots at work, and the increasing deployment of artificial intelligence (AI). Such technologies have been directly responsible for substantial job destruction, sometimes contributing to significant employment decline in certain industries, ranging from textile production to complex electrical equipment manufacturing (OECD, 2017[10]). At the same time, by increasing productivity and raising incomes, they have generated additional demand for goods and services that has given rise to even more jobs (see Box 2.1 for a fuller discussion of the mechanisms through which technological progress destroys and creates jobs). Recent research indicates that the digital revolution has contributed significantly to job creation: 4 out of 10 jobs were created in digitally-intensive industries over the past decade (OECD, 2019[23]).

Technological progress has also contributed to higher female employment. Since women have historically borne the brunt of domestic work, increased productivity in home production (e.g. thanks to washing machines, dishwaters, etc.) is among the factors that may have contributed to the increase in their participation in the labour market. Moreover, in the past, automation has disproportionately impacted jobs typically held by men (e.g. factory workers, construction workers), while jobs in which women are overrepresented (e.g. health workers, service workers) have been buffered to a larger extent (OECD, 2017[24]). This trend, however, is changing. Recent OECD work shows that the expected risk of job displacement due to automation in the coming decades does not show significant differences by gender (OECD, 2017[24]).

Similarly, trade openness has historically gone hand-in-hand with increasing employment, despite the disruptive effects that import competition has had on specific industries. In a review of 14 multi-country econometric studies on the relationship between trade and economic performance, Newfarmer and

Sztajerowska (2012[25]) find no negative impacts of trade on job quantity. On the contrary, greater openness to trade can play an important role in creating better jobs, increasing wages in both rich and poor countries, and improving working conditions. The risk of focusing on aggregate outcomes, however, is to overlook that technological progress and trade openness have not benefited all workers equally and have had strong negative impacts on certain industries and regions. This is a key challenge facing policy makers and represents one of the central issues highlighted in this report.

---

**Box 2.1. How does technology destroy and create jobs? Understanding the forces at play**

As technological progress marches on, celebrity entrepreneurs like Bill Gates and Richard Branson have echoed Keynes' alarms over technological unemployment (Gates, 2017[26]; Branson, 2017[27]). While it is true that workers are displaced by new technologies, there are various channels through which technology may actually boost employment and, historically, net changes in employment have been positive in the long run. Recent OECD work finds that 40% of jobs created between 2005 and 2016 were in digitally intensive industries (OECD, 2019[23]).

A variety of evidence supports concerns that automation will cause job displacement. Recent technological progress, particularly in artificial intelligence (AI), is rapidly extending the range of tasks machines can perform and, according to some analysis, this may put a significant share of jobs at risk of automation (as discussed above). A decline in the labour share of national income across the OECD has also been attributed in part to technological change. Increasing market shares are being captured by firms that employ relatively little labour in their production process (see the discussion on "superstar firms" and "winner-takes-most dynamics" below), and in some countries it is becoming more common for companies to be organised as networks of contractors and sub-contractors who substitute some of their permanent employees (Autor et al., 2017[28]; Weil, 2014[29]). In fields like manufacturing, where a relatively large share of routine jobs are prone to automation, many workers have seen their jobs change radically or disappear altogether (Autor, Dorn and Hanson, 2013[30])

Despite these developments, prominent labour economists point to a range of countervailing forces through which technology creates new jobs. This may help to explain why, despite the displacement effects of technological progress, employment in OECD countries has historically increased on average. This framework is based on recent work by Autor and Salomons (2018[31]), Acemoglu & Restrepo (2018[32]), Acemoglu & Restrepo (2017[33]), Bessen (2017[34]).

First, technological progress can generate more jobs than it destroys within a given industry. Taking a historical perspective that spans the last two centuries, Bessen (2017[34]) clearly shows that a number of industries, including textiles, steel and automotive, experienced strong employment growth during periods of rapid technological progress and productivity growth, which could have been feared to cause a net job loss. A modern example from one specific industry is the technology developed by ride-hailing apps, which can help to improve the matching process between drivers and passengers and thus reduce the cost of ride-hailing services. By making it more convenient and cheaper for customers to use this form of transport, those apps may expand the market, creating additional demand and more jobs than they destroy (though some concerns may exist about the quality of the new jobs, as discussed in the next section). Some evidence in support of this hypothesis exists in the United States (e.g. Hathaway & Muro (2016[35])), but further investigation will be required to prove it conclusively and for a wider range of markets.

Another possibility is that by increasing productivity and reducing prices, certain technologies have a positive impact on employment in industries other than the ones when they are deployed (Autor and Salomons, 2018[31]). By increasing productivity and decreasing consumer prices in one industry, such technologies boost consumer income and increases demand (and employment) in other industries. An example, in this case, are large supermarket chains, which introduced a new business model that generated considerable economies of scale and led to lower prices, allowing consumers to increase their spending in other industries.

Thirdly, automation can lower input costs for downstream industries, leading to output and employment growth in those industries. A clear example, in this case are bulk suppliers of consumer and producer goods which exploit technology that facilitates transport, packaging, inventory management, etc. to lower prices. This helps buyers to save on per-item costs and enables downstream companies to lower their own prices increasing demand for their goods, and allowing them to hire more people.

The three channels above all operate by increasing productivity and generating new income that can be used to expand consumption. Similar examples can be found throughout the economy and span a range of industries. In addition, entirely new jobs may be created as a result of innovation, either to complement machine capabilities within existing occupational categories (e.g. new types of teachers who blend in-class and computer-based learning) or in entirely new fields (e.g. social media managers, internet of things architects, AI experts, user-experience (UX) designers, etc.). This framework is also consistent with recent empirical work by Moretti (2012[36]; 2010[37]) who shows that the creation of jobs in the ICT sector can have large multiplier effects in local labour markets (for each additional job in a high tech company in a local community, five additional jobs outside high-tech are created in the same community).

While the mechanisms above may lead to an overall increase in employment, the importance of public policy to cushion the displacement effects of technology should not be downplayed, particularly because such risks are not distributed evenly across countries, regions, and socio-demographic groups. Rather, the displacement effects of automation have a disproportionate impact on certain industries, regions and disadvantaged groups, while new jobs are often generated elsewhere and may not be accessible to displaced workers. For example, the initial wave of industrial robots primarily affected manufacturing processes, and workers who generally perform routine non-cognitive tasks (Autor, 2015[38]). While new job opportunities primarily arose in the service sector (as discussed below). If current trends continue, the already-high levels of inequality that characterise many OECD countries may worsen, which will, in turn, stunt potential consumption, productivity, and economic growth (OECD, 2015[39]).

Another megatrend that is expected to affect jobs in the coming decades is the transition towards a low-carbon economy. In light of growing concerns about climate change and global warming, a number of countries have committed to strategies for limiting average global temperature increases to 1.5 degrees Celsius above pre-industrial levels (United Nations, 2016[40]). This will result in job losses in industries involving carbon-intensive emissions but create jobs in new forms of greener energy production and in energy conservation. Estimates of total job reallocation, however, suggest that the transition towards a green economy will have relatively low impacts on total job quantity — the difference between job creation and job destruction amounts to about 0.3% of employment in OECD countries and 0.8% in non-OECD countries (Château, J., Bibas and Lanzi, 2018[41]; Botta, 2018[42]; Château, Saint-Martin and Manfredi, 2011[43]).[11] In fact, the overall impact on employment might be positive. The greenness of jobs index (goji) developed using German data, for instance, suggests that Germany's transition to a greener economy has been correlated with higher employment growth and a slight increase in wages (Janser, 2018[44]). Yet, as for the impact of trade openness, the estimated job losses from green policies will be concentrated in specific industries and types of work, possibly fostering inequality (as discussed in the previous section).

### 2.2.2. Is this time different? The recent wave of anxiety regarding automation

While the historical evidence suggests that broad technological unemployment and a large negative impact of globalisation on overall employment are unlikely, the most recent wave of anxiety regarding automation is fuelled by the perception that technological change is faster paced and broader based than in the past, making more jobs automatable than previously thought (Brynjolfsson and McAfee, 2011[3]; Mokyr, Vickers and Ziebarth, 2015[4]). Some authors have even argued that in some cases automation may be excessive, with firm leaders inefficiently over-investing in adopting the latest technologies, and under-investing in preparing for the jobs of tomorrow and helping workers prepare for them, with the consequence of generating negative externalities for society at large (Acemoglu and Restrepo, 2017[45]; Acemoglu and Restrepo, 2018[32]).

In light of these concerns, several authors have attempted to predict what share of jobs may be automated as a result of new technologies permeating the workplace. A widely cited analysis in this field is the one by Frey and Osborne (2017[20]), who estimate that almost half of all jobs (47%) in the United States are at risk of being substituted by computers or algorithms within the next 10 to 20 years. These estimates are constructed using experts' assessment of the probability that different occupations can be automated.[12] Critics of these large estimates argue that occupations as a whole are unlikely to be automated, as not all workers in the same occupation perform the same tasks and hence face the same risk of their jobs being automated (Autor and Handel, 2013[46]). For example, the job of one worker may involve more face-to-face interaction or autonomy than the job of another worker in the same occupation. This may partly explain why the predictions of Frey and Osborne about the pattern and depth of job automation have not yet shown up in the labour market (Manning, forthcoming).[13]

### 2.2.3. The latest OECD results show that around 14% of jobs are at risk of complete automation but many more will be affected by deep changes

An alternative approach to estimate the number of jobs at risk of automation is to directly analyse the task content of individual jobs instead of the average task content within each occupation (Arntz, Gregory and Zierahn, 2016[47]; Nedelkoska and Quintini, 2018[21]).[14] Using this approach, the OECD estimates that the share of jobs at high risk of automation (i.e. those with a probability of being automated of at least 70%) is around 14%, on average, across the OECD (Figure 2.6). The figures for individual countries range from 6% in Norway to 34% in the Slovak Republic. These figures, however, only capture potential job destruction and do not account for the (possibly larger) number of jobs that technology generates (see Box 2.1; and Box 2.2 for a focus of this discussion on emerging economies).

In addition, a large share of existing jobs may change substantially in the way they are carried out. The OECD estimates that 32% of jobs, on average across the OECD, may see a large share of their tasks be automated while entirely new tasks may emerge (Figure 2.6). The analysis also highlights that the risk of automation is higher among low-skilled workers, which may further increase disparities in the labour market (Nedelkoska and Quintini, 2018[21]).

While the risk of automation may not be as high as thought by some, it is essential to recognise that there is considerable uncertainty around these estimates. The consequence of such uncertainty is that responsible policy making should be prepared for a range of possible future outcomes and aim to increase the resilience of the labour market in the face of future transformations. In this regard, providing workers with adequate training opportunities throughout their careers will play a crucial role. According to the OECD Survey of Adult Skills (PIAAC), more than 50% of the adult population, on average in 28 OECD countries, can only carry out the simplest set of computer tasks, such as writing an email and browsing the web, or have no ICT skills at all (OECD, 2016[48]). Existing systems of adult education are often unable to bridge disparities among workers and may, in fact, contribute to widen them, as higher-skilled workers typically receive more training (OECD, 2013[49]). How to make adult learning systems more effective and inclusive is the subject of Chapter 6.

## Figure 2.6. Jobs at risk of automation in OECD countries

Share of jobs which are at a high risk of automation or a risk of significant change (%)

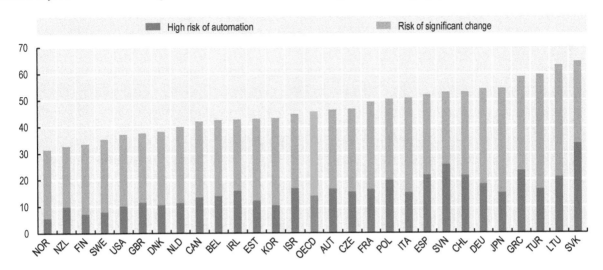

Note: Jobs are at high risk of automation if the likelihood of their job being automated is at least 70%. Jobs at risk of significant change are those with the likelihood of their job being automated estimated at between 50 and 70%. Data for Belgium correspond to Flanders and data for the United Kingdom to England and Northern Ireland.

Source: OECD calculations based on the Survey of Adult Skills (PIAAC) (2012), http://www.oecd.org/skills/piaac/; and Nedelkoska, L. and G. Quintini (2018[21]), "Automation, skills use and training", OECD Social, Employment and Migration Working Papers, No. 202, https://doi.org/10.1787/2e2f4eea-en.

StatLink 🔗 http://dx.doi.org/10.1787/888933966046

---

### Box 2.2. Technological unemployment in emerging economies: slow change but large risks looming on the horizon

The literature on the impact of automation on jobs is largely focused on advanced economies. Emerging economies, however, have very different initial conditions, including a different occupational mix, higher costs of information and communication technologies (ICT) capital, and greater skills shortages (Maloney and Molina, 2016[50]). The key question is whether, in such a context, the job opportunities created by new technologies will outweigh the loss of manufacturing jobs due to automation.

Based on their current stage of development, emerging economies face a higher predicted risk of automation. As economies develop, the industry mix of employment follows a predictable path, shifting labour from low-productivity activities, often in agriculture, to higher-productivity activities, mostly in the manufacturing and in the service sectors. In most emerging economies, agriculture and low value-added industries still make up a large share of employment. Hence, estimates based on occupations (The World Bank, 2016[51]) and more recent ones based on tasks (Nedelkoska and Quintini, 2018[21]) or work activities (McKinsey Global Institute, 2017[52])[15] show that emerging economies face a higher risk of automation than more advanced ones. However, the picture is mixed and varies by income level, with countries like China, the Russian Federation, Turkey and Mexico facing a higher proportion of jobs that are potentially at risk of automation.

Nevertheless, while many jobs are "technically automatable", automation may not be yet economically attractive in many emerging economies. As many emerging economies still have a productive structure biased towards small and medium-sized enterprises (SMEs), the resources that are necessary for costly investments in advanced technology are out of reach for most entrepreneurs. Furthermore, the incentive to innovate is dampened by skills shortages and by the relative abundance of cheap unskilled labour in young and rapidly expanding populations.

**Figure 2.7. The potential cost savings from using robots are significant in some emerging economies**

Projected labour-cost savings from adoption of advanced industrial robots (%, 2025)

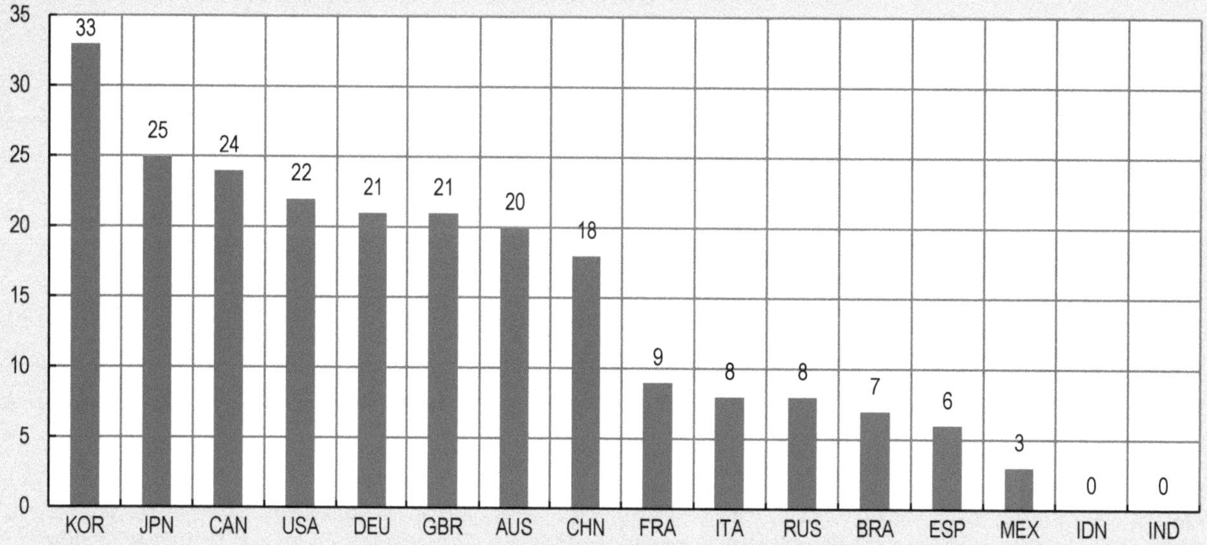

Source: The Boston Consulting Group (2015[53]), *The Shifting Economics of Global Manufacturing: How a Takeoff in Advanced Robotics Will Power the Next Productivity Surge*, https://www.slideshare.net/TheBostonConsultingGroup/robotics-in-manufacturing.

StatLink 🔗 http://dx.doi.org/10.1787/888933966065

The potential disruptions, however, could be significant. As the cost of industrial robots continues to decline and labour costs increase, the cost savings of using technology to replace labour are starting to become significant also in emerging economies. While the Boston Consulting Group predicts that countries with very low labour costs and expanding young workforces like India and Indonesia will not benefit from replacing humans with robots in the near future, such savings will amount to more than 5% in countries like the Russian Federation and Brazil, reaching up to 18% in China by 2025 (Figure 2.7). In addition, re-shoring of production to advanced economies may contribute to job losses in emerging markets. Although the evidence on re-shoring is still limited and mixed, some signs of this process are already visible, as a number of manufactures are choosing to relocate their production nearer their domestic markets (De Backer et al., 2016[54]). Increasing labour costs and the falling cost of technology may continue to fuel this process, potentially leading some emerging countries to experience premature deindustrialisation, which may leave them in a middle-income trap (Rodrik, 2016[55]). Depending on their occupational and industrial makeup (and on their stage of development), different countries will be impacted at different points in time. Policy makers in emerging economies should start preparing well in advance. Given the lack of adequate safety nets and retraining systems, the effects on workers' welfare may be significant and foster increased social tensions.

Source: Alonso-Soto (forthcoming[56]), *Technology and the future of work in emerging economies: What is different?*

### 2.2.4. The mere existence of a new technology does not imply that it will become pervasive and replace humans at work

An important caveat that needs to be attached to any estimate on the risk of job loss due to automation is that technological diffusion depends on a host of factors that may speed it up or slow it down. Failing to recognise the impact of these different forces may mean falling prey to *technological determinism*, the idea that technology determines the development of society, its labour market, social structure, and cultural values. While this is certainly true to some extent, other factors, including active policy making and social preferences, play a crucial role. The fact that a technology exists does not necessarily imply that it will spread and change the way people live, and more specifically, the way people work. In fact, existing evidence reveals that the spread of technology is highly heterogeneous across countries, industries, and firms. Constraints to broader technology diffusion may help explaining why technological progress has not translated into productivity gains in recent decades (OECD, 2018[57]).

A number of factors may favour or hinder the spread of different technologies. Above all, market forces driving the relative prices of capital and labour play an important role in determining the profitability of investing in labour-replacing technologies. Countries with relatively low labour costs, for instance, have witnessed a slower process of automation and, also for that reason, do not display a similar pattern of job polarisation as higher industrialised countries (OECD, 2017[10]).

Institutional norms and regulations – for example, product and labour market regulations as well as safety, medical and ethical standards – may prevent certain technologies from becoming prominent in certain countries. Recent OECD evidence shows that certain labour market institutions, including the rate of unionisation and employment protection legislation (EPL), can mediate the effects of technology and globalisation on job polarisation – the fall in the share of middle-skilled jobs relative to low- and, most prominently, high-skilled jobs (OECD, 2017[10]).[16]

Finally, consumer and societal preferences, as well as ethical norms, will play a crucial role in determining the diffusion of labour-replacing technology. In this regard, an interesting example comes from Eurobarometer data on people's preferences regarding the deployment of robots in different industries. While the majority of respondents would be happy for robots to be used in areas such as manufacturing and space exploration, the views are much more negative regarding the use of robots in health care and education.

These countervailing trends of market forces, institutional frameworks, and consumer preferences argue against technological determinism: the mere existence of a technology does not imply that it will necessarily become pervasive nor that it will be adopted to replace humans at work (rather than to complement them).

### 2.2.5. While the number of employed workers may not have fallen, an increasing number of them are under-employed

While overall employment might not be negatively affected by the megatrends, there has been a rise in under-employment.[17] Much like employment, changes in under-employment are generally cyclical. However, the gradual post-industrial growth of industries facing volatile demand even over the very short term (such as accommodation and food services) has exposed more workers to the risk of fewer and more variable hours (see Chapter 3). There is some evidence that the global financial crisis has exacerbated this shift. Under-employment rose sharply in many countries hit hard by the crisis, and has been slow to return to pre-crisis levels.

The risk of under-employment has increased for all workers in recent times, but, on average across the OECD, the increase has been larger for the young and those with low or medium education (Chapter 3). Across countries, women remain at a much higher risk of under-employment than men, but men – and in particular those with less than tertiary education – have seen significant increases in the probability of being under-employed. Whereas trends in under-employment among women have varied across countries, men have experienced increases in almost all of the countries examined.

## 2.3. Job quality: A future of better opportunities or increased risks for workers?

Technological progress can improve job quality by increasing productivity and earnings, reducing exposure to dangerous, unhealthy and tedious tasks, as well as by granting many workers greater flexibility, autonomy, and work-life balance. New technology may also allow greater use of high-performance work practices that are typically associated with greater job satisfaction. In addition, globalisation and international trade can help "export" better working conditions through greater integration in global value chains (GVCs).

However, the greater job instability that often characterises new, non-standard forms of employment (including, but not exclusively, in the so-called "gig economy" – see Box 2.3) may result in a loss of well-being for workers in the absence of policies which guarantee adequate rights and protections for these workers (see Chapter 4). This is an important concern in countries where non-standard forms of work are proliferating and where firms increasingly rely on networks of contractors and sub-contractors, rather than on their permanent workforce, to perform many functions (giving rise to the definition of the "fissured workplace").[18, 19]

---

### Box 2.3. What are new forms of work?

"Non-standard" employment is an umbrella term, which typically covers all temporary, part-time and self-employment arrangements, i.e. everything deviating from the "standard" of full-time, open-ended employment with a single employer – see e.g. OECD (2014[58]).

However, people generally have something more specific in mind when they talk about "new forms of employment" and the resulting challenges in the context of the future of work. Often, what falls in the category of "new forms of employment" are situations in which workers are less well covered than standard employees by existing labour market regulations and social protection programmes – partly because they have developed at the fringes of existing legislation. For example, this tends to exclude "traditional" part-time and temporary work because the rights and benefits for these forms of employment are now broadly in line with those of full-time and permanent workers. Traditional forms of self-employment may also not be seen as a "new" form of employment because it is accepted that there is an element of entrepreneurial risk – i.e. in return for potentially high rewards, there is a greater element of risk that does not need to be insured against by society.

In contrast, "new" forms of work is often used to refer to: platform work (i.e. transactions mediated by an app or a website which matches customers with workers who provide services); temporary contracts of very short duration; contracts with no guaranteed and/or unpredictable working hours (on-call and zero-hours work); and own-account work more generally (i.e. self-employed workers with no employees) – see Chapter 4.

---

Technology and globalisation may also have an adverse impact on working conditions. By facilitating closer monitoring of workers, new technologies may reduce workers' autonomy and increase the risk of job strain. Such adverse impacts may be further worsened by import competition, which may increase the risk of a "race to the bottom" in terms of labour standards and job quality, counteracting the positive effects of international trade on job quality mentioned above.[20] Overall, the net impact of globalisation on job-quality worldwide is difficult to identify precisely and may differ across countries.

This section discusses the different forces that are likely to affect the quality of jobs in the future of work. In doing so, it connects with the broader OECD agenda on job quality, which resulted in the release of the OECD Job Quality framework (OECD, 2014[58]). It shows that while the megatrends can potentially have positive impacts on key dimensions of job quality, these gains have not been uniform across the workforce, especially in non-standard jobs.

### 2.3.1. Wages have been stagnating for a large share of the population over the past decade

Both trade openness and technological progress have contributed to increase workers' earnings and living standards, on average. However, for large segments of the labour force, earnings in recent years have been stagnating despite a recovery in employment after the global economic and financial crisis (OECD, 2018[22]). In OECD countries, annual growth in nominal hourly wages dropped from 4.8% on average in the pre-crisis period to 2.1% in recent years. Real wage growth decreased by 1 percentage point over the same period. Salary dynamics in low-pay jobs have been a key driver of the overall decline in wage growth. In particular, there has been a significant worsening in average earnings of part-time jobs relative to those of full-time jobs, which is associated with the rise of involuntary part-time employment in a number of countries, discussed below.

### 2.3.2. Jobs have become less stable

Another key dimension of job quality is labour market security, which is closely linked to job stability. Recent OECD work shows that over the past two decades job stability has decreased on average, although with considerable differences across countries – as discussed in Chapter 3 and in Falco, Green and MacDonald (forthcoming[59]). The evidence in this respect is nuanced, but clear. Average job tenure, a direct indicator of job stability, measuring the amount of time spent in one's current job, has increased on average. This is, however, the result of an ageing population, as a larger share of older workers in the workforce is mechanically associated with higher average tenure-levels. Once ageing is accounted for, job stability has decreased in the majority of OECD countries. The trend is particularly evident among less educated workers and it is not exclusively concentrated among youth. Prime-age and older workers with lower levels of education have also experienced increased instability in their jobs. Chapter 3 discusses this trend in detail and investigates whether decreased job stability can be ascribed to increased risks for workers or better opportunities for mobility and career progression.

### 2.3.3. The impacts of globalisation on job quality are mixed

Turning to the link between trade and job quality, a number of competing factors are at play. On the one hand, trade openness may be conducive to higher earnings. Indeed, there is evidence that export-driven industries tend to pay higher wages.[21] On the other hand, with regard to job security, greater openness to trade and integration in GVCs may lower it by increasing the risk of job displacement due to offshoring or outsourcing (Acemoglu and Autor, 2010[60]; OECD, 2017[10]). For example, when Chinese factories began undercutting production in the United States, workers in the affected industries faced a higher risk of job loss (Autor, Dorn and Hanson, 2013[30]), resulting in higher job insecurity and, therefore, lower overall job quality.

The megatrends can also impact job quality by directly influencing working conditions and the quality of the working environment. With regard to trade, the main risk is that firms use GVCs to jettison workers in countries with high labour standards and move production to areas where labour standards are lower. For example, if welders in Germany see their jobs go to emerging economies with lower health and safety standards, global job quality may fall. Such concerns find some support in the literature, but the existing evidence is still too limited to draw firm conclusions.[22] On the other hand, globalisation and international trade can help "export" better working conditions, especially as multinational companies face increasing consumer pressure and closer international scrutiny of their work environment (OECD, 2008[61]). If the latter effect could be strengthened, international trade could effectively widen global access to good jobs. The OECD Guidelines for Multinational

Enterprises and the OECD Due Diligence Guidance for Responsible Business Conduct are prime examples of instruments aimed at improving labour standards through global supply chains (OECD, 2011[62]; 2018[63]).

### 2.3.4. Technological progress has historically helped improve working conditions

Technological progress has considerable potential to improve working conditions. Across a number of industries, tasks have been automated that formerly required hard physical labour, were often performed in strenuous or even dangerous conditions, and could increase stress and alienation.

One clear illustration of how onerous tasks may disappear is the transformation of agriculture. Between 1991 and 2017, the share of global employment in this sector fell from 43.3% to 26.5% (ILO, 2018[64]), thanks to massive diffusion of productivity-enhancing technologies, ranging from tractors and combine harvesters to more recent innovations such as robo-pickers of fruits and vegetables (ILO, 2018[65]). Many agricultural jobs were of very low quality, involving physically onerous and repetitive tasks, sometimes combined with abusive working conditions (ILO, 2015[66]) and little access to social protection, training opportunities and collective representation. Similarly, technology currently helps workers to perform some of the most dangerous and hazardous tasks in the manufacturing and construction sectors. This welcome development directly contributes to improving working conditions and safety at work.

### 2.3.5. But greater use of technology can also have a negative impact on job quality in certain occupations

In some cases, however, technology in the workplace can reduce job quality. For instance, greater use of computers and digital technologies to standardise and monitor tasks may limit workers' autonomy and independence, two key markers of high-quality employment (Weil, 2014[29]; OECD, 2014[58]), but the literature is not unanimous in finding evidence of these negative aspects. Menon et al. (2018[67]), for example, find evidence of a positive effect of computer use on autonomy in Europe. Some authors have been discussing new forms of "digital Taylorism" in which employees enjoy very limited control over their work – for a survey, see Gallie (2013[68]). Many cases of such developments exist throughout the economy, for example in industries like retail and logistics. Employees who work in the warehouses of large logistics companies can be micro-managed (e.g. receiving instructions via headphones) and their productivity can be closely monitored, raising pressure and stress. Looking ahead, some firms are assessing the possibility of introducing wearable devices that would allow close monitoring of workers' movements on the company floor. Such tight control standards have generated much controversy as they can directly harm job quality.[23]

Perverse effects of technology on autonomy and discretion are not limited to low-skilled workers. Recent studies find that interconnected devices afford professionals greater control over the pace and organisation of their work, but also create the expectation of constant availability by colleagues and clients, reducing discretion (Mazmanian, Orlikowski and Yates, 2013[69]). Some countries have reacted against these changes. France, for instance, recently passed a law that requires companies with more than 50 employees to grant workers the "right to disconnect" (by not expecting them to respond to emails) outside of regular working hours (de Guigné, 2016[70]).[24] At the same time, some executives have embraced new technologies for enabling "work-life integration" and improved flexibility (Lebowitz, 2018[71]). However, the literature is not unanimous in highlighting the negative aspects of technology on working conditions.

### 2.3.6. Platform work: greater flexibility vs digital Taylorism

The rise of platform work has thrown a spotlight on the impact of technological progress on job quality. Platform work encompasses a broad range of activities, which have in common the use of online platforms to connect the demand and supply of particular services.[25] The services provided by digital labour platforms can be broadly distinguished as services performed digitally (i.e. micro tasks, clerical and data entry, etc.)

or services performed on-location (i.e. transport, delivery, housekeeping, etc.), as outlined in a recent report by the Joint Research Centre of the European Commission (Biagi et al., 2018[72]). In some cases, the function of the platform goes beyond its mediating role and includes providing workers with an online environment and with the necessary tools to conduct their work.

One of the positive aspects of platform work is the increased efficiency of the matching process, which may help to alleviate problems such as frictional unemployment and skills mismatches. In many OECD countries, unemployment coexists with firms recurrently complaining about not being able to find workers to fill vacancies. Platforms can help employers find workers for tasks that their existing employees cannot perform (Manyika et al., 2015[73]). Another positive aspect of platform work, often cited by workers, is greater flexibility. In the EU Collaborative Economy and Employment (COLLEEM) survey, flexibility was the most cited motivation for engaging in platform work (Biagi et al., 2018[72]). In countries with a high incidence of informal employment, platform work can represent a route to formalisation (Box 2.4).

However, work through platforms can sometimes impose severe limitations to workers' autonomy, which may have negative impacts on their job quality and well-being. While platform workers are often classified as self-employed and can in principle choose their own hours, demand may de facto be highly concentrated in certain parts of the day. Many workers cannot set their own pay rate, which is imposed by the platform, and face restrictions over other aspects of their work organisation, including the use of uniforms and stringent instructions regarding the way the work is carried out. Finally, platform work allows for close monitoring and levels of micro-management that would be difficult to attain in the absence of the new technologies (but which are by no means exclusive to platform work, as exemplified by the case of retail and logistics discussed above). For instance, employers can use monitoring software by companies like Crossover, which takes periodic photos through the user's webcam to verify freelancer productivity (Solon, 2017[74]). And workers who do not perform well can be automatically excluded (see also Chapter 4).

While some of these factors may generate greater efficiency and productivity, benefiting consumers (chiefly through lower prices, as well as higher service quality and availability), the result is that some if not much platform work may in fact be far from flexible and may not provide workers with the autonomy and discretion they might wish for.

The potential downsides of certain types of platform work are not limited to the risk of job strain and poor working conditions but also include the risk of low (and uncertain) earnings. Some platforms, for instance, operate globally across very different labour markets. This might induce a race to the bottom in workers' pay.[26] Moreover, since platform workers are frequently classified as self-employed, they also face challenges with regard to the adequacy of social protection, collective representation, and employment protection. These problems are not unique to platform work and they may apply to a different degree to many non-standard workers (i.e. those with contracts that fall outside the "standard" of full-time permanent employment). As such, they will be discussed below. While the jury is still out on the potential advantages and drawbacks of platform work, it is important to underscore that the risks for job quality are not inevitable and can be overcome through careful policy action.

### 2.3.7. Work through platforms is still a limited phenomenon

How big is employment in the platform economy? Existing evidence in this respect is still scant and imprecise, largely because standard labour force surveys do not capture the phenomenon effectively. The available data, however, indicates that this segment of the labour market is still very small.

A recent survey of 14 European countries indicates that less than 2% of the entire labour force, on average, mentions platform work as their primary activity (Biagi et al., 2018[72]). Furthermore, this is likely to be an overestimate due to the features of the survey design, which is based on an online tool that tends to over-represent the most technologically savvy part of the population. Most of the other existing studies covering a range of countries have typically produced estimates that vary between 0.5% and 3% of the labour force

– see OECD (2018[6]) for a survey of the literature). The most recent evidence from the United States, for example, indicates that platform workers accounted for 1% of total employment in May 2017 (BLS, 2018[75]).

---

**Box 2.4. New forms of work in emerging economies: A gateway to formalisation?**

Work through digital platforms is becoming increasingly important in emerging economies. Well-known international platforms such as Uber, Cabify, and Airbnb are becoming more established in the emerging world. For example, Uber's second largest market is Brazil and there were nearly 50 000 registered drivers and two million active users in Chile by 2017 (African Development Bank Group et al., 2018[76]). In addition, there is a growing number of active local companies in these markets (Sundararajan, 2017[77]).

To date, the debate surrounding platform work has largely focused on more advanced economies, where the emergence of platforms has sparked concerns about precarisation of labour, challenges for social protection and, more generally, for job quality (see Section 2.3.6).

Similar concerns apply in emerging economies, but one additional element plays an important role in those countries: the high incidence of informal employment (OECD, 2015[78]). In such a context, the platform economy may constitute an opportunity for many workers to formalise, since it can reduce the costs of formalisation and improve monitoring of economic activity through the digitalisation of transactions.

A good example of the potential benefits of platform work for formalisation is from Indonesia, a country where almost 60% of the workforce is working in the informal sector (OECD, 2015[78]) and where at least a third of formal jobs are of poor quality (Fanggidae, Sagala and Ningrum, 2016[79]). In a recent study, Fanggidae, Sagala and Ningrum (2016[79]) interviewed 205 drivers of "*ojek*" (motorcycle taxis) active on one of the rental platforms available in Jakarta (mainly "GoJek" and "Grab Bike"). Although limited in time and space, the results of the study show that platform work is not always synonymous with worse working conditions. Notably, the study highlights the role played by the platforms in facilitating access to social protection for workers. For example, GoJek offers help to its drivers to subscribe to the government health insurance program, while at Grab Bike workers are automatically enrolled in the government's professional insurance programme.

While this is only one example and additional research in this area is needed, it clearly highlights that by reducing the costs of formalisation, platforms can be an important bridge towards formality. Policy makers could go further and mandate platforms to collect personal income taxes and social security contributions on behalf of the workers (OECD, 2019[80]).

Of course, platform work is not a panacea for the problem of informality, if anything because the sector is still very small. Curbing informality in emerging economies requires a comprehensive three-pronged approach that not only aims to reduce the costs of formalisation, but also increase it perceived benefits (e.g. by improving service delivery, and linking social security contributions to the benefits received) and improves enforcement mechanisms (see OECD (2015[78]) for a detailed discussion).

Source: Alonso-Soto (forthcoming[56]), *Technology and the future of work in emerging economies: What is different?*

---

Figure 2.8. The rapid growth of online work has recently slowed down

Index time series (May 2016 = 100; monthly average) of new vacancies posted on the five largest English-language online labour platforms

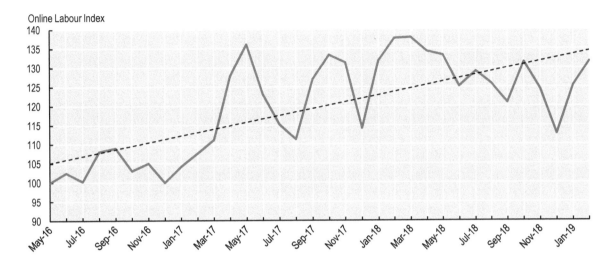

Source: http://ilabour.oii.ox.ac.uk/online-labour-index/. For further details, see Kässi, O. and V. Lehdonvirta (2016[81]), "Online Labour Index: Measuring the Online Gig Economy for Policy and Research", Munich Personal RePEc Archive.

StatLink ᵐᵍᵖ http://dx.doi.org/10.1787/888933966084

Also, while the platform economy may have grown fast, there are signs that its growth may already have started to slow down. Data produced by the Oxford Internet Institute provides an indication of the growing importance of online work (one type of platform work which is carried out entirely online). This Online Labour Index (OLI) is based on real-time data from five of the world's largest English-language online labour platforms (Kässi and Lehdonvirta, 2016[81]). Despite its limitations and its focus on one particular kind of platform work, the indicator provides an indication of recent trends. Between May 2016 and May 2017 platform work grew by over a third. Since then, however, there was strong volatility and a flattening of the long-term trend (Figure 2.8).

Most vacancies are posted from OECD countries, particularly in the United States, but the majority of workers are based in non-OECD countries, with India being a particularly important player (OECD, 2018[82]). This global dimension of platform work and the risk of a race to the bottom in terms of labour standards for certain segments of this market indicate that coordinated action among countries is required.

### 2.3.8. More generally, non-standard work constitutes an important policy concern

The recent interest in the (still small) platform economy risks detracting from a more general and relevant issue: the significant (and in some countries growing) incidence of non-standard work more generally, and its potentially negative implications for job quality. Non-standard forms of employment encompass all forms of work that deviate from the "standard" of full-time, open-ended contracts with a single employer (see Box 2.3 for a detailed explanation). They include, therefore, workers with temporary jobs, part-time contracts, and those who are self-employed. Non-standard jobs are not necessarily of lower quality than standard jobs. The work of a high-skilled professional, for instance, may be non-standard since it falls into the category of self-employment, but might be characterised by high and stable earnings, as well as by good working conditions. Across countries, however, an association exists between many forms of non-standard work and poorer job quality, in the form of lower wages, less employment protection, reduced (or no) access to employer and social benefits, greater exposure to occupational safety and health risks, lower investments in lifelong learning, and low bargaining power of workers – e.g. OECD (2014[58]). For this reason, monitoring trends in non-standard work becomes crucial to assess developments in job quality. In the majority of OECD countries, non-standard work encompasses a significant share of the labour force (over a third), but recent trends have not been uniform.

### 2.3.9. Temporary employment has risen in one half of OECD countries, with a very marked upward trend in some of them

In around half of OECD countries, there has been a long-term upward trend in temporary employment. The growth of fixed-term employment has been particularly marked in countries like France, Italy, Luxembourg, the Netherlands, Poland, Portugal, the Slovak Republic, and Spain prior to the crisis (Figure 2.9). In the countries where the share of fixed-term contracts has fallen, the reduction has typically been small (with the exception of Greece, Japan, and Turkey). The share of contracts of very short duration (zero to three months) in fixed-term employment, a category that often concerns policy makers, shows a somewhat heterogeneous trend. In just over half of OECD countries, this share has increased. Yet, with the exception of the Baltic countries and Belgium, in the countries where it decreased, that trend was essentially due to the expansion of fixed-term contracts of longer duration.[27] Finally, employment through temporary work agency (TWA) has grown in most OECD countries.[28] Since the expansion of fixed-term employment has occurred in several countries prior to the 2000s, it is important to remark that it may only be partly attributable to the megatrends analysed in this report, and may in fact be the result of policy choices that facilitated the diffusion of temporary contracts.

**Figure 2.9. Temporary employment has risen in one half of OECD countries**

Fixed-term employment as a share of dependent employment, all ages

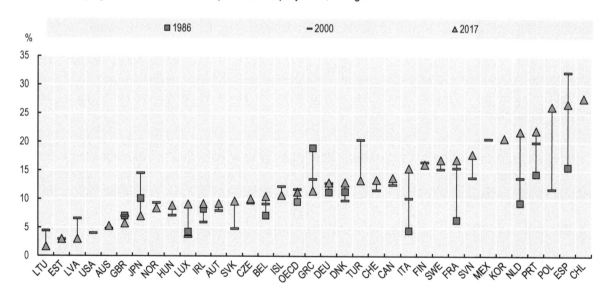

Note: Data are for 1987 instead of 1986 for the Netherlands and Spain; 2001 instead of 2000 for Australia, Poland and the United States.
Source: OECD Employment Database, www.oecd.org/employment/database.

StatLink ꝏꜱ⯑ http://dx.doi.org/10.1787/888933966103

### 2.3.10. Part-time has grown and it is increasingly involuntary

Part-time employment has risen in most OECD countries over the past few decades, with a few notable exceptions including Iceland, Poland and Sweden (Figure 2.10). This is often viewed positively, especially since the rise in part-time employment has been associated with more women entering the labour market, and it has allowed individuals to find a better work-life balance. For some workers, however, part-time employment is involuntary and reflects the difficulty to find full-time jobs. Chapter 3 offers a discussion of this phenomenon within a broader analysis of under-employment.

The share of involuntary part-time in total part-time dependent employment has risen in two thirds of OECD countries for which data are available, although there have been declines in countries like Belgium, Poland and in Germany (since 2010). While in some countries this increase in involuntary part-time will have been partly crisis-related (e.g. Portugal, Spain, Italy and Greece), in most countries one can observe a longer-term trend increase.[29]

Figure 2.10. Part-time employment has generally increased

Part-time employment as a share of dependent employment, all ages

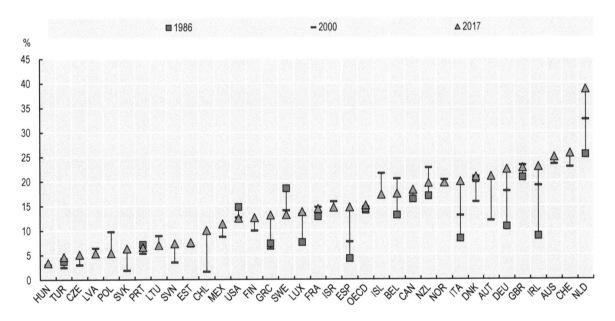

Note: Part-time employment is defined using a common cut-off of 30 hours per week usually worked in the main job. Data are for 1988 (instead of 1986) for Turkey; 1985 (instead of 1986) for Sweden, Spain and the Netherlands; and 2001 (instead of 2000) for Australia.
Source: OECD Employment Database, www.oecd.org/employment/database.

StatLink ⧉ http://dx.doi.org/10.1787/888933966122

### 2.3.11. Short part-time and on-call labour have risen in many countries

In around one-half of OECD countries with available data, there has also been a rise in "short part-time" (i.e. individuals working 20 hours per week or less) (Figure 2.11).[30] The share of short part-time is particularly high in the Netherlands (21% of dependent employment), Denmark (15%), Switzerland (13%) and Australia (13%). In some countries, there has been a fall in the share of short part-time, including Australia, Latvia, Poland, the United Kingdom, and the United States. When interpreting these trends, one should bear in mind that in some countries the rise of short part-time may be an enabling factor for some workers seeking greater flexibility (e.g. to cope with family responsibilities, combine work and study, etc.). The available data do not allow a clear distinction between these different interpretations.

This rise might be partly driven by increases in very atypical contracts (on-call and zero-hour work), but the evidence in this respect is mixed.[31] Many countries have special forms of atypical part-time contracts which either involve very short part-time hours or no established minimum hours at all – such as "on-call" work and "zero-hour" contracts (Messenger and Wallot, 2015[83]) – and several of these have experienced rapid growth in recent years. In Australia, one in four workers is a casual worker, and over half of casual employees report having no guaranteed hours (Campbell, 2018[84]). In Italy, there were around 295 000 workers employed by means of an "on call" contract in 2016 (INPS, 2017[85]).[32] In the Netherlands, according to a study commissioned by the ILO, on-call work is the fastest-growing type of flexible work arrangement. In 2016, there were 551 000 on-call workers in the Netherlands, making up about 8% of the workforce (Burri, Heeger-Hertter and Rossetti, 2018[86]).[33] In the United Kingdom, nearly 3% of people in employment (about 900 000 people) said that they were on a zero-hour contract at the end of 2016.[34] This figure represents a 29% increase over that of 2014 (ONS, 2017[87]; Adams and Prassl, 2018[88]).[35] In the Republic of Ireland, a 2015 study roughly approximates the employed population reporting variable hours at 5.3% – acknowledging that this population may include permanent and temporary workers whose hours vary (O'Sullivan et al., 2016[89]).[36]

**Figure 2.11. Short part-time is on the rise in many countries**

Short part-time employment as a share of dependent employment, all ages

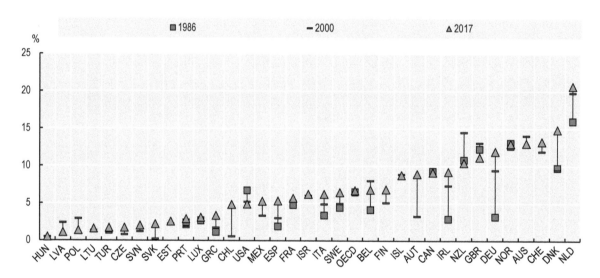

Note: Data are for 1987 instead of 1986 for Spain, Sweden and the Netherlands; 1989 instead of 1986 for Norway; and 2001 instead of 2000 for Australia. Short part-time is defined as usually working 1-19 hours per week.
Source: OECD Employment Database, www.oecd.org/employment/database.

StatLink http://dx.doi.org/10.1787/888933966141

### 2.3.12. Self-employment is on a long-term downward trend, with some notable exceptions

There has been a long-term decline in self-employment as a share of total employment across the OECD over the past four decades, which can be observed in the majority of countries (Figure 2.12). This may be surprising and in contrast with the perception that new technologies and work models ought to facilitate the rise of independent work. Much of this trend, however, is related to the long-term decline in the agricultural sector, which predominantly occurred during the earlier part of the period. Since 2000, the incidence of self-employment has remained stable in the majority of countries.

Yet in some countries, there have been increases in self-employment, particularly in recent years. These countries include the Netherlands, the Slovak Republic and the United Kingdom.[37] On the one hand, growing self-employment could be viewed as a sign of booming entrepreneurship. On the other hand, it can be linked to more precarious working conditions that may reduce job quality. This risk is particularly high for the self-employed without employees (also known as own-account workers or solo self-employed). There is no clear trend across OECD countries in the share of own-account workers in total employment in recent decades, but there have been substantial increases in countries like the Netherlands, the Czech Republic, the Slovak Republic and the United Kingdom (OECD, 2018[6]).

**Figure 2.12. Self-employment is on a long-term downward trajectory**

Self-employment as a share of total employment, all ages

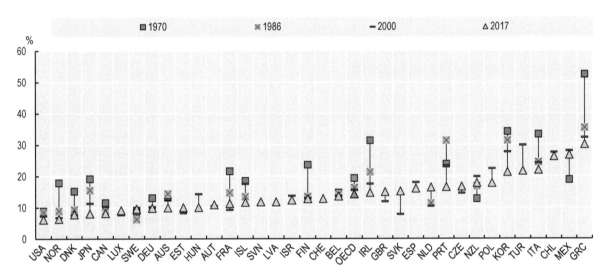

Note: Data are for 1971 instead of 1970 for New Zealand and Greece; 2003 instead of 2000 for Luxembourg; and 2015 instead of 2017 for Latvia.
Source: OECD Employment Database, www.oecd.org/employment/database.

StatLink http://dx.doi.org/10.1787/888933966160

### 2.3.13. Dependent self-employment and false self-employment are becoming more common

Own-account work is a particular challenge in cases where individuals are financially dependent on a single employer. These are the so-called economically "dependent" self-employed who earn most of their income from just one client. The reason these are a group of interest to policy makers is that they tend to be in a vulnerable position vis-à-vis their client and may need special protections put in place (especially since they will not have access to the usual benefits and protections that employees do).[38] Available data from the European Working Conditions Survey show that in around two thirds of countries, dependent self-employment rose between 2010 and 2015 (OECD, 2018[6]).

A closely related concept to dependent self-employment is that of false self-employment. This is a situation where a worker is not only financially dependent on one or several clients, but he/she is also in a situation of subordination with no or limited control over the work (e.g. in the form of mandated working hours, restrictions to the way work is carried out, the place of work, etc.). In other words, despite the worker is classified as self-employed by the parties (e.g. in a written contract between employers and workers), the characteristics of their relationship closely mirror those of an employment relationship (see Chapter 4). Obtaining an internationally comparable measure of false self-employment presents clear challenges due to differing statistical proxies and data availability. Despite the potential limitations, however, the evidence from the European Working Conditions Survey suggests that false self-employment has increased in the majority of EU countries between 2010 and 2015 (OECD, 2018[6]).[39]

### 2.3.14. While some forms of employment may be new, the key policy challenges are as old as non-standard work itself

In light of the evidence presented in this section, non-standard forms of work (especially very atypical ones such as on-call work), and low-quality work more generally, require further policy action. The objective, however, should not be to regulate them out of existence or to impose overly stringent regulation, since a diversity in employment contracts remains an important tool to allow firms to adapt to changing market conditions and to give workers greater flexibility in managing their work-life balance. The goal of policy action should be primarily to avoid abuse and to increase the quality of non-standard jobs.

### 2.3.15. The line between salaried work and self-employment is increasingly blurred, posing a key challenge for regulators

One issue which has received considerable public, policy and legal attention in recent years is the correct classification of workers who appear to fall somewhere in the grey zone between dependent and self-employment. Workers in the platform economy are a classic example of the potential ambiguity that may give rise to controversy. Platform workers are typically classified as own-account workers. However, like employees, they often have limited control over their work (for instance, in some cases they cannot fix prices, they are required to wear uniforms, they cannot choose the order of their tasks, etc.). The problem, however, is not limited to the platform economy – many hairdressers, plumbers, and gardeners have faced similar challenges in the past. In some cases, the issue may be that these workers are falsely classified as self-employed in order to avoid regulation, or to access preferential tax treatment. But this is not always the case. In many instances, employer-worker relationships are genuinely difficult to classify and may require a revision of the legislation and, in particular, of what it means to be "an employee", "self-employed" and/or "an employer". Even where individuals are correctly classified and genuinely self-employed, there may be a case for government intervention to improve their labour market outcomes, for example because these workers find themselves in a situation of monopsony (and are price takers) or are in a situation of economic dependency. Some countries have address this challenge by giving subgroups of these individuals access to some, though usually not all, of the rights and protections granted to employees (advantages and disadvantages of different approaches are discussed in Chapter 4). Aside from the need to resolve potential ambiguities in classification, governments should consider policy avenues to give non-standard workers greater access to collective representation, better training opportunities, and stronger social security, as well as adequate employment protection (as discussed in Chapters 4 to 7).

## 2.4. Inclusiveness: Preventing a more unequal future of work

The ongoing labour market transformations do not affect all workers equally. Some people have greatly benefited from the new opportunities arising in a changing world of work. Many others have seen their jobs disrupted or destroyed by those forces. As a result, in the absence of adequate support, they have experienced significant losses of well-being. Allowing all workers to benefit from future opportunities represents the single most important challenge that policy makers face. Failing to attain this objective is likely to result in deeper social cleavages, which may foster tensions, jeopardise well-being, and generate political upheavals.

### 2.4.1. While overall employment has been growing, some industries have dramatically declined

While overall employment has continued to grow in the face of major structural transformations, as documented above, entire sectors of the economy have declined as a result of the megatrends, leading to considerable job losses and to major disruption in the lives of many workers. Recent work by the OECD documents trends in employment across broad economic industries (OECD, 2017[10]). It shows a clear imbalance: over the past two decades, with new employment predominantly created in service industries, while manufacturing has typically shrunk (Figure 2.13). This trend has contributed to increase disparities between different groups of workers, as it has been partly responsible for the polarisation of the labour market.[40]

The transition towards a low-carbon economy is exacerbating some of these trends. Primary industries, such as mining, and high-emission industries in manufacturing are the ones that will be most negatively affected by the transition. The estimated impacts of a relatively moderate carbon tax policy is the elimination of 8% of employment related to fossil fuels mining and electricity generation by 2035 (Château, J., Bibas and Lanzi, 2018[41]). While new jobs will also be created as a result of the greening of the economy, they will typically be in different industries, often in different regions, and they may frequently require different skill sets compared to the jobs that were lost. In the absence of adequate re-training programmes, the new jobs may be simply out of reach for displaced workers.

### Figure 2.13. The decline of the manufacturing sector

Percentage change in total employment within industry for selected OECD countries, 1995 to 2015

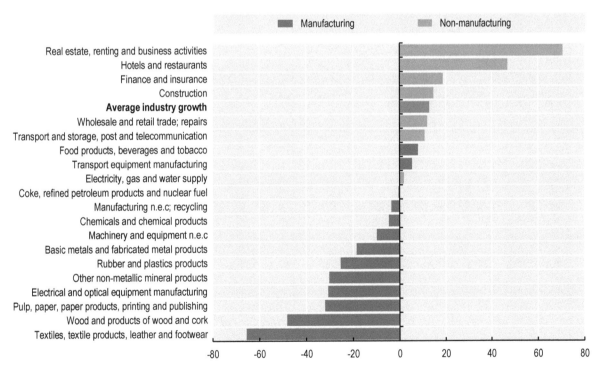

Note: The figure depicts the percentage changes in total employment by industry (by two-digit ISIC Rev.3 classification). The results are obtained by pooling together employment in each industry across all the countries analysed. The average industry growth (red bar) is a simple unweighted average of changes in total employment across industries.

Source: OECD (2017[90]), "How technology and globalisation are transforming the labour market", in *OECD Employment Outlook 2017*, https://doi.org/10.1787/empl_outlook-2017-7-en.

StatLink ᴹᴷ http://dx.doi.org/10.1787/888933966179

An ageing population has made the prospect of displaced workers an even more significant concern. In the short-term, this may lead to an increased risk of long-term unemployment among specialised older workers, who have a more difficult time retraining and finding work with comparable wages (OECD, 2005[91]; OECD, 2018[22]). As life expectancy increases and the retirement age has been rising in many OECD countries, workers who are dismissed from manufacturing jobs in their 40s or 50s may still have two or more decades of active working life ahead of them. One potential reason for optimism, however, is that educational attainment in the workforce has been growing over time and older workers are increasingly well-educated, which should make them better equipped for career changes.

The need to help displaced workers through difficult transitions is a pressing policy issue. Effective safety nets in the face of job displacement are a key piece of the policy response. Activation measures that intervene early and possibly prior to dismissal are equally important (OECD, 2018[22]). Timely and effective action requires identifying the workers who are most in need of support and design tailored assistance programmes (see Chapter 7). Another crucial element is how to help workers to update their skills and acquire new competences (see Chapter 6).

### 2.4.2. The labour market has become more polarised

Another transformation that is upending the labour market of advanced economies is job polarisation. Over the past decades, the share of middle-skilled jobs has decreased relative to the share of workers in high- and low-skilled occupations (Autor, Katz and Kearney, 2006[92]; Goos and Manning, 2007[93]; Goos, Manning and Salomons, 2009[94]; OECD, 2017[10]).[41] In almost all countries for which data are available, this process has resulted in an overall shift of employment towards high-skilled occupations (Figure 2.14).[42]

Figure 2.14. The labour market is polarising

Percentage point change in share of total employment, 1995 to 2015

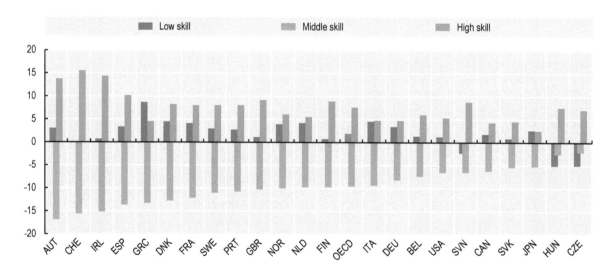

Note: High-skilled occupations include jobs classified under the ISCO-88 major groups 1, 2, and 3., that is, legislators, senior officials, and managers (group 1), professionals (group 2), and technicians and associate professionals (group 3). Middle-skilled occupations include jobs classified under the ISCO-88 major groups 4, 7, and 8, that is, clerks (group 4), craft and related trades workers (group 7), and plant and machine operators and assemblers (group 8). Low-skilled occupations include jobs classified under the ISCO-88 major groups 5 and 9, that is, service workers and shop and market sales workers (group 5), and elementary occupations (group 9).
Source: OECD (2017[90]), "How technology and globalisation are transforming the labour market", in *OECD Employment Outlook 2017*, https://doi.org/10.1787/empl_outlook-2017-7-en.

StatLink 🔗 http://dx.doi.org/10.1787/888933966198

What are the drivers of job polarisation? The decline of the manufacturing sector has been partly responsible, since many manufacturing jobs are also in the middle of the pay distribution, but it does not account for the entire change. In fact, the majority of polarisation is due to the loss of middle-skilled jobs *within* industries (OECD, 2017[10]). The forces of technological change and globalisation have both played a major role in fostering polarisation. Middle-skilled jobs have been the most prone to automation and offshoring, due to their highly routine nature, which makes them relatively easy to codify into a set of instructions that could either be carried out by a machine or by a worker abroad.

The relative importance of technological progress and globalisation in driving job polarisation is the subject of a lively debate. It is a difficult question to answer, since the two megatrends complement and reinforce each other. Recent OECD work attempts to address the issue. It shows that the penetration of ICT in a given industry bears the strongest correlation with its polarisation, while the role of globalisation is less clear-cut (OECD, 2017[10]; Breemersch, Damijan and Konings, 2017[95]). This implies that raising barriers to trade may have limited effects in reducing job losses in declining industries when the effects of automation are also at play. It is important to remark, however, that the evidence varies across countries, and a growing literature documents the adverse impacts of import competition from countries like China on local labour markets, which should not be downplayed (Autor, Dorn and Hanson, 2013[30]). It is also important to note that technology-induced job-polarisation does not necessarily imply that workers will be displaced. Rather, it may occur as the result of a lower share of young labour market entrants taking middle-skilled jobs and older workers in these jobs retiring (Dauth et al., 2017[96]; Green, forthcoming[97]).

The impacts that globalisation had on the labour market of OECD countries over the past decades were closely linked to the rapid integration of major global players, most notably China, in GVCs. This led to what some commentators have called the "great doubling" of the world labour supply (Freeman, 2007[98]). As the success of China was largely driven by low-cost, labour-intensive manufacturing, the rise of China's exports put middle and low-skilled labour in many OECD countries under pressure in terms of their jobs and wages – see e.g. Autor, Dorn and Hanson (2013[30]) – and fuelled their perception of being left behind by globalisation. Going forward, the integration of more countries with expanding populations in GVCs will continue to have important consequences for the labour market, but the effects may not be as dramatic and will likely be different compared to the past. Emerging economies nowadays are indeed also producing a growing pool of high-skilled workers who are competing in the global labour market.

In the policy debate it is often assumed that the decline in the share of middle-skilled occupations has led to a decline in the share of middle-pay jobs. However, this is not the case for two main reasons (Chapter 3). First, many of the high-skilled jobs (whose share has increased in all countries) also pay mid-level wages. Second, there have been changes in the propensity of all occupations (including both high- and low-skilled ones) to pay middle-level wages, which, overall, have tended to increase the share of middle-pay jobs.

The complex interaction of these transformations has affected the fortunes of different workers differently (see Chapter 3). In particular, on average across the OECD, young people without tertiary education have seen increases in the probability of being neither in education nor employment as well as increases in the probability of being in low-pay jobs for those who do find employment. In addition, while women remain at much higher risk of non-employment, men have seen increases in non-employment in most countries. Women also remain more likely to be in low-pay jobs and less likely to be in high-pay ones, despite an improvement in the probability of being in middle-pay jobs.

### 2.4.3. Labour market changes may contribute to the growing sense of frustration and discontent among the middle class

Job polarisation is frequently associated with the perception that the middle class in advanced economies is being squeezed (OECD, 2016[99]; Manfredi and Salvatori, forthcoming[100]; OECD, 2019[101]). That is because middle-skilled jobs have been traditionally associated with middle-class households and the relative decline of those jobs has sparked concerns that an important source of income for the middle-class may be drying up.[43] A squeezed middle class is a key policy concern because it directly implies that economic opportunities are less equally shared and that opportunities for social mobility may have decreased.

Recent OECD work shows that job polarisation per se has *not* resulted in a decline in the share of workers who are in middle-income households (Manfredi and Salvatori, forthcoming[100]). In fact, the share of workers in middle-income households has not changed significantly over the past 20 years, although there are differences across countries.[44] This is because the decline of middle-skilled jobs (plant and machine operators, assemblers, clerical, and craft occupations) has been mostly compensated by an increase in high-skilled jobs (technicians and associate professionals, managerial and professional occupations) which are also commonly found in middle-income households.[45] In addition, the fraction of high-skilled workers who are in middle-income household has also increased. The combination of these trends implies that the skill composition of the middle class has changed considerably, as the share of high-skilled workers has increased more in middle-income households than in the economy as a whole (OECD, 2019[101])

### 2.4.4. A tale of broken promises?

The overall conclusion is that some jobs are increasingly failing to deliver the same income status and the same labour market security as in the past. Middle-skilled occupations no longer guarantee middle-class status, and high-skilled jobs no longer give workers automatic access to the higher echelons of the income distribution (OECD, 2019[101]). This may be a cause of significant frustration especially for workers who made their occupational choices at a time when these trends were not yet clear, and found their labour market outcomes falling short of their expectations.

This type of phenomenon may help to explain the growing sense of preoccupation and discontent registered in many OECD countries, which spans well beyond people in the lowest tiers of the income distribution and increasingly encompasses middle-class households. A recent report by the UK Resolution Foundation, for instance, paints a detailed picture across occupations and shows that some public-sector jobs such as teachers, lecturers, the police, and armed forces, which used to be typical middle-class occupations, were among those recording the largest decline in relative position in the income distribution (Corlett, 2016[102]).

### 2.4.5. A shrinking share of national income is going to workers

A trend that is related to increasing economic inequality and to growing discontent in many OECD countries is the falling share of national income that goes to workers in the form of labour earnings, while the share that goes to capital owners has been increasing. Over the past two decades, the aggregate labour share fell by 3.5 percentage points (from around 71.5% to 68%) in the 24 countries covered by a recent OECD study (OECD, 2018[22]). Within the same period, the economy witnessed a decoupling between real median wages and productivity, with the latter growing much faster than the former.[46] If real median earnings had perfectly tracked productivity over the period, they would have been 13% higher at the end of it (Figure 2.15). In other words, contrary to previous decades, the productivity gains generated by the economy have not resulted in broadly shared wage gains for all workers (Schwellnus, Kappeler and Pionnier, 2017[103]).

The labour share, however, has not been falling uniformly across countries. While it fell by about 8 percentage points in the United States and by nearly 6 percentage points in Japan, it remained broadly constant or increased in about half of the covered OECD countries, including France, Italy and the United Kingdom.[47] These differences partly reflect cross-country differences in business cycle developments. Schwellnus et al. (2018[104]) show that an increase in the output gap of 1% reduces the labour share by 0.5 percentage points. However, structural reforms in a number of areas, including product and labour market institutions, as well as collective bargaining, also emerge as significant determinants of labour share developments and may partly explain cross-country differences (Schwellnus et al., 2018[104]).

Technological progress and (to a lesser extent) globalisation can explain most of the contraction in the labour share (OECD, 2018[22]). Capital-augmenting technological progress or technology-driven declines in relative investment prices reduce the labour share by fostering labour-capital substitution and increasing overall capital intensity. Globalisation can have similar effects. Offshoring and import competition typically lead to job displacement in relatively labour-intensive tasks and hence increase the capital intensity of the production process, but such impacts have been less marked. Furthermore, these dynamics do not impact all industries equally and low-skilled workers are more likely to be negatively affected. In industries with a predominance of routine tasks, the substitution of capital for labour in response to declines in relative investment prices is particularly pronounced. A higher share of high-skilled workers, on the other hand, reduces the substitution of capital for labour even in industries with a high incidence of routine tasks.[48]

Figure 2.15. Real median wages have decoupled from labour productivity

Indices, 1995 = 100

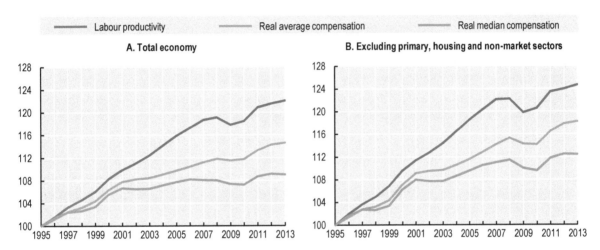

Note: Gross domestic product (GDP) weighted average of 24 countries (two year moving averages ending in the indicated years). 1995-2013 for Finland, Germany, Japan, Korea and the United States; 1995-2012 for France, Italy and Sweden; 1996-2013 for Austria, Belgium and the United Kingdom; 1996-2012 for Australia and Spain; 1997-2013 for the Czech Republic, Denmark and Hungary; 1997-2012 for Poland; 1996-2010 for the Netherlands; 1998-2013 for Norway; 1998-2012 for Canada and New Zealand; 1999-2013 for Ireland; 2002-11 for Israel; 2003-13 for the Slovak Republic. In Panel A, all series are deflated by the total economy value added price index. In Panel B, all series are deflated by the value added price index excluding the primary, housing and non-market industries. The industries excluded in Panel B are the following (International Standard Industry Classification – ISIC – rev. 4 classification): (1) Agriculture, Forestry and Fishing (A), (2) Mining and quarrying (B), (3) Real estate activities (L), (4) Public administration and defence, compulsory social security (O), (5) Education (P), (6) Human health and social work activities (Q), (7) Activities of households as employers (T), and (8) Activities of extraterritorial organisations and bodies (U).
Source: OECD (2018[22]), *OECD Employment Outlook 2018*, Fig. 2.1, http://dx.doi.org/10.1787/empl_outlook-2018-en. Based on OECD National Accounts Database, http://dx.doi.org/10.1787/data-00727-en; OECD Earnings Distribution Database, http://dx.doi.org/10.1787/data-00302-en.

StatLink ᛗᔕᕬ http://dx.doi.org/10.1787/888933966217

### 2.4.6. Winner-takes-most dynamics, superstar firms, and the falling labour share

The fall in the labour share is also connected to the phenomenon of "winner-takes-most" – the process through which the most productive firms in the economy capture an overwhelming share of the market (Rosen, 1981[105]; Frank and Cook, 1995[106]; Autor et al., 2017[28]). This is itself a result of technological progress and globalisation. Thanks to a fall in ICT costs and transport costs, increased access to consumer data, as well as a reduction in tariffs, firms have been increasingly able to access global markets. This has increased enormously the potential for economies of scale. The result is that the most productive firms in the economy (the so-called "superstar" firms) are now significantly larger than the most productive firms were decades ago, which implies that their labour share declines (as the value added share of fixed labour overhead costs declines and/or their mark-up increases). As a consequence, a significant increase in industry concentration has been recorded in both Europe and North America between 2000 and 2014 (Bajgar et al., forthcoming[107]). Furthermore, as the market share of the best firms increases, production is reallocated towards them (and, therefore, towards a production process with a lower labour share). Recent OECD work supports this view. Winner-takes-most dynamics have contributed to the fall of the labour share both through a decline in labour shares among leading firms and through the allocation of market shares towards those firms (OECD, 2018[22]). The most important implication for policy makers is that they should maintain a strong focus on competition policy to ensure that superstar firms do not engage in anti-competitive behaviours and that the markets they operate in remain contestable. Doing so will not only benefit consumers and workers. It will also be beneficial for small businesses, for whom accessing highly concentrated markets may become prohibitive.

### 2.4.7. Increasing market concentration in certain industries sparks new worries of growing monopsony power

Rising concentration in the product market, which partly results from winner-takes-most dynamics, is becoming an increasingly important policy concern. De Loecker and Eeckhout (2017[108]) show that company mark-ups are increasing. Calligaris et al. (2018[109]) demonstrate that this phenomenon is particularly evident in the digitally intensive industries, where winner-takes-most dynamics are most prominent. High mark-ups are a sign of greater market power as firms are able to charge higher prices (or to offer lower wages) the higher their share of the total market is.

Increasing market concentration is also bringing back concerns about possible monopsony in the labour market, a situation where a company dominates the market and can keep wages low since it faces little (or no) competition for workers. A classic case of monopsony from the past is the "company town", such as coal mining communities in rural areas. More recent research and the development of search-and-matching models have shown that different kinds of frictions may give rise to monopsony. For instance, limited information about available jobs, constraints on geographical mobility of workers, and skills mismatches, may be contributing factors. Regulations can also play a perverse role. Non-compete covenants and occupational licenses, as well as health and pension benefits that are linked to specific jobs, for instance, can contribute to lock workers in and lock other workers out of better remunerated jobs (see Chapter 4). In addition, declining trade union membership and weaker collective bargaining institutions can further reduce workers' bargaining power and increase monopsony power (see Chapter 5).

The policy discussion on monopsony, however, is still relatively limited. This is due partly to difficulties in documenting the phenomenon and partly to the *modus operandi* of competition policy. Despite the measurement challenges, some recent papers on the United States document growing labour market concentration. Azar, Marinescu and Steinbaum (2017[110]) use data from a large online job board and show that higher concentration is associated with lower posted wages.[49] Benmelech, Bergman and Kim (2018[111]) measure employment concentration and its effect on wages using Census data for manufacturing industries over a long time horizon. They show that, there is a negative relation between local-level employer concentration and wages, which is more pronounced at high levels of concentration. They also find that exposure to greater import competition from China is associated with more concentrated labour markets. The open question is to what extent such trends are also visible in other OECD countries (see Chapter 4 for a more extensive discussion of evidence and policy issues).[50]

### 2.4.8. The effects of the megatrends are geographically concentrated and contribute to regional disparities

While inequality between countries in per-capita GDP and labour productivity have decreased over the past two decades (especially in Europe), within-country inequality (i.e. inequality between different regions in the same country) remain large and have even grown (OECD, 2018[112]).

Geographical disparities are particularly clear between rural and urban areas. While average business creation rates are 13% (of the total number of existing firms) in predominantly urban regions, it is only 10.9% in predominantly rural ones.[51] More importantly, urban and rural areas display very different sectoral composition and characteristics of new firms. Urban areas tend to attract more knowledge-intensive firms, which are likely to have the best future prospects (OECD, 2018[112]).

The megatrends have contributed to growing regional imbalances (OECD, 2018[113]). The adverse effects of import competition and offshoring, as well as the labour-displacing impacts of new technologies, are particular strong in regions with the highest concentration of firms in routine-intensive industries. A classic example is the Midwest and the Great Lakes region of the United States (nowadays often referred to as the "rust belt"), where the decline of previously very prominent manufacturing industries (such as the automotive industry), led to the disruption of the regional economy. Similar trends are ongoing across the OECD, with countries facing a geographically unequal distribution of jobs at risk of automation. A common pattern is that capital-city regions tend to face the lowest risk of automation, while peripheral regions (often characterised by a stronger presence of mature manufacturing industries) have a higher share of automatable jobs (OECD, 2018[113]). The transition towards a greener economy amplifies these trends. Population ageing and outmigration exacerbate the economic challenges faced by such regions and further reduce their productive potential.

A growing literature documents the impact of the megatrends on local labour markets. Autor, Dorn and Hanson (2013[30]), for instance, show in the context of the United States that when a local labour market was more exposed to import competition from China (because it accounted for a larger share of national employment in industries that faced heavy import competition), it experienced a 4.5% fall in manufacturing employment and a decline in the employment rate by 0.8 percentage points, relative to a less exposed local labour market. A number of other studies show similar findings in different countries and reveal that when the industries most affected by import competition are clustered in specific regions, employment losses in those regions can be significant (Dauth, Findeisen and Suedekum, 2014[114]; Balsvik, Jensen and Salvanes, 2015[115]; Donoso, Martín and Minondo, 2015[116]).

A key problem is the speed at which job losses occur. If jobs were lost gradually and the phenomenon was spread over a wide geographical area, workers could more easily find new opportunities and might even benefit from job turnover as new jobs may be created in more productive firms (OECD, 2018[112]). However, a growing literature indicates that job losses due to the megatrends, and particularly to trade, are highly concentrated and take a long time to be offset by local job growth in other firms or industries (OECD, 2017[117]).

The very unequal effects of the megatrends across regions has contributed to a marked "geography of discontent," with an increasing concentration in specific regions of feelings of dissatisfaction with trade, immigration, and economic inequality (OECD, 2018[112]; OECD, 2017[118]) . The failure of economists and policy makers to acknowledge the pitfalls of globalisation for certain regions and communities has contributed further to international scepticism of international trade, and – more holistically – policy advice from elites (Krugman, 2018[119]).

In light of this evidence, policy makers face a difficult dilemma. Trade is beneficial to the national economy (as discussed above), but can have long-lasting negative effects in some regions (and for specific groups of workers). In order to generate shared prosperity, trade integration needs to be accompanied by timely policy action to help the areas, industries, and workers that risk falling behind. Protectionist policies that aim to restrict trade to protect specific industries or regions, however, risk having detrimental effects for the rest of the economy. Reducing trade would reduce living standards in the long run by limiting productivity gains from specialisation, slowing down innovation, and leading to higher prices for consumers – for an extensive discussion of specific policies to help reducing regional imbalances, see the policy discussion in OECD (2018[112]).

### 2.4.9. The megatrends may contribute to further inequality in the labour market without opportune policy action

The transformations brought about by technological progress, globalisation, and demographic change have been accompanied by a worrying trend across many OECD countries: a rise in income inequality. Today, across OECD countries, the top 10% of adults by income have incomes that are 9.4 times the amount of the poorest 10% (OECD, 2018[120]). Only one generation ago, the ratio was seven to one (Figure 2.16 shows the divergence of bottom and top incomes over the past three decades). Wealth distribution figures are even starker, with the top 10% holding the same amount of wealth as the bottom 90% combined—and only 3% of wealth held by 40% of the population. Such inequalities in wealth and income translate into other forms of inequality of opportunity, including in the domain of education and health (Andersen, 2015[121]; Chetty et al., 2016[122]). Ultimately, these large inequalities lead to lower mobility for individuals and lower productivity for economies (OECD, 2015[39]; OECD, 2018[120]).

Figure 2.16. Income inequality is growing rapidly

Real income trends at the bottom, middle and top of the income distribution since the 1980s, OECD-17

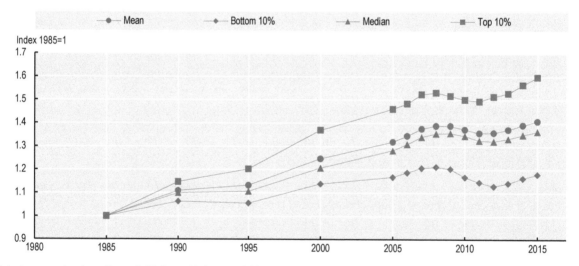

Note: Income refers to real household disposable income. OECD-17 refers to the unweighted average of the 17 OECD countries for which data are available: Canada, Denmark, Finland, France, Germany, Greece, Israel, Italy, Japan, Luxembourg, Mexico, the Netherlands, New Zealand, Norway, Sweden, the United Kingdom and the United States. Some data points have been interpolated or use the value from the closest available year.
Source: OECD Income Distribution Database, http://oe.cd/idd.

*StatLink* ⫘⫘ http://dx.doi.org/10.1787/888933966236

Policy makers and experts increasingly agree that inequality constitutes a key policy challenge that can severely hamper the functioning of economies and societies. Income inequality has been at the top of the policy agenda at the OECD with its *Inclusive Growth* initiative, as well as in other International Organisations.[52] A Pew Research Center survey of general publics across the world found that at least half of the respondents in each European country surveyed had serious concerns about income inequality

(Pew Research Center, 2013[123]). In addition, a survey of over 10 000 opinion leaders in developing countries found that over 50% ranked income inequality as "a very big problem." Within the countries surveyed, Mexican and Colombian leaders were the most concerned (Guo, 2017[124]).

These findings mirror the conclusions of a growing literature showing that high inequality can harm productivity and reduce social mobility, hampering growth and fostering discontent. Recent OECD work shows that by preventing large segments of society from investing in human capital, inequality may reduce productivity and growth (OECD, 2015[39]). Furthermore, while one often-cited rationale for tolerating inequality is to motivate workers to reap the rewards of their achievements, the chances of someone doing better than one's parents are lower in more unequal societies. There is not a single example of a country with high economic inequality and high mobility in the OECD (OECD, 2018[120]). Instead, inequality seems to snowball across generations, as the wealthiest create and sustain both literal and figurative gated communities around high-quality education, health care, and political influence (OECD, 2016[125]; OECD, 2015[39]; Epp and Borghetto, 2018[126]).

The ongoing labour market transformations are linked to the deepening of market income inequalities and, without significant policy changes, the trend is likely to continue. Skill-biased technological progress may continue to increase the earnings of the top earners, who possess the necessary skills and capital, widening the gap with the most disadvantaged. Furthermore, new technologies and access to the global market facilitate the rise of a few superstar firms with increasing market power and growing profits. At the same time, workers' bargaining power is weakening (see also Chapter 5) and new forms of precarious employment are expanding (also due, in many industries, to an increasingly "fissured production process", whereby tasks are farmed out to contractors and sub-contractors, as opposed to employees, as discussed by Weil and Goldman (2016[127]) and Weil (2014[29])). As a result, there is a risk that incomes and wealth will become even more concentrated, and social mobility may well fall further (OECD, 2018[120]). Demographic changes can further exacerbate this gap. Without effective policy action, increasing income inequality may cumulate over the course of longer lifespans to create an elderly underclass (OECD, 2017[12]).

However, the cross-country evidence on rising inequality also shows that there is nothing inevitable about its rise. Policies and institutions matter and can play and important role in mitigating the impact of new technologies, globalisation, and population ageing on inequality.

### Box 2.5. Structural transformation and the challenge of growing disparities in emerging economies

Structural transformation has supported economic growth and reduced poverty in emerging economies. The move from low productivity, labour-intensive activities to higher productivity, capital- and skill-intensive ones is at the heart of economic development.

However, structural transformation has been associated with job polarisation, though the process has not been uniform across countries (Figure 2.17). India, the Russian Federation and Brazil are experiencing a dominant shift in employment to more skilled occupations (upskilling), while other countries like China, Mexico, South Africa and Turkey are undergoing a relative growth in low-skilled occupations.[53] The data also show that in some countries polarisation has not occurred (e.g. Argentina and Peru have experienced an increase in the share of middle-skilled jobs relative to the share of workers in high- and low-skilled occupations). Moreover, unlike in more advanced economies (OECD, 2017[10]), job polarisation in emerging economies is predominantly the result of shifting employment from less polarised industries (agriculture, but also manufacturing in some countries) to more polarised service industries, with polarisation within industries playing a less important role (Alonso-Soto, forthcoming[56]).

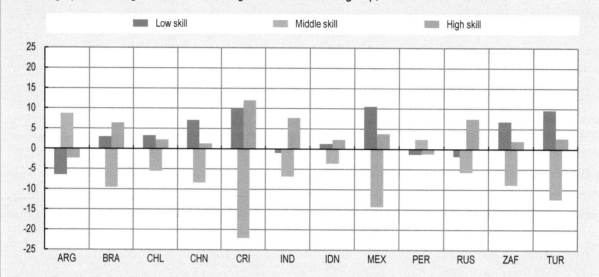

**Figure 2.17. Labour markets are polarising in many emerging economies too**

Percentage points change in share of working adults in each skill group, mid-1990s to mid-2010s[1]

Note: High-skilled occupations include jobs classified under the ISCO-88 major groups 1, 2, and 3, that is, legislators, senior officials, and managers (group 1), professionals (group 2), and technicians and associate professionals (group 3). Middle-skilled occupations include jobs classified under the ISCO-88 major groups 4, 6, 7, and 8, that is, clerks (group 4), skill agricultural and fisheries workers (group 6), craft and related trades workers (group 7), and plant and machine operators and assemblers (group 8). Low-skilled occupations include jobs classified under the ISCO-88 major groups 5 and 9, that is, service workers and shop and market sales workers (group 5), and elementary occupations (group 9).

1. 2004-17 for Argentina, 1995-2015 for Brazil, 1996-2009 for Chile, 2000-10 for China, 1997-2010 for Costa Rica, 1994-2012 for India, 2007-15 for Indonesia, 1995-2017 for Mexico, 2002-17 for Peru, 1997-2017 for Russian Federation, 1996-2007 for South Africa and 2001-10 for Turkey.

Source: ILO KILM, www.ilo.org/kilm, except China (Chinese Census, http://www.stats.gov.cn/english/statisticaldata/censusdata/).

*StatLink* ⟦≋⟧ http://dx.doi.org/10.1787/888933966255

From an historical perspective, structural transformation helped reduce poverty in emerging economies as a large part of employment shifted from low-pay low-productivity agricultural jobs to better-paid jobs in the manufacturing and service sectors (Baymul and Sen, 2017[128]). Yet, automation and job polarisation may now contribute to further increase inequality in emerging economies. First, certain groups of workers are increasingly exposed to the risk of job displacement due to automation. This is likely to be higher for low-skilled workers in manufacturing sectors where jobs with a high routine content are prevalent (Alonso-Soto, forthcoming[56]). Second, the ongoing transformation is linked with two specific drivers of inequality in emerging economies: informal employment and the persistently large geographical differences in economic performances (OECD, 2011[129]). On the one hand, the growing share of service-sector jobs may contribute to increase informality, as it is associated with the rise of non-standard forms of work. On the other hand, new jobs tend to be created in urban areas and in different regions compared to those that are disappearing, fostering the already high regional divides and the urban-rural gaps in emerging economies (OECD, 2018[112]). These changes are occurring against the backdrop of the already high levels of inequality that characterise emerging economies. The lower coverage and generosity of social protection systems, along with a tax system that delivers only modest redistribution makes these challenges even harder to tackle.

*Source*: Alonso-Soto (forthcoming[56]), *Technology and the future of work in emerging economies: What is different?*

## 2.5. Concluding remarks

This chapter provides an overview of the impact of a number of megatrends (technological progress, globalisation and demographic change) on the labour market and highlights the key challenges for policy makers. A key conclusion is that, despite all the uncertainties about the speed and depth of the ongoing changes, a jobless future is highly unlikely. Certain tasks (and, in some cases, entire jobs) are disappearing, but others are emerging, and overall employment has been growing. Going forward, the main challenge will lie in managing the transition of workers, industries, and regions towards new opportunities that will open up in a changing world of work. Perhaps more worrying are the prospects for job quality. Real wages for many workers have stagnated in a number of countries over most of the past decade, and job stability has been declining. Moreover, different forms of non-standard employment are growing in a number of countries.

While a diversity in employment contracts is welcome as a way of responding to different needs by companies and especially workers, important policy challenges remain in providing high-quality jobs to non-standard workers. There is also a risk that existing inequalities in earnings and incomes may widen further. Finally, and most importantly, the costs of the adjustments are not shared equally. Workers from certain sub-groups and regions are at greater risk of job displacement and suffer disproportionately from poor job quality. Failing to address such growing disparities might result in deeper social cleavages, with adverse implications for growth, productivity, well-being, and social cohesion.

The transformations documented in this chapter are already happening. Indeed, some of them have been under way for decades already, but policy responses have been insufficient or too slow to address them. The new emphasis generated by the debate on the future of work is therefore welcome as a call for further, decisive policy action.

Most importantly, the negative consequences of certain structural changes, which are occurring in the labour market, are not inevitable. Policy can and should play an important role in shaping the future of work. Steering these changes will require a whole-of-government approach, as identified in the new OECD Jobs Strategy (OECD, 2018[6]), engaging with the social partners and civil society. Key roles will be played by skills policy, the inclusiveness of employment and social protection, and the effectiveness of social dialogue to ensure that all parties have their voices heard in the policy debate. However, identifying the appropriate policy responses will depend crucially on having good evidence on how the world of work is changing. This evidence and its implications for how policy makers can steer the economy in the direction of better jobs for all will be the subject of the following chapters.

## References

Abel, W., S. Tenreyro and G. Thwaites (2018), "Monopsony in the UK", *CEPR Discussion Paper*, No. 13265, CEPR, London. [142]

Abraham, K. et al. (2017), "Measuring the Gig Economy: Current Knowledge and Open Issues", http://conference.iza.org/conference_files/Statistic_2017/abraham_k16798.pdf (accessed on 27 June 2017). [139]

Acemoglu, D. and D. Autor (2010), "Skills, Tasks and Technologies: Implications for Employment and Earnings", No. 16082, National Bureau of Economic Research (NBER), Cambridge, MA, http://www.nber.org/papers/w16082 (accessed on 13 August 2018). [60]

Acemoglu, D. and P. Restrepo (2018), "Artificial Intelligence, Automation and Work", No. 24196, National Bureau of Economic Research, Cambridge, MA, http://www.nber.org/papers/w24196 (accessed on 10 August 2018). [32]

Acemoglu, D. and P. Restrepo (2017), *Robots and Jobs: Evidence from US Labor Markets*, National Bureau of Economic Research, Cambridge, MA, http://dx.doi.org/10.3386/w23285. [33]

Acemoglu, D. and P. Restrepo (2017), "Secular Stagnation? The Effect of Aging on Economic Growth in the Age of Automation", *American Economic Review*, Vol. 107/5, pp. 174-179, http://dx.doi.org/10.1257/aer.p20171101. [16]

Acemoglu, D. and P. Restrepo (2017), "The Race Between Man and Machine: Implications of Technology for Growth, Factor Shares and Employment", *American Economic Review*, https://economics.mit.edu/files/14458 (accessed on 10 August 2018). [45]

Adams, A. and J. Prassl (2018), "Zero-Hours Work in the United Kingdom", *Conditions of Work and Employment Series*, No. 110, International Labour Office, Geneva, http://www.ilo.org/wcmsp5/groups/public/---ed_protect/---protrav/---travail/documents/publication/wcms_624965.pdf (accessed on 4 June 2018). [88]

African Development Bank Group et al. (2018), *The Future of Work: Regional Perspectives*, African Development Bank Group, Asian Development Bank, European Bank for Reconstruction and Development, Inter-American Development Bank, http://dx.doi.org/10.18235/0001059. [76]

Alonso-Soto, D. (forthcoming), "Technology and the future of work in emerging economies: What is different?", *OECD Social, Employment and Migration Working Papers*, OECD Publishing, Paris. [56]

Andersen, T. (2015), "Human Capital, Inequality and Growth", No. 007, European Commission, Luxembourg, http://ec.europa.eu/economy_finance/publications/. (accessed on 10 August 2018). [121]

Arntz, M., T. Gregory and U. Zierahn (2016), "The Risk of Automation for Jobs in OECD Countries: A Comparative Analysis", *OECD Social, Employment and Migration Working Papers*, No. 189, OECD Publishing, Paris, http://dx.doi.org/10.1787/5jlz9h56dvq7-en. [47]

Autor, D. (2015), "Why Are There Still So Many Jobs? The History and Future of Workplace Automation", *Journal of Economic Perspectives*, Vol. 29/3, pp. 3-30, http://dx.doi.org/10.1257/jep.29.3.3. [38]

Autor, D., D. Dorn and G. Hanson (2013), "The China Syndrome: Local Labor Market Effects of Import Competition in the United States", *American Economic Review*, Vol. 103/6, pp. 2121-2168, http://dx.doi.org/10.1257/aer.103.6.2121. [30]

Autor, D. et al. (2017), "The Fall of the Labor Share and the Rise of Superstar Firms", *NBER Working Papers, No. 23396*, https://www.nber.org/papers/w23396. [28]

Autor, D. and M. Handel (2013), "Putting Tasks to the Test: Human Capital, Job Tasks, and Wages", *Journal of Labor Economics*, Vol. 31/S1, pp. S59-S96, http://dx.doi.org/10.1086/669332. [46]

Autor, D., L. Katz and M. Kearney (2006), "The Polarization of the U.S. Labor Market", *American Economic Review*, Vol. 96/2, pp. 189-194, http://dx.doi.org/10.1257/000282806777212620. [92]

Autor, D. and A. Salomons (2018), *Is automation labor-displacing? Productivity growth, employment, and the labor share*, Brookings Institution, Washington, DC, https://www.brookings.edu/wp-content/uploads/2018/03/1_autorsalomons.pdf (accessed on 13 August 2018). [31]

Azar, J., I. Marinescu and M. Steinbaum (2017), *Labor Market Concentration*, National Bureau of Economic Research, Cambridge, MA, http://dx.doi.org/10.3386/w24147. [110]

Azar, J. et al. (2018), "Concentration in US Labor Markets: Evidence From Online Vacancy Data", *NBER Working Papers*, No. 24395, NBER, Cambridge, MA, http://dx.doi.org/10.3386/w24395. [141]

Bajgar, M. et al. (forthcoming), "Industry Concentration in Europe and North America", *OECD Science, Technology and Industry Working Papers*, OECD Publishing, Paris. [107]

Balsvik, R., S. Jensen and K. Salvanes (2015), "Made in China, sold in Norway: Local labor market effects of an import shock", *Journal of Public Economics*, Vol. 127, pp. 137-144, http://dx.doi.org/10.1016/J.JPUBECO.2014.08.006. [115]

Baymul, C. and K. Sen (2017), "What do we know about the relationship between structural transformation, inequality and poverty?", *ESRC GPID Research Network Working Paper*, No. 2. [128]

Benmelech, E., N. Bergman and H. Kim (2018), *Strong Employers and Weak Employees: How Does Employer Concentration Affect Wages?*, National Bureau of Economic Research, Cambridge, MA, http://dx.doi.org/10.3386/w24307. [111]

Bessen, J. (2017), "Automation and jobs: When technology boosts employment", *Law & Economics Paper*, http://www.bu.edu/law/faculty-scholarship/working-paper-series/ (accessed on 6 September 2018). [34]

Biagi, F. et al. (2018), *Platform Workers in Europe Evidence from the COLLEEM Survey*, European Commission, Luxembourg, http://dx.doi.org/10.2760/742789 (accessed on 17 July 2018). [72]

BLS (2018), *Electronically mediated work: new questions in the Contingent Worker Supplement*, http://dx.doi.org/10.21916/mlr.2018.24. [75]

Botta, E. (2018), "A Review of "Transition Management" Strategies: Lessons for advancing the green low-carbon transition", *Issue note for the GGSD 2018 Forum on "Inclusive Solution for the green Economy"*, https://issuu.com/oecd.publishing/docs/ggsd_2018_issuepaper_transition_man. [42]

Branson, R. (2017), "Experimenting with universal basic income", *Virgin*, https://www.virgin.com/richard-branson/experimenting-universal-basic-income (accessed on 8 August 2018). [27]

Breemersch, K., J. Damijan and J. Konings (2017), "Labour Market Polarization in Advanced Countries: Impact of Global Value Chains, Technology, Import Competition from China and Labour Market Institutions", *OECD Social, Employment and Migration Working Papers*, No. 197, OECD Publishing, Paris, http://dx.doi.org/10.1787/06804863-en. [95]

Broad Institute (2018), *Questions and Answers about CRISPR*, Broad Institute, https://www.broadinstitute.org/what-broad/areas-focus/project-spotlight/questions-and-answers-about-crispr (accessed on 13 August 2018). [13]

Browne, M. (2018), "Cashier-free tech makes debut in San Francisco", *Supermarket News*, https://www.supermarketnews.com/retail-financial/cashier-free-tech-makes-debut-san-francisco (accessed on 24 August 2018). [7]

Brynjolfsson, E. and A. McAfee (2014), *The second machine age : work, progress, and prosperity in a time of brilliant technologies*, W. W. Norton & Company, http://books.wwnorton.com/books/the-second-machine-age/ (accessed on 21 June 2018). [8]

Brynjolfsson, E. and A. McAfee (2011), *Race against the machine : how the digital revolution is accelerating innovation, driving productivity, and irreversibly transforming employment and the economy*, Digital Frontier Press. [3]

Burri, S., S. Heeger-Hertter and S. Rossetti (2018), *On-call work in the Netherlands: trends, impact, and policy solutions*, International Labour Organization (ILO), Geneva, http://www.ilo.org/travail/info/working/WCMS_626410/lang--en/index.htm (accessed on 6 June 2018). [86]

Calligaris, S., C. Criscuolo and L. Marcolin (2018), "Mark-ups in the digital era", *OECD Science, Technology and Industry Working Papers*, No. 2018/10, OECD Publishing, Paris, https://dx.doi.org/10.1787/4efe2d25-en. [109]

Campbell, I. (2018), "On-call and related forms of casual work in New Zealand and Australia", http://www.labourlawresearch.net/sites/default/files/papers/IainILO.pdf (accessed on 6 June 2018). [84]

Château, J., R. Bibas and E. Lanzi (2018), "Impact of green growth polices on labour markets and wage income distribution: a general equilibrium application to climate and energy policies", *OECD Environment Working Paper, forthcomiing*. [41]

Château, J., A. Saint-Martin and T. Manfredi (2011), "Employment Impacts of Climate Change Mitigation Policies in OECD: A General-Equilibrium Perspective", *OECD Environment Working Papers*, No. 32, OECD Publishing, Paris, http://dx.doi.org/10.1787/5kg0ps847h8q-en. [43]

Chetty, R. et al. (2016), "The Association Between Income and Life Expectancy in the United States, 2001-2014", *JAMA*, Vol. 315/16, p. 1750, http://dx.doi.org/10.1001/jama.2016.4226. [122]

Corlett, A. (2016), *Robot wars Automation and the labour market*,
https://www.resolutionfoundation.org/app/uploads/2016/07/Robot-wars.pdf (accessed on
24 September 2018).
[102]

Dauth, W., S. Findeisen and J. Suedekum (2014), "The rise of the East and the Far East:
German labor markets and trade integration", *Journal of the European Economic Association*,
Vol. 12/6, pp. 1643-1675, http://dx.doi.org/10.1111/jeea.12092.
[114]

Dauth, W. et al. (2017), "German Robots - The Impact of Industrial Robots on Workers",
*Discussion Paper Series*, No. No. DP12306, CEPR,
https://papers.ssrn.com/sol3/papers.cfm?abstract_id=3039031 (accessed on
26 November 2018).
[96]

Davies, R. and K. Vadlamannati (2013), "A race to the bottom in labor standards? An empirical
investigation", *Journal of Development Economics*, Vol. 103, pp. 1-14,
http://dx.doi.org/10.1016/J.JDEVECO.2013.01.003.
[138]

De Backer, K. et al. (2016), "Reshoring: Myth or Reality?", *OECD Science, Technology and
Industry Policy Papers*, No. 27, OECD Publishing, Paris,
https://dx.doi.org/10.1787/5jm56frbm38s-en.
[54]

de Guigné, A. (2016), "De nouvelles règles sur le temps de travail le 1er janvier 2017", *Le
Figaro*, http://www.lefigaro.fr/emploi/2016/12/26/09005-20161226ARTFIG00178-de-
nouvelles-regles-sur-le-temps-de-travail-le-1erjanvier-2017.php (accessed on
24 August 2018).
[70]

De Loecker, J. and J. Eeckhout (2017), *The Rise of Market Power and the Macroeconomic
Implications*, National Bureau of Economic Research, Cambridge, MA,
http://dx.doi.org/10.3386/w23687.
[108]

Deloitte (2017), *Smart everything, everywhere: Mobile consumer survey 2017*,
https://landing.deloitte.com.au/rs/761-IBL-328/images/tmt-mobile-consumer-survey-
2017_pdf.pdf?utm_source=marketo&utm_medium=lp&utm_campaign=tmt-mobile-consumer-
survey-2017&utm_content=body (accessed on 13 August 2018).
[137]

Donoso, V., V. Martín and A. Minondo (2015), "Do Differences in the Exposure to Chinese
Imports Lead to Differences in Local Labour Market Outcomes? An Analysis for Spanish
Provinces", *Regional Studies*, Vol. 49/10, pp. 1746-1764,
http://dx.doi.org/10.1080/00343404.2013.879982.
[116]

Epp, D. and E. Borghetto (2018), *Economic Inequality and Legislative Agendas in Europe*,
https://enricoborghetto.netlify.com/working_paper/EuroInequality.pdf (accessed on
16 August 2018).
[126]

Falco, P., D. MacDonald and A. Green (forthcoming), "Are jobs becoming less stable?", *OECD
Social, Employment and Migration Working Papers*, OECD Publishing, Paris.
[59]

Fanggidae, V., M. Sagala and D. Ningrum (2016), *On-Demand Transport Workers in indonesia:
Toward understanding the sharing economy in emerging markets*,
http://www.justjobsnetwork.org (accessed on 1 March 2019).
[79]

Frank, R. and P. Cook (1995), *The winner-take-all society : how more and more Americans compete for ever fewer and bigger prizes, encouraging economic waste, income inequality, and an impoverished cultural life*, Free Press, https://bepl.ent.sirsi.net/client/en_US/default/search/detailnonmodal/ent:$002f$002fSD_ILS$0 02f0$002fSD_ILS:856060/ada (accessed on 31 July 2018).   [106]

Freeman, R. (2007), "The great doubling: The challenge of the new global labor market", in *Ending Poverty in America: How to Restore the American Dream*.   [98]

Frey, C. and M. Osborne (2017), "The future of employment: How susceptible are jobs to computerisation?", *Technological Forecasting and Social Change*, Vol. 114, pp. 254-280, http://dx.doi.org/10.1016/J.TECHFORE.2016.08.019.   [20]

Gallie, D. (2013), ""Skills, Job Control and the Quality of Work: The Evidence from Britain (Geary Lecture 2012)", *The Economic and Social Review*, Vol. 43/3, Autumn, pp. 325-341, https://www.esr.ie/article/view/41/33 (accessed on 17 July 2018).   [68]

Gates, B. (2017), "We should tax the robot that takes your job - YouTube", https://www.youtube.com/watch?v=nccryZOcrUg (accessed on 8 August 2018).   [26]

Goos, M. and A. Manning (2007), *Lousy and lovely jobs: The rising polarization of work in Britain*, https://www.mitpressjournals.org/doi/pdf/10.1162/rest.89.1.118 (accessed on 21 September 2018).   [93]

Goos, M., A. Manning and A. Salomons (2009), "Job Polarization in Europe", *American Economic Review*, Vol. 99/2, pp. 58-63, http://dx.doi.org/10.1257/aer.99.2.58.   [94]

Green, A. (forthcoming), "Where are Middle-skill Workers Going?", *OECD Social, Employment and Migration Working Papers*.   [97]

Guo, J. (2017), "Many around the world worry about inequality, especially women", *The Data Blog*, https://blogs.worldbank.org/opendata/many-around-world-worry-about-inequality-especially-women (accessed on 8 August 2018).   [124]

Harari, Y. (2016), *Homo Deus: A Brief History of Tomorrow*, Harvill Secker, London.   [147]

Hathaway, I. and M. Muro (2016), *Tracking the gig economy: New numbers*, Brookings, https://www.brookings.edu/research/tracking-the-gig-economy-new-numbers/ (accessed on 11 June 2018).   [35]

ILO (2018), *Global Commission on the Future of Work: Technology for social, environmental, and economic development*, https://www.ilo.org/wcmsp5/groups/public/---dgreports/---cabinet/documents/publication/wcms_618168.pdf (accessed on 13 August 2018).   [65]

ILO (2018), *International Labour Organization, ILOSTAT database*, https://data.worldbank.org/indicator/SL.AGR.EMPL.ZS (accessed on 17 December 2018).   [64]

ILO (2015), *Decent and Productive Work in Agriculture*, ILO, https://www.ilo.org/wcmsp5/groups/public/---ed_emp/---emp_policy/documents/publication/wcms_437173.pdf (accessed on 23 August 2018).   [66]

INPS (2017), *Il mercato del lavoro: verso una lettura integrata*, Italy, https://www.inps.it/docallegatiNP/Mig/Allegati/Rapporto_Mercato_del_Lavoro_2017.pdf (accessed on 6 June 2018).   [85]

Jackson, E., A. Looney and S. Ramnath (2017), *The Rise of Alternative Work Arrangements: Evidence and Implications for Tax Filing and Benefit Coverage*, https://www.treasury.gov/resource-center/tax-policy/tax-analysis/Documents/WP-114.pdf (accessed on 6 September 2018). [136]

Janser, M. (2018), "The greening of jobs in Germany First evidence from a text mining based index and employment register data", http://doku.iab.de/discussionpapers/2018/dp1418.pdf (accessed on 29 August 2018). [44]

Kässi, O. and V. Lehdonvirta (2016), *Online Labour Index: Measuring the Online Gig Economy for Policy and Research*, Paper presented at Internet, Politics & Policy 2016, 22-23 September, Oxford, UK. [81]

Katz, L. and A. Krueger (2016), *The Rise and Nature of Alternative Work Arrangements in the United States, 1995-2015*, National Bureau of Economic Research, Cambridge, MA, http://dx.doi.org/10.3386/w22667. [135]

Keynes, J. (1931), "Economic Possibilities for our Grandchildren", http://www.econ.yale.edu/smith/econ116a/keynes1.pdf (accessed on 26 July 2018). [1]

Krugman, P. (2018), *Globalization: What Did We Miss?*, https://www.gc.cuny.edu/CUNY_GC/media/LISCenter/pkrugman/PK_globalization.pdf (accessed on 2 August 2018). [119]

Lebowitz, S. (2018), "Top execs in banking, retail, and tech are saying they don't practice work-life balance — because they found something better", *Business Insider France*, http://www.businessinsider.fr/us/jp-morgan-chase-cmo-other-execs-value-work-life-integration-2018-6 (accessed on 24 August 2018). [71]

Lippoldt, D. (ed.) (2012), *Policy Priorities for International Trade and Jobs*, https://www.oecd.org/site/tadicite/50258009.pdf (accessed on 26 July 2018). [133]

Lordan, G. and D. Neumark (2018), "People versus machines: The impact of minimum wages on automatable jobs", *Labour Economics*, Vol. 52, pp. 40-53, http://dx.doi.org/10.1016/J.LABECO.2018.03.006. [134]

Maloney, W. and C. Molina (2016), "Are automation and trade polarizing developing country labor markets, too ?", *Policy Research working paper*, No. WPS 7922, World Bank Group, Washington, D.C, http://documents.worldbank.org/curated/en/869281482170996446/Are-automation-and-trade-polarizing-developing-country-labor-markets-too (accessed on 11 September 2018). [50]

Manfredi, T. and A. Salvatori (forthcoming), "Job polarisation and the changing work profile of the middle-income class", *OECD Social, Employment and Migration Working Papers*. [100]

Manyika, J. et al. (2015), *A Labor Market that Works: Connecting talent with opportunity in the digital age*, McKinsey Global Institute, http://www.mckinsey.com/mgi. (accessed on 14 August 2018). [73]

Martins, P. (2018), "Making their own weather? Estimating employer labour-market power and its wage effects", *QMUL Working Papers*. [143]

Mazmanian, M., W. Orlikowski and J. Yates (2013), "The Autonomy Paradox: The Implications of Mobile Email Devices for Knowledge Professionals", *Organization Science*, Vol. 24/5, pp. 1337-1357, http://dx.doi.org/10.1287/orsc.1120.0806. [69]

McKinsey Global Institute (2017), *A future that works: Automation, employment, and productivity*, http://www.mckinsey.com/mgi. (accessed on 26 July 2018). [52]

Melville, J., J. Kaiser and E. Brown (2017), *Silicon Valley Competitiveness and Innovation Project-2017 Report*, Silicon Valley Leadership Group; Silicon Valley Community Foundation, http://www.coecon.com (accessed on 2 August 2018). [17]

Menon, S., A. Salvatori and W. Zwyseni (2018), "The effect of computer use on job quality Evidence from Europe", *OECD Social, Employment and Migration Working Papers*, No. 200, OECD, https://doi.org/10.1787/1815199X. [67]

Messenger, J. and P. Wallot (2015), *The diversity of "marginal" part-time employment*, International Labour Office, Geneva, http://www.ilo.org/wcmsp5/groups/public/---ed_protect/---protrav/---travail/documents/publication/wcms_375630.pdf (accessed on 31 May 2018). [83]

Mokyr, J., C. Vickers and N. Ziebarth (2015), "The History of Technological Anxiety and the Future of Economic Growth: Is This Time Different?", *Journal of Economic Perspectives*, Vol. 29/3, pp. 31-50, http://dx.doi.org/10.1257/jep.29.3.31. [4]

Moretti, E. (2012), *The new geography of jobs*, Houghton Mifflin Harcourt. [36]

Moretti, E. (2010), "Local Multipliers", *American Economic Review*, Vol. 100/2, pp. 373-377, http://dx.doi.org/10.1257/aer.100.2.373. [37]

Nedelkoska, L. and G. Quintini (2018), "Automation, skills use and training", *OECD Social, Employment and Migration Working Papers*, No. 202, OECD Publishing, Paris, http://dx.doi.org/10.1787/2e2f4eea-en. [21]

Newfarmer, R. and M. Sztajerowska (2012), "Trade and Employment in a Fast-Changing World", in Lippoldt, D. (ed.), *Policy Priorities for International Trade and Jobs*, https://www.oecd.org/site/tadicite/50286917.pdf (accessed on 26 July 2018). [25]

O'Sullivan, M. et al. (2016), *Zero Hours Work in Ireland: Prevalence, drivers, and the role of law*, University of Limerick, Ireland, https://www.jurinst.su.se/polopoly_fs/1.281559.1462519131!/menu/standard/file/Zero%20Hours%20Work%20in%20Ireland%20Prevalence%2C%20Drivers%20and%20the%20Role%20of%20the%20Law.pdf. [89]

OECD (2019), *Going Digital: Shaping Policies, Improving Lives*, OECD Publishing, Paris, https://dx.doi.org/10.1787/9789264312012-en. [23]

OECD (2019), *Policy Responses to New Forms of Work*, OECD Publishing, Paris, https://doi.org/10.1787/0763f1b7-en. [80]

OECD (2019), *Trade in goods and services* (indicator), https://dx.doi.org/10.1787/0fe445d9-en (accessed on 11 January 2019). [11]

OECD (2019), *Under Pressure: The Squeezed Middle Class*, OECD Publishing, Paris, https://doi.org/10.1787/689afed1-en. [101]

OECD (2018), *A Broken Social Elevator? How to Promote Social Mobility*, OECD Publishing, Paris, http://dx.doi.org/10.1787/9789264301085-en. [120]

OECD (2018), *Good Jobs for All in a Changing World Of Work: The OECD Jobs Strategy*, OECD Publishing, Paris, https://doi.org/10.1787/9789264308817-en. [6]

OECD (2018), *International Migration Outlook 2018*, OECD Publishing, Paris, https://dx.doi.org/10.1787/migr_outlook-2018-en. [19]

OECD (2018), *Job Creation and Local Economic Development 2018: Preparing for the Future of Work*, OECD Publishing, Paris, https://dx.doi.org/10.1787/9789264305342-en. [113]

OECD (2018), "OECD Due Diligence Guidance for Responsible Business Conduct", http://mneguidelines.oecd.org/OECD-Due-Diligence-Guidance-for-Responsible-Business-Conduct.pdf. [63]

OECD (2018), *OECD Employment Outlook 2018*, OECD Publishing, Paris, http://dx.doi.org/10.1787/empl_outlook-2018-en. [22]

OECD (2018), "Online Work in OECD countries", *Policy Brief on the Future of Work*, OECD, Paris, http://www.oecd.org/els/employment/online-work-in-oecd-countries-2018.pdf. [82]

OECD (2018), *Productivity and Jobs in a Globalised World: (How) Can All Regions Benefit?*, OECD Publishing, Paris, http://dx.doi.org/10.1787/9789264293137-en. [112]

OECD (2018), *Report for the Meeting of the OECD Council at Ministerial Level Meeting of the OECD Council at Ministerial Level "Going digital in a multilateral world"*, http://www.oecd.org/mcm/documents/C-MIN-2018-6-EN.pdf. [57]

OECD (2018), "The Opioids Epidemic in OECD Countries - Better Prevention and Effective Control", *Paper presented at the 24th Session of the OECD Health Committee*, OECD, Paris. [15]

OECD (2017), *Geography of Discontent A look back at the OECD Forum 2017 session*, https://www.oecd-forum.org/users/50593-oecd/posts/20331-geography-of-discontent. [118]

OECD (2017), "Going Digital: The Future of Work for Women", *Policy Brief on The Future of Work*, OECD, Paris, https://www.oecd.org/employment/Going-Digital-the-Future-of-Work-for-Women.pdf. [24]

OECD (2017), "How technology and globalisation are transforming the labour market", in *OECD Employment Outlook 2017*, OECD Publishing, Paris, https://dx.doi.org/10.1787/empl_outlook-2017-7-en. [90]

OECD (2017), "How to make trade work for all", in *OECD Economic Outlook, Volume 2017 Issue 1*, OECD Publishing, Paris, http://dx.doi.org/10.1787/eco_outlook-v2017-1-3-en. [117]

OECD (2017), *International Migration Outlook 2017*, OECD Publishing, Paris, https://dx.doi.org/10.1787/migr_outlook-2017-en. [18]

OECD (2017), *OECD Employment Outlook 2017*, OECD Publishing, Paris, https://dx.doi.org/10.1787/empl_outlook-2017-en. [10]

OECD (2017), *OECD Science, Technology and Industry Scoreboard 2017: The digital transformation*, OECD Publishing, Paris, http://dx.doi.org/10.1787/9789264268821-en. [9]

OECD (2017), *Preventing Ageing Unequally*, OECD Publishing, Paris,
https://dx.doi.org/10.1787/9789264279087-en. [12]

OECD (2016), *Making Cities Work for All: Data and Actions for Inclusive Growth*, OECD
Publishing, Paris, http://dx.doi.org/10.1787/9789264263260-en. [125]

OECD (2016), "Skills for a Digital World", *Policy Brief on The Future of Work*, OECD Publishing,
Paris, https://www.oecd.org/els/emp/Skills-for-a-Digital-World.pdf. [48]

OECD (2016), *The squeezed middle class in OECD and emerging countries-myth and reality*,
https://www.oecd.org/inclusive-growth/about/centre-for-opportunity-and-equality/Issues-note-
Middle-Class-squeeze.pdf. [99]

OECD (2015), *In It Together: Why Less Inequality Benefits All*, OECD Publishing, Paris,
https://dx.doi.org/10.1787/9789264235120-en. [39]

OECD (2015), *OECD Employment Outlook 2015*, OECD Publishing, Paris,
https://dx.doi.org/10.1787/empl_outlook-2015-en. [78]

OECD (2014), *OECD Employment Outlook 2014*, OECD Publishing, Paris,
http://dx.doi.org/10.1787/empl_outlook-2014-en. [58]

OECD (2013), *OECD Skills Outlook 2013: First Results from the Survey of Adult Skills*, OECD
Publishing, Paris, https://dx.doi.org/10.1787/9789264204256-en. [49]

OECD (2012), *OECD Employment Outlook 2012*, OECD Publishing, Paris,
http://dx.doi.org/10.1787/empl_outlook-2012-en. [140]

OECD (2011), *Divided We Stand: Why Inequality Keeps Rising*, OECD Publishing, Paris,
https://dx.doi.org/10.1787/9789264119536-en. [129]

OECD (2011), *OECD Guidelines for Multinational Enterprises, 2011 Edition*, OECD Publishing,
Paris, https://dx.doi.org/10.1787/9789264115415-en. [62]

OECD (2008), "Do Multinationals Promote Better Pay and Working Conditions?", in *OECD
Employment Outlook 2008*, OECD Publishing, Paris, https://doi.org/10.1787/empl_outlook-
2008-7-en. [61]

OECD (2005), "Trade-adjustment costs in OECD labour markets: a mountain or a molehill?", in
*OECD Employment Outlook 2005*, OECD Publishing, Paris,
http://www.oecd.org/els/emp/36780847.pdf. [91]

OECD (forthcoming), *Online Platforms: What Are They and How Are They Changing Economies
and Societies?*, OECD Publishing, Paris. [146]

ONS (2017), *People in employment on a zero-hours contract*,
https://www.ons.gov.uk/employmentandlabourmarket/peopleinwork/earningsandworkinghours
/articles/contractsthatdonotguaranteeaminimumnumberofhours/mar2017#summary
(accessed on 4 June 2018). [87]

Pew Research Center (2018), *In Advanced and Emerging Economies Alike, Worries About Job
Automation*. [5]

Pew Research Center (2016), *Public Predictions for the Future of Workforce Automation*. [132]

Pew Research Center (2013), *The global consensus: Inequality is a major problem*, FactTank, http://www.pewresearch.org/fact-tank/2013/11/15/the-global-consensus-inequality-is-a-major-problem/ (accessed on 8 August 2018). [123]

Republican Party (1928), *Republican Party Platforms: Republican Party Platform of 1928*, http://www.presidency.ucsb.edu/ws/index.php?pid=29637 (accessed on 30 July 2018). [2]

Rodrik, D. (2016), "Premature deindustrialization", *Journal of Economic Growth*, Vol. 21/1, pp. 1-33, http://dx.doi.org/10.1007/s10887-015-9122-3. [55]

Rosen, S. (1981), *The Economics of Superstars*, American Economic Association, http://dx.doi.org/10.2307/1803469. [105]

Sanders, R. (2016), "Genetic switch could be key to increased health and lifespan", *Berkeley News*, http://news.berkeley.edu/2016/05/03/genetic-switch-could-be-key-to-increased-health-and-lifespan/ (accessed on 13 August 2018). [14]

Schank, T., C. Schnabel and J. Wagner (2008), *Higher Wages in Exporting Firms: Self-Selection, Export Effect, or Both? First Evidence from German Linked Employer-Employee Data*, http://ftp.iza.org/dp3359.pdf (accessed on 24 September 2018). [131]

Schwellnus, C., A. Kappeler and P. Pionnier (2017), "Decoupling of wages from productivity: Macro-level facts", *OECD Economics Department Working Papers*, No. 1373, OECD Publishing, Paris, http://dx.doi.org/10.1787/d4764493-en. [103]

Schwellnus, C. et al. (2018), "Labour share developments over the past two decades: The role of technological progress, globalisation and "winner-takes-most" dynamics", *OECD Economics Department Working Papers*, No. 1503, OECD Publishing, Paris, https://dx.doi.org/10.1787/3eb9f9ed-en. [104]

Sokolova, A. and T. Sorensen (2018), "Monopsony in Labor Markets: A Meta-Analysis", *IZA Discussion Paper*, No. 11966, IZA, Bonn, http://ftp.iza.org/dp11966.pdf (accessed on 8 January 2019). [144]

Solon, O. (2017), "Big Brother isn't just watching: workplace surveillance can track your every move", *The Guardian*, https://www.theguardian.com/world/2017/nov/06/workplace-surveillance-big-brother-technology (accessed on 14 August 2018). [74]

Sundararajan, A. (2017), "Capitalismo Colaborativo", in *Integration and Trade Journal 21 (42, August): Robot-lution: The Future of Work in Latin American Integration 4.0*, https://publications.iadb.org/en/integration-and-trade-journal-volume-21-no-42-august-2017-robot-lucion-future-work-latin-american. [77]

The Boston Consulting Group (2015), *The Shifting Economics of Global Manufacturing: How a Takeoff in Advanced Robotics Will Power the Next Productivity Surge*, https://www.slideshare.net/TheBostonConsultingGroup/robotics-in-manufacturing (accessed on 11 September 2018). [53]

The World Bank (2016), *World Development Report 2016: Digital dividends*, International Bank for Reconstruction and Development / The World Bank, Washington, DC, http://dx.doi.org/10.1596/978-1-4648-0728-2. [51]

UNICEF (2017), *OPV costs*, https://www.unicef.org/supply/files/OPV.pdf (accessed on 31 July 2018). [130]

United Nations (2016), *The Paris Agreement*, https://unfccc.int/process-and-meetings/the-paris-agreement/the-paris-agreement (accessed on 22 August 2018). [40]

Weil, D. (2014), *The Fissured Workplace: Why Work Became So Bad for So Many and What Can Be Done to Improve it.* [29]

Weil, D. and T. Goldman (2016), "Labor Standards, the Fissured Workplace, and the On-Demand Economy", in *Perspectives on Work*, http://www.fissuredworkplace.net/assets/Weil_Goldman.pdf (accessed on 10 August 2018). [127]

Wheeler, D., H. Wong and T. Shanley (2009), *Science and practice of pediatric critical care medicine*, Springer, https://books.google.fr/books?id=3p7jezlQ0zgC&pg=PA11&redir_esc=y#v=onepage&q=polio&f=false (accessed on 8 August 2018). [145]

## Notes

[1] A previous survey by the Pew Research Center also highlighted that people in the United States are significantly more pessimistic about the labour market in general than about their own jobs. While 65% of respondents reported that 50 years from today automation will have taken over "much" of the work currently done by humans, 80% of them thought their own job would still exist in that time frame (Pew Research Center, 2016[132]). While it might be tempting to dismiss such evidence as inconsistent, workers' perceptions are an important driver of their decisions and well-being. As such, they should be further investigated.

[2] The chapter has greatly benefited from the collaboration of Karen Scott.

[3] A similar progression has been recorded in other countries. For example, today roughly 9 in 10 people own smartphones in Australia, Norway, the Netherlands, Ireland, and Luxembourg (Deloitte, 2017[137]).

[4] While this might sound like a very significant rise, however, it is important to bear in mind that the diffusion of other transformational technologies in the past might may have been even faster in some cases. It is also important to remark that the continuation of recent trends is not assured and a number of factors will play an important role, including consumer preferences and policy choices (as discussed in Section 2.2.4).

[5] In advanced economies, workers are concerned about job opportunities lost to offshoring and services outsourcing, as well as about the increased vulnerability associated with job and income volatility from global competition. Workers in many emerging economies worry about the adverse consequences of trade liberalisation, lagging employment opportunities for growing labour forces, and competition from other emerging economies (OECD, 2012[133]). A more general concern expressed by workers in all countries (advanced and emerging alike) is that globalisation is contributing to increased income inequality and poorer working conditions for many, and particularly the lower-skilled in developed economies.

[6] For example, at the start of the 20th century, polio was "the number one dreaded disease" by paediatricians—today the average cost of treatment is less than USD 20 cents (Wheeler, Wong and Shanley, 2009[145]; UNICEF, 2017[130]).

[7] This process, however, will not necessarily be automatic, and policy makers should carefully monitor the possible emergence of barriers and market failures that might hinder such positive developments.

[8] In *Homo Deus*, Yuval Noah Harari speculates that such medical advancements will likely extend lifespans—and that 150-year-olds may be only decades away from possibility, if not the new norm. (Harari, 2016[147]).

[9] In countries with a young and growing workforce, the opposite is likely to happen as the middle class expands and rapid urbanisation takes place. The challenge in this case will be to harness the full potential of this demographic dividend, ensuring that youth have the skills and opportunities for gainful employment, with positive implications for economic growth.

[10] https://esa.un.org/unpd/wpp/

[11]The analysis models the consequences of implementing a USD 50/tCO2 uniform tax on CO2 emissions resulting from economic activities – excluding emissions from land use, land-use change and forestry

(LULUCF) – for all regions in the world. Job creation and job destruction are calculated relative to employment in 2011 (Château, J., Bibas and Lanzi, 2018[41]).

[12] The experts classify a sample of 70 occupations (the training set) into automatable and non-automatable on the basis of the following question: "Can the tasks of this job be sufficiently specified, conditional on the availability of big data, to be performed by state of the art computer-controlled equipment". The authors then use information on the engineering bottlenecks – the human tasks that cannot be automated – associated with those 70 occupations (contained in the O*NET dataset) to assign a probability of automation to all other occupations in the US economy.

[13] Between 2012 and 2017, employment that Frey and Osborne classified as having a "high probability of automation" did grow more slowly, but their predictions explained less than 2% of changing employment levels.

[14] Following these initial studies, a task-based approach has been gaining traction in the literature. The McKinsey Global Institute, for instance, carried out a similar analysis and concluded that about 45% of tasks are at risk of automation but only about 5% of jobs risk full automation given current technology (McKinsey Global Institute, 2017[52]).

[15] The World Bank (2016) estimates are constructed using experts' assessment of the probability that different occupations can be automated and follow the same methodology as Frey and Osborne (2017). Nedelkoska and Quintini (2018), while also departing from Frey and Osborne's analysis, directly explore the task content of individual jobs instead of the average task content within each occupation. Finally, McKinsey (2017) assesses the technical potential for automation through an analysis of the component activities of each occupation. The authors break down about 800 occupations into more than 2,000 activities, and determine the performance capabilities needed for each activity based on the way humans currently perform them. Finally, they further break down each activity into 18 capabilities and assess the technical potential for automation of those capabilities.

[16] The minimum wage can also play a role in affecting the incidence of job automation, but the process is still poorly understood and constitutes the subject of a lively debate. Though the conventional wisdom has been that minimum wages have minimal impact on employment, one recent study based on United States data found that states that raised the minimum wage saw more workers in automatable jobs become unemployed. The same study suggests that higher-skilled workers in those states found better work opportunities after minimum wages were increased (Lordan and Neumark, 2018[134]). Before drawing firm conclusions, however, this subject will need further investigation.

[17] As in Chapter 3, under-employed workers are defined as workers whose main job is part-time and who report either that they could not find a full-time job or that they would like to work more hours. In different contexts, under-employment may be defined differently (e.g. it may refer to problems of skills mismatch).

[18] Non-standard (or atypical) forms of employment encompass all forms of work that deviate from the "standard" of full-time, open-ended contracts with a single employer. They include, therefore, workers with temporary jobs, part-time contracts, and those who are self-employed.

[19] Such a transformation is typically more visible in countries that experience a more significant shift of employment from manufacturing to service sectors (which are more amenable to this type of work organisation). It also represents a more important concern in countries that exhibit stronger job polarisation, where a larger share of service-sector jobs may attract low earnings (as discussed in the next section).

[20] Through the offshoring of jobs from advanced economies to developing countries with more lax labour regulations, the net effect of globalisation on job quality worldwide may in fact be negative.

[21] Such impacts, however, may be driven by the selection of more productive firms into the export sector and identifying causal impacts is challenging (Schank, Schnabel and Wagner, 2008[131]).

[22] In a study covering 135 countries, Davies and Vadlamannati (2013[138]) show evidence of a race to the bottom in labour standards as countries compete to attract foreign direct investment. Crucially, the effect occurs through laxer enforcement of existing standards and would not be easily solved through additional regulation.

[23] Some of this concerns are counterbalanced by the possibility that occupations with substantial monitoring and micro-management of workers' actions may be among the most automatable, and could therefore shrink in coming decades. This question would deserve further scrutiny.

[24] *Code du Travail*, Art. L2242-17.

[25] The OECD defines a platform as a "digital service that facilitates interactions between two or more distinct but interdependent sets of users (whether firms or individuals) who interact through the service via the Internet" (OECD, forthcoming[146]).

[26] Available evidence is nevertheless insufficient to draw firm conclusions in this respect.

[27] Estimates discussed in this subsection and not presented in Figure 2.9 are based on labour force statistics and are available from the OECD Secretariat upon request.

[28] TWA employment is defined here as the employment of workers with a contract under which the employer (i.e. the agency), within the framework of its business or professional practice, places the employee at the disposal of a third party (i.e. the user firm) in order to perform work (i.e. the assignment) under supervision and direction of that user firm by virtue of an agreement for the provision of services between the user firm and the agency. It should be noted that some TWA workers have open-ended contracts (with compensation for non-assignment periods).

[29] Estimates discussed in this subsection and not presented in the figures are based on OECD labour force statistics.

[30] The ILO uses the following definitions: "substantial part-time" (21-34 hours per week); "short part-time" (20 hours or less); and "marginal part-time" (fewer than 15 hours per week).

[31] On-call work, which includes the case of zero-hour contracts, is a type of agreement under which the employer can call the employee when work is available, and which therefore entails a flexible amount of working hours.

[32] In Italy, on-call contracts (*lavoro a chiamata o intermittente*) set the parameters for employers to call in a worker over a given period of time, even on short notice. For a 20% wage premium, the employer can enforce a worker's guarantee to work if called in. On-call workers in Italy receive similar protections to regular workers, including holidays, social insurance and parental leave.

[33] In the Netherlands, on-call workers may sign either *min-max contracts*, with a specified range of hours per week, or *zero-hour contracts*, with no specified number of hours. In turn, both these contract types can fall into one of two categories: i) preliminary agreements, which do not require employers to offer work or workers to accept it; and ii) future work obligation contracts, which commit employers to offer available

work and employees to accept it. Those who sign the less-regulated "preliminary contract" have no employment rights except during the hours that the employer calls them to work. Their entitlements to hours-based benefits (e.g. leave, unemployment insurance) are limited relative to workers with guaranteed hours. Further, on-call workers in some cases are explicitly excluded from collective labour agreements – for example, agreements for gas stations and laundromats exclude on-call workers from holiday pay, paid sick leave, pension funds, and training days.

[34] Employers in the United Kingdom are not required to provide any minimum working hours for individuals hired on zero-hour contracts, and workers are not obliged to accept any work offered. Their rights and protections will depend on whether they are classified as workers or as employees. In most cases, they will be classified as workers, in which case they are only entitled to certain basic employment rights. Since May 2015, exclusivity clauses (i.e. clauses which prevent an employee from accepting work from another employer) in zero-hour contracts have been banned. Since January 2016, workers have been able to claim compensation at an employment tribunal if they are punished or dismissed for looking for work elsewhere.

[35] It is possible that part of this increase is due to increased awareness among workers about what contract they are on, given the (often negative) press coverage which zero-hour contracts have received in the United Kingdom. In addition, however, zero-hour contracts are considered as suitable job offers by the PES, therefore forcing workers to take them up.

[36] In the Republic of Ireland, *if-and-when contracts* cover cases in which the worker has zero set hours and is not formally required to maintain availability to work (i.e. he/she can work "if and when" mutually amenable). Another, less commonly used type of contract is the *zero-hour contract*, which requires the worker to maintain availability to work if called by the employer. While zero-hour contract workers are usually considered employees, workers who are on if-and-when contracts are not generally recognised as employees under Irish law and thus they have neither the right to minimum pay nor employee protections (as prescribed by the Organisation of Working Time Act).

[37] However, in some countries (particularly the United States), there has been some concern that traditional labour force surveys are underestimating the rise in new forms of self-employment (Katz and Krueger, 2016[135]; Jackson, Looney and Ramnath, 2017[136]; Abraham et al., 2017[139]).

[38] Only a few countries have official (legal) definitions of dependent self-employment and, where these exist, they tend to differ (see Chapter 4). Estimating the extent of dependent self-employment is further complicated by the fact that standard labour force and household surveys do not permit the identification of such workers.

[39] Using the European Working Conditions Survey, false self-employed workers can be defined as own account workers who generally only have one client and also cannot change at least two of the following: i) the order of their tasks; ii) their method of work; and iii) the speed or rate of work.

[40] Manufacturing industries are typically less polarised than service industries. Their relative decline, therefore, contributes to overall polarisation, though it is not its main driver (for the most part, the polarisation process is due to *within-industry* polarisation). For a detailed discussion, see OECD (2017[10]).

[41] Following previous analysis on job polarisation (OECD, 2017[10]), high-, middle-, and low-pay occupations (alternatively referred to as high-, middle-, and low-skilled, respectively) are defined using the International Standard Classification of Occupations (ISCO-88). Low skill workers are those holding a job in sales and service and elementary occupations (ISCO 5 and 9); medium skill workers are those holding a job in clerical, craft, plant and machine operators and assemblers occupations (ISCO 4,7 and 8). High

skill workers are those holding a job in managerial, professional, technicians and associate professionals occupations (ISCO 1, 2 and 3). Skilled agricultural workers are excluded from the analysis.

[42] In Switzerland and a few Eastern European countries the share of low-skilled jobs also decreased. The results are based on the analysis published in Chapter 3 of the *Employment Outlook 2017* (OECD, 2017[10]), where additional details can be found on the methodological choices made to calculate polarisation (which, include, for instance, devising a statistical method to fix documented breaks in the occupational classification that occurred in several countries over the period analysed).

[43] Middle-class households are those with net disposable income between 75% and 200% of the median household income in a given country.

[44] For instance, the proportion of working adults in the middle class shrank by more than 4 percentage points in Denmark, Canada, the United States, and Germany, while it grew by more than 4 percentage points in France, Ireland, and Hungary. It should also be remarked that while the squeeze may not be visible from an earnings perspective, it may be the result of rising costs for middle-class households (OECD, 2019[101]).

[45] It should also be remarked that, while it might not explain the perceived squeeze of the middle-class, job polarisation may be linked to the growing sense of insecurity associated with many jobs (documented in Chapter 3). Most importantly, while the declining middle-skilled jobs are predominantly associated with full-time open-ended (i.e. standard) contracts, the growth in high- and low-skilled jobs is mainly associated with non-standard employment (OECD, 2015[39]).

[46] This was partly due to the falling labour share (which captures the decoupling of average wages from productivity) and partly to increases in wage inequality (which captures the decoupling of median wages from average wages).

[47] The period analysed, however, includes a protracted crisis. Previous OECD work shows that between 2000 and 2009 the labour share also decreased in those countries (OECD, 2012[140]).

[48] This is because high-skilled workers may be more difficult to substitute and can be more easily re-employed in non-routine tasks.

[49] In Azar et al (2018[141]), the same authors refine the analysis by estimating labour market concentration across nearly all occupations and for every commuting zone in the United States using data from Burning Glass Technologies (BGT).

[50] Available evidence however shows that a significant fraction of employment is in highly concentrated labour markets in the United Kingdom and Portugal (Abel, Tenreyro and Thwaites, 2018[142]; Martins, 2018[143]). Moreover, in many OECD countries, a large number of studies have also estimated low residual labour supply elasticities – measuring how easily workers switch to a different employer in reaction to wage changes in a specific firm – which is typically considered as evidence of labour market monopsony – see e.g. Sokolova and Sorensen (2018[144]).

[51] The percentage of business births is even lower (9.3%) in remote rural regions (those not in the vicinity of an urban agglomeration with at least 50 000 inhabitants).

[52] For additional details on the OECD Inclusive Growth initiative, see http://www.oecd.org/inclusive-growth/.

[53] Upon interpreting these results, it is important to bear in mind that the methodology is sensitive to changes in the range of years and to whether agricultural employment is included or not in the analysis - see (Alonso-Soto, forthcoming[56]) for additional details.

# 3 The future of work: New evidence on job stability, under-employment and access to good jobs

The complex interplay of globalisation, technological and demographic changes is generating many new opportunities but also challenges for many workers across the OECD. This chapter provides new evidence on three selected topics that have featured prominently in the debate on the future of work: job stability, under-employment and changes in the share of well-paid jobs. The results point to worsening labour market outcomes for those with less than tertiary education and for the young in several countries. In fact, young workers with less than tertiary education stand out as a group that has experienced a pronounced decline in fortunes across a large number of countries. This raises a two-fold challenge. First, policies must promote better opportunities for school-leavers entering the labour market. Second, policies are needed to improve job prospects for the generation of young people who have faced a very tough labour market environment in the past decade.

---

The statistical data for Israel are supplied by and under the responsibility of the relevant Israeli authorities. The use of such data by the OECD is without prejudice to the status of the Golan Heights, East Jerusalem and Israeli settlements in the West Bank under the terms of international law.

# In Brief

## Key findings

The complex interplay of globalisation, technological and demographic changes is generating many new opportunities but also challenges for many workers across the OECD. Identifying who is likely to benefit and who may lose out of these deep changes is essential to inform policies contributing to the development of a more inclusive labour market.

This chapter provides new information on three selected topics related to both the quality and quantity of jobs that have featured prominently in the debate on the future of work, but for which hard evidence has been limited – job stability, under-employment and changes in the share of well-paid jobs. First, it investigates whether jobs have truly become less stable and, if so, whether these changes are linked to an increase in the mobility of workers between jobs or between jobs and non-employment. Second, the chapter examines whether there is a growing risk of under-employment (the extent to which people would like to work more hours than they currently do) rather than technologically driven unemployment. More specifically, it looks at how the risk of under-employment has evolved for different socio-demographic groups, as the growth of the service sector, low-skill occupations and atypical forms of employment have contributed to its overall increase in several countries. Finally, the chapter investigates how the chances of getting a middle-paid job have changed for different groups. Again, a key issue here may be that, rather than being confronted by a jobless future, some groups in the labour market may be facing a future where it will be harder to find a well-paid job.

A key finding of the analysis is that the labour market experiences of many young people and of those with less than tertiary education have worsened over the past decade. In fact, the young with less than tertiary education have been particularly affected by these changes, as the share experiencing under-employment, non-employment and low-pay has increased. While these changes have affected different countries to varying degrees, only two countries (Germany and Poland) have not seen a worsening of any of these indicators for young people with less than tertiary education. The evidence suggests that these patterns are unlikely to be only a hangover of the recent global economic crisis.

There is also a clear gender dimension. While the absolute risks of both under-employment and non-employment remain higher for women, the risk of non-employment for men has increased in most countries (particularly for those with less than tertiary education). Men with less than tertiary education have also experienced proportionally large increases in the risk of under-employment. But women remain more likely to be in low-paid jobs and less likely to be in high-paid ones, despite an improvement in the probability of being in middle-paid jobs.

More specifically, the key findings of the chapter are as follows.

### Job stability

- Since 2006, across the OECD, average job stability (as measured by job tenure, the length of time spent in the current job) has increased in a number of countries. This is, however, a compositional effect due to the increase in the share of older workers who tend to have longer job tenure. Once this change in the composition of the workforce is taken into account, job tenure actually declined in most countries.

- These changes have not affected all workers equally. The largest declines in tenure have occurred for low-educated workers (i.e. those without an upper secondary qualification).

- There is some evidence that the decline in job tenure stems from the fact that workers move more frequently between jobs rather than from jobs to non-employment. However, the magnitudes of these changes are small and there are many differences between countries.

## Under-employment

- The incidence of under-employment has increased in many countries over the past decade. While the business cycle explains a large part of these changes, more structural and persistent changes have also played a role, including the growth of the service sector, the growing employment share of low-skilled occupations and the spread of non-standard forms of employment with no guaranteed hours.

- Again, some workers have been more affected than others. Across the OECD, the largest increases in the risk of under-employment have occurred for young people and those with less than tertiary education. Because under-employed workers suffer many disadvantages, these changes represent a substantial challenge on the road to more inclusive labour markets.

- Across the OECD, women remain much more likely to be under-employed than men (8% vs 3.2%), but under-employment has grown faster among men in most countries, with larger increases affecting those with less than tertiary education.

## Job polarisation and jobs of different pay levels

- In most countries, the share of middle-paid jobs has increased despite the decline in the employment share of middle-skilled occupations (i.e. job polarisation). However, the decline in the share of middle-skilled occupations has meant that the workers without tertiary education are increasingly moving into low-skilled occupations or out of work entirely.

- On average across the OECD, there have been small increases in the probability of low-paid employment for the young and for workers with medium education. But there has been a pronounced deterioration in the labour market position of the young with less than tertiary education in many countries. In particular, among those who have left education, there have been widespread increases in the incidence of non-employment and of low pay for those in employment.

- Low-paid employment has increased also among highly educated young people in some countries. On average across the OECD, they are now more likely to be in low-paid jobs than in high-paid ones.

## Introduction

This chapter provides new evidence on selected topics relating to both the quality and quantity of work that have featured prominently in the debate on the future of work. In particular, the chapter looks at recent changes in job stability, under-employment and the availability of jobs at different pay levels.

A common conjecture in the debate on the future of work is that job stability might be decreasing as firms adopt business models that favour ad-hoc, short-term hires of workers over traditional long-term employment relationships. On the one hand, this could lead to increased job insecurity and volatile labour income if the job changes involved are largely involuntary for workers. On the other hand, a decline in average job tenure might be the result of increased job hopping by workers, which could lead to better working conditions. Each scenario requires a different policy approach. Therefore, Section 3.1 documents changes in job stability and offers new evidence on the evolution of job-to-job flows and the risk of involuntary separation for different groups of workers.

The second issue discussed in Section 3.2 is that of under-employment (i.e. the extent to which people are working fewer hours than they would like). As argued in Chapter 2, employment losses resulting from job automation are not likely to be as large as has sometimes been suggested. Nevertheless, there has been a process of de-industrialisation and a growth in service sector employment, where low-skilled and less stable jobs are more common. This structural change may contribute to a permanent shift to higher under-employment even if it does not result in a jobless future. Under-employment has already been advanced as an explanation for weak aggregate wage growth over the last decade (OECD, 2018[1]), but it is also a challenge because under-employed workers are at a considerable disadvantage in the labour market: they receive lower wages and experience worse working conditions than similar workers in full-time or voluntary part-time employment (MacDonald, forthcoming[2]). If under-employment is more common for certain groups than for others, it could further increase disparities in the labour market. Understanding how under-employment affects different groups of workers is therefore crucial to inform policies that seek to make work more inclusive in the future.

The third issue addressed in Section 3.3 concerns the risk that jobs are becoming not only more polarised in terms of skill levels (as documented in Chapter 2) but also in terms of pay. A key concern is whether countries are seeing a decline in the share of the middle-paid jobs, which have typically underpinned the living standards of the middle class (OECD, 2019[3]). To address the lack of evidence on this important policy issue, Section 3.3 investigates whether job polarisation has eroded the share of middle-paid jobs. The analysis yields a picture of the changing relationship between occupational skill levels and pay levels and how this has affected different types of workers.

## 3.1. Are jobs becoming less stable?

In the debate on what the future of work may look like, a common prediction is that lifetime employment will gradually disappear. Instead, job mobility will increase and people will make more frequent transitions into and out of employment and between jobs, which may involve a different employment status (e.g. employee versus self-employment).

A number of megatrends appear to be pushing towards a decline in job stability, which might constitute a positive or a negative development for workers. Rapid advancements in Information Communication Technology (ICT) boost labour mobility by facilitating job search, by encouraging new business models that rely on outsourcing to a greater extent, and by fostering opportunities for independent work and weakening the traditional employer-employee relationship (see also Chapter 2 and Chapter 4). The forces of globalisation play an equally important role. They increase the risk of job displacement by exposing workers to international competition, and they expand the set of available opportunities by granting workers access to the global labour market. In addition, workers' preferences vis-à-vis employment, flexibility, and independent work are changing and constitute another fundamental driver of labour mobility (Prising, 2016[4]). The rise of the platform economy and of "gig work" epitomises these transformations, and feeds the anxiety that an increasing number of jobs will be shorter-lived.

Are jobs truly becoming less stable? To answer this question, this section uses data on workers who have left education to analyse trends in job stability and labour market mobility across 30 countries over the past decade.[1] Section 3.1.2 investigates whether the observed changes in tenure reflect increasing flows of workers between jobs, or rather between jobs and non-employment.

### 3.1.1. Job stability has decreased for all age groups

Overall job stability (as measured by average job tenure) has remained stable or has even risen slightly over the past decade in most OECD countries (Figure 3.1). However, after adjusting for changes in the age, education and gender composition of the workforce, tenure has declined on average. The difference between the unadjusted and the adjusted change in tenure is largely due to population ageing which increases the proportion of older workers (with usually longer average job tenure) relative to younger ones. This has been reinforced by recent reforms, including the termination of early-retirement schemes and increases in the official retirement age in several OECD countries, which have led to higher labour force participation at older ages (OECD, 2014[5]).

After adjusting for changes in the demographic structure, job tenure decreased by 4.9% (or around five months) on average (Figure 3.1).[2] This modest change masks considerable variation across OECD countries. Nineteen out of thirty countries saw a decrease in tenure (the Czech Republic experienced almost no change). Tenure decreased by more than 17% in Sweden, Luxembourg and Lithuania, while it increased significantly in countries such as Spain and Latvia. Part of the observed decline in average tenure might be driven by the recovery as workers find new jobs with lower tenure. However, while the limited time period makes it difficult to isolate the effect of the cycle, the average decline in tenure across the OECD is larger when adjusting for the cycle.[3] This suggests that the main effect of the cycle over the period considered has been to increase job tenure, consistent with the observation that the crisis disproportionally destroyed jobs with low tenure.

**Figure 3.1. Job stability has decreased in the majority of countries after accounting for population ageing**

Percentage change in job tenure for workers not in education, unadjusted and adjusted, 2006 to 2017[1]

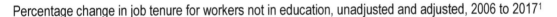

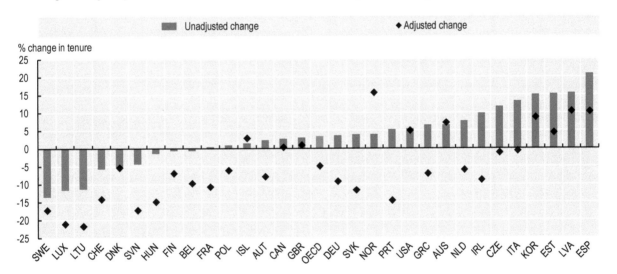

Note: The OECD average is the unweighted average of the displayed countries. The *unadjusted change* is the percentage change in average tenure between 2006 and 2017. The *adjusted change* shows the estimated changes once controlling for the composition of the labour force by age, gender and education. The methodology is similar to the one used by Farber (2010[6]).
1. Data for 2017 refer to 2016 for Australia, Germany, and the United States, and to 2014 for Korea.
Source: European labour force survey (EU-LFS), German Socio-Economic Panel (GSOEP), Household, Income and Labour Dynamics in Australia (HILDA) Survey, Korean Labor & Income Panel Study (KLIPS), Canadian Labour Force Survey, and the United States Current Population Survey (CPS) Tenure Supplement.

StatLink ᴍꜱᴸ http://dx.doi.org/10.1787/888933966274

*The largest declines in job stability have occurred for workers with low education*

The decline in job stability was larger for low-educated workers (i.e. with less than upper-secondary education)[4] than for other education groups (Figure 3.2). This was the case for all age groups, with the exception of younger male workers where the decline in tenure was almost identical for all education groups.

Over two-thirds of the OECD countries in the sample saw reductions in tenure for workers with low education (see Annex Figure 3.A.1). The reductions in tenure were in some cases large, exceeding 30% in the Slovak Republic, Lithuania, Hungary, Sweden and Poland. In contrast, Norway and Australia, along with Estonia and Latvia, saw workers without an upper-secondary qualification experience increases in tenure of over 15%.

Figure 3.2. The largest declines in job stability have occurred for low-educated workers

Percentage change in job tenure (years) by gender, age and education, 2006 to 2017[1]

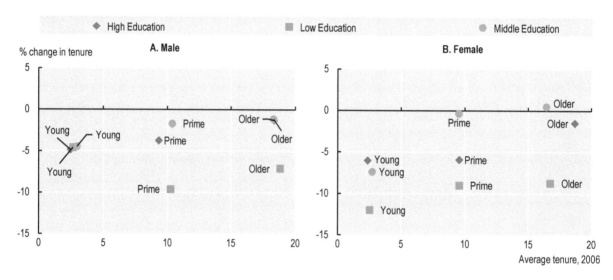

Note: Each data point is the unweighted average of the countries included in the analysis, excluding Korea due to data quality. The x-axis is the observed average tenure in 2006 and the y-axis is the percent change in average tenure between 2006 and 2017. Young workers are aged 15 to 29 years, prime-aged workers are aged 30 to 54, and older workers are aged 55 to 69.
1. Data for 2017 for Australia, Germany, and the United States refer to 2016.
Source: European labour force survey (EU-LFS), German Socio-Economic Panel (GSOEP), Household, Income and Labour Dynamics in Australia (HILDA) Survey, Canadian Labour Force Survey, and the United States Current Population Survey (CPS) Tenure Supplement.

StatLink 🔗 http://dx.doi.org/10.1787/888933966293

### 3.1.2. Decreasing job tenure may be the result of increased job mobility

Changes in job stability can be linked to more transitions between jobs or between jobs and non-employment. To gauge the relative importance of these different mechanisms, this section studies changes in different types of flows in the labour market.

To assess whether there has been an increase in moves across jobs, the section uses data on yearly transitions from job to job. An increase in this type of transition is often interpreted in the literature as a positive development since the evidence indicates that switching jobs is typically associated with opportunities for career progression and wage gains (Topel and Ward, 1992[7]; Hahn et al., 2018[8]).[5] However, job changes might not be voluntary and might not necessarily lead to better outcomes (for example, for workers who move because their fixed-term contract is ending). Unfortunately, the data available do not allow this distinction to be tested.

To assess whether changes in job tenure are linked to increases transitions into non-employment, the section considers: i) transitions from jobs to non-employment (excluding transitions into education); and ii) changes in the probability of moving into unemployment involuntarily, i.e. as a result of a layoff or the end of a contract of limited duration.

## Figure 3.3. Job-to-job flows and transitions out of work differ significantly across the OECD

Percentage point changes in rate of transition out of a job into either another job or non-employment, 2006 to 2017[1]

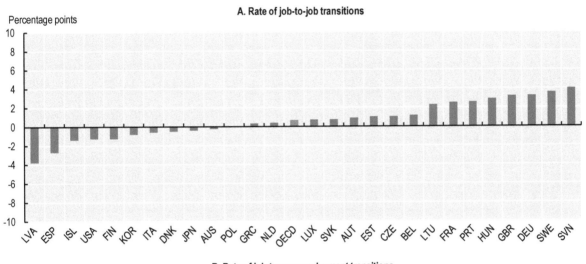

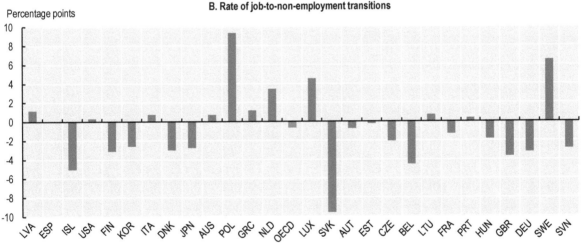

Note: The OECD average is the unweighted average of all depicted countries. Values have been adjusted for compositional changes. Norway has been excluded for reasons of data quality.
1. Data for 2017 refer to 2016 for Australia, Germany, and the United States, and to 2014 for Korea.
Source: European labour force survey (EU-LFS), German Socio-Economic Panel (GSOEP), Household, Income and Labour Dynamics in Australia (HILDA) Survey, Korean Labor & Income Panel Study (KLIPS), and the United States Current Population Survey (CPS) Tenure Supplement.

StatLink 🔗 http://dx.doi.org/10.1787/888933966312

*The evidence that the decline in tenure is due to higher mobility between jobs is mixed across countries*

Over the past decade, job-to-job flows have increased in over one-half of 27 countries after adjusting for demographic changes (Figure 3.3).[6,7] At the same time, transitions to non-employment fell over the period in most countries. This suggests that the observed declines in tenure are generally linked to increased mobility between jobs rather than between jobs and non-employment. This was particularly evident in Germany, Slovenia, and the United Kingdom. However, in ten countries, the rate of job-to-job movements fell, with the largest drops recorded in Latvia, Spain, Finland, Iceland, and the United States.

*The risk of involuntary entry into unemployment has remained stable on average across countries*

Over the same period, the share of workers who became unemployed involuntarily (as a result of a layoff or of the end of a contract of limited duration) did not change on average across the OECD, but there were important cross-country differences. After adjusting for demographics, the likelihood of workers becoming unemployed involuntarily increased significantly in countries like the Netherlands, Italy, Greece, Latvia, and Spain, while it fell most prominently in Sweden, France, Germany and Poland (Figure 3.4).

Five of the 12 countries with an increase in the risk of involuntary separations (Figure 3.4) also experienced a decline in job-to-job flows (Figure 3.3). These are Italy, Australia, Denmark, Spain and Latvia. Hence, changes in mobility in these countries appear to be linked to increased risk and uncertainty for workers.[8] Conversely, among the twelve countries with declining risk of involuntary separation, all but two (Iceland and Finland) saw an increase in job-to-job flows. Some of the largest drops in involuntary separations and increases in job-to-job flows were observed in Sweden, Germany, France, Great Britain and Hungary.

**Figure 3.4. Involuntary separations show very different trends across countries**

Percentage point change in probability of an involuntary separation in the past 12 months leading to unemployment, 2006 to 2017[1]

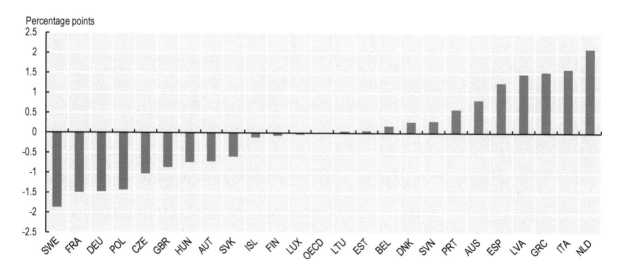

Note: The OECD average is the unweighted average of all depicted countries. Values have been adjusted for compositional changes. Norway has been excluded for reasons of data quality.
1. Data for 2017 refer to 2016 for Australia and Germany.
Source: European labour force survey (EU-LFS), German Socio-Economic Panel (GSOEP), Household, Income and Labour Dynamics in Australia (HILDA) Survey.

*StatLink* 📊 http://dx.doi.org/10.1787/888933966331

*Increases in the risk of involuntary unemployment disproportionately affected men*

While the changes in involuntary separations were small on average across the OECD, men generally saw larger increases than women. Among men, the increases were of similar magnitude (always below half a percentage point) across education and age groups with two notable exceptions (Figure 3.5). In fact, older workers with high education and younger male workers with low education saw declines in the rate of involuntary separation of just over half a percentage point.

Among women the picture is mixed, with a negative relationship between a group's pre-crisis rate of involuntary separation and their associated post-crisis change. Younger women with middle and low education had the highest rates of pre-crisis involuntary separations. They also saw the largest fall post-crisis with rates declining by 0.5 and 1.2 percentage points, respectively. Older and prime-age women with middle- and low-education experienced modest to no declines in the rate of involuntary separation. High-educated workers of all age groups – who had the lowest pre-crisis rates – experienced increases in the rate of involuntary separation similar to their male counterparts.

**Figure 3.5. Men saw the largest increase in the risk of involuntary entry into unemployment**

Percentage point change in likelihood of involuntary separation, 2006 to 2017[1]

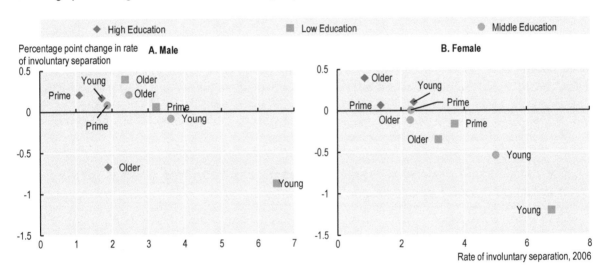

Note: Each data point is the unweighted average of the countries included in the analysis. Data for Norway is excluded from the average due to data quality issues.
1. Data for 2017 refer to 2016 for Australia and Germany.
Source: European labour force survey (EU-LFS), German Socio-Economic Panel (GSOEP), Household, Income and Labour Dynamics in Australia (HILDA) Survey.

*StatLink* 🔗🔗 http://dx.doi.org/10.1787/888933966350

*Overall, the cross-country picture is mixed and lower stability has not necessarily been associated with increased mobility between jobs*

The hypothesis that job stability is decreasing as the result of increased mobility between jobs finds some support across the OECD. Adjusted for compositional changes, tenure is down on average, while transitions to non-employment are down and job-to-job transitions are up. However, the magnitudes of these changes are small and they are a result of significant heterogeneity across countries rather than a clear trend. A trend does emerge among demographic groups. Workers without an upper-secondary diploma experienced the largest decrease in job stability.

These findings point to the need for careful policy interventions to ensure that workers who are affected by increased job insecurity can count on adequate safety nets, effective (and, where possible, pre-emptive) activation policies, and sufficient opportunities for training and re-skilling. Even when declining tenure is linked to greater mobility between jobs (which could, potentially be a positive trend), policies need to ensure that the fragmentation of careers does not penalises workers in terms of access to social protection or training.

## 3.2. Not unemployed, but under-employed?

The future of work may not be characterised by greater unemployment (see Chapter 2), but will it be one of greater under-employment? This section shows that under-employment has increased in a number of countries in recent times. While heavily affected by the business cycle, under-employment is also linked to persistent structural changes in the labour market. In particular, the incidence of under-employment is higher in the service sector and within low-skill occupations (MacDonald, forthcoming[2]; Valletta, Bengali and van der List, forthcoming[9]), both of which have been growing in recent decades (OECD, 2017[10]).

Under-employed workers are at a particular disadvantage in the labour market.[9] They tend to receive lower hourly wages and experience worse working conditions than similar workers in full-time or voluntary part-time employment (MacDonald, forthcoming[2]). Understanding how under-employment affects different groups of workers is therefore crucial to inform policies to promote inclusive labour markets.

This section provides new evidence on how the risk of under-employment has evolved in recent times for different groups of workers, using data from 33 OECD countries and Colombia from 2006 to 2017. Under-employed workers are defined as workers whose main job is part-time and who report either that they could not find a full-time job or that they would like to work more hours.[10] Throughout the section, people still studying are excluded from the analysis to ensure that the results are not driven by an increasing number of students seeking part-time employment.

### 3.2.1. The incidence of under-employment varies across countries and has increased more in those hit hardest by the crisis

The level of under-employment varies considerably across countries (Figure 3.6). On average in OECD countries in 2017, about a third of all part-time workers were under-employed, amounting to around 5.5% of all employees. Italy, Spain, and Australia had 10% or more of employees in under-employment. At the other end of the spectrum, the figure was less than 2% for Colombia, Japan, Estonia, Turkey, Hungary and the Czech Republic.

The Great Recession certainly played an important role in pushing up under-employment in some countries. Under-employment rose in Ireland, Italy, Greece, and Spain, which had been hit particularly hard by the Great Recession, by an average of 6.2 percentage points, much higher than the 1.1 percentage points OECD average.[11] In fact, the increases in these countries drive a large share of the overall increase. Without these four countries, the average increase of the remaining ones is 0.4 percentage points.

Nevertheless, levels of under-employment remained higher in 2017 than in 2006 in a number of countries that had long been on a recovery path or had only marginally been affected by the recession (for example in Australia, France, the Netherlands, the United Kingdom, and the United States). This suggests that some of the increase observed is driven by persistent structural changes over and above the temporary fluctuations of the business cycle.

**Figure 3.6. The majority of countries have seen increases in under-employment, but particularly those hit hardest by the crisis**

Percentage share of dependent workers in under-employment, 2006 and 2017 (or latest year)[1]

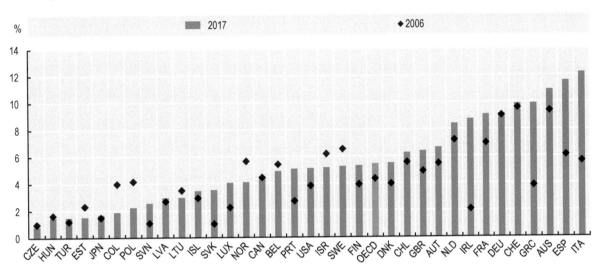

Note: The OECD average is the unweighted average of the countries depicted. Under-employed workers are in part-time employment (working 30 hours or less per week) who report either that they could not find a full-time job or that they would like to work more hours.
1. Data for 2017 refer to 2016 for Australia, Germany, and Japan, 2015 for Chile and Turkey, and 2011 for Israel. Data for 2006 refer to 2007 for Colombia and 2009 for Chile.
Source: European labour force survey (EU-LFS), German Socio-Economic Panel (GSOEP), United States Current Population Survey (CPS), Canadian Labour Force Survey, Turkey Labour Force Survey, Japan Household Panel Survey (JHPS/KHPS), Colombian *Gran encuesta integrada de hogares* (GEIH), Chilean National Socio-Economic Characterization Survey (CASEN), Israel Labour Force Survey, Household, Income and Labour Dynamics in Australia (HILDA) Survey.

StatLink 🔗 http://dx.doi.org/10.1787/888933966369

### 3.2.2. The rise in under-employment also reflects permanent structural changes

Across the OECD, under-employment exhibits a positive trend even after accounting for the economic cycle, as shown by the dashed line in Figure 3.7.[12] The convergence between the adjusted and unadjusted trends in recent years suggests that under-employment is unlikely to recede much further, unless labour markets become particularly tight as in the years immediately before the recession.

The main structural change contributing to the positive trend adjusted for the economic cycle is the slow but steady growth of the service sector. Figure 3.7 shows that the trend adjusted for the change in the industrial mix is much flatter than the one adjusted for the cycle only. The increasing difference between the two lines since the recession suggests that the importance of the expanding service sector in driving the increase in under-employment has grown in recent times. These results are in line with those obtained for the United States by Valletta, Bengali and Van Der List (forthcoming[9]).

**Figure 3.7. Under-employment exhibits an increasing trend even after adjusting for the cycle**

Percentage point change in the under-employment rate across the OECD since 2001, adjusted for cyclical and structural factors

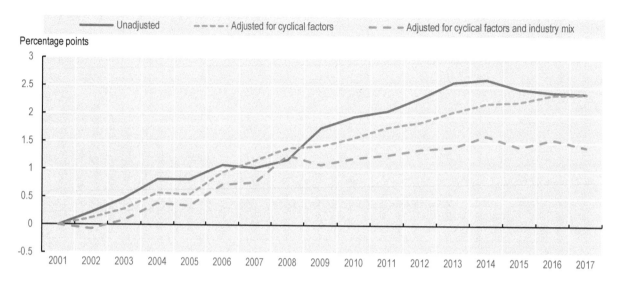

Note: Time trend shown with reference the baseline level in 2001. The Figure presents unconditional and conditional time trend from a GLM regression model with a logit link. The unconditional model controls for country differences. The model adjusting for cyclical factors adds unemployment and its square to the model. The industry mix is represented by the share of employment in the "Accommodation and food" and the "Arts and leisure" sectors. The results are robust to using a broader definition of the service sector. Estimates are weighted by the average employment for each country over the period. Values are presented as average marginal effects. The model does not include Turkey or Colombia due to data constraints. Similar results are obtained when countries are not weighted by employment, or when a measure of output gap is used to account for the cycle.
Source: OECD calculations.

StatLink 🔗 http://dx.doi.org/10.1787/888933966388

Some parts of the service sector have a much higher incidence of under-employment than manufacturing. For example, in 2017 "Accommodation and food services" had a share of under-employed workers of around 12.2%, against only 1.8% in manufacturing (Figure 3.8). One explanation for such large difference is that firms in these sectors often favour part-time employment as a way of dealing with demand variation over the day (Euwals and Hogerbrugge, 2006[11]). In this context, since the choice of a part-time arrangement is driven by the employer's preference rather than the worker's, it is more likely to result in involuntary part-time. This argument suggests that under-employment might be particularly important in labour markets where workers have a weak bargaining position vis-à-vis their employers (Chapter 4 further discusses the issue of monopsony power).

Other factors associated with the growth of under-employment are the increasing employment share of low-skilled occupations and the spread of non-standard forms of employment (MacDonald, forthcoming[2]). The increase in the share of low-skilled occupations (which is linked to the expansion of the service sector) is a well-known trend affecting a large number of countries across the OECD – see OECD (2017[10]) and Section 3.3. Chapter 2 discusses the emergence of very atypical part-time contracts, like on-call or zero-hours contracts, where people are not guaranteed any fixed hours or, indeed, any hours at all.

As the structural changes behind the increase in under-employment are likely to continue into the future, it is likely that under-employment will continue to affect a significant (and possibly increasing) number of workers.

Figure 3.8. Under-employment is more common in service sectors

Figure 3.8. Under-employment is more common in service sectors

Percentage share of dependent workers indicating under-employment, by broad industry. Unweighted OECD average, 2006 and 2017 (or latest year)[1]

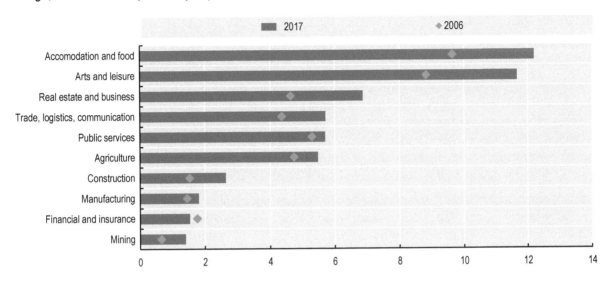

Note: The OECD average is an unweighted average. Under-employed workers are in part-time employment (working 30 hours or less per week) who report either that they could not find a full-time job or that they would like to work more hours. Industries are broadly grouped according to a modified NACE Rev.2 A10 classification structure. The category of "Agriculture" broadly corresponds to NACE Rev.2 Section A; "Trade, Logistics, Communications" broadly corresponds to Sections G, H, and J; "Public Services" broadly corresponds to Sections O, P, and Q; and "Arts and leisure" broadly corresponds to Sections R, S, T, and U.
1. Data for 2017 refer to 2016 for Australia, Germany, and Japan, 2015 for Chile and Turkey, and 2011 for Israel. Data for 2006 refer to 2007 for Colombia and 2009 for Chile.
Source: European labour force survey (EU-LFS), German Socio-Economic Panel (GSOEP), United States Current Population Survey (CPS), Canadian Labour Force Survey, Turkey Labour Force Survey, Japan Household Panel Survey(JHPS/KHPS), Colombian *Gran encuesta integrada de hogares* (GEIH), Chilean National Socio-Economic Characterization Survey (CASEN), Israel Labour Force Survey, Household, Income and Labour Dynamics in Australia (HILDA) Survey.

StatLink ᵐˢ🔗 http://dx.doi.org/10.1787/888933966407

### 3.2.3. Under-employment has increased more for youth and those with less than tertiary education

The prevalence of under-employment has increased more for young workers and those with a low or medium level of education (Figure 3.9). Within all age groups of both genders, those with lower education have seen larger increases in the risk of under-employment. And, within all educational groups for both men and women, younger workers have seen larger increases than older ones with one exception. This is the group of prime-age, low-educated women who have seen an increase in the probability of under-employment larger than their younger colleagues and, indeed, than almost any other group (just over 4 percentage points). Overall, three of the four groups with the largest increases include young (male and female) workers with less than tertiary education. For all of these groups the increase is larger than 3.0 percentage points.

By country, young people have seen an increase in the probability of under-employment in 23 of the 34 countries considered in this analysis (see Annex Figure 3.A.2). The average increase for the young among all countries was 2.4 percentage points, but fifteen countries have seen larger increases, and in three (Greece, Italy and, Spain) the increase exceeded 10 percentage points.

### 3.2.4. Women remain much more likely to be under-employed than men, despite higher than average increases for low-educated men

The share of workers who are under-employed increased by about 1 percentage point for both women and men, but women had much higher initial levels. In 2017, under-employment as a share of dependent workers was almost 8% for women (of all education levels and ages) and only 3.2% for men. For some of the education and age groups reported in Figure 3.9, women's relative position has improved only because men's conditions have deteriorated more (for example among young workers with lower education).

While under-employment remains higher among women, its incidence has grown in particular among male workers with less than tertiary education. Among prime-aged male workers with low education, the incidence of under-employment almost doubled from 2.7% in 2006 to 5.1% in 2017. Meanwhile, for low educated young male workers, it increased by almost 80%, reaching 9.7%. Among male workers with medium education, the young ones saw a two-fold increase (from 3.0% to 6.1%), and those in the prime-working age group an increase of 79% (from 1.3% to 2.4%).

Men have seen an increase in the probability of under-employment in 28 of the 34 countries considered (with decreases in Colombia, Poland, Lithuania, Latvia, and Hungary) see Annex Figure 3.A.3. The fortunes of women varied more across countries, as their risk of under-employment actually declined in 13 of the 34 countries. Furthermore, in five of the six countries in which men saw the largest increases in the probability of under-employment (that is, the Slovak Republic, Italy, Spain, Greece and Ireland) women experienced even larger increases. Denmark was an exception, with men experiencing a larger increase.

**Figure 3.9. The young and those with low education have seen the largest increases in under-employment**

Change in the percentage share of under-employed dependent workers, by age, gender and level of education, unweighted OECD average for 2006-17 (or latest year)[1]

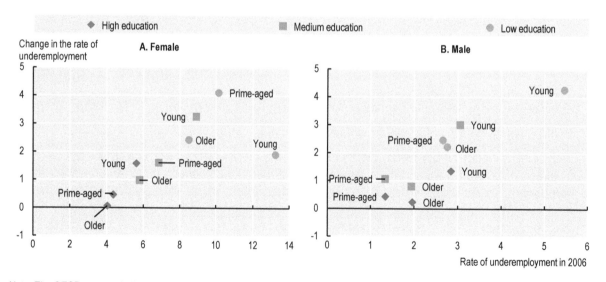

Note: The OECD average is the unweighted average of the countries depicted. Under-employed workers are in part-time employment (working 30 hours or less per week) who report either that they could not find a full-time job or that they would like to work more hours.
1. Data for 2017 refer to 2016 for Australia, Germany, and Japan, 2015 for Chile and Turkey, and 2011 for Israel. Data for 2006 refer to 2007 for Colombia 2009 for Chile.
Source: European labour force survey (EU-LFS), German Socio-Economic Panel (GSOEP), United States Current Population Survey (CPS), Canadian Labour Force Survey, Turkey Labour Force Survey, Japan Household Panel Survey(JHPS/KHPS), Colombian *Gran encuesta integrada de hogares* (GEIH), Chilean National Socio-Economic Characterization Survey (CASEN), Israel Labour Force Survey, Household, Income and Labour Dynamics in Australia (HILDA) Survey.

StatLink ᴍꜱᴾ http://dx.doi.org/10.1787/888933966426

### 3.3. Job polarisation and access to good jobs

The share of middle-skilled occupations has declined in most OECD countries in recent decades (OECD, 2017[10]). A major policy concern is that this might be causing a decline in the number of middle-paid jobs that have typically underpinned the living standards of the middle class. This worry is often echoed in the press (Yglesias, 2014[12]; Elliot, 2017[13]) as well as in the academic and policy debate on the fortunes of the middle class in recent times (Vaughan-Whitehead, Vazquez-Alvarez and Maître, 2016[14]; Pew Research Center, 2015[15]). However, the share of middle-paid jobs might hold up if low- or high-skilled occupations increasingly pay wages close to the median. While job polarisation has received much attention in the academic and policy debate on the future of work, there is surprisingly little evidence on whether the share of middle-paid jobs has held up or not.

Therefore, this section brings new evidence to bear on this issue, using data from up to 32 countries from 2006 to 2016.[13] The choice of the time period is constrained by the need to have reliable data on wages for a large number of countries. Jobs are classified into high, middle or low skill depending on the occupation they belong to. The classification adopted is the same as in OECD (2017[10]) and much of the earlier literature cited therein.[14] The distribution of jobs into high, middle, or low pay is based on how their hourly wage compares to the median hourly wage in a given year. Following the OECD standard definition,[15] low-paid jobs are those paying less than two thirds of the median wage, while high-paid jobs are those paying more than 1.5 times the median wage.[16]

#### 3.3.1. The decline in the share of middle-skilled jobs has not led to a decline in the share of middle-paid workers

Labour markets across the OECD continued to polarise in the last decade, with most of the decline in the middle-skilled occupations compensated by growth in high-skilled ones (see Annex Figure 3.A.4). This followed a known trend dating back at least to the 1990s (OECD, 2017[10]), which accelerated during the economic crisis (Green, forthcoming[16]). Between 2006 and 2016 the share of middle-skilled jobs declined in all 31 countries considered, except Luxembourg.[17] On average, the decline was just over 5 percentage points and was entirely compensated by an increase in the share of high-skilled occupations.

To investigate how job polarisation has affected the share of middle-paid jobs, Figure 3.10 presents a decomposition of changes in the total share of low-paid, middle-paid and high-paid jobs into two components. The first component is the "job polarisation effect". This is driven by changes in the relative size of different occupations. For example, one might expect that the decline in the share of middle-skilled jobs – which also tend to be middle-paid jobs – might have pushed the share of middle-paid jobs down. The second component is driven by changes in the propensity of different occupations to pay medium wages. For example, the share of middle-paid jobs might increase as a result of an increases in the proportion of high- or low-skilled jobs paying medium wages. Because this would amount to a "shift" in the distribution of these occupations towards middle-pay, this is referred to as "occupational shift" in this analysis.

*The share of middle-paid jobs has increased in most countries despite the decline in the share of middle-skilled occupations*

Far from decreasing, the share of middle-paid jobs increased by nearly 2 percentage points on average across the 31 countries considered (Panel B of Figure 3.10).[18] In 2016, the average share of middle-paid jobs across all countries was 60%, ranging from 45% in Lithuania to 77% in Denmark. Increases took place in 18 countries, with the largest increases of more than 10 percentage points seen in Hungary, Poland and Greece. Among the 13 countries where the share of middle-paid jobs declined, the average change was just under -2 percentage points. Spain saw the largest decline (-7 percentage points) followed by Estonia

(-4 percentage points). A decrease also occurred in Australia (-3 percentage points) but this was accounted for by an increase in the share of high-paid jobs rather than in the share of low-paid jobs.

Overall, job polarisation explains a small part of the change in the share of middle-paid jobs. Instead, changes in the propensity of different occupations to pay medium wages account for most of the changes. This is the case regardless of whether the share of middle-paid jobs is increasing or decreasing. On average across all countries, job polarisation reduced the share of middle-pay occupations by 0.8 percentage points, but changes in the propensity of all occupations to pay medium-level wages added over 2.5 percentage points, resulting in a total net increase of just under 2 percentage points.[19]

*The share of high-paid jobs has not grown as fast as the share of high-skilled occupations*

Job polarisation has generally contributed to increasing the share of high-paid jobs across countries, but a decline in the propensity of different occupations to pay high wages has limited the growth of high-paid jobs (Panel C of Figure 3.10). On average, job polarisation contributed 1.3 percentage points to the growth of high-paid occupations, but the second component subtracted 1.8 percentage points, resulting in a net small decline of -0.5 percentage points. In other words, the share of high-paid jobs has generally grown less than would have been expected given the shift of the occupational structures towards high-skilled occupations. This pattern is observed in the vast majority of countries.[20] In 2016, the average share of high-paid jobs (relative to each country's median wage) was 21% across all countries, ranging from 11% in Denmark to 29% in Portugal.

On average across the 31 countries, the share of low-paid jobs has declined by 1.3 percentage points (Panel A of Figure 3.10). About 0.5 percentage points of this is explained by the fact that high-skilled occupations have grown more than the other occupations. The remaining 0.8 percentage points is explained by a decline in the propensity of different occupations to pay low wages. The decline in the share of low-pay employment occurred in 20 of the 31 countries considered.

*The polarisation of the occupational structure has not led to a hollowing out of the pay distribution*

The main conclusion of this analysis is that job polarisation has not resulted in a decline in the share of middle-paid jobs and an increase in the share of high-paid jobs, as might have been expected. Instead, changes in the propensity of different occupations to pay medium-wages have tended to increase the share of middle-paid jobs and decrease that of high-paid ones.

These results point to a changing association between occupational skill levels and relative pay levels which are likely to affect workers in different ways, generating winners and losers. Identifying who these might be is not trivial. In fact, as the propensity of different occupations to pay wages of different levels changes, so do the characteristics of the workers employed in them. This is in part driven by socio-demographic trends, such as increasing female labour force participation, ageing and increasing educational attainment. But the propensity of different groups to work in different occupations is also changing (see Box 3.1).

Hence, to identify those who have lost ground in the midst of all these changes, the next section looks at how the chances of being in a low-paid job have evolved for men and women of different age groups and education levels.

# Figure 3.10. Job polarisation explains a small part of the change in the share of middle-paid jobs

Percentage point changes in the share of jobs by level of pay between 2006 and 2016

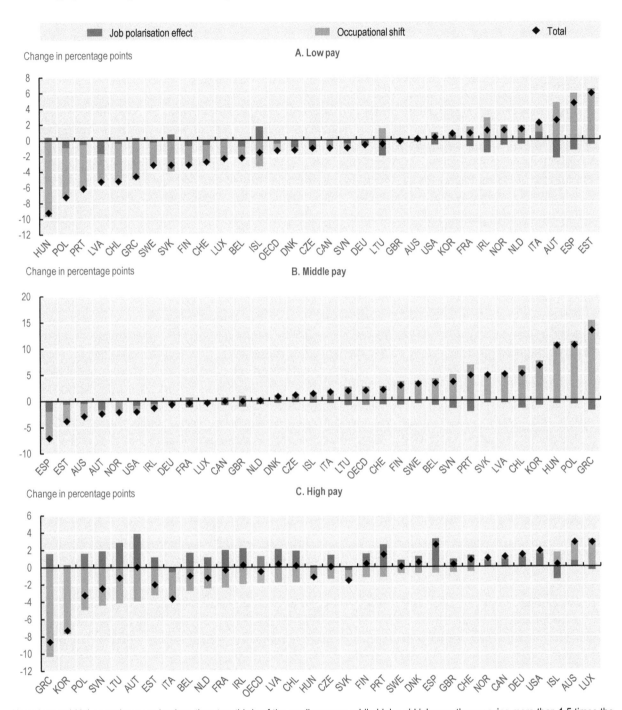

Note: Low-paid jobs are those paying less than two thirds of the median wage, while high-paid jobs are those paying more than 1.5 times the median wage. The OECD average is the unweighted average of all displayed countries. The time period covered is 2006-16, except for Korea (2006-14), Australia (2006-15). Greece, Portugal and Latvia (2007-16), Italy (2007-15), Switzerland (2008-15). Chile, Canada, Ireland and Luxembourg (2006-15), and Iceland (2006-13).

Source: EU statistics on income and living conditions survey (EU-SILC), German Socio-Economic Panel (GSOEP), Household, Income and Labour Dynamics in Australia (HILDA) Survey, Korean Labor & Income Panel Study (KLIPS), Canadian Labour Force Survey, Chilean National Socio-Economic Characterization Survey (CASEN), and CPS Merged Outgoing Rotation Groups (MORG) for the United States.

StatLink ⟨⟩ http://dx.doi.org/10.1787/888933966445

Where are the workers going who typically would have been employed in middle-skilled occupations? This is a key question for understanding the consequences of job polarisation for workers. Its answer may also illuminate what policies, if any, should be implemented to counter any ill effects of job polarisation.

Although the destruction of middle-skilled jobs might cause distress for workers who held those jobs, this need not be the case. Workers may be able to quickly reskill or work with their employers to transition to high-skilled occupations. Part of the loss of middle-skilled jobs may also occur through a process of attrition as workers in these jobs retire and fewer workers are hired to replace them. Alternatively, workers losing these jobs may only be able to find work in low-skilled occupations, or faced with diminished pay and opportunities, they may decide to exit employment entirely.

Recent OECD research provides the first comparative evidence on how the decline in the share of middle-skilled occupations has affected workers with less than tertiary education, who account for the majority of workers in middle-skilled occupations. (Green, forthcoming[16]). Previous studies have examined individual countries (Jaimovich, Siu and Cortes, 2017[17]; Bachmann, Cim and Green, 2018[18]; Maczulskij and Kauhanen, 2017[19]; Salvatori, 2018[20]).

From the mid-1990s to the mid-2010s across the OECD[21], the share of all working-age men (whether in employment or not) with middle-education who are in a middle-skilled occupation declined by 2.9 percentage points from 40.4% to 37.5%, while the share working in low-skilled employment rose from 11.3% to 15.4%. Middle-educated women experienced an even larger shift from middle-skilled employment to low-skilled employment. Their share in middle-skilled jobs dropped by 6.0 percentage points from 22.6% to 16.6% while their share in low-skilled occupations increased from 18.1% to 28.0%. Part of this increase was driven by an increase in women's labour force participation. The employment-to-population ratio of middle-educated women increased by 4 percentage points over this period.

The proportion of low-educated men working in low-skilled employment also increased from 12.0% to 14.8% while their share in middle-skilled occupations declined by 7.8 percentage points. Over the same period, their share in non-employment rose from 47.1% to 53.3% (see also Section 3.3.3 as well).

The share of low-educated women in middle-skilled employment fell 5.5 percentage points from 19.2% to 14.7%, while their share in low-skilled employment rose by almost the same magnitude from 17.2% to 22.4%. The proportion of low-educated women in employment did not change over this period.

To summarise, there has been a substantial decline in middle-skilled jobs for workers with less than tertiary education. Employment in these middle-skilled occupations provided many workers with a good standard of living. Their decline has meant that workers without a college degree who previously would have held these jobs are increasingly moving into low-skilled occupations, or out of work entirely.

### 3.3.2. The probability of low-paid employment has increased for some groups of workers

On average, all workers, irrespective of age, education and gender, have seen a decline in the probability of high pay, with the largest decline affecting workers with high education (Figure 3.11).[22] For all groups this has translated in an increase in the probability of middle pay, but for some also the probability of low-paid employment has increased slightly. In particular, while the probability of low-paid employment has declined on average for both men and women,[23] the results differ across education and age groups.

Figure 3.11. The probability of being in a high-paid job has declined across demographic groups

Percentage point change in the share of jobs by level of pay and by age, gender and level of education between 2006 and 2016, OECD average

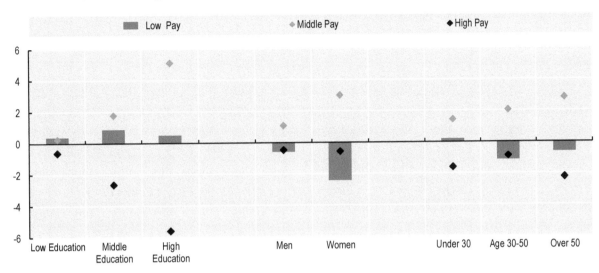

Note: The OECD average is the unweighted average of all countries included in Figure 3.10 and Mexico. Low-paid jobs are those paying less than two thirds of the median wage, while high-paid jobs are those paying more than 1.5 times the median wage. The time period covered is 2006-16, except for Korea (2006-14), Australia (2006-2015). Greece, Portugal and Latvia (2007-16), Italy (2007-15), Switzerland (2008-15). Chile, Canada, Ireland and Luxembourg (2006-15), and Iceland (2006-13).
Source: EU statistics on income and living conditions survey (EU-SILC), German Socio-Economic Panel (GSOEP), Household, Income and Labour Dynamics in Australia (HILDA) Survey, Korean Labor & Income Panel Study (KLIPS), Canadian Labour Force Survey, Chilean National Socio-Economic Characterization Survey (CASEN), ENOE longitudinal survey for Mexico and CPS Merged Outgoing Rotation Groups (MORG) for the United States.

StatLink ꜛꜱ꜔ http://dx.doi.org/10.1787/888933966464

*The incidence of low pay increased more for the young and those with medium education*

All education groups saw an increase in the probability of being in low-paid jobs across the OECD between 2006 and 2016.[24] The changes are all very small, with the largest one reaching a mere 0.8 percentage points for workers with middle-education.[25] The small average changes are the result of very different patterns across countries.[26]

On average, across countries, low- and medium-educated workers have seen more of a shift towards low pay than those with high education. The low-educated saw an increase in the probability of low pay in 18 of the 32 countries (average increase: 4 percentage points), and the medium-educated in 23 (average increase: 3 percentage points) (see Annex Figure 3.A.5). In just over half of the countries (17), these two groups together experienced a net shift of employment towards low-paid jobs. The impact of these shifts across the pay distribution on wage differentials by level of education is discussed in Box 3.2.

By age, an increase in the probability of low pay on average across countries was only recorded for the youngest age group, albeit a very small one (0.2 percentage points, Figure 3.11).[27] The increase occurred in 15 of the 32 countries (average of 6.5 percentage points) and in 13 of these resulted in a net shift of young people to low pay. By contrast, for workers aged 30 to 50 the probability of being in low pay declined on average across the OECD by just over 1 percentage point, increasing in only eight countries (see Annex Figure 3.A.6).

Hence, while these changes have affected different countries to varying degrees, the results point to a small increase on average in the probability of working in low-paid jobs for young workers and those with less than tertiary education. These pattern are not driven by increasing enrolment in education as they are obtained excluding those in education and are confirmed when the sample is restricted to full-time workers. This motivates a closer look at the fortunes of young workers with different levels of education.

*The probability of low-paid employment has increased for young people with medium education*

Young people with low and medium level education both saw shifts of their employment towards low pay. For brevity, Panel A of Figure 3.12 reports the results for those with medium education. On average, this group saw a larger increase in the probability of low pay than young workers with low education (2.6 percentage points vs 0.3). Also, they are a larger and more stable group that has been at the centre of the policy debate in many countries in recent years.[28]

The probability that a young person with medium education is in a low-paid job increased by 2.6 percentage points on average across countries. This was accompanied by similar declines in the probability of middle- and high-paid employment (-1.1 percentage points and -1.5 percentage points respectively) – with similar patterns between genders. As a result, the share of young workers with medium education who hold a low-paid job reached 38% in 2016.[29]

The probability of low-paid employment increased for young workers with medium education in two-thirds (19) of the countries. The average increase in these countries was 8 percentage points (against a decline of 6.6 percentage points in the remaining countries). In six countries, the increase was larger than 10 percentage points (France, Norway, Spain, Austria, Denmark, and Estonia). Among the countries were the probability declined, three had changes in excess of 10 percentage points (Sweden, Poland, and Hungary).

*In many countries, even young people with high education have seen an increase in the probability of low-paid employment*

Young people with a high-level of education also saw increases in the probability of low-paid employment in many countries (Panel B of Figure 3.12). On average, the increase was 3.5 percentage points across the OECD, accounting for over half of the 6.5 percentage points decline in the probability of high pay. As a result, on average across the OECD, young highly educated people are now more likely to be in low-paid jobs than in high-paid ones (21% vs 14.5%). This was the case in 18 countries already in 2006 – which were joined by Slovenia, Iceland and Austria in 2016.

The increase in the probability of low pay for young people with a high-level of education occurred in as many as 22 countries. This resulted in a net shift of employment to low pay in 13 countries. In 17 countries, the net shift was towards middle pay. Luxembourg was the only country with a net shift of employment towards high pay for this group. The largest increases in the probability of low pay were in Portugal (16 percentage points), Ireland (17 percentage points) and Spain (20 percentage points), while the largest increases in the probability of middle pay were in the Czech Republic (14 percentage points), Sweden (16 percentage points) and Hungary (26 percentage points).

## Figure 3.12. Young workers with middle education have seen a shift towards low-paid employment in many countries

Percentage point change in the share of jobs by level of pay by level of education between 2006 and 2016

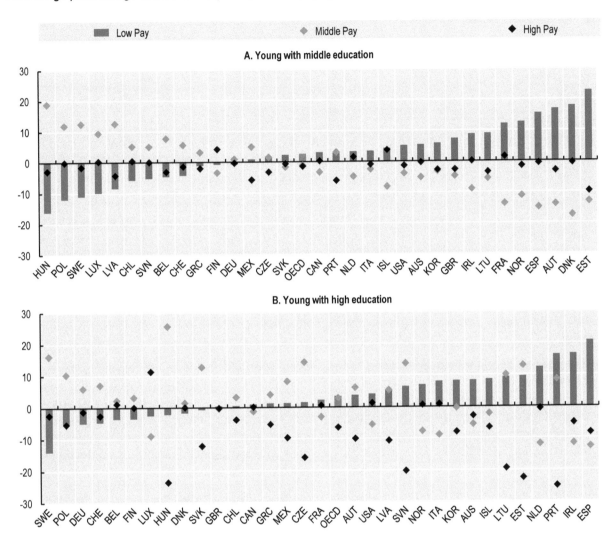

Note: The OECD average is the unweighted average of all countries shown. Low-paid jobs are those paying less than two thirds of the median wage, while high-paid jobs are those paying more than 1.5 times the median wage. The time period covered is 2006-16, except for Korea (2006-14), Australia (2006-15). Greece, Portugal and Latvia (2007-16), Italy (2007-15), Switzerland (2008-15). Chile, Canada, Ireland and Luxembourg (2006-15), and Iceland (2006-13).

Source: EU statistics on income and living conditions survey (EU-SILC), German Socio-Economic Panel (GSOEP), Household, Income and Labour Dynamics in Australia (HILDA) Survey, Korean Labor & Income Panel Study (KLIPS), Canadian Labour Force Survey, Chilean National Socio-Economic Characterization Survey (CASEN), ENOE longitudinal survey for Mexico and CPS Merged Outgoing Rotation Groups (MORG) for the United States.

StatLink ⟹ http://dx.doi.org/10.1787/888933966483

### 3.3.3. The risk of being out-of-employment after leaving education has increased for some groups

The changes in the types of jobs by skill and pay level documented in the previous section raise the possibility that some groups might be struggling to find jobs. For example, Beaudry et al. (2016[21]) argue that the increasing influx of high-educated workers into lower-skilled occupations has pushed more low-educated workers out of employment. Therefore, this section documents changes in the probability of being out-of-employment for workers aged 20 to 60 who have left education.

Box 3.2. The evolution of the wage premium for tertiary education

The contemporaneous occurrence of job polarisation and educational upgrading means the distribution of different educational groups across occupations and, more broadly, the pay distribution is changing (see Section 3.3.2 and Box 3.1). How are these changes affecting the wage premium for tertiary education relative to those with secondary education?

Between 2006 and 2016, the average wage premium across OECD countries with available data for tertiary education declined by about 3.3 percentage points (Figure 3.13).[30] There is, however, some variation across countries. Overall, the premium declined in 21 of the 32 countries considered here, but only in 12 was the change larger than 5 percentage points. Six countries experienced declines of at least 10 percentage points (Greece, Poland, Chile, Slovenia, Hungary and Portugal). Five countries had positive or negative changes of less than 1 percentage points (France, Luxembourg, Canada and Latvia). In three countries the premium increased by more than 5 percentage points (Belgium, the United Kingdom and Estonia).

Job polarisation and other compositional changes account for about 40% of the decline in the average premium. When holding occupation, age and gender characteristics constant, the average decline across all countries is 2.1 percentage points. In general, this adjusted estimate is lower than the unadjusted one in the countries with falling premia, especially among those with larger changes. Even among the countries with an overall increase in the wage premium, compositional changes have often tended to push the wage premium down as indicated by the fact that the (positive) adjusted estimate is larger than the unadjusted one.

Differences in wage dynamics across occupations have also played a major role in driving changes in the educational premium in most countries. This is largely because average wage growth between 2006 and 2016 was particularly weak in high-skilled occupations, which tend to employ a high share of workers with high education. Indeed, once differences in occupational wage growth are also accounted for, the average change in the education premium across the 32 countries is positive (1.5 percentage points), remaining negative in only 12 countries (and less than 1 percentage point in two of these, Australia and Italy).

Differences in occupational wage growth have played a particularly important role in the countries with the largest declines in the unadjusted education premium. Among the five countries with the largest declines, controlling for occupation, age and gender, and occupational wage growth reduces the estimated fall in the premium by more than 80% in three (Portugal, Slovenia, and Poland) and by around 60% in the remaining two (Hungary and Chile). The average decline among these countries goes from 18 to around 4 percentage points.

The education wage premium within occupational groups has been stable or increasing on average across countries. In particular, it remained stable within high-skill occupations but increased by about 3 percentage points within low and middle skill occupations. In all three cases, the premium declined in fewer than half of the countries considered.

In summary, while workers with tertiary education retain an earning advantage across the OECD (OECD, 2018[22]), over the past decade the education wage premium fell in a number of countries. This was driven in part by the fact that an increasing number of workers with tertiary education are found in occupations that do not pay high wages. The major driver of the fall has actually been the poor performance of wages of high-skill occupations, which still employ a large share of the highly educated group. The evidence of falling education wage premia within occupations is much weaker. This suggests that, in general, all occupations have been able to absorb the increasing supply of workers with high-education and that low- and middle-skilled occupations in particular might be undergoing a process of upskilling in at least some countries.

## Figure 3.13. Changes in the education wage premium across countries

Percentage points change in the wage premium of workers with tertiary education relative to those with secondary education between 2006 and 2016

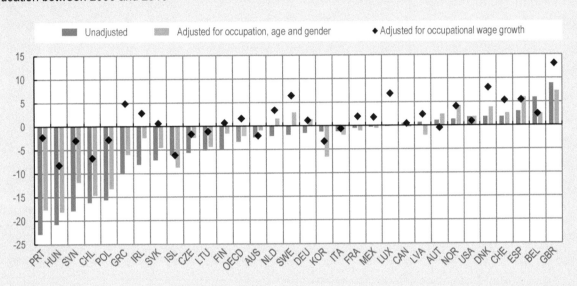

Note: The reported values are approximate changes in percentage points obtained from country-specific regressions of log of wages on the relevant covariates The OECD average is the unweighted average of all countries shown. Low-paid jobs are those paying less than two thirds of the median wage, while high-paid jobs are those paying more than 1.5 times the median wage. The time period covered is 2006-16, except for Korea (2006-14), Australia (2006-15). Greece, Portugal and Latvia (2007-16), Italy (2007-15), Switzerland (2008-15). Chile, Canada, Ireland and Luxembourg (2006-15), and Iceland (2006-13).
Source: EU statistics on income and living conditions survey (EU-SILC), German Socio-Economic Panel (GSOEP), Household, Income and Labour Dynamics in Australia (HILDA) Survey, Korean Labor & Income Panel Study (KLIPS), Canadian Labour Force Survey, Chilean National Socio-Economic Characterization Survey (CASEN), ENOE longitudinal survey for Mexico and CPS Merged Outgoing Rotation Groups (MORG) for the United States.

StatLink ⬛ᴵˢᴸ http://dx.doi.org/10.1787/888933966502

### The risk of non-employment has increased for men but decreased for women

On average, the share of men who have left education and are not employed has risen (2 percentage points), with larger increases among those with lower levels of education. Among women, the increases have been limited to the young (of all education levels) and to those aged 30 to 50 with low education (Figure 3.14). Indeed, on average across all countries the share of all women who have left education but are not working has declined by 3 percentage points.

**Figure 3.14. The young with low and medium education suffered the largest increases in the probability of non-employment**

Percentage point change in the probability of not being in employment for people who have left education, by age, gender and level of education, unweighted OECD average between 2006 and 2016

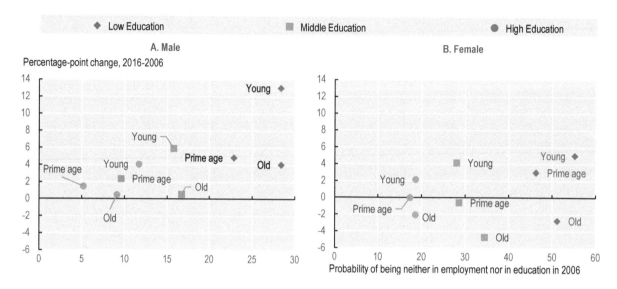

Note: The OECD average is the unweighted average of all countries reported in Figure 3.12. The sample is restricted to people who have left education and are aged 20 to 60. Young are aged 20-30, prime age between 30 to 50 and old from 50 to 60. The time period covered is 2006-2016, except for Korea (2006-2014), Australia (2006-2015). Greece, Portugal and Latvia (2007-2016), Italy (2007-2015), Switzerland (2008-2015). Chile, Canada, Ireland and Luxembourg (2006-2015), and Iceland (2006-2013).
Source: EU statistics on income and living conditions survey (EU-SILC), German Socio-Economic Panel (GSOEP), Household, Income and Labour Dynamics in Australia (HILDA) Survey, Korean Labor & Income Panel Study (KLIPS), Canadian Labour Force Survey, Chilean National Socio-Economic Characterization Survey (CASEN), ENOE longitudinal survey for Mexico and CPS Merged Outgoing Rotation Groups (MORG) for the United States.

*StatLink* 〰️🖹 http://dx.doi.org/10.1787/888933966521

The probability of non-employment increased in 26 of the 32 countries for men and decreased in as many countries for women. In all, except four countries (Poland, Slovenia, Slovakia and Estonia), the position of women relative to men improved. Nevertheless, women remain much more likely to be in non-employment than men (on average 27.7% vs 15.8% in 2016).

*Young people with low and medium education suffered the largest increases in the probability of non-employment*

For both men and women who have left education, the probability of non-employment rose most for young people, especially for those with low education.[31][32] In fact, young men with low education experienced the largest increase of all groups (13 percentage points). Women with high education had the smallest increase among the young (2 percentage points).[33] When the changes are computed by age group only (pooling together both genders and all education levels), it is only the young who have experienced an increase in non-employment (4 percentage points) on average across the OECD.[34]

The probability of a young person being out-of-employment after leaving education increased in 25 of the countries considered (see Annex Figure 3.A.7). The average increase across all countries was 4 percentage points, while the other two age groups saw small declines. The increases were above 10 percentage points in five countries (Iceland, Ireland, Italy, Greece, Spain) and below 1 percentage point in Estonia, Belgium and Korea. Among the seven countries where the probability of a young person in non-employment decreased, the largest changes were seen in Germany (4 percentage points), the Czech Republic (5 percentage points) and Poland (10 percentage points). The United States, the United Kingdom and the Slovak Republic saw small negative changes of less than 1 percentage point.

The other groups to have experienced increases in the probability of non-employment of a magnitude comparable to those of the young were all low-education groups (Figure 3.14).

### *The fortunes of the young have been declining*

The results of this section point to a deterioration of the position of young people in the labour market, which has affected in particular those with less than tertiary education. In fact, the incidence of non-employment has increased among young people who have left education in most countries, with larger increases among those with less than tertiary education. In addition, young workers with medium or low education have also seen widespread increases in the probability of being in low-paid jobs when they do find employment. There are only two countries in which neither of these results hold, i.e. Germany and Poland.

Even young people with high education have seen a worsening of their labour market situation in several countries. Strikingly, following a fall in the probability of being in high-paid jobs, a larger share of them is now found in low-paid than in high-paid jobs on average across the OECD.

While there is some variation in the size of the changes across countries, the main conclusions of this section apply to a large number of countries. These countries were affected to varying degrees by the economic crisis and by 2016 most had been on a recovery path for years. While it is certainly the case that the prolonged and deep recession has played a role in exacerbating the changes in some countries, the results suggest that overall the broad patterns documented in this section cannot be dismissed as the mere temporary product of the recession in all countries. Indeed, most of these results hold on average across the OECD also when adjusting for the economic cycle, even though this evidence can only be seen as tentative since the limited time span covered by the data makes it difficult to isolate the effect of the cycle.[35]

## 3.4. Concluding remarks

Understanding how the ongoing transformations of the labour market are affecting different workers is essential to design policies to help make the labour market more inclusive in the future. This chapter has presented new evidence in three key areas of policy relevance, namely job stability, under-employment and the availability of jobs of different pay levels.

While the results differ somewhat between the three topics and across countries, the evidence point to a deterioration of labour market conditions on average across the OECD for two groups, namely the young and those with less than tertiary education. The workers who belong to both of these groups, i.e. the young with less than tertiary education, stand out as those who have seen a deterioration in most of the outcomes considered here and across a large number of countries.

In particular, over the past decade or so, there have been widespread increases in the risk of not being in employment or of being in low-pay employment or under-employment for young people with less than tertiary education. While these changes have affected different countries to varying degrees, only two (Germany and Poland) have not seen a worsening of any of these indicators.[36] More highly educated youth have generally fared better than their less-educated peers, but even they have seen increases in the probability of low-pay employment in a number of countries.

These patterns are unlikely to be the short-lived product of the recent global financial crisis. While the OECD countries have been affected by the crisis to a different degree, the majority have been on a recovery path for several years by now and yet the deterioration of labour market conditions for youth is still present in the data. The main conclusions also stand when attempting to adjust for the cycle in spite of the limited time span covered by the data. Overall, therefore, the findings of this chapter point to significant challenges on the road to more inclusive labour markets.

The policy challenges raised by the declining fortunes of young people are twofold. First, there is the need to improve opportunities for the new cohorts entering the labour market. Second, there is the issue of the cohorts of young people who have already suffered worse labour market outcomes than previous generations. A large body of literature has shown that the conditions at the time of labour market entry have a lasting impact on wage and career trajectories over the life cycle.[37] This point illustrates that even if part of the changes documented in this chapter are the product of the crisis, they represent a significant policy issue for the future. Helping the cohorts who have faced the tougher environment of the past decade to improve their situation in the future will therefore be a major challenge for inclusive policies.

From a gender perspective, men have seen an increase in the risk of non-employment and under-employment in a number of countries. Nevertheless, the risks of both under-employment and non-employment remain higher for women. Women also remain more likely to be in low-paid jobs and less likely to be in high-paid ones, despite an improvement in the probability of being in middle-paid jobs. While there is a need to better understand the reasons behind the deteriorating labour market outcomes of men, policies to address gender imbalances remain a key priority to build more inclusive labour markets (OECD, 2018[1]).

The scale of the policy challenge at hand requires a multifaceted response. Skill policies can play an important role in improving the labour market experiences of new entrants, as well as supporting career progression for older cohorts. Given the increase in mobility discussed in this Chapter, skills policies will need to adapt to ensure that training programmes also reach those in less stable careers (see Chapter 6). Strengthening social dialogue and better employment regulation can help address imbalances in the employment relationship that may have an adverse impact on more vulnerable workers (see Chapter 4 and 5). Finally, the heightened job insecurity documented in this chapter calls for a review of existing social protection systems to prevent more and more workers from falling through the cracks (see Chapter 7).

# References

Bachmann, R., M. Cim and C. Green (2018), "Long-run Patterns of Labour Market Polarisation: Evidence from German Micro Data", *Ruhr Economic Papers*, No. 748, RWI. [18]

Beaudry, P., D. Green and B. Sand (2016), "The Great Reversal in the Demand for Skill and Cognitive Tasks", *Journal of Labor Economics*, Vol. 34/S1, pp. S199-S247, http://dx.doi.org/10.1086/682347. [21]

Brunner, B. and A. Kuhn (2013), "The impact of labor market entry conditions on initial job assignment and wages", *Journal of Population Economics*, Vol. 27/3, pp. 705-738, http://dx.doi.org/10.1007/s00148-013-0494-4. [26]

Burgess, S. et al. (2003), "The class of 1981: the effects of early career unemployment on subsequent unemployment experiences", *Labour Economics*, Vol. 10/3, pp. 291-309, http://dx.doi.org/10.1016/S0927-5371(02)00138-0. [25]

Elliot, L. (2017), *Robots will not lead to fewer jobs – but the hollowing out of the middle class*, The Guardian, https://www.theguardian.com/business/2017/aug/20/robots-are-not-destroying-jobs-but-they-are-hollow-out-the-middle-class (accessed on 11 September 2018). [13]

Euwals, R. and M. Hogerbrugge (2006), "Explaining the Growth of Part-time Employment: Factors of Supply and Demand", *Labour*, Vol. 20/3, pp. 533-557, http://dx.doi.org/10.1111/j.1467-9914.2006.00352.x. [11]

Farber, H. (2010), "Job Loss and the Decline in Job Security in the United States", in Abraham, K., J. Spletzer and M. Harper (eds.), *Labor in the New Economy*, University of Chicago Press, http://www.nber.org/chapters/c10822 (accessed on 28 July 2017). [6]

Goos, M., A. Manning and A. Salomons (2009), "Job Polarization in Europe", *American Economic Review*, Vol. 99/2, pp. 58-63, http://dx.doi.org/10.1257/aer.99.2.58. [27]

Green, A. (forthcoming), "Where are Middle-skill Workers Going?", *OECD Social, Employment and Migration Working Papers*, OECD Publishing, Paris. [16]

Hahn, J. et al. (2018), *Job Ladders and Growth in Earnings, Hours, and Wages \**, https://468ca243-a-0c9971f9-s-sites.googlegroups.com/a/asu.edu/hjanicki/job_ladder_earnings.pdf (accessed on 15 November 2018). [8]

Jaimovich, N., H. Siu and M. Cortes (2017), "Disappearing Routine Jobs: Who, How, and Why?", *Journal of Monetary Economics*, Vol. 91, pp. 69-87. [17]

Liu, K., K. Salvanes and E. Sørensen (2016), "Good skills in bad times: Cyclical skill mismatch and the long-term effects of graduating in a recession", *European Economic Review*, Vol. 84, pp. 3-17, http://dx.doi.org/10.1016/J.EUROECOREV.2015.08.015. [24]

MacDonald, D. (forthcoming), "Underemployment: Quantity, Quality, and Inclusiveness", *OECD Social, Employment and Migration Working Papers*, OECD Publishing, Paris. [2]

Maczulskij, T. and M. Kauhanen (2017), "Where do workers from declining routine jobs go and does migration matter?", *Työpapereita Working Papers*, No. 314, Labour Institute for Economic Research. [19]

OECD (2019), *Under Pressure: The Squeezed Middle Class*, OECD Publishing, Paris, https://dx.doi.org/10.1787/689afed1-en. [3]

OECD (2018), "How does the earnings advantage of tertiary-educated workers evolve across generations?", *Education Indicators in Focus*, No. 62, OECD Publishing, Paris, https://dx.doi.org/10.1787/3093362c-en. [22]

OECD (2018), *OECD Economic Outlook, Volume 2018 Issue 2: Preliminary version*, OECD Publishing, Paris, https://dx.doi.org/10.1787/eco_outlook-v2018-2-en. [1]

OECD (2017), *OECD Employment Outlook 2017*, OECD Publishing, Paris, http://dx.doi.org/10.1787/empl_outlook-2017-en. [10]

OECD (2014), "Post-crisis pension reforms", in *OECD Pensions Outlook 2014*, OECD Publishing, Paris, https://doi.org/10.1787/pens_outlook-2014-5-en. [5]

Pew Research Center (2015), *The American middle class is losing ground*, https://www.pewsocialtrends.org/2015/12/09/the-american-middle-class-is-losing-ground/. [15]

Prising, J. (2016), *Four changes shaping the labour market*, The World Economic Forum, https://www.weforum.org/agenda/2016/01/four-changes-shaping-the-labour-market/ (accessed on 8 December 2017). [4]

Salvatori, A. (2018), "The anatomy of job polarisation in the UK", *Journal for Labour Market Research*, Vol. 52/1, p. 8, http://dx.doi.org/10.1186/s12651-018-0242-z. [20]

Schwandt, H. and T. von Wachter (2019), "Unlucky Cohorts: Estimating the Long-Term Effects of Entering the Labor Market in a Recession in Large Cross-Sectional Data Sets", *Journal of Labor Economics*, Vol. 37/S1, pp. S161-S198, http://dx.doi.org/10.1086/701046. [23]

Topel, R. and M. Ward (1992), "Job Mobility and the Careers of Young Men", *The Quarterly Journal of Economics*, Vol. 107/2, pp. 439-479, http://dx.doi.org/10.2307/2118478. [7]

Valletta, R., L. Bengali and C. van der List (forthcoming), "Cyclical and Market Determinants of Involuntary Part-Time Employment", *Journal of Labor Economics*. [9]

Vaughan-Whitehead, D., R. Vazquez-Alvarez and N. Maître (2016), "Is the world of work behind middle-class erosion?", *Chapters*, pp. 1-61, https://ideas.repec.org/h/elg/eechap/17301_1.html (accessed on 31 January 2018). [14]

Yglesias, M. (2014), *Robots won't destroy jobs, but they may destroy the middle class*, Vox, https://www.vox.com/2014/8/23/6057551/autor-job-polarization (accessed on 11 September 2018). [12]

# Annex 3.A. Additional results

Annex Figure 3.A.1. Change in adjusted tenure by country and level of education

Percentage change in job tenure (years) by gender, age and education, 2006 to 2017[1]

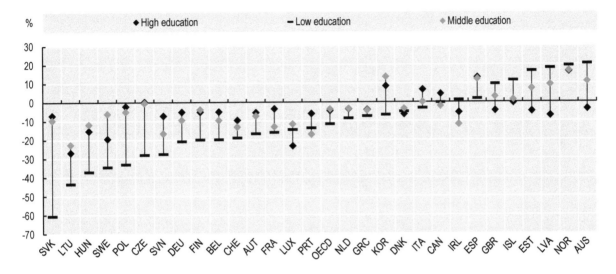

Note: The OECD average is the unweighted average of the displayed countries. Data are adjusted to control for the composition of the labour force by age, and gender. High education workers have completed a tertiary education. Middle education workers have achieved an upper secondary education and possibly some additional education but less than a bachelor degree. Workers with low education have not completed upper secondary education.

1. Data for Australia, Germany, and the United States are from 2016.

Source: European labour force survey (EU-LFS), German Socio-Economic Panel (GSOEP), Household, Income and Labour Dynamics in Australia (HILDA) Survey, Canadian Labour Force Survey, and the United States Current Population Survey (CPS) Tenure Supplement.

StatLink ᎁᏚᒪ http://dx.doi.org/10.1787/888933966540

Annex Figure 3.A.2. Young workers are more likely to be under-employed

Percentage change in the share of dependent workers who indicate they are under-employed, by age, 2006-17 (or latest year)[1]

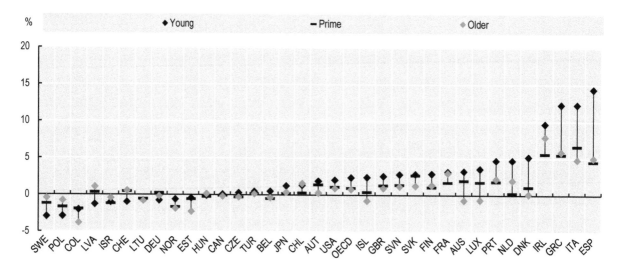

Note: The OECD average is the unweighted average of the countries depicted. Under-employed workers are in part-time employment (working 30 hours or less per week) who report either that they could not find a full-time job or that they would like to work more hours. Young workers are those aged 15 to 29, prime-aged workers are aged 20 to 54, and older workers are aged 55 to 69. The analysis excludes students.

1. Data for Australia, Germany, and Japan are from 2016. Data for Chile and Turkey are from 2015, while Israel data is from 2011. Colombia data for 2006 is from 2007, while Chile uses data from 2009.

Source: European labour force survey (EU-LFS), German Socio-Economic Panel (GSOEP), United States Current Population Survey (CPS), Canadian Labour Force Survey, Turkey Labour Force Survey, Japan Household Panel Survey(JHPS/KHPS), Colombia GEIH, Chilean National Socio-Economic Characterization Survey (CASEN), Israel Labour Force Survey, Household, Income and Labour Dynamics in Australia (HILDA) Survey.

*StatLink* 衊⬚ http://dx.doi.org/10.1787/888933966559

## Annex Figure 3.A.3. Change in under-employment by country and gender

Percentage point change in share of dependent workers who indicate they are under-employed, by gender, 2006-17 (or latest year)[1]

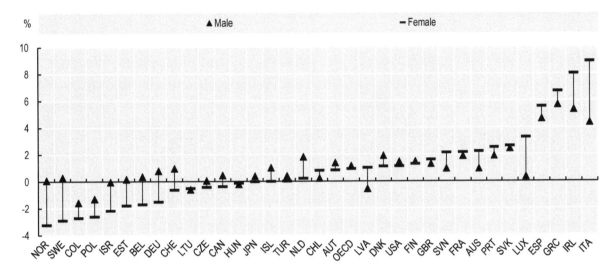

Note: The OECD average is the unweighted average of the countries depicted. Under-employed workers are in part-time employment (working 30 hours or less per week) who report either that they could not find a full-time job or that they would like to work more hours. The analysis excludes students.

1. Data for 2017 refer to 2016 for Australia, Germany, and Japan, 2015 for Chile and Turkey are from 2015, and 2011 for Israel. Data for 2006 refer to 2007 for Colombia data and 2009 for Chile.

Source: European labour force survey (EU-LFS), German Socio-Economic Panel (GSOEP), United States Current Population Survey (CPS), Canadian Labour Force Survey, Turkey Labour Force Survey, Japan Household Panel Survey(JHPS/KHPS), Colombian *Gran encuesta integrada de hogares* (GEIH), Chilean National Socio-Economic Characterization Survey (CASEN), Israel Labour Force Survey, Household, Income and Labour Dynamics in Australia (HILDA) Survey.

StatLink 🔗 http://dx.doi.org/10.1787/888933966578

Annex Figure 3.A.4. Jobs by occupation have continued to polarise between 2006 and 2016

Percentage point change in occupational employment shares, 2006-16

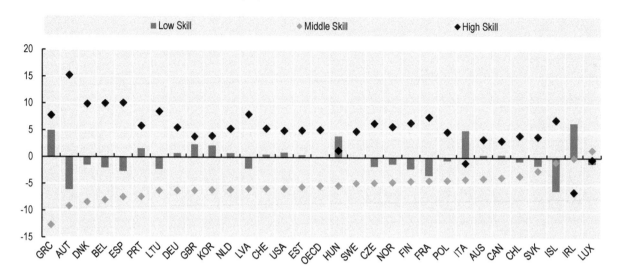

Note: High-skill occupations are managers, professionals and technicians (ISCO88 codes: 1, 2 and 3). Middle skill occupations are clerks, machine operatives and crafts (codes: 4, 7 and 8). Low-skill occupations are sales and service occupations and elementary occupations (codes: 5 and 9). The OECD average is the unweighted average of all displayed countries. The time period covered is 2006-16, except for: Korea (2006-14), Australia (2006-15). Greece, Portugal and Latvia (2007-2016), Italy (2007-15), Switzerland (2008-15). Chile, Canada, Ireland and Luxembourg (2006-15), Iceland (2006-13)

Source: EU statistics on income and living conditions survey (EU-SILC), German Socio-Economic Panel (GSOEP), Household, Income and Labour Dynamics in Australia (HILDA) Survey, Korean Labor & Income Panel Study (KLIPS), Canadian Labour Force Survey, Chilean National Socio-Economic Characterization Survey (CASEN), and CPS Merged Outgoing Rotation Groups (MORG) for the United States.

StatLink ᐧᐧ᠊ᐢᐧᐧ http://dx.doi.org/10.1787/888933966597

Annex Figure 3.A.5. The risk of low pay has increased for employees with low and medium education in a number of countries

Percentage point change in distribution of jobs by pay level for workers with a low or medium level of education, 2006-16

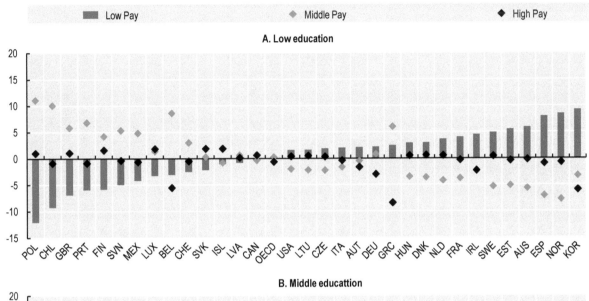

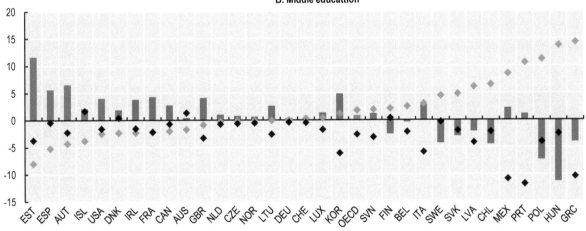

Note: The OECD average is the unweighted average of all countries shown. Low-paid jobs are those paying less than two thirds of the median wage, while high-paid jobs are those paying more than 1.5 times the median wage. The time period covered is 2006-16, except for: Korea (2006-14), Australia (2006-15). Greece, Portugal and Latvia (2007-16), Italy (2007-15), Switzerland (2008-15). Chile, Canada, Ireland and Luxembourg (2006-15), Iceland (2006-13).
Source: EU statistics on income and living conditions survey (EU-SILC), German Socio-Economic Panel (GSOEP), Household, Income and Labour Dynamics in Australia (HILDA) Survey, Korean Labor & Income Panel Study (KLIPS), Canadian Labour Force Survey, Chilean National Socio-Economic Characterization Survey (CASEN), ENOE longitudinal survey for Mexico and CPS Merged Outgoing Rotation Groups (MORG) for the United States.

StatLink ▒▒▒ http://dx.doi.org/10.1787/888933966616

Annex Figure 3.A.6. Young workers have shifted more towards low pay than older ones in some countries

Percentage point change in the distribution of jobs by pay level for younger and prim-age workers, 2006-16

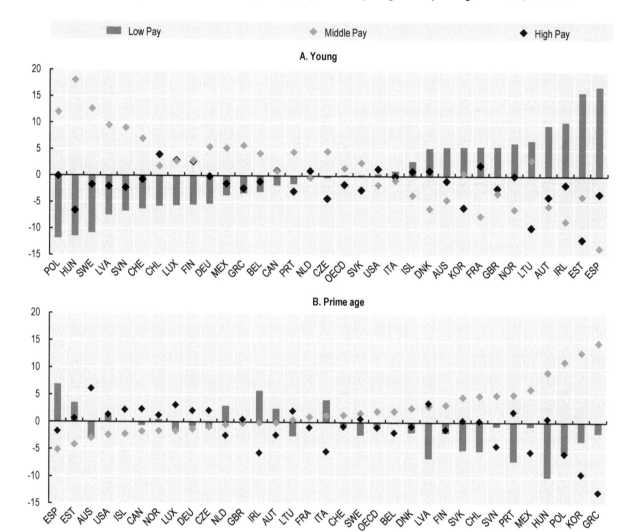

Note: The OECD average is the unweighted average of all countries shown. Low-paid jobs are those paying less than two thirds of the median wage, while high-paid jobs are those paying more than 1.5 times the median wage. Young people are aged 16 to 30 and prime age 31-50. The time period covered is 2006-16, except for: Korea (2006-14), Australia (2006-15). Greece, Portugal and Latvia (2007-16), Italy (2007-15), Switzerland (2008-15). Chile, Canada, Ireland and Luxembourg (2006-15), Iceland (2006-13).

Source: EU statistics on income and living conditions survey (EU-SILC), German Socio-Economic Panel (GSOEP), Household, Income and Labour Dynamics in Australia (HILDA) Survey, Korean Labor & Income Panel Study (KLIPS), Canadian Labour Force Survey, Chilean National Socio-Economic Characterization Survey (CASEN), ENOE longitudinal survey for Mexico and CPS Merged Outgoing Rotation Groups (MORG) for the United States.

StatLink ᵐˢᴾ http://dx.doi.org/10.1787/888933966635

## Annex Figure 3.A.7. The risk of being out of employment has risen most for youth who have left education

Percentage point changes in the probability of not being in employment for people who have left education aged 20 to 60 by age, 2006-2016

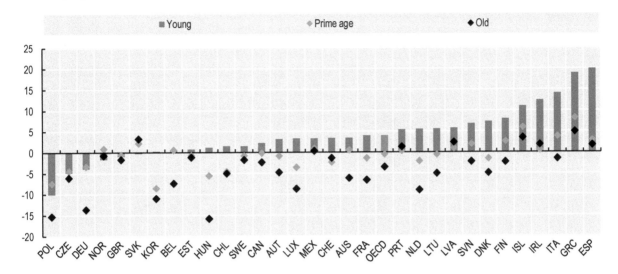

Note: The OECD average is the unweighted average of all countries shown. Young people are aged 20 to 30, prime age between 31 to 50 and old from 51 to 60. The time period covered is 2006-2016, except for: Korea (2006-14), Australia (2006-15). Greece, Portugal and Latvia (2007-16), Italy (2007-15), Switzerland (2008-15). Chile, Canada, Ireland and Luxembourg (2006-15), Iceland (2006-13).

Source: EU statistics on income and living conditions survey (EU-SILC), German Socio-Economic Panel (GSOEP), Household, Income and Labour Dynamics in Australia (HILDA) Survey, Korean Labor & Income Panel Study (KLIPS), Canadian Labour Force Survey, Chilean National Socio-Economic Characterization Survey (CASEN), ENOE longitudinal survey for Mexico and CPS Merged Outgoing Rotation Groups (MORG) for the United States.

StatLink ⫍ᴍˢ⫍ http://dx.doi.org/10.1787/888933966654

Notes

[1] Choosing an earlier start data does not qualitatively affect the results, and allows consistency with other sections in the Chapter.

[2] The result is obtained by means of a regression analysis that identifies changes in job tenure between 2006 and 2017, controlling for workers' age as well as for their level of education and gender.

[3] Compared with the model that controlled for only demographic shifts, the model controlling for the business cycle (output gap) estimated that tenure had fallen by an additional 4.4 percentage points since 2006. Tenure adjusted for the cycle fell in Canada, Estonia, the Czech Republic, Latvia, and the United Kingdom, whereas tenure adjusted only for demographics had increased in these countries. Controlling for the cycle did not change the direction of adjusted tenure in any countries where adjusted tenure fell when controlling for demographics.

[4] High education workers have completed a tertiary education. Middle education workers have achieved an upper secondary education and possibly some additional education but less than a bachelor degree. Workers with low education have not completed upper secondary education.

[5] The available measures of job-to-job transitions capture movements between jobs across consecutive calendar years. Transitions from one year to the next may in fact conceal one (or several) transitions in and out of employment that occur over the course of the reference year. For example, a worker who was employed in the previous year may have experienced a period out of employment before finding the current job, but will be recorded has having experienced a job-to-job transition since job status is recorded yearly. The measure, therefore, should not be interpreted literally as an indicator of direct transitions from a job to another, but rather as a measure of transitions that involve short periods of non-employment between jobs.

[6] The analysis follows the same technique used for correcting changes in tenure for demographic changes.

[7] Note that the countries included in the analysis of employment flows does not perfectly match the set of countries examined in the previous tenure analysis due to data limitations. In particular, the flows analysis excludes Canada, Ireland, Norway and Switzerland, and includes Japan.

[8] There are differences among these countries of course. For example, the changes documented for Denmark here are generally small, and this country is the one with the highest job-to-job transition rate among all those considered in this analysis.

[9] The term underemployment is sometimes used to refer to workers who are employed in jobs that requires lower qualifications or skills than they possess. As made clear in the text, this section focuses exclusively on underemployment as involuntary part-time employment.

[10] For a discussion of measurement issues related to underemployment see (MacDonald, forthcoming[2]).

[11] The unweighted OECD average increased from 4.3% in 2006 to 5.4% in 2017.

[12] The results reported adjust for the cycle by including a quadratic in unemployment, but the results are qualitatively the same if using a quadratic in output gap. The results reported only control for the share of employment in the service sectors with a high incidence of underemployment, but unsurprisingly the results are very similar when controlling for the overall share of employment in the broader service sector.

[13] Reliable and comparable data are only available for a handful of countries prior to 2006. At the time of writing, most of the datasets used in the analysis were available up to 2016 at most. The variables considered in this section typically display little year-on-year variation, so it is unlikely that adding one additional year of data would make a substantial difference. In addition, investigations conducted for the analysis in Sections 3.1 and 3.2 (which use different datasets) indicate that the same main patterns are found when using either 2017 or 2016 as end years.

[14] High skill occupations are managers, professionals and technicians (ISCO88 codes: 1, 2 and 3). Middle skill occupations are clerks, machine operatives and crafts (codes: 4, 7 and 8). Low skill occupations are sales and service occupations and elementary occupations (codes: 5 and 9). The ISCO88 category 6 ("skilled agricultural and fishery workers") are not included in the analysis. This grouping is line with previous practice in the international literature. See OECD (2017[10]) and references therein. Typically, this literature uses average occupational wages as proxy for skills – see for example Goos et al. (2009[27]) for an example covering multiple countries. When using the wage data employed in this Chapter, the average ranking of occupations across countries does indeed reflect the splitting of occupations into low, middle, and high skill groups adopted in this analysis and other contributions.

[15] See http://www.oecd.org/employment/emp/employmentdatabase-earningsandwages.htm.

[16] The wage distribution used is that of all employees. However, the main conclusions presented in the analysis also hold when only full-time employees are used to compute median wages.

[17] Mexico is excluded from this part of the analysis due to inconsistencies in the occupational classification over time.

[18] As discussed above, middle-paid jobs here are defined as those with wages between 66% and 150% of the median. The finding that the share of middle-paid jobs has not seen a widespread decline across countries holds even when adopting more restrictive definitions of middle-paid jobs. In particular, when eight smaller groups are used (66-80%, 81-90%, and so on until 140-150% of the median), all except one group (jobs with wages between 1.3 times and 1.4 times the median) have seen increases in their share of total employment on average across the 31 countries considered here. Hence, it is clear that, regardless of the precise definition, there has not been a widespread decrease in the share of middle-paid jobs across countries mirroring the ubiquitous decline in the share of middle-skilled jobs that characterises job polarisation.

[19] The generally small and negative contribution of job polarisation to changes in the share of middle-pay occupations is the result of two partially offsetting forces. The first is the decline in the share of middle-skill occupations that has tended to push the share of middle-paid jobs down. The second is the increase in the share of high-skill jobs that has contributed to the growth of middle-paid jobs because a substantial fraction of these jobs also pays medium-level wages.

[20] Among the 19 countries where high-paid jobs gained shares, the average growth was less than 1 percentage point. The largest increases occurred in Spain (2.5 percentage points), Luxembourg (2.7 percentage points) and Australia (2.8 percentage points). Only in seven countries was the increase in the share of high-paid jobs in line with (or larger than) the growth expected given the general shift towards high-skill occupations. These countries are Norway, Canada, Germany, the United States, Iceland, Austria and Luxembourg. Among the 12 countries with a declining share of high-paid jobs, the average change was -2.6 percentage points, with the largest values recorded in Italy (-3.4 percentage points), Korea (-7.2 percentage points) and Greece (-8.6 percentage points). All of these countries experienced substantial declines in the propensity of different occupations to pay high wages.

[21] The countries include all OECD members, which are also members of the European Union, as well as Switzerland, Norway, Iceland and the United States. The analysis uses the following datasets: European labour force survey (EU-LFS), The German Socio-Economic Panel (SOEP) for Germany, and the Current Population Survey (CPS) for the United States.

[22] The apparent discrepancies between the within-group changes reported in Figure 3.11 and those reported in Figure 3.10 (for the OECD average) are due to the role played by compositional changes. For example, the aggregate decline in the share of workers in high-paid jobs seen for the OECD average in Figure 3.10 is smaller than any of the declines seen for each of the three education groups in Figure 3.11 because the composition of the workforce has shifted towards groups that are more likely to be in high-paid jobs (i.e. older and more educated workers).

[23] Despite the larger decline in the probability of being in low-pay employment, women remain much more likely to be in low-paid jobs than men (23% vs 16%) and much less likely to be in high-paid jobs (17% vs 25%).

[24] As referenced in note 22, the apparent discrepancies between the overall (small) decline in the fraction of workers in low pay ( see OECD average in Figure 3.11) and the increase within each of the three education groups (Figure 3.12) is due to the fact the changes in the composition of the workforce have favoured groups that tend to be less concentrated in low pay. A formal decomposition indicates that educational upgrading (i.e. a compositional shift towards workers with higher levels of education) has pushed the share of low-paid workers down by 1.6 percentage points, while the increase propensity of each education group to be in the low-paid employment has added 0.3 percentage points with a net decline of 1.3 percentage points.

[25] By 2016, the average share employed in low-paid jobs was 37% for the low-education group, 23% for the medium-education group, and 10% for the high-education group.

[26] One concern is that the changes in the performance of different education groups over time might reflect changes in the unobserved composition of these groups. However, robustness checks show that qualitatively similar results are observed when a single cohort of worker (aged 25 to 45 in 2006 and 35 to 55 in 2016) with a given education level is followed over time. Since the level of education of this cohort is roughly stable over the observation period, this attenuates the concern that the main results might mostly be driven by selection effects.

[27] The average share of young workers in low pay employment was 35% in 2016, but only 15% and 16% respectively for workers between 30 and 50 and for older workers.

[28] In the data used in this analysis, the proportion of young people in employment who have low education declined from 22% to 17% between 2006 and 2016 on average across the OECD. The proportion of young people in employment with medium education remained stable at around 47-48%. Such stability makes it implausible that the results reported here stem only or even mostly from the fact that young workers with less than tertiary education are increasingly negatively selected. In fact, as discussed in the main text, the probability of low-paid employment has increased even for young workers with tertiary education in several countries. Moreover, the result in Figure 3.11 show that in the aggregate all education groups have seen some increase in the probability of low-paid employment. Taken together these results point to a generalised change in labour market conditions rather than to a change in selection affecting one particular group. See also note 26 for an additional check that suggests that selection into education levels is unlikely to play a significant role in explaining any of the patterns described here.

[29] As noted above in the text, only workers whose main economic status is in employment are considered. This attenuates the concern that the results presented might be driven by young people in education taking up part-time jobs. In addition the results on the increase probability of low pay employment for young workers (in general and in particular with low and medium education) hold even when restricting the sample to workers in full-time employment only. This further reduces the risk of the results being heavily affected by young people still in education.

[30] These estimates are obtained from country-specific regressions of log of wage on the relevant covariates. The reported estimates are therefore in log points and can be interpreted as percentage point changes approximately.

[31] Note that the figures reported here are not NEET rates, i.e. the proportion of all young people (aged 15-29) who are not in employment, education or training. As described in the main text, the analysis focuses on changes in the incidence of non-employment among those who have left education and the young are defined as workers aged 20 to 30. In addition, due to the data sources used in this analysis, the definition of the employment status also differs from that used in the construction on NEET rates which typically rely on ILO definitions of employment from labour force survey data. Here, for most countries, the definition of employment is instead based on self-reported main economic status.

[32] A possible observation is that part of the increase in non-employment rates for young people with lower levels of education might be due changes in the composition of this group since, as more people stay in education for longer, those who leave education earlier are increasingly those with poorer labour market prospects. While this analysis cannot rule out this possibility entirely, two facts suggest that the increase in the probability of non-employment for young people who have left education is unlikely to be driven by selection. First, as discussed in note 28, the stability of the share of young people in employment who have medium education suggests that it is unlikely that the composition of this group has changed significantly over this period of time. Second, the deterioration of labour market outcomes described in this section and elsewhere in this chapter is stronger for those with less than tertiary education, but does affect young workers with tertiary education as well (and in fact other age groups are also affected to some extent). While changes in selection may perhaps help explain some of the differences between groups, the fact that the observed changes are not limited to specific subgroups suggests that selection is unlikely to be the main force at play. Finally, it is worth emphasising that even when the deterioration of the labour market conditions for a specific group can be ascribed to changes in its composition driven by selection mechanisms, this remains an important issue that poses a challenge for policies aiming at promoting a more inclusive labour market.

[33] Young women with high education remain more likely to be in non-employment than their male counterparts (21% vs 16%).

[34] This figure is effectively a weighted average of the figures for the six young groups reported in Figure 3.14.

[35] In particular, the average increase in the probability of low pay for the young with medium education across the OECD are robust to controlling either for the output gap or the unemployment rate. The increase in the probability of non-employment for young people who have left education is robust to the inclusion of the unemployment rate, but not to the output gap.

[36] In particular, Germany and Poland are the only two countries in which the young have not seen an increase in the probability of underemployment, nor in that of non-employment, nor have the young with medium education experienced an increase in the probability of low-pay employment.

[37] See, among others, Liu et al. (2016[24]), Burgess et al. (2003[25]), Schwandt et al. (2019[23]), Brunner and Kuhn (2013[26]) and references therein.

# 4 Labour market regulation 4.0: Protecting workers in a changing world of work

This chapter discusses the role of labour market regulations to adequately protect workers in a changing world of work. A key focus of the chapter is on employment status – a critical area because it acts as a gateway to various worker rights and protections. Ensuring the correct classification of workers is therefore a key first step to ensure access to labour and social protection, collective bargaining and lifelong learning. For some workers, however, there is genuine ambiguity about employment status as they find themselves somewhere in the "grey zone" between dependent and self-employment. While arguing that this grey zone should be kept as small as possible, the chapter examines the rationale and policy options for extending certain labour rights and protections to these workers. Finally, the chapter discusses the role of regulations in addressing abuses of monopsony power and rebalancing bargaining power between employers/clients and workers.

The statistical data for Israel are supplied by and under the responsibility of the relevant Israeli authorities. The use of such data by the OECD is without prejudice to the status of the Golan Heights, East Jerusalem and Israeli settlements in the West Bank under the terms of international law.

# In Brief

## Key findings

Labour market regulation plays an important role in protecting workers, but a number of developments are challenging its role. First, the emergence of new forms of work poses a challenge to regulations largely designed for full-time, permanent employees working for a single employer. Second, there is increasing evidence of (and in some cases growth in) unbalanced power relationships between workers and their employers, which calls for a reassessment of how regulation can address both the consequences and sources of such power imbalances.

This chapter examines the role of labour market regulation in protecting workers in a changing world of work, and ensuring that firms that follow the rules are not put at a disadvantage. More specifically, it looks at the role of regulation in operationally defining employment status, extending protections beyond standard employees and rebalancing power asymmetries between employers/clients and workers. Its main findings are:

- Clearly defining the employment status of workers (e.g. the distinction between the self-employed and employees) in labour market regulation and enforcing it are crucial. Employment status acts as a gateway to various worker rights and protections – including employment and social protection, but also access to training and collective bargaining – see Chapters 5 to 7.

- Policy and law enforcement should minimise opportunities and incentives for the misclassification of workers. Certain employers may deliberately misclassify workers in an attempt to avoid employment regulation, tax obligations and workers' representation, as well as to shift risks onto workers and/or gain a competitive advantage; and others may do so by mistake. Similarly, workers may choose among different employment forms in order to benefit from a better tax regime or simply avoid taxes – but at the risk of losing labour and social protections. Such misclassification therefore harms individuals, but also leaves firms that properly classify their workers at a competitive disadvantage, and damages public finances.

- Regulations or guidelines for determining employment status may need to be clarified, revised and/or harmonised. This would help reduce the size of the "grey zone" between self-employment and dependent employee status – i.e. workers who share certain characteristics of both forms of employment. Reducing the size of the grey zone would reduce uncertainty for both workers and employers, and reduce litigation.

- For workers who remain in the grey zone, where there is genuine ambiguity about their employment status, governments should seek to extend rights and protections. These workers have some of the characteristics of employees and, like them, they may find themselves in an unbalanced power relationship since employers often have a higher degree of control over the employment relationship than they do. At the same, they may be deprived of most of the standard rights and protections afforded to employees because they are usually classified as self-employed.

- Labour market regulations should be adapted so that workers in the grey zone can benefit, at least partially, from: fair pay, working time regulations, occupational health and safety, anti-discrimination legislation, as well as some form of employment protection. This will involve identifying those groups that need protection and clarifying who bears responsibility as an

- employer towards these workers. Not all protections can be extended to these workers in the "grey zone". Chapters 5 to 7 discuss how this could be done for social protection, collective bargaining and training.

- Imbalances in power relationships between employers and workers (including many self-employed workers) can also emerge (or be worsened) when workers have few or no outside options and much lower bargaining power than employers (a situation usually called monopsony power in the labour market). There is growing empirical evidence that monopsony is important in many labour markets and that high market concentration of a few firms is associated with significantly lower pay and worse working conditions.

- Such situations can be made worse when workers are unable to organise and bargain collectively, which is usually the case for self-employed workers who tend to be banned from collective bargaining by antitrust regulation (see Chapter 5).

- The abuse of monopsony power in the labour market and its sources can be addressed by better regulation and more effective enforcement. This includes: i) extending coverage of labour market regulations to address the effects of monopsony on workers' well-being; ii) more aggressively enforcing rules against employers colluding in the labour market e.g. through non-poaching agreements; iii) limiting the scope of non-compete agreements; and iv) using labour market regulation to redress information asymmetries between employers and workers. A comprehensive policy strategy to reduce labour market frictions and enhance job mobility would also help lessen the sources of monopsony power.

## Introduction

New, non-standard forms of work have received much attention in recent media, legal and policy debates – see for example ILO (2019[1]). Barely a day goes by without a newspaper article either praising or demonising work in the "platform" economy (in which workers provide services through online platforms), and many court cases are ongoing in which workers are challenging their employment status – giving the impression that employment regulation is increasingly out of date and policy makers unsure how to react. A recent OECD/European Commission survey confirms that addressing the issues raised by new forms of work is a major policy concern among member states (OECD, 2019[2]). However, these discussions are not limited to technology-induced forms of employment (i.e. platform work); they also cover other non-standard employment, such as on-call labour and own-account work more generally (see Chapter 2 for an overview of what is meant by new forms of work).

Underlying these debates is a fear that the standard, full-time and dependent employment relationship is under pressure and that, in the future, many individuals will be working in "flexible" work arrangements with little employment and social protection, few benefits and rights, and limited access to training. According to this view, the nature of firms is also changing and a growing number of them act as "intermediaries" in the production and delivery of products and services, rather than as producing firms in their own right. Consequently, firms will seek out new business models and engage in a "race to the bottom" in which working conditions become the basis for competition, rather than the quality or value of the product or service they provide. Such scenarios, if ever realised, would undermine many of the foundations on which welfare states were built last century, and would require a serious re-thinking of labour market, social and skills policies and institutions, as well as of traditional labour relations and social dialogue.

However, the debate has a tendency to get ahead of the facts, and policy makers should be careful to base any decisions they make on evidence rather than anecdotes, as well as on a balanced consideration of all the arguments.

First, it is important to remember that new, non-standard forms of work often emerge in response to the real needs of both employers and workers. For example, companies need to have sufficient flexibility to adjust workforces and working hours in response to fluctuating and unpredictable demand. Workers may be seeking greater flexibility to fit work around caring responsibilities and/or leisure in order to achieve a better work-life balance. Many workers also want more independence in the way they organise their work and hours. Diversity (and continuous innovation) in employment contracts allows both employers and workers to escape the constraints of a "one-size-fits-all" approach and find arrangements that are in the best interest of both. It is equally important to point out that "non-standard" employment (which is what many new forms of work are) does not necessarily equate to poor quality employment. Indeed, standard jobs can be low quality, while non-standard ones can be high quality. In fact, across the OECD, most individuals in temporary and part-time contracts now have access to similar rights and benefits as standard employees (although, this does not rule out that there might be practical barriers in exerting these rights and accessing benefits for temporary and part-time workers, and that their job might still be more precarious and of lower quality). Moreover, many high-tech professionals sell their services as independent contractors, and new digital intermediaries such as online platforms have made it possible for them to reach more rapidly a much larger, often worldwide, market.

Second, despite the fact there has been rapid growth in some "new", forms of work like platform work and zero-hours contracts, they remain small as a share of total employment (see Chapter 2). Standard, full-time, permanent employment still remains the norm across the OECD (i.e. it accounts for the majority of all employment), even if non-standard employment as a whole may represent a relatively large share of all employment. There are several reasons for the continuing appeal of more stable, permanent employment arrangements. From the workers' side, such contracts provide more certainty and allow them to plan ahead in both their private and professional lives. From the firms' perspective, permanent contracts allow them to attract and retain talent (by increasing loyalty), which reduces hiring and training costs, and increases the pay-off from investing in staff (which raises productivity). Consequently, there is no logical reason to believe that standard work will completely disappear in the near future.

However, while the growth in non-standard employment may sometimes have been overstated and the concerns regarding their intrinsic job quality exaggerated, there are some important issues which policy makers need to address.

The first of these is the question of employment status. Many "new" forms of work have emerged in the grey zone between employee and self-employed status. This raises questions as to which labour rights and protections apply to these workers and whether or not such forms of work are being used merely to avoid costs and regulations at the expense of job quality. More broadly, there is an issue of worker vulnerability and power imbalance vis-à-vis employers, regardless of employment status – which is the second key issue that governments may need to address. The vulnerabilities inherent in the employment relationship can become more acute when workers have no means of organising and bargaining collectively (see Chapter 5), as well as in labour markets characterised by monopsony power. The third and final issue concerns the international aspects of some work in the platform economy, which offers great opportunities for some workers but also risks a race to the bottom in working conditions for others.

While many of these issues have come to the fore as a result of the rise in the platform economy, they are not necessarily new and apply to many pre-existing non-standard forms of work too. Policy makers should therefore ensure that any reforms also cover other forms of non-standard work.

This chapter will discuss each of these policy challenges in turn. Section 4.1 reviews issues related to worker classification and explores options for addressing false self-employment. It also considers how to identify workers in the grey zone between employee and self-employed status, where genuine ambiguity remains but there may be a need to extend certain labour rights and protections. Section 4.2 discusses policy options for extending protection beyond standard employees. Section 4.3 examines power imbalances and the role of labour market monopsony. Section 4.4 briefly discusses the role of international competition in the platform economy and Section 4.5 provides concluding remarks and sets out some policy directions.

## 4.1. Employment status: A gateway to workers' rights and protections

One issue that has recently received a lot of attention in media, legal and policy circles is that of how to define a worker's employment status. In particular, there have been a number of high-profile tribunal cases in which workers have challenged their status as "self-employed" and argued for more rights and benefits, in line with what employees would get.

The reason why employment status matters so much (and hence why there is so much at stake in these court cases) is that it determines access to worker rights, benefits and protections. As an employee, one will generally be entitled to the minimum wage (where it exists), working time regulations and overtime pay, holidays, sickness and accidents insurance, unemployment benefits, protection against unfair dismissal and discrimination.[1] This will not usually be the case for self-employed workers (see Figure 4.1). Getting employment status right therefore matters from a worker's perspective.

**Figure 4.1. Worker classification and coverage of labour law protection**

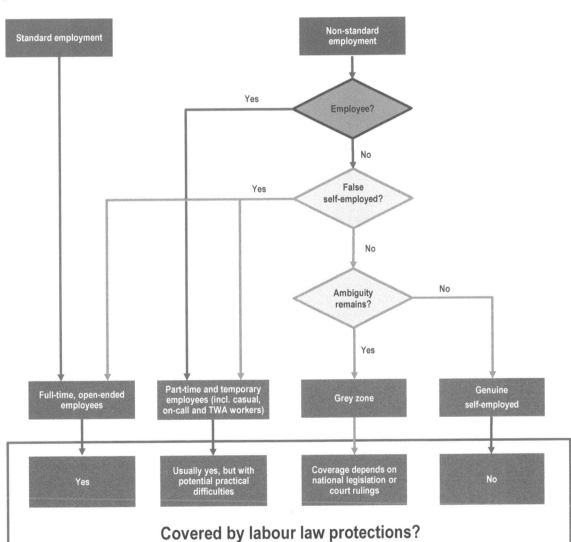

Note: The figure maps standard and non-standard employment into the different categories of workers whose classification is discussed in this chapter. Diamonds correspond to classification decisions that can be taken either by the parties (e.g. stipulated in a written contract between employers and workers) or by adjudicators (courts or enforcement agencies). Grey diamonds and lines refer to decisions that are most often taken by adjudicators. The bottom rectangles refer to coverage of labour law.

Ensuring workers are correctly classified also matters for employers and society more generally. Employers want to avoid situations where competitors gain an advantage simply because they avoid taxes and regulations by disguising employment relationships with their workers as self-employment. From a government perspective, traditional employment is an important source of public revenue, accounting for a greater share of taxes per capita than self-employment. Employment misclassification can result in a significant loss of revenues. For example, in the United States, the Department of Labor has estimated that between 10-30% of workers are misclassified and that this could have a significant impact on tax revenue (Brumm, 2016[3]) and the Government Accountability Office placed the tax gap due to worker misclassification at USD 44.3 billion for the tax years 2008-2010 (GAO, 2017[4]). In the United Kingdom, Her Majesty's Revenue and Customs (HMRC) has estimated that the self-employed account for GBP 5 billion of the GBP 7 billion uncollected tax gap for self-assessment tax income – but this includes also the effects of under-reporting of income and error (Adam, Miller and Pope, 2017[5]). Such erosion of the tax base will have an impact on everyone in society, including businesses attempting to reduce their tax obligations.

The purpose of this section is to bring some clarity to these debates, and to help policy makers think through the issues and the associated policy responses. A key conclusion is that it is important to distinguish between cases of false self-employment and those cases where genuine ambiguity might exist, because this has implications for how policy makers should address the situation.

### 4.1.1. Tackling false self-employment: Ensuring that individuals are correctly classified

False self-employment (also sometimes referred to as disguised, sham, bogus or pseudo self-employment) refers to cases where individuals are classified as self-employed but, to all intents and purposes, work as employees (see Figure 4.1 above). The deliberate misclassification by employers of workers in an attempt to avoid employment regulation, fiscal obligations, workers' representation, as well as to shift risks onto workers and/or gain a competitive advantage, should be cracked down on. Similarly, workers' misclassification of themselves as self-employed to avoid taxes should be addressed. As discussed above, misclassification harms individuals, but also may put firms that follow the rules at a disadvantage and risks creating a hole in public finances.

To successfully fight false self-employment, firms and workers first need to be clear about the rules and regulations. Most countries have in place tests and criteria for assessing employment relationships (Box 4.1) and government action should ensure that firms and workers are aware of, and understand these rules (as well as the spirit in which they were written). For example, in the United States, the Department of Labor published guidance in 2015 to help with the classification of employees and independent contractors.[2] Australia has launched an "Independent Contractors Decision Tool" which helps firms, based on a series of questions they need to answer, identify whether their workers should be classified as a contractor or as an employee.

Governments should also consider making it easier/less costly for workers to challenge their employment status, for example by: placing the burden of proof on the employer (rather than on the employee)[3], reducing court fees[4], simplifying procedures[5], reducing the risks to workers, and/or protecting workers against potential retaliation. Some platforms have tried to get workers to sign arbitration agreements under which they waive the right to sue them in court. In the United States, the National Labor Relations Board had initially argued that such waivers violated labour law (Waas et al., 2017[7]) – however, a recent decision of the Supreme Court ruled against this position, at least as regards class actions.[6]

It is important to allow labour authorities and/or unions to take cases to court. For an individual, filing a complaint with a court is typically expensive and the outcome is uncertain. In addition, workers may worry about retaliation from their employer and losing their job. In some countries, the labour authority has some power to enforce compliance with labour laws – although this is usually limited and does not include the possibility of ordering a civil remedy or taking a claim to court without the consent of the aggrieved worker(s). In Australia, Chile, Poland, Spain and the United States, however, the labour authority can seek for a civil remedy on behalf of the aggrieved workers even in the absence of consent, particularly in cases where an important public interest is concerned (OECD, 2014[8]). In Sweden, trade unions can take employers to court on behalf of the worker (Williams and Lapeyre, 2017[9]).

---

### Box 4.1. Tests and criteria for determining employment status

In practice, the question of whether individuals should be treated as employees or self-employed is often determined by courts. In most countries, the term "employee" is not defined in legislation or, even where it is, leaves broad room for judicial discretion (Davidov, Freedland and Countouris, 2015[6]). In many cases, an employee is defined circularly as "someone who is employed by an employer".

In general, employee status tends to be decided based on the principle of "primacy of facts" – i.e. regardless of what is stipulated in the contract of employment, it is the actual facts of the working relationship which matter to determine whether the person is genuinely self-employed or not (see Figure 4.1 above).[7] One of the reasons for looking at the facts of the relationship rather than at what is stipulated in the contract is that there may be inequality of bargaining power between workers and employers – and the latter are more likely to be able to determine what is written in the employment contract (see Section 4.3).

To assess the employment relationship, a number of tests/criteria are used. In a few civil law countries, these criteria tend to be enshrined in law and there will be a presumption of an employment relationship if these criteria are met, with the burden of proof put on the employer to show that this is not the case. In most countries, however, (including common law countries), judges base their rulings on certain tests developed by case law.

There will be differences in the number of criteria used in these tests. For example, in Canada, courts sometimes use a fourfold test, while in the United States courts have tended to use a 13- or even 20-factor test (Davidov, Freedland and Countouris, 2015[6]). The ILO's recommendation concerning the employment relationship lists 14 factors.

Notwithstanding these differences, the actual tests/criteria used are very similar across countries.[8] Financial dependence of the individual on the client is one of the aspects considered. However, financial dependence is usually not sufficient for employee status to be established. In most countries, there also needs to be an element of subordination of the worker (and control from the client). This may be assessed on the basis of several criteria, including: the worker's integration in the organisation; the extent to which the worker controls his/her conditions of work (including the place and time of work); who provides the tools, materials or machines; the regularity of payments; the extent to which the worker takes on financial/entrepreneurial risk; and whether or not the work must be carried out personally by the worker. There are differences across countries (but also within countries across judges and over time) on the relative emphasis placed on control versus dependency.

---

Strengthening the penalties for firms not complying with legislation could also help address false self-employment. Where consequences of abuse are minimal, firms may have little incentive to correctly classify workers. Policy options include: requalification of the employment relationship; imposing retroactive payment of taxes and social security contributions; imposing greater penalties if firms continue to breach the law in repeated comparable cases; and extending the application of tribunal judgments beyond the plaintiffs and to the entire workforce in a similar situation.[9] In cases where responsibility can easily be passed on because there are multiple customers or contractors (e.g. in multi-party employment relationships), governments can hold the entire chain jointly and severally liable ("chain liability") if labour regulations are broken. This was done in the Netherlands in 2016, when the Act Combating Bogus Self-Employed came into force.[10]

Actions to facilitate legal challenges and increase penalties should be combined with efforts to strengthen the labour inspectorate's capacity to monitor and detect breaches, e.g. increased responsibilities and resources (including the number of inspectors), innovative methods to inspect those working from home/on platforms (e.g. new technological tools), and training. Some countries (e.g. Ireland, Spain and Greece) are also targeting inspection efforts on particular sectors or geographical areas known to have a greater prevalence of false self-employment (OECD, 2019[2]). The extra costs involved should be balanced against the potential revenue gains from clawing back taxes and social security contributions lost as a result of misclassification.

Because social security and tax authorities have strong incentives to ensure the right classification of workers, it might also make sense to ensure that they coordinate their efforts with other enforcement authorities. In the United States, for example, the Internal Revenue Service has made employment tax compliance, including repressing misclassification of workers as independent contractors, an enforcement priority and coordinates its actions with those of the Department of Labor (Internal Revenue Service, 2005[10]; Keneally, Saleski and Engell, 2015[11]). Similarly, in Sweden, the tax agency played a pivotal role in inducing many platforms to accept employer status (Söderqvist, 2018[12]).

In parallel to strengthening the penalties for misclassification, governments should seek to reduce any incentives for firms and workers to misclassify employment relationships as self-employment.[11] In some countries, tax and/or employment regulation have created incentives for employers and/or individuals to shift away from standard employee relationships to self-employment, or other non-standard forms of employment. For example, in Italy, the legislation introduced in 1997 and 2003 to legalise temporary work agencies and collaboration agreements may have led to an increase in self-employed workers who are in fact in an employer-employee-like relationship, but are classified as own-account workers (OECD, 2015[13]). In Australia, employers have an incentive to use casual workers who fall back on tax-financed benefits rather than on employer-sponsored benefits (OECD, 2018[14]). Further examples for the Netherlands and the United Kingdom are discussed in Box 4.2. Some of these incentives were not deliberate, but many countries have in the past introduced specific advantages/benefits in order to encourage self-employment/entrepreneurship.

Some countries have tried to address these incentives in an attempt to make independent worker status more neutral compared with employee status. For example, a tax reform was introduced in the Czech Republic in 2004 to halt the spread of "false" self-employment, although it was overturned in 2007. While it remains difficult to isolate the effect of policy reforms from other factors, the incidence of own-account work increased less in the Czech Republic than in the Slovak Republic during this period (OECD, 2008[18]). In Austria, concerns that independent contractors (*freie Dienstnehmer*) would be used by employers to evade taxes and regulations led the government to gradually integrate them into the social protection system and, since 2008, they pay the same social security contributions as standard employees (OECD, 2018[14]). In Italy, the pension contribution rates for employers and workers in the case of dependent self-employment (*collaboratori*) have been gradually increased since 2012, with the aim of reducing incentives for misclassification (OECD, 2019[2]). In Latvia, the micro-enterprise tax has been increased from 9% to 15%, and the maximum turnover has been reduced in 2018, to try and crack down on bogus self-employment (Golubeva, 2018[19]).

Policy makers could also consider measures to encourage hiring on standard contracts by making them more attractive relative to non-standard employment relationships. Making standard employment more attractive could be achieved by easing the obligations or enhancing the flexibility associated with standard contracts for employers – while still ensuring an adequate level of protection for workers. For example, as part of its 2015 labour market reform, Italy provided a temporary amnesty from fines to employers who convert existing self-employed contracts into standard, open-ended employment contracts (Williams and Lapeyre, 2017[9]).[12] In the Netherlands, the government aims to encourage small and medium-sized businesses to hire on open-ended contracts by reducing sick pay obligations (OECD, 2019[2]).

A recent OECD study analyses the tax treatment of the different employment forms in a set of eight countries, in order to assess to what extent the tax system contributed to the rising shares of non-standard work (Milanez and Bratta, 2019[15]). The authors find that tax treatment differentials cause total employment costs between employees and the self-employed to vary. As a result, non-wage costs are often higher for standard employees than for the self-employed and, at times, this differential may be large enough to shift employer-employee preferences toward self-employment.

The situation in the Netherlands and the United Kingdom provides two case studies of how policy choices have created strong incentives for choosing self-employment over other employment forms.

In the *Netherlands*, self-employed workers are not subject to most social security contributions and non-tax compulsory payments (e.g. pension payments). In addition, unincorporated self-employed workers are eligible for two reductions in the personal income tax (PIT) tax base: i) a self-employment deduction of EUR 7 280 for those who work more than 1 225 hours annually; and ii) an SME exemption equal to 14% of the gross wage, net of the aforementioned self-employment deduction. As a result, total employment costs are around 30% higher for traditional employees than for the self-employed at the average wage (Milanez and Bratta, 2019[15]).

This arrangement shifts pension and insurance costs to the individual. Although the self-employed may self-insure by purchasing private insurance or increasing pension contributions, many do not. For example, in the Netherlands, only one in three own-account workers takes out insurance against incapacity (Ministerie van Financiën, 2015[16]). In addition to this tax incentive, until recently, procedures for declaring employment status to the tax office facilitated growth in self-employment. Workers in a weak bargaining position were encouraged by employers to declare themselves as self-employed, and the employer risked little because the responsibility for declaring the correct employment status was on the worker. Under a new system introduced in 2016, the burden of misclassification is on the employer – who will be liable for all insurance and tax payments if the contractor is found to be an employee. However, enforcement of this new measure is pending following a very negative reaction from various stakeholders, including the self-employed themselves.

In the *United Kingdom*, the government funds an effective self-employment subsidy of GBP 5.1 billion, or GBP 1 240 per person per year (UK Parliament, 2017[17]). Initially, the tax differential aimed to promote entrepreneurship – but the policy fails to target this population effectively. Instead, it incentivises people to identify as self-employed so they can save money, without commensurate reduction in benefits: in the United Kingdom, the difference in benefits entitlement between employees and the self-employed is limited to contribution-based jobseeker's allowance or statutory maternity/paternity/adoption/shared parental pay (see also Chapter 7). The implication is that regular workers subsidise the self-employed since they pay higher contributions without a commensurate increase in benefits (Adam, Miller and Pope, 2017[5]).

### 4.1.2. Workers in the grey zone between self- and dependent employment

In most cases where individuals are falsely self-employed, courts will be able to determine this relatively easily using the criteria and tests described in Box 4.1. However, there are also cases where the issue is less clear, and where a genuine ambiguity may remain (see Figure 4.1 above). Some workers share characteristics of the self-employed (for example, they can choose when and where to work; they use their own equipment); but they also share characteristics of employees (e.g. they cannot set their own rates of pay, they may have to wear a uniform, they cannot be replaced in executing their tasks by someone else).

This issue of the "grey zone" between employee and self-employed status has gained prominence in recent times as a result of the rise of the platform economy and the numerous court cases which have ensued from it.[13] In one such case, the judge recognised the ambiguity and stated that "The jury [...] will be handed a square peg and asked to choose between two round holes."[14] However, the issue of the "grey zone" is by no means a new challenge. As far back as 1944, Justice Wiley Blount Rutledge of the US Supreme Court stated that "Few problems in the law have given a greater variety of application and conflict than the cases arising in the borderland between what is clearly an employer-employee relationship and what is clearly one of independent entrepreneurial dealing".[15] Some researchers even trace the issue back to Roman law (Rubinstein, 2012[20]). In all likelihood, this grey zone will always exist – although its boundaries and scope may vary over time as new business models emerge, technology advances, court practices change and policy changes interact with all of these. Indeed, while there were hopes that many of the court cases against platforms would settle the issue once and for all, in practice the decisions of these cases have been inconsistent in both Europe and the United States (Cherry and De Stefano, 2018[21]).

From a policy perspective, this grey zone matters because workers who find themselves in it share some characteristics with dependent employees. Because of this, they will also share some of the vulnerabilities of employees. However, because these workers tend to be classified as self-employed, they will not benefit from most of the rights and protections given to employees. As a result, it can be argued that some of these rights and protections should be extended to workers in the grey zone. Indeed, workers in a situation of dependence and/or subordination are by definition in a position of unequal bargaining power,[16] and one of the key objectives of labour law is to redress such inequality (and/or its consequences). The challenges for policy makers are to identify who are the workers in the grey zone and decide which labour laws and protections should be extended to them (and how).

In a first instance, the size of the grey zone should be managed and kept to a minimum. In some cases, regulations or guidelines for determining employment status may need to be clarified, revised and/or harmonised[17]. This would help reduce uncertainty for both workers and employers, and reduce litigation (Linder, 1999[22]). For example, in recent years, many countries have laid down criteria aimed at better circumscribing the status of a self-employed worker and distinguishing it from that of an employee – e.g. Belgium in 2006. In doing so, countries face a trade-off between simple rules and broad guidelines (Box 4.3). Simple rules provide clear and unambiguous decisions about employment status, but risk excluding certain workers who may also need labour protections. Broad guidelines leave considerable discretion to adjudicators (enforcement officers or judges) with the potential to extend protection to a much larger group of workers (but at the risk of introducing a greater element of uncertainty and arbitrariness).

---

**Box 4.3. Simple versus complex rules for establishing employment status**

In a few countries, the criteria used for determining employment status define very precise, simple and unambiguously applicable rules. For example, in Italy, there is a rebuttable presumption of an employment relationship in all cases of contract for services if at least two of the following conditions hold: i) the relationship lasts for more than eight months within the same year; ii) associated worker's compensation represents more than 80% of the total compensation earned by the worker within the year; and iii) the worker has his/her work space at the employer's offices.[18] If a relationship meets at least two of these criteria, then the contract will be re-classified as an employment contract and the worker will be entitled to all the rights, benefits and obligations of a standard employee.[19] Similarly, in Greece, an individual supplying work to primarily one employer for a period of nine consecutive months is assumed to be in dependent employment.

While simple rules like these make it relatively straightforward to determine employment status, they inevitably leave unprotected a number of other workers sharing some of the characteristics of dependent employees. Also, strict rules are easier to work around, and such an approach does not take into account new forms of employment that might emerge.

In most other countries, the tests developed through statutory law, guidelines for enforcement agencies or jurisprudence are more complex. The key difference with respect to simple, automatic rules is that all different factors must be jointly assessed in a holistic way. For example, in Canada, labour inspectors and health and safety officers are explicitly instructed to examine all aspects of the relationship and take into account the different factors, bearing in mind that they do not represent an exhaustive list and that their relative weight depends on the particular facts and circumstances of each case (Employment and Social Development Canada, 2006[23]).

The advantage of an ex post, holistic evaluation of the different factors characterising employee and self-employment status resides in its flexibility, which in practice allows for protection to be extended to a much larger group of workers who do not share all the characteristics of dependent employees but who are nonetheless quite similar to them. Precisely defining what it means to be an employee may, in fact, be impossible.[20]

However, by leaving large discretion to adjudicators to appreciate the specificity of each case and the weight to be given to different factors, this approach inevitably introduces a degree of uncertainty and arbitrariness.[21] There is, in fact, a large empirical literature showing that different judges in the same jurisdiction tend to have persistent appraisal differences – see e.g. Waldfogel (1998[24]) and Aizer and Doyle (2015[25]). Thus, if the same case had been assigned to a different adjudicator, the probability of a different outcome is typically high (Fischman, 2014[26]). While this problem can be lessened by resorting to panels of adjudicators, the evidence suggests that it persists even in panels of randomly assigned judges, and cases decided by unanimous vote are no proof of the absence of inconsistency across panels (Fischman, 2011[27]).

Adjudicators in social and labour law also face these problems – see e.g. Autor et al. (2017[28]); Ichino and Pinotti (2012[29]); Breda et al. (2017[30]). As regards detecting employee misclassification, given the genuine ambiguity in the status of workers that has been uncovered in many of the court cases, it is no surprise that apparently similar situations have yielded different outcomes within the same jurisdictions (Davidov, Freedland and Countouris, 2015[6]). This setting may not be ideal for both businesses and workers. Employers would be confronted with a relatively high level of legal uncertainty and, possibly, unexpected changes of legal standards, thereby increasing their potential costs. Workers would find the enforcement of their rights being partially dependent on random events, such as the assignment of the court to a judge with favourable or unfavourable attitudes. This suggests that protections of workers should not be uniquely dependent on being granted employee status by adjudicators and should be, at least partially, extended to all situations where genuine ambiguity remains (see Figure 4.1 above).

An equally important task for policy makers is to clarify who, in triangular employment arrangements (such as those involving a user-firm, a subcontractor and a worker employed by the latter but providing services to the former within its premises) and those involving intermediaries (like many of those in the platform economy), is the employer and who, therefore, bears the responsibility for complying with labour market regulation. In such arrangements, there is a strong argument for clarifying obligations and, where necessary, spreading them across multiple legal entities – for example by holding the intermediaries and the clients jointly and severally liable, or by imposing liability on the intermediary and only subsidiary liability on the client (Box 4.4).

---

### Box 4.4. Identifying who is an employer

Much of the discussion around new forms of work centres around the question of who is an employee, and who is not. A closely related (though less discussed) question is who is an employer, and who is not. This is particularly complicated in multi-party (or triangular) employment relationships, such as those observed in Temporary Agency Work (TWA) and subcontracting, but also in many of the new working arrangements that are emerging in the platform economy.

The question in such set-ups is who is responsible for worker rights and protections. In the case of TWA work – which was initially banned or heavily restricted in many countries (Countouris et al., 2016[31]) – the employment relationship is generally assumed to be between the worker and the agency, and the latter is therefore responsible for ensuring labour law is complied with. That being said, there might also be a legal requirement for the user company to guarantee certain worker rights and protections including, for example, health and safety at work, and to be jointly responsible for others together with the agency (OECD, 2014[8]).

The platform economy has complicated this landscape even further, and it is not clear to what extent the TWA experience might be a useful example for regulating platform work (Lenaerts et al., 2018[32]) – although the TWA model seems to have been accepted by many platforms in Sweden (Söderqvist, 2018[12]) and several platforms worldwide have taken the initiative to treat their workers as employees (Cherry and Aloisi, 2017[33]). Platforms usually argue that they are not employers but mere intermediaries providing the infrastructure for the worker to find clients. However, it is sometimes hard to argue that clients themselves should be considered to be the employer. Platform work typically involves a multiplicity of clients and tasks of a very short duration, even if these tasks are sometimes carried out on the premises of the client. At the same time, many platforms exert significant control over workers (through ratings systems, the management of payments, the withholding of information about clients, controlling the way work is carried out, the deactivation of accounts, etc.)

In some cases, where clear responsibilities cannot be assigned, there may therefore be an argument for platforms and users to bear joint and several liability for worker rights, so that a worker can claim against both or either. In other cases, the user might be argued to bear subsidiary liability – i.e. the worker can claim against the user in those cases where the platform does not comply with the regulation. Along similar lines, some authors have argued that the question of who is responsible for worker rights and protections should be analysed from the perspective of what are the key employer functions – from hiring workers to setting their rates of pay (Prassl and Risak, 2016[34]). The outcome of such an approach would equally be that employment law obligations are spread across multiple legal entities, rather than ascribed to a single employer in the classical sense of the term.

---

For those workers who are left in the grey zone (and therefore tend to be excluded from much of the scope of existing labour law), legislators should consider how (and which) labour rights and protections could be extended. Indeed, clarifying and stating as precisely as possible the scope of the law is unlikely to eliminate the grey zone entirely and hence the uncertainty for workers and employers. Many countries have identified specific groups of workers to which certain parts of the labour law are to be applied but with different approaches, each with their advantages and disadvantages. Some countries have identified very specific occupations; others have focused on the economically dependent self-employed; and still others have relied on vaguer (but broader) definitions. Each of these are discussed below.

Some countries have identified very specific occupations to which certain labour rights and protections have been extended. For example, in France, the following occupations are presumed to have an employment relationship under certain conditions: performing artists (also in Spain), models, professional journalists, and sales representatives and travelling salespersons (Pedersini, 2002[35]; ILO, 2005[36]). In

Mexico, there are similar legal provisions for sales representatives, insurance salespersons, travelling salespersons, sales promoters and similar categories.

In several countries, policy attention has focused on the "dependent" self-employed (Box 4.5). A specific income threshold is usually set. In Spain, the economically dependent self-employed (*trabajador autónomo económicamente dependiente* – TRADE) need to rely on a single client for at least 75% of their income. In Portugal, an individual is considered dependent self-employed when at least 50% of their yearly income comes from one single client (*regime dos trabalhadores independentes e que prestam serviços maioritariamente a uma entidade contratante*). In Germany, workers are "employee-like" persons (*arbeitnehmerähnliche Person*) if they: i) work on the basis of a contract for service or a contract for work and services for other persons; ii) do so personally and essentially without collaboration with employees; and iii) receive 50% of their income from a single client (33% for artists, writers and journalists). In Canada, there is no fixed threshold, but "dependent contractors" cover "those non-employment work relationships that exhibit a certain minimum economic dependency, which may be demonstrated by complete or near-complete exclusivity".[22] Similarly, in Sweden, there is no precise definition, but dependent contractors (*jämställda/beroende uppdragstagare*) include "any person who performs work for another and is not thereby employed by that other person but who occupies a position of essentially the same nature as that of an employee" (Rönnmar, 2004[37]).

While the definition of dependent self-employed in all these countries is similar, the purpose of the category varies significantly. In Portugal, it opens up access to social protection (unemployment insurance, parental benefits, sickness and invalidity protection, as well as old age and survivors pensions). In Germany, employee-like persons have freedom of association, the right to collective bargaining, and the right to minimum leave of four weeks (Däubler, 2016[38]). In both Canada and Sweden, dependent contractors also have a right to collective bargaining and need to be given reasonable notice of the termination of the contractor relationship. In Spain, the TRADE category has access to a wide range of rights and protections, including: minimum wage, annual leave, entitlements in case of wrongful termination, leave for family or health reasons, and the right to collective bargaining (Cherry and Aloisi, 2017[33]).

Other countries have relied on a vaguer definition of an intermediate (or "third worker") category to which some of the rights and protections of employees have been extended, though not all. These third worker categories often combine elements of financial dependency with elements of control/subordination. For example, in the United Kingdom, the statutory category of "worker" was introduced to broaden the reach of employment regulations and to include individuals who had been excluded from employee status by a judiciary taking a very narrow interpretation of the term. The worker category is not precisely defined but is intended to cover any individual who works under a contract to provide a personal service, independently of whether he/she has a contract of employment. These workers are entitled to protection against discrimination under the Equality Act 2010 – implying also a right to equal treatment with standard employees in basic working conditions. In addition, they are covered by selected labour regulations including those on working time, holiday pay and the minimum wage. They may also be entitled to sick pay and parental pay, though they do not benefit from minimum notice periods, health and safety provisions, protection against unfair dismissal and redundancy pay. In addition, they are responsible for their own social security contributions and tax (like the self-employed). While the original intention of the worker category was to broaden the reach of protective employment regulations to a greater number of workers, the creation of this separate category of workers may have shifted the objective of litigation down from obtaining employee status to merely obtaining worker status – as has been evidenced in recent court cases involving ride-sharing services.[23]

## Box 4.5. The incidence of dependent self-employment

The "dependent" self-employed are usually defined as those own-account workers who rely for a large share of their income on a single client/employer. This can be a useful category to focus on in order to extend labour rights and protections to certain workers in the grey zone. But how important is this category of workers?

Measuring dependent self-employment is complicated given that: i) only a few countries have official definitions of dependent self-employment and, where these exist, they tend to differ; and ii) standard labour force and household surveys do not permit the identification of such workers.

Based on a special module of the European Union Labour Force Survey (EULFS), it is possible to get some estimates of the incidence of dependent self-employment, defined here as those own-account workers who generally have one dominant client. In many countries, dependent self-employment represents a non-negligible fraction of total self-employment (16%, on average) – Figure 4.2.[24] Moreover, according to data from the European Working Conditions Survey, this share has risen between 2010 and 2015 across the countries covered by around 20%.

### Figure 4.2. The incidence of own-account workers who generally have one dominant client

As a percentage of the self-employed, 2017

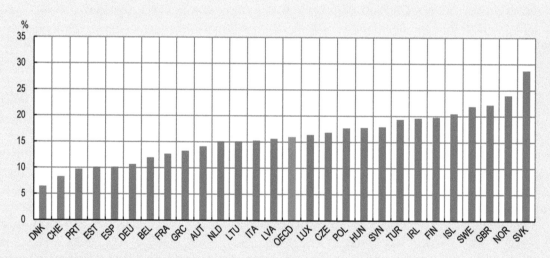

Note: OECD: unweighted average of countries shown.
Source: OECD calculations based on the EU Labour Force Survey, Eurostat.

StatLink 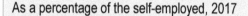 http://dx.doi.org/10.1787/888933966673

In Italy, the "semi-subordinate" worker category (*lavoro parasubordinato*) – covering *co.co.co* and *co.co.pro* contracts[25] – was initially created to increase flexibility in the labour market and to reduce labour costs. These were self-employed workers characterised by: a certain continuity and length of the working arrangement; the individual nature of the service being provided; and some subordination to the client. These workers had access to employer-financed social protection (employers paid a reduced rate). In addition, the rules for termination of these contracts were less stringent than those of employees (OECD, 2014[8]). In the Italian case, the creation of the *semi-subordinate* worker category created clear incentives for employers to replace "standard" employees with workers in the less protected (and cheaper) intermediate category (Liebman, 2006[39]; Muehlberger, 2007[40]). In response to this situation, recent reforms in Italy have all but abolished these contracts (Cherry and Aloisi, 2017[33]). Both in terms of social protection and termination of contracts, the rules are gradually being aligned with those of employees on fixed-term contracts.

These two examples from Italy and the United Kingdom illustrate the dangers inherent in creating an intermediate category of worker where the boundaries of this category are vaguely defined or where it is created to introduce more flexibility in the labour market. The spirit of reforms to employment and social protection regulation should be to extend rights and broaden the reach of these regulations to vulnerable workers who were previously excluded, and not to create opportunities to take rights and protections away from workers who previously had them.

These potential pitfalls of creating a third worker category should be borne in mind in the context of the platform economy, which has changed the shape and size of the "grey zone" between employee and self-employed status, and which has spurred some to suggest a third worker category to cover those workers. In particular, creating a third worker category with vague boundaries would create a significant potential for downgrading. In the United States, Harris and Krueger (2015[41]) have argued for an "independent worker" category which would qualify for many, though not all, of the benefits and protections that employees receive, including the freedom to organise and collectively bargain, civil rights protections, tax withholdings, and employer contributions for payroll taxes. However, they would not qualify for hours-based benefits, including overtime or minimum wage requirements, nor for unemployment insurance benefits. In France, the government has introduced the idea of voluntary charters, which platforms would draw up and which would set out the rights and protections of platform workers. The French idea is an interesting one because it allows the government to buy time in terms of deciding on a certain policy action, while at the same time ensuring more rights and protections for these workers. The risk, however, is that these rights and protections will be set unilaterally by platforms (without consulting workers) at a low level of protection. Moreover, the lack of common protection standards across charters may reduce mobility and therefore heighten the monopsony power of platforms and exert downward pressure on pay (see Section 4.3 below). And a further concern is that, if they are not time-bound, they will end up forming a permanent third worker category (or, rather, multiple third worker categories) with diminished rights. Ideally, therefore, the charters should be seen as a temporary experiment from which governments can learn. In the longer-term, more sustainable solutions should be envisaged and the risk of creating a permanent third "platform" worker category should be avoided. New regulations should be flexible and broad enough to encompass various types of employment, regardless of the means through which work is obtained.

Alternative solutions could also be imagined to extend labour regulations to a greater number of workers in the grey zone. One approach would be to clarify as much as possible the definitions of "employee" and "self-employed", and to treat everyone in the "grey zone" as an "employee" as far as labour law is concerned (until and unless it can be proved that these workers are properly self-employed).[26] [27] This was a route followed by the California Supreme Court in a recent case.[28] Also, in Sweden, a Supreme Court decision dating back to 1996[29] concluded that, because the circumstances were ambiguous and it was difficult to make a clear judgement, the ruling went in favour of the plaintiff and an employment relationship was assumed (Åberg, 2016[42]). This could be the default position, while allowing specific parts of the law to create exceptions for those rights and protections which are more difficult (if not impossible) to extend to self-employed workers. For example, while it may be relatively straightforward to extend health and safety regulations as well as anti-discrimination laws to all own-account workers, it becomes much more difficult to do so for minimum wage legislation and working time regulations. These issues are discussed further in Section 4.2 below.

## 4.2. Extending rights and protections beyond standard employees

Self-employed workers are not usually covered by the same rights and protections as employees (see Figure 4.1 above). The key reason for this is that the self-employed are considered to be business undertakings, taking on their own risks in return for the prospect of earning profits. In principle, they do so with total autonomy, which is not the case for employees. In fact, the key reason why employment relationships are usually governed by labour law is to protect workers from the potential abuse of bargaining power and asymmetric control of information in the hands of the employer. The self-employed usually do not have access to the same social protection either (for example, they are often excluded from unemployment insurance) because the odds of losing one's income depend on their sole efforts and decisions, and as such are considered to be part of the entrepreneurial risk they take on. Finally, because they are considered to be business undertakings, the self-employed are usually banned from collective bargaining as well, since this would be akin to price-fixing under competition law.

Yet, as argued in Section 4.1.2, there are a number of self-employed workers who share some (though not all) of the characteristics of dependent employees and for whom it might make sense to extend some of the rights and protections that employees benefit from (see Figure 4.1 above). Chapters 5 to 7 address the questions of how social protection and collective bargaining, but also training programmes, could be extended to these workers. The remainder of this section discusses some key aspects of labour market regulation and the extent to which (and how) they might be extended to workers in the "grey zone". The section highlights that there are often significant practical difficulties in extending labour rights and protections to these workers – although these challenges are greater for some parts of the labour law than for others. In some cases, there might be a need to adapt existing regulations so that they can be applied to workers in the grey zone. More generally, the same policy issues may apply also to non-standard employees (such as those with an on-call or a zero-hour contract) who are in principle covered by labour law protections but are confronted to practical difficulties in exerting their rights (see Figure 4.1 above). Of course, a balanced approach is necessary to avoid that excessively burdensome regulations end up unduly curbing entrepreneurial activity and innovation.

### 4.2.1. Fair pay

For employees in standard employment arrangements, a legally binding minimum wage and collectively negotiated wage floors can help to prevent exploitation and address in-work poverty. Many studies of minimum wage impacts find that small increases in the minimum wage from a moderate level have no negative employment effects. This is contrary to standard theory but consistent with monopsony power and could suggest that there is some scope to set a minimum wage that exceeds the wage that would otherwise prevail in the labour market without harming employment levels (Card and Krueger, 2015[43]) – see also Annex 4.A.

Yet workers in the grey zone between dependent and self-employment (and, sometimes, other non-standard workers) are usually excluded from such arrangements. For example, neither minimum wages nor collectively negotiated wage floors tend to cover self-employed workers, who are considered "businesses" and are often paid per task that they complete (as opposed to the time-based compensation which most employees receive). While it may not be appropriate/necessary to introduce a minimum wage for many self-employed workers (e.g. entrepreneurs, highly paid freelancers or the "liberal professions"), there are many low-paid workers who will find themselves in the grey zone and/or who will face situations of monopsony power and bargaining asymmetry (see Sections 4.1.2 and 4.3). In those cases, it might be worth considering how mechanisms to achieve fair pay could be extended.

One way to extend minimum wage legislation to cover such workers would be to identify a group of workers in the grey zone (e.g. the dependent self-employed or certain occupations) and require employers to pay the equivalent of the minimum wage to individuals working on a piece rate basis. Piece rate legislation already exists in many countries as part of their minimum wage legislation and generally requires that employers pay individuals the equivalent of the minimum wage, regardless of the basis on which they are rewarded (i.e. by unit of time, or by unit of output).[30] Employers are therefore expected to estimate the average productivity of piece rate workers and ensure that the average individual working at the average speed would earn the equivalent of the minimum wage. In most cases, such legislation is restricted to employees, and so the challenge lies in extending this to other vulnerable workers, including those in the grey zone between dependent and self-employment.

Proposals to introduce minimum rates for some groups of self-employed workers are being discussed in a number of countries. In the United Kingdom, it has been proposed by both the Taylor Review (BEIS, 2017[44]) and the Resolution Foundation (D'Arcy, 2017[45]). In the Netherlands, a legislative proposal has been put forward for the introduction of a minimum wage for the self-employed without employees and a revision of legislation to allow them to set minimum rates collectively (PvdA, 2017[46]). In Germany, a motion on the income of freelancers and solo self-employed, which also includes the demand for minimum fees, has been introduced in the federal parliament (Deutscher Bundestag, 2016[47]). In Poland, minimum wage legislation has recently (1 January 2017) been extended to work carried out under services agreements (*umowy zlecenia, umowy o świadczenie usług*). In particular, this covers individuals hired under services contracts and self-employed service providers who are not employers themselves or who do not contract work out to other parties. However, persons working under so-called specific task agreements (*umowy o dzieło*) are not covered, nor are providers of personal care services and service providers who determine the place and time of their services themselves and work on commission (OECD, 2019[2]).

While extending minimum wage legislation to some sub-groups of the self-employed may seem both desirable and (in theory) feasible, there are significant practical difficulties in doing so. These include: deciding what types of self-employed workers should be covered; defining who the employer is (which is particularly difficult in triangular working arrangements, see Box 4.4 above)[31]; measuring the average productivity of workers[32] (especially for non-standard tasks); determining what counts as work[33,34]; and how to deal with work carried out across national borders (see Section 4.4 below). However, it is not impossible to overcome these difficulties. Since January 2018, for example, New York City has imposed a minimum wage for Uber and Lyft drivers.

Some voluntary initiatives have already been taken by a number of platforms to put a minimum floor under wages. For example, Favor, an on-demand delivery service in the United States, guarantees its drivers a minimum hourly wage. While its "runners" are paid by task, Favor will make up the difference if they do not meet the pay guarantee (Kessler, 2016[48]). Upwork has a global minimum wage of USD 3 per hour for tasks that pay by the hour. In the United Kingdom, Prolific also has a minimum wage per hour. In Australia, the online job-posting platform AirTasker has reached an agreement with unions to recommend minimum rates of pay to its users (Patty, 2017[49]) – although the platform does not guarantee this minimum pay (Kaine, 2017[50]). Some other websites, like the Czech Topdesigner.cz and the Spanish adtriboo.com, have set a minimum or even a fixed price for certain tasks, based on the average number of hours that workers spend on them (European Parliament, 2016).

However, because of the practical difficulties involved in extending minimum wage legislation to self-employed workers, alternative (or complementary) solutions could be sought for strengthening the pay of these workers. One of the most promising avenues might be to extend collective bargaining rights to certain groups of self-employed workers who find themselves in the grey zone between dependent and self-employment and, therefore, in situations of unequal power relationships. Canada, Germany and Sweden are examples of countries which have done this. One key challenge, however, is to ensure that labour market and competition policy are aligned on this issue – this is discussed more extensively in Chapter 5.

### 4.2.2. Regulating working time

Traditional concerns around working time have centred on the issues of excessive working hours. This is why labour legislation usually contains rules limiting working hours and requiring periods for rest and recuperation, including weekly rest and paid annual leave. It is difficult to see how some of these regulations might be extended to own-account workers who, in theory, choose their own working hours – even though, in practice, many (including those in the platform economy) often have limited ability to choose their own hours of work (Lehdonvirta, 2018[51]). Poor bargaining power combined with fierce competition between workers means that they may need to remain on-call if they do not want to lose out when new jobs/tasks are advertised. Moreover, in the case of certain micro-task platforms, workers spend as much time searching for tasks as they do in performing them (Kingsley, Gray and Suri, 2015[52]). Some platforms have introduced their own working hour limits (e.g. CloudFactory sets upper and lower limits on the amount of work each worker can complete in a week) and workers have adopted their own informal practices such as daily routines and quota setting to manage their time (Lehdonvirta, 2018[51]). Data collected through platforms can help in monitoring working time. However there are many complications with extending working time protections to such workers, including the fact that many of them have several clients/employers at any particular point in time, and therefore monitoring overall working time (and allocating responsibility) may be very difficult if not impossible. Again, certain exceptions could be envisaged for the economically dependent self-employed (e.g. minimum leave for employee-like persons in Germany) – but this may exclude many platform workers since they typically work for several clients at the same time (unless employer responsibilities are partially attributed to platforms – see Box 4.4).[35] An alternative would be to focus on certain occupations.

For some workers, there are concerns about the unpredictability of working hours and/or the unwillingness of employers to guarantee a set number of working hours in the contract as they seek a maximum amount of flexibility to respond to fluctuating demand. This is an issue that goes beyond workers in the grey zone and relates to variable- and zero-hours contracts. Many countries have made reforms in this area in recent years (Box 4.6).

---

#### Box 4.6. Regulating variable- and zero-hours contracts

Many countries have special forms of atypical part-time employment contracts (or clauses within contracts) which either involve very short part-time hours or no established minimum hours at all. Some examples of these atypical part-time work arrangements include: casual workers in Australia, on-call contracts (*lavoro a chiamata o intermittente*) in Italy, min-max contracts and zero-hour contracts in the Netherlands, on-call contracts in New Zealand, zero-hour work in the United Kingdom, and if-and-when contracts and zero-hour contracts in Ireland. Many of these atypical part-time contracts have experienced rapid growth in recent years.

In response to concerns about the consequences of unpredictability in working hours on workers' overall earnings, earnings volatility and their ability to plan ahead, there have been a number of reforms in recent years. This has particularly been the case for so-called "zero-hour" contracts. Reforms undertaken include: restricting the use of such contracts to situations where employers truly have a variable need for labour (Finland); requiring employers to provide information (such as the minimum number of hours) upfront or in the employment contract (Finland, Ireland and Norway); requiring advance notice of work schedules (Finland, Ireland, Netherlands, Norway and Oregon in the United States) or adjusting the contracted hours to reflect hours actually worked (Ireland); giving employees the right to request a more predictable contract after a certain period of time (Australia and the United Kingdom); compensation in case workers are called in but sent home again without work (Ireland) or in case they are expected to remain available outside guaranteed hours (New Zealand); and introducing provisions for sick pay and for compensation in cases of termination of employment

(Finland). In addition, in the United Kingdom, there was a recent public consultation on introducing a higher minimum wage for such types of contracts to discourage their (over-) use (OECD, 2019[2]).

To a large extent, the concerns around variable-hours/on-call contracts derive from asymmetries in bargaining power between workers and employers. That is why some measures aim to strengthen the bargaining power of workers through, for example, the banning of exclusivity clauses (i.e. contract clauses which forbid workers from working for other employers – in the United Kingdom and a proposal in the Netherlands) or removal of obligations on the employee to accept work where the employer does not offer guaranteed hours (e.g. in New Zealand where firms must offer compensation for such availability). However, in some cases, countries have undermined the bargaining position of workers – for example, by expecting the unemployed to take up variable- (or zero-) hours contracts to be eligible for unemployment benefits (Kenner, 2017[53]).

### 4.2.3. Occupational safety and health

Some of the issues relating to working time also apply to occupational safety and health (OSH). Many new forms of work tend to transfer responsibilities for OSH from the employer to individual workers, who often lack the training or resources to take appropriate measures to ensure that their working conditions and the working environment are safe. Sometimes, strong competition between workers may result in corners being cut and unnecessary risks being taken. At the same time, labour inspectorates are often not adequately prepared to deal with these new forms of employment, which are often harder to reach, where it is not always clear that the existing legislation applies, and where the support from unions is often lower (Walters, 2017[54]). This makes it easier for such workers to avoid existing regulations like, for example, the need to obtain medical certificates in certain professions. Again, this is to some extent an issue of unbalanced bargaining power between employers and workers – although individuals themselves may also be short-sighted and/or want to avoid costs and regulations. In addition, there are the same difficulties in identifying the liable party due to the triangular nature of some relationships and the short nature of some of these tasks.

New forms of work also bring new or increased risks. For example, many platform activities are in the transport sector, where the risk of accidents is elevated. Recent evidence suggests that the arrival of ridesharing is associated with an increase of 2%-3% in the number of motor vehicle fatalities and fatal accidents as a result of increased congestion and road utilisation (Barrios, Hochberg and Yi, 2018[55]). There are also risks associated with online work – both physical and psychosocial, such as visual fatigue; musculoskeletal problems; work-related stress; chronic job and income insecurity; and isolation.

Again, the question of employment status is critical here as OSH regulation often only applies to employees. Special provisions for the dependent self-employed or certain occupations could be envisaged, while information campaigns and training could help strengthen OSH among own-account workers more generally. On the social protection side, some countries are beginning to think about how insurance for accidents at work might be extended to some previously excluded workers. For example, France has recently expected certain platforms to provide such insurance to some of their workers: if workers earning more than EUR 5 100 per year voluntarily insure themselves against the risk of occupational accidents or illness, the platform must provide reimbursement. The voluntary charters which France is considering might also lead to improved OSH for certain platform workers.

### 4.2.4. Anti-discrimination

Because of its potential negative impact on inclusiveness and basic human rights, but also on productivity, measures to tackle discrimination in the labour market on the basis of race, gender, religion, political opinion, socio-economic background, etc. have been put in place in all OECD countries (OECD, 2008[18]).

The emergence of the platform economy has an ambiguous effect on the ability to protect workers from discrimination. To the extent that platforms promote anonymity, they might help address discrimination. However, where such anonymity is not guaranteed, discrimination may be worse because of the lack of regulation and enforcement – see Edelman, Luca and Svirsky (2017[56]) for evidence of racial discrimination on Airbnb; Galperin and Greppi (2017[57]) for geographical discrimination on Nubelo (one of the largest Spanish-language online labour platforms); and Galperin, Cruces and Greppi (2017[58]) for evidence of gender discrimination, also on Nubelo. Moreover, while algorithms may offer the promise of removing human judgment and bias from decisions, there is some evidence that, in fact, they may reinforce human prejudice and embed biases of their own – see, for example, Sweeney (2013[59]) for such evidence on ads by Google AdSense.

This emerging evidence suggests that governments should think carefully about how non-discrimination laws might be extended to online platforms and independent workers more generally. Calls for labour platforms to collect (and publish) data on outcomes for various groups could be one step in the right direction. Focusing on certain occupations or the dependent self-employed could be another way of extending anti-discrimination legislation – see Section 4.1.2. In most European countries, anti-discrimination laws already cover the self-employed; exceptions include Lithuania and the United Kingdom, where they are not fully covered (European Commission, 2017[60]).

### 4.2.5. Employment protection

When workers have employee status, employment protection legislation usually protects them against unjustified breach of contract obligations on the part of employers, including remedies for unfair dismissal and wage theft. With rare exceptions, these rights are not contractible, in the sense that the employee cannot give them up upon signing the employment contract – see e.g. OECD (2013[61]).

However, these labour law protections do not extend to most contracts for services and/or intermediation contracts (such as terms of conditions for using platform apps), where the scope for contractible provisions is much larger. Yet, in a number of cases, wage and working conditions are set unilaterally by the platform (or the intermediary) or the requester (i.e. individual or company who posts tasks), with no scope for individual workers to negotiate any of the items in the terms of conditions that must be accepted in order to begin or continue working.[36] For example, on certain micro-task platforms, requesters can refuse completed tasks without providing a reason, in which case the worker receives no pay – see e.g. Kingsley, Gray and Suri (2015[52]). Even with direct transactions, without platform intermediation, not getting paid for completed tasks is a challenge for many providers of work services – see e.g. Berg et al. (2018[62]). Similarly, terms of conditions of digital intermediation services often establish that the platform can deactivate a worker's account without providing a justification, sometimes even without previous warning – see e.g. Ross (2015[63]), Kingsley, Gray and Suri (2015[52]), Kaltner (2018[64]), and Marcano (2018[65]).

The absence of adequate, simplified mechanisms of dispute resolution reinforces the asymmetry in the control of the relationship.[37] Filing complaints with courts is expensive and long, and usually not attractive for workers in the case of small claims. In the case of micro-task platforms, these barriers are largely prohibitive, since the value of each task corresponds to very small amounts of money.

Building in some kind of simplified dispute resolution system for platform workers would therefore be desirable. For example, platforms could be required to provide a dispute resolution process that places the burden on the client to demonstrate that the work has not been completed (to the required standard) and allows workers a reasonable time to re-do rejected tasks – see e.g. Silberman (2018[66]). Similarly, platforms could be required to communicate swiftly the reason for account deactivation to the worker. The statement of reasons should identify the objective grounds for the deactivation decision, based on the grounds set out in advance in the platform's terms and conditions, and reasonably refer to the relevant specific circumstances that led to that decision. That statement could also be set to define the limits of the possible legal dispute, in the sense that no additional griefs could be raised by the platform in the case of a lawsuit.[38] A proposal for a regulation in this sense is under discussion at the European Parliament (European Commission, 2018[67]) and, in a recent court case involving a ride-hailing service[39], the settlement included an agreement that, in the future, workers would receive a hearing before an arbitrator prior to any dismissal (Kovács, 2017[68]).

Simplified dispute resolution systems must be designed in such a way to guarantee impartiality. Standard private out-of-court arbitration may not be a solution, however, because in situations where the arbitrator has frequent interactions with one party, there is potential for abuse and the advantage of neutrality may be lost due to a conflict of interest (US House of Representatives, 2009[69]).[40] Such a situation tends to be more frequent in cases opposing individuals to large corporations, not least because the latter are more accustomed with the arbitration process.[41] This suggests that an alternative dispute resolution system could be more effective if provided or supervised by an administrative agency. In New York City, for example, the Freelance Isn't Free Act (FIFA) is intended to protect freelancers from non-payment. Among FIFA's protections is the requirement that hiring parties provide a written contract to freelancers for any work exceeding USD 800 over a 120-day period. Freelancers can bring a complaint to an administrative agency, which is empowered to issue payment orders as well as civil penalties. Alternatively, simplified dispute resolution systems could rely on social partners. For example, in the temporary work industry, there are a number Ombuds and arbitration schemes managed by social partners that could represent interesting models in the case of tripartite relationships (World Employment Confederation, 2018[70]). In the platform industry, indeed, three German platforms and the German Crowdsourcing Association drafted, in 2015, a Crowdsourcing Code of Conduct and established, in 2017, in conjunction with five other platforms and IG Metall, an "Ombuds office" to enforce the Code of Conduct and resolve disputes between workers and signatory platforms – see Berg et al. (2018[62]) and Chapter 5.[42]

## 4.3. Monopsony power, labour market efficiency and worker vulnerability

Many workers, including many self-employed workers, face an unbalanced power relationship vis-à-vis their employer/client, which makes them vulnerable and potentially in need of the protections that are normally granted to employees only (see the previous section). Unbalanced power relationships tend to emerge because employers/clients often have a higher degree of control over the relationship than workers (discussed in Section 4.1.2 above) and because the latter may have few or no outside options, giving rise to a degree of labour market monopsony (see Box 4.7). In many situations, employers' power (often referred to as buyer power in the industrial organisation literature) is not compensated by sufficient bargaining power on the side of the workers and may, therefore, lead to lower employment and pay as well as poor working conditions. This is a particular challenge for self-employed workers who are often banned from collective bargaining by antitrust regulation (see Chapter 5).

> ### Box 4.7. What labour market monopsony means in the labour literature
>
> The labour economics literature often defines as *labour market monopsony* a situation in which employers' power as buyer of labour services is not compensated by sufficient workers' bargaining power, and workers have low or no outside options. Strictly speaking, the term "monopsony" refers to the extreme case in which one buyer dominates a specific upstream market and, in order to maximise its profits, can fix input purchases and prices below the level that maximises social welfare. The term "oligopsony" would more correctly refer to cases where few firms dominate buying in a market, and can affect input prices by reducing input purchases in that market. In the case of platforms, which face a multi-sided market, certain studies consider an operational concept of "intermediation power" (Bundesministerium für Wirtschaft und Energie, 2018[71]). Yet, the literature often refers to labour market monopsony to indicate any of these situations with respect to a specific segment of the labour market (Manning, 2003[72]; Bhaskar, Manning and To, 2002[73]). See also Annex 4.A for a more extensive discussion.

Unbalanced power relationships affect not just the self-employed, but workers more generally – including employees (but, in particular, workers who are in precarious employment). There are a number of policy options to tackle an imbalance of power in employment: i) collective voice can be strengthened or extended to workers previously excluded (see Chapter 5); ii) labour market regulation can be used to counteract the ill effects of power imbalances (as discussed in the previous section); and/or iii) these imbalances can be addressed directly, tackling the abuse of monopsony power and its sources. The three options are not mutually exclusive. As the first two options are treated elsewhere, this section briefly focuses only on the third option, with particular reference to non-standard forms of work – Annex 4.A provides a more extensive discussion of both existing evidence on labour market monopsony and related policies to address it.

There is a growing literature showing that, in some OECD countries, a significant fraction of employment is in highly concentrated labour markets – see e.g. Azar et al. (2018[74]), Abel, Tenreyro and Thwaites (2018[75]) and Martins (2018[76]). In specific labour markets of many OECD countries, a large number of studies have also estimated low residual labour supply elasticities – measuring how easily workers switch to a different employer in reaction to wage changes in a specific firm – which is typically considered as evidence of labour market monopsony – see e.g. Manning (2003[72]), Sokolova and Sorensen (2018[77]), and Naidu, Posner and Weyl (forthcoming[78]). While most of this evidence typically refers to employees, there are some studies quantifying the extent to which own-account workers, including platform workers, may be exposed to monopsony power. For example, Dube et al. (forthcoming[79]) provide evidence that workers on Amazon Mechanical Turk can have a residual labour supply elasticity as low as 0.1, while Chevalier et al. (forthcoming[80]) find values comprised between 1 and 2 for Uber drivers. Both estimates are clear evidence of strong buyer power in these labour markets. Although more evidence on the market for platform work is required, when compared with previous results in the literature for employees in many labour markets – see Annex 4.A, these figures suggest that certain platform workers are even more exposed to labour market monopsony than most ordinary employees.

Labour market monopsony (or, more generally, excess employers' buyer power in the market for labour) can have a negative impact on prices – i.e. pay and benefits – and quantities – overall employment. Recent evidence suggests that high concentration in the labour market depresses wages and increases the wedge between pay and productivity. Labour market monopsony also appears to inefficiently reduce labour demand and employment, particularly at the bottom of the wage distribution, although the evidence is somewhat more indirect (see Annex 4.A).

Labour market monopsony is also a source of concern for business. On the one hand, a lack of competition in the labour market (for example through abuse of non-compete clauses by competitors – see the next section) may imply that innovative companies might be prevented from exploiting new opportunities. On the other hand, insufficient enforcement of competition law may disadvantage those firms that abide by the rules with respect to competitors engaging in illicit behaviours.

### 4.3.1. Enforcing regulation to address labour market monopsony

Excess monopsony power can be addressed by better regulations and more effective enforcement of these regulations. In fact, to date, enforcement agencies have paid somewhat less attention to labour market power and firms' ability to pay workers less than their marginal productivity than to product market power.

Fighting against labour market collusion is one of the areas where further action is needed – see Annex 4.A for more extensive discussion of existing regulations. In most jurisdictions, competition law forbids collusion among buyers of intermediate goods or services, including labour services – see e.g. Blair and Wang (2017[81]). Illicit collusion occurs, for example, when companies competing for the same type of workers agree on refraining from hiring those employed by the others (so-called "no-poaching agreements") or, except in the framework of collective bargaining (see Chapter 5), when firms competing in the same labour market agree to apply a common compensation policy to employees or independent contractors (wage collusion).

General statistics on collusion are difficult to collect, since figures on those illicit behaviours that escape investigation are typically not available. Anecdotal evidence suggests, however, that the phenomenon is far from negligible – see e.g. Krotoski et al. (2018[82]). Statistics on non-poaching covenants exist for franchising agreements, where these covenants are not necessarily unlawful (see Annex 4.A). Krueger and Ashenfelter (2018[83]) estimate that more than 50% of major franchise companies in the United States use no-poaching clauses in their franchising agreements.

Providing explicit guidance about labour market collusion is crucial to guide and set priorities for enforcement agencies. For example, US antitrust authorities have issued guidelines that explicitly refer to collusion in the labour market, present clear examples of illicit behaviours, and underline the importance of fighting them for their effects in the labour market (US Department of Justice and Federal Trade Commission, 2016[84]). Whistleblower protection is also needed for effective enforcement, since collusion is often discovered based on information provided by insiders (Dyck, Morse and Zingales, 2010[85]; Yeoh, 2014[86]). Specific protection is particularly essential in the case of independent contractors who usually are not covered by dismissal legislation provisions concerning whistleblowing – see e.g. OECD (2014[8]). Last, but not least, enforcement agencies should also be able to provide adequate sanctions for collusive behaviours.

Potentially colluding companies, however, could avoid unlawful labour market collusion by simply merging, thereby raising their buyer power in the labour market – see e.g. Marinescu and Hovenkamp (forthcoming[87]). More generally, if merging firms would together form the dominant buyer in the labour market, the merged entity would likely use its buyer power to reduce quantities and prices in that market, similarly to what non-merging colluding companies would do. Yet, one difficulty in assessing the impact of mergers on buyer power in the labour market has to do with the shortage of specific tools to analyse labour competition and, in particular, the difficulty of identifying the relevant market. Another difficulty is the evaluation of merger effects when merging firms are not direct competitors in downstream product markets.[43] This is an area in which more research is needed and more investment in developing adequate tools by governments and enforcement authorities would be welcome.

Another area of possible policy action concerns non-compete covenants, which are contract clauses preventing workers from working for a competitor after they separate from the employer. In most countries, non-compete agreements are lawful and justified by the need to protect trade secrets and specific investment in the employment relationship by the employer (such as certain types of training and investment in knowledge). Yet, recent evidence suggests that employers may use these clauses in order to limit effectively the outside options of their workers. A number of cases, for example, have concerned low-skilled workers involved in production of standardised products, such as sandwich making, and with little access to company tacit knowledge. Starr, Prescott and Bishara (2018[88]) estimate that almost 30 million US workers are currently covered by non-compete agreements, and that many of these agreements are imposed broadly on workers with less than a bachelor's degree, often with low income or no access to trade secrets.

A particular type of non-compete covenant is represented by the restrictions imposed on certain platform workers to continue a direct relationship with their client off the platform without paying a disproportionately high fee (Berg et al., 2018[62]). This constraint is particularly binding in the case of unilateral changes to the terms of service provided by the platform. In fact, the specific relationship that is sometimes created between a given worker and a given client on certain platforms implies a high opportunity cost for workers if they cannot quit the platform without losing their clients, which often forces them to accept unfavourable changes in the terms of conditions.[44]

In order to fight against non-compete agreements in situations where they are most likely used only to reduce workers' outside options, governments could consider establishing a rebuttable presumption of abusive use (or even banning them), in the case of certain type of positions, pay levels or skill requirements, for which a clear justification, such as the protection of trade secrets, seems implausible.

Where non-compete clauses are enforceable, governments could also consider banning "blue-pencilling" by courts – i.e. situations where courts can redraft unreasonable covenants in order to make them enforceable. In fact, this practice creates incentives to draft unenforceable, extensive clauses only to discourage uninformed workers from seeking alternative job offers. Last, but not least, since workers who are victim of abuses rarely initiate private damage actions, enforcement agencies, including labour inspectorates, should take a leading role and have the possibility of imposing sanctions or taking the case to courts for imposing them (see Annex 4.A for more discussion of current practices and issues in OECD countries).

Finally, one of the reasons why workers often have low bargaining power and few outside options is that they have much less information than employers. Workers often have only a vague idea of their rights, in particular if they are employed with a non-standard contract. For example, when signing a contract (or accepting terms and conditions) workers may not fully understand the obligations they are committing to (or the rights they are waiving). Regulation could therefore make sure that all contracting parties are fully aware of their rights and responsibilities. For example, certain scholars have suggested that governments should invest in a dedicated service for independent contractors, and in particular platform workers, offering general advice and counsel about their employment rights (Balaram, Warden and Wallace-Stephens, 2017[89]).

Lack of pay transparency may also increase monopsony power. Shortage of information about alternative opportunities reduces workers' ability to change jobs or leverage outside opportunities to negotiate for higher pay (and better working conditions) (Harris, 2018[90]). Digital technologies have the potential to improve this type of information asymmetry, as workers can access a large number of job offers and compare them, thereby reducing search costs (see below). Yet, in many platforms, workers have few tools to search for available alternatives and have to spend much time searching for them (Kingsley, Gray and Suri, 2015[52]; Berg et al., 2018[62]). To improve pay transparency in the platform economy, employers and platforms could be required to publish information about the average pay per task, as well as on the average time taken to complete a task (which would help workers make more informed decisions about which tasks to accept).

One specific problem related to digital intermediation concerns the information which platforms collect on workers. For example, most platforms have a rating system for workers, which evaluates their performance history and which is supposed to improve service quality for the requester. However, the ratings algorithms often lack transparency (Rosenblat and Stark, 2016[91]). This informational asymmetry allows requesters or platforms to exclude certain workers from certain tasks, based on their ratings, while workers are unable to identify and refuse tasks proposed by bad requesters, who typically do not pay regularly or are inclined to provide negative assessments (Kingsley, Gray and Suri, 2015[52]). To address these issues, governments could consider regulating the ratings system by imposing rating symmetry (so called "five-for-five" policies) and algorithm transparency to platforms.

### 4.3.2. *Other interventions to reduce frictions*

Labour market monopsony tends to emerge in situations where there are few, large firms, and where frictions in the labour market, preventing workers from easily switching jobs in response to changes in wages or working conditions, are considerable – see e.g. Manning (2011[92]). All types of non-regulatory interventions to reduce frictions in the labour market are likely to contribute to lessen monopsony power in that market. A comprehensive strategy of simultaneously tackling all barriers to potential job mobility in the labour market should be developed (OECD, 2018[93]).

Interventions favouring geographical mobility play a crucial role. Existing evidence suggests that labour markets tend to be more concentrated in rural areas and/or areas where economic activity is more dispersed (Azar et al., 2018[74]; Rinz, 2018[94]). For example, housing policies could promote geographical mobility of workers to help people move to the regions where the best jobs are available. Similarly, occupational licensing should be used judiciously and standards should be harmonised across regions (and countries, where applicable) as much as possible, insofar as in some countries licensing has acted as a barrier to mobility, without clear benefits in terms of better service quality, consumer health or safety – see OECD (2018[93]) for further discussion. The same arguments apply to national (and international) recognition of competences and acquired skills – see Chapter 6.

Technological developments are improving the efficiency of the matching process. In many OECD countries, unemployment coexists with firms complaining about not being able to find suitably skilled workers to fill vacancies. Digital platforms can help employers find workers for tasks that their existing employees cannot perform, thereby enlarging the labour market by expanding opportunities in it – see Chapter 2. Similarly, digital intermediaries, such as commercial job boards, can provide access to a large number of vacancies and worker profiles, significantly reducing search costs for both workers and employers. The possibility of working from a distance made possible by digital technologies also allows workers in rural areas accessing jobs and tasks that before were precluded to them. However, in platform-mediated interactions, there is a potential for adverse selection and asymmetric concealment of information, which may require the development of institutions to certify the information provided by users (Autor, 2009[95]). Moreover, in certain cases, there is a risk of a race to the bottom because of competition from world regions with much lower labour standards and pay level in real terms (see Section 4.4 below)

Digital technology is also transforming the way the Public Employment Service (PES) and other placement providers operate, making it easier to exploit information about vacancies and jobseekers, thereby improving the matching process and reducing market frictions. By automating a number of tasks, digitalisation also allows the PES to concentrate resources on activities requiring personal interactions and more discretionary task actions. There are limits to what digitalisation can achieve in this field, however. While benefit applications and vacancy registration are easy to digitalise, it may be more difficult to do so for other services, such as personalised counselling and training. In addition, safeguards must be introduced in new, heavily digitalised systems to avoid creating a digital divide by handicapping more disadvantaged jobseekers (OECD, 2015[96]).

Promoting job mobility also requires making social protection more portable and less linked to a specific job or employer (see Chapter 7). In that respect, relying on voluntary provision of social protection entitlements by employers or intermediaries such as platforms (see e.g. Section 4.2 above) might not be a wise idea in the long-run. In fact, the lack of portability of employer-provided social protection plans may reduce mobility and therefore heighten the monopsony power of employers and intermediaries, exerting downward pressure on pay.

Specific features of certain platforms can also create obstacles to job mobility. For example, payment or remuneration in a moneyless form like bitcoins and vouchers are relatively common on certain platforms (Kingsley, Gray and Suri, 2015[52]) and tie the worker to the platform. Similarly, personal work histories, such as personal ratings, are usually lost upon changing platform (Berg et al., 2018[62]). Given that platforms de facto favour workers with good ratings, the loss of individual ratings represents a strong barrier to worker mobility, and may limit competition for workers across platforms. Governments could therefore consider further interventions to enhance worker mobility across platforms such as regulating moneyless payments and facilitating the portability of personal ratings.

## 4.4. International competition

Labour law tends to apply to the national or regional labour market, and it faces serious limitations when work is performed across national borders. Yet, with the rise of the platform economy, an increasing number of workers provide services internationally. As the ILO puts it, "digital labour platforms provide new sources of income to many workers in different parts of the world, yet the dispersed nature of the work across international jurisdictions makes it difficult to monitor compliance with applicable labour laws" (ILO, 2019, p. 44[1]). Clients and employers can be based in one country, the platform in another, and the workers in yet another. In those cases, it is not obvious what law should apply, if any, or how it should be enforced. In addition, when countries start regulating the platform economy, there is a risk that they will do so in very different ways which can not only cause difficulties for the platforms themselves, but could also result in a race to the bottom among countries trying to attract work through the platform economy (Cherry and De Stefano, 2018[21]). In such a context, it becomes very difficult to regulate working conditions and international cooperation becomes indispensable.

In the context of the European Union (EU), there is some precedent in terms of regulating cross-border work. While the EU legislation allows for choice, the default position is to apply the law of the country in which the employee is carrying out the work.[45] Furthermore, recognising the imbalance in power relations between employers and employees, the choice of national law regime may not "have the result of depriving the employee of the protection afforded to him by provisions that cannot be derogated from by agreement under the law that, in absence of choice, would have been applicable" – Rome Convention of 1980, Rome I Article 6(1). In short, the choice of law allows some flexibility, but not at the expense of worker rights.

In most cases, however, platform workers are likely to have a contract for services (and not an employment contract) – in which case the above regulations do not apply. In the case of a contract for services, European law – Rome I Article 4(1) – again gives as the prioriy "the law of the country where the service provider has his habitual residence" or, failing that, "the law of the country where the party required to effect the characteristic performance of the contract has his habitual residence" – Article 4(2). However this will do little to protect the working conditions of platform workers (unless national regulations have specific provisions in place).

Given the limitations of the above regulations as far as platform workers are concerned, some have argued for further regulation at the EU level in the form of a "platform work directive" (Risak, 2018[97]). This could set out a list of rights for platform workers, regardless of their employment status. However, such a directive would still only apply to workers based in the EU and would not solve the problem of a possible race to the bottom in working conditions with countries outside the EU. It is also important to point out that for many genuinely self-employed and highly skilled platform workers such regulation would be less necessary, as they are typically less vulnerable and their activities could genuinely be seen as international trade in services between undertakings.

For the more vulnerable self-employed platform workers in the grey zone, voluntary initiatives and/or self-regulation might offer a solution (at least temporarily). Some initiatives have already sprung up. For example, the Dynamo Guidelines for Academic Requesters aim to encourage academics using Amazon Mechanical Turk to be good employers and pay fair wages – but there is currently no way of enforcing these guidelines (Salehi et al., 2015[98]). In Germany, the Crowdsourcing Code of Conduct has been signed by eight platforms, and there is now an Ombuds Office for workers to turn to in case they think they have been treated unfairly by one of the platforms that signed up to the Code of Conduct – see Silberman (2018[99]) and Section 4.2 above. For Mechanical Turk, there are also plans to set up a voluntary pledge for requesters to sign, and which would appear as a badge next to their name for workers to see. At the international level, the G20 countries have committed to "promoting decent work in the platform economy" (Labour 20, 2018[100]). While such efforts are at a very early stage, it is possible to envisage a set of guidelines for countries and platforms to sign up to and which might have a similar impact as the OECD Guidelines for Multinational Enterprises, which have promoted responsible business conduct in global supply chains.[46]

## 4.5. Concluding remarks

This chapter has examined how labour market regulation could be extended and adapted to adequately protect workers in a changing world of work, and to ensure that firms that respect these regulations are not at a disadvantage to their competitors. Employment status acts as a gateway to various rights and protections. Ensuring the correct classification of workers (and tackling misclassification) is therefore a key first step to ensure that those in new forms of work have access to labour and social protection, as well as to collective bargaining and lifelong learning. For some workers, however, there is genuine ambiguity about employment status as they find themselves somewhere in the "grey zone" between dependent and self-employment. In addition to urging policy makers to try and reduce the size of this grey zone as much as possible, the chapter discusses the rationale and policy options for extending certain labour rights and protections beyond standard employees. Tackling power imbalances between employers/clients and workers also involves addressing abuses of monopsony power, e.g. by fighting labour market collusion by employers, limiting the scope of non-compete covenants and redressing inequalities in the information available to employers and workers. Nevertheless, these issues could also be addressed, and the position of many workers improved, through social dialogue and collective bargaining (Chapter 5), skill policies (Chapter 6) and social protection measures (Chapter 7).

While this chapter has discussed policy options to extend labour rights and protections beyond standard employees, it is important to underline that a balanced approach is needed. New forms of work often emerge in response to the real needs of both employers and workers. Diversity (and continuous innovation) in employment contracts gives both employers and workers the necessary flexibility to find arrangements which are in the best interests of both. The objective of policy should therefore be to accommodate these changes without abandoning the aim of protecting the weakest and ensuring fundamental rights for all.

> ### Box 4.8. Policy directions
>
> Governments should ensure that all workers in the labour market have access to an adequate set of rights and protections, regardless of their employment status or contract type, and guarantee a level playing field among firms by preventing some from gaining a competitive advantage by avoiding their obligations and responsibilities.
>
> In the area of labour market regulation, countries should:
>
> - Tackle false self-employment by:
>   - Ensuring that employers and workers are aware of, and understand, existing regulations;
>   - Making it easier and less costly for workers to challenge their employment status;
>   - Strengthening the penalties for firms misclassifying workers;
>   - Strengthening the capacity of labour inspectorates to monitor and detect breaches;
>   - Reducing incentives for firms and workers to misclassify employment relationships as self-employment in order to avoid/reduce taxes and regulations.
> - Reduce the size of the "grey zone" between self- and dependent employment by revising, updating and/or harmonising definitions of what it means to be an employee and/or a self-employed person in order to make these definitions as clear as possible and reduce uncertainty for both workers and employers.
> - Extend rights and protections to those workers left in the "grey zone" (i.e. where genuine ambiguity in employment status exists) by a combination of:

- o Identifying and targeting specific groups of workers to which certain labour rights and protections could be extended;

- o Deciding which labour rights and protections to (at least partially) extend (e.g.: fair pay, working time protections, occupational health and safety, anti-discrimination and employment protection) and whether and how they should be adapted;

- o Where necessary, clarifying and/or assigning employer duties and responsibilities in the case of triangular employment relationships (including platform work), which may require spreading such responsibilities across multiple legal entities.

- At the international level, build on the recent G20 commitment to promote decent work in the platform economy and consider ways of improving the working conditions of workers with little say over their remuneration and working conditions who provide services globally – including best practice principles or guidelines, which countries and/or platforms could sign up to.

Addressing power imbalances between employers/clients and workers also requires enhancing collective bargaining and social dialogue (see Chapter 5) and tackling labour market monopsony. Options that could be considered to fight against abuses of monopsony power include:

- Fighting labour market collusion, for example by providing explicit guidance on illicit behaviours, setting priorities for enforcement agencies and ensuring adequate whistleblower protection;

- Limiting the scope of non-compete covenants, including in contracts for services – particularly for certain types of jobs, pay levels or skill requirements, where they are most likely to be used to reduce competition in the labour market;

- Reducing the incentives for broad or unlawful non-compete agreements, by banning court redrafting of unreasonable covenants to make them enforceable, and by appropriately sanctioning the abuse of illicit clauses;

- Favouring the development of new tools and instruments to better analyse the effects of mergers and anti-competitive conduct in the labour market;

- Redressing inequalities in the information available to employers and workers by ensuring that workers are fully aware of their rights and responsibilities, improving pay transparency in the labour market and enhancing symmetry of treatment of workers and requesters on online platforms, including as regards mutual evaluations.

# References

Abel, W., S. Tenreyro and G. Thwaites (2018), "Monopsony in the UK", *CEPR Discussion Paper*, No. 13265, CEPR, London.  [75]

Åberg, A. (2016), *Working in a Cross-Border Situation - A Study on the Concepts of Employment and Self-Employment*, Lund University, https://lup.lub.lu.se/student-papers/search/publication/8876224 (accessed on 13 December 2018).  [42]

Adams, A. and J. Prassl (2018), "Zero-Hours Work in the United Kingdom", *Conditions of Work and Employment Series*, No. 110, International Labour Office, Geneva, http://www.ilo.org/wcmsp5/groups/public/---ed_protect/---protrav/---travail/documents/publication/wcms_624965.pdf (accessed on 4 June 2018).  [161]

Adam, S., H. Miller and T. Pope (2017), "Tax, legal form and the gig economy", in *The Institue for Fiscal Studies (IFS) Green Budget*, The Institute for Fiscal Studies (IFS), https://www.ifs.org.uk/uploads/publications/comms/R124_Green%20Budget_7.%20Tax%2C%20legal%20form%20and%20gig%20economy.pdf (accessed on 8 June 2018).  [5]

Adler, S. (2006), *General Report on non-competition clauses (covenants not to compete) in labour contracts*, https://www.ilo.org/wcmsp5/groups/public/---ed_dialogue/---dialogue/documents/meetingdocument/wcms_159933.pdf (accessed on 20 November 2018).  [143]

Aizer, A. and J. Doyle (2015), "Juvenile Incarceration, Human Capital, and Future Crime: Evidence from Randomly Assigned Judges *", *The Quarterly Journal of Economics*, Vol. 130/2, pp. 759-803, http://dx.doi.org/10.1093/qje/qjv003.  [25]

Ashenfelter, O., H. Farber and M. Ransom (2010), "Modern Models of Monopsony in Labor Markets: A Brief Survey", *IZA Discussion Paper*, No. 4915, IZA, Bonn, https://papers.ssrn.com/sol3/papers.cfm?abstract_id=1599013 (accessed on 18 November 2018).  [108]

Association of Corporate Counsel (2018), *Multi-Country Survey on Covenants Not to Compete*, Association of Corporate Counsel, Washington, D.C., https://www.gtlaw.com/en/-/media/files/insights/alerts/2018/3/gtnoncompeteeuroinfopak.pdf.  [173]

Autor, D. (ed.) (2009), *Studies of Labor Market Intermediation*, The University of Chicago Press, Chicago, Ill.  [95]

Autor, D. et al. (2017), "The Fall of the Labor Share and the Rise of Superstar Firms", *NBER Working Papers*, No. 23396, NBER, Cambridge, MA, http://dx.doi.org/10.3386/w23396.  [115]

Autor, D. et al. (2017), "Disability Benefits, Consumption Insurance, and Household Labor Supply", *NBER Working Papers*, No. 23466, NBER, Cambridge, MA, https://www.nber.org/papers/w23466.pdf (accessed on 22 October 2018).  [28]

Azar, J., I. Marinescu and M. Steinbaum (2017), "Labor Market Concentration", *NBER Working Papers*, No. 24147, NBER, Cambridge, MA, http://dx.doi.org/10.3386/w24147.  [105]

Azar, J. et al. (2018), "Concentration in US Labor Markets: Evidence From Online Vacancy Data", *NBER Working Papers*, No. 24395, NBER, Cambridge, MA, http://dx.doi.org/10.3386/w24395.  [74]

Balaram, B., J. Warden and F. Wallace-Stephens (2017), *Good Gigs - A fairer future for the UK's gig economy*, RSA, https://www.thersa.org/globalassets/pdfs/reports/rsa_good-gigs-fairer-gig-economy-report.pdf (accessed on 31 May 2018).  [89]

Barkai, S. (2017), "Declining labor and capital shares | London Business School", London Business School, https://www.london.edu/faculty-and-research/academic-research/d/declining-labor-and-capital-shares (accessed on 23 October 2018).  [114]

Barrios, J., Y. Hochberg and H. Yi (2018), "The Cost of Convenience: Ridesharing and Traffic Fatalities", http://dx.doi.org/10.2139/ssrn.3271975.  [55]

BEIS (2017), *Good work: the Taylor review of modern working practices*, Department for Business, Energy & Industrial Strategy, https://www.gov.uk/government/publications/good-work-the-taylor-review-of-modern-working-practices (accessed on 4 June 2018).  [44]

Bell, B., P. Bukowski and S. Machin (2018), "Rent Sharing and Inclusive Growth", *IZA Discussion Papers*, No. 12060, IZA, http://www.iza.org.  [116]

Benmelech, E., N. Bergman and H. Kim (2018), "Strong Employers and Weak Employees: How Does Employer Concentration Affect Wages?", *NBER Working Paper*, No. 24307, NBER, Cambridge, MA, http://dx.doi.org/10.3386/w24307.  [111]

Berg, J. et al. (2018), *Digital labour platforms and the future of work: Towards decent work in the online world*, International Labour Organization, https://www.ilo.org/global/publications/books/WCMS_645337/lang--en/index.htm (accessed on 6 November 2018).  [62]

Bhaskar, V., A. Manning and T. To (2002), "Oligopsony and Monopsonistic Competition in Labor Markets", *The Journal of Economic Perspectives*, Vol. 16/2, pp. 155-174, http://www.jstor.org/stable/2696501.  [73]

Blair, R. and J. Harrison (2010), *Monopsony in Law and Economics*, Cambridge University Press, Cambridge, http://dx.doi.org/10.1017/cbo9780511778766.  [109]

Blair, R. and W. Wang (2017), "Buyer cartels and private enforcement of antitrust policy", *Managerial and Decision Economics*, Vol. 38/8, pp. 1185-1193, http://dx.doi.org/10.1002/mde.2857.  [81]

Bork, R. (1993), *The Antitrust Paradox (second edition)*, Free Press.  [149]

Breda, T. et al. (2017), "Prud'hommes : peut-on expliquer la disparité des décisions ?", *Les notes de l'IPP* 29, https://www.ipp.eu/wp-content/uploads/2017/11/n29-notesIPP-nov2017.pdf (accessed on 24 October 2018).  [30]

Brumm, F. (2016), *Making Gigs Work The new economy in context*, University of Illinois - Urbana Champaign, https://blogs.illinois.edu/files/6232/430823/98170.pdf (accessed on 1 June 2018).  [3]

Bundesministerium für Wirtschaft und Energie (2018), *Modernisierung der Missbrauchsaufsicht für marktmächtige Unternehmen*, Bundesministerium für Wirtschaft und Energie, Berlin, https://www.bmwi.de/Redaktion/DE/Publikationen/Wirtschaft/modernisierung-der-missbrauchsaufsicht-fuer-marktmaechtige-unternehmen.html (accessed on 14 December 2018).  [71]

Cahuc, P., F. Postel-Vinay and J. Robin (2006), "Wage Bargaining with On-the-Job Search: Theory and Evidence", *Econometrica*, Vol. 74/2, pp. 323-364, http://dx.doi.org/10.1111/j.1468-0262.2006.00665.x. [139]

Caldwell, S. and O. Danieli (2018), "Outside Options in the Labor Market", *Mimeo*, Harvard University, https://scholar.harvard.edu/danieli/publications/outside-options-labor-market (accessed on 10 December 2018). [140]

Calligaris, S., C. Criscuolo and L. Marcolin (2018), "Mark-ups in the digital era", *OECD Science, Technology and Industry Working Papers*, No. 2018/10, OECD Publishing, Paris, https://dx.doi.org/10.1787/4efe2d25-en. [170]

Capobianco, A. and P. Gonzaga (2017), "Algorithms and competition: Friends or foes?", *CPI Antitrust Chronicle* 08/2017, https://www.competitionpolicyinternational.com/wp-content/uploads/2017/08/CPI-Capobianco-Gonzaga.pdf (accessed on 9 December 2018). [124]

Card, D. and A. Krueger (2015), *Myth and measurement : the new economics of the minimum wage*, Princeton University Press, https://press.princeton.edu/titles/10738.html (accessed on 5 November 2018). [43]

Carlton, D., M. Israel and M. Coleman (2014), "Buyer Power in Merger Review", in Blair, R. and D. Sokol (eds.), *The Oxford Handbook of International Antitrust Economics*, Oxford University Press, Oxford. [146]

Carstensen, P. (2012), "Buyer Power and the Horizontal Merger Guidelines: Minor Progress on an Important Issue", *University of Pennsylvania Journal of Business Law*, Vol. 14/3, https://scholarship.law.upenn.edu/jbl/vol14/iss3/4 (accessed on 16 November 2018). [171]

Cherry, M. and A. Aloisi (2017), "'Dependent Contractors' in the Gig Economy: A Comparative Approach", *American University Law Review*, Vol. 66/3, http://digitalcommons.wcl.american.edu/aulr (accessed on 14 December 2018). [33]

Cherry, M. and V. De Stefano (2018), "A Labour Law Perspective on Conflict of Laws", in Pretelli, I. (ed.), *Conflict of Laws in the Maze of Digital Platforms*, Schultess, Zurich. [21]

Chevalier, J. et al. (forthcoming), "The Value of Flexible Work: Evidence from Uber Drivers", *Journal of Political Economy*, http://dx.doi.org/10.1086/702171. [80]

Chopra, R. (2018), "Keynote of Federal Trade Commissioner Rohit Chopra", in *Conference on Monopoly, Monopsony, and the Labor Market: Diminishing Worker Power in an Era of Market Concentration*, The Economic Policy Institute, Washington, D.C., https://openmarketsinstitute.org/events/monopoly-monopsony-labor-market-diminishing-worker-power-era-market-concentration/ (accessed on 14 December 2018). [155]

Countouris, N. et al. (2016), *Report on temporary employment agencies and temporary agency work*, International Labour Office, Geneva, http://www.ilo.org/publns (accessed on 28 November 2018). [31]

D'Arcy, C. (2017), *The minimum required? Minimum wages and the self-employed*, Resolution Foundation, https://www.resolutionfoundation.org/app/uploads/2017/07/The-minimum-required.pdf (accessed on 5 November 2018). [45]

Däubler, W. (2016), "Challenges to Labour Law", *Pravo. Zhurnal Vysshey shkoly ekonomiki* 1, pp. 189-203, http://dx.doi.org/10.17323/2072-8166.2016.1.201.215. [38]

Davidov, G. (2002), "The Three Axes of Employment Relationships: A Characterization of Workers in Need of Protection", *University of Toronto Law Journal*, Vol. 52, https://papers.ssrn.com/sol3/papers.cfm?abstract_id=555998 (accessed on 21 November 2018). [163]

Davidov, G., M. Freedland and N. Countouris (2015), "The Subjects of Labor Law: 'Employees' and Other Workers", in Finkin, M. and G. Mundlak (eds.), *Research Handbook in Comparative Labor Law*, Edward Elgar, https://papers.ssrn.com/sol3/papers.cfm?abstract_id=2561752 (accessed on 2 November 2018). [6]

Davies, A. (2009), "Sensible Thinking About Sham Transactions: Protectacoat Firthglow Ltd v Szilagyi * [2009] EWCA Civ 98; [2009] IRLR 365", *Industrial Law Journal*, Vol. 38/3, pp. 318-328, http://dx.doi.org/10.1093/indlaw/dwp017. [169]

De Loecker, J. and J. Eeckhout (2018), "The Rise of Market Power and the Macroeconomic Implications", *NBER Working Paper, Revised 2018 version resubmitted to the Quarterly Journal of Economics*, No. 23687, NBER, Cambridge, MA, http://www.janeeckhout.com/wp-content/uploads/RMP.pdf (accessed on 12 December 2018). [113]

Deutscher Bundestag (2016), *Arbeit 4.0 – Arbeitswelt von morgen gestalten*, http://dipbt.bundestag.de/dip21/btd/18/102/1810254.pdf (accessed on 5 November 2018). [47]

Dobson, P. and R. Inderst (2007), "Differential Buyer Power and the Waterbed Effect: Do Strong Buyers Benefit or Harm Consumers?", *European Competition Law Review*, Vol. 28/7, pp. 393-400, https://ueaeprints.uea.ac.uk/26139/ (accessed on 21 November 2018). [144]

Dube, A. et al. (forthcoming), "Monopsony in Online Labor Markets", *American Economic Review: Insights*, http://www.aeaweb.org/articles?id=10.1257/aeri.20180150&&from=f (accessed on 15 January 2019). [79]

Dyck, A., A. Morse and L. Zingales (2010), "Who Blows the Whistle on Corporate Fraud?", *The Journal of Finance*, Vol. 65/6, pp. 2213-2253, http://dx.doi.org/10.1111/j.1540-6261.2010.01614.x. [85]

Edelman, B., M. Luca and D. Svirsky (2017), "Racial Discrimination in the Sharing Economy: Evidence from a Field Experiment", *American Economic Journal: Applied Economics*, Vol. 9/2, pp. 1-22, http://dx.doi.org/10.1257/app.20160213. [56]

Employment and Social Development Canada (2006), "Determining the Employer/Employee Relationship - Canada Labour Code", *Interpretations, Policies and Guidelines*, No. IPG 069, Government of Canada, Ottawa, https://www.canada.ca/content/dam/canada/employment-social-development/migration/documents/assets/portfolio/docs/fr/edsc/lois_reglements/travail/interpretations_politiques/index/069.pdf (accessed on 23 October 2018). [23]

European Commission (2018), *Proposal for a regulation of the European Parliament and of the Council on promoting fairness and transparency for business users of online intermediation services, 2018/0112(COD)*, European Commission, Brussels, https://eur-lex.europa.eu/legal-content/EN/TXT/PDF/?uri=CELEX:52018PC0238&from=EN (accessed on 5 December 2018). [67]

European Commission (2017), *A comparative analysis of non-discrimination law in Europe 2017*, [60]
European Commission, Brussels, http://dx.doi.org/10.2838/52129.

European Commission (2011), *Guidelines on the applicability of Article 101 of the Treaty on the* [182]
*Functioning of the European Union to horizontal co-operation agreements (2011/C 11/01)*,
European Commission, Brussels.

European Commission (2004), *Guidelines on the assessment of horizontal mergers under the* [147]
*Council Regulation on the control of concentrations between undertakings (2004/C 31/03)*,
European Commission, Brussels.

Fischman, J. (2014), "Measuring Inconsistency, Indeterminacy, and Error in Adjudication", [26]
*American Law and Economics Review*, Vol. 16/1, pp. 40-85,
http://dx.doi.org/10.1093/aler/aht011.

Fischman, J. (2011), "Estimating Preferences of Circuit Judges: A Model of Consensus Voting", [27]
*The Journal of Law and Economics*, Vol. 54/4, pp. 781-809, http://dx.doi.org/10.1086/661512.

Freedland, M. and N. Kountouris (2011), *The Legal Construction of Personal Work Relations*, [164]
Oxford University Press, http://dx.doi.org/10.1093/acprof:oso/9780199551750.001.0001.

Galperin, H., G. Cruces and C. Greppi (2017), "Gender Interactions in Wage Bargaining: [58]
Evidence from an Online Field Experiment", *SSRN*, http://dx.doi.org/10.2139/ssrn.3056508.

Galperin, H. and C. Greppi (2017), "Geographical Discrimination in Digital Labor Platforms", [57]
https://annenberg.usc.edu/sites/default/files/2017/11/27/Geographical%20Discrimination%20
Galperin%20%26%20Greppi.pdf (accessed on 1 June 2018).

GAO (2017), *Employment Taxes - Timely Use of National Research Program Results Would* [4]
*Help IRS Improve Compliance and Tax Gap Estimates*, United States Government
Accountability Office, https://www.gao.gov/assets/690/684162.pdf (accessed on
7 January 2019).

Garmaise, M. (2009), "Ties that Truly Bind: Noncompetition Agreements, Executive [133]
Compensation, and Firm Investment", *Journal of Law, Economics, and Organization*,
Vol. 27/2, pp. 376-425, http://dx.doi.org/10.1093/jleo/ewp033.

Golubeva, M. (2018), *Tax reforms not enough for changing the game?*, [19]
http://ec.europa.eu/social/main.jsp?langId=en&catId=89&newsId=9040&furtherNews=yes
(accessed on 2 November 2018).

Gomulkiewicz, R. (2015), "Leaky Covenants-Not-to-Compete as the Legal Infrastructure for [174]
Innovation", *UC Davis Law Review*, Vol. 49/1, pp. 251-304,
https://lawreview.law.ucdavis.edu/issues/49/1/Articles/49-1_Gomulkiewicz.pdf (accessed on
4 December 2018).

Green, T. (2015), "The shifting landscape of restrictive covenants in Oklahoma", *Oklahoma City* [175]
*University Law Review*, Vol. 49/2, pp. 449-480, http://wallethub.com/edu/best-cities-to-start-a-
business/2281/#complete-rankings (accessed on 5 December 2018).

Gurkaynak, G., A. Guner and C. Ozkanli (2013), "Competition Law Issues in the Human [117]
Resources Field", *Journal of European Competition Law & Practice*, Vol. 4/3, pp. 201-214,
http://dx.doi.org/10.1093/jeclap/lpt017.

Haar, B. (2018), "Regulation through litigation - Collective redress in need of a new balance between individual rights and regulatory objectives in Europe", *Theoretical Inquiries in Law*, Vol. 19/2, http://dx.doi.org/10.1515/til-2018-0007. [121]

Hara, K. et al. (2017), "A Data-Driven Analysis of Workers' Earnings on Amazon Mechanical Turk", Cornell University, http://arxiv.org/abs/1712.05796 (accessed on 1 June 2018). [162]

Harris, B. (2018), *Information Is Power Fostering Labor Market Competition through Transparent Wages*, The Hamilton Project, https://www.brookings.edu/wp-content/uploads/2018/02/es_2272018_information_is_power_harris_pp.pdf (accessed on 6 November 2018). [90]

Harrison, J. (2012), "Complications in the Antitrust Response to Monopsony", in Sokol, D. and I. Lianos (eds.), *The Global Limits of Competition Law*, Stanford University Press, http://dx.doi.org/10.11126/stanford/9780804774901.003.0005. [156]

Harris, S. and A. Krueger (2015), "A Proposal for Modernizing Labor Laws for Twenty-First-Century Work: The `Independent Worker'", *Discussion Papers*, No. 2015-10, The Hamilton Project, http://www.hamiltonproject.org/assets/files/modernizing_labor_laws_for_twenty_first_century_work_krueger_harris.pdf (accessed on 31 May 2018). [41]

Herrera Anchustegui, I. and J. Nowag (2017), "How the Uber & Lyft Case Provides an Impetus to Re-Examine Buyer Power in the World of Big Data and Algorithms", *Lund University Legal Research Paper Series Lund Comp Working Paper*, No. 01/2017, Lund University, http://dx.doi.org/10.2139/ssrn.2998688. [160]

Hershbein, B. and C. Macaluso (2018), "Labor Market Concentration and the Demand for Skills", *IDSC of IZA Workshop: Matching Workers and Jobs Online*, 21-22 September 2018, Bonn, http://conference.iza.org/conference_files/DATA_2018/macaluso_c26795.pdf (accessed on 8 January 2019). [112]

Hershbein, B., C. Macaluso and C. Yeh (2018), "Concentration in U.S. local labor markets: evidence from vacancy and employment data", *mimeo*, University of Illinois, Urbana-Champaign, https://sites.google.com/site/clamacaluso/research. [107]

Hovenkamp, H. (forthcoming), "Whatever Did Happen to the Antitrust Movement?", *Notre Dame Law Review*. [148]

Ichino, A. and P. Pinotti (2012), "La roulette russa dell'Articolo 18", *lavoce.info*, https://www.lavoce.info/archives/27539/la-roulette-russa-dellarticolo-18/ (accessed on 24 October 2018). [29]

Illinois Attorney General (2018), *Attorney General Madigan reaches settlement with WeWork to end use of overly broad non-competes*, Press Releases of the Illinois Attorney General, http://illinoisattorneygeneral.gov/pressroom/2018_09/20180918.html (accessed on 18 September 2018). [181]

ILO (2019), *Work for a brighter future – Global Commission on the Future of Work*, International Labour Organization, Geneva, https://www.ilo.org/wcmsp5/groups/public/---dgreports/---cabinet/documents/publication/wcms_662410.pdf (accessed on 21 February 2019). [1]

ILO (2005), *The employment relationship. International Labour Conference, 95th Session, 2006, Report V (1).*, ILO, https://www.ilo.org/global/publications/ilo-bookstore/order-online/books/WCMS_PUBL_9221166112_EN/lang--en/index.htm (accessed on 7 December 2018). [36]

Inderst, R. and G. Shaffer (2008), "Buyer Power in Merger Control", in American Bar Association (ed.), *Issues in Competition Law*, American Bar Association, Chicago, Ill. [145]

Internal Revenue Service (2012), "Voluntary Classification Settlement Program, Announcement 2012-45", *Internal Revenue Bulletin* 2012-51, https://www.irs.gov/irb/2012-51_IRB#ANN-2012-45 (accessed on 29 November 2018). [167]

Internal Revenue Service (2005), *Independent Contractor or Employee?*, Internal Revenue Service, Washington, D.C., https://www.irs.gov/pub/irs-pdf/p1779.pdf (accessed on 29 November 2018). [10]

Irani, L. and S. Silberman (2013), *Turkopticon: Interrupting Worker Invisibility in Amazon Mechanical Turk*, ACM, https://cloudfront.escholarship.org/dist/prd/content/qt10c125z3/qt10c125z3.pdf (accessed on 6 November 2018). [158]

Jacobson, J. (2013), "Monopsony 2013: What's the Latest on (Too) Low Prices?", *61st Spring Meeting of the Section of Antitrust Law, American Bar Association*, 12 April 2013, Washington, D.C. [153]

Johnstone, R. et al. (2012), *Beyond employment : the legal regulation of work relationships*, The Federation Press, https://www.federationpress.com.au/bookstore/book.asp?isbn=9781862878891 (accessed on 22 November 2018). [165]

Kaine, S. (2017), *All care and no responsibility: Why Airtasker can't guarantee a minimum wage*, The Conversation, http://dx.doi.org/10.1111/rego.12122. [50]

Kaltner, J. (2018), "Employment Status of Uber and Lyft Drivers: Unsettlingly Settled", *Hastings Women's Law Journal*, Vol. 29/1, pp. 29-54, https://repository.uchastings.edu/cgi/viewcontent.cgi?article=1403&context=hwlj (accessed on 12 December 2018). [64]

Keneally, K., C. Saleski and C. Engell (2015), *All Employers Face Independent Contractor, Employment Tax Scrutiny*, https://www.forbes.com/sites/janetnovack/2015/06/24/all-employers-face-independent-contractor-employment-tax-scrutiny/#1116972c6ea8 (accessed on 29 November 2018). [11]

Kenner, J. (2017), "Inverting the flexicurity paradigm: the United Kingdom and zero hours contracts", in Ales, E., O. Deinert and J. Kenner (eds.), *Core and contingent work in the European Union*, Hart Publishing, Oxford. [53]

Kessler, S. (2016), *Could A Minimum Wage Work In The Gig Economy?*, Fast Company, https://www.fastcompany.com/3058599/could-a-minimum-wage-work-in-the-gig-economy (accessed on 5 November 2018). [48]

Kingsley, S., M. Gray and S. Suri (2015), "Accounting for Market Frictions and Power Asymmetries in Online Labor Markets", *Policy & Internet*, Vol. 7/4, pp. 383-400, http://dx.doi.org/10.1002/poi3.111. [52]

Knable Gotts, I. (ed.) (2018), *The Private Competition Enforcement Review - Edition 11 - The Law Reviews*, Law Business Research Ltd., London, https://thelawreviews.co.uk/edition/1001145/the-private-competition-enforcement-review-edition-11 (accessed on 19 November 2018). [122]

Korean Fair Trade Commission (2009), *Guidelines for Concerted Practice Review*, Korean Fair Trade Commission , Seoul. [172]

Kovács, E. (2017), "Regulatory Techniques for 'Virtual Workers'", *Hungarian Labour Law E-Journal*, Vol. 2017/2, http://www.hllj.hu (accessed on 14 December 2018). [68]

Krotoski, M. et al. (2018), *No-Poaching Agreements and Antitrust Laws: What Global Employers Should Know*, Morgan Lewis, https://www.morganlewis.com/events/tech-mayrathon-no-poaching-agreements-and-antitrust-laws-what-global-employers-should-know (accessed on 13 December 2018). [82]

Krueger, A. and O. Ashenfelter (2018), "Theory and Evidence on Employer Collusion in the Franchise Sector", *NBER Working Paper*, No. 24831, National Bureau of Economic Research, http://dx.doi.org/10.3386/w24831. [83]

Krueger, A. and E. Posner (2018), *A Proposal for Protecting Low-Income Workers from Monopsony and Collusion*, Brookings, Washington, D.C., http://www.hamiltonproject.org/assets/files/protecting_low_income_workers_from_monopsony_collusion_krueger_posner_pp.pdf (accessed on 25 October 2018). [123]

Labour 20 (2018), *L20 Statement to the G20 Labour And Employment Ministers' Meeting*, G20, Argentina 2018, https://www.g20.org/sites/default/files/media/l20declarationen.pdf (accessed on 3 December 2018). [100]

Lehdonvirta, V. (2018), "Flexibility in the Gig Economy: Managing Time on Three Online Piecework Platforms", *New Technology, Work and Employment*, https://papers.ssrn.com/sol3/papers.cfm?abstract_id=3099419 (accessed on 1 June 2018). [51]

Lenaerts, K. et al. (2018), *Online Talent Platforms, Labour Market Intermediaries and the Changing World of Work*, https://www.ceps.eu/system/files/CEPS_IZA_OnlineTalentPlatforms.pdf (accessed on 28 November 2018). [32]

Liebman, S. (2006), *Employment situations and workers' protection - Italy*, http://ilo.org/wcmsp5/groups/public/---ed_dialogue/---dialogue/documents/genericdocument/wcms_205366.pdf (accessed on 5 June 2018). [39]

Linder, M. (1999), "Dependent and Independent Contractors in Recent U.S. Labor Law: An Ambiguous Dichotomy Rooted in Simulated Statutory Purposelessness", *Comparative Labor Law & Policy Journal*, Vol. 187, https://ir.uiowa.edu/cgi/viewcontent.cgi?referer=https://www.google.fr/&httpsredir=1&article=1010&context=law_pubs (accessed on 4 December 2018). [22]

Lipsitz, M. and M. Johnson (2018), "Why Are Low-Wage Workers Signing Noncompete Agreements?", *American Economic Association Annual Meeting*, 5-7 January 2018, Philadelphia, PA., https://www.aeaweb.org/conference/2018/preliminary/1515. [138]

Luz, R. and G. Spagnolo (2017), "Leniency, collusion, corruption, and whistleblowing", *Journal of Competition Law & Economics*, Vol. 13/4, pp. 729-766, http://dx.doi.org/10.1093/joclec/nhx025. [120]

Manning, A. (2011), "Imperfect Competition in the Labor Market", in Ashenfelter, O. and D. Card (eds.), *Handbook of Labor Economics*, Elsevier, http://dx.doi.org/10.1016/s0169-7218(11)02409-9. [92]

Manning, A. (2003), *Monopsony in motion : imperfect competition in labor markets*, Princeton University Press, https://press.princeton.edu/titles/7522.html (accessed on 25 October 2018). [72]

Manning, A. and B. Petrongolo (2017), "How Local Are Labor Markets? Evidence from a Spatial Job Search Model", *American Economic Review*, Vol. 107/10, pp. 2877-2907, http://dx.doi.org/10.1257/aer.20131026. [103]

Marcano, I. (2018), "E-hailing and Employment Rights: The Case for an Employment Relationship Between Uber and its Drivers in South Africa", *Cornell International Law Journal*, Vol. 51, pp. 273-295, https://www.lawschool.cornell.edu/research/ILJ/upload/Marcano-note-final.pdf (accessed on 5 December 2018). [65]

Marinescu, I. and H. Hovenkamp (forthcoming), "Anticompetitive Mergers in Labor Markets", *Indiana Law Journal*, http://dx.doi.org/10.2139/ssrn.3124483. [87]

Marinescu, I. and R. Rathelot (2018), "Mismatch Unemployment and the Geography of Job Search", *American Economic Journal: Macroeconomics*, Vol. 10/3, pp. 42-70, http://dx.doi.org/10.1257/mac.20160312. [104]

Martins, P. (2018), "Making their own weather? Estimating employer labour-market power and its wage effects", *QMUL Working Papers 95*, Queen Mary University London, http://webspace.qmul.ac.uk/pmartins/CGRWP95.pdf (accessed on 9 November 2018). [76]

Marx, M. (2011), "The Firm Strikes Back", *American Sociological Review*, Vol. 76/5, pp. 695-712, http://dx.doi.org/10.1177/0003122411414822. [135]

Marx, M. and L. Fleming (2012), "Non-compete Agreements: Barriers to Entry ... and Exit?", *Innovation Policy and the Economy*, Vol. 12, pp. 39-64, http://dx.doi.org/10.1086/663155. [157]

Marx, M., D. Strumsky and L. Fleming (2009), "Mobility, Skills, and the Michigan Non-Compete Experiment", *Management Science*, Vol. 55/6, pp. 875-889, http://dx.doi.org/10.1287/mnsc.1080.0985. [134]

Meritas (2017), *Employee Non-Compete Agreements in Europe, Middle East and Africa*, Meritas, Minneapolis, Minn., http://www.meritas.org. [127]

Milanez, A. and B. Bratta (2019), "Taxation and the future of work: How tax systems influence choice of employment form", *OECD Taxation Working Papers*, No. 41, OECD Publishing, Paris, https://dx.doi.org/10.1787/20f7164a-en. [15]

Ministerie van Financiën (2015), *IBO Zelfstandigen zonder personeel*, Rijksoverheid, https://www.rijksoverheid.nl/documenten/rapporten/2015/10/02/eindrapport-ibo-zelfstandigen-zonder-personeel (accessed on 18 March 2019). [16]

Motta, M. and T. Rønde (2002), "Trade Secret Laws, Labor Mobility, and Innovations", *CEPR Discussion Paper*, No. 3615, CEPR, London, https://ideas.repec.org/p/cpr/ceprdp/3615.html. [129]

Muehlberger, U. (2007), "Work on the Border Between Employment and Self-Employment", in *Dependent Self-Employment*, Palgrave Macmillan UK, London, http://dx.doi.org/10.1057/9780230288782_2. [40]

Naidu, S., E. Posner and E. Weyl (forthcoming), "Antitrust Remedies for Labor Market Power", *Harvard Law Review*. [78]

New York State Attorney General (2018), *A.G. Underwood Announces Settlement With WeWork To End Use Of Overly Broad Non-Competes That Restricted Workers' Ability To Take New Jobs*, Press Releases of the New York State Attorney General, https://ag.ny.gov/press-release/ag-underwood-announces-settlement-wework-end-use-overly-broad-non-competes-restricted (accessed on 18 September 2018). [176]

New York State Attorney General (2018), *Non-Compete Agreements In New York State Frequently Asked Questions What is a non-compete agreement? Are non-competes legal?*, New York State Attorney General, New York, N.Y., https://ag.ny.gov/sites/default/files/non-competes.pdf (accessed on 21 November 2018). [177]

Nicandri, A. (2011), "The Growing Disfavor of Non-Compete Agreements in the New Economy and Alternative Approaches for Protecting Empoyers' Proprietary Information and Trade Secrets", *University of Pennsylvania Journal of Business Law*, Vol. 13/4, https://scholarship.law.upenn.edu/jbl/vol13/iss4/6 (accessed on 11 December 2018). [126]

OECD (2019), *Policy Responses to New Forms of Work*, OECD Publishing, Paris, https://doi.org/10.1787/0763f1b7-en. [2]

OECD (2018), *Good Jobs for All in a Changing World of Work: The OECD Jobs Strategy*, OECD Publishing, Paris, https://dx.doi.org/10.1787/9789264308817-en. [93]

OECD (2018), *OECD Employment Outlook 2018*, OECD Publishing, Paris, http://dx.doi.org/10.1787/empl_outlook-2018-en. [101]

OECD (2018), *Taxi, ride-sourcing and ride-sharing services - Background Note by the Secretariat, DAF/COMP/WP2(2018)1*, OECD, Paris, https://one.oecd.org/document/DAF/COMP/WP2(2018)1/en/pdf. [159]

OECD (2018), *The Future of Social Protection: What Works for Non-standard Workers?*, OECD Publishing, Paris, https://dx.doi.org/10.1787/9789264306943-en. [14]

OECD (2017), *Algorithms and Collusion: Competition Policy in the Digital Age*, OECD, Paris, http://www.oecd.org/daf/competition/Algorithms-and-colllusion-competition-policy-in-the-digital-age.pdf. [125]

OECD (2017), *OECD Employment Outlook 2017*, OECD Publishing, Paris, https://dx.doi.org/10.1787/empl_outlook-2017-en. [118]

OECD (2015), *In It Together: Why Less Inequality Benefits All*, OECD Publishing, Paris, https://dx.doi.org/10.1787/9789264235120-en. [13]

OECD (2015), *OECD Employment Outlook 2015*, OECD Publishing, Paris, http://dx.doi.org/10.1787/empl_outlook-2015-en. [96]

OECD (2014), *OECD Employment Outlook 2014*, OECD Publishing, Paris, https://dx.doi.org/10.1787/empl_outlook-2014-en. [8]

OECD (2013), *OECD Employment Outlook 2013*, OECD Publishing, [61]
https://doi.org/10.1787/empl_outlook-2013-en (accessed on 8 January 2018).

OECD (2008), *OECD Employment Outlook 2008*, OECD Publishing, Paris, [18]
https://dx.doi.org/10.1787/empl_outlook-2008-en.

Office of the Attorney General of the State of Illinois (2018), *Non-Compete Agreements:* [178]
*Frequently Asked Questions*,
http://www.illinoisattorneygeneral.gov/rights/Non_Compete_Agreements.pdf (accessed on
21 November 2018).

Office of the Washington State Attorney General (2018), *AG Ferguson's initiative to end no-* [179]
*poach clauses nationwide continues with four additional chains*, Press Release of the Office
of the Washington State Attorney General, http://www.atg.wa.gov/news/news-releases/ag-
ferguson-s-initiative-end-no-poach-clauses-nationwide-continues-four (accessed on
21 November 2018).

Patty, A. (2017), *Airtasker and unions make landmark agreement to improve pay rates and* [49]
*conditions*, The Sunday Morning Herald,
https://www.smh.com.au/business/workplace/airtasker-and-unions-make-landmark-
agreement-to-improve-pay-rates-and-conditions-20170427-gvtvpo.html (accessed on
5 November 2018).

Pedersini, R. (2002), *'Economically dependent workers', employment law and industrial* [35]
*relations*, Eurofound,
https://www.eurofound.europa.eu/publications/report/2002/economically-dependent-workers-
employment-law-and-industrial-relations (accessed on 7 December 2018).

Prassl, J. and M. Risak (2016), "Uber, Taskrabbit, & Co: Platforms as Employers? Rethinking the [34]
Legal Analysis of Crowdwork", *Oxford Legal Studies Research Paper*, No. 8/2016,
https://papers.ssrn.com/sol3/papers.cfm?abstract_id=2733003 (accessed on
28 November 2018).

Prescott, J., N. Bishara and E. Starr (2016), "Understanding noncompetition agreements: The [141]
2014 noncompete survey project", *Michigan State Law Review*, Vol. 2016/2, pp. 369-464,
https://digitalcommons.law.msu.edu/cgi/viewcontent.cgi?article=1163&context=lr (accessed
on 13 December 2018).

PvdA (2017), *Een Verbonden Samenleving - Verkiezingsprogramma 2017*, Partij van de Arbeid, [46]
https://www.pvda.nl/wp-
content/uploads/2017/02/PvdAVerkiezingsprogramma2017EenVerbondenSamenleving.pdf
(accessed on 5 November 2018).

Pynnonen, B. (1994), "Ohio and Michigan Law on Postemployment Covenants Not to Compete", [180]
*Ohio State Law Journal*, Vol. 55, pp. 215-235,
https://kb.osu.edu/bitstream/handle/1811/64679/OSLJ_V55N1_0215.pdf (accessed on
23 November 2018).

Qiu, Y. and A. Sojourner (2019), "Labor-Market Concentration and Labor Compensation", *IZA* [110]
*Discussion Paper*, No. 12089, IZA, Bonn.

Rauch, J. (2016), "Dynastic entrepreneurship, entry, and non-compete enforcement", *European* [131]
*Economic Review*, Vol. 86, pp. 188-201, http://dx.doi.org/10.1016/j.euroecorev.2015.12.004.

Rinz, K. (2018), "Labor Market Concentration, Earnings Inequality, and Earnings Mobility", [94] *CARRA Working Paper*, No. 2018-10, US Census Bureau, https://www.census.gov/library/working-papers/2018/adrm/carra-wp-2018-10.html (accessed on 8 January 2019).

Risak, M. (2018), *Fair Working Conditions for Platform Workers Possible Regulatory Approaches* [97] *at the EU Level*, http://www.fes.de/ipaBestellungen/Kontakt:info.ipa@fes.de (accessed on 30 November 2018).

Rönnmar, M. (2004), *The personal scope of labour law and the notion of employee in Sweden*, [37] https://lup.lub.lu.se/search/publication/617804 (accessed on 23 November 2018).

Rosenblat, A. and L. Stark (2016), "Algorithmic Labor and Information Asymmetries: A Case [91] Study of Uber's Drivers", *International Journal of Communication*, Vol. 10, pp. 3758-3784, https://ijoc.org/index.php/ijoc/article/view/4892/1739.

Rosenthal, R. (2018), *Employee non-competes: a state by state survey*, Howard & Howard, Las [142] Vegas, Nev., http://nevadalaw.info/wp-content/uploads/2018/01/Employee-Non-Competes-50-State-Survey.pdf (accessed on 13 December 2018).

Ross, H. (2015), "Ridesharing's House of Cards: O'Connor v. Uber Technologies, Inc. and the [63] Viability of Uber's Labor Model in Washington", *Washington Law Review*, Vol. 90, pp. 1431-1469, https://digital.law.washington.edu/dspace-law/bitstream/handle/1773.1/1489/90WLR1431.pdf (accessed on 12 December 2018).

Rubin, P. and P. Shedd (1981), "Human Capital and Covenants Not to Compete", *The Journal of* [128] *Legal Studies*, Vol. 10/1, pp. 93-110, http://www.jstor.org/stable/724227.

Rubinstein, M. (2012), "Employees, Employers, and Quasi-Employers: An Analysis of [20] Employees and Employers Who Operate in the Borderland between an Employer-and-Employee Relationship", *NYLS Legal Studies Research Paper*, No. 12/13 40, https://papers.ssrn.com/sol3/papers.cfm?abstract_id=2047484 (accessed on 4 January 2019).

Salehi, N. et al. (2015), *We Are Dynamo: Overcoming Stalling and Friction in Collective Action* [98] *for Crowd Workers*, ACM Press, — April 18 - 23, 2015, http://dx.doi.org/10.1145/2702123.2702508.

Salop, S. (2010), "Question: What is the Real and Proper Antitrust Welfare Standard? Answer: [152] The True Consumer Welfare Standard", *Loyola Consumer Law Review*, Vol. 22/3.

Schwartz, M. (2004), *Should Antitrust Assess Buyer Market Power Differently Than Seller* [150] *Market Power?*, US Department of Justice, Washington DC, https://www.justice.gov/atr/should-antitrust-assess-buyer-market-power-differently-seller-market-power (accessed on 22 November 2018).

Silberman, S. (2018), *Ombuds Office of the Crowdsourcing Code of Conduct*, Presentation given [99] to Sharers and Workers, Brussels, http://wtf.tw/etc/bru/slides.pdf (accessed on 4 December 2018).

Silberman, S. (2018), "Rights for Platform Workers", *IG Metall Crowdsourcing Project Discussion* [66] *Papers*, IG Metall.

Sims, R. (2018), *Address to the 2018 Annual RBB Economics Conference*, Speeches of the Chairman of the Australian Competition and Consumer Commission, https://www.accc.gov.au/speech/address-to-the-2018-annual-rbb-economics-conference#ref10 (accessed on 30 November 2018). [154]

Söderqvist, F. (2018), "Sweden: will history lead the way in the age of robots and platforms?", *Policy Network*, https://policynetwork.org/opinions/essays/sweden-will-history-lead-way-age-robots-platforms/ (accessed on 29 November 2018). [12]

Sokolova, A. and T. Sorensen (2018), "Monopsony in Labor Markets: A Meta-Analysis", *IZA Discussion Paper*, No. 11966, IZA, Bonn, http://ftp.iza.org/dp11966.pdf (accessed on 8 January 2019). [77]

Starr, E. (forthcoming), "Consider This: Training, Wages, and the Enforceability of Covenants Not to Compete", *Industrial and Labor Relations Review*, http://dx.doi.org/10.1177/0019793919826060. [137]

Starr, E., J. Prescott and N. Bishara (2018), "Noncompetes in the U.S. Labor Force", *University of Michigan Law & Econ Research Paper*, No. 18-013, http://dx.doi.org/10.2139/ssrn.2625714. [88]

Starr, E., J. Prescott and N. Bishara (2016), "Noncompetes and Employee Mobility", *University of Michigan Law & Econ Research Paper*, No. 16-032, http://dx.doi.org/10.2139/ssrn.2858637. [136]

Stewart, A. and J. Stanford (2017), "Regulating work in the gig economy: What are the options?", *The Economic and Labour Relations Review*, Vol. 28/3, pp. 420-437, http://dx.doi.org/10.1177/1035304617722461. [166]

Sweeney, L. (2013), "Discrimination in Online Ad Delivery", http://dataprivacylab.org/projects/onlineads/1071-1.pdf (accessed on 1 June 2018). [59]

UK Parliament (2017), *Self-employment and the gig economy*, Committee on Work and Pensions, UK Parliament, https://publications.parliament.uk/pa/cm201617/cmselect/cmworpen/847/84705.htm (accessed on 8 June 2018). [17]

US Department of Justice and Federal Trade Commission (2016), *Antitrust Guidance For Human Resource Professionals (October 2016)*, U.S. Department of Justice and the Federal Trade Commission, Washington, D.C., https://www.ftc.gov/public-statements/2016/10/antitrust-guidance-human-resource-professionals-department-justice (accessed on 15 November 2018). [84]

US Department of Justice and Federal Trade Commission (2016), *Antitrust Red Flags for Employment Practices*, US Department of Justice and Federal Trade Commission , Washington, D.C., http://go.usa.gov/xkdrq. (accessed on 16 November 2018). [119]

US Department of Justice and Federal Trade Commission (2010), *Horizontal Merger Guidelines (08/19/2010)*, U.S. Department of Justice and the Federal Trade Commission, Washington, D.C., https://www.justice.gov/atr/horizontal-merger-guidelines-08192010 (accessed on 14 November 2018). [106]

US House of Representatives (2009), "Arbitration or arbitrary: the misuse of mandatory arbitration to collect consumer debts", *Hearing before the Subcommittee on Domestic Policy of the Committee on Oversight and Government Reform, July 22, 2009* Serial 111-125, https://www.gpo.gov/fdsys/pkg/CHRG-111hhrg64915/pdf/CHRG-111hhrg64915.pdf. [69]

Waas, B. et al. (2017), *Crowdwork – A Comparative Law Perspective*, http://www.hugo-sinzheimer-institut.de/fileadmin/user_data_hsi/Veroeffentlichungen/HSI_Schriftenreihe/Waas_Liebman_Lyubarsky_Kezuka_Crowdwork.pdf (accessed on 1 June 2018). [7]

Waldfogel, J. (1998), "Does inter-judge disparity justify empirically based sentencing guidelines?", *International Review of Law and Economics*, Vol. 18/3, pp. 293-304, http://dx.doi.org/10.1016/S0144-8188(98)00013-1. [24]

Walters, D. (2017), *An Inspector Calls? Achieving regulatory compliance on OHS in times of change*, Tööinspektsioon, Tallinn, http://ti.ee/fileadmin/user_upload/failid/dokumendid/Meedia_ja_statistika/Teavitustegevus/SLIC/David_Walters.pdf (accessed on 2 December 2018). [54]

Wank, R. (1999), *Workers' Protection - National Study for Germany for the ILO*, ILO, https://www.ilo.org/wcmsp5/groups/public/---ed_dialogue/---dialogue/documents/genericdocument/wcms_205364.pdf (accessed on 4 December 2018). [168]

Webber, D. (2015), "Firm market power and the earnings distribution", *Labour Economics*, Vol. 35, pp. 123-134, http://dx.doi.org/10.1016/j.labeco.2015.05.003. [102]

Werden, G. (2007), "Monopsony and the Sherman act: consumer welfare in a new light", *Antitrust Law Journal*, Vol. 74/3, pp. 707-737, http://www.jstor.org/stable/27897564. [151]

Wickelgren, A. (2018), "A novel justification for legal restrictions on non-compete clauses", *International Review of Law and Economics*, Vol. 54, pp. 49-57, http://dx.doi.org/10.1016/j.irle.2017.10.004. [132]

Williams, C. and F. Lapeyre (2017), "Dependent self-employment: Trends, challenges and policy responses in the EU", *Employment Working Paper*, No. 228, ILO, http://ilo.org/wcmsp5/groups/public/---ed_emp/documents/publication/wcms_614176.pdf. [9]

World Employment Confederation (2018), *Compendium of voluntary initiatives promoting ethical recruitment practices by the national federations of the World Employment Confederation*, World Employment Confederation, Brussels, http://www.wecglobal.org/uploads/media/WEC_Compendium_Final.pdf. [70]

Yeoh, P. (2014), "Whistleblowing: motivations, corporate self-regulation, and the law", *International Journal of Law and Management*, Vol. 56/6, pp. 459-474, http://dx.doi.org/10.1108/ijlma-06-2013-0027. [86]

Younge, K., T. Tong and L. Fleming (2014), "How anticipated employee mobility affects acquisition likelihood: Evidence from a natural experiment", *Strategic Management Journal*, Vol. 36/5, pp. 686-708, http://dx.doi.org/10.1002/smj.2237. [130]

# Annex 4.A.  Labour market monopsony: Evidence and regulation

Many workers face an unbalanced power relationship vis-à-vis their employer. This emerges because employers have a much higher degree of control over the relationship than workers (employers take hiring, firing and other organisational decisions and often may fix pay and working conditions) and because the latter may have few or no outside options. In many situations, employers' buyer power is not compensated by sufficient bargaining power on the side of the workers – in particular in the absence of collective bargaining – and may, therefore, lead to lower employment and pay as well as worse working conditions.

The labour economics literature often defines as *labour market monopsony* a situation in which employers' buyer power is not compensated by sufficient workers' bargaining power and workers have low or no outside options. Strictly speaking, the term "monopsony" refers to the extreme case in which one buyer dominates a specific upstream market and, in order to maximise its profits, can fix input purchases and prices below the level that maximises social welfare. The term "oligopsony" would more correctly refer to cases where few firms dominate buying in a market. Yet, the literature often refers to labour market monopsony to indicate any of these situations with respect to a specific segment of the labour market (Manning, 2003[72]; Bhaskar, Manning and To, 2002[73]).

This annex briefly summarises existing evidence on labour market monopsony and discusses instruments to tackle the abuse of employers' buyer power and its sources. Other policy instruments, which are not primarily intended to address labour market monopsony, could nonetheless affect its sources and/or effects. These are discussed in Section 4.3 in the main text and in Chapter 5.

## Empirical evidence on labour market monopsony and its effects

There is a growing literature demonstrating that labour market competition is far from perfect. The early literature tended to attribute a key role to collective bargaining and labour market institutions in limiting competition in the labour market – e.g. OECD (2018[101]) and Chapter 5. Recent academic work, however, has begun to point out the key role played by labour market concentration and, more generally, buyer power in the labour market – in particular in the absence of collective bargaining.

A large number of studies for specific labour markets have estimated that workers cannot easily switch to a different employer in reaction to wage changes in a specific firm (i.e. residual labour supply elasticities are low) – see e.g. Manning (2003[72]), Webber (2015[102]), Naidu, Posner and Weyl (forthcoming[78]), and references cited therein. These studies typically find residual labour supply elasticities that are close to, or smaller than 5.[47] They have usually been found to be smaller in America than in Europe, but even in the latter they tend to remain within single digits (Sokolova and Sorensen, 2018[77]). Single-digit elasticities are usually considered as evidence of labour market monopsony.[48] While most of this evidence refers to employees, there is some evidence that residual labour supply elasticities are even lower for some independent contractors, including certain platform workers – see Section 4.3 in the main text.

Manning and Petrongolo (2017[103]) and Marinescu and Rathelot (2018[104]) have shown that both UK and US labour markets are very local, in the sense that job searches decline rapidly with distance. Using "scraped" data on online job postings from thousands of websites, Azar, Marinescu and Steinbaum (2017[105]) and Azar et al. (2018[74]) find that the average local US labour market – as defined at the level of the sixth digit of occupational classification within the same commuting zone – is highly concentrated, that is more concentrated than the threshold triggering concern of lack of competition according to the US horizontal merger guidelines (US Department of Justice and Federal Trade Commission, 2010[106]).[49] Recent evidence for Portugal shows lower levels of concentration in this country (Martins, 2018[76]). Yet, the most reliable measures suggest that more than 15% of Portuguese employment is exposed to a higher level of labour market concentration than the above-mentioned threshold. Other studies for the United States and the United Kingdom have used a definition of the relevant labour market based on the industry and commuting zone. These studies find that about 25% of employment in both countries is in a local labour market with a level of concentration close or above the high-concentration threshold (Hershbein, Macaluso and Yeh, 2018[107]; Abel, Tenreyro and Thwaites, 2018[75]; Rinz, 2018[94]).

Market power in the markets for inputs (including labour) can have a negative impact on prices – i.e. wages and benefits – and quantities – overall employment, see e.g. Manning (2003[72]), Ashenfelter, Farber and Ransom (2010[108]) and Blair and Harrison (2010[109]). Azar, Marinescu and Steinbaum (2017[105]) and Azar et al. (2018[74]) find that employer concentration has a significant depressing effect on posted wages, while Hershbein, Macaluso and Yeh (2018[107]), Martins (2018[76]) and Qiu and Sojourner (2019[110]) find a negative relationship between concentration and pay using actual wages. Rinz (2018[94]) finds that this association is stronger at the lower tail of the earnings distribution, while Webber (2015[102]) estimates that residual labour supply elasticities are smaller and have a stronger effect on earnings at the bottom of the earnings distribution. Abel, Tenreyro and Thwaites (2018[75]) find that higher levels of labour market concentration are associated with lower pay especially amongst workers not covered by a collective bargaining agreement. Benmelech, Bergman and Kim (2018[111]) show that the negative relationship between concentration and actual wages becomes steeper over time, while the link between productivity growth and wage growth is stronger when labour markets are less concentrated. Hershbein and Macaluso (2018[112]) find that highly concentrated labour markets tend to have greater demand for skilled rather than unskilled labour. Qiu and Sojourner (2019[110]) estimate that workers in concentrated labour markets are less likely to be covered by employer-sponsored health insurance. Finally, evidence on lack or limited effects of the minimum wage on employment (when the former is not too high) is also considered as evidence of employment-depressing effects of monopsony, at least at the lower tail of the pay distribution – see e.g. Manning (2011[92]) and Card and Krueger (2015[43]) .

Recent research has also explored the link between market power in product markets and labour markets, finding that increasing price-cost margins have gone hand in hand with declining labour shares and decreasing workers' bargaining power (De Loecker and Eeckhout, 2018[113]; Barkai, 2017[114]; Autor et al., 2017[115]; Bell, Bukowski and Machin, 2018[116]), suggesting that buyer power in the labour market may be associated with some degree of market power in the product market, with possible implications also for consumer welfare.[50]

## Enforcing regulation to address labour market monopsony

To date, regulators have paid somewhat less attention to labour market power and firms' ability to pay workers less than their marginal productivity than to product market power. There are four areas of action, in which legislators and enforcement authorities (including labour inspectorates and antitrust authorities) could consider taking a more active role in many countries: i) no-poaching agreements and wage-setting collusion; ii) non-compete clauses; iii) mergers; and iv) information asymmetries between employers and workers. These will be discussed one-by-one below.

### No-poaching agreements and labour market collusion

In most jurisdictions, competition law forbids collusion among buyers of intermediate goods or services – see e.g. Blair and Wang (2017[81]). The labour market is no exception in this respect. Firms can collude in the labour markets in several ways. For example, companies competing for the same type of professionals can agree on refraining from hiring or making job offers to workers employed by the others (so-called "no-poaching agreements"), thereby limiting the outside options of their employees or independent contractors. Alternatively, firms competing in the same labour market may agree to apply a common compensation policy to employees or independent contractors, thereby preventing market forces to raise wages as the result of supply and demand (wage collusion). Collusion, however, can occur in more elusive ways: for example, buyers can simply meet and discuss compensation and hiring policies, thereby reaching de facto an arrangement without formal agreement (US Department of Justice and Federal Trade Commission, 2016[84]). To be considered illicit, a collusive agreement does not need to concern direct competitors in the downstream output market[51], nor does it need to have an adverse impact on final consumer prices.[52]

General statistics on collusion are difficult to collect, since figures on those illicit behaviours that escape investigation are typically not available. Anecdotal evidence suggests however that the phenomenon is far from negligible: US Deputy Assistant Attorney General for Civil Antitrust, Barry Nigro, said recently that he found "shocking how prevalent agreements have become between companies not to solicit or hire each others' employees" – cited in Krotoski et al. (2018[82]).

Only a few jurisdictions have been significantly active in fighting labour market collusion. A number of cases of collusion in the labour market have been adjudicated by US courts and antitrust authorities in recent years – see e.g. Marinescu and Hovenkamp (forthcoming[87]) for a number of examples. In a few of these cases, illegal agreements have concerned collusion on compensation of independent contractors or employees on very atypical work arrangements.[53] Similar cases have been adjudicated in some other jurisdictions, notably in France, the Netherlands, Spain, and the United Kingdom.[54] However, law enforcement authorities and courts in most OECD countries have been somewhat less aggressive in fighting labour market collusion – see e.g. Gurkaynak, Guner and Ozkanli (2013[117]); and Blair and Wang (2017[81]). This heterogeneity may partially reflect the inherent difficulty of distinguishing tacit collusion agreements from lawful co-ordination among employers in countries with co-ordinated or branch-level collective bargaining (Gurkaynak, Guner and Ozkanli, 2013[117]; OECD, 2017[118]; 2018[101]).

Providing explicit guidance about labour market collusion is crucial to guide and set priorities for action of enforcement agencies. In fact, the greater number of cases in the United States is likely to be also the result of the explicit guidance provided by US antitrust authorities (US Department of Justice and Federal Trade Commission, 2016[84]; 2016[119]). The issued guidelines explicitly refer to collusion in the labour market, present clear examples of illicit behaviours, and underline the importance of fighting collusion in order to help "actual and potential employees through higher wages, better benefits, or other terms of employment" (US Department of Justice and Federal Trade Commission, 2016, p. 2[84]).[55] By contrast, in other jurisdictions, guidelines typically refer to any type of joint-cooperation agreements, with examples from both cooperation in production and cooperation in input purchasing, at the risk of diluting the importance of fighting illicit agreements in the labour market.[56]

Providing adequate whistleblower protection is also crucial for effective action by enforcement agencies (Dyck, Morse and Zingales, 2010[85]; Yeoh, 2014[86]). As information which allows the identification of collusion agreements is often confidential and can be passed to enforcement agencies only by insiders, whistleblower protection is needed, in particular in the case of independent contractors who usually are not protected by dismissal legislation provisions covering whistleblowing – see e.g. OECD (2014[8]).

Enforcement agencies should also be able to provide adequate sanctions for illicit behaviours. Deterrence of possible future collusive behaviours from other companies would not be exerted if those caught up colluding are simply ordered to stop. Nevertheless, adequate leniency programmes, offering immunity to the first cartel member that blows the whistle, may play an important role – see e.g. Luz and Spagnolo (2017[120]).

Private actions seeking redress in courts should be seen as a complement rather than a substitute to public enforcement actions in deterring collusive behaviour. Beyond public enforcement by antitrust authorities, most OECD legislations allow private damage actions initiated by the victims of collusive behaviour (Blair and Wang, 2017[81]). However, individual employees often do not have the resources or incentives to sue employers for this type of antitrust violations because an antitrust suit is usually much more costly than the individual damage. By contrast, an antitrust claim concerning product markets is usually brought by a large firm claiming conspicuous compensation for damages resulting from the anticompetitive practices of a rival. Hence, private damage actions concerning labour market collusion would often require collective actions. In most countries, however, private collective actions are frequently subject to strict requirements as regards the parties that have the legal standing to initiate a claim – for example, associations and non-governmental organisations often do not have such standing, see e.g. Haar (2018[121]) and Knable Gotts (2018[122]). In turn, this may limit the capacity of filing such claims for independent contractors in the absence of representative trade unions (see also Chapter 5). Class actions may also impose considerable costs and risks on the initiating third parties or law firms, in the absence of previous infringement sanctions by antitrust authorities (Krueger and Posner, 2018[123]). As a result, collective claims usually follow the investigation of antitrust authorities.

The development of algorithms and artificial intelligence is opening up new opportunities for collusion, including in the labour market. Firms can indeed independently design algorithms to signal and coordinate a common compensation policy as well as to monitor and retaliate against deviators without any explicit communication (Capobianco and Gonzaga, 2017[124]). This is all the more likely in the labour markets for independent contractors and platform work, where in essentially all countries there is no legal constraint to adjust downward compensation for similar tasks over time. However, it is not obvious that the effect of algorithms is necessarily that of facilitating collusion. For example, if the use of different algorithms leads to cost asymmetry across companies, collusion might be difficult to sustain, due to the inherent difficulties of finding a focal point to coordinate and, as a consequence, of the low incentives for the most efficient firms to collude (OECD, 2017[125]). Moreover, it is not obvious how regulation can be adapted to allow enforcement agencies fighting effectively against this type of collusion without curbing innovation and depressing the growth of the digital economy (Capobianco and Gonzaga, 2017[124]). More research is still needed in this area.

A question that remains open is whether no-poaching clauses among franchisees should be considered unlawful. Krueger and Ashenfelter (2018[83]) estimate that more than 50% of major franchise companies in the United States use no-poaching clauses in their franchising agreements. Collusion agreements are typically defined as illicit pacts across different organisations, while franchisees are usually considered as part of the same organisation. Yet, when several franchisees are the dominant employer in a labour market, a no-poaching rule has clear anti-competitive effects in that market (Krueger and Posner, 2018[123]). Several cases involving franchisees are under examination by US courts, but typically concern situations in which franchisees are totally independent in terms of staffing decisions.[57]

### Non-compete covenants

Non-compete covenants are clauses in contracts that prevent workers from working for a competitor after they separate from the employer (and should be distinguished from moonlighting clauses that prevent employees from performing work for a competitor during the term of their employment).[58] Sometimes the literature distinguishes between "non-compete" and "garden leave" clauses, the difference being that in the latter the worker is compensated after separating from the employer for the period of validity of the covenant while in the former she is not – see e.g. Nicandri (2011[126]). As in many countries and states a clause without worker compensation is not enforceable – see e.g. Meritas (2017[127]), for the purpose of this chapter, the term "non-compete covenant" or "non-compete agreement" refers to both type of clauses.

In most countries, non-compete agreements are lawful and justified by the need to protect trade secrets and specific investment in the employment relationship by the employer (such as certain types of training and investment in knowledge).[59] These clauses are often considered to have a positive impact on innovation, in particular when companies cannot protect their investment in knowledge through patents or other types of contracts. Yet, the literature is far from conclusive on this matter, in particular due to the possible impact of restrictive covenants on knowledge spillovers – see e.g. Rubin and Shedd (1981[128]); Motta and Rønde (2002[129]); Younge, Tong and Fleming (2014[130]); Rauch (2016[131]) and Wickelgren (2018[132]).

Non-compete covenants, however, can also be used as a legal instrument to increase monopsony power in the labour market. The evidence on litigation suggests that employers may use these clauses in order to limit effectively the outside options of their workers, for example by preventing them from taking up similar jobs even in companies with which they do not compete in practice.[60] Consequently, non-compete clauses typically result in lower wages and job mobility – see e.g. Garmaise (2009[133]), Marx, Strumsky and Fleming (2009[134]); Marx (2011[135]); Starr, Prescott and Bishara (2016[136]) and Starr (forthcoming[137]).

More striking, recent cases have concerned low-skilled workers involved in production of standardised products, such as sandwich making, and with little access to company tacit knowledge.[61] More generally, available evidence suggests that non-compete covenants are pervasive in low-skilled jobs. For example, Lipsitz and Johnson (2018[138]) show that non-compete clauses are more common among minimum wage hairdressers than among those working for a higher wage. More striking, Starr, Prescott and Bishara (2018[88]) estimate that almost 30 million US workers are currently covered by non-compete agreements, and that many of these agreements are imposed broadly on workers with less than bachelor's degree, often with low income or no access to trade secrets. This is even more challenging since low-skilled workers tend to be more vulnerable to monopsony than high-skilled workers: in particular, they often have fewer outside options and less bargaining power since they have less access to transportation, well-situated housing markets and job information – see e.g. Cahuc, Postel-Vinay and Robin (2006[139]) and Caldwell and Danieli (2018[140]).

In order to fight against non-compete agreements in situations where they are most likely used only to reduce competition in the labour market, governments could consider banning them, or establishing a rebuttable presumption of abusive use, in the case of certain type of positions, pay levels or skill requirements, for which a clear justification, such as the protection of trade secrets, seems implausible. A number of US states have introduced or are considering legislation limiting the use of non-compete clauses in particular for low-wage workers. For example, Massachusetts enacted a provision of this type for all covenants signed after October 2018 concerning either low-pay employees or low-skill jobs, with few exceptions.[62] Similar provisions exist in three European legislations (Austria, Belgium and Luxembourg), where non-compete clauses are banned for workers earning less than a specified threshold that is close to, or even above, the median wage of full-time employees.[63] Similarly, in the United Kingdom, the 2015 Small Business, Enterprise and Employment Act, by making exclusivity clauses for zero-hours contracts unlawful, has arguably resulted in a ban of restrictive covenants concerning future employment for these contracts.[64] However, in most countries and states, while some restriction on the scope of restrictive covenants is often imposed, notably in terms of duration after separation and worker compensation during that period, a presumption (rebuttable or not) of abusive use is not made on the basis of the type of position, the level of pay or the skill requirements of the job. Instead, courts typically assess the reasonableness of non-compete agreements on a case-by-case basis (Meritas, 2017[127]). Moreover, regulations limiting the applicability of non-compete clauses often concern only employment relationships and do not extend to any type of contracts for services.[65]

Private actions initiated by workers themselves are rare and under-deterring. Even when restrictive covenants are unenforceable or unlawful according to statutory or case law, they may still be included in employment or service contracts as a way to put pressure on uninformed workers. In fact, costly private actions by workers would most often result in simply waving unlawful covenants, with no additional gain for plaintiff workers (Krueger and Posner, 2018[123]). As a result, private litigation cases are typically initiated by the employer aiming to enforce a restrictive covenant, rather than by employees hoping to waive them. Moreover, in most cases, workers are likely to honour these clauses by renouncing to search for certain jobs without consulting counsel or challenging the clause in court. For example, 19% of employees in California and North Dakota report having signed a non-compete clause, despite the fact that these clauses are legally not enforceable in these states (Prescott, Bishara and Starr, 2016[141]), suggesting that employers consider them having a mobility deterrence effect despite their formal lack of enforceability.[66] Public guidance and counselling which clarify, in simple terms, under what conditions a non-compete clause is enforceable and lawful, can partially palliate this problem.[67]

Governments should also consider a ban on "blue-pencilling" – i.e. situations where courts redraft unreasonable or unlawful covenants in order to make them enforceable. When legislation allows "blue-pencilling", workers are not guaranteed that restrictive covenants would be rendered void in the event of litigation, even when these clauses are clearly unenforceable as drafted. In such cases, employers could simply insert broad, unreasonable covenants not to compete in their employment contracts to put pressure on employees, to subsequently retreat to a narrower, more reasonable construction in the event of litigation. For example, a clause could state that the worker cannot accept alternative employment in an unreasonably long list of countries or regions, and the court could simply delete a few of them (or ask the company to delete a few of them) from the covenant to make the clause enforceable.[68] For this reason, blue-pencilling has been rejected by courts in a few jurisdictions, such as Nebraska, Vermont, Virginia and Wisconsin (Rosenthal, 2018[142]) and, more recently, the United Kingdom.[69] Yet, it is acceptable practice in many others, including a number of European countries – see e.g. Adler (2006[143]).

To the extent that private legal actions do not appear to exert an adequate deterring effect against the abuse of non-compete covenants with the intention of restricting mobility in the labour market, government and enforcement authorities should take a leading role in this area. For example, the attorneys general of the US states of New York and Illinois have recently been very active in investigating unreasonably broad or unlawful restrictive covenants, often reaching settlements involving significant sanctions with infringing companies.[70] To be effective, however, enforcement agencies, including labour inspectorates, should have the possibility of imposing sanctions or taking the case to courts for imposing them. In particular, administrative sanctions could be considered in the case of inclusion of non-compete clauses in an employment contract for a type of job for which they are explicitly banned – such as for workers and independent contractors whose remuneration is below the enforceability threshold in those countries for which this threshold is defined in the law (see above).

### Mergers and anti-competitive conduct

Mergers can also have the effect of increasing employers' buyer power in the labour market. In fact, if merging firms would together form the dominant buyer in an input market, the merged entity would likely use its buyer power to reduce quantities and prices in that input market, thereby increasing its profits. For this to occur, merging firms do not need to compete in the same downstream product market. For example, in the extreme case in which merging local input buyers sell their products in perfectly competitive markets, such as in markets for homogeneous tradable goods where prices are fixed by world demand and supply (such as markets for raw materials), the merger would not affect downstream product prices. Yet, in this case, the merger may generate significant welfare losses due to its impact in the input market – see e.g. Dobson and Inderst (2007[144]) and Marinescu and Hovenkamp (forthcoming[87]).

More generally, however, the merging firm could potentially pass part of the input price reduction onto downstream output prices, making final consumers gain from the merger, which implies that the welfare gain in the output market could offset the welfare loss in the input market. However, the actual pass-on of the reduction of input prices on downstream output prices will depend on a number of factors, including the degree of competition in the output markets, the degree of bargaining power of input suppliers and the type of outside options available to them – see e.g. Inderst and Shaffer (2008[145]) and Carlton, Israel and Coleman (2014[146]). In particular, worker bargaining power or good outside options for the workers are necessary conditions for a pass-on of any reduction in wages on downstream output prices. But, in the absence of collective bargaining, these conditions are unlikely to hold in many labour markets,[71] where workers are capacity constrained – i.e. they cannot indefinitely extend their working time – and have a strong financial dependence on their employer – see e.g. Inderst and Shaffer (2008[145]) and Naidu, Posner and Weyl (forthcoming[78]).

In many jurisdictions, guidelines for antitrust authorities are cautious in considering the effects of mergers on input markets based on their possible effects on prices and quantities in those markets, even when likely effects on the downstream product markets are minor or absent. For example, EU guidelines suggest that the evaluation by antitrust authorities of a merger must be based on its possible effects in the final product market – see e.g. European Commission (2004[147]). In other jurisdictions, merger guidelines are more explicit on the fact mergers between input purchases should be mainly assessed by examining their impact in the relevant input market. For example, the US horizontal merger guidelines explicitly indicate that enforcing agencies should not "evaluate the competitive effects of mergers between competing buyers strictly, or even primarily, on the basis of effects in the downstream markets in which the merging firms sell" (US Department of Justice and Federal Trade Commission, 2010, p. 33[106]). US enforcement authorities and US courts have applied this principle in a few investigations of mergers of buyers of agricultural products,[72] but cases of mergers with suspected monopsonistic effects in the labour market have rarely been investigated – see e.g. Hovenkamp (forthcoming[148]) and Naidu, Posner and Weyl (forthcoming[78]).[73]

One difficulty in assessing the impact of mergers on buyer power in the labour market has to do with the shortage of specific tools to analyse labour competition and, in particular, the difficulty of identifying the relevant market. This stands in stark contrast with the tools available to examine competition in specific output markets. While the recent literature has suggested a few practical methods – see e.g. Naidu, Posner and Weyl (forthcoming[78]), more research in this area and more investment in developing adequate tools by governments and enforcement authorities would be welcome.

Another difficulty in assessing the impact of mergers on buyer power in the labour market is the evaluation of their effects in the downstream markets when merging firms are not direct competitors in those downstream markets – see e.g. Marinescu and Hovenkamp (forthcoming[87]) for a few hypothetical examples. Certain scholars have suggested that a merger increasing concentration in the labour market may be harming the final consumer even if concentration in downstream markets does not pass the threshold level suggesting anti-competitive effects, although the size of the effect is hardly identifiable. For this reason, Krueger and Posner (2018[123]) suggest to introduce in the legislation a rebuttable presumption of anti-competitive effects on consumer welfare when a merger increases concentration in the labour market above a given threshold level. A connected debate – more philosophical but loaded with many implications in this area – turns around whether worker welfare should also be included in the definition of "consumer welfare" (which typically guides antitrust authorities) and, if not, to what extent enforcement authorities should also consider other welfare losses beyond those affecting the final consumer – see e.g. Bork (1993[149]); Schwartz (2004[150]); Werden (2007[151]); Salop (2010[152]); Jacobson (2013[153]); Sims (2018[154]); Chopra (2018[155]) and Hovenkamp (forthcoming[148]).[74]

Finally, effectively addressing other types of monopsonistic conduct in the labour market, such as predatory price-bidding,[75] might be more difficult, in particular if courts and enforcement authorities adopt cautious behaviours to avoid over-deterrence – that is inefficient deterrence of conduct whose anti-competitive effects are offset by efficiency gains. In this case, antitrust authorities and courts may apply very strict tests that may fail in the presence of both monopsony in the upstream market and oligopoly in the downstream market. For example, if a predator in the input market has monopoly power in the output market, it may be able to sell its output at a price higher than its costs despite paying more than the marginal revenue for the input market in which it is pricing predatorily. In this case, the predator is making temporary smaller gains but no losses. Requiring temporary losses as evidence of predatory price-bidding[76] may fall short of identifying the most important cases – see e.g. Harrison (2012[156]). More research in this area is needed.

## Informational asymmetries

One of the reasons why workers often have low bargaining power and few outside options is that they have much less information than employers. Workers often have only a vague idea of their rights and are uncertain about what they can legitimately ask for, in particular if they are employed with a non-standard contract on which information may be less abundant. For example, when signing a contract (or accepting terms and conditions) workers may not fully understand the obligations they are committing to (or the rights they are waiving). Even after signing the contract or accepting a job offer, and therefore, in some cases, having turned down alternative offers, workers may be pressed for signing covenants giving away specific rights without a clear understanding of their implications. For example, based on a survey of over 1 000 US engineers, Marx (2011[135]) finds that over two-thirds of those who signed a non-compete clause were asked to do so only after having accepted the job offer, and sometimes after having started working.

Regulation could therefore make sure that all contracting parties are fully aware of their rights and responsibilities. In the United Kingdom, the government's response to the Taylor Review ("Good Work") (BEIS, 2017[44]) includes plans to ensure that all workers receive information from day one on their working relationship, and what rights they are entitled to (OECD, 2019[2]). In the same line, a regulation proposal under discussion at the European parliament provides that terms and conditions for the use of intermediation services should be drafted in clear and unambiguous language which is easily understood by an average user (European Commission, 2018[67]). Similarly, in Oregon, regulations stipulate that non-compete clauses should be made clear before negotiating compensation, so that giving up future options could be traded off against pay (Marx and Fleming, 2012[157]). And the recently adopted Fair Work Week Act in the same state stipulates that large corporations in selected sectors (retail, food and hospitality) must provide a new employee with a written good faith estimate of the employee's work schedule at the time of hire. Certain scholars have suggested, more generally, that governments should invest in a dedicated service for independent contractors, and in particular gig workers, offering general advice and counsel about their employment rights (Balaram, Warden and Wallace-Stephens, 2017[89]).

Lack of pay transparency may also increase monopsony power. Shortage of information about alternative opportunities reduces workers' ability to change jobs or leverage outside opportunities to negotiate for higher pay (and better working conditions) – see e.g. Harris (2018[90]). Digital technologies have the potential to improve this type of information asymmetry, as workers can access a large number of job offers and compare them, thereby reducing search costs. Yet, in many platforms, workers have few tools to search for available alternatives and have to spend much time searching for them (Kingsley, Gray and Suri, 2015[52]; Berg et al., 2018[62]).

To improve pay transparency in the platform economy, employers and platforms could be required to publish information about the average pay per task, as well as on the average time taken to complete a task (which would help workers make more informed decisions about which tasks to accept).[77] In addition, tools could be designed to help workers find requesters who pay well, and avoid those who pay poorly. However, the devil is in the details: publishing information on pay policies without making it easily accessible by workers could facilitate collusion among requesters, even in the absence of an explicit agreement among them (see above in this section). In practice, some websites and online communities have already sprung up which help workers find well-paying requesters. For example, the social networks Turkopticon and TurkerView allow Turkers (crowdworkers offering work on Amazon Mechanical Turk) to help one another with information and share experiences about their employers (Irani and Silberman, 2013[158]).

One specific problem related to digital intermediation concerns the information that platforms collect on workers. For example, most platforms have a rating system for workers, which evaluates their performance history and is supposed to improve service quality for the requester. However, the ratings algorithms, which are based on inputs from the requesters or on other productivity parameters (such as task acceptance rates and average delivery lags), often lack transparency (Rosenblat and Stark, 2016[91]) and workers sometimes have no clear information on how to improve their ratings (Berg et al., 2018[62]). In addition, certain platforms do not allow workers to rate requesters and/or to ask for the reason of a bad evaluation. This informational asymmetry allows requesters or platforms to exclude certain workers from certain tasks, based on their ratings, while workers are unable to identify and refuse tasks proposed by bad requesters, who typically do not pay regularly or are inclined to provide negative assessments, which results in lower average pay and heightened worker stress (Kingsley, Gray and Suri, 2015[52]). Even though some collective workers' initiatives such as Turkopticon or FairCrowdWork.org have been recently developed to, inter alia, deal with this problem, there is probably scope for regulating the ratings system by imposing rating symmetry (the so-called "five-for-five" policies, in which workers and employers rate each other on the same scale) and transparency in algorithms on platforms.

The information accumulated by platforms could also give rise to exclusionary practices that are illicit under either anti-discrimination or competition law. For example, while independent contractors should be able to work for different platforms, the latter, by digitally tracking the former, can punish those who also work for the competitor, or alternatively engage in targeted predatory price-bidding by proposing different fees or compensation packages to these workers, thereby potentially excluding competitors from the labour market – see e.g. OECD (2018[159]). To the extent that pay, rating and task allocation algorithms are not transparent, these illicit behaviours might be extremely difficult to identify by enforcement authorities (Herrera Anchustegui and Nowag, 2017[160]).

## Notes

[1] As well as access to training programmes, freedom of association and the right to bargain collectively.

[2] A similar guide for tax purposes is available on the website of the US Internal Revenue Service (Internal Revenue Service, 2005[10]).

[3] Some countries, like France (*présomption de salariat*) and the Netherlands, presume an employment contract when a number of criteria are met. In the Netherlands, for example, if a worker has worked on a regular basis for his or her employer for a period of three months (or at least 20 hours a month), then a contract of employment is automatically presumed (Davidov, Freedland and Countouris, 2015[6]). In Belgium, there is a presumption of an employment contract (subject to certain criteria) in certain "at-risk" sectors including caretaking/security, construction, transport, cleaning, agriculture and horticulture. In Ontario (Canada), the Employment Standards Act was amended in 2017 to put the burden of proof on the employer in cases where a contractor claims to be an employee. See also the online annex to OECD (2014[8]) for other examples of presumption of an employment relationship.

[4] In the United Kingdom, for example, the introduction in July 2013 of launch and hearing fees of GBP 1 200 for an individual bringing a claim to the employment tribunal has led to a drop in claims of over 70%, which has affected disproportionately the bottom end of the claim distribution (Adams and Prassl, 2018[161]).

[5] Portugal introduced a new, simplified judicial procedure to target the growth of bogus self-employment through changes in 2013 and 2017. It provides workers with a speedier court decision recognising the existence of an employment relationship.

[6] Epic Systems Corp. v. Lewis, 138 S. Ct. 1612 (2018).

[7] That being said, practice by judges will vary across countries and time. In some countries, for example, courts have tended to pay more attention to what is written in the employment contract (Davidov, Freedland and Countouris, 2015[6]).

[8] Differences across countries tend to stem primarily from differences in practice rather than differences in theory (Davidov, Freedland and Countouris, 2015[6]).

[9] In most cases, the decision of a tribunal will apply only to the plaintiff. To some extent, this will act as a deterrent to firms because it could create a precedent which would have an impact on similar cases in the future. However, the deterrent might remain limited if the outcome of the tribunal only applies to the few workers who brought the case in the first place (especially because many of these cases settle). The deterrent would be much greater if, once a case is decided, people in the same situation can make a liability claim that would automatically apply.

[10] A complementary strategy consists in providing incentives to employers who have misclassified workers to seek settlement with the administration in exchange of a partial relief on penalties. In the United States for example, the Voluntary Classification Settlement Program (VCSP) provides substantial partial relief from federal employment taxes for eligible taxpayers who agree to treat workers prospectively as employees. In exchange, the employer pays 10% of the employment tax liability that would have been due if those workers were classified as employees in the most recent year. Moreover the employer is not liable for any interest and penalties on the liability and is not subject to an employment tax audit with respect to

the worker classification of the class or classes of workers for prior years (Internal Revenue Service, 2012[167]).

[11] There may be broader issues here than false self-employment. Where incentives are so strong as to lead to an "inefficiently high" level of self-employment, this could lead to a misallocation of labour resources as well as undermining social protection systems (particularly where lower-risk individuals choose to become self-employed and are allowed to opt out of parts of the social protection system, leaving only the "bad risks" behind and resulting in an increased reliance on social assistance, see also Chapter 7). In addition, to the extent that the self-employed participate less in training, very high levels of self-employment could act as a drag on productivity.

[12] However, the problem with amnesties is that they create an expectation of further amnesties and therefore can encourage future deviations, except if they are introduced simultaneously with a real change in legislation that makes the reduction of sham arrangements more durable.

[13] See e.g. Berwick v. Uber Technologies, Inc., CGC-15-546378, Cotter v. Lyft, Inc., Dkt. No. 94, 60 F. Supp. 3d 1067 (N.D. Cal. 2015); Dynamex Operations West, Inc. v. Superior Court, 4 Cal.5th 903 (2018); O'Connor v. Uber Technologies Inc., Case No. 14-16078 (9th Cir. 2018); Uber B.V. & Ors v Aslam & Ors UKEAT/0056/17/DA; Kaseris v Rasier Pacific V.O.F [2017] FWC 6610; or Cass. soc., 28 novembre 2018, n° 17-20.079.

[14] Cotter v. Lyft, Inc., Dkt. No. 94, 60 F. Supp. 3d 1067 (N.D. Cal. 2015).

[15] NLRB v. Hearst Publ'ns, Inc., 322 U.S. 111, 121 (1944).

[16] The employer generally drafts the contract and can use this to deny employment rights to individuals who would otherwise be employees (Davies, 2009[169]).

[17] If countries have several employment tests and/or definitions, which vary across legal/policy areas (labour, tax, social protection), then there may be a case for harmonising them, as this could contribute to possible confusion. Even small differences across tests can result in very different results (Rubinstein, 2012[20]). For example, in the United States, the tests for defining employee status range from the broadest "suffer or permit" test, passing through the hybrid and the "ABC" tests, to the narrowest common law test (Waas et al., 2017[7]).

[18] As introduced by Act 92/2012.

[19] For a while, Germany also had a definition of employee for social security reasons which consisted of four criteria. If all four criteria were fulfilled, the person was classified as an employee; if none were fulfilled then the person was self-employed; and if two out of four criteria were met, the person would be presumed to be an employee for social protection purposes (Wank, 1999[168]).

[20] Lord Wedderburn described the test used by courts to identify employees as an "elephant test" – "an animal too difficult to define but easy to recognise when you see it" (Davidov, 2002[163]).

[21] Allowing for court discretion in the identification of employment relationships risks leading to results which the legislature may not appreciate. An interesting historical example is the Taft-Hartley Act of 1947, in which the US legislature reacted to a series of Supreme Court judgments from 1944 through 1947, which adopted an economic reality of dependence test instead of the common-law agency (control) test to ascertain employee status (Davidov, Freedland and Countouris, 2015[6]). This resulted in far more workers

being classified as employees than congress liked, and the definition of employee in the National Labor Relations Act was subsequently amended to explicitly exclude independent contractors.

[22] McKee v. Reid's Heritage Homes Ltd., (2009) ONCA 916.

[23] Judgement of 28 October 2010, Aslam v. Uber, London Employment Tribunal: 2202550/2015, paragraph 97.

[24] Or 2.2% of total employment.

[25] The co-ordinated and continuous collaboration contract (*collaborazioni coordinate e continuative* – co.co.co.); and the project-based collaboration contract (*contratto di collaborazione a progetto* – co.co.pro., abolished since January 2016).

[26] In practice, this would be equivalent to defining the third worker category as a "residual category" capturing those cases where employment tests fail to come to clear conclusions about employment status.

[27] An alternative approach which has been proposed is more radical, but would perhaps also encounter greater practical difficulties. The idea put forward is to no longer tie labour protections to employment status, but rather apply them to anyone performing work (Freedland and Kountouris, 2011[164]; Johnstone et al., 2012[165]; Stewart and Stanford, 2017[166]; Linder, 1999[22]).

[28] See Dynamex Operations West, Inc. v. Superior Court, 4 Cal.5th 903 (2018), in which the court stated that delivery drivers should be considered as employees if at least one of the factors in the ABC test does not hold, thereby reversing the standard common law approach.

[29] NJA 1996 s 311.

[30] Two interesting variations exist in the United Kingdom and in the Netherlands. In the United Kingdom, there is a certain margin around the national minimum wage to allow even slower workers to earn a "fair rate". Employers are required to monitor the average number of tasks/pieces completed per hour worked and divide this by 1.2. The hourly minimum wage rate should then be divided by that number to estimate the fair rate for each piece of work completed. In the Netherlands, in cases where work is difficult to supervise and the employees have a certain degree of freedom to organise their work, employers can ask for an exemption to the national piece rate legislation and, instead, pay a sectorally-determined piece rate.

[31] One option is to make all parties jointly and severally liable for making sure that the worker is paid a fair wage. For example, in the Netherlands, the Act on Combatting Sham Arrangements came into force in January 2016. The law states that, in case of multiple customers/contractors, the entire chain is liable to make the correct payment of the agreed wage (supply chain liability).

[32] This is an area where technological developments and the rise of the platform economy could potentially offer a solution since they present unprecedented opportunities for data collection which, in turn, could be used to calculate average productivity. This would help overcome some of the challenges traditionally encountered with piece rate pay.

[33] For example, should platform workers be paid for the time that they have an app open and/or the time they spend waiting/searching for tasks? While the answer may depend on the particular type of work considered, the general response would probably be no – otherwise workers could simply log on to several platforms at the same time and be paid for waiting on each one of them. The hourly pay of platform workers also depends on whether the time working on tasks that are rejected is taken into account (Hara et al., 2017[162]). In a well-functioning market, such time would be accounted for in the rates that gig and

self-employed workers set, so in their calculation of minimum piece rates employers should probably factor those in as well. Similarly, the expenses incurred by platform workers when performing gigs should be compensated for.

[34] In Poland, the parties to an agreement covered by the new minimum wage legislation may agree on the method of determining the number of hours worked by the service provider. If they do not do so, it is for the service provider to indicate the number of hours worked. However, this rule does not apply to service providers who are temporary work agency workers, in which case, the number of hours worked is determined by the user undertaking.

[35] In some cases, where there is a specific risk of injury to the worker or to others, working time regulations have already been extended to self-employed workers. For example, in accord with the EC Road Transport Directive, self-employed drivers are subject to the 48-hour average working week and other provisions of working time regulations.

[36] These terms purport to govern issues such as how and when crowd workers will be paid, how work will be evaluated and what recourse workers have (or do not have) when things go wrong.

[37] In turn, this asymmetry in the control of the relationship can enhance monopsony power by the platform or the requesters (see the next section).

[38] This is standard practice in the case of the dismissal of an employee in many countries – see e.g. OECD (2013[61]).

[39] O'Connor v. Uber Technologies, Inc.

[40] Formal arbitration is also not necessarily shorter and less expensive than resolution by court.

[41] See e.g. In re National Arbitration Forum Trade Practices Litig, 704 F. Supp. 2d 832 (D. Minn. 2010). See also Virtualpoint Inc. v. Poarch Band of Creek Indians, C.D. Cal., No. 8:15-cv-02025, (2016).

[42] The Ombuds office consists of a board of five people – one worker, one trade union representative, one platform employee, one representative of the Crowdsourcing Association, and a neutral chair – and resolves disputes by consensus.

[43] Furthermore, an open question remains on how to weigh the effects in labour and downstream product markets, in the cases where they are of opposite sign – see the discussion in Annex 4.A.

[44] This is neither new nor platform-specific. In fact, it applies in principle to any triangular relationship between a client, an intermediary and an independent contractor, if the intermediary is not committed to maintain the same conditions of service but the client and the independent contractor commit on refraining from engaging in a direct relationship.

[45] When there is an employment relationship, Article 6 of the Rome Convention of 1980 allows parties to choose the applicable law and, in the absence of such choice, "the contract shall be governed by the law of the place in which the employee habitually carries out his work in performance of the contract or, in the absence of such a place, the law of the place in which he was engaged".

[46] http://www.oecd.org/corporate/mne/.

[47] Most studies typically estimate residual labour supply elasticities for employees comprised between 0.5 and 5 – see e.g. Sokolova and Sorensen (2018[77]) and Naidu, Posner and Weyl (forthcoming[78]).

[48] By contrast, a competitive market would require a residual labour supply elasticity close to infinity.

[49] Azar et al. (2018[74]) find that the average level of concentration (the Herfindahl-Hirschman Index) in a market defined as a commuting zone by SOC-6 occupation by quarter is 3953. This figure is well above the 2500 threshold triggering concern of lack of competition that is mentioned in the horizontal merger guidelines of the US antitrust authorities – Department of Justice, Antitrust Division, and Federal Trade Commission (US Department of Justice and Federal Trade Commission, 2010[106]). Certain scholars even suggest that, due to search frictions, in the absence of worker bargaining power, negative welfare effects of buyer power arise at lower levels of concentration than in the case of product market power – see e.g. Carstensen (2012[171]), but this position is far from being consensual in the literature – see e.g. Schwartz (2004[150]).

[50] On trends in price-cost margins, see also Calligaris, Criscuolo and Marcolin (2018[170]).

[51] See e.g. California v. eBay, Inc., case No. 5:12cv05874, Document 85 (N.D. Cal. 2015) concerning an alleged handshake agreement entered into between senior executives of two companies specialised in different markets (accounting and tax preparation software and online auctions) but competing for a similar workforce.

[52] For example, the European Court of Justice has condemned a wage-fixing agreement among Dutch telecommunications operators while underlining the lack of evidence of harm to the final consumer: "in order to find that a concerted practice has an anti-competitive object, there does not need to be a direct link between that practice and consumer prices." Case C-8/08 T-Mobile Netherlands BV v Raad van Bestuur van de Nederlandse Mededingingsautoriteit [2009] ECR I-4529, [39].

[53] See e.g. Your Therapy Source, LLC; Neeraj Jindal; and Sheri Yarbray , FTC File No. 171 – 0134, concerning therapist staffing companies colluding on rates paid to physical therapists in the Dallas/Fort Worth area (the case was concluded with a settlement in July 2018); and Beltran v. Noonan et al, Civil Action No. 14-cv-03074, U.S. District Court D. Colo., concerning sponsors agencies conspiring to fix compensation for *au pairs* throughout the United States (a settlement on this case was agreed in January 2019).

[54] See e.g. Cass. soc., 2 mars 2011, n° 09-40.547, concerning the no-poaching agreement between two information technology companies in France; Cass., com., 13 février 2001, 98-21.078, concerning a wage-fixing agreement among French temporary work agencies; JAR 2010/145, Gerechtshof's-Hertogenbosch 04-05-2010, BM3366, HD-200.056.33, concerning human resource agreements among a few Dutch hospitals with the purpose of restricting competition for practitioners, including independent contractors; Expediente S/0120/08, concerning a no-poach agreement among eight Spanish companies in the road freight transport industry; and Kores Manufacturing Co Ltd v Kolok Manufacturing Co Ltd [1959] Ch.108, concerning an agreement among two British competitors that required each other's consent in case of one company recruiting the other's employee. See also endnote 52.

[55] Certain scholars argue that anti-collusion legislation may however be too rigid, thereby backfiring on both wages and employment, since companies may be reluctant to disclose their wage rules even to their own employees. The argument is that the asymmetry of information between employers and workers might increase monopsony power – see e.g. Harris (2018[90]) and the discussion of information asymmetries below in this section.

[56] See for example Korean Fair Trade Commission (2009[172]) and European Commission (2011[182]).

57 See e.g. Yi v. SK Bakeries, LLC et al, U.S. District Court W.D. Wash., case number 3:18-cv-05627; Maurella v. H&R Block Inc. et al., U.S. District Court N.D. Ill., case number 1:18-cv-07435; and The State of Washington v. Jersey Mike Franchise System Inc. et al., KCSC, Wash., case number 18-2-25822-7). The attorney general of the US state of Washington is particularly aggressive in fighting no-poaching agreements among franchisees (Office of the Washington State Attorney General, 2018[179]).

58 Moonlighting covenants are usually enforced in most countries. Nonetheless, they can be particularly problematic in contracts that do not guarantee a minimum of hours of work, such as zero-hours contracts.

59 California, which bans non-compete clauses altogether, represents the best known exception (Section 16600 of the California Business and Professions Code). Similar provisions exist in few other US states, such as North Dakota, and Oklahoma (Gomulkiewicz, 2015[174]; Green, 2015[175]), and Mexico (Association of Corporate Counsel, 2018[173]). Michigan also used to have similar legislation but it was repealed in 1985 (Pynnonen, 1994[180]).

60 See for example Shores v. Global Experience Specialists, Inc., 134 Nev. Adv. Op. 61 (Aug. 2, 2018), concerning a sale agent at an event management company who signed non-compete covenant preventing him from taking a similar job in any US state, including those in which the company had no affiliates.

61 A famous case involved a fast-food company preventing its workers from taking up jobs in any capacity within two miles of any of its stores at any employer "who derived at least ten percent of revenues business from the sale of categories of products such as 'deli-style' sandwiches, for two years [and] anywhere in the United States." (People v. Jimmy John's Franchises LLC, Circuit Court of Cook County, 2016-CH-07746). The company agreed to a settlement and suppressed the clause (Office of the Attorney General of the State of Illinois, 2018[178]).

62 More precisely, the 2018 Massachusetts Noncompetition Agreement Act provides that non-compete covenants are enforceable only on "exempt" employees under the Fair Labor Standards Act, which means that they must earn more than a given threshold, have guaranteed minimum pay independently of their effectively-worked hours, and have executive, professional or high-level administrative duties, with few exceptions for specific jobs.

63 Art. 1 § 36 Angestelltengesetz (AngG – Employees Act), for Austria, art. 65 §2 of the Loi du 3 juillet 1978 for Belgium, and art. L-125-8 Code du Travail, for Luxembourg. In Luxembourg, the labour code in principle only regulates clauses that prevent employees from starting a new business competing with that of their previous employer. However, an appeal court ruling effectively extended this regulation to other types of non-compete clauses in 2014 – Cour d'Appel de Luxembourg, arrêt du 13 novembre 2014 (n°39706 du rôle).

64 The official explanatory notes accompanying the reform state that the Act "provides that a provision in a zero-hours contract which prohibits the worker from doing work under any other arrangement is unenforceable", without explaining whether work is provided during or after the contract is terminated (http://www.legislation.gov.uk/ukpga/2015/26/notes/division/5/11 note 844). Yet, it remains to be seen how courts will interpret this provision in practice.

65 For example, the 2018 Massachusetts Noncompetition Agreement Act explicitly defines non-compete clauses as agreements between an employer and an employee, for the purpose of the act. Standard common law principle remain applicable to independent contractors.

66 See also the discussion in Kolani v. Gluska, 75 Cal. Rptr. 2d 257 – Cal: Court of Appeal, 2nd Appellate Dist., 7th Div. 1998.

[67] As done, for example, by the offices of the attorney general of the US states of Illinois and New York (Office of the Attorney General of the State of Illinois, 2018[178]; New York State Attorney General, 2018[177]).

[68] See e.g. Cour d'Appel de Luxembourg, 6 avril 2017, n°39706 du role.

[69] See e.g. Egon Zehnder Ltd v Tillman [2017] EWHC 1278 (Ch).

[70] See e.g. People v. Check into Cash of Illinois LLC, Circuit Court of Cook County, 2017-CH-14224; People v. Jimmy John's Franchises LLC, Circuit Court of Cook County, 2016-CH-07746; as well as Illinois Attorney General (2018[181]), New York State Attorney General (2018[176]) and the cases cited there.

[71] As shown by the low estimated values of the residual labour supply elasticity – see the previous section in this annex. When workers can bargain collectively, possible welfare effects will depend on the capacity of bargaining parties to achieve the outcome that would be pursued by a vertically-integrated firm in the downstream market – an outcome that may depend on a number of institutional settings – see e.g. Inderst and Shaffer (2008[145]) and OECD (2017[118]; 2018[101])

[72] See e.g. United States v. Cargill Inc. and Continental Grain Co., U.S. District Court D.D.C., case number 99-1875 (GK), final judgement 29 July 2000. The merger of two major grain traders was refused despite the absence of allegations of harm to the final consumer, since grain prices to national processors are determined in world markets.

[73] The labour market for health practitioners represents the most notable exception – see e.g. United States of America and the State of Texas v. Aetna, Inc. and The Prudential Insurance Company of America 1999 WL 1419046 (N.D. Texas); and United States v. Anthem, Inc., 855 F.3d 345, 356 (D.C. Cir. 2017).

[74] The difference between the U.S. and EC horizontal merger guidelines (see above) could also result of different answers given by legislators to these questions (US Department of Justice and Federal Trade Commission, 2010[106]; European Commission, 2004[147]). See also the discussion above concerning standards for fighting collusion and the literature cited there.

[75] Predatory bidding occurs when the dominant buyer temporarily raises the price of inputs to exclude weaker competitors and then recover its costs by lowering it.

[76] See for example the doctrine imposed by the US Supreme Court in Weyerhaeuser Company v. Ross-Simmons Hardwood Lumber Company, 549 U.S. 312 (2007), as regards predatory price-bidding.

[77] While not directly related to the platform economy, the existing piece rate legislation in the United Kingdom already requires that a notice be issued before the start of the pay reference period, with a clear reference to the expected mean hourly output rate of the task in question.

# 5 Facing the future of work: How to make the most of collective bargaining

The purpose of this chapter is to identify the role of labour relations in shaping the future of work. The discussion starts by reviewing how social dialogue, and collective bargaining in particular, can be complementary and flexible tools along with labour market regulation to foster a more rewarding and inclusive future of work. This is followed by a discussion of what type of government intervention may be required to keep bargaining systems fit for purpose and make the most of collective bargaining in a changing world of work. Finally, the chapter reviews how existing institutions and social partners are adjusting to the new challenges in the labour market, as well as the role of emerging actors and new practices.

# In Brief

## Key findings

Collective bargaining and social dialogue can help addressing the challenges posed by a changing world of work. As demographic and technological changes unfold, collective bargaining can allow companies to adjust wages, working time, work organisation and tasks to new needs in a flexible and pragmatic manner. It can help shaping new rights, adapting existing ones, regulating the use of new technologies, providing active support to workers transitioning to new jobs and anticipating skills needs.

Yet, the number of workers who are members of unions and covered by collective agreements have declined in many OECD countries. In addition, increases in different forms of non-standard employment in a number of countries pose a challenge to collective bargaining, as non-standard workers are under-represented by trade unions. This under-representation reflects both practical difficulties in organising non-standard workers and the historical focus of collective bargaining on standard employees, but also legal obstacles to collective bargaining for some non-standard workers such as the self-employed. Indeed, while labour law grants all *salaried* employees – whether in a standard or non-standard relationship – an undisputed legal right to collective bargaining, for workers usually classified as self-employed this right may be seen as infringing competition law. This is the case even though the International Labour Organisation (ILO) Convention on the right to organise and bargain collectively refers to *workers* in general. In this context, this chapter argues that:

- Enforcing the correct classification of workers and fighting misclassification is of particular importance in ensuring that workers benefit from the protection and rights to which they are entitled.

- However, a significant number of workers may still fall in a "grey zone" between the usual definitions of employee and self-employed, where genuine ambiguity exists about their employment status. For those workers, who share vulnerabilities with salaried employees, and for some self-employed workers in unbalanced power relationships, adapting existing regulations to extend collective bargaining rights may be necessary. For instance, several OECD countries have already sought to grant collective bargaining rights to some of these workers through tailored interventions in the labour law or explicit exemptions to the law prohibiting cartels.

While each country's history, situation and regulatory settings are different, this chapter argues that, despite the above-mentioned challenges, collective bargaining systems can still play a key role in promoting inclusive labour markets for workers and a level-playing field for all companies, including new ones. For example:

- Social partners have developed strategies to reach potential members in non-standard forms of work, first in challenging workers' status and classification, but also through lobbying on behalf of non-standard workers, adapting their bargaining practices to be more inclusive, or engaging in initiatives aimed at strengthening these workers' voice. In some OECD countries, unions have adapted their legal status to allow self-employed workers to become members, while others have created dedicated branches for non-standard workers. New independent unions have also been created.

- New vehicles for representing workers' interests have been developing in some OECD countries, such as Worker Centers or the Freelancers Union in the United States, or co-operatives of workers in some European countries. Yet, while these forms of workers' organisations can improve links and communication between non-standard workers, they cannot replace unions. In particular, they do not have the legal mandate to bargain collectively on behalf of their members or the ability to deliver on negotiated agreements. Therefore, they can complement unions rather than be a substitute for them; co-operation between traditional and new forms of workers' organisation is now emerging in some contexts.

- Employers' organisations are also being put to the test by changes to the world of work. They have an interest in ensuring a level playing field for their members in the face of new competitors, who may circumvent existing labour regulations – for instance, digital platforms often consider themselves as matchmakers rather than employers.

- Successful examples of bargaining in the temporary work agency sector (which emerged as an innovative form of employment decades ago) or in sectors where non-standard work is common, such as the cultural and creative industries, have proven that systems are able to adjust to cover different and new forms of work.

- A few innovative collective agreements have also recently been signed in European OECD countries between unions and companies – including digital platforms, but they remain very limited. Platforms have taken some initiatives to allow workers to express their concerns and pre-empt the introduction of new legislation on the way they operate.

## Introduction

Over the last three decades, collective bargaining and social dialogue systems have been facing a combination of major challenges resulting from technological and organisational changes, globalisation, the decline of the manufacturing sector, the expansion of non-standard forms of work and population ageing (see Chapter 2).[1] In addition, policy reforms leading to a decentralisation of bargaining systems, combined with a near general long-term decline in union membership rates and increasing individualisation of the employment relationship, led to a further weakening of collective bargaining. Since 1985, trade union membership has halved on average across OECD countries, while coverage of collective agreements signed at the national, sector or firm level has gone down by one-third – see OECD (2017[11]) for a detailed discussion of these trends.

The weakening of labour relations poses serious challenges for workers' rights, benefits and protections. It also increasingly leaves employers and employers' organisations without a clear counterpart for discussions on sector- or firm-specific issues. While this may reduce labour conflicts or increase firm's flexibility in some contexts, it may also lead to other forms of social conflict, such as boycotts or social media campaigns, and other types of regulation, as the scope for "self-organisation" among employers and workers on the ground is reduced.

While collective bargaining and social dialogue face increasing challenges in a changing world of work, they can nonetheless help address its increasing complexity and diversity. There are many examples showing that social partners and collective bargaining systems can adjust, develop new strategies and reshape existing institutions. In particular, they can contribute to addressing the realities of global markets, increased competition and fragmentation of production, and ensure that all workers and companies, including small and medium-sized enterprises, reap the benefits of technological innovation, organisational changes and globalisation (European Commission, 2018[2]).

In this context it is important to acknowledge the potential flexibility offered by social dialogue and collective bargaining in seeking solutions to issues of common concerns[2] and to discuss how they can complement public policies in social protection systems, life-long learning schemes and the regulation of employment relationships (ILO, 2019[3]). This chapter focuses on the role of collective bargaining as a "fundamental principle and right at work"[3] and a key labour market institution that allows reaching mutually beneficial agreements about work organisation and conditions, and provides room for interactions between social partners. However, the precise role played by collective bargaining in shaping the future of work will depend on national institutional settings, practices and traditions (OECD, 2018[4]).

This chapter builds on the analysis on the functioning of collective bargaining systems in OECD (2017[1]) as well as their role for good labour market performance in OECD (2018[4]), and reviews the ongoing debate on the role of labour relations in a changing world of work. In particular, this chapter assesses the extent to which existing models remain fit for purpose, and discusses how traditional actors can adjust to the new challenges.[4] Section 5.1 illustrates how collective bargaining can complement public policies in strengthening labour market security and adaptability. Section 5.2 discusses adaptations to existing regulations that may be required to ensure that all workers in vulnerable situations get adequate worker representation and access to collective bargaining. Section 5.3 discusses the strategies developed by social partners to reach out to those in non-standard and new forms of work and business. Section 5.4 reviews other forms of labour organisation that are emerging in some OECD countries and their relations with the more traditional ones.

## 5.1. Collective bargaining in a changing world of work

### 5.1.1. Collective agreements can be flexible tools to address some of today's and tomorrow's challenges

Through collective bargaining and social dialogue, trade unions (simply called "unions" hereafter) play a crucial role articulating and pressing demands for higher wages, as well as representing the collective interests of workers more generally and facilitating an exchange between workers and their employers on various aspects of the working life (Freeman and Medoff, 1984[5]).

Depending on national regulatory settings as well as actual practices and traditions, unions' access to information, consultation and participation in decision making at the workplace can also enhance occupational health and safety and improve work organisation – e.g. by fostering high performance work practices, such as team work, autonomy, task discretion, mentoring, job rotation, and applying new learning (OECD, 2016[6]). Through collective agreements, in particular sector-level agreements that also allow covering small and medium-sized enterprises, collective bargaining can also help spreading best practices in terms of personnel management, training, health and safety, technology usage, insurance, or retirement packages.

When undertaken in a constructive spirit, accommodating the need for balancing inclusiveness and flexibility (OECD, 2018[7]), and within a framework that guarantees the respect of fundamental labour rights and a balance in bargaining power, collective bargaining can help companies respond to demographic and technological change. Collective bargaining allows them to adapt pay, working time, work organisation and jobs themselves, to new needs, in a more flexible and pragmatic – but yet fair – manner than that entailed by changing labour law.

Recent agreements in some OECD countries show that new issues related to work-life balance, increased flexibility around working time arrangement, or regulation of the use of new technological tools, are gaining ground in collective bargaining – see European Commission (2018[2]).

In France for instance the "right to disconnect", i.e. the right not to read and answer work-related emails and calls outside working hours, was provided in 2014 in a sectoral agreement for business consulting, followed by the wholesale trade sector in 2016. These agreements introduce "an obligation to disconnect distant communication tools". Similar provisions have been signed at firm level, for instance by the insurance company AXA, the energy company Areva and the telecommunication company Orange. The HR Director of Orange then published a very influential report on digital transformation and quality of life at work (Mettling, 2015[8]). The report was the basis for a law in 2017 which acknowledged the "right to disconnect" among the topics of mandatory annual negotiations with unions. In the absence of an agreement, employers have to draft a charter in consultation with the works council or the employee representatives.

Similar agreements including the recognition of the right to turn off company phones or to not answer work-related calls outside working hours have been signed at company level. Volkswagen was first in 2012 by preventing email exchanges on its internal servers between 6.15pm and 7am. AXA and the Spanish Trade Union Confederation of Workers' Commissions (CCOO) also concluded a similar agreement in 2017 in Spain.

There are also signs that the more general issues of work-life balance and working time flexibility are gaining prominence in collective agreements, possibly reflecting changes in workers' preferences and company recognition of the negative impact of job strain on productivity (Saint-Martin, Inanc and Prinz, 2018[9]). In 2018, in the region of Baden Württemberg in Germany, a landmark agreement in the metalworking sector has introduced the possibility for workers to reduce their working week from the standard 35 hours to 28 hours, while preserving the right to return to full-time work. In return, firms have obtained the flexibility to offer more 40-hour-a-week contracts to workers who wish to work more.

Similar arrangements have been negotiated in other sectors in Germany: Deutsche Bahn, Deutsche Post as well as local transports in Bavaria negotiated similar agreements giving the choice between more money and more time off as means to improve work-life-balance. "À-la-carte models" in sectoral agreements in Denmark and the Netherlands (Ibsen and Keune, 2018[10]) also give individual employees significant flexibility to choose between money and time.

Finally, unions and employers are engaging in "algorithm negotiations", i.e. they are including as a subject of bargaining the use of artificial intelligence, big data and electronic performance monitoring ("people analytics") in the workplace, as well as their implications for occupational health and safety, privacy, evaluation of work performance and hiring and firing decisions (De Stefano, 2018[11]). Several collective agreements have started regulating the use of technology not only in monitoring workers but also in directing their work (Moore, Upchurch and Whittaker, 2018[12]).

### 5.1.2. Collective bargaining can complement public policies in enhancing labour market security and adaptability

The OECD's work on displaced workers (OECD, 2018[4]) has highlighted the significant role that collective bargaining, in particular at the sectoral level, can play in enhancing labour market security[5] and strengthening workers' labour market adaptability. As evolving demands for products and services as well as technological change are quickly affecting skills needs, social partners can provide active support to workers displaced from their existing jobs to help them back into good jobs.

The Swedish Job Security Councils (JSCs) are one of the most notable examples of this (OECD, 2015[13]). They provide support and guidance to displaced workers, even before displacement occurs, as well as access to training and reskilling opportunities in the case of plant closures and mass layoffs. JSCs allow companies and unions to trade exemptions from the "last in, first out"[6] rule for collective dismissals in exchange for a timely[7] and effective reallocation of displaced workers (Engblom, 2017[14]). JSCs are jointly owned by employers' organisations and unions (the government has no role). Their funding (which comes entirely from employers) is negotiated in collective agreements along with wage increases and unions frequently hold back on the latter to safeguard JSC funding. JSCs also illustrate the advantage of sector level bargaining[8], which allows to distribute the risks and the accompanying costs of displacement over an entire sector. All workers covered by a collective agreement are covered by the JSC, including non-union members. To be eligible, workers need to have worked in their company for at least 12 months. JSCs are a complement to the Public Employment Service (PES). They can provide a top-up to unemployment benefits as well as coaching, training and upskilling services. A similar model to the Job Security Councils exists in Austria, where Outplacement Labour Foundations provide assistance, guidance, reskilling solutions and practical training to displaced workers. They also provide extended unemployment insurance, especially to those workers most in need.

Beyond supporting displaced workers, the social partners can also play a role in anticipating skills needs. Unions and employers' organisations are involved in skills assessment and anticipation exercises in a majority of OECD countries (OECD, 2016[15]). For instance, the JSCs' upskilling services are partly based on a skills barometer which they run twice a year and which allows JSCs to anticipate skills needs. In addition to "outplacement" foundations, Austria also has Inplacement Labour Foundations which have a more forward-looking element and help companies/sectors obtain qualified personnel in case of shortage. Because Labour Foundations are owned by the social partners, skills needs can be identified swiftly. In Germany, a 2016 agreement in the metal, engineering and technology sector titled "Training and qualification for industry 4.0 – managing change successfully", committed to analysing all vocational and lifelong training programmes offered by the industry to assess their adequacy to the growing use of data exchange and automation in manufacturing. More generally, in several OECD countries, social partners are represented on sectoral skills councils, which produce industry-specific long-term projections to ensure that current qualifications meet future demand for skills (OECD, 2019[16]).

Crucially, the social partners can help ensure that workers get enough life-long training to adapt to ongoing changes. As discussed in Chapter 6, equipping workers with the right skills in a context of technical and occupational changes is a key challenge for shaping a future of work that is more inclusive and rewarding. Access to life-long training for workers can be negotiated and secured in collective agreements and is an increasingly important issue of collective bargaining. For instance in 2016, unions in the metal sector in Italy traded lower-than-expected wage increases for a new provision at the sector level, ensuring a minimum amount of employer-supported yearly training to all workers, irrespective of the company they work for.[9] In Denmark, a national-level tripartite agreement was signed in 2017 that specifically focused on adult and continuing training. It included a series of initiatives over four years to increase and improve the access to and the quality of adult learning. In particular, the agreement set up a new "reconversion fund" of around EUR 53 million allowing workers to undertake further training on their own initiative. Yet there exists a substantial margin for improving the inclusion of training provisions in collective bargaining: on average in OECD countries, only about 15% of firms are covered by an agreement containing provisions on training[10] (OECD, 2019[16]). One way of ensuring a broad-based access to training and lifelong learning for workers in the future of work is to promote collective bargaining over these programmes.

The social partners can also play an important role in managing and funding training programmes, as well as contributing to their design and their evaluation. Table 5.1 shows that social partners play a significant role in managing and funding training programmes in several OECD countries. A particularly interesting case is that of the O&O funds (*Opleidings- en Ontwikkelingsfonds*) in the Netherlands, which are financed primarily through a compulsory payroll levy fixed by collective agreement. O&O funds provide lifelong learning to workers to keep them "up-to-date" and ready to find new jobs in the future. The funds also promote campaigns on the importance of training, and finance or kick-start projects on the ground. Again, a constant exchange between social partners allows O&O funds to anticipate skill needs.

**Table 5.1. How much are social partners' involved in training programmes in OECD countries?**

| | Country | | | |
|---|---|---|---|---|
| 1) Trade unions and / or employers finance some ad hoc training initiatives | Australia<br>Chile<br>Czech Republic | Estonia<br>Finland | Latvia<br>Norway | United Kingdom<br>United States |
| 2) Employers pay a compulsory training levy to a government fund | Canada (QB)<br>Ireland | Korea<br>Poland | Spain | |
| 3) Social partners are in charge of managing training funds[1] | Austria<br>Belgium<br>Denmark | France<br>Germany<br>Greece | Iceland<br>Italy<br>Luxembourg | Netherlands<br>Sweden<br>Switzerland |

Note: QB: Québec. "Training" in this table refers both to vocational training and lifelong learning. Categories 1 to 3 are not mutually exclusive. Countries are classified based on social partners' highest level of engagement on average across industries. This means that countries in category 3 might also belong to categories 1 or 2 (and those in category 2 could belong to category 1). For instance, in France, there is a compulsory levy on medium and large firms (to finance the *Compte Personnel de Formation*), but social partners are further involved in the funding and managing of training funds – hence France appears in category 3. In addition, in countries in categories 1 or 2, social partners may also manage a training fund in *one* specific sector: this is the case in Spain and the United States, where social partners manage training funds in the construction sector. However, these examples are not representative of the situation in the whole country.
1. At least in several sectors. Depending on countries, funds can be compulsory or voluntary, and they can be mandated by law or agreed upon through collective bargaining.
Source: OECD Policy Questionnaires on Collective bargaining as well as information collected in the context of the OECD project on "Getting skills right: promoting workforce adaptability".

Finally, in several countries (for instance in the Czech Republic, Finland, Luxembourg, Slovenia or the United Kingdom), the social partners also act as direct training providers – see OECD (2019[16]) and Chapter 6 for a detailed discussion of the role of social partners for adult learning and the importance of ensuring the quality of the training offered.

In a time of rapid change and despite the decline in membership and coverage, the role of social partners in finding tailor-made solutions, managing transitions, anticipating and filling skills needs may, therefore, be increasingly important. Moreover, Klindt (2017[17]) argues that investing in skills is not only useful to strengthen labour market adaptability and to help workers in case of displacement, but it is also a winning strategy for union renewal. Partnership with employers can be a revitalisation strategy for weak unions to attract new members, but also for more established unions to keep their roots in the local community.

### 5.1.3. But challenges are accumulating…

Over the last three decades, collective bargaining systems have been under increasing pressure: the proportion of union members among employees in the OECD fell from 30% in 1985 to 16% in 2016, while the proportion of employees covered by collective agreements declined from 45% to 32%.[11] The rise of different forms of non-standard work in a number of OECD countries discussed in Chapter 2 poses an additional challenge to collective bargaining, as non-standard workers are less likely to be unionised than standard workers (Figure 5.1). With the exception of Israel, this is the case even when controlling for composition effects (linked to gender, age, education, industry, occupation, firm size and part-time vs. full-time employment).[12] On average, when controlling for composition effects, the ratio of trade union density among non-standard workers relative to standard workers is not significantly higher in countries where trade union density among standard workers is higher and is remarkably similar across countries in all three panels.[13] This suggests that the lower unionisation of non-standard workers does not depend on country-specific characteristics but rather reflects difficulties in organising non-standard workers that are inherent to the non-standard status itself.

## Figure 5.1. Non-standard workers are underrepresented by trade unions

Actual and adjusted ratio of trade union density among non-standard workers relative to standard workers (%), latest available year

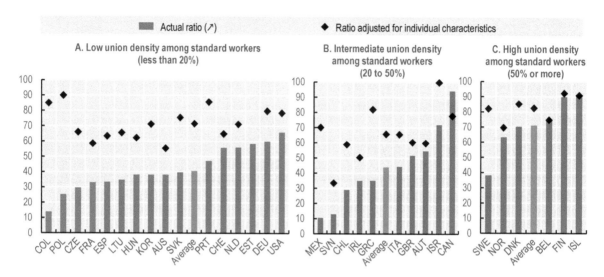

Note: Countries are grouped by degree of unionisation among standard workers. Figures refer to 2010-12 for Greece and the Slovak Republic; 2013 for France; 2015 for Germany and Hungary; 2016 for Finland; 2014-16 for Austria, Belgium, the Czech Republic, Denmark, Iceland, Israel, Italy, Lithuania, the Netherlands, Norway, Poland, Portugal, Slovenia, Spain and Switzerland; 2017 for Canada, Chile, Colombia, Estonia, Ireland, Korea, Sweden, the United Kingdom and the United States; and 2018 for Australia and Mexico. Average is the unweighted average of countries shown in each panel (excepted Estonia in Panel A).

Non-standard workers are those without an open-ended employment contract. The precise categories of workers included in the chart differ across countries (for further details see Annex 5.A). The adjusted ratio for individual characteristics is based on the marginal effect of being in a non-standard form of work relative to being in an open-ended contract calculated from a probit regression controlling for sex, age groups, educational levels, industry, public vs private sector (except for Ireland), occupation, firm size (except for the United States) and full-time vs. part-time employment. The data necessary for this adjustment are not available for Estonia.

The correlation between the adjusted ratio and trade union density among standard workers is weak (0.39) and statistically significant at the 5% level but becomes statistically insignificant (and even weaker, 0.24) when excluding Finland and Iceland.

Source: OECD estimates based on the Labour Force Survey (LFS) for Canada, the Encuesta de Caracterización Socioeconómica Nacional (CASEN) for Chile, the Gran Encuesta Integrada de Hogares (GEIH) for Colombia, the Finnish Working Life Barometer (FWLB) for Finland, the Enquête statistique sur les ressources et conditions de vie (SRCV) for France, the German Socio-Economic Panel (SOEP) for Germany, the Quarterly National Household Survey (QNHS) for Ireland, the Encuesta Nacional de Ocupación y Empleo (ENOE) for Mexico, the Labour Force Survey (LFS) for the United Kingdom, the Current Population Survey (CPS), May Supplement for the United States and the European Social Survey (ESS) for all other European countries not listed above (excepted Estonia, Hungary and Sweden) and Israel. For Australia, Estonia (actual ratio only), Hungary, Korea and Sweden, actual ratios are based on data provided by national statistical authorities: Characteristics of Employment (COE) Survey for Australia, Labour Force Survey (LFS) for Hungary, Economically Active Population Survey (EAPS) for Korea and Labour Force Survey (LFS) for Sweden, while adjusted ratios are OECD estimates based on the Household, Income and Labour Dynamics in Australia (HILDA) for Australia, the European Social Survey (ESS) for Estonia, Hungary and Sweden and the Korean Labor and Income Panel Study (KLIPS) for Korea.

StatLink 🔍 http://dx.doi.org/10.1787/888933966692

In particular, non-standard workers face practical difficulties and legal obstacles in joining unions (see Section 5.1.4 below). Their lower unionisation rates may also be the result of unions historically focusing on standard workers' needs, rather than those of non-standard ones. Insider-outsider theories have argued that unions may not only neglect the interest of outsiders (e.g. the unemployed, low-skilled, youth, and those in non-standard employment) but may even accept the development of temporary and part time employment as a buffer for their members (insiders with full-time permanent contact), thereby increasing the duality of labour markets (Saint-Paul, 1996[18]; Bertola, 1999[19]; Lindbeck and Snower, 1986[20]).

However, empirical evidence for these theories is partial and mixed: OECD (2018[7]) shows that while temporary employment does not vary across different bargaining systems, it is higher in countries with higher bargaining coverage. This is in line with the finding by Salvatori (2009[21]) who looks at 21 European countries and shows that unionised workplaces are more likely to use temporary employment. But these results are contrasted by others; for instance, Gramm and Schnell (2001[22]) and Autor (2003[23]) do not find corresponding evidence when looking at temporary agency work in the United States. Furthermore, other research based on the content of collective agreements shows that the fact that unions take into account the concerns of agency workers does not necessarily depend on their membership composition (Benassi and Vlandas, 2016[24]).

The general decline in trade union density is also sometimes interpreted as resulting from changing attitudes and preferences among workers, in particularly those from younger generations. However, as shown in Box 5.1 below, lower rates of unionisation among young workers cannot be interpreted as signalling a change of preferences away from collective action, or a rejection of trade unions per se. In fact, Box 5.1 shows that support for collective action and trust in unions is higher among young people compared with older workers in a majority of countries.

Even if traditional forms of labour relations are under increasing pressure, the need for collective expression and representation of workers and employers' interests will not fade away as young workers enter the labour market in new types of jobs. The alternative to collective bargaining is, indeed, not individual bargaining but either state regulation or no bargaining at all, as only few employees can effectively negotiate their terms of employment with their employer (OECD, 2017[1]).

Finally, extending the coverage of job-related benefits (minimum wages, health plans, unemployment benefits, etc.) to non-standard workers (see Chapters 4 and 7) or improving their job mobility prospects is not a functional equivalent to guaranteeing access to collective bargaining. As highlighted before, collective bargaining is not only a fundamental right, but also a flexible tool that can be mobilised by workers as well as employers to address work-related challenges (including some that cannot be currently anticipated) at national, sectoral or company-level.

---

### Box 5.1. Are young workers turning their noses up at unions?

Trade-union density is particularly low among young workers and has fallen by more than the rate for older workers since 2000 in close to half of the countries shown in Figure 5.2. According to some, this pattern reflects the different preferences of younger generations (Blanchflower, 2007[25]). Young workers have been described as more individualistic than older ones (Berry and Mcdaniel, 2018[26]), and less prone to engage in collective action. Alternatively, some say that they favour environmental and consumer organisations, thus crowding out unions (Inglehart, 1997[27]). Yet another argument sometimes made is that younger workers find unions unattractive and old-fashioned. Unions themselves have taken up this last argument (Vandaele, forthcoming[28]). Could systematically different preferences among young workers explain their lower rates of unionisation?

Using available longitudinal survey data on attitudes, it is hard to find clear evidence supporting this hypothesis. As shown in Figure 5.3 (Panels A and B), in a majority of countries, respondents aged 20-34 are more attached to both individual freedom *and* solidarity with others than those aged 35-54. Young respondents are also more supportive of collective actions such as attending a demonstration or raising funds for a social or political cause than their older peers in most countries (Panels C and D). Finally, the proportion of 20-34 year olds who are members of environmental (8.4%) or consumer organisations (6.5%) is on par with that of older respondents (9.5% and 7.7%) (World Value Survey, 2010-2014, see appendix for details). In addition, contrary to the "crowding out" hypothesis,

Ebbinghaus et al. (2011[29]) find that such engagement is in fact positively associated with union membership.

Moreover, in contrast with commonly held ideas about young workers disliking unions, confidence in trade unions is higher among young workers than among older ones in 23 out of 32 countries (Figure 5.4, Panel A). These measures are consistent with various country case studies: for instance, Bryson et al. (2005[30]) found a substantial frustrated demand for unionisation among young workers in Canada, the United Kingdom and the United States.

**Figure 5.2. Trend in union density among youth aged 20-34 in selected OECD countries**

Young-to-adults ratio of union density, 2000's and latest year available (%)

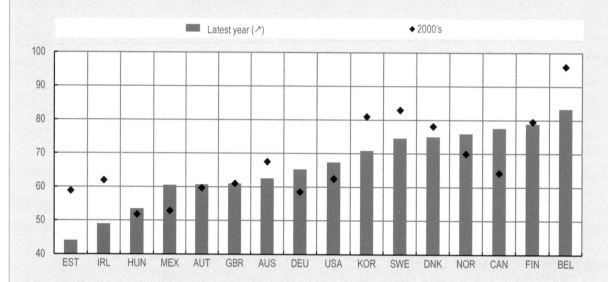

Note: Trade union density by age group for Austria, Belgium, Denmark, Finland, Germany, Norway and Sweden have been adjusted for the overall trade union density by using the share of age groups in total union membership and total number of employees. Estimates based on the European Social Survey (due to size of the sample or of subcategories in certain countries) may be imprecise and are only reproduced to illustrate common patterns across OECD countries. 2000's refers to 2000 for Australia, Canada, Estonia, Sweden, the United Kingdom and the United States; 2001 for Germany; 2002 for Austria, Belgium, Denmark, Finland and Norway; 2003 for Ireland; 2004 for Hungary (second quarter) and Korea; and 2005 for Mexico. The latest year available is 2014 for Denmark; 2015 for Germany and Hungary (second quarter); 2016 for Austria, Belgium, Finland and Norway; 2017 for Canada, Estonia, Ireland, Sweden and the United Kingdom; and 2018 for Australia, Korea, Mexico and the United States. Youth refers to employees aged 20-34 and adults to those aged 35-54.
Source: OECD estimates based on the European Social Survey (ESS) for Austria, Belgium, Denmark and Norway, the Labour Force Survey (LFS) for Canada, the Finnish Working Life Barometer (FWLB) for Finland, the German Socio-Economic Panel (SOEP) for Germany, the Quarterly National Household Survey (QNHS) for Ireland, the Encuesta Nacional de Ocupación y Empleo (ENOE) for Mexico, and the Current Population Survey Merged Outgoing Rotation Groups (CPS-MORG) for the United States. Data provided by national statistical authorities based on the Survey of Employee Earnings, Benefits and Trade Union Membership (EEBTUM) and the Characteristics of Employment (COE) Survey for Australia, the Labour Force Survey (LFS) for Estonia, the Labour Force Survey (LFS) for Hungary, the Economically Active Population Survey (EAPS) for Korea, the Labour Force Survey for Sweden, and the Labour Force Survey for the United Kingdom.

StatLink ᵐˢᴾ http://dx.doi.org/10.1787/888933966711

In these latter two countries, higher trust in trade unions among young workers is associated with a higher perception of unions' indispensability in protecting workers' rights. However, in two-thirds of the countries represented in Figure 5.4 (Panel B), young workers appear less convinced than older ones that workers need strong unions to protect their interests. This leads to a surprising pattern in countries like Denmark, France, Latvia, Lithuania, Slovenia, or Sweden, where young respondents are more confident in unions than older respondents but less convinced that workers need them to protect their rights. Explaining these contradictory patterns is beyond the scope of this box. However, these data do *not* support strong claims about young workers' weaker interest in collective action driving the age-related membership differential.

## Figure 5.3. Individual values and support for collective action among young people

Young-to-adults ratios

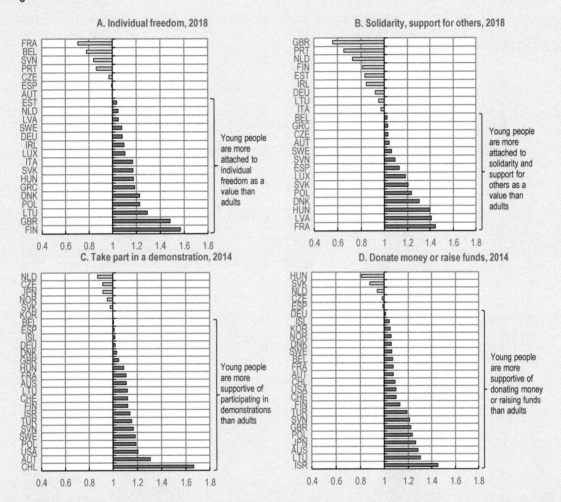

Note: Statistics in Panels A and B are based on a question about respondents' three most important personal values. In Panels C and D, statistics refer to individuals who ever participated or might participate in particular collective actions. See Annex 5.B for further details.
Source: OECD calculations based on the Standard Eurobarometer 89, March 2018 (Panels A and B) and the International Social Survey Programme (ISSP) 2014, Citizenship module II (Panels C and D).

StatLink ᵐˢᴸ http://dx.doi.org/10.1787/888933966730

If not preferences, then what could explain this differential? Structural labour market factors are good candidates for an explanation. Indeed, young workers tend to work in sectors characterised by weak union presence, which limits their opportunity to join unions in the first place. They are also disproportionately employed on non-standards contracts, which reduces the benefits and increases the costs of union membership (Ebbinghaus, Göbel and Koos, 2011[29]). Annex Figure 5.B.1 in Annex 5.B shows that composition effects provide a partial answer to the puzzle of young people's lower unionisation. When controlling for various factors including gender, educational level, type of contract (temporary vs open-ended), industry, public vs private sector, occupation, firm size and full-time vs. part-time employment, the gap in young-to-adult union membership is reduced in all countries studied. However, it is closed in none. Composition effects significantly close the gap in the United States, Canada, or France but explain relatively little in the United Kingdom or Germany – while a differential of around 30% remain in these last three countries. While non-standard employment has developed in the last two decades, composition effects are not explaining a larger part of the membership differential in recent years compared with the 2000s.

**Figure 5.4. Trust and perceived necessity of trade unions among young people aged 20-34**

Young-to-adults ratios

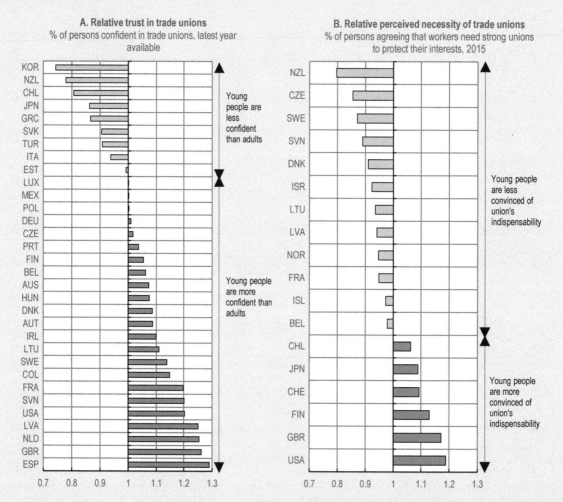

Note: Youth refers to persons aged 20-34 and adults to those aged 35-54. The latest year available in Panel A refers to 2010 for Japan and Korea; 2011 for Chile, New Zealand and the United States; 2012 for Colombia and Mexico; 2016 for Australia; and 2018 for all the European countries. In Panel B, Belgium refers to Flanders only and age groups for Denmark refer to youth aged 26-35 and adults aged 36-55. For further details, see Annex 5.B.
Source: Panel A: OECD calculations based on the Australian Election Study (AES) for Australia, Eurobarometer 89.1, March 2018 for the European countries, and the World Value Survey (WVS) for all other countries. Panel B: OECD calculations based on the International Social Survey Program (ISSP) 2015, Work Orientation module IV and the Pew research Center Poll (march 2015) for the United States.

StatLink ⬛ http://dx.doi.org/10.1787/888933966749

Another prevalent explanation in the literature is that union density is lower among young workers because they have not yet had a chance to evaluate the benefit of union membership. Looking at data from 24 countries, Givan and Hipp (2012[31]) find a positive correlation between union membership and perception of unions' efficacy. Exposure to union benefit and union membership would be part of one positive self-reinforcing loop. Yet because of their limited labour market experience, young workers might have a limited awareness of unions and their purpose (Keune, 2015[32]) – in other words the probability that they have not yet entered that loop is high. According to Bryson et al. (2005[30]), the membership differential is not all that surprising when considering that union membership is an experience good: it can only be properly valued after one has been exposed to it.

Beyond differences in work experiences, authors argue that young workers also face higher entry barriers to unionisation. Supply-side constraints such as employers' resistance to unionism, the lack of dedicated recruitment efforts from unions (Vandaele, 2012[33]), or the relatively high cost of membership rates might also explain the lower unionisation of young workers.

### 5.1.4. ...and there are legal obstacles to overcome

Beyond individual-level barriers, the organisation and representation of some non-standard forms of employment is hindered by concrete legal obstacles. If ILO Convention 98 on the right to organise and bargain collectively refers to workers in general[14], in practice, the right to bargain for non-salaried workers is subject to legal discussion as possibly infringing the application of antitrust regulations (Aloisi, 2018[34]; Linder, 1999[35]).

As illustrated in Figure 5.5, while salaried workers face only practical difficulties in exercising their collective rights (see Section 5.3 and Section 5.4 below), workers in the "grey zone" between dependent employment and self-employment (see Chapter 4 and Box 5.2 below) as well as genuine self-employed workers, who might nonetheless be in unbalanced power relationships with their employer/client, may also be barred from bargaining collectively due to laws prohibiting cartels, which tend to consider them as "undertakings" (Daskalova, 2018[36]).

Traditionally, the primary objective of competition law has been to defend consumers from anti-competitive practices by sellers. When this objective came into contradiction with the labour law objective of protecting workers, courts and legislators have intervened to clarify legal interactions. In particular, courts have detailed the conditions under which collective bargaining could be exempt from the cartel prohibition established in competition law. For instance, the US Clayton Antitrust Act of 1914 states that "the labor of a human being is not a commodity or article of commerce". Therefore, "labor (…) organizations, instituted for the purposes of mutual help, [should not] be held or construed to be illegal combinations or conspiracies in restraint of trade, under the antitrust laws" (§7 Clayton Act, 15 U.S.C. § 18). In EU competition law, the clarification came from the Court of Justice in the so-called Albany case (C-67/96) – which arose from a dispute between a company and a pension fund regulated by a collective agreement in 1999. In this instance, the European Court of Justice also ruled that collective agreements for employees fall outside the scope of competition law.[15]

However, as forms of work become more heterogeneous and self-employment increases, especially in the context of platform-mediated services, new challenges face courts and legislators. The standard approach in antitrust enforcement has often been to consider all self-employed workers as undertakings and therefore any collective agreement reached by self-employed workers – including those in the "grey zone" and self-employed workers in an unbalanced power relationship – as a cartel.

In Ireland, for instance, the national competition authority decided in 2004 that self-employed actors could not set tariffs and contract terms collectively.[16] In the Netherlands, in 2006 and 2007, associations representing freelance workers in the performing arts sector and an association representing orchestras signed an agreement that included a minimum fee for self-employed musicians temporarily replacing orchestra members. Reacting to this, the Dutch competition authority issued a reflection document warning that the setting of minimum tariffs by a union representing the self-employed was a price-fixing scheme contrary to competition law.[17] Following this statement, the employer association withdrew from the agreement (Daskalova, 2018[36]). The argument that collective bargaining for self-employed workers was incompatible with competition law has also been used in the United States by Uber to challenge a 2017 ordinance by the City of Seattle that allowed drivers to unionise and bargain together.[18]

**Figure 5.5. Access to collective bargaining for different forms of employment, current situation**

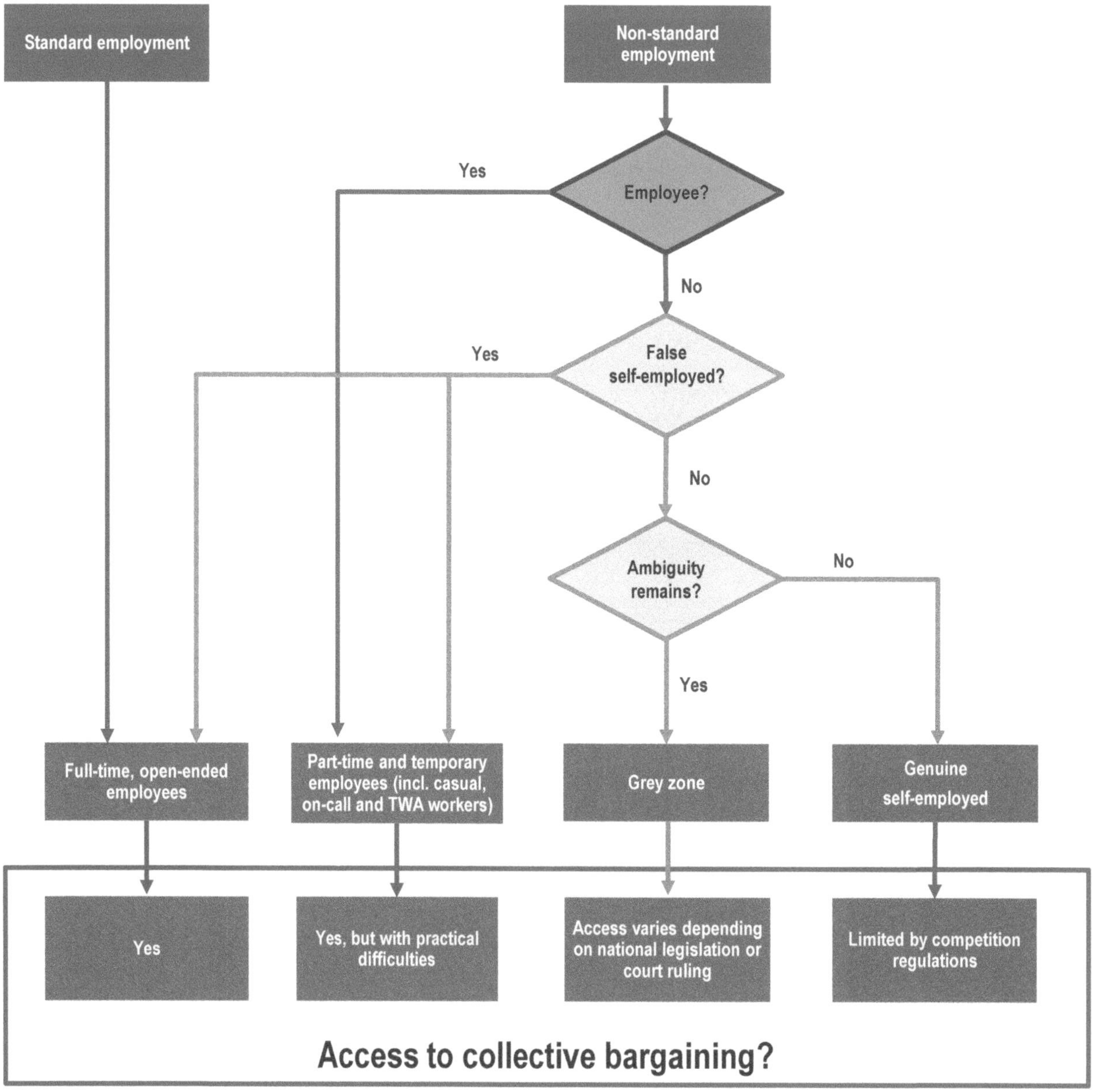

Note: The figure is an adapted version of Figure 4.1 in Chapter 4 for collective bargaining access. It maps standard and non-standard employment into the different categories of workers. Diamonds correspond to classification decisions that can be taken either by the parties (e.g. stipulated in a written contract between employers and workers) or by adjudicators (courts or enforcement agencies). Grey diamonds refer to decisions that are most often taken by adjudicators. The bottom rectangles refer to access to collective bargaining.

---

**Box 5.2. Who are the workers in the grey zone?**

In most cases where individuals are falsely classified by the parties as self-employed (e.g. in a written contract between employers and workers), courts will be able to determine this relatively easily using the criteria and tests that have been developed in statutory legislation or jurisprudence (see Figure 5.5). In establishing whether a worker is an employee, courts typically look at: financial dependence; control and subordination; the worker's integration in the organisation; who provides the tools, materials or machines; the regularity of payments; the extent to which the worker takes on financial/entrepreneurial risk; the degree of discretion over the continuation of the relationship, etc.

However, there are also cases where a genuine ambiguity remains since test criteria may point in different directions. These cases fall in a "grey zone" between self- and dependent employment. Workers in this grey zone, who are usually formally classified as self-employed, share a number of characteristics with dependent employees, usually resulting in an unbalanced power relationship with their employer/client. There is therefore a case for extending to them certain rights and protections usually granted to employees by labour law.

Countries have taken different routes to extend rights and protections to workers in the grey zone. Some countries have identified very specific occupations to which certain labour rights and protections have been extended. Other countries have focussed on the specific category of workers who are dependent on one employer/client for most of their income (the so-called "dependent" self-employed).

A handful of countries have relied on a vaguer definition of an intermediate category (or "third worker category") to which some of the rights and protections of employees have been extended. While this solution potentially covers a larger set of workers, it also increases the danger that the objective of litigation is shifted down from obtaining employee status to merely obtaining worker status, and that it could be used to downgrade the degree of protection of workers that would have otherwise been classified as employees.

Finally, another approach consists in treating everyone in the grey zone as an employee as far as certain aspects of labour law are concerned. In practice, this would be equivalent to defining a "residual category" capturing those cases where employment tests fail to come to clear conclusions about self-employment status. Although so far no country has systematically adopted this approach, it was followed in a couple of cases by the supreme courts of both California and Sweden. The latter concluded that, because the circumstances of the relationship were ambiguous and it was difficult to make a clear judgement, an employment relationship would be assumed (see Chapter 4 for a more extensive discussion).

---

The case of the Dutch substitute musicians was brought to the European Court of Justice (ECJ) which in 2014 ruled that, while genuine self-employed should continue to be seen as "enterprises", the so-called "false self-employed" are not to be considered undertakings for the purpose of competition rules (Daskalova, 2018[36]; Aloisi, 2018[34]).[19] If, on the one hand, the ECJ left the door open to agreements signed on behalf of the false self-employed (Ankersmit, 2015[37]), it also left to legislators and lower courts the challenge of distinguishing genuine self-employment and entrepreneurship from false self-employment.

In addition, workers in the grey zone who share some of the vulnerabilities inherent to an employee status but are not false self-employed are still barred from accessing bargaining following that ruling. Moreover, the ruling also forbids collective bargaining for genuinely self-employed workers that nevertheless are in unbalanced power relationship vis-à-vis their employer/client.

As forms of work continue to diversify, the question of access to collective bargaining for new technology-induced forms of employment (i.e. platform work – see Chapter 2) and other forms of work in the "grey zone", such as dependent self-employment – where a self-employed worker's income is dependent on only one or a few clients – is a key contemporary challenge for labour relations (ILO, 2019[3]).

## 5.2. Adapting regulations to more diverse forms of employment

In light of the legal obstacles discussed in the previous section, legislators may have a role to play to adapt existing rules to the changing world of work and extend the legal access to collective bargaining to a larger share of workers, notably to workers in the "grey zone" as well as to some self-employed workers in unbalanced power relationship.

The European Committee of Social Rights of the Council of Europe has recently argued that in establishing collective bargaining rights "it (is) not sufficient to rely on distinctions between worker and self-employed. (…) Where providers of labour have no substantial influence on the content of contractual conditions, they must be given the possibility of improving the power imbalance through collective bargaining".[20]

Granting bargaining rights to workers in the "grey zone" and to self-employed workers in unbalanced power relationships may not only be desirable for fairness consideration, but also for efficiency reasons. Indeed, as discussed in Chapter 4 (see, in particular, Annex 4.A), disproportionate buyer power not compensated by sufficient bargaining power on the workers' side (including when these workers are self-employed) may lead to suboptimal employment and wage outcomes, as well as poor working conditions (Daskalova, 2018[36]). In this context, extending the right to bargain, or lifting the prohibition to collectively bargain on a case-by-case basis could improve both equity and efficiency of the market.[21]

In practice, the main difficulty is to identify some criteria for providing access to collective bargaining to avoid giving unregulated freedom to own-account self-employed workers – that is, self-employed without employees – to form cartels (even small ones), as this could have clear negative consequences for consumer welfare. Typically, the numerous existing cases of, for example, plumbers or professional services agreeing about sharing local markets or colluding to set prices should be prevented.[22]

Adapting regulations to allow workers in the "grey zone" and certain self-employed workers in unbalanced power relationships to bargain collectively is part of a broader framework to protect workers and address concerns like that of disproportionate employer market power discussed in other chapters. Giving these workers the possibility to voluntary "exit", i.e. to find another job (in terms of the skills they possess but also of restrictions to mobility in labour contracts) if their "voice" is not heard would also contribute to strengthen their bargaining power (see also Chapter 4).[23]

The following sections discuss some options which have been considered in OECD countries to grant bargaining rights to non-standard workers formally classified as self-employed but who share some characteristics with dependent employees and are in an unequal power relationship with their employer.

### 5.2.1. Enforcing the correct classification of the employment relationship

As discussed in Chapter 4, ensuring a correct classification of workers and fighting against misclassification is critical to enforce existing regulations and provide access to collective bargaining to workers who would otherwise be unjustly excluded. This has been a strategy frequently pursued by unions to include all non-standard forms of work into existing collective agreements (see Section 5.3) as providing a first step to access collective bargaining and a direct gateway to social and employment protection. However, even if all workers were correctly classified, there would still be an issue of bargaining rights for those workers in the grey zone, who cannot be easily classified, and for workers who are genuinely self-employed, but are in an unbalanced power relationship vis à vis certain buyers, with limited options to provide services to other buyers.

### 5.2.2. Tailoring labour law to grant access to bargaining to workers in the grey zone

Some OECD countries have given the right to bargain collectively to some workers in the grey zone by including them in an extended definition of who is an employee, as far as the labour relations legislation are concerned. This is the approach favoured since the mid-1960s in Canada, where the federal and many provincial labour relations legislations regarding collective bargaining explicitly includes "dependent contractors"[24] in its definition of employees, allowing for their inclusion in the same bargaining unit[25] as permanent full-time employees and usually with the same collective agreements (while it is uncommon for dependent contractors to have a separate collective agreement from permanent employees, this is legally permissible).[26]

In other OECD countries, specific categories of workers in the "grey zone", such as dependent contractors in Korea, *parasubordinati* in Italy, *Arbeitnehmerähnliche Personen* in Germany, *workers* in the United Kingdom, *TRADE* in Spain or, since January 2019, any "person working for money"[27] in Poland, are included in collective bargaining (or in the case of Spain they can sign specific "professional interests agreements", *acuerdos de interés profesional*) even if they are not formally employees.

### 5.2.3. Exempting specific forms of self-employment or sectors/occupations from the prohibition to bargain collectively

A complementary policy option explored by some governments consists in lifting the prohibition to bargain collectively for some workers who are genuinely self-employed, but are nonetheless in situations of power asymmetry vis-à-vis their customer/employer. This is the case when self-employed workers are facing employers/clients with a disproportionate buyer or monopsony power, while their outside options are limited (see Chapter 4 and below). Examples of such genuinely self-employed workers who might nonetheless be in unbalanced power relationships include for instance freelance musicians, actors, performing artists, or journalists – for whom the possibility of lifting the bargaining prohibition has been discussed in several countries – and granted in some.

Such objectives could be pursued either by adopting a pragmatic approach vis a vis groups of self-employed most exposed to unbalanced power relationships or by introducing explicit legal exemptions from the enforcement of the prohibition to bargain collectively.

In many cases, regulators and enforcement authorities have taken a case-by-case approach to avoid a strictly procedural analysis of cases involving those workers with little or no bargaining power and exit options. Moreover, in several countries (e.g. in France, Italy, Spain, etc.), independent unions of platform workers are de facto negotiating working conditions for their members even if they are classified as self-employed without any intervention from national antitrust authorities. The risk associated with this route is that it potentially creates uncertainty since it could be reversed without any legislative reform.

Another avenue that has been followed by a few OECD countries is to introduce explicit exemptions to the cartel prohibition for certain forms of self-employed, sectors or occupations (Daskalova, 2018[36]). In 2017, the Irish Parliament amended the Competition Act to include voice-over actors, session musicians and freelance journalists among the occupational categories that have the right to negotiate. Furthermore, it also opened the possibility to access collective bargaining for "fully dependent self-employed"[28] and not only "false self-employed" workers (as per the ECJ 2014 ruling – see above). Under Irish law, trade unions have to apply for the exemption, prove that the workers they want to represent fall in one of these two classes, and show that their request will have "no or minimal economic effect on the market in which the class of self-employed worker concerned operates", nor "lead to or result in significant costs to the State".

The 2017 Irish amendment has attracted many criticisms and is currently debated in the ILO. Irish employers as well as the International Organisation of Employers, on the one hand, expressed their concern about the lack of clarity in the criteria used to identify "fully dependent" and "false" self-employed workers. They also contested the lack of employer consultation in determining those criteria – currently the law states that the Government makes the decision in consultation with a trade union only.[29] On the other hand, those in favour of extending bargaining rights to self-employed workers experiencing power imbalance find the dependency criteria too stringent (a platform worker can work for more than two platforms and still be economically dependent). The condition of "no or minimal economic effect on the market" is also seen as a potentially insurmountable practical limit for workers (De Stefano and Aloisi, 2018[38]).

The Australian Competition and Consumer Act also allows businesses to collectively negotiate with suppliers or customers if the Australian Competition and Consumer Commission considers that collective bargaining would result in overall public benefits. The Australian Competition and Consumer Commission is currently undertaking a public consultation process regarding the creation of a class exemption for collective bargaining by small businesses (including independent contractors). A class exemption for collective bargaining would effectively provide a "safe harbour", so businesses that met eligibility criteria could engage in collective bargaining without breaching the competition law and without seeking approval from the Australian Competition and Consumer Commission.

Legal exemptions for specific categories of self-employed also exist in other OECD countries. In 1996, the US Department of Justice and Federal Trade Commission jointly ruled that physician networks which "collectively agree on prices or price-related terms and jointly market their services" do not infringe anti-cartel regulation provided that "they constitute 20% or less of the physicians in each physician specialty in the relevant geographic market" – 30% if they are part of non-exclusive network[30] – see DOJ/FTC (1996[39]).

In practical terms, targeted exemptions by sector or occupation are not always easy to define and apply; the list may need frequent updating, and the potential reversal of exemptions is a source of legal uncertainty for workers and businesses alike.[31]

In addition, as outlined before, small cartels can induce suboptimal outcomes for consumers. For that reason any exemptions aimed at granting bargaining rights to self-employed in situations of power imbalance should be based on a comprehensive costs-benefits analysis. One way to focus on workers in real need of access to collective bargaining would be to prioritise exemptions to those groups of self-employed workers that are likely to have few outside options.

Overall, granting some exemptions from the prohibitions to bargain to some self-employed in particular sectors or occupations is an option worth exploring and evaluating further.[32]

## 5.3. How can social partners enhance collective bargaining and social dialogue in non-standard and new forms of work?

Beyond legal obstacles, trade unions in most countries face a series of practical difficulties to organise and negotiate collective agreements on behalf of non-standard workers. These difficulties are partly linked to some of the intrinsic characteristics of non-standard work, such as frequent turnover and a limited attachment to a single workplace, and to the negative implications of these characteristics, e.g. reluctance to organise for fear of future retaliation, or a limited awareness of bargaining rights. Both the ILO Committee on Freedom of Association (CFA) and Committee of Experts on the application of Conventions and recommendations (CEACR) examined various cases and circumstances in which non-standard workers were restricted in the exercise of the right to freedom of association and the right to collective bargaining (ILO, 2016[40]).

In addition, in the past, some unions may have tended to focus primarily on standard employees.[33] Yet, there are now examples of unions which are making efforts in several OECD countries to reach out to new potential members, in particular non-standard and young workers, by adapting their strategies and changing their structure – see Benassi and Dorigatti (2014[41]) or Durazzi, Fleckenstein and Lee (2018[42]).

More generally, social dialogue and collective bargaining systems have demonstrated their ability to adjust to cover different and new types of employment relationships in a number of cases. The development of collective bargaining in the temporary work agency sector, for instance, illustrates how social partners have addressed challenging issues such as the regulation of triangular working relations – see Box 5.4 below and WEC and Uni Global (2018[43]). Instances of collective bargaining and social dialogue initiatives in the cultural and creative industry provide examples of how labour relations can develop in sectors with a high share of non-standard workers (Box 5.3). Both cases can provide inspiration for enhancing social dialogue and collective bargaining for workers in new forms of employment such as platform work, or for workers in the "grey zone" more generally.

### 5.3.1. Unions are diversifying their strategies to reach potential members

Trade unions are pursuing several strategies to extend their reach to non-standard forms of employment, and notably the most vulnerable ones. In most OECD countries, unions' main approach to reach new members has been to focus on challenging workers' status (i.e. reclassifying them as discussed before). For several decades, unions have been trying to bring non-standard workers under the umbrella of a standard contract through judicial reclassification – see Linder (1999[35]) for examples of reclassifications in the United States of grocery baggers, adult entertainment workers, drug testing subjects, "lessee" taxicab drivers, fruit pickers, and truck drivers.

More recently, the issue of classification has taken a new prominence with digital platforms. In the United Kingdom, for instance, the union GMB representing private hire drivers took the case of Uber drivers to an Employment Tribunal, which reclassified self-employed Uber drivers into workers covered by minimum wage legislation, and legal provisions for holiday pay and breaks.[34] Tribunals in Italy[35], France[36] and the Netherlands[37] recently took similar decisions. Moreover, even before these recent rulings, the risk of re-classification had led platforms in France and Italy to accept to open discussions or negotiations with recognised unions or workers' representatives (see Section 5.4.2).

Another strategy has been to lobby for public policy interventions restricting the use of non-standard forms of employment or enhancing the quality of these jobs at either national or local level. In Korea, for instance, trade unions and civil society organisations created the "Alliance for Nonstandard Workers" in 2000, which in 2006 succeeded in pushing the Government to limit the use of fixed-term contracts and outlaw discrimination based on employment status[38] (Fleckenstein and Lee, 2018[44]).

Unions in some cases have also changed bargaining practices to ensure better outcomes for non-standard workers. For instance, the Korean Confederation of Trade Unions launched its "solidarity wage" initiative in 2013, which promoted lump-sum pay increases rather than percentage increases with the explicit aim of "closing the wage gap between standard and nonstandard workers" (Durazzi, Fleckenstein and Lee, 2018[42]).

Finally, unions are also exploring other ways to strengthen workers' voice, either by putting pressure on employers – as in the United States through "corporate campaigns" to gain recognition or conclude an agreement (McCartin, 2014[45]), or by designing new means of organisation and information-sharing for non-standard workers. For instance, the German metal-worker union *IG Metall*, the Austrian union confederation, together with the Austrian Chamber of Labour, and the Swedish trade union *Unionen*, launched one of the first cross-border union initiatives to support platform work with the website *faircrowd.work* which provides information and advice to platform workers and in particular ratings of working conditions on different online platforms based on surveys of workers (see Section 5.4.3 for a discussion on the use of new technologies to strengthen workers' rights).

## Box 5.3. Collective bargaining in the creative sector

In the creative sector, where the incidence of freelance work is high, issues related to collective association and right to bargain are far from new. In the 1920s and 1930s, the status of writers in Hollywood production studios was being argued over. Studios initially favoured hiring writers as employees, who could not claim intellectual property rights under the Copyright Act of 1909 (Fisk, 2018[46]). But after the 1935 National Labour Relations Act had granted employees the right to organise, studios attempted to contest writers' unionisation right in courts. This led the National Labour Relations Board to confirm in 1937 that freelance writers, like writers under contract, had the right to bargain (Fisk, 2018, p. 186[46]). Over time, and with frequent detours through the courts, other crafts emulated the writers' example in forming their "guilds" and the phenomenon expanded beyond the film industry to radio, television and theatre. The current system is characterised by high union density and a bargaining culture akin to that of some corporatist European countries. Each guild engages in multi-employer bargaining in a way that resembles pattern bargaining – the Writers' Guild usually sets the mark for others (Kleingartner, 2001[47]). Studios now recognize unions as useful negotiating partners (Frommer, 2003[48]).

In other cases, access to collective bargaining for creative workers depended on the introduction of special statuses. A 1920 law allowed Austrian freelance journalists to collectively negotiate their fees (Fulton, 2018[49]). Changes to French labour law in the 1970s granted journalists and performing artists the status of employees for matters of collective bargaining. In Germany, the Collective Bargaining Act of 1949 was amended in 1974 to cover "employee-like" persons; criteria defining access to this status are relaxed for writers and journalists. In Denmark, since 2002, unions can bargain on behalf of journalists, scenographers, and graphic designers classified as "freelance wage earners".

Moreover, in 1980, the United Nations Educational, Scientific and Cultural Organization (UNESCO) adopted the Recommendation concerning the Status of the Artist, which "recognises the right of artists to be organised in trade unions or professional organisations that can represent and defend the interests of their members" (UNESCO, 1980[50]). In response to this recommendation, Canada passed in 1995 the *Status of the Artist Act*, which allows self-employed artists to be recognised and certified by the Canadian Industrial Relations Board (CIRB) as an artists' association with the exclusive right to negotiate collective agreements with producers.

When freelance creatives cannot access collective bargaining, trade unions and professional associations often offer advisory recommended minimum fees or rates lists (ILO, 2014[51]). For instance, the Dutch professional association of graphic designers (BNO) developed guidelines for minimum fees, and its Italian counterpart (AIAP) set up a fee guide. Guidelines also cover subjects such as work organisation and working hours. Collecting societies have been set up to handle the payment of royalties to writers, photographers, musicians or actors flowing from copyrights legislation (Gherardini, 2017[52]). Unions have set up lists to warn freelance workers about bad payers, e.g. the "ask-first" list set up by the British media and entertainment union BECTU in the film industry (Charhon and Murphy, 2016[53]).

Finally, co-operatives have emerged to provide solutions to some of the challenges faced by precarious freelance artists. Typically, these structures will formally hire artists, who thereby gain access to social security programmes – including unemployment insurance. Pooling resources, cooperatives also guarantee a regular pay to freelance artists, smoothing out the payment delays they frequently face. Workers are still entirely independent in finding and managing their projects. They pay a fee equivalent to a percentage of their earnings and can access a range of business services. Some of these cooperatives were set up by unions (in Denmark, the Danish association of professional technicians, *Teknisk Landsforbund*, created the Danish Technology and Design Freelance Bureau in 1992), while others emerged from private initiatives – such as the Brussels-based SMart created in 1998, see Section 5.4 (Gherardini, 2017[52]).

### 5.3.2. Unions are adapting their own organisation and structure

In several OECD countries, unions have opened their membership to non-standard workers, including the self-employed, and have started campaigning for the rights of platform workers. In Sweden, *Unionen*, a white-collar union, has been open to the self-employed since 1998. In Germany, *IG Metall*, the largest trade union amended its statutes in 2015 to allow the self-employed to join.

In other countries, unions have established separate branches specifically for the self-employed. According to a survey by the European Trade Union Confederation (Fulton, 2018[49]), the *Unión General de Trabajadores* (UGT) in Spain, the *Confederazione Italiana Sindacati Lavoratori* (CISL) in Italy and the *Federatie Nederlandse Vakbeweging* (FNV) in the Netherlands – where self-employment has experienced a very significant increase (Baker et al., 2018[54]) – are the most notable examples.

Furthermore, some unions have also set up specific branches or union-affiliated guilds for non-standard forms of work in general. Since 1998, the largest Italian union, *Confederazione Generale Italiana del Lavoro* (CGIL), has a specific branch *Nuove Identità di Lavoro* (NiDIL) devoted to non-standard workers. In the United States, the National Taxi Workers Alliance is the first member of the AFL-CIO, the US federation of trade unions, representing independent contractors. In Slovenia, *Sindikat prekarcev*, which is part of the main union confederation (ZSSS – Association of Free Trade Unions of Slovenia), has sought to represent "non-classical workers" since 2016.

Finally, some independent unions have been created, especially in the private hire or food delivery sectors. The most notable case is the one of the Independent Worker Union of Great Britain (IWGB), which is not affiliated to the Trade Union Confederation but has scored a series of significant victories in tribunals and negotiations with platforms. In Italy, food couriers have set up their own associations, which are not affiliated to any established union but are recognised as the counterparts to food-delivery platforms. In France, private hire drivers have set up an independent union. Similar developments have been observed in Belgium, Germany, the Netherlands and Spain (Vandaele, 2018[55]).

### 5.3.3. Employers' organisations are slowly adjusting

Employers, business and employers' organisations are the other key actors of collective bargaining. OECD (2017[1]) has shown that membership to employer organisations (at least in those countries for which time series are available) shows a remarkable stability which sharply contrasts with the fall observed in trade union density.

Yet, according to the International Organisation of Employers (IOE, 2017, p. 46[56]), "employers and business organisations will be affected too [by the megatrends presented in Chapter 2] as the concept of dependent employment comes under discussion" and their role has to evolve from one of support to one of provider of advice, representation and concrete solutions.

ILO ACT EMP and IOE (2019[57]) also highlight the need for employers' organisations to improve their representativeness, reaching out to underrepresented or emerging economic actors, and in particular giving "a seat at the table" to small and medium enterprises. Accordingly, some existing employers' organisations are currently trying to expand their reach to new members. For instance, the Iberico American Federation of Young Entrepreneurs (FIJE), which covers 150 000 young entrepreneurs in 20 countries, aims to foster youth membership in employers' organisations through networking, training, and representation activity.

Moreover, employers' organisations face the rapid emergence of new sectors and industries based on new business models. The development of new businesses outside of the coordinated and organised framework of traditional employers' organisations creates a challenge for the latter, who have an interest in ensuring a level playing field for their members against new competitors who may circumvent existing labour regulations. In addition, as these new industries emerge, traditional organisations are challenged by the fact that companies can choose to associate through more informal arrangements, based on temporary projects or issues, to represent their interests, particularly in highly local labour markets. Efforts to reach out to underrepresented companies by employers' organisations include the development of new services and tailored solutions for companies whose business models does not (yet) fall under a clear-cut regulatory framework (IOE, 2017[56]; ILO ACT EMP and IOE, 2019[57]).

Reaching a balance between the needs of their historical members and those of the new digital platform companies, however, may in some cases not be an easy challenge for traditional employers' organisations (Johnston and Land-Kazlauskas, 2018[58]). For instance, platforms often see themselves as a matchmaker, not as an employer (see Chapter 4).[39] This makes identifying the bargaining counterpart more challenging.

Yet, the experience with temporary work agencies (see the discussion in Box 5.4) shows that this is not an insurmountable obstacle if there is a will to negotiate or a threat of public intervention in the absence of an agreement. In Italy, for instance, a group of major food delivery companies announced in July 2018 the creation of a new employers association to represent their business and negotiate with the Government and the couriers associations. In Slovakia, Uber has become a member of the National Union of Employers and the professional association of information technology (IT) companies (ITAS).

Beyond the difficulty of organising new entrants on the employers' side, traditional employers' organisations are also threatened by the weakening of workers' representation. In the Netherlands, AWVN, an employers' association, released a report in 2018 where it expressed its concerns about the sustainability of the Dutch bargaining model in the absence of strong workers' involvement (AWVN, 2018[59]). AWVN proposed two options to strengthen the direct representation of employees. The first option is to let employees elect their representatives in the bargaining process at company or sector level (currently unions represent workers without a formal election). For each vote, the union would receive a small fee, e.g. EUR 10, as a compensation for the costs of bargaining. The second option is to offer newly hired employees a trial union membership for a period of one year for free or for a sharply reduced contribution. Employers would encourage this by providing extensive information when hiring people and unions would offer a reduced membership rate. To determine which option works better, AWVN has proposed to trial them in a number of companies.

---

### Box 5.4. Collective bargaining and temporary agency work

Including non-standard workers and platform workers in particular in collective bargaining requires some degree of organisation among workers but also a clear identification of the employer. In the case of a triangular relationship such as the one between a contractor, a platform and a customer, it may be difficult to identify the real employer, and consequently, the bargaining counterpart. While platforms are a recent development and, so far, limited in scope, triangular employment relationships are not new. Temporary work agency (TWA) workers are hired by an agency and assigned for work into a user firm (OECD, 2013[60]). However, a key difference between TWAs and platforms is that agency workers have an employment contract, while most platform workers are (rightly or wrongly) classified as self-employed (WEC and Uni Global, 2018[43]).

In the early stages of their development, TWA were considered as disruptive as the platforms of today and were highly contested or even banned in a number of countries. Governments intervened to regulate the sector and collective agreements now represent an important means of regulation of this industry in many OECD countries (Eurofound, 2008[61]) despite very low levels of unionisation. Today collective agreements covering TWA workers are negotiated in several OECD countries (see Table 5.2). In some countries, agency work is simply included in the reference sector (or firm) level collective agreement applicable to the user firm (for instance, in Finland or Spain). In other countries, specific agreements are signed directly with temporary work agencies (for instance, in Australia or Italy), either at the industry level or within agencies.

In Europe, the European directive on temporary agency work regulating TWAs introduced the principle of equal treatment with workers in the user company in order to establish a level-playing field. As the directive opened the possibility for collective agreements to diverge from a blanket equal treatment approach, provided certain quality conditions are respected such as the right to an adequate level of protection, TWAs felt encouraged by the law to engage in collective bargaining (IDEA Consult, 2015[62]). Hence, in several European countries, collective agreements are now used as a tool to co-define the regulation of the sector. Notably, in Germany labour law allows to derogate from the principle of equal pay when agency workers are on an open-ended contract with the agency and paid fully in-between assignments. However, until 2008 the responsibility for regulating agency work laid with works councils and not unions or collective agreements. Therefore, the German metal-worker union IG Metall launched a campaign to recruit agency workers and, at the same time, set a common bargaining floor across companies. This campaign led to an industry-wide agreement on equal pay for agency workers in the steel sector in 2010 followed by a collective agreement for the metal and electronics industry in 2012 (Benassi, 2016[63]). Collective agreements covering TWA work are also used to establish specific funds for training, pensions and sickness leave (as in Belgium, France, Italy and the Netherlands), which are often more generous than those offered to employees with a fixed-term contract. Finally, collective agreements in the TWA industry have been used to set up specific bodies to protect health and safety at work for workers in the agency sector such as the Dutch "*Stichting Arbo Flexbranche*" (STAF).

Table 5.2. Collective agreements for temporary work agency workers

| | Country | | | | | |
|---|---|---|---|---|---|---|
| None or very rare | Canada | Czech Rep. | Japan | Latvia | Mexico | United States |
| Covered by an agreement if applicable to user firm | Colombia Estonia Finland | Greece Hungary Iceland | Ireland Korea Lithuania | New Zealand Poland Portugal | Slovenia Spain Slovak Rep. | United Kingdom |
| Covered by an agreement with temporary work agency | Australia Austria[1] Belgium | Chile Denmark France | Germany Israel Italy | Luxembourg Netherlands | Norway Sweden | Switzerland Turkey |

1. In Austria, the specific agreement for temporary agency workers applies only if the provisions in the agreement covering the user firm are less favourable for workers.
Source: OECD Policy Questionnaires on Collective Bargaining.

### 5.3.4. A few innovative agreements have been signed in Europe

Unions' engagement with platforms on behalf of non-standard workers has paid off in some cases, with the signature of a few collective agreements in Europe. In Sweden, for instance, the transportation start-up Bzzt has signed an agreement with the Swedish Transport Workers union (Johnston and Land-Kazlauskas, 2018[58]). In Denmark Hilfr.dk, a platform for private home cleaning services, signed a collective agreement in April 2018 with the trade union 3F. The agreement grants platform workers sick pay, holiday allowance and a contribution to their pension.

In Austria, the transport and services union *vida* announced in April 2017 the creation of a work council (*Betriebsrat*) for the couriers of Foodora, which would be able to negotiate a collective agreement on working conditions. In April 2018, an agreement establishing a European Work Council at Delivery Hero, a publicly listed online food-delivery service based in Berlin (Foodora is owned by Delivery Hero), was signed. It includes a provision to have employee representatives on the supervisory board.

## 5.4. Increased pressure and new challenges have led to the emergence of non-traditional initiatives

The erosion of union membership and collective bargaining coverage, as well as the insufficient representation of some types of workers and businesses have led to the emergence of other initiatives by new actors such as platforms as well as non-traditional forms of labour organisations aimed at defending workers' interests. In some respects, new forms of labour movements can be considered as functional equivalents to "traditional" unions by helping to reduce information asymmetries, collectively mobilising workers and potentially increasing bargaining power as well as supporting litigations and class actions (Silberman and Irani, 2016[64]). However, a closer look reveals that they also serve different, non-bargaining related purposes and have different organisational structures.

### 5.4.1. A new mutualism

Notable examples of non-traditional organisations to represent workers' collective interests may be found in the United States with the development of Worker Centers[40] (representing low-wage, and mainly immigrant workers) or the Freelancers Union (representing high skilled independent contractors).[41] Similar developments have been observed in Canada with the Freelance Union representing self-employed media and communications workers or the Workers' Action Centre, which advocates on behalf of workers in non-standard forms of employment, in Ontario as well as in Europe, where worker co-operatives have developed. These initiatives echo in some respects the spirit of mutual organisations that in the 19th century represented the first form of work organisation and provided workers with basic insurances and mutual help.[42]

These organisations are legally distinct from traditional unions but there may be a formal or informal connection (Manheim, 2017[65]). Worker Centers in the United States tend to have both different cultures and fewer legal restrictions on their activities than traditional unions and thus are viewed by some as "organising laboratories" where innovative strategies can be formed and tested (Fine, 2006[66]). While the traditional union movement has had mixed views about these non-union worker organisations, it has increasingly embraced them and has invited some to join the AFL-CIO, the US federation of trade unions (Gaus, 2011[67]).

One strategy Worker Centers have used to organise workers has been creating and/or enforcing legal workplace standards.[43] Worker Centers have also engaged in direct action against employers, often through strikes.[44] In addition, Worker Centers have used consumer pressure throughout the supply chain to change employer behaviour.[45] Service delivery, from language classes for recent immigrants to low-cost portable benefits provided for independent contractors by the Freelancers Union, are another way Worker Centers and similar non-union workers' organisations respond to workers' needs.

These organisations have also used their political resources to push several pieces of legislation, leading many companies to raise wages and standards (Fine, 2005[68]). However, for the most part, this model has struggled to achieve scale and sustainable funding (Strom, 2016[69]).

Another type of actor has emerged in a number of countries: co-operatives organising self-employed workers and providing them with a range of services. One of the most established is SMart, which was founded in Belgium in 1998 as an association of creative and cultural freelance workers and then transformed itself into a non-profit co-operative (Graceffa, 2016[70]). SMart is currently present in nine European countries and has extended to other sectors beyond creative work. In exchange for a fee, it provides self-employed workers with a wide range of services, including help with invoicing and the declaration of income; getting paid as an employee (and therefore gaining access to social protection); debt collection; salary advancement (through a mutual guarantee fund); and access to training and co-working spaces.

SMart is based on a participatory process: all members are invited to participate in the general assembly, and all profits are reinvested. SMart, and other similar workers cooperatives, do not usually[46] bargain on behalf of their members. Occasionally they publicly voice the concerns of freelancers and advocate on their behalf, but this is not their primary goal. The model proposed by SMart is not uncontroversial and has been criticised by some unions as it "legitimises grey zones" instead of fighting them (Xhauflair, Huybrechts and Pichault, 2017[71]).

Setting aside their non-profit nature, this type of co-operative is akin to for-profit umbrella companies which process invoices and pool risks among freelancers, offering them sick, maternity and holiday pay as well as legal counselling. Such for-profit umbrella companies exist in several countries and notably in Belgium, France ("*portage salarial*"), the Netherlands ("payroll company"), Norway (*"Egenanstillingsförrettning"*), Sweden ("*Egenanställningsföretag*"), the United Kingdom and the United States (Arvas, 2011[72]) and they cover a wide range of individual professionals in many sectors.

### 5.4.2. Platforms are also taking some actions

In addition to worker-led initiatives, some platforms have also started taking action to address platform workers' limited access to representation and social dialogue. As highlighted before, the risk of re-classification as well as government initiatives have led some platforms to enter into negotiations with worker representatives in several countries.[47] In Italy, following a government threat of worker reclassification by decree in summer of 2018, food delivery platforms have agreed to start negotiating with rider associations over working conditions. Although these negotiations have not yet led to concrete results, the example mentioned above of the Danish platform Hilfr.dk shows that such negotiations can sometimes lead to agreements.

Beyond formal bargaining, platforms have taken initiatives aimed at giving workers the possibility to express their concerns. Uber, for example, embraced the creation of the New York City Independent Drivers' Guild (IDG).[48] The IDG cannot negotiate on behalf of drivers, but it allows channelling their concerns through monthly meetings with the company's management.

Social dialogue, if not formal bargaining, has also emerged as the outcome of government's engagement with platforms to address some of the issues related to platform work. In France, a legal provision encouraging platforms to publish "social responsibility charters" online and as appendixes to workers' contract is currently being discussed. Such charters would state the platforms' policy on a variety of issues including the prevention of occupational risks, professional development, measures to guarantee a "decent income" to workers, as well as rules framing the communication of changes to working conditions. Along the same lines, but based on the initiative of a crowdworking platform, a code of conduct has been established in Germany and signed in 2017 by eight Germany-based platforms.

Platforms' initiatives have thus tended to develop outside of the realm of traditional collective bargaining institutions rather than within them. For instance while the representation of platforms in traditional employer organisations is still limited, dedicated associations have emerged in some countries such as the *Deutscher Crowdsourcing Verband* in Germany. Rather than engaging in bargaining with platform workers, some platforms have focused on offering solutions to emerging issues (around e.g. occupational insurance) while preventing the risks of re-classification. This has taken various forms, from setting up partnerships with professional associations (as Uber has done with the Association of Independent Professionals and the Self-Employed in the United Kingdom) offering workers preferential deals on various goods and services, to providing free or discounted occupational insurance covers.

This approach, exchanging benefit provision for protection against reclassification is advocated by Uber which suggests the creation of legislative "safe harbours", "to ensure that the provision of benefits or training could not be used as a factor in employment classification claims" (Uber, 2018[73]). In other words, platform-led initiatives tend to revolve around direct benefit provision driven by the risk of reclassification.

However, this approach raises the question of co-ordination between different platforms and the portability of workers' protection, as these initiatives are taken at the level of individual platforms (see the discussion in Chapter 4). They also raise the question of the unilateral nature, since they are not the result of dialogue between different stakeholders (including workers).

### 5.4.3. New technologies can also strengthen workers' voice

The digital technology used by platforms can also be mobilised to organise workers and improve job quality. A good example of this is Turkopticon, an all-volunteer website that started as a class project by two computer scientists turned labour organisers (Silberman and Irani, 2016[64]). For the past 10 years, Turkopticon has allowed workers on Amazon Mechanical Turk, a platform where online workers are hired for small tasks, to review the "requesters" (individuals or companies posting tasks to be executed by workers). It helps workers to identify "bad" requesters, who tend to pay late or never, and to find good ones.[49] Other websites facilitating the organisation of workers include Coworker.org, which helps workers to create company-specific networks to collect data and to aggregate their demands into coherent campaigns.

Instant messaging applications, social media groups, online fora as well as online polls play a very important role for workers who do not share a common physical workplace and lack the ability to discuss work issues face-to-face with each other. These technologies allow them to exchange information about clients and tasks, warn each other about scams, discuss best practices and set informal price norms, and to co-ordinate actions. It also provides community support. Such online communities of remote gig workers sometimes become linked to institutionalised unions, but they also exist in contexts lacking an institutionalised labour movement – see e.g. Wood, Lehdonvirta and Graham (2018[74]) on online communities of micro-workers and online freelance workers in Nigeria, South Africa, Kenya, the Philippines, Malaysia and Vietnam.

Technological innovations also open up new possibilities to protect the relatively weaker party in an employment/contractual relationship. For instance, the platform Bitwage uses Blockchain technology[50] to make international payments of remote contractors faster and more trustworthy.

Finally, the same algorithms, big data and basic AI tools which are used by large companies to manage human resources could also be used by unions to mine information about their members and guide their actions. In many OECD countries, business registry data are also used by trade unionists to gauge how companies are performing when deciding whether to ask for wage increases or for the negotiation of a new collective agreement. New data and statistical tools would allow unions to use information on the state of business faster and more efficiently.[51]

In other words, some technological innovations represent an opportunity to foster social dialogue and extend it to non-standard workers. One way in which governments could help social partners to seize this opportunity would be through the setting up of common knowledge platforms to share practices and experiences among actors.

### 5.4.4. Non-traditional actors can complement but not substitute for social partners

While non-traditional workers' organisations can help improve working conditions for a greater number of non-standard workers, they cannot completely substitute for labour unions. Differences in new actors' prerogatives compared to those of traditional unions include: i) the legal ability to bargain collectively on behalf of their members and to sign an agreement; ii) the ability to guarantee the enforcement of this agreement; and iii) the benefit (in some countries) of information and consultation rights that reduce information asymmetries vis-à-vis employers, and play and instrumental role in the definition and strengthening of unions' bargaining position. Non-traditional organisations can engage in actions such as boycotts, petitions, and thus strengthen workers' voice; but this might not lead to an agreement.

Further, in some cases, non-traditional actors are not even interested in doing so. These organisations are often professional associations, which are created to provide services, to coalesce individuals around a common identity and to help with networking, but not necessarily to negotiate nor sign formal collective agreements.

However, they might help bridge some of the perceived mismatch between the professional identity of independent workers and traditional unions (King, 2014[75]). Saundry, Stuart and Antcliff (2012[76]) have shown how freelance networks in the British audio-visual industry were more successful than unions in creating a sense of identity and community among freelance workers, but lacked the resources to achieve industrial relations successes and the legal framework to sign and guarantee the validity and binding nature of collective agreements. By "linking networks to reservoir of expertise and influence" (Saundry, Stuart and Antcliff, 2012, p. 282[76]), unions were able to build on them to secure progress for these workers. More generally, new forms of workers' organisations can coalesce non-standard workers whom traditional unions have a harder time reaching out to, for practical and historical reasons. In that sense, these new initiatives can complement rather than substitute for traditional actors. The combination of efforts from both traditional and new actors is necessary to fully address the challenges posed by the evolving world of work, and should be encouraged.

## 5.5. Concluding remarks

While the practice of collective bargaining reflects cultural and social norms as well as institutional variation and therefore differs considerably across OECD countries, this chapter argues that it can play an important role in addressing some of the labour market challenges driven by technological and demographic changes and increased global competition.

When social partners work co-operatively and anticipate new challenges, collective bargaining can support and usefully complement public policies. This is particularly the case for the regulation of new forms of work, the anticipation and meeting of skills needs, and the design of measures to help workers with the transition to new jobs. Collective bargaining, at both sectoral and firm levels can also help companies to adapt, through tailor-made agreements and adjustments in the organisation of work to meet their specific needs. Finally, collective bargaining and social dialogue can help workers to make their voice heard in the design of national, sectoral or company-specific strategies and ensure a fair sharing of the benefits brought by new technologies and more globalised markets.

The contribution of collective bargaining to shaping the future of work crucially depends on workers and firms being able and willing to associate and negotiate mutually satisfying binding agreements. However, since the 1980s bargaining coverage and membership of trade unions have declined sharply in most countries. The rise of different forms of non-standard work in a number of OECD countries discussed in Chapter 2 poses an additional challenge to collective bargaining, as non-standard workers are less likely to be unionised than standard workers.

Unions are trying to expand their membership to workers in non-standard forms of employment and develop new strategies to negotiate with employers. Meanwhile, new forms of collective organisation are emerging, although they tend to serve different purposes and have different organisational structures. Employers' organisations are also having to deal with the development of new forms of business and the weakening of their traditional counterparts. The examples of successful collective agreements in the temporary work agency sector and in the cultural and creative industries, even in countries where unions have generally low membership, show that collective bargaining can adjust to different and new types of employment relationships.

Legislation may also need to change to take account of the development of a wider variety of forms of employment and business, which are very different to those of 50 years ago when many of the current

OECD bargaining systems took form. It is therefore important to address the issue of worker classification to ensure that employment contracts match the real nature of the employment relationship. In addition, regulators and enforcement authorities need to reflect on how workers in the grey area between dependent and self-employment and those self-employed in situations of strong power imbalance vis-à-vis their client/employer can be empowered to negotiate and organise collectively.

This chapter has presented several national policies and initiatives taken by employers, unions and new forms of workers' organisation to adapt to the challenges arising from the outlook for the future of work. Even though, for most of them, rigorous evaluation is lacking, these initiatives can still provide useful inspiration in other contexts.

---

### Box 5.5. Policy directions

While each country's situation and traditions are different, a well-functioning system of labour relations can contribute to shaping a more rewarding and inclusive future of work. Depending on the national context, policy makers should consider:

- Promoting national consultations and discussions on the future of work with both social partners and other organisations representing workers and employers to establish a joint diagnosis about challenges, and share practices among actors on new initiatives and technological innovation through common knowledge platforms.

- Leaving scope for collective bargaining and incentivising self-regulation among actors on these issues by making a limited but strategic use of legislative interventions (as exemplified in the case of the temporary work agencies sector in several countries).

- Ensuring broad-based access to training and lifelong learning by promoting collective bargaining over these issues.

- Accompanying the efforts of unions and employers' organisations to expand their membership to non-standard forms of work and new forms of business without discouraging the emergence of other forms of organisation.

Enforcing the correct classification of workers' employment status and fighting misclassification is the first step in ensuring that workers have access to collective bargaining. Yet, there would still be scope for potential adaptation of existing regulations to allow collective bargaining for workers in the grey zone and for the self-employed who have little influence on the content of their contractual conditions. Options to be considered include:

- Enlarging the definition of "employee" in labour law, as far as labour relations legislation is concerned, to specific groups of workers in the grey zone; and

- Introducing exemptions to the prohibition of bargaining collectively for specific groups of workers or occupations, in case where power imbalances are likely to be more important.

---

# References

Aloisi, A. (2018), "Non-standard workers and collective bargaining: Legal challenges, practical difficulties, and successful responses", mimeo. [34]

Ankersmit, L. (2015), *Albany revisited: The Court directs NCA to carry a more social tune*, European Law Blog, https://europeanlawblog.eu/tag/c-41313-fnv-kunsten-informatie-en-media/ (accessed on 21 November 2018). [37]

Arthurs, H. (1965), "The Dependent Contractor: A Study of the Legal Problems of Countervailing Power", *The University of Toronto Law Journal*, Vol. 16/1, p. 89, http://dx.doi.org/10.2307/825096. [85]

Arvas, F. (2011), *Umbrella Companies in Europe. A study on their growth behaviors and job-creation.*, MBA Henley Business School. [72]

Autor, D. (2003), "Outsourcing at Will: The Contribution of Unjust Dismissal Doctrine to the Growth of Employment Outsourcing", *Journal of Labor Economics*, Vol. 21/1, pp. 1-42, https://doi.org/10.1086/344122. [23]

AWVN (2018), *Wegwerkzaamheden. Tien ideeën voor de wereld van werk - AWVN*, AWVN, Den Haag. [59]

Baker, M. et al. (2018), "To what extent do policies contribute to self-employment?", *OECD Economics Department Working Papers*, No. 1512, OECD Publishing, Paris, https://dx.doi.org/10.1787/74c044b1-en. [54]

Benassi, C. (2016), *Extending solidarity rather than bargaining concessions: the IG Metall campaign for agency workers*, ETUI Policy Brief No. 1/2016, Brussels. [63]

Benassi, C. and L. Dorigatti (2014), "Straight to the Core - Explaining Union Responses to the Casualization of Work: The IG Metall Campaign for Agency Workers", *British Journal of Industrial Relations*, Vol. 53/3, pp. 533-555, http://dx.doi.org/10.1111/bjir.12079. [41]

Benassi, C. and T. Vlandas (2016), "Union inclusiveness and temporary agency workers: The role of power resources and union ideology", *European Journal of Industrial Relations*, Vol. 22/1, pp. 5-22, http://dx.doi.org/10.1177/0959680115589485. [24]

Berry, C. and S. Mcdaniel (2018), *Young people and trade unionism in the hourglass economy*, Unions 21, http://www.unions21.org.uk (accessed on 6 November 2018). [26]

Berryhill, J., T. Bourgery and A. Hanson (2018), "Blockchains Unchained: Blockchain Technology and its Use in the Public Sector", *OECD Working Papers on Public Governance*, No. 28, OECD Publishing, Paris, https://dx.doi.org/10.1787/3c32c429-en. [84]

Bertola, G. (1999), "Microeconomic perspectives on aggregate labor markets", in Ashenfelter, O. (ed.), *Handbook of Labor Economics*, Elsevier, https://econpapers.repec.org/bookchap/eeelabchp/3-45.htm (accessed on 7 February 2018). [19]

Blanchflower, D. (2007), "International Patterns of Union Membership", *British Journal of Industrial Relations*, Vol. 45/1, pp. 1-28. [25]

Bryson, A. et al. (2005), "Youth-adult differences in the demand for unionization: Are American, British, and Canadian workers all that different?", *Journal of Labor Research*, Vol. 26/1, pp. 155-167, http://dx.doi.org/10.1007/BF02812227. [30]

Charhon, P. and D. Murphy (2016), *The Future of Work in the Media, Arts & Entertainment Sector: Meeting the Challenge of Atypical Working*, Euro FIA, EFJ, FIM and UNI MEI, https://www.fim-musicians.org/wp-content/uploads/atypical-work-handbook-en.pdf (accessed on 26 October 2018). [53]

Creighton, B. and S. McCrystal (2016), "Who is a 'Worker' in International Law?", *Comparative Labor Law and Policy Journal*, Vol. 37/3, pp. 691-725. [87]

Daskalova, V. (2018), "Regulating the New Self-Employed in the Uber Economy: What Role for EU Competition Law?", *German law journal*, Vol. 19/3, pp. 461-508. [36]

De Stefano, V. (2018), ""Negotiating the algorithm": Automation, artificial intelligence and labour protection", *Employment Working Paper*, No. 246, ILO, Geneva. [11]

De Stefano, V. and A. Aloisi (2018), "Fundamental Labour Rights, Platform Work and Human-Rights Protection of Non-Standard Workers", in Bellace, J. and B. ter Haar (eds.), *Labour, Business and Human Rights Law*, Edward Elgar Publishing Ltd., https://dx.doi.org/10.2139/ssrn.3125866. [38]

DOJ/FTC (1996), *Statements of Antitrust Enforcement Policy in Health Care*, https://www.ftc.gov/sites/default/files/attachments/competition-policy-guidance/statements_of_antitrust_enforcement_policy_in_health_care_august_1996.pdf (accessed on 21 November 2018). [39]

Drahokoupil, J. and A. Piasna (2019), *Work in the platform economy: Deliveroo riders in Belgium and the SMart arrangement*, ETUI. [83]

Dube, A. et al. (forthcoming), "Monopsony in Online Labor Markets", *American Economic Review: Insights*. [82]

Durazzi, N., T. Fleckenstein and S. Lee (2018), "Social Solidarity for All? Trade Union Strategies, Labor Market Dualization, and the Welfare State in Italy and South Korea", *Politics & Society*, Vol. 46/2, pp. 205-233, http://dx.doi.org/10.1177/0032329218773712. [42]

Ebbinghaus, B., C. Göbel and S. Koos (2011), "Social capital, 'Ghent' and workplace contexts matter: Comparing union membership in Europe", *European Journal of Industrial Relations*, Vol. 17/2, pp. 107-124, http://dx.doi.org/10.1177/0959680111400894. [29]

Engblom, S. (2017), "Employment Protection, Collective Bargaining, and Labour Market Resilience - The Swedish Transition Agreements", mimeo. [14]

Eurofound (2008), *Temporary agency work and collective bargaining in the EU*, European Foundation for the Improvement of Living and Working Conditions, Dublin. [61]

European Commission (2018), *Employment and Social Developments in Europe 2018*, Publications Office of the European Union, Luxembourg. [2]

Fine, J. (2006), *Worker centers : organizing communities at the edge of the dream*, ILR Press/Cornell University Press. [66]

Fine, J. (2005), "Community Unions and the Revival of the American Labor Movement", *Politics & Society*, Vol. 33/1, pp. 153-199, http://dx.doi.org/10.1177/0032329204272553. [68]

Fisk, C. (2018), "Hollywood Writers and the Gig Economy", *University of Chicago Legal Forum*, Vol. 2017/Article 8, https://chicagounbound.uchicago.edu/cgi/viewcontent.cgi?article=1595&context=uclf (accessed on 26 October 2018). [46]

Fleckenstein, T. and S. Lee (2018), "Organised Labour, Dualisation and Labour Market Reform: Korean Trade Union Strategies in Economic and Social Crisis", *Journal of Contemporary Asia*, pp. 1-21, http://dx.doi.org/10.1080/00472336.2018.1536762. [44]

Freeman, R. and J. Medoff (1984), *What do unions do?*, Basic Books, New York. [5]

Frommer, G. (2003), "Hooray for... Toronto? Hollywood, collective bargaining, and extraterritorial union rules in an era of globalization", *Journal of Labor and Employment Law*, Vol. 6/1, pp. 55-120, https://www.law.upenn.edu/journals/jbl/articles/volume6/issue1/Frommer6U.Pa.J.Lab.%26Emp.L.55(2003).pdf (accessed on 26 October 2018). [48]

Fulton, L. (2018), *Trade Unions protecting self-employed workers*, ETUC, Brussels. [49]

Gaus, M. (2011), *Taxi Workers Become a Union—Officially*, Labor Notes, http://labornotes.org/blogs/2011/10/taxi-workers-become-union%E2%80%94officially (accessed on 20 November 2018). [67]

Gherardini, A. (2017), *So many, so different! Industrial relations in the creative sectors*, IR-CREA report for the European Commission. [52]

Givan, R. and A. Hipp (2012), "Public Perceptions of Union Efficacy", *Labor Studies Journal*, Vol. 37/1, pp. 7-32, http://dx.doi.org/10.1177/0160449X11429264. [31]

Graceffa, S. (2016), *Refaire le monde...du travail : une alternative à l'ubérisation de l'économie*, Éditions Repas. [70]

Gramm, C. and J. Schnell (2001), "The use of flexible staffing arrangements in core production jobs", *Industrial and Labor Relations Review*, Vol. 54/2, pp. 245-258, http://journals.sagepub.com/doi/pdf/10.1177/001979390105400203 (accessed on 21 February 2018). [22]

Haucap, J., U. Pauly and C. Wey (2001), "Collective wage setting when wages are generally binding. An antitrust perspective", *International Review of Law and Economics*, Vol. 21/3, pp. 287-307, http://dx.doi.org/10.1016/s0144-8188(01)00061-8. [81]

Horowitz, S. (2013), *What is New Mutualism?*, Freelancers Union, https://blog.freelancersunion.org/2013/11/05/what-new-mutualism/ (accessed on 20 November 2018). [80]

Ibsen, C. and M. Keune (2018), "Organised Decentralisation of Collective Bargaining : Case studies of Germany, Netherlands and Denmark", *OECD Social, Employment and Migration Working Papers*, No. 217, OECD Publishing, Paris, https://dx.doi.org/10.1787/f0394ef5-en. [10]

IDEA Consult (2015), *How temporary agency work compares with other forms of work*. [62]

ILO (2019), *Work for a brighter future – Global Commission on the Future of Work*, International Labour Office, Geneva. [3]

ILO (2016), *Non-standard employment around the world: Understanding challenges, shaping prospects*, International Labor Office, Geneva. [40]

ILO (2014), *Employment relationships in the media and culture industries*, International Labour Office, Sectoral Activities Department,, http://www.ilo.org/publns. (accessed on 25 October 2018). [51]

ILO ACT EMP and IOE (2019), *Changing Business and Opportunities for Employer and Business Organizations*, ILO Bureau for Employers' Activities and International Organization of Employers, Geneva. [57]

Inglehart, R. (1997), *Modernization and postmodernization : cultural, economic, and political change in 43 societies*, Princeton University Press, https://press.princeton.edu/titles/5981.html (accessed on 19 November 2018). [27]

IOE (2017), *IOE Brief: Understanding the future of work*, IOE, Geneva. [56]

Johnston, H. and C. Land-Kazlauskas (2018), "Organizing On-Demand: Representation, Voice, and Collective Bargaining in the Gig Economy", *Conditions of Work and Employment Series*, No. 94, ILO. [58]

Keune, M. (2015), *Trade unions and young workers in seven EU countries*, ADAPT-Association for International and Comparative Studies in Labour Law and Industrial Relations, http://www.adapt.it/younion/ (accessed on 13 November 2018). [32]

Kleingartner, A. (2001), "Collective Bargaining: Hollywood Style", *New Labor Forum*, Vol. 9/Fall - Winter, pp. 113-121, https://www.jstor.org/stable/pdf/40342321.pdf?refreqid=excelsior%3A2d94f2167ffaf020cc454 6379b36ec73 (accessed on 26 October 2018). [47]

Klindt, M. (2017), "Trade union renewal through local partnerships for skill formation", *Transfer: European Review of Labour and Research*, Vol. 23/4, pp. 441-455, http://dx.doi.org/10.1177/1024258917727403. [17]

Lindbeck, A. and D. Snower (1986), "Wage Setting, Unemployment, and Insider-Outsider Relations", *American Economic Review*, Vol. 76/2, pp. 235-239, http://www.jstor.org/stable/1818771. [20]

Linder, M. (1999), "Dependent and Independent Contractors in Recent U.S. Labor Law: An Ambiguous Dichotomy Rooted in Simulated Statutory Purposelessness", *Comparative Labor Law & Policy Journal*, Vol. 21/1. [35]

Manheim, J. (2017), *The Emerging Role of Worker Centers in Union Organizing: An Update and Supplement*, U.S. Chamber of Commerce, Washington, D.C. [65]

McCartin, J. (2014), *Bargaining for the Future: Rethinking Labor's Recent Past and Planning Strategically for Its Future a report by initially drafted with*, Kalmanovitz Initiative for Labor and the Working Poor, Georgetown University. [45]

Mettling, B. (2015), *Transformation numérique et vie au travail*. [8]

Moore, P., M. Upchurch and X. Whittaker (2018), *Humans and Machines at Work: Monitoring, Surveillance and Automation in Contemporary Capitalism*, Palgrave Macmillan, London. [12]

OECD (2019), *Getting Skills Right: Making adult learning work in social partnership*, OECD, Paris, http://www.oecd.org/employment/emp/adult-learning-work-in-social-partnership-2019.pdf. [16]

OECD (2019), *Policy Responses to New Forms of Work*, OECD Publishing, Paris, https://doi.org/10.1787/0763f1b7-en. [78]

OECD (2018), "Back to work: lessons from nine countries case studies of policies to assist displaced workers", in *OECD Employment Outlook 2018*, OECD Publishing, https://doi.org/10.1787/empl_outlook-2018-8-en. [4]

OECD (2018), "The role of collective bargaining systems for good labour market performance", in *OECD Employment Outlook 2018*, OECD Publishing, Paris, https://dx.doi.org/10.1787/empl_outlook-2018-7-en. [7]

OECD (2017), "Collective bargaining in a changing world of work", in *OECD Employment Outlook 2017*, OECD Publishing, Paris, https://dx.doi.org/10.1787/empl_outlook-2017-8-en. [1]

OECD (2016), *Getting Skills Right: Assessing and Anticipating Changing Skill Needs*, Getting Skills Right, OECD Publishing, Paris, https://dx.doi.org/10.1787/9789264252073-en. [15]

OECD (2016), *OECD Employment Outlook 2016*, OECD Publishing, Paris, https://dx.doi.org/10.1787/empl_outlook-2016-en. [6]

OECD (2015), *Back to Work: Sweden: Improving the Re-employment Prospects of Displaced Workers*, OECD Publishing, Paris, http://dx.doi.org/10.1787/9789264246812-en. [13]

OECD (2014), "Non-regular employment, job security and the labour market divide", in *OECD Employment Outlook 2014*, OECD Publishing, Paris, https://dx.doi.org/10.1787/empl_outlook-2014-7-en. [86]

OECD (2013), *OECD Employment Outlook 2013*, OECD Publishing, Paris, http://dx.doi.org/10.1787/empl_outlook-2013-en. [60]

OECD (forthcoming), *Collective Bargaining in a Changing World of Work*, OECD Publishing, Paris. [79]

Ott, E. (ed.) (2014), *Protecting and Representing Workers in the Gig Economy: the Case of the Freelancers Union*, Cornell University Press. [75]

Prassl, J. (2018), *Collective Voice in the Platform Economy: Challenges, Opportunities, Solutions*, ETUC, https://www.etuc.org/sites/default/files/publication/file/2018-09/Prassl%20report%20maquette.pdf (accessed on 10 December 2018). [77]

Saint-Martin, A., H. Inanc and C. Prinz (2018), "Job Quality, Health and Productivity: An evidence-based framework for analysis", *OECD Social, Employment and Migration Working Papers*, No. 221, OECD Publishing, Paris, https://dx.doi.org/10.1787/a8c84d91-en. [9]

Saint-Paul, G. (1996), *Dual labor markets : a macroeconomic perspective*, MIT Press, https://mitpress.mit.edu/books/dual-labor-markets (accessed on 7 February 2018). [18]

Salvatori, A. (2009), "What Do Unions Do to Temporary Employment?", *IZA Discussion Paper*, No. 4554, http://ftp.iza.org/dp4554.pdf (accessed on 26 January 2018). [21]

Saundry, R., M. Stuart and V. Antcliff (2012), "Social Capital and Union Revitalization: A Study of Worker Networks in the UK Audio-Visual Industries", *British Journal of Industrial Relations*, Vol. 50/2, pp. 263-286, http://dx.doi.org/10.1111/j.1467-8543.2011.00850.x. [76]

Silberman, M. and L. Irani (2016), "Operating an employer reputation system: Lessons from Turkopticon, 2008-2015'", *Comparative Labor Law & Policy Journal*, Vol. 37/3. [64]

Strom, S. (2016), *Organizing's Business Model Problem*, The Century Foundation, https://tcf.org/content/report/organizings-business-model-problem/?agreed=1&agreed=1 (accessed on 20 November 2018). [69]

Uber (2018), *White Paper on Work and Social Protection in Europe*, https://ubernewsroomapi.10upcdn.com/wp-content/uploads/2018/02/Uber-White-Paper-on-Work-and-Social-Protections-in-Europe.pdf (accessed on 10 December 2018). [73]

UNESCO (1980), *Recommendation concerning the Status of the Artist*. [50]

Vandaele, K. (2018), "Will Trade Unions Survive in the Platform Economy? Emerging Patterns of Platform Workerss Collective Voice and Representation in Europe", *SSRN Electronic Journal*, http://dx.doi.org/10.2139/ssrn.3198546. [55]

Vandaele, K. (2012), "Youth representatives' opinions on recruiting and representing young workers: A twofold unsatisfied demand?", *European Journal of Industrial Relations*, Vol. 18/3, pp. 203-218, http://dx.doi.org/10.1177/0959680112452692. [33]

Vandaele, K. (forthcoming), "How Can Trade Unions in Europe Connect with Young Workers?", in O'Reilly, J. et al. (eds.), *Youth labor in transition inequalities, mobility, and policies in Europe*, Oxford Unversity Press, https://global.oup.com/academic/product/youth-labor-in-transition-9780190864798?cc=fr&lang=en&# (accessed on 13 November 2018). [28]

WEC and Uni Global (2018), *Online Talent Platforms, Labour Market Intermediaries and the Changing World of Work*, Independent study prepared by CEPS and IZA for the World Employment Confederation-Europe and UNI Europa, Brussels. [43]

Wood, A., V. Lehdonvirta and M. Graham (2018), *Workers of the Internet Unite? Online Freelancer Organisation Among Remote Gig Economy Workers in Six Asian and African Countries*, https://papers.ssrn.com/sol3/papers.cfm?abstract_id=3211803 (accessed on 28 November 2018). [74]

Xhauflair, V., B. Huybrechts and F. Pichault (2017), "How Can New Players Establish Themselves in Highly Institutionalized Labour Markets? A Belgian Case Study in the Area of Project-Based Work", *British Journal of Industrial Relations*, Vol. 56/2, pp. 370-394, http://dx.doi.org/10.1111/bjir.12281. [71]

# Annex 5.A. Union density and forms of employment: Sources and additional material

In Figure 5.1, standard and non-standard workers correspond, as closely as possible, to the categories displayed in Figure 5.5 with the notable exception of part-time jobs: in general, standard employment refers to wage and salary workers (both full-time and part-time) with an open-ended contract; non-standard employment includes, as far as possible, casual or occasional work, job provided by a temporary work agency or through a prime contractor enterprise (which subcontract their employees to a third part), independent contractors, interns or apprentices, self-employed without autonomy and, for some emerging economies, informal employment.

However, given the heterogeneity of the data sources used (see Annex Table 5.A.1), the scope of questions available relating to the contractual forms of employment, the nature of the job and of union affiliation (generally restricted only to workers identified as employees), non-standard forms of employment do not necessary cover all these categories.

In four countries (Canada, Estonia, Hungary and Korea), the data available do not allow to go beyond the simple distinction between permanent and temporary employment as defined in the OECD Employment Database (for further details see specific definitions in Table 3 of the sources, coverage and definitions of Labour Force Statistics in OECD countries)[52] and do not include dependent self-employed.

Temporary work agency workers (in addition to fixed-term contracts or project workers and sometimes interns and apprentices) are clearly identifiable for seven countries (Chile, Finland, France, Germany, Ireland, Sweden and the United Kingdom) and provide a better definition of the open-ended contract category, which in this case excludes all potential temporary work agency workers working under an open-ended contract.

The United States is a particular case due to the use of an alternative definition of temporary jobs based on the third definition of the contingent workers (as defined by the BLS). Contingent workers include wage and salary workers not expecting their jobs to last and the incorporated self-employed (without paid employees) if they expect their employment to last for an additional year or less. In addition to this criterion, alternative employment arrangements (temporary work agency workers, fixed-term contracts, project contracts and independent contractors) are included as such irrespective of the excepted duration of their contract.

The informal employment, in addition to the listed categories above, constitute an independent category for some emerging economies. In the case of Colombia, this category covers all workers without a written contract and, for Mexico, all workers classified as in an informal job (based on the official definition TIL1 provided by the INEGI).

The European Social Survey (ESS) allows identifying the self-employed without autonomy as those without full control on the organisation of the work to be done or the decisions about the activities of the organisation.

The Australian survey Characteristics of Employment (COE) allows identifying the self-employed without autonomy as independent contractors who are not able to have more than one active contract, to subcontract their own work and are under the authority of somebody else on how to do their work.

Annex Table 5.A.1. Non-standard forms of employment included in Figure 5.1.

| Country | Source | Contract of limited duration | FTC | Project contracts | TWA | Occasional workers | Independent contractors | Informal workers | Self-employed without autonomy |
|---|---|---|---|---|---|---|---|---|---|
| Australia | COE² | | • | • | • | • | | | • |
| | HILDA | | • | | • | • | | | • |
| European countries¹ | ESS | • | | | | | | | • |
| Canada | LFS | • | | | | | | | |
| Chile | CASEN | | • | | • | | | | |
| Colombia | GEIH | | • | | • | | | • | |
| Estonia | LFS² | • | | | | | | | |
| Finland | FWLB | | • | | • | | | | |
| France³ | SRCV | | • | | • | | | | |
| Germany³ | SOEP | | • | | • | | | | |
| Hungary | LFS² | • | | | | | | | |
| Ireland³ | QHNS | | • | | • | | | | |
| Korea | EAPS² | • | | | | | | | |
| | KLIPS | | • | • | • | • | • | | |
| Mexico | ENOE | | • | • | | | | • | |
| Sweden³ | LFS² | | • | • | • | | | | |
| United Kingdom³ | LFS | | • | | • | | | | |
| United States | CPS | | • | • | • | • | • | | |

TWA: temporary work agency workers; CASEN: Encuesta de Caracterización Socioeconómica Nacional; COE: Characteristics of Employment Survey ; CPS: Current Population Survey, May Supplement ; EAPS: Economically Active Population Survey; ENOE: Encuesta Nacional de Ocupación y Empleo; ESS: European Social Survey; FWLB: Finnish Working Life Barometer; GEIH: Gran Encuesta Integrada de Hogares; HILDA: Household, Income and Labour Dynamics in Australia; KLIPS: Korean Labor and Income Panel Study; LFS: Labour Force Survey; QHNS: Quarterly National Household Survey; SOEP: German Socio-Economic Panel; SRCV: Enquête statistique sur les ressources et conditions de vie.

1. Austria, Belgium, the Czech Republic, Denmark, Greece, Hungary, Iceland, Israel, Italy, Lithuania, the Netherlands, Norway, Poland, Portugal, the Slovak Republic, Slovenia, Spain, Sweden and Switzerland.

2. Data kindly provided by the national statistical office.

3. Interns/apprentices are available for this country as a separate form of employment (not shown in this table).

Note: For Australia, Hungary, Korea and Sweden, the actual ratio refers to the national estimates provided by the national statistical authorities while the adjusted ratio is an estimate based on alternative microdata available (HILDA, ESS, KLIPS and ESS, respectively).

**Contract of limited duration**: contracts for which both employer and employee agree that its end is decided by objective rules (usually written down in a work contract of limited life). These rules can be a specific date, the end of a task, or the return of another employee who has been temporarily replaced. Typical cases are: employees in seasonal employment; employees engaged first by an agency or employment exchange and then hired to a third party to do a specific task (unless there is a written work contract of unlimited life); employees with specific training contracts.

**Fixed-term contracts (FTC)**: A fixed-term contract is a contractual relationship between an employee and an employer that lasts for a specified period.

**Project contracts**: fixed-term contracts where the end date is defined by the completion of a particular project or task.

**Temporary work agency (TWA) workers**: an employee with a contract (of limited or unlimited duration) under which the employer (i.e. the agency) places that employee at the disposal of a third party (i.e. the user firm) in order to engage in work under supervision and direction of that user firm through an agreement for the provision of services between the user firm and the agency.

**Occasional workers**: Employees who worked on an irregular basis over the year. This may include on-call workers, seasonal workers, casual workers.

**Interns/apprentices**: contracts with a period of work experience offered by an organisation for a limited period of time.

**Informal workers**: Employees are considered to have informal jobs if their employment relationship is, in law or in practice, not subject to national labour legislation, income taxation, social protection or entitlement to certain employment benefits. For Colombia, this category includes all workers with no written contract of no contract at all and in the case of Mexico, this refers to the national definition of informal employment (the so-called TIL1 measure).

**Self-employed without autonomy**: own-account self-employed who typically work for one (or more) client-firm(s) with limited autonomy.

## Annex Figure 5.A.1. Estimated trade union density for standard workers

Percentage of standard employment, latest available year

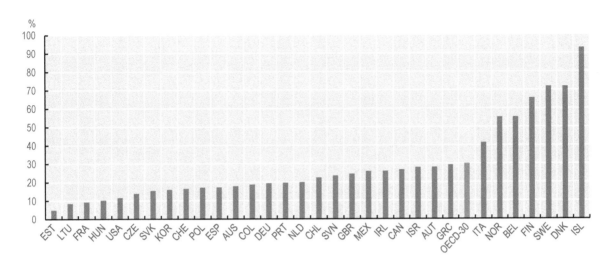

Note: Standard employment: Employees with an open-ended contract. Trade union density of standard form of employment have been adjusted for the overall trade union density by using the share of standard workers in total union membership and total number of employees. Estimates refer to 2010-12 for Greece and the Slovak Republic; 2013 for France; 2015 for Germany and Hungary; 2016 for Finland; 2014-16 for Austria, Belgium, the Czech Republic, Denmark, Iceland, Israel, Italy, Lithuania, the Netherlands, Norway, Poland, Portugal, the Slovak Republic, Slovenia, Spain and Switzerland; 2017 for Canada, Chile, Colombia, Estonia, Ireland, Korea, Sweden, the United Kingdom and the United States; and 2018 for Australia and Mexico. OECD-30 is the unweighted average of countries shown (not including Colombia, Estonia, Iceland, Latvia, Luxembourg, New Zealand and Turkey).

Source: OECD estimates based on results from the Characteristics of Employment (COE) Survey provided by the Australian Bureau of Statistics for Australia, the Labour Force Survey (LFS) for Canada, the Encuesta de Caracterización Socioeconómica Nacional (CASEN) for Chile, the Gran Encuesta Integrada de Hogares (GEIH) for Colombia, results from the Labour Force Survey (LFS) provided by Statistics Estonia for Estonia, the Finnish Working Life Barometer (FWLB) for Finland, the Enquête statistique sur les ressources et conditions de vie (SRCV) for France, the German Socio-Economic Panel (SOEP) for Germany, results from the Labour Force Survey (LFS) provided by the Hungarian Central Statistical Office for Hungary, the Quarterly National Household Survey (QNHS) for Ireland, results from the Economically Active Population Survey (EAPS) provided by Statistics Korea for Korea, the Encuesta Nacional de Ocupación y Empleo (ENOE) for Mexico, results from the Labour Force Survey (LFS) provided by Statistics Sweden for Sweden, the Labour Force Survey (LFS) for the United Kingdom, the Current Population Survey (CPS), May Supplement for the United States and the European Social Survey (ESS) for all other European countries and Israel.

*StatLink* 🔗📊 http://dx.doi.org/10.1787/888933966768

Annex Figure 5.A.2. Non-standard workers in the private sector are also underrepresented by trade unions

Actual and adjusted ratio of trade union density among non-standard workers relative to standard workers in the private sector (%), latest available year

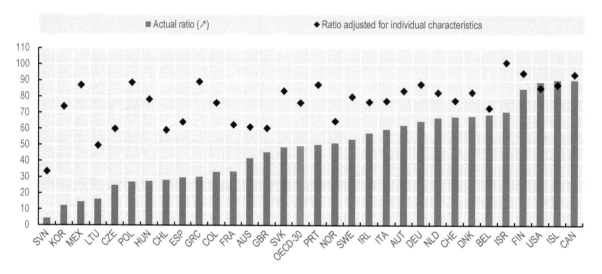

Note: 2010-12 for Greece and the Slovak Republic; 2013 for France and Korea; 2015 for Germany; 2016 for Australia and Finland; 2014-16 for Austria, Belgium, the Czech Republic, Denmark, Hungary, Iceland, Ireland, Israel, Italy, Lithuania, the Netherlands, Norway, Poland, Portugal, Slovenia, Spain, Sweden and Switzerland; 2017 for Canada, Chile, Colombia, the United Kingdom and the United States; and 2018 for Mexico. OECD-30 is the unweighted average of countries shown (not including Colombia, Estonia, Iceland, Latvia, Luxembourg, New Zealand and Turkey).

Non-standard workers are those without an open-ended employment contract. The adjusted ratio for individual characteristics is based on the marginal effect of being in a non-standard form of work relative to being in an open-ended contract calculated from a probit regression controlling for sex, age groups, educational levels, industry, occupation, firm size (except for the United States) and full-time vs. part-time employment.

Source: OECD estimates based on the Household, Income and Labour Dynamics in Australia (HILDA) for Australia, the Labour Force Survey (LFS) for Canada, Encuesta de Caracterización Socioeconómica Nacional (CASEN) for Chile, the Gran Encuesta Integrada de Hogares (GEIH) for Colombia, the Finnish Working Life Barometer (FWLB) for Finland, the Enquête statistique sur les ressources et conditions de vie (SRCV) for France, the German Socio-Economic Panel (SOEP) for Germany, the Korean Labor and Income Panel Study (KLIPS) for Korea, the Encuesta Nacional de Ocupación y Empleo (ENOE) for Mexico, the Labour Force Survey (LFS) for the United Kingdom, the Current Population Survey (CPS), May Supplement for the United States and the European Social Survey (ESS) for all other European countries and Israel.

*StatLink* 🔗 http://dx.doi.org/10.1787/888933966787

# Annex 5.B. Additional material on youth and collective actions

Annex Figure 5.B.1. Trend in union density among youth aged 20-34 in selected OECD countries

Young-to-adults ratio of union density, 2000's and latest year available (%)

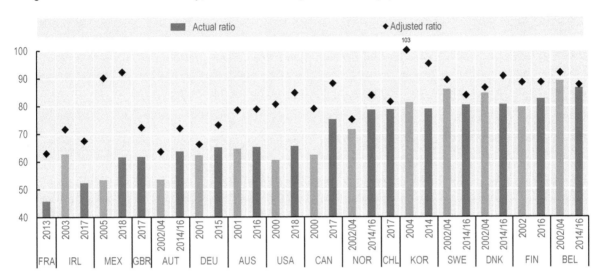

Note: The adjusted ratio for individual characteristics is based on the marginal effect of youth (aged 20-34) relatively to adults (aged 35-54) from a probit regression controlling for temporary job (excepted for the United States), sex, educational levels, industry, public vs private sector (except for Austria, Belgium, Ireland, Norway and Sweden), occupation, firm size (except for the United States) and full-time vs. part-time employment. Youth in education have been excluded in the different samples used in the regressions (although this was not possible for Finland, the United States, and countries with estimates based on the European Social Survey as a source). Countries are ordered by ascending order of the actual ratio for the latest year available.
Source: OECD estimates based on the Household, Income and Labour Dynamics in Australia (HILDA) for Australia, the labour force survey (LFS) for Canada, the Encuesta de Caracterización Socioeconómica Nacional (CASEN) for Chile, the Finnish Working Life Barometer (FWLB) for Finland, the Enquête statistique sur les ressources et conditions de vie (SRCV) for France, the German Socio-Economic Panel (SOEP) for Germany, the Quarterly National Household Survey (QNHS) for Ireland, the Korean Labor and Income Panel Study (KLIPS) for Korea, the Encuesta Nacional de Ocupación y Empleo (ENOE) for Mexico, the Labour Force Survey (LFS) for the United Kingdom, the Current Population Survey (CPS), May Supplement for the United States and the European Social Survey (ESS) for Austria, Belgium, Denmark, Norway and Sweden.

StatLink ᐧᐧᐧ http://dx.doi.org/10.1787/888933966806

## Individual values and support for collective action among young people

Statistics shown in Figure 5.3. Panels A and B are based on the occurrence of "individual freedom" and "solidarity and support for others" taken from the list of the three most important personal values of youth aged 20-34 and adults aged 35-54. The Question is labelled as follows in the Eurobarometer: "In the following list, which are the three most important values for you personally?"

Statistics reported in Figure 5.3. Panels C and D are calculated as the proportion of youth aged 20-34 and adults aged 35-54 who declared either that they engaged in the past / in the recent past / or that they would in the future engage in the following actions: attending a demonstration, donating money or raising funds for a particular social or political cause. The question in the ISSP 2014, Citizen Module II is labelled as follows: "Here are some different forms of political and social action that people can take. Please indicate, for each one, whether you have done any of these things in the past year, whether you have done it in the more distant past, whether you have not done it but might do it or have not done it and would never, under any circumstances, do it". For the two following forms or political and political actions: "Took part in a demonstration (any kind of demonstration)" and "Donated money or raised funds for a social or political activity".

Figures on perceived necessity of trade unions (Figure 5.4. Panel B) refer to the share of persons who consider that "workers needs strong trade unions to protect their interest". For the United States, this corresponds to the percentage of persons feeling that the decline in union representation over the last 20 years has been mostly bad for working people ("As you may know, over the past twenty years there has been a large reduction in the percentage of workers who are represented by unions. Do you think this reduction in union representation has been mostly good for working people or mostly bad for working people?"). Age groups correspond to persons aged 20-34 for youth and aged 35-54 for the adults, except for Denmark (26-35 and 36-55, respectively). Belgium refers to Flanders only.

## Trust and perceived necessity of trade unions

### Annex Table 5.B.1. Trust in trade unions: Sources and definitions

| Country | Source | Year | Question used | Possible answers | Statistics reported (% of persons) |
|---|---|---|---|---|---|
| Australia | Australian Election Study | 2016 | How much confidence do you have in trade unions? | Scale in four categories: 1. A great deal of confidence; 2. Quite a lot of confidence; 3. Not very much confidence; 4. None at all | A great deal or quite a lot of confidence |
| Austria, Belgium, the Czech Republic, Denmark, Estonia, Finland, France, Germany, Greece, Hungary, Ireland, Italy, Latvia, Lithuania, Luxembourg, the Netherlands, Poland, Portugal, the Slovak Republic, Slovenia, Spain, Sweden, Turkey and the United Kingdom | Eurobarometer 89.1 | 2018 | Could you please tell me for trade unions, whether the term brings to mind something very positive, fairly positive, fairly negative or very negative? | Scale in four categories: 1. Very positive; 2. Fairly positive; 3. Fairly negative; 4. Very negative | Very positive or fairly positive |
| Chile, Colombia, Japan, Korea, Mexico, New Zealand and the United States | World value Survey | 2010 (JPN, KOR); 2011 (CHL, NZL, USA); 2012 (COL, MEX) | How much confidence you have in labour unions? | Scale in four categories: 1. A great deal of confidence; 2. Quite a lot of confidence; 3. Not very much confidence; 4. None at all | A great deal or quite a lot of confidence |

## Annex Figure 5.B.2. Trust in trade unions

Percentage of population by age group

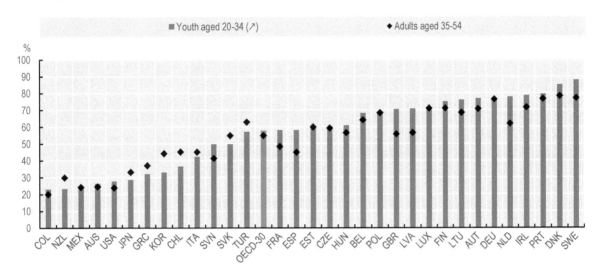

Note: For further details, see Annex Table 5.B.1. OECD-30 is the unweighted average of countries shown (not including Canada, Colombia, Iceland, Israel, Norway and Switzerland).
Source: OECD calculations based on the Australian Election Study (AES) for Australia, Eurobarometer 89.1, March 2018 for the European countries, and the World Value Survey (WVS) for all other countries.

StatLink 🔗 http://dx.doi.org/10.1787/888933966825

## Annex Figure 5.B.3. Perceived necessity and trust in trade unions

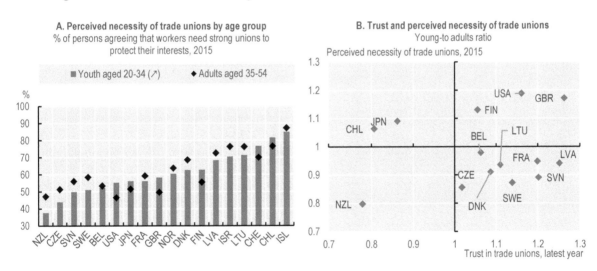

Note: Youth refers to persons aged 20-34 and adults to those aged 35-54, except for Denmark (26-35 and 36-55, respectively). Belgium refers only to Flanders. For further details on trust in trade unions, see Annex Table 5.B.1.
Source: OECD calculations based on the International Social Survey Programme (ISSP) 2015, Work orientation module IV and the Pew Research Center, March 2015 Political Survey for the United States.

StatLink 🔗 http://dx.doi.org/10.1787/888933966844

## Notes

[1] OECD (forthcoming[79]) looks at the issue of the drivers of the decline in trade union density in more depth.

[2] Collective bargaining and social dialogue are two distinct forms of action in which social partners engage. Social dialogue includes all kind of negotiation, consultation or, simply, exchange of information at any level between employers and workers. Social dialogue is often voluntary and can be formal (such as "works councils" in Germany) or informal (such as informal exchanges on the workplace or declarations of intent at national level). Collective bargaining is a formal process which is in most cases based on a (national) legal framework defining the rights and obligations of the bargaining parties and which, following a period of negotiation, generally leads to legally binding collective agreements.

[3] As set, together with the "right to organise", by the ILO Convention No. 98.

[4] The analysis in this chapter builds on the answers to the OECD Policy Questionnaires on Collective Bargaining (OECD, 2017[1]) updated in late 2018 to reflect the latest changes as well as on a number of interviews and exchanges with academics, policy-makers, trade unionists and representatives of employer organisations. The last section also builds on the responses to the Questionnaire on Policy Responses to New Forms of Work (OECD, 2019[78]).

[5] For instance, in some OECD countries, the so-called "Ghent system" countries, the social partners play a key role in directly managing the unemployment insurance system.

[6] "Last in, first out" is a policy used to prioritise layoffs by seniority.

[7] Workers at risk of layoff are supported well before the layoff actually occurs.

[8] See OECD (2017[1]) and OECD (2018[7]) for a detailed discussion on the functioning of different systems of collective bargaining as well as their impact on labour market performance.

[9] The agreement, however, has largely failed to materialise so far, as companies, but also local unions, struggle to implement the new possibility opened by the sectoral agreement.

[10] Although there is a large cross-country variation, from almost no firms covered by training provisions in Central and Eastern European countries to only about 10% in Finland or Denmark to 79% in France (OECD, 2019[16]). Moreover, it is important to note that firms may also provide training in the absence of collective agreements.

[11] Source: OECD/ICTWSS Database.

[12] The patterns presented in the figure are not affected when focusing on private sector employees only (see Annex Figure 5.A.2).

[13] The correlation between the adjusted ratio of trade union density among non-standard workers relative to standard workers and trade union density among standard workers is weak (0.39) and not strongly significant; it becomes insignificant (and even weaker, 0.24) when excluding the Finnish and Icelandic cases.

[14] According to the ILO Committee of Experts on the Applications of Conventions and Recommendations (CEACR), "the entitlement to these right should not be based on the existence of an employment relationship, which is often non-existent". The recent report of the ILO Global Commission on the Future of Work also states that "all workers must enjoy (…) the right to collective bargaining" (ILO, 2019, p. 12[3]).

[15] While economists have discussed how insider companies, i.e. companies already operating in the market, can use the extensions of collective agreements to raise outsider rivals' costs or increase entry barriers – see e.g. Haucap et al. (2001[81]), – such anticompetitive behaviours result from deliberate *employers'* strategy, not from unions' bargaining power. As such, they do not contradict legal arguments exempting labour organisations from antitrust regulations, which consider collective bargaining from the perspective of *workers*. In fact, Haucap et al. (2001[81]) argue that, in some cases, a strong labour union can serve as an efficiency enhancing countervailing power to employers' associations.

[16] Decision No E/04/002 (Case COM/14/03) Agreements between Irish Actors' Equity SIPTU and the Institute of Advertising Practitioners in Ireland concerning the terms and conditions under which advertising agencies will hire actors

[17] Dutch Competition Authority (*Nederlandse Mededingingsautoriteit*), *Cao-tariefbepalingen voor zelfstandigen en de Mededingingswet: visiedocument* (Collective labour agreements determining fees for self-employed and the competition law: a reflection document), 2007.

[18] United States Court of Appeals for the Ninth Circuit, No. 17-35640.

[19] This case is often referred to as the FNV Kunsten case (Case C-413/13). The case was also brought to the ILO Committee of Experts on the application of Conventions and recommendations (CEACR) which reiterated that Convention No. 98 "establishes the principle of free and voluntary collective bargaining and the autonomy of bargaining parties" (ILO, 2016[40]).

[20] Collective Complaint No. 123/2016 ICTU v. Ireland, decision adopted on 12 September 2018, paragraph 38.

[21] In addition, as discussed in the annex of Chapter 4, a current debate in the field of competition law revolves around whether worker welfare should be included in the definition of "consumer welfare", which guides the action of antitrust authorities, and whether the latter's analyses should consider welfare losses beyond those affecting the final consumer.

[22] For instance, U.S. v. Joseph P. Cuddigan, et al., U.S. District Court D.R.I., Civil Action N.3843, 15 June 1970.

[23] Although when the pool of available workers is extremely large (e.g. in the case of crowdsourcing platform workers such as Amazon Mechanical Turk), increasing exit options through competition might not be enough. Indeed these workers have an extremely low residual labour supply elasticity – as low as 0.1 according to Dube et al (forthcoming[82]). When taking into account the supply response of all their competitors and the fact that the pool of available workers stretches worldwide, they have little choice but to accept evolving prices.

[24] A dependent contractor is defined as follows: a) a person, whether or not employed under a contract of employment, b) and whether or not furnishing tools, vehicles, equipment, machinery, material, or any other thing owned by the dependent contractor, c) who performs work or services for another person for compensation or reward, d) on such terms and conditions that the dependent contractor is in a position of economic dependence upon, and under an obligation to perform duties for, that person, e) more closely

resembling the relationship of an employee than that of an independent contractor (Section 1 Labour Relations Act Ontario).

[25] Employers can dispute the composition of the bargaining unit (i.e. the group of employees that the union/bargaining agent is certified to represent in collective bargaining). Such disputes will be settled by the Canada Industrial Relations Board (CIRB) during the certification process and before collective bargaining begins. During the certification process, the employer or union may contest the inclusion or exclusion of any job classification or position from the bargaining unit. The CIRB will review the evidence and determine the group of employees/bargaining unit that is appropriate for collective bargaining. In making such a determination, the CIRB has significant discretion, and will look beyond job titles/classifications and examines the actual duties of the persons concerned. If a collective agreement covers dependent contractors and a dispute arises concerning whether an individual is a dependent or independent contractor, the CIRB will also examine the evidence by looking beyond the job title/classification and make a decision. The CIRB's decision is subject to judicial review, initially by the Federal Court of Canada.

[26] The origins of this approach were in arguments by a law professor in the 1960s (Arthurs, 1965[85]) that collective bargaining is a way of addressing a power imbalance and, due to similarities between dependent contractors and employees, they should be eligible for unionisation. Many Canadian jurisdictions adopted the definition of dependent contractor in the following decade.

[27] A person who works for money is either an employee or a person providing work for remuneration on a different basis that the employment relationship as long as he/she does not employ any other persons to perform this type of work, irrespective of the legal basis of employment, and has such rights and interests related to performing the work which may be represented and defended by a trade union.

[28] The Irish law defines precisely the two cases: A "*false self-employed worker*" is an individual who (a) performs for a person the same activity or service as an employee of the other person, (b) has a relationship of subordination, (c) is required to follow the instructions of the other person regarding the time, place and content of his or her work, (d) does not share in the other person's commercial risk, (e) has no independence as regards the determination of the time schedule, place and manner of performing the tasks assigned, and (f) for the duration of the contractual relationship, forms an integral part of the other person's undertaking. A "*fully dependent self-employed worker*" is an individual (a) who performs services for another person (whether or not the person for whom the service is being performed is also an employer of employees) under a contract (whether express or implied, and if express, whether orally or in writing), and (b) whose main income in respect of the performance of such services under contract is derived from not more than two persons (Competition (Amendment) Act 2017).

[29] Collective complaint procedure, Council of Europe, Irish Congress of Trade Unions v. Ireland Complaint No 123/2016; IOE submission, https://rm.coe.int/123casedoc4-en-observations-by-the-ioe/16808b127f

[30] Physicians or hospitals in a non-exclusive provider network are allowed to offer medical services outside of the network itself.

[31] For instance, in 2010 in New Zealand, following an industrial dispute in the film industry, the government passed an amendment to the Employment Relations Act effectively preventing all workers in the film industry (considered independent contractors) to enter into collective bargaining. The current government has declared its intention to restore the right to engage in collective bargaining for film industry workers.

[32] A more radical approach to ensure that all self-employed workers experiencing power imbalance have the right to negotiate their own terms of employment – with no precedent in OECD countries and in conflict

with most existing regulations – is discussed in the academic literature (Creighton and McCrystal, 2016[87]; De Stefano and Aloisi, 2018[38]) and among trade unions (Fulton, 2018[49]). This consists in reversing the current presumption that self-employed workers do not only provide labour but also services by means of an independent business organisation that they actually own and manage – which justifies their exclusion from collective bargaining. In this approach, the burden of proof would be shifted onto those who propose the restriction, in particular regulation enforcement authorities. The main argument used in support of this approach is that "the right to bargain applies to all workers with the sole possible exception of those explicitly excluded by the text of ILO Convention No. 87 and No. 98" (notably, armed forces and the police) and "self-employed workers are not among those excluded and, therefore, the Conventions are deemed as fully applicable to them" (De Stefano and Aloisi, 2018, pp. 14-15[38]). A reversal of the burden of the proof would however conflict with most existing antitrust regulations and it would likely increase the burden for antitrust authorities that would have to check ex post the validity of a large number of agreements. Moreover, while aimed at ensuring that all workers in unbalanced power relationship are covered, the reversal of the burden of the proof may be exploited more effectively by relatively stronger and more organised groups of workers.

[33] For instance, in September 2004, the Hyundai Heavy Industry company union was expelled from the Korean Metal Workers' Union (a member of the Korean Confederation of Trade Unions, KCTU) precisely because of their discriminatory stance toward nonstandard workers (Durazzi, Fleckenstein and Lee, 2018[42]).

[34] Aslam & Ors v Uber BV & Ors [2016] EW Misc B68 (ET) (28 October 2016).

[35] Ruling 26/2019, *Corte d'Appello di Torino*, R.G.L. 468/2018. In the first instance, the judges rejected the request of re-classification. The *Corte di Cassazione* will take the final decision.

[36] Ruling of 10 January 2019, *Cour d'Appel de Paris,* RG 17/04674. Also in this case, the *Cour de Cassation* will take the final decision.

[37] Ruling of 15 January 2019, *Rechtbank Amsterdam*, case nb. 7044576 CV EXPL 18-14762 and 7044576 CV EXPL 18-14763.

[38] While outlawing discrimination clearly benefits "outsiders", strategies aimed at limiting the use of non-standard forms of employment might backfire against "outsiders" by reducing their job opportunities (OECD, 2014[86]).

[39] The issue of the status of platforms has been the subject of a series of recent court cases throughout OECD countries. In 2017, the European Court of Justice (case 434/15) found that Uber acts as a transportation service provider rather than a mere technological intermediary between customers and independent service providers and that "it exercises a certain control over the quality of the vehicles, the drivers and their conduct, which can, in some circumstances, result in their exclusion". In 2018, the French *Cour de Cassation* (Cass. soc., 28 *novembre* 2018, n° 17-20.079) concluded that the power to apply sanction and to monitor rides constituted a bond of subordination linking the platform TakeEatEasy and the drivers working for it, which justified considering the platform as an employer. See also Chapter 4 for other references.

[40] Between 1990 and 2017, the number of worker centers in the United States increased from 5 to 240, though membership is hard to estimate.

[41] The discussion on the United States in this section owes much to David Madland whose inputs are gratefully acknowledged.

[42] The founder of the Freelancers Union explicitly referred to a "new mutualism" (Horowitz, 2013[80]).

[43] For example, the campaign in New York by Domestic Workers United to extend basic legal protections such as overtime pay to domestic workers; the Restaurant Opportunities Center's efforts to end subminimum wage work for tipped employees and their suits against lawbreaking employers; and the "Freelance isn't Free" legislation pushed by the Freelancers Union.

[44] For example, strikes at Walmart were organised by the worker center Organization United for Respect at Walmart.

[45] One of the most successful examples of this is the Coalition of Immokalee Workers' effort to improve working conditions for farmworkers picking tomatoes sold by prominent retailers.

[46] Although an interesting example is the commercial negotiation conducted in 2016 by SMart in Belgium. Namely, SMart negotiated as an *employer*, on behalf of those of its employees who were also food-delivery riders on the side. SMart signed a convention with the platforms Deliveroo and TakeEatEasy in which they committed to guarantee riders shifts of three hours minimum and to be paid by the hour and not by the delivery. In addition, riders were given a formal *employment* contract. However, this example also highlights the limits to this type of negotiation: it had led to a non-binding commercial convention, but Deliveroo unilaterally decided to revert to payment by the delivery with self-employed riders in 2017 (Drahokoupil and Piasna, 2019[83]).

[47] However, Prassl (2018[77]) argues that platforms remain resistant to collective bargaining in many cases. For instance, in the United Kingdom, Deliveroo successfully fought the union recognition request from the Independent Workers Union of Great Britain (IWGB), on the basis that workers were independent contractors who could not collectively bargain.

[48] In 2016, Uber agreed to the formation of a workers' organisation in New York City, organised by a local branch of the International Association of Machinists and Aerospace Workers – while drivers are classified as independent contractors and thus outside of the provisions of the US National Labor Relations Act.

[49] Other websites, such as TurkerView and TurkerHub, offer similar possibilities and are run by Amazon Mechanical Turk workers themselves.

[50] Blockchain technology is a form of distributed ledger technology that acts as an open and trusted record (i.e. a list) of transactions from one party to another (or multiple parties) that is not stored by a central authority. Instead, a copy is stored by each user running Blockchain software and connected to a Blockchain network, also known as a node. Therefore, nobody can tamper with the ledger and everyone can inspect it (Berryhill, Bourgery and Hanson, 2018[84]).

[51] The Swedish white-collar union *Unionen* is, for instance, exploring how to use data to reduce members churn and keep a high membership. *Unionen* is also testing how data on workers requests of support can be used to "nowcast" (i.e. predict the very near future or near past) the state of a company or a region (the intuition being that when the business goes well, the number of requests of support tends to be lower and vice-versa). This would allow them to better target their efforts.

[52] http://www.oecd.org/els/emp/LFS Definitions - Tables.pdf.

# 6 Making adult learning systems future-ready for all

This chapter discusses the key role of adult learning in ensuring that all individuals can successfully navigate a changing labour market. It provides an overview of how several megatrends are changing job content and skill requirements. It identifies groups of adults that may face difficulties adapting to these changes unless they participate in re-skilling and up-skilling programmes. It also singles out workers in non-standard employment arrangements who face a number of challenges in obtaining training. For each group, the chapter discusses policy options to raise participation in training based on the specific barriers they face, be it the low quality of available training or a lack of motivation, time, money or employer support.

# In Brief

## Key findings

The skills required to enter and progress in the labour market are undergoing profound changes as a result of megatrends such as technological progress, new trade patterns and population ageing. This process is driven by shifts not only in the occupational structure of employment but also in changing skill requirements within each occupation.

Technological progress and the associated changes in work organisation are reshaping most occupations by altering the job tasks involved, with a rising demand for high-level cognitive and complex social-interaction skills. More jobs are part of global value chains, in which the different stages of production are spread across countries. Consequently, in advanced countries, high-level skills are becoming increasingly important for companies to specialise in the most technologically advanced activities. In parallel, employment relationships are changing as a result of these megatrends, leading to a rise in non-standard work and a reduction in job stability. More training opportunities will therefore be needed to facilitate labour mobility, but adult learning provision must also become more flexible and less tied to the traditional model of employer-provided training. Finally, population ageing means that individuals will need to maintain and update their skills over longer working lives. It is also likely to lead to a change in skill needs due to the associated shifts in demand for goods, services and qualified labour – notably healthcare professionals and elderly care personnel.

Initial education systems have a key role to play in providing young people with the skills required for a successful entry into the labour market. However, deep and rapid changes in technology make it difficult for initial education to equip young people with the knowledge and capabilities that they will need throughout their work life.

Adult learning systems that allows adults, whether working or looking for work, to maintain and upgrade their skills are therefore essential to harness the benefits that the megatrends will bring about by preventing skills depreciation and obsolescence and facilitating transitions from declining jobs and sectors to those that are expanding.

However, most adult training systems are ill equipped for this challenge. Participation in training varies widely, but what is common across all OECD countries is that those who need training the most, train the least. These groups include the low skilled, older adults, displaced workers, those whose jobs are most at risk from automation, as well as non-standard workers. In addition, training is not always of good quality and aligned to the needs of the labour market.

The key findings of the chapter include:

- Unless urgent action is taken, the low skilled, workers in jobs at high risk of automation, older adults and displaced workers – i.e. workers who have lost their jobs for economic reasons and/or in mass layoffs – are likely to be left behind. They tend to work in shrinking sectors and occupations and are generally ill equipped with the skills required in emerging jobs and businesses.

- Workers in non-standard forms of employment have more difficulties accessing training compared to standard employees. This is the case for part-time employees, own-account workers and those in temporary jobs – either on fixed-term contracts or temporary agency workers.

- Only one in five adults who do not participate in training report that there were learning opportunities that they would have wanted to take up. The remainder are either not motivated to participate in training, have not been offered meaningful training options or are discouraged by the barriers they face. This issue is particularly pressing for the low skilled, older workers, workers in jobs at high risk of automation and displaced workers. Conversely, more workers in non-standard forms of employment are willing to train than among full-time permanent employees, although they are still few.

- Many adults still face several barriers to access adult learning opportunities. Lack of time for personal or work reasons is by far the main barrier cited by adults who would like to participate in training but do not. Time constraints are a major impediment for high-skilled adults and own-account workers but are also a significant barrier for other groups, except for the unemployed and displaced workers, who presumably have more time on their hands. Financial constraints are the main barrier for these two groups.

- Most employers who do not train admit that they prefer to recruit new staff rather than provide training for their existing workforce. Others cite high training costs and a lack of time for staff to participate as major barriers. Moreover, among firms that do train, only about half do so for at least 50% of their workforce – which prompts the questions of whether firms' training reaches the most disadvantaged workers.

Action on the adult learning front is urgent. In view of the scope and the speed of the changes taking place, adjustments at the margins are unlikely to be sufficient and a significant overhaul of adult learning policies is needed to make adult learning systems future-ready for all.

- There are different policy options for countries to ensure that vulnerable groups and non-standard workers have access to adequate adult learning opportunities. These revolve around building a learning culture among firms and individuals, removing the barriers to training that disadvantaged groups face, tackling unequal access to training based on employment status, encouraging firms to train groups at risk, and making training rights portable between jobs and spells out of work.

- Increasing access to training for under-represented groups will not automatically address the skills challenges of a changing world of work. The scaling up of training provision needs to focus on programmes that are of good quality and aligned to labour market needs.

- Finally, adult learning needs to receive adequate and sustainable funding to function well – with contributions by the government individuals, and firms – as well as governance arrangements that can help countries to make different parts of adult learning systems work well together.

## Introduction

In a rapidly changing world of work, adult learning systems are under strain. Skill demands have been gradually, but consistently, shifting towards a more intensive use of cognitive and interpersonal skills under the combined forces of technology and globalisation. In this context, there is an urgent need to scale up and strengthen training opportunities for adults to keep their skills up to date or acquire new ones over longer working lives.

Low-skilled adults[1] are likely to bear the brunt of changes in skill needs unless they can engage in high-quality reskilling and upskilling programmes. Similarly, as new forms of work emerge at the border between self-employment and employee status, it is important to ensure that this does not translate into growing inequality in access to training based on employment status.

While some countries are better prepared than others to address these changes, all face challenges – be it on participation, inclusiveness, financing or relevance and quality of the training provided (OECD, 2019[1]). On average, two in five adults (40%) participate in job-related formal and non-formal training in any given year,[2] and this often only involves training for only few hours, according to data from the Survey of Adult Skills (PIAAC). The figure ranges from 20% or less in Greece, Italy and Turkey to just short of 60% in New Zealand and Norway, pointing to a need for a significant scaling-up in several countries to catch up with the best performers.[3]

If participation in training varies widely across OECD countries, what is common to all countries is that it remains very unequally distributed. Participation is especially low amongst those most in need of new or additional skills and among the rising number of workers in non-standard employment arrangements (see Chapters 2 and 4). To give a few examples, participation by low-skilled adults is a staggering 40 percentage points below that of high-skilled adults, in the OECD on average. Older adults are 25 percentage points less likely to train than 25-34 year-olds. Workers whose jobs are at high risk of automation are 30 percentage points less likely to engage in adult learning than their peers in less exposed jobs. Only 35% of own-account workers participate in training yearly compared with 57% of full-time permanent employees. A better understanding of the specific barriers faced by these groups is essential to design effective measures adapted to their needs.

This chapter builds on recent OECD work on the functioning, effectiveness and resilience of adult learning systems across countries (Box 6.1) and focusses on disadvantaged groups most affected by the changes that the future of work will bring. The chapter is structured as follows. Section 6.1 looks at how various megatrends are changing job content and skill requirements. Section 6.2 identifies groups of adults who are under-represented in training and discusses the barriers to participation they face, such as motivation, time or money. For each group, Section 6.3 discusses policy options to increase participation in training based on the specific barriers they face. Section 6.4 discusses the potential role of individual learning accounts and Section 6.5 highlights the importance of aligning training to labour market needs, building governance structures involving all relevant stakeholders, and ensuring adequate and equitable financing mechanisms.

---

Box 6.1. OECD work on the functioning, effectiveness and resilience of adult learning systems across countries

Over the past few years, the OECD has undertaken an ambitious programme of work on the functioning, effectiveness and resilience of adult learning systems across countries. This includes:

- A new dashboard on Priorities for Adult Learning (PAL). The dashboard facilitates cross-country comparisons of the future-readiness of adult learning systems. It presents a set of internationally comparable indicators along seven dimensions: i) urgency; ii) coverage; iii) inclusiveness; iv) flexibility and guidance; v) alignment with skill needs; vi) perceived training impact; and vii) financing (OECD, 2019[2]).

- The report Getting Skills Right: Future-Ready Adult Learning Systems. The report highlights key emerging challenges in adult learning and presents examples of policy initiatives put in place in OECD countries. The report also features concrete policy recommendations to help OECD

---

countries increase the future readiness of their adult learning systems in a changing world of work (OECD, 2019[1]).

- Three booklets on specific aspects of getting adult learning systems ready for the future, including "Engaging low-skilled adults in learning", "Creating responsive adult learning systems" and "Making adult learning work in social partnership". Each booklet outlines seven concrete actionable principles for stakeholders involved in adult learning policies. These actionable principles draw on existing evidence and provide insights on how to translate policy recommendations into practice by highlighting promising initiatives in OECD and emerging countries (OECD, 2019[3]; 2019[4]; 2019[5]).

- The OECD is also engaging with individual countries to help them address their specific challenges and priorities in making adult learning systems future ready. In addition to providing country-specific suggestions, these studies also add to the evidence base on how to make adult learning systems more responsive and effective.

## 6.1. How megatrends are influencing the demand and supply for skills

The demand for skills in the labour market is undergoing substantial change as a result of technological progress, globalisation and population ageing. In parallel, developments such as rising levels of educational attainment, higher labour market participation of women, and greater migration flows are altering the supply of skills.

Technological progress is reshaping the content and tasks of many occupations. In 2013, Frey and Osborne (2017[6]) interviewed experts to identify occupations that were at high risk of automation based on their task content over the following two decades. High-level cognitive tasks as well as complex social interaction skills were found to be crucial bottlenecks to automation. As a result, jobs are likely to become more intensive in these tasks as new technologies are adopted in the workplace to automate more repetitive ones.

Looking at the presence and frequency of these bottleneck tasks in individual jobs, Nedelkoska and Quintini (2018[7]) find that, on average across OECD countries, about 14% of jobs could change so dramatically as to disappear entirely and an additional 32% could change significantly. Occupations at low risk of automation correspond to those where high-level cognitive skills and complex social interactions are required most frequently, and the opposite is true for occupations at high risk (Figure 6.1) (Nedelkoska and Quintini, 2018[7]).[4]

Based on these findings, one can expect technological change to impact skill requirements through changes in the nature and content of jobs. On the one hand, it would affect employment composition as the share of jobs at high risk of automation decreases as automation takes place. On the other, the content of remaining jobs – those not at risk of disappearing entirely but still affected by automation – is likely to change in favour of bottleneck tasks as more routine tasks are automated.[5]

Shortages in bottleneck skills and surpluses in skills that are highly automatable are already emerging (Figure 6.2). Exploiting detailed information on skill requirements, the OECD Skills for Jobs database shows a gradual intensifying over the past decade of shortages in high-level cognitive skills (e.g. reasoning, fluency of ideas and originality) and the skills needed in complex social interactions (e.g. written and oral communication and time sharing skills).

## Figure 6.1. Risk of automation and skill content of jobs, OECD average

Task frequency by occupation, top ten and bottom ten occupations by risk of automation

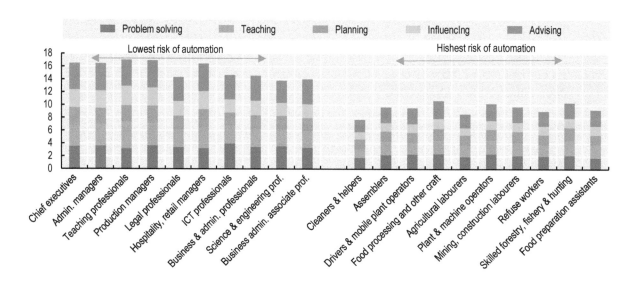

Note: For each task, frequency is measured on a 5-point scale, ranging from 1 Never to 5 Every day. The value reported is the average frequency of respondents in each occupation. The ranking by risk of automation is derived from Nedelkoska, L. and G. Quintini (2018), "Automation, skills use and training", OECD Social, Employment and Migration Working Papers, No. 202, https://doi.org/10.1787/2e2f4eea-en.
Source: OECD calculations based on the Survey of Adult Skills (PIAAC) (2012, 2015), http://www.oecd.org/skills/piaac/.

StatLink ᵐˢᴾ http://dx.doi.org/10.1787/888933966863

## Figure 6.2. Trends in skill shortages and surpluses, OECD unweighted average, 2004-17

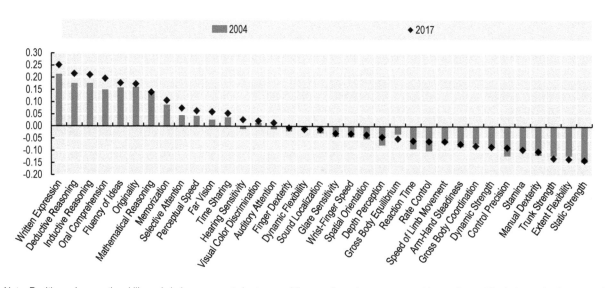

Note: Positive values on the skill needs index represent shortages, while negative values correspond to surpluses. The index varies between -1 and +1. The maximum value represents the strongest shortage observed across OECD (31) countries and skill areas.
Source: OECD Skills for Jobs database, www.oecdskillsforjobsdatabase.org.

StatLink ᵐˢᴾ http://dx.doi.org/10.1787/888933966882

Technological change is also leading to substantial adjustments in how work is organised and the adoption of new business models. Across the OECD and EU countries, a significant proportion of workers are in workplaces that have introduced new technologies and/or undergone significant restructuring in the way jobs and tasks are carried out (Figure 6.3). Ongoing changes in work organisation include the adoption of high performance work practices and engagement of workers through mechanisms such as teamwork, employee's voice, workers' autonomy, multitasking and problem-solving. These management and organisational changes can foster skills use in the workplace but require more emphasis on workplace learning and workers with strong cognitive skills and motivation to learn (OECD, 2016[8]).

### Figure 6.3. Share of workers in changing workplaces, 2015

Percentage of workers in workplaces that have introduced new technologies and/or undergone significant restructuring in the way jobs and tasks are carried out, EU countries

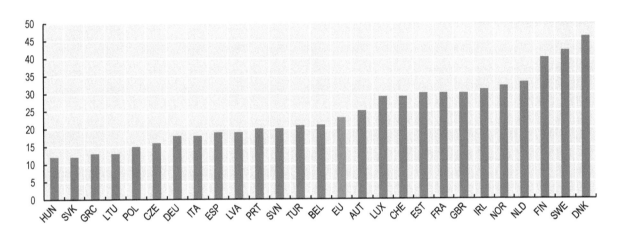

Note: Share of working answering affirmatively to the following question: During the last three years, has there been a restructuring or reorganisation at the workplace that has substantially affected your work?
Source: European Working Condition Survey, 2015, https://www.eurofound.europa.eu/surveys/european-working-conditions-surveys.

StatLink 🔗 http://dx.doi.org/10.1787/888933966901

Indeed, countries that underwent substantial restructuring in the workplace (e.g. Finland, Sweden or Denmark and Estonia) have stronger shortages in administration and management knowledge as well as in other key skills requiring workers to develop autonomy in making decisions and independence in the organisation of tasks.[6] Similarly, there is a positive correlation between organisational change and shortages of skills such as co-ordination with others and ability to lead others (see Figure 6.4).

In parallel, as highlighted in Chapter 2, the share of some non-standard forms of employment, such as temporary, part-time, own-account and platform workers, is increasing in many OECD countries, and across economic sectors and occupations.[7] Not only does this change skill requirements – potentially raising the need for self-organisation and self-management skills – and make training particularly important to facilitate labour mobility, but it also shifts the responsibility for skills acquisition from employers to the workers themselves.

Figure 6.4. Organisational change and changing skill needs, EU countries

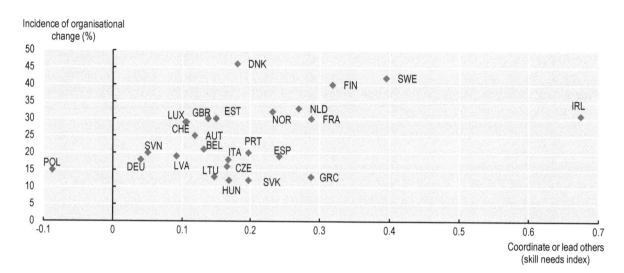

Note: Positive values on the skill needs index represent shortages, while negative values correspond to surpluses. The index varies between -1 and +1. The maximum value represents the most acute shortage observed across OECD (31) countries and skill areas.
Source: European Working Conditions Survey (2015), OECD Skills for Jobs database (2017), www.oecdskillsforjobsdatabase.org.

StatLink 🔟🔣🔲 http://dx.doi.org/10.1787/888933966920

Similar changes in skill requirements are brought about by globalisation. Over the past decade, the discussion on international trade has moved away from the concept of globalisation – whereby the entire production of goods was being offshored to developing countries to take advantage of lower labour costs – and towards the participation in global value chains – *i.e.* the offshoring of specific stages of the production process. In this context, the set of tasks performed by workers at each given skill level and the intensity with which they are performed is likely to change (Acemoglu and Autor, 2010[9]). Evidence suggests that moving up global value chains raises the demand for high-level skills which are crucial for countries to specialise in the most technologically advanced industries and in complex business services (OECD, 2017[10]). For instance, Becker, Ekholm and Muendler (2013[11]) find that offshoring firms have relatively more domestic jobs involving non-routine and interactive tasks.

Demographic change is also raising challenges for adult learning systems. In the context of increasing life expectancy and reforms to keep pension systems financially sustainable, working lives are likely to become longer and job changes more frequent as people retire later. Thus, adult learning will become even more important in the future. Furthermore, the shrinking number of young people entering the labour market relative to the number retiring has already contributed to significant shortages of qualified labour in some countries. The ageing of the baby boom generation is also leading to a substantial rise in the elderly population and consequently to shortages in healthcare professionals and long-term care personnel in many countries. Indeed, the OECD Skills for Jobs database (OECD, 2017[12]) shows that healthcare and personal care related skills are in shortage in the large majority of countries, and the most acute shortages of healthcare professionals are found in countries experiencing more rapid population ageing. Finally, population ageing is likely to contribute to further shifts in the structure of the economy, as demand for goods and services changes to accommodate the preferences of older consumers, indirectly affecting the occupational structure of employment and skill needs of employers.

## 6.2. Some groups are more affected than others

The changes in skill requirements described above have the potential to affect all workers. However, the growing demand for high-level cognitive skills and complex social interaction skills suggests that low-skilled adults working in jobs that are very intensive in simple and repetitive tasks are likely to bear the brunt of these changes. Many of them are at risk of losing their jobs as a result of automation. Others – denoted displaced workers in this chapter – will already be unemployed following dismissals for economic reasons.[8] In all cases, the adults concerned are likely to need retraining for different jobs in different sectors, making the task particularly hard (OECD, 2019[13]; European Commission, 2018[14]).

Age plays a key role in the context of continuous skill development, particularly when it overlaps with low skills, jobs at high risk of automation or in sectors undergoing structural change. Older adults are likely to experience significant skills obsolescence, particularly in the context of technological change, unless further training is available to upgrade what they learnt in initial education. At the same time, incentives for adults to train and for employers to provide training opportunities tend to decline with age as there is less time to recoup the investment made before retirement (Martin, 2018[15]; OECD, 2017[16]).

With the share of workers in non-standard contractual arrangements rising in some countries, the challenges faced by this group in maintaining and updating their skills are receiving significant attention. As training is often provided by employers, workers with less attachment to the labour market have more difficulties accessing it. This is likely to be the case for temporary, part-time and own-account workers, including platform workers.

Despite their greater need for up-skilling and re-skilling, these groups receive less training than their counterparts. The largest differences are observed between low and high skilled adults and between adults in jobs at high and low risk of automation, but a significant gap also exists between older adults and younger people (Figure 6.5). Workers in non-standard contracts receive significantly less training than their counterparts in full-time permanent jobs, lending support to the concern that these workers find it particularly difficult to access training because of the lack of attachment to an individual employer. This is particularly the case for own-account workers.

One should be careful in interpreting the differences in the incidence of training between groups presented in Figure 6.5 as a causal relationship. Differences in training incidence by contract type are particularly difficult to analyse because, at any given point in time, less skilled workers are both less likely to have a regular open ended contract and less likely to participate in job-related training. To the extent that ability is not accounted for in simple descriptive statistics, one might incorrectly attribute the observed training pattern to contract type while, in fact, this might reflect differences in unobserved ability at least partly. Similar arguments apply to the other groups discussed above.

In light of these considerations, and given that many of the groups in Figure 6.5 are overlapping, running a pooled cross-country regression using PIAAC data of the probability of participating in job-related training on a set of individual, job and firm characteristics provides a way of better isolating the effect of each factor.[9] The results presented in Table 6.1 confirm the descriptive relationships highlighted in Figure 6.5. Both educational attainment and proficiency in literacy are positively associated with the likelihood of participating in training for adults as well as workers, while controlling for other individual (and employer's) characteristics. The effect is twice as large when the unemployed and the inactive are included suggesting that skill levels are more crucial determinants of these groups' participation in training than of the participation of workers. The risk of automation is also a very strong predictor of the probability of training participation: workers in jobs at high risk of automation train less than their counterparts in jobs at low risk. Participation in training decreases with age. In terms of employment status, employees are the group participating the most in training.

### Figure 6.5. Participation in job-related training by group, OECD average

Share of adults (age 16-65) in each group that participate in training, 2012/2015

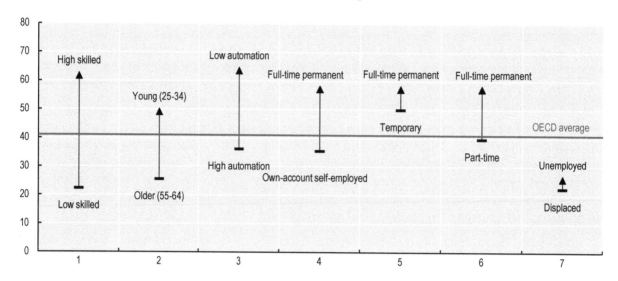

Note: Share of adults who participated in formal or non-formal job-related training over the previous 12 months. Data refer to 2012 for most countries, except for Chile, Greece, Israel, Lithuania, New Zealand, Slovenia and Turkey where they refer to 2015. Low (high) skilled refers to adults who score at level 1 or below (levels 4 or 5) on the PIAAC literacy scale. High (low) automation refers to adults at high (low) risk of automation. Own-account workers are the self-employed without employees. Temporary refers to workers on fixed term or temporary work agency contracts. Part-time refers to adults who work less than 30 hours per week. Full-time permanent are adults in full-time jobs with an indefinite work contract. Unemployed refers to all unemployed who have not been dismissed for economic reasons in their last job; displaced refers to unemployed adults who have been dismissed for economic reasons in the last job. The OECD average (40%) refers to the unweighted average participation in job-related training among all adults among OECD countries participating in the Survey for Adult Skills (PIAAC).
Source: Survey of Adult Skills (PIAAC) (2012, 2015), http://www.oecd.org/skills/piaac/.

*StatLink* ᵃₛₗ http://dx.doi.org/10.1787/888933966939

The results in Table 6.1 also confirm that own-account workers and the unemployed receive significantly less training than employees in open-ended contracts, once other socio-demographic characteristics are controlled for. This is also the case for part-time workers.

Conversely, for fixed-term and temporary agency workers there is no statistically-significant difference with employees in open-ended contracts, suggesting that individual characteristics play a bigger role than their contract type in determining their likelihood of participation.[10] However, this may hide further heterogeneity across types of training and firms characteristics. For instance, Fialho, Quintini and Vandeweyer (forthcoming[17]) find that fixed-term and temporary-agency workers receive less non-formal training[11] but more formal training[12] than their counterparts on open-ended contracts. This is probably due to the fact that formal training tends to be of a general nature and less likely to be employer-sponsored. Temporary workers may invest in formal training – by paying out of their own pocket or using available public funding – to compensate for the reduced amount of training they receive at work. They may also use temporary work as a short-term source of financing for expensive education courses and search for open-ended contracts after graduation: the causality in this case would run from formal training participation to temporary contract status.

Further evidence by the OECD (OECD, 2014[18]) shows a negative and statistically significant relationship between temporary contract status and participation in employer-sponsored[13] non-formal training in the vast majority of OECD countries for which data is available.

## Table 6.1. Incidence of training and willingness to participate, by socio-demographic characteristics

Marginal effects from probit regressions

| | All adults | All employees | All workers | Willingness to train – employees who did not train |
|---|---|---|---|---|
| Female | -0.011** | -0.023*** | -0.039*** | 0.043 |
| Age (ref=16-24) | | | | |
| 25-34 | 0.009 | -0.003 | -0.001 | -0.026 |
| 35-54 | -0.022* | -0.037* | -0.038** | -0.037 |
| 55-64 | -0.075*** | -0.100*** | -0.097*** | -0.064*** |
| Education (number of years) | 0.030*** | 0.014*** | 0.019*** | 0.005** |
| Employment status (ref=employees) | | | | |
| Own-account worker | -0.110*** | | -0.100*** | |
| Self-employed with employees | -0.094*** | | -0.102*** | |
| Displaced | -0.135*** | | | |
| Unemployed | -0.135*** | | | |
| Out of the labour force | -0.259*** | | | |
| Literacy proficiency score | 0.009*** | 0.007*** | 0.007*** | 0.008*** |
| Firm size (ref=1-10 employees) | | | | |
| 11-50 employees | | 0.035*** | | -0.030*** |
| 51-250 employees | | 0.063*** | | -0.005 |
| 251-1000 employees | | 0.092*** | | -0.006 |
| 1000 employees or more | | 0.109*** | | -0.025 |
| Growing firm | | 0.037*** | | 0.016 |
| Private sector | | -0.052*** | | -0.061*** |
| Part-time job | | -0.051*** | | 0.003 |
| Contract type (ref=open-ended contract) | | | | |
| Fixed-term contract | | 0.013 | | 0.011 |
| Temporary work agency contract | | 0.007 | | 0.057 |
| Apprenticeship or training contract | | 0.281*** | | 0.016 |
| No contract | | -0.041** | | -0.008 |
| Other | | 0.069** | | 0.013 |
| Risk of automation | | -0.214*** | -0.276*** | -0.118*** |
| High performance work practices at work | | 0.052*** | | -0.014 |
| Country Dummies | Yes | Yes | Yes | Yes |
| Occupation Dummies | No | Yes | Yes | Yes |
| Industry Dummies | No | Yes | Yes | Yes |
| Observations | 148386 | 75231 | 91391 | 33238 |
| Pseudo R2 | 0.201 | 0.180 | 0.167 | 0.093 |

Note: The dependent variable "willingness to train" is constructed to take value 1 if the employee did not participate in training but would have liked to and 0 if the employee did not participate in training and there were no learning activities that he/she wanted to participate. The regression includes additional controls for marital status, dependent children, country of birth, tenure and experience required. Occupation and industry dummies are included at the 1-digit level. The table reports marginal effects, i.e. percentage change in the outcome variable following a change in the relevant explanatory variable. Marginal effects for categorical variables refer to a discrete change from the base level. Proficiency in literacy is measured on a 500-point scale but is divided by 10 for presentational purposes. *, **, ***: statistically significant at the 10%, 5%, and 1% level, respectively.
Source: OECD Secretariat calculations based on the Survey of Adult Skills, PIAAC (2012, 2015).

StatLink ᵐˢᵖ http://dx.doi.org/10.1787/888933967205

Finally, among other factors, firms characteristics such as size, growth potential and sector also affect the changes of training participation, with larger firms, growing firms and firms operating in the public sector providing more training, ceteris paribus.

The reasons for lower participation of disadvantaged groups in training are complex and can come from either the demand (participants) or the supply (training provision) side. On average in the OECD, only 19% of adults who did not participate in training over the previous 12 months report that there were learning opportunities that they would have wanted to take up.

In this chapter, the term *willingness to train* will denote the likelihood that workers had learning opportunities that they wanted to take up but could not. Willingness to train varies across under-represented groups defined above (Figure 6.6). Low-skilled adults, workers in jobs at high risk of automation and older workers are significantly less willing to train than their counterparts, and so are dismissed workers although the difference is smaller. The willingness to train is also low for workers in non-standard forms of employment who, nevertheless, seem to have more appetite for training than full-time permanent employees.

Many reasons could explain why so many adults have low willingness to train, including the poor quality of the training offers they receive (or more generally lack of support from their employer), poor attitudes to learning, a lack of information on training opportunities, lack of understanding of the benefits that can derive from training, or the perception that existing barriers to participation are unsurmountable.

### Figure 6.6. Willingness to train by group, OECD average

Share of adults (age 16-65) in each group who did not participate in training but would have liked to, 2012, 2015

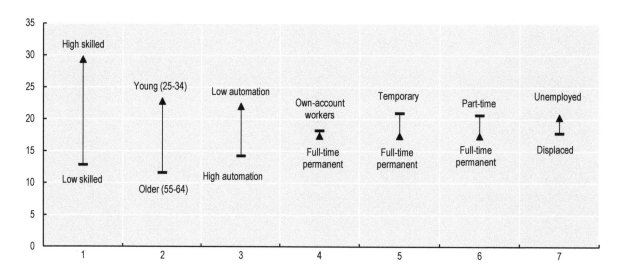

Note: Share of adults who did not participate in training but report that, over the previous 12 months, there were learning activities that they would have wanted to participate in. Data refer to 2012 for most countries, except for Chile, Greece, Israel, Lithuania, New Zealand, Slovenia and Turkey where they refer to 2015. Low (high) skilled refers to adults who score at level 1 or below (levels 4 or 5) on the PIAAC literacy scale. High (low) automation refers to adults at high (low) risk of automation. Own account workers are the self-employed without employees. Temporary refers to workers on fixed term or temporary work agency contracts. Part-time refers to adults who work less than 30 hours per week. Full-time permanent are adults in full-time jobs with an indefinite work contract. Unemployed refers to all unemployed who have not been dismissed for economic reasons in their last job; displaced refers to unemployed adults who have been dismissed for economic reasons in the last job.

Source: Survey of Adult Skills (PIAAC) (2012, 2015), http://www.oecd.org/skills/piaac/

StatLink ᵃˢ⁾ http://dx.doi.org/10.1787/888933966958

Table 6.1 attempts to shed light on the factors determining the willingness to train. The dependent variable is constructed to take value 1 if the employee did not participate in training but would have liked to and 0 if the employee did not participate in training and there were no learning activities that he/she wanted to participate in. Results confirm that the willingness to participate in training is affected by individual, family, job and firm characteristics. It increases with educational attainment and skill level while it declines with age, suggesting that personal motivation may play a role. It is lower in jobs at high risk of automation and in jobs in the private sector which tend to receive less training overall, lending credit to the idea that the lack of willingness to train may have to do with the lack of valuable and interesting training options. On the other hand, the willingness to train among non-participants is lower in larger firms despite the fact that larger firms generally provide more opportunities to train.

Another key challenge to training participation is that even adults who would be willing to train in principle do not do so because they face several barriers. Lack of time for personal or work reasons is by far the main barrier cited by adults who would like to participate in training but do not. This tends to be the main barrier for all the groups considered, except for the unemployed and displaced workers who presumably have more time on their hands (Figure 6.7). For the latter, the main barrier turns out to be financial. The lack of pre-requisites – most likely minimum qualification requirements – represents a hurdle for about 11% of low-skilled adults and 8% displaced workers. For those who report that there were learning opportunities that they would have wanted to take up, lack of employer support does not stand out as a key barrier to training, although this is likely to be due to the fact that many of the adults considered are not in an employment relationship. This is the case for many low-skilled and older adults, for the unemployed and displaced workers as well as for own-account workers.

## Figure 6.7. Reasons for not training by group, OECD average

Reasons for not training among adults (age 16-65) who did not train but would have liked to, by group, 2012, 2015

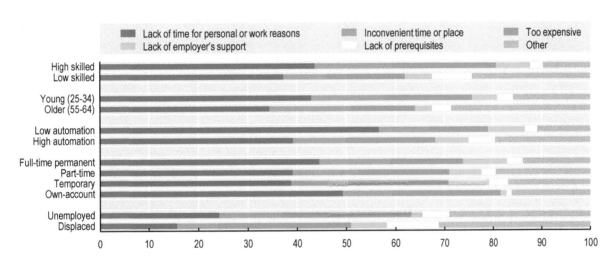

Note: Share of adults who participate in formal or non-formal job-related training over the previous 12 months. Data refer to 2012 for most countries, except for Chile, Greece, Israel, Lithuania, New Zealand, Slovenia and Turkey where they refer to 2015. Low (high) skilled refers to adults who score at level 1 or below (levels 4 or 5) on the PIAAC literacy scale. High (low) automation refers to adults at high (low) risk of automation. Own-account workers are the self-employed without employees. Temporary refers to workers on fixed term or temporary work agency contracts. Part-time refers to adults who work less than 30 hours per week. Full-time permanent are adults in full-time jobs with an indefinite work contract. Unemployed refers to all unemployed who have not been dismissed for economic reasons in their last job; displaced refers to unemployed adults who have been dismissed for economic reasons in the last job. Lack of time for personal or work reasons refers to lack of time due to "being too busy at work" or due to "childcare or family responsibilities".
Source: Survey of Adult Skills (PIAAC) (2012, 2015) http://www.oecd.org/skills/piaac/

StatLink ᵐˢᵖ http://dx.doi.org/10.1787/888933966977

Participation is also influenced by the supply of training by firms. The European Continuing Vocational Training Survey (CVTS) provides some insights into how many firms train and the reasons for not training or for not training more. Analysis of CVTS data shows that the share of training firms has increased gradually over the past decade. However, today like in the past, smaller firms tend to train less than larger firms: the share of training firms with 10 to 49 employees – the smallest category covered by CVTS – is almost 35 percentage points lower than the share of training firms with 250 employees or more (Figure 6.8), confirming the results presented in Table 6.1. It is worth noting that while many firms train, only about half of the firms that provide training do so for at least 50% of their workforce. This prompts the questions of whether training provided by firms actually reaches the most disadvantaged workers.[14]

### Figure 6.8. Training provision by firm size, EU28, 2005-15

Share of firms that provide CVT training and share of firms that provide CVT training to at least 50% of their employees

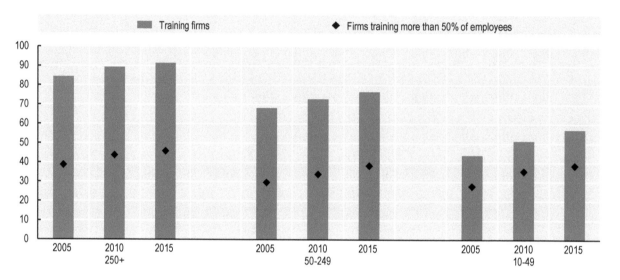

Note: Data excludes firms with less than 10 employees. CVT: continuing vocational training.
Source: Eurostat (2019[19]), CVTS Database – Eurostat, https://ec.europa.eu/eurostat/web/education-and-training/data/database.

StatLink ᵐˢᵖ http://dx.doi.org/10.1787/888933966996

The vast majority of employers who do not train cite the fact that continuing vocational training (CVT) is not necessary because: either existing qualifications are considered sufficient or initial vocational training – such as apprenticeships for younger employees – is preferred. The other key reasons are reported in Figure 6.9. A preference for recruiting over training existing employees, the cost of training and the workload of employees leaving little time to train are the most frequently cited reasons for not training. A similar ranking applies to firms that already provide training to justify why they do not train more. Despite the expectation that costs and time might be a bigger issue for smaller firms, the ranking of barriers to training provision does not vary much by firm size. This could be due to fact that CVTS excludes the smallest firms for which the pattern of barriers might differ more markedly.

Firms' training efforts may also vary across different industries, reflecting the fact that each industry may face different training needs. For instance, industries vary in the speed with which new technologies are developed and adopted, giving rise to different reskilling needs. Differences in training efforts may also reflect differences in sectoral collective bargaining arrangements around training, training cultures, and the skill-intensity of jobs in the industry.

Figure 6.9. Reasons for not providing training or limiting training provision, by firm size, EU 28

Percentages

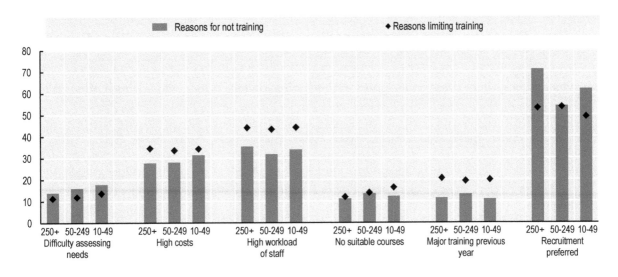

Note: Multiple choices allowed. Data excludes firms with less than 10 employees.
Source: Eurostat (2019[19]), CVTS Database – Eurostat, https://ec.europa.eu/eurostat/web/education-and-training/data/database.

StatLink 🔗 http://dx.doi.org/10.1787/888933967015

Figure 6.10. Adults' participation in training, by industry

Share of adults (16-65) in each industry that participate in training, OECD average, 2012/2015

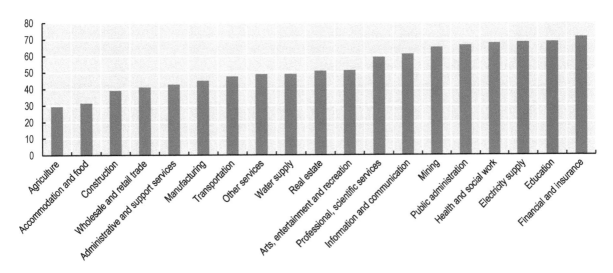

Note: Share of adults who participate in formal or non-formal job-related training over the previous 12 months. Data refer to 2012 for most countries, except for Chile, Greece, Israel, Lithuania, New Zealand, Slovenia and Turkey where they refer to 2015.
Source: Survey of Adult Skills (PIAAC) (2012, 2015), http://www.oecd.org/skills/piaac/

StatLink 🔗 http://dx.doi.org/10.1787/888933967034

Across OECD countries on average, participation to training is lowest in the agriculture, accommodation and food sectors, where around 30% of workers train in a given year, and highest in the financial and insurance, education, and electricity supply sectors, where around 70% of workers train in a given year (Figure 6.10).

Training needs also vary across regions – requiring different policy responses. For example, regions with a high level of adoption of new technologies may need to reskill many workers to cope with automation (OECD, 2018[20]). Conversely, in regions experiencing structural adjustment problems, adult learning policies that try to upskill workers for the future of work will fail to succeed if they are not complemented by regional development policies that favour entrepreneurship and increasing the value-added content of existing firms.

## 6.3. Encouraging participation in adult learning by under-represented groups

The analysis presented in the previous section identifies the groups of adults most likely to bear the brunt of the changes in skill needs, assesses their willingness to train and explores barriers to training participation.

Overall, the analysis suggests that in order to increase access to training, it will be crucial for countries to implement policies that enhance the willingness to train of individuals, tackle barriers to training related to lack of time, money or prerequisites for entry, and encourage firms to train groups at risk. Several policy options exist to address these challenges. For example:

- *To enhance the willingness to train of individuals*, countries can strengthen career guidance that helps adults navigate different training options available; raise awareness on the benefits of learning, for example through awareness campaigns; and ensure that wages more closely reflect productivity gains resulting from training participation. Taken together, these measures may help foster a learning culture and a mind-set for learning among adults.

- *To tackle lack of time*, countries can provide flexible training options, delivered online or outside of working hours (during week-ends or evenings), so that training can fit into busy schedules. Modular training options can also allow adults to learn at their own pace by completing self-contained (and shorter) learning modules that together ultimately lead to a full qualification. Education and training leave – mandated by law or negotiated through collective bargaining – is another policy option that allows workers to take time off work to train.

- *To tackle financial constraints*, countries can provide free training programmes, and/or develop financial incentives that help adults meet the direct cost of training (e.g. subsidies, tax deductions), and cover the opportunity costs of not working (e.g. through wage replacement schemes).

- *To address the lack of prerequisites*, the recognition of prior learning allows (low-qualified) adults to have the skills they have learnt through work experience certified. This formal recognition allows them to access those adult learning programmes that impose entry requirements.

- *To encourage employers to provide training to groups at risk*, countries can introduce financial incentives that lower the cost of organising training and implement policies to provide better information to firms about the benefits of training and the availability of training opportunities.

While policies along these lines already exist in many OECD countries (OECD, 2019[11]), it is crucial that they do not exclude disadvantaged groups and that they are designed in a way that allows disadvantaged groups to benefit. The following sections describe policy initiatives for each group, with a particular focus on addressing the barriers outlined in Section 6.2.[15]

It is noteworthy that, in order to be effective, these policies need to be considered together and not in isolation. For example, because lack of time is a key barrier for training participation for many adults, any adult learning policy, in order to be effective, needs to make time for training. Similarly, without enhancing the willingness to train and building a culture of learning, take-up of adult learning programmes may be low irrespective of costs or quality. Adult learning programmes that do not provide sufficient financial assistance for adults and firms to meet the cost of training may also end up being ineffective. Finally, because it is challenging to take up training while working full-time, a culture of learning can only be fostered with the support of employers.

### 6.3.1. Low-skilled adults

In all OECD countries, low-skilled adults are less likely to train than the high skilled, although the difference between the two groups varies across countries. The gap in participation between high and low-skilled adults in largest in Denmark, Germany, and Turkey where it is around 50 percentage points. It is lowest in Greece where participation in adult learning is very low for both high- and low-skilled adults (Figure 6.11).

**Figure 6.11. Differences in training participation and willingness to train between low and high-skilled adults, by country, 2012, 2015**

Percentage point difference in training participation and willingness to train, high-skilled minus low-skilled adults (age 16-65)

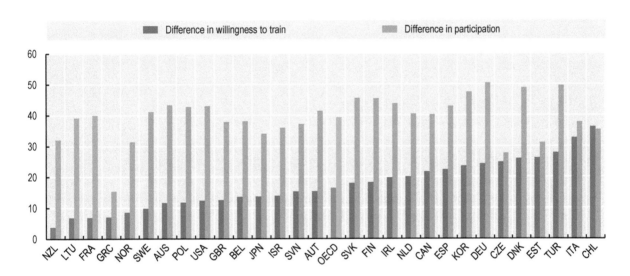

Note: The difference in willingness to train is the percentage point difference in the share of adults who did not participate in training but would have liked to (positive values indicate that this share is higher for high-skilled adults than for low-skilled adults). The difference in participation is the percentage point difference in the share of adults who participated in training over the previous 12 months (positive values indicate that this share is higher for high-skilled adults than for low-skilled adults).
Source: Survey of Adult Skills (PIAAC) (2012, 2015), http://www.oecd.org/skills/piaac/.

StatLink ᐧᐧᐧ http://dx.doi.org/10.1787/888933967053

The low skilled are also less willing to train than high skilled adults, although this gap varies significantly across the OECD. For example, in Chile and Italy, the low-skilled who did not take part in training are over 30 percentage points less likely to report that they would have liked to train than their high-skilled counterparts (Figure 6.11). However, this difference is less than 10 percentage points in New Zealand, Lithuania, France, Greece, Norway and Sweden.

*Improving the willingness to train among low-skilled adults*

Reaching out to the low-skilled and raising awareness of the benefits of learning is crucial to engage them more proactively in training. While public awareness campaigns on adult learning have been implemented in many OECD countries over the past years, they have often proved ineffective in reaching out to the low-skilled (OECD, 2019[5]; European Commission/EACEA/Eurydice, 2015[21]).[16]

To address this challenge, several OECD countries have started to put in place more proactive initiatives to reach the low-skilled in the places they frequent regularly – such as workplaces, kindergartens and schools, and public spaces (OECD, 2019[5]) (see Box 6.2).

More than other population groups, the low-skilled may find it challenging to identify their training needs and navigate the plethora of adult learning options available to them. Several countries across the OECD have taken steps to offer targeted career guidance to help the low-skilled identify their needs and the training programmes that are most appropriate for them (see Box 6.2).

Another key challenge is that the low-skilled often have experienced failure in their initial education and may find returning to the classroom unattractive. Ensuring that adult learning is delivered in innovative ways (e.g. outside of classroom settings) and that it is closely linked to the context of the learner (e.g. their workplace), is key to ensure that low-skilled adults are motivated to train and that training meets their needs. Some OECD countries have started to explore more innovative ways to deliver learning for the low-skilled (see Box 6.2).

---

Box 6.2. Improving the willingness to train of the low-skilled

**Reaching out to the low-skilled in innovative ways:**

- In the *United Kingdom*, Unionlearn uses Union Learning Representatives (ULRs) to reach out to workers in workplaces and provides training to about 250 000 workers every year, including many low-qualified workers (Stuart et al., 2016[22]; Stuart et al., 2013[23]).

- In *Vienna* (Austria), the project *Mama lernt Deutsch!* provides basic skills courses for mothers with low-qualifications and for whom German is not their first language, and takes place in their child's educational institution (OECD, 2019[5]).

- In *Brussels* (Belgium), Formtruck is a mobile information centre on training opportunities, which aims to engage with low-qualified jobseekers in public locations, e.g. at events, parks and public squares. Since its introduction in 2017, the truck has been used around 20 times per year. There are no evaluations on the effectiveness of this approach (OECD, 2019[5]).

**Career guidance targeted to the low-skilled:**

- In *Iceland*, Lifelong Learning Centres provide education counselling with a focus on the adults with low-qualifications. Guidance services are provided by highly qualified counsellors, who typically have a degree in education and vocational counselling. Every year Lifelong Learning Centres conduct around 10 000 guidance-counselling sessions with low-qualified people (OECD, 2019[5]).

- The *European project GOAL* (Guidance and Orientation Interventions for Low-Educated Adults) ran between February 2015 and January 2018 in a number of OECD countries – e.g. Flanders (Belgium), Czech Republic, Iceland, Lithuania, the Netherlands and Slovenia – with the aim to develop and expand educational guidance services for adults without upper secondary education. The project had four primary objectives: (i) enhancing partnerships and networks with other organisations serving the target groups; (ii) engaging in outreach activities designed to bring guidance services to those target groups; (iii) defining the competences which counsellors require

---

to enable them to address the specific needs of GOAL clients; and (iv) developing and effectively using guidance tools tailored to low-educated adults. The evaluation of the programme emphasises two findings: (i) partnerships can ensure that guidance addresses the full range of issues faced by adults, but also comes with coordination costs; (ii) there is no one-size-fits-all approach to providing advice and guidance, and the type of guidance provided must be tailored to the individual needs and context of the adult (Carpentieri et al., 2018[24]; OECD, 2019[5]).

**Delivering training in innovative ways:**

- In *Norway*, Skills Plus Work combines work and basic skill training – e.g. reading, writing, numeracy and digital skills. Guidance for the design of programmes is provided in the form of profiles of basic job-related skills for different professions, learning materials and national standards for basic skills for adults. Since 2006, the programme has supported more than 30 000 adults in acquiring reading, writing, numeracy and digital skills (OECD, 2019[5]).

- In *Germany* the project eVideoTransfer, co-funded by the Germany Ministry of Education, offers mobile learning opportunities for workers with low basic skills. The programme combines industry-specific and basic skills training. In order to ensure that those with low basic digital skills can participate, a learning module was developed on how to use mouse and keyboard (OECD, 2019[5]).

### *Making training more accessible to the low-skilled*

The importance of barriers to training for the low-skilled, such as lack of time (due to work or family reasons), financial constraints and entry requirements, varies across countries. The lack of time due to work reasons plays a central role in Korea while it is cited as a barrier by just 10% of adults who did not train in France (Figure 6.12). Lack of time due to family constraints play a major role in Turkey where it appears to be more important than lack of time due to work constraints. Financial constraints are a key barrier to training among the low-skilled in Estonia, France, Greece and Slovenia. Finally, the lack of prerequisites represents a sizeable barrier for the low-skilled particularly in Chile, Finland and Slovenia. This variation across countries partly reflects different situations in each country such as attitudes to training but also differences in policy settings.

### *Dealing with entry requirements*

Most low-skilled adults are low-qualified and only hold lower-secondary educational qualification. Despite this, many among them have gained knowledge and competences through years of work experience. For this group, the recognition of prior learning can be particularly valuable to ensure access to training courses with entry-level requirements.

The recognition of prior learning can help to re-engage individuals in training and limit the time and costs needed to complete a formal credential. Recognition programmes can also help individuals improve their labour mobility by providing proof to a new employer of the skills they have obtained informally (OECD, 2019[1]).

### Figure 6.12. Reasons why the low-skilled do not train, by country

Share of adults (age 16-65) citing each reason for not training among low-skilled adults who did not train but would have liked to, by country, 2012, 2015

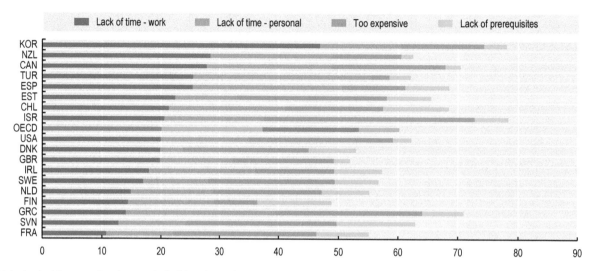

Note: Lack of time – work, refers to a lack of time due to "being too busy at work". Lack of time – personal refers to a lack of time due to childcare of family responsibilities. Only countries with at least 10 observations are shown in the figure.
Source: Survey of Adult Skills (PIAAC) (2012, 2015) http://www.oecd.org/skills/piaac/.

*StatLink* 㾎᷑ http://dx.doi.org/10.1787/888933967072

But while programmes for the recognition of prior learning exist in most OECD countries, they can often be too difficult to navigate for the low-qualified, due to complex procedures, or the high number of complementary classes needed to obtain a final certification. To facilitate take-up, some OECD countries have put in place guidance services that support the low-qualified throughout the process of having their skills recognised and certified (Box 6.3).

---

#### Box 6.3. Broadening the use of recognition prior learning among adult with low qualifications

- In *France*, in recent years, the system for the recognition and certification of skills (*Validation des acquis de l'expérience – VAE*) has been made more accessible for the low-qualified. Firms have an obligation to inform their workers about VAE every second year, in the context of their mandated professional development assessment (*Entretien professionnel*) (Mathou, 2016[25]). Adults also have access to specific VAE leave.

- In *Portugal*, *Qualifica Centres* target low-qualified adults among other groups, and the recognition of prior learning is embedded in their overall guidance offer. One key characteristic of the programme is that the low-qualified receive assistance throughout the whole skills recognition procedures. In 2017, 28 804 adults enrolled in recognition procedures and 10 157 received a certificate (OECD, 2019[5]).

---

*Making time for training or making training less time-consuming*

More than other groups, many low-skilled adults are busy with work and family responsibilities and lack the time to participate in lengthy training programmes (Fouarge, Schils and de Grip, 2013[26]). The lack of financial means to pay for childcare or take time off work aggravates the situation for the low-skilled who tend to work in low-wage jobs.

Modular training, which divides a learning programme into self-contained and certified modules, can encourage the low skilled to find the time to learn at their own pace. Several OECD countries have been taking steps to provide modular training options to adults, although these programmes are generally not targeted specifically to the low-skilled (Box 6.4).

Digital and online training programmes can also help make time for training, broadening access to training while containing training costs. However, these training options have limitations, because many low-skilled people (especially adults with low digital skills) may find it more difficult to access them.

Education and training leave, *i.e.* a regulatory instrument which sets out the conditions under which workers may be granted time away from work for leaning purposes, is another policy tool to ensure that adults – including the low-skilled – have the right to put aside sufficient time for training (OECD, 2019[1]).

Although education and training leave exists in many OECD countries, take-up tends to be low, especially for the low-skilled. Indeed, adults with low skills are often in low-wage blue-collar jobs with limited bargaining power *vis-à-vis* their employer and may feel reluctant to ask for education and training leave. Employers themselves – that in many OECD countries (e.g. Italy) are not obliged to accept the training leave request – may be reluctant to grant education and training leave to the low-skilled, especially if it is to upskill for a different job with another employer. Finally, it can be particularly challenging for a financially-constrained, low-skilled worker to actually use education and training leave, if adequate financial support (e.g. in the form of wage compensation during training; or subsidies to cover the direct costs of training) is not provided.

---

Box 6.4. Modular training to accommodate time constraints

- In *Denmark*, learners are able to combine modules from different types of adult learning programmes – e.g. ALMPs, basic skills courses, higher education, VET and non-formal liberal education programmes – to obtain a formal qualification (OECD, 2019[1]).

- In *Flanders* (Belgium), Centres for Adult Education (*Centra voor Volwassenonderwijs*, CAE) provide education in a wide range of skills such as technical skills and languages. The courses are fully modular: after completing a module, the learner receives a partial certificate, and after completing an entire programme, the learner receives a formal certificate recognised by the Flemish government (OECD, 2019[27]).

- In *Mexico*, the Model for Life and Work Programme (MEVyT)[17] allows low-skilled adults to gain qualification through different modules at initial, intermediate (primary education) and advanced (lower secondary education) level (OECD, 2019[5]).

- In *Switzerland*, modular programmes have started to develop in the mid-1990s and today are available throughout the adult learning sector. Adults can take part in individual modules or combine different modules to form a full training programme (OECD, 2019[1]).

---

### *Reducing the financial barrier to training*

Financial constraints can be particularly important for the low-skilled and may prevent them from participating in training. In fact, the low-skilled often alternate between work and periods of unemployment, have low-quality jobs with limited access to employer-sponsored training, and/or are in low-wage jobs which leave them little financial resources to invest in training. When they train, their investment in training – in terms of time and cost – does not always pay off in terms of better, higher paid jobs.[18]

To address these challenges, many OECD countries have put in place a number of measures – e.g. training vouchers, allowances, fully-funded training programmes – specifically targeted to the low-skilled with a view to make training more affordable for them (Box 6.5). These schemes include programmes for the employed and the unemployed with low skills.

---

Box 6.5. Making training more affordable for the low-skilled

- In *France*, the individual learning account (*Compte Personnel de Formation*) provides more generous credits to the low-skilled, i.e. EUR 800 per year against EUR 500 for the rest of the labour force (see Section 6.4) (OECD, forthcoming[28]).

- In *Estonia*, the public employment services offer a Degree Study Allowance to employed and unemployed adults with insufficient or outdated skills, who may have trouble finding a job or be at risk of redundancy. The monthly allowance is only paid for skills that are in demand according to the analysis of sectoral skill needs conducted by the Estonian Qualifications Authority, and the amount is income dependent (OECD, 2019[1]).

- In *Sweden*, an education entry grant was introduced in mid-2017, targeting low-qualified unemployed persons aged 25-56. It consists of approximately EUR 210 per week that can be received for 50 weeks and allows adults to study at the primary or secondary levels (European Commission, 2019[29]).

- In the *United Kingdom*, from 2020 onwards, low-skilled adults will have access to fully-funded digital skills programmes, in line with the already existing maths and English programmes (OECD, 2019[1]).

- In the *United States*, unemployed low-skilled adults have access to training vouchers – called Individual Training Accounts (ITAs) – for training programmes that prepare participants for work in in-demand sectors (OECD, forthcoming[28]).

---

*Encouraging employers to provide training to the low-skilled*

Employers may be reluctant to train the low-skilled, or support them to undertake training. They may prefer to focus training efforts on higher-skilled workers, for whom they can expect to reap greater returns on investments, and/or they might find it less costly to hire high-skilled people rather than upskill existing low-skilled employees (Figure 6.9).

In this context, encouraging firms to train low-skilled workers – e.g. by lowering the cost of training them – is key. Many policy measures across the OECD focus on encouraging employers to hire and then train the low-skilled – often through financial incentives. An interesting example of such a programme was the *Emplois d'avenir* (Jobs of the Future) in France. Until early 2018, the programme encouraged firms to hire low-skilled, unemployed, youth for a period of three years. The government covered 75% of the wage costs (paid at the minimum wage) on the condition that the employer provided a tutor to help train the young person. However, a recent evaluation shows that to be beneficial to workers in the medium run, the received training needs to lead to a certification (Cahuc, Carcillo and Minea, forthcoming[30]). Similar programmes exist in Greece (training voucher for young unemployed aged 18-24), Italy (*Tirocini in Garanzia Giovani*), Wallonia and the Flanders (Belgium – *Formation Alternée* and the *Programme de Transition Professionnelle*, which also targets the low-skilled) (OECD, 2017[31]).

### 6.3.2. Workers with jobs at high risk of automation

Workers in jobs at high risk of automation[19] may need to retrain to learn how to handle the introduction of new technologies, or to find a less automatable job either within the same sector/occupation or in a different one.

Several OECD countries already have programmes in place to re-train workers in firms facing major technological disruption. These measures aim to identify workers at risk and ensure that they acquire the skills needed to keep up with the changes brought about by digitalisation, automation, and the introduction of new technologies (Box 6.6).

Other OECD countries are also going in a similar direction, although adult learning measures are still in a pilot phase. For example, in the UK, the National Retraining Scheme is being put in place to respond to changes in the economy and support people to progress in work and redirect their careers. In the pilot phases of the project, some intensive user research is being carried out on the needs of employers and employees in jobs at risk of automation or industries in decline.

---

Box 6.6. Identifying and training workers at risk of automation

- In *Australia*, a Stronger Transitions Package was introduced in 2018 to support individuals in five regions impacted by structural change to transition to new jobs and prepare for the jobs of the future. The package includes a pre-redundancy skills and training support component, which can provide targeted services such as comprehensive skills assessments; job search preparation; resilience training; language, literacy and numeracy support; digital literacy training; financial management information; exploring self-employment options; health and wellbeing support, and industry awareness experiences (OECD, 2019[1]).

- In *Austria*, Outplacement Labour Foundation (*Arbeitsstiftung*) programmes have been introduced by the social partners to support workers in the case of structural changes through appropriate labour market policies. These foundations can be set up by one or multiple employers, but also at the sector and regional level when specific regions or sectors are affected by major staff cuts. The programmes are co-financed by local labour actors, including the public employment service (PES) and the affected employers. Funding is available to cover training costs, allowances for course-related additional cost, and active job-search assistance and career guidance costs (OECD, 2019[1]).

- *Luxembourg* launched in 2018 the Digital Skills Bridge, which helps employees in companies facing major technological disruption to find new placement opportunities (whether within or outside the company) and acquire new professional skills – either transversal, digital, or industry-related – to fit the requirements of the new identified position (Luxembourg Government, 2019[32]).

- In *Estonia*, in May 2017 the PES implemented "Work and Study", a programme that offers a training card (voucher) for employed persons at risk of unemployment (e.g. due to skills obsolescence); and a training grant for employers who wish to improve the skills of their employees at risk of losing their job after the introduction of new technologies (Estonian Unemployment Insurance Fund, 2019[33]).

---

### 6.3.3. Displaced workers

Many displaced workers are at risk of long-term unemployment or inactivity and yet as a group their participation in training is relatively low (see Figure 6.5). Many left sectors that are shrinking or disappearing – not just due to automation but to structural change more generally. As a result, they require intensive retraining to be able to reintegrate the labour market in a different sector and occupation – particularly the low-skilled among them.

To avoid long unemployment spells and facilitate rapid job reinsertion, re-training needs to take place quickly during the notice period or right after dismissal. Across OECD countries, generally during the notice period attention is devoted to documenting workers' skills and exploring potential training options, while training starts only after a long period of unemployment (OECD, 2018[34]). That being said, some OECD countries have been taking steps to train dismissed workers promptly, during the notice period or soon after displacement occurs (Box 6.7).

On top of early interventions during the notice period or shortly after dismissal, dismissed workers in some OECD countries receive preferential training support during unemployment. For example, in France, displaced workers are entitled to sign a professional employability agreement (*contrat de sécurisation professionnelle*)[20] and are able to access more personalised and intensive re-training assistance from the public employment service (PES) than is generally available to unemployment insurance benefit recipients (OECD, 2018[34]).

Displaced workers may also continue to receive preferential training support even after they have reintegrated the labour market, in a view to encourage their continuous upskilling. For example, in France, no minimum seniority is required to access paid education and training leave for dismissed workers who have found a new job and who have not trained since dismissal.

---

**Box 6.7. Early interventions for displaced workers**

- In *Sweden*, Job Security Councils provide transition services – such as advice, training, business start-up support – to dismissed workers often before the dismissals actually take place (OECD, 2018[34]).

- In *Finland*, the Change Training (*MuutosKoulutus*) programme offers re-training options to dismissed workers during nine months starting from the day of their work obligation ends (Eurofound, 2018[35]). Firms pay 20% of the training cost, and the remaining 80% is covered by the PES. However, the actual PES support that workers can access at an early stage (i.e. before actual dismissal) appears to be limited, presumably mostly due to a lack of resources (OECD, 2016[36]).

- In *Ontario* (Canada), when layoffs concern 50 or more employees, workers can access activation measures (sometimes including re-training) through the Rapid Re-employment and Training Service (OECD, 2015[37]).

---

### 6.3.4. Temporary workers

As the share of temporary workers – namely workers under fixed-term and temporary work agency (TWA) contracts – is large and, in some countries, increasing (see Chapter 2), ensuring that they participate in adult learning represents a major policy priority.

While temporary workers train less than full-time workers across the OECD on average, it has to be acknowledged that gaps in training participation are lower than for other groups (e.g. low-skilled versus high-skilled) (Figure 6.5). Moreover, as discussed in Section 6.2, these differences tend to be due to socio-demographic characteristics as opposed to contractual status itself. This is particularly the case for participation in formal training, often provided by educational institutions, while contractual status carries an important weight in the participation in non-formal training, often provided by employers.

Overall, there are large differences across countries, with gaps in participation between temporary and full-time employees spanning from under 5 percentage points in Ireland, Israel, Lithuania and New Zealand to 15 percentage points or more in Belgium, Japan, the Netherlands and the Slovak Republic (Figure 6.13). In four countries – Austria, Greece, Denmark, and the United States – the gap is positive.[21]

Substantial differences exist not only across countries but also within countries between employees on different types of temporary contracts themselves. Indeed, unlike workers with fixed-term contracts, often TWA workers benefit from targeted adult learning programmes.

Unlike other population groups, temporary workers are significantly more likely to report that they were willing to train than full-time permanent workers. This is true across all OECD countries, with the exception of Australia, Israel and Korea (Figure 6.13). Time and cost are the most frequently cited barriers to training participation for employees in temporary contracts in most OECD countries. Lack of support from the employer appears to play a major role in Turkey as well as in the Netherlands, Poland and Denmark (Figure 6.14).

**Figure 6.13. Differences in training participation and willingness to train between temporary and full-time permanent workers, by country, 2012, 2015**

Percentage point difference in training participation and willingness to train, full-time permanent workers minus temporary workers (age 16-65)

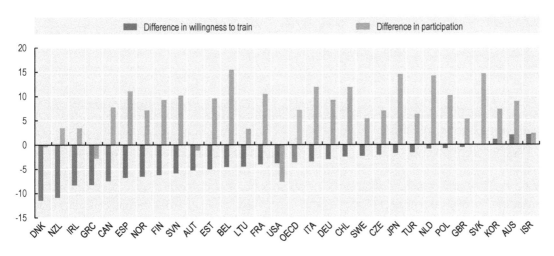

Note: The difference in willingness to train is the percentage point difference in the share of adults who did not participate in train but would have liked to (positive values indicate that this share is higher for full-time permanent employee than for temporary workers). The difference in participation is the percentage point difference in the share of adults who participated in training over the previous 12 months (positive values indicate that this share is higher for full-time permanent employees than for temporary workers).
Source: Survey of Adult Skills (PIAAC) (2012, 2015), http://www.oecd.org/skills/piaac/.

StatLink ᵐˢᵖ http://dx.doi.org/10.1787/888933967091

### Equal treatment: rights, entitlements and representation

Many OECD countries include non-discrimination rules in their legal frameworks, with a view to promote equal training rights between permanent workers and workers on fixed-term contracts. For example, in Poland, the Labour Code states that fixed-term and permanent employees shall be treated equally as regards to the promotion and access to training. Similarly, in Greece, the legal framework states that employers should facilitate fixed-term workers' access to appropriate training opportunities, with a view to strengthen their skills, improve their career development, and enhance their professional mobility.[22]

### Figure 6.14. Reasons why temporary workers do not train, by country

Reasons for not training among temporary workers (age 16-65) who did not train but would have liked to, 2012, 2015.

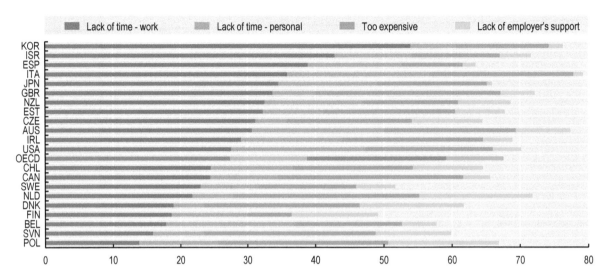

Note: Lack of time for work, refers to a lack of time due to "being too busy at work". Lack of time – personal refers to a lack of time due to childcare of family responsibilities. Only countries with at least 10 observations are shown in the figure.
Source: Survey of Adult Skills (PIAAC) (2012, 2015), http://www.oecd.org/skills/piaac/.

StatLink ᵀᵗˢ⁴ http://dx.doi.org/10.1787/888933967110

Similarly, several OECD countries have also taken steps to ensure that the legal framework establishes equal training rights between permanent and TWA workers. For example, the German law on TWA workers is based on the principle of equal treatment, including on training opportunities (Finn, 2016[38]). Similarly, in Belgium, TWA workers have access to the paid education and training leave as standard employees (IDEAconsult, 2015[39]). In France, individual learning accounts (*compte personnel de formation*) are open to all, including to TWA workers (see Section 6.4).[23] Equal training rights are also often agreed through collective agreements. For example, in France, the temporary agency work employers' confederation (PRISME) and the five main union organisations, signed an agreement[24] in 2007, which establishes that both the agency and the user companies should promote equal training as a means for equality of opportunities (Ebisui, 2012[40]) – see also Chapter 5.

Despite these positive examples, there are still significant challenges to ensuring that temporary workers benefit from adult learning policies as much as permanent workers. Indeed, some adult learning measures explicitly exclude temporary workers altogether. For example, in Canada, the Job Training Grant – a programme which offers firms funding towards the cost of training their workers – is reserved to the training of permanent staff (Busby and Muthukumaran, 2016[41]). Similarly, in the United Kingdom, TWA workers are not entitled to education and training leave.

Even when equal rules are in place in the legal framework, in several countries, collective bargaining may still stipulate different on-the-job-training rights for temporary and permanent workers in the same sector (OECD, 2018[42]). For example, in Italy, the collective agreement for the metalwork industry has recently established an individual training right of 24 hours in the period 2017-2019 (see Chapter 5) – but the right is reserved to permanent workers only and excludes temporary staff.

Moreover, temporary workers often lack representation – *i.e.* there are virtually no unions dedicated to represent the interests of temporary workers as such, irrespective of the economic sector they belong to.

While there are several reasons for this (see Chapters 4 and 5), lack of representation results into temporary workers having little room to negotiate better training rights and more adequate training opportunities through collective bargaining.

Even when equal training rights are in place through legislation and/or collective bargaining agreements, entitlements are often based on tenure, which in practice excludes many temporary workers with contracts of short duration. To give one example, in some OECD countries education and training leave entitlements are provided to workers after a minimum tenure within the company (e.g. five years in Italy, two in Norway, six months in Sweden) (OECD, 2019[1]).

Finally, holding a temporary job may imply having weaker training rights in case of unemployment, compared to standard employees, hence less access to training provided by public employment services. Indeed, while in many OECD countries, displaced workers often receive preferential training support, there do not seem to be similar measures for the unemployed whose previous (temporary) contract was not renewed. For example, in Sweden, Job Security Councils – which provide transition services to dismissed workers – are available to employees who have been employed for a minimum period (normally over one year) on a permanent (not temporary) contract (Eurofound, 2018[43]).

### Targeted programmes

All else being equal, many employers still prefer to invest in the training of permanent employees, who are expected to stay with the company for longer, and from whom they can expect to reap greater benefits from their skills investments.

This may be particularly true in countries with dual labour market, with significant differences in dismissal legislation between temporary and permanent workers (e.g. Spain, Italy, France), and where firms hire temporary contracts in sequence to bypass conversion rules (Cabrales, Dolado and Mora, 2014[44]). In these contexts, reforming EPL to address labour market segmentation may have the spillover effect of encouraging firms to train temporary workers.

As equal rules may not be sufficient to ensure that temporary workers access training opportunities at least as much as permanent workers, there may also be a need to target adult learning programmes more specifically on them. Apart from a few notable exceptions, most adult learning measures in place across the OECD do not provide particular targeting to workers with fixed-term contracts, and are – at best – open to both fixed-term and permanent staff.

One example of adult learning policy specifically targeted to fixed-term workers is implemented in France. By law, when a fixed-term contract ends, the firm must pay an indemnity to the worker ("*Prime de précarité*"), equal to at least 10% of the total pay the worker received during the entire duration of the contract. However, if the firm can prove that it sponsored/provided training to the fixed-term worker, the indemnity's minimum amount goes down to 6%. This programme should, at least in principle, provide firms with an incentive to train fixed-term workers, although no evaluation of the programme was conducted so far.

If targeted training support is limited for fixed-term workers, many initiatives are in place for TWA workers. Temporary work agencies themselves often provide training opportunities for workers.[25] For example, staffing companies such as Adecco, Randstad, and Manpower offer thousands of online courses for their staff (Spermann, 2016[45]). Several studies show how training provided by TWAs can lead to good employment outcomes in the longer-term (Ehlert, 2012[46]) and can improve the productivity of workers (De Grip, 2012[47]).

In addition to the training programmes provided directly by TWAs, many OECD countries – such as Austria, Belgium, France, Italy, the Netherlands, Spain, and Switzerland – have set up dedicated training funds to finance the training of TWA workers (Box 6.8).

In OECD countries where training funds are not in place, the training of TWA workers can be partly financed through public resources (Voss et al., 2013[48]). In Germany, for example, vouchers co-financed by public employment services can be used to finance TWA workers' training (Spermann, 2016[45]).

---

**Box 6.8. Training funds for temporary work agency workers**

Many OECD countries have set up dedicated training funds to finance the training of temporary work agency (TWA) workers. Examples of these training funds include *Forma.Temp* in Italy; the *FAF-TT* in France; the Training and Development Foundation for the Flex-sector (*STOOF*) in the Netherlands; *Fonds de Formation pour les Intérimaires* (FFI) in Belgium; and *Temptraining* in Switzerland. The funds are mainly financed by compulsory contributions paid by TWAs (Voss et al., 2013[48]), and more than EUR 500 million is invested by these funds every year in the skills of TWA workers (WEC, 2016[49]).

These training funds provide specific services for TWA workers, such as training vouchers, career guidance, and wage replacement schemes during training. For example, *Forma.Temp* in Italy has developed a training voucher system which provides EUR 5 000 worth of training to TWA workers. The voucher is accompanied with guidance and information support (*e.g.* on training opportunities available), which is provided by local *Forma.Temp* branches or through a dedicated electronic platform[26] (OECD, 2019[50]). To give another example, in Switzerland, *Temptraining* provides financial support to TWA workers, by covering training costs and reimbursing for lost earnings during training.

---

### 6.3.5. Own-account workers

Own-account workers, *i.e.* self-employed workers without employees, often fall between the cracks of adult learning measures that are typically conceived for dependent employees or the unemployed who can rely on training initiatives by their employers or the public employment service.[27]

While willingness to train remains generally close to that of full-time permanent employees, in all OECD countries own-account workers are less likely to train, with the size of the gap varying significantly across countries (Figure 6.15), possibly reflecting different policies towards this group of workers.[28] The largest participation gap is found in the Netherlands, where only 18% of own-account workers train compared to 72% of full-time permanent employees. At the other extreme, the smallest difference is found in Italy where 32% of own-account workers train compared with 33% of full-time permanent employees.

*Barriers to training for own-account workers*

Own-account workers face two major, and partly interlinked, barriers to learning: they lack time and do not have the financial means to train (Figure 6.7). These barriers are often more important for them than for full-time permanent workers and most other groups which are under-represented in training. The cost of training appears to represent a particularly important barrier in Canada, Israel and the United States. And while the lack of time is a major barrier in most countries, it is particularly acute in Korea and the Czech Republic (Figure 6.16).

*Adapting the legislative and collective bargaining framework*

Own-account workers often have fewer training rights than employees. Indeed, in virtually all OECD countries own-account workers (and the self-employed more generally) are not covered by most of the provisions of labour law (see Chapter 4). Therefore, they do not benefit from the training rights set in labour laws as employees do.

Moreover, unlike employees, own-account workers often lack representation, and therefore are not entitled to training rights negotiated through collective bargaining (see Chapter 5). Indeed, legal restrictions often prevent bargaining for own-account workers (and the self-employed more generally). For example, in the Netherlands, self-employed workers (including own-account workers) remain outside the reach of collective agreements on topics related to education and training (Bekker and Posthumus, 2010[51]).

**Figure 6.15. Differences in training participation and willingness to train between own-account workers and full-time permanent employees, by country, 2012, 2015**

Percentage point difference in training participation and willingness to train, full-time permanent employees minus own-account workers (age 16-65)

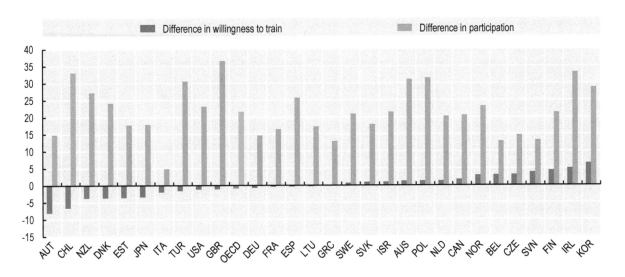

Note: The difference in willingness to train is the percentage point difference in the share of adults who did not participate in training but would have liked to (positive values indicate that this share is higher for full-time permanent employee than for own-account workers). The difference in participation is the percentage point difference in the share of adults who participated in training over the previous 12 months (positive values indicate that this share is higher for full-time permanent employees than for own-account workers).
Source: Survey of Adult Skills (PIAAC) (2012, 2015), http://www.oecd.org/skills/piaac/.

StatLink ᐧᒪᔕᐧ http://dx.doi.org/10.1787/888933967129

While practically no business representation exists for own-account workers as such, in some OECD countries own-account workers can voluntary enrol in professional associations or public representation bodies (see Chapter 5), which often provide a number of services for the skills development of their members (see Box 6.9). Other than providing training to members, these associations often also operate as pressure groups to influence policymaking – at state and local levels – in all areas of interest for own-account workers, including training (Pedersini and Coletto, 2010[52]).

On top of national initiatives, some cross-national organisations have started to emerge, too. For example, SMart – a cooperative dedicated to the needs of freelancers which was created in Belgium in 1998 and is now active in 9 European countries – offers discounted training to members among other services (Lejeune, 2017[53]) (see Chapter 5).

### Figure 6.16. Reasons why own-account workers do not participate in training, by country

Reasons for not training among own-account workers (age 16-65) who did not train but would have liked to, 2012, 2015

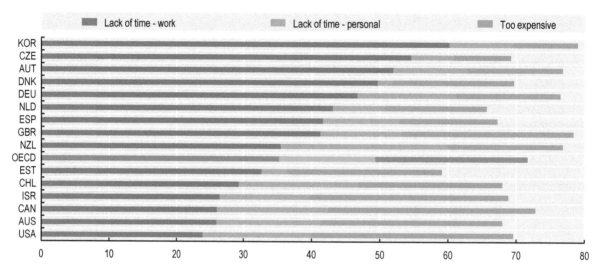

Note: Lack of time for work, refers to a lack of time due to "being too busy at work". Lack of time – personal refers to a lack of time due to childcare of family responsibilities. Only countries with at least 10 observations are shown in the figure.
Source: Survey of Adult Skills (PIAAC) (2012, 2015), http://www.oecd.org/skills/piaac/.

StatLink http://dx.doi.org/10.1787/888933967148

---

### Box 6.9. Training for own-account workers through professional associations

- In *Austria*, membership in one-person company's union includes a training package.[29]
- In *Italy*, the freelancers association ACTA provides free or discounted training courses for members. ACTA has also elaborated several proposals to support the training of freelancers, which have been presented to parliamentary committees on adult learning, and which have pushed some regions to finance training opportunities for the self-employed (Bologna, 2016[54]).
- In *Luxembourg*, self-employed workers registered with a professional association (e.g. Chamber of Trade, Chamber of Agriculture), are offered training guidance and advice (European Commission, 2010[55]).
- In the *Netherlands*, several organisations represent the needs of solo-entrepreneurs and some offer training to members (Jansen, 2017[56]).
- In *Portugal*, self-employed who are part of a chamber of commerce and professional chambers, can be given assistance with regards to training (Eurofound, 2017[57]).
- In the *United Kingdom*, Equity – one of the oldest unions for self-employed entertainment professionals – developed a professional pension scheme for its members which also provides access to training courses (Eurofound, 2017[57]).
- In the *United States*, trade unions for Hollywood writers and movie professionals provide training for members (WEC, 2016[49]).

*Putting time aside for training*

As shown in Figure 6.16, lack of time is a key barrier to training for own-account workers in many OECD countries. Long working hours may prevent own-account workers from investing in training and developing strategies for the longer term. Moreover, they may also have to invest considerable time looking for the next job assignment, which further diminishes their time available for training.

There are several policy tools OECD countries can put in place to help own-account workers put aside sufficient time off work for training. While education and training leave is available in many OECD countries for employees, it is not always clear whether own-account workers can also benefit. Moreover, to be meaningful for them, it is fundamental that education and training leave is paid or accompanied by adequate income support measures. One good practice example can be found in Luxembourg, where education and training leave is available not only to employees but also to own-account workers and those in liberal professions (provided they have been registered with social security for at least two years), and includes a financial compensation paid by the state based on the income of the previous tax year.[30]

Providing flexible training arrangements is also key for allowing own-account workers to find the time to combine work with training. Some OECD countries offer adult learning opportunities that are specifically conceived for the needs of the self-employed, and are delivered in flexible ways, *e.g.* outside of regular working hours. For example, in Flanders (Belgium), the Flemish agency for Entrepreneurial Training *(Syntra Flanders)* is developing 'innovative entrepreneurship programmes', which provide flexible training options, including evening or week-end courses, specifically targeted to the self-employed population.

*Making training more affordable*

As highlighted in Figure 6.16, the cost of training is another major barrier to training for the own-account workers in several OECD countries. This is not surprising, considering that own-account workers often have no or limited access to public financial support for training, typically conceived for employees or the unemployed population. Those who work regularly for the same employers are also less likely to receive employer-sponsored training as employers tend to privilege investment in the skills of their employees instead. As a result, the own-account workers often have to pay for training themselves (Bologna, 2016[54]).

Some OECD countries have financial incentives in place that apply to own-account workers and the self-employed more generally (e.g. tax deductions, subsidies). Tax deductions are one of the most common tools to support training for the own-account workers. In many OECD countries (e.g. Belgium, Italy, the United Kingdom), professional development and training expenses are accounted as business costs and therefore are tax deductible. However, there are often restrictions on the type of training that that is eligible for deduction, e.g. on the type of training courses, or on the type of skills developed.

Subsidies are another tool sometimes used by OECD countries to financially support the training of own-account workers. They are rarely conceived exclusively to benefit the own-account workers population, or as a means to address their specific needs. At best, they are targeted to the self-employed alongside other vulnerable population groups (e.g. the subsidy BRAWO in Belgium), or are open to all individuals regardless of their employment status (e.g. reimbursement of training costs to prepare federal exams in Switzerland; Individual Learning Accounts in France).

Another key approach adopted across the OECD to help the own-account workers meet the cost of training, is to make certain subsidies dependent on the payment of social security contributions (e.g. *Contribution à la Formation Professionnelle*, in France), or conditional on enrolment in an employment insurance plan (e.g. Korea, and some schemes in Austria and Belgium) (see Box 6.10).

Putting in place voluntary saving schemes that can be accessed for training purposes is another measure countries can put in place to help own-account workers put money aside for training. However, the international experience seems to suggest that when withdrawals are not bound to finance training, and if individuals are not assisted in their choices, savings are rarely used for training. For example, in the Netherlands, the Dutch Life Course Savings Scheme allowed own-account workers/freelancers[31] to save tax free, however training was the least mentioned reason to participate and most individuals chose to use their funds to retire early instead (OECD, 2018[42]).

Finally, on top of direct training costs, own-account workers also face high opportunity costs of not working. Unlike employed workers, own-account workers most likely have to forgo paid employment opportunities in order to access training. To address this challenge, some OECD countries (e.g. Austria, Finland, Luxembourg), have put in place subsidies to help own-account workers sustain their incomes during training.

Despite these positive efforts, today many of the financial incentives available to employees and the unemployed are still not available to own-account workers (and the self-employed more generally). To address this challenge, some OECD countries (e.g. Ireland, France) have already been taking steps to extend eligibility criteria of existing financial incentives also to the self-employed.

Box 6.10 provides some policy examples on tax deductions, subsidies, employment insurance plans, and wage replacement schemes implemented in OECD countries to help the self-employed meet the cost of training.

---

Box 6.10. Making training more affordable for the self-employed (including own-account)

**Tax deductions**

- In *Belgium*, the self-employed are eligible for tax deductions for training expenses, provided they can show that the training is necessary to perform the job (OECD, 2019[27]).
- In the *United Kingdom*, the self-employed can claim a tax deduction for training that maintains or updates existing skills, while training that introduces new skills is regarded as a capital cost and therefore does not qualify for tax relief (HR Tresury, 2018[58]).
- In 2017 *Italy* introduced a Jobs Act for Autonomous Workers, which allows the self-employed to deduct certain training (e.g. post-graduate studies, professional training, conferences and seminars) and skills certification expenditures from their taxes (for a maximum of EUR 10 000 and EUR 5 000 respectively per year) (Casano et al., 2018[59]).

**Subsidies**

- In *Belgium*, the training subsidy BRAWO[32] is an initiative from the German speaking community which subsidises one third of training costs (for a maximum of EUR 1 000) and is targeted to several vulnerable groups, including the self-employed and freelancers (Allinckx and Monico, 2016[60]).
- In *Switzerland*, since January 2018, all individuals (including the self-employed) who have taken training to pass a federal examination can receive a reimbursement of training costs after the exam has taken place.[33]

**Employment insurance plans**

- In *France*, independent workers (such as craftsmen and traders) and micro-entrepreneurs have to pay a social security contribution for professional development, which allows them to receive funding for training (OECD, 2018[42]).
- In *Vienna* (Austria), the *Waff Training Account* provides training grants to certain workers – including the "new self-employed" (*i.e.* holders of a 'contract for work' without a trade licence) provided they are insured under the Commercial Social Security Act (OECD, 2019[61]).

---

- In *Wallonia* (Belgium), certain workers – including the self-employed – can have access to the *Chèque-Formation* to co-finance training (OECD, 2017[31]), and the number of cheques available per year depend on employment status alongside other criteria. In order to benefit, the self-employed need to be affiliated to the *Institut national d'Assurances sociales pour travailleurs indépendants.*
- In *Korea*, the self-employed who have voluntarily subscribed to employment insurance can have access to a skills development subsidy, which covers 60-100% of training costs (depending on the economic sector) and a training allowance of KWR 18 000 (approximately EUR 15) per day (OECD, 2014[62]).

**Extending financial incentives to the self-employed**

- In *France*, since January 2018, entitlements to the Individual Learning Account is extended to independent workers (see Section 6.4) (OECD, forthcoming[28]).
- In *Ireland*, in 2017, Springboard+ (a programme originally conceived for the unemployed population which offers free courses leading to qualification) was extended to the self-employed who want to upskill in certain sectors (Biopharma/Med Tech, and ICTs).[34]

**Wage replacement schemes**

- In *Austria* the Skilled Workers' Grant[35] provides incomes (from three months to three years) to a number of target groups, including the self-employed, who are enrolled in full-time training (OECD, 2017[31]).
- In *Finland*, the Adult Education Allowance provides an income support during training not only to employees but also to self-employed persons who attend training (OECD, 2019[1]).
- In *Luxembourg*, the government provides wage compensation to self-employed workers taking education and training leave (European Commission, 2010[55]).

*Providing skills advice and guidance*

On top of providing financial support for training, ensuring that own-account workers have access to skills advice services is also crucial to help them navigate through the available training options and accompany them in their training choices.

One key challenge is that, unlike employees, own-account workers have no or limited access to skills advice provided by employers, firms' HR departments, and/or trade unions; and the self-employed may not benefit from guidance services offered by the PES, which are often reserved to the unemployed.

Recognising these challenges, some OECD countries are already taking steps to ensure that skills advice and guidance are also available to own-account workers. These efforts focus mainly on extending skills advice and guidance services provided by the PES (see Box 6.11). Similar efforts in this direction have been undertaken by professional associations (see Box 6.9).

### 6.3.6. Platform workers

Platform workers face specific challenges in accessing training. In many OECD countries, they are considered as self-employed and as such, they often have to organise their own training and professional development, hence the policies highlighted for the own-account workers would also apply to this group (Box 6.7).

> ### Box 6.11. Skills advice and guidance services for the self-employed (including own-account)
>
> - In *Flanders* (Belgium), both employees and self-employed workers can apply to the PES for career guidance vouchers (*loopbaancheques*). Workers must pay EUR 40 per voucher, which entitles them to 4 hours of career guidance with a mandated career coaching centre of their choice. Workers are eligible for 2 vouchers every six years (OECD, 2019[27]).
> - In *Germany*, the Federal Employment Agency has recently enhanced the range of counselling services available for all adults (including the self-employed), going beyond the traditional focus given to the unemployed population (OECD, 2019[61]).
> - In *Italy*, law 81/2017 establishes the possibility to extend PES consultation services also to autonomous workers, although implementation is still ongoing (Casano et al., 2018[59]).
> - In *Latvia*, the PES provides career consultations free of charge not only to the unemployed, but also to the self-employed.[36]

However, platform workers face additional challenges compared with other self-employed. For instance, there is a significant legal uncertainty surrounding the gig economy in many OECD countries. As a result, platform workers may find it challenging to navigate training rights and opportunities available to them. More than other self-employed, platform workers may be working to tight deadlines or on low piece-rates for micro-tasks (European Parliament, 2016[63]), which may leave them little time for training. This is particularly true for platform workers on low incomes, who may need to work longer hours in order to make ends meet and may not be able to take time off for training. In addition, many platform or gig workers have little scope for career development within the platform they work for, which may discourage both platforms and workers themselves to invest in training.

Although international comparable surveys do not yet allow to adequately identifying platform workers, recent ad hoc research conducted in some OECD countries can help to shed light on their specific barriers to training. For example, a recent survey conducted among platform workers in the United Kingdom suggests that eight in ten platform workers face obstacles to develop new skills in the future. The most frequently quoted barriers for participation are affordability (41%), lack of employers' training opportunities (35%), lack of time due to work commitments (26%), and lack of time due to family responsibilities (21%) – while only a minority of all respondents (14%) say they lack the motivation to train (CIPD, 2017[64]).[37]

One key challenge OECD countries are currently facing is to encourage platforms to invest in the training of their workers (France Stratégie, 2018[65]). So far, training offered by platforms has been scant and often limited to induction, training on how to best carry out the work, or at best training that allows the worker to perform the job (e.g. online language courses; basic computer skills). For example, *Uber* instructs drivers to streamline and to improve the quality of service; and has recently started offering free access to *Babbel* or *Duolingo*,[38] to help workers newly arrived in the country to improve their language skills. *Samasource* trains vulnerable people in basic computer skills and employs them to complete computer-based work. Overall, however, today these remain stand-alone examples, that can hardly count as systematic training efforts by platforms (OECD, 2016[66]). Indeed, a study conducted among gig workers in the United Kingdom confirms that platforms rarely offer training opportunities to their workers (Broughton et al., 2018[67]). Moreover, the coverage and quality of these training efforts remain unknown.

In this context, only few OECD countries have started adapting the legal framework and impose training obligations to platforms. In France, in 2016 the *Loi Travail* requires platforms to pay employers contributions' for training, cover expenses for the recognition of prior learning, and provide a training indemnity for all gig workers above a certain revenue (OECD, 2018[68]). More recently, the law "For the freedom to choose one's professional future" ("*Pour la liberté de choisir son avenir professionnel*") adopted in August 2018 and currently under discussion, would require platforms to financially contribute to the *Individual Learning Account* (see Section 6.4) when workers earn at least half of the minimum wage per month. Moreover, the new law would give platforms the possibility to establish a charter, *i.e.* a written agreement with the worker, which determines workers' rights, including on training and skills development (OECD, 2019[61]).

Workers' reputation plays a key role in having access to jobs in the platform economy. In this respect, skills certification is particularly important to make gig workers' competences visible to potential platforms, and ultimately result in better employment opportunities. Recent research shows that completing a skills certificate increases freelancers' earnings, by making their skills more visible to employers and decreasing employer uncertainty (Kässi and Lehdonvirta, 2019[69]). Skills certification is also important to avoid that workers undertake similar training several times when working with different platforms.

On top of skills certification, reputation (e.g. measured through clients' evaluations and assessments) can provide, de facto, a client-based certification of skills. While most platforms have client evaluations in place, one key challenge going forward will be to attach the property to the individual gig worker, who should be able to leave the platform with it (see Chapter 4).

Going forward, it will also be important that individuals have the skills to take advantage of the job opportunities that the platform economy can offer if they wish to. Indeed, participation in crowd working requires access to internet and certain digital skills, yet today not all individuals have the digital skills required to benefit – e.g. the low-skilled, older workers (European Parliament, 2016[63]; De Stefano, 2016[70]). To address this challenge, some OECD countries and states (e.g. California and Israel) are taking steps to help individuals to train for the jobs in the platform economy (Box 6.12).

---

**Box 6.12. Training adults for the jobs in the platform economy**

- In *California* (United States) a pilot programme "Self-Employment Pathways in the Gig Economy" is being implemented in community colleges, and offers classes focused on the pros and cons of platforms, advice on creating and optimising an online profile, and provides professional strategies for finding and performing jobs in the platform economy (OECD, 2019[1]).
- In *San Francisco* (United States) the Office of Economic and Workforce Development collaborated with Samaschool (a non-profit organisation) to launch a pilot program - Bridge to Employment - that provides support to aspiring gig workers. The goal is to help individuals take advantage of the gig economy to gain experience, develop skills, and earn additional incomes. The programme includes a series of free interactive training modules and videos on topics unique to independent work, and provides in-person assistance (OECD, 2019[1]; OECD, 2018[68]).
- In *Israel*, the government – in cooperation with non-government organisations (NGOs) – runs a few small pilot programmes that aim to train and provide guidance to workers who use the platform economy. A new training model offers target vulnerable populations (people with disabilities, Arab women), to learn how to use online trading platforms and to make a living at the global online market (OECD, 2019[61]).

---

### 6.3.7. Part-time workers

Part-time workers tend to participate less in training than full-time employees (Figure 6.5). Evidence across OECD countries shows that workers holding part-time jobs face a penalty compared with full-time workers in terms of training, even after controlling for observable characteristics (OECD, 2010[71]). Evidence from several OECD countries – e.g. Japan (Hara, 2014[72]); Switzerland (Backes-Gellner, Oswald and N. Tuor, 2011[73]) – also corroborates that working part-time constitutes a serious disadvantage in access to training.

Lower participation in training may reflect, in some cases, part-timers' individual preferences and less commitment to career goals. However, low participation may also be the result of the fact that employers are less willing to invest in training part-time workers, as the return is lower than for full-time workers (OECD, 2010[71]).

In many OECD countries, equal-treatment laws have been introduced in the past two decades to ensure that part-time workers receive working conditions – including on training opportunities – comparable to full-time workers. The principle of equal treatment for full- and part-time work is detailed in the ILO Part-Time Work Convention (1994) and the European Working Time Directive (2001).

Since then, OECD countries have progressively included equal-treatment laws in their national legislations, often specifying equal rights with regards to training. In Japan, for example, the 2008 Part Time Work Act establishes that employers should give equal training opportunities to part- and full-time workers (Ebisui, 2012[40]; ICLG, 2018[74]). Similarly, in Greece, a law enacted in 2010 establishes that part-time workers have the same rights to participate in vocational training activities as full-time employees. Overall, evidence from OECD countries shows that part-timers' access to training improved after the introduction of equal treatment laws[39] (OECD, 2010[71]).

Despite these efforts, part-timers still fall between the cracks of many adult learning policies. One key challenge is that often training rights are built on the number of hours worked – which means that part-time workers typically take more time to accrue the same training rights as full-time employees. For example, in France the number of training credits accumulated by part-time employees in the Individual Learning Account depends on the number of hours worked. Similarly, in countries such as Belgium and Luxembourg, education and training leave entitlements for part-time workers are calculated based on the number of hours worked (UCM, 2017[75]).

Another key challenge is that part-time workers often cannot fully benefit from training programmes provided by the PES. Indeed, many of these training opportunities are reserved to "full-time" jobseekers/unemployed who do not work at all, and exclude part-time employees who would be willing to acquire new skills. In some OECD countries, activation (including training) programmes may be mandatory for "full time" jobseekers/unemployed, but only voluntary for part-timers (Fagan et al., 2014[76]). Or, training may require full-time participation, that makes attendance difficult for part-time workers – as has been the case for some training programmes in Mexico (OECD, 2010[71]). Finally, in some OECD countries (e.g. Czech Republic, Slovak Republic, Sweden, Switzerland) activation and training support is limited to certain categories of part-time workers, such as involuntary part-timers, or part-timers with incomes below a certain threshold (Fagan et al., 2014[76]) – which in practice excludes many part-time workers from many of the training opportunities available.

One way OECD countries can further improve training for part-timers, is by ensuring that adult learning programmes target this group of workers more specifically or give them priority access. For example, in Japan, the "Job-Card system" allows job-hopping part-timers – among other groups – to participate in training and record theirs skills in the job card, with a view to facilitate transition to a more stable job (Hara, 2014[72]). In Latvia, a EU-funded programme *Izaugsme un nodarbinātība* – which covers training fees and provides career guidance and validation of skills – gives priority access to a number of vulnerable groups, including part-time employees. Despite these positive examples, overall targeted training efforts for part-time workers remain scant across the OECD.

*The glass half-full: could part-time work help workers train?*

Some OECD countries have put in place mechanisms to incentivise full-time workers to work part-time in order to train. In some OECD countries, – such as Austria, Belgium, France, Korea, New Zealand, Norway, Portugal, Sweden, (OECD, 2010[71]; ILO, 2016[77]) – full-time workers have specific rights to request part-time work to pursue education or training. For example, in 2013 Austria introduced the educational part-time work (*BildungSteilzeit*) which allows full-time workers to work part-time (25-50% of working time) to pursue education and training – for a period of four months to two years – and receive a monetary compensation by the PES (Rathgeb, 2016[78]). In other OECD countries, similar rights are set in collective agreements. For example, in Germany, collective agreements in the metal and electrical industries have set a right for part-time work for allowing part-time training (German Federal Ministry of Labour and Social Affairs, 2017[79])

### 6.3.8. Older adults

Older adults across the OECD participate less in training than younger adults (Figure 6.17). The largest differences are found in Austria, Belgium, Korea and the Netherlands where they exceed 30 percentage points. The smallest differences are observed in Israel, the Slovak Republic and the United States, where they are below 15 percentage points.

Older adults have also lower willingness to train than younger adults. This gap is particularly high in Denmark where it reaches 20 percentage points, and is lower than 5 percentage points in Turkey, Korea, and Japan (Figure 6.17). Lack of willingness to train among older adults may be due to a mix of limited interest in training and limited training offers received. In fact, proximity to retirement age may discourage older people from seeking training opportunities and firms to invest in the skills development of older workers.

**Figure 6.17. Differences in training participation and willingness to train between young and older adults, by country, 2012, 2015**

Percentage point difference in training participation and willingness to train, young adults (age 25-34) minus older adults (age 55-64)

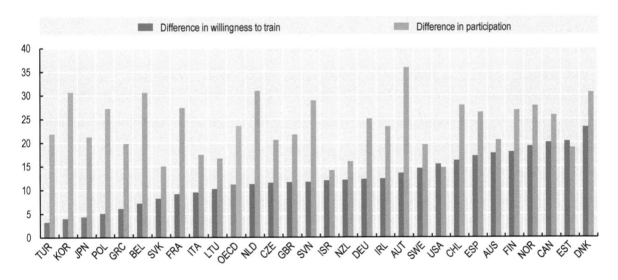

Note: The difference in willingness to train is the percentage point difference in the share of adults who did not participate in training but would have liked to (positive values indicate that this share is higher for young adults than for older adults). The difference in participation is the percentage point difference in the share of adults who participated in training over the previous 12 months (positive values indicate that this share is higher for young adults than for older adults).
Source: Survey of Adult Skills (PIAAC) (2012, 2015), http://www.oecd.org/skills/piaac/.

StatLink ᐉᓯᔭ http://dx.doi.org/10.1787/888933967167

Even older adults who would be willing to train in principle face several obstacles in doing so (Figure 6.18).[40] Lack of time for work reasons is most frequently cited barrier to training, particularly so in Australia, Korea and Sweden. Cost appears to pay a major role in Israel, Slovenia and the United States.

A lack of prerequisites – due to outdated skills or to lower levels of formal education – appear to be an issue in Chile and Estonia.

**Figure 6.18. Reasons why older adults do not participate in training, by country**

Reasons for not training among older adults (age 55-64) who did not train but would have liked to, by country, 2012, 2015

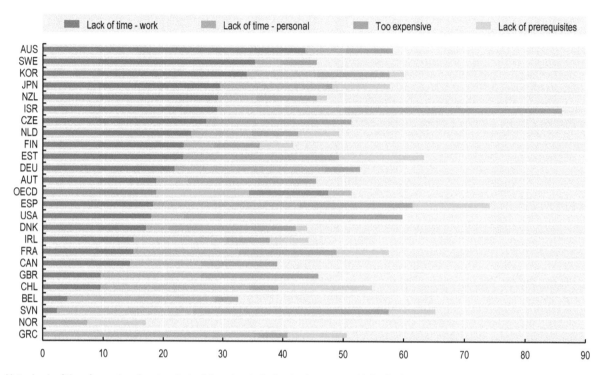

Note: Lack of time for work, refers to a lack of time due to "being too busy at work". Lack of time – personal refers to a lack of time due to childcare of family responsibilities.
Source: Survey of Adult Skills (PIAAC) (2012, 2015), http://www.oecd.org/skills/piaac/.

StatLink 🔗 http://dx.doi.org/10.1787/888933967186

Training needs to be made more attractive for older workers and their employers. Longer working lives resulting from increases in retirement age adopted in many OECD countries, are expected to strengthen the willingness of firms to train older workers and encourage older workers to invest in their skills development.

Additional adult learning measures can be implemented to enhance firms' willingness to train older workers. One policy option is to reduce the cost of training older workers relative to other employees, for example through financial incentives targeted to firms that train older workers (Box 6.13).

Efforts on the firm side need to be complemented by adequate mechanisms to support the interest and motivation of older adults to invest in their skills. In this context, targeted career advice and guidance services can help older adults understand the benefits of learning and make informed decisions about their investment in further skill development (Box 6.13).

Targeted training support is important not only for older employees but also for those who are unemployed, for example because they were made redundant. Redundancy may be particularly challenging for older people, whose skills may be obsolete and who may need intensive re-training and guidance to be able to find a new job. Canada offers several programmes specifically for older and/or long-tenured displaced workers (Box 6.13).

**Career advice and guidance services targeted to older adults**

- Since mid-2018, *Australia* has been trialling a new programme "Career Transition Assistance" for job-seekers aged 50 and above in five regions, with the perspective of national roll-out for everyone aged 45 and above in 2019. The programme will combine tailored career assistance and functional digital literacy training using different types of technology (OECD, 2019[1]).

- In the *Netherlands*, workers aged 45 and more can participate in subsidised career development guidance (*Ontwikkeladvies*). These guidance activities help older workers understand the future prospects of their current job, and give insight into their skills profile and career opportunities. Participants develop a personal development plan that describes the actions that will be taken to ensure employment until retirement age (OECD, 2019[1]).

- In *Korea*, Job Hope Centres offer re-employment services for vulnerable individuals aged 40, including counselling and guidance services for older workers who need (re)training before starting their job search, and often lack the basic ICT skills needed to use online services. Almost 30 000 people benefited from this programme in 2017 (OECD, 2018[80]).

**Encouraging employers to train older workers**

- In *Estonia*, there is a training grant for employers to train employees upon changing circumstances, or to train a worker previously registered as long-term unemployed within one year of the start of employment. Subsidises equal 50% of training costs, but are higher (at 80%) for certain disadvantaged groups including older workers (Estonian Unemployment Insurance Fund, 2019[33]).

- In *Germany*, the public employment agency supports training of low-skilled and older workers in SMEs through the programme *WeGebAU*. SMEs receive a 75% subsidy to the training costs of workers 45 years of age and older, while micro-enterprises (with less than 10 employees) receive a 100% subsidy. Evaluations of the programme find that it helps participants to increase their time spend in employment, although it has no effect on wages and the probability of receiving benefits later on (Dauth, 2017[81]; OECD, 2019[1]).

- In *Luxembourg*, private sector companies can receive training aid up to 15% of the yearly amount invested in training, while 35% of salary expenses of trained employees are subsidies for certain workers, including workers older than 45 (Luxembourg Government, 2019[82]).

- In *Slovenia*, the "Comprehensive Support for Companies for Active Ageing of Employees Programme" provides financial incentives for employers to prepare action plans and strategies for better management of older workers as well as financial incentives for older workers for upskilling (aged above 45). Capacity building workshops for HR managers and CEOs are organised to build their competencies for effective human resource management of ageing workforce (OECD, 2017[83]).

**Programmes for older/long-tenured displaced workers in *Canada***

- The federal-provincial/territorial cost-shared programme Targeted Initiative for Older Workers (TIOW) is specifically designed to support retraining for unemployed older workers (aged 55-64), living in small communities which have been affected by high unemployment, significant downsizing/closures, unfulfilled employer demand and/or skills mismatches (OECD, 2015[37]).

- The Career Transition Assistance (CTA), temporarily introduced during the economic crisis, extended duration of Employment Insurance benefits to up to two years for eligible long-tenured displaced workers who participate in longer-term training; and earlier access to Employment

Insurance regular benefits for displaced workers investing in their own training using all or part of their severance package (OECD, 2015[37]).[41] More recently, as of fall 2018, eligible EI claimants who lose their jobs after several years in the workforce will have more opportunities to continue to receive EI benefits while taking a self-funded full-time training.

- In Ontario (Canada), the Second Career programme provides training assistance to older or long-tenured workers affected by economic restructuring to help them train for new careers in high-demand fields (OECD, 2015[37]).

## 6.4. Can individual learning accounts make adult learning accessible to a broader group of adults?

Individual learning accounts (ILAs) have sometimes been touted as an alternative and more radical way of overhauling the adult learning system. These are schemes that provide an individual with resources he/she can use to take-up training of his/her own initiative. One of the key objectives of real ILAs is also to make training right portable/transferable from jobs to jobs, which is particularly important in the context of the future of work.

They can be "real" individual accounts – financed by the state, the individual and/or the employer – where rights/saving for training are accumulated over a certain period of time, or voucher schemes which support training through direct governmental payments, sometimes with a contribution from the participant.

ILA schemes aim to make individuals more responsible for their training, and more autonomous in defining their skills needs and finding training opportunities among a set of courses offered by providers competing against one another. In many countries, these schemes aim to reduce inequalities in access to training, either directly by restricting access to under-represented groups or indirectly by motivating competing training organisations to propose training modalities more adapted to the needs of under-represented groups and by attaching training rights to individuals rather than jobs. The latter is particularly important for workers in new forms of work and on non-standard employment contracts more generally: by making training rights portable between jobs and from one employment status to another, ILAs de facto broaden training rights to workers who have a limited attachment to their employer.

However, while many countries are looking at ILAs for their potential to broaden training participation, this was not the original objective of most of these schemes. Indeed, when several countries introduced ILAs in the 1990s, they were aimed at promoting competition amongst training providers to improve the match between individual needs and service provision and improve value for money in training provision. Policy makers hoped that this could be achieved by providing choice to the individuals on which training they receive and who delivers it. This needs to be kept in mind when drawing conclusions on how successful ILAs have been so far in engaging under-represented groups in training. Box 6.14 provides an overview of existing schemes including a description of the sources of funding, training content and quality and governance arrangements.

### Box 6.14. Individual Learning Accounts in OECD countries and beyond

Several countries have introduced Individual Learning Account (ILAs) schemes since the 1990s. Although many are officially called "individual learning/training account", in reality most function as vouchers and "real" ILAs are quite rare. Current voucher schemes include the *Opleidingscheques* in Flanders (Belgium), the *Bildungspraemie* in Germany, the *Cheque Formação* in Portugal, the Individual Training Accounts (ITA) in Scotland, the *Chèque annuel de formation* in Geneva Canton (Switzerland), the ITA in the United States. The *Bildungskonto* in Upper Austria functions almost as a voucher scheme, although application is made after training completion. "Real" ILAs currently exist only in France (*Compte Personnel de Formation*) since 2015 and in Singapore (SkillsFuture Credits) since 2016, and some were piloted on a very limited scale in Michigan, Maine and Washington in the United States (Lifelong Learning Accounts, LiLAs) and in some Canadian Communities (*learn$Save*) in the 2000s. The recent French reform (*Loi de 2018 pour la liberté de choisir son avenir professionnel*) places the *Compte Personnel de Formation* (CPF) at the centre of the adult training system and significantly reforms its governance.

Most ILA schemes are based on a principle of cost-sharing between the individual undertaking training and the government. Schemes in Austria, Germany, Flanders and Portugal require some degree of financial participation by individuals. To compensate for the potential disincentive introduced by co-financing for some under-represented groups, some schemes (e.g. the *Bildungskonto* in Austria) require a smaller financial contribution from them. Employers are more rarely directly involved, with employee/employer co-financing being a founding principle only in the LiLA scheme in the United States. In France, the *CPF* is financed through a training levy on medium and large firms, so that employers are involved. Other schemes, such as the ITAs in Scotland and the United States, the Geneva and Singapore schemes are fully financed from public money.

To ensure the use of ILAs, transparency and administrative simplicity are crucial. The current reform of the French *CPF* involves a significant simplification of access procedure, notably through increased reliance on a web application that provides information on the account and on the training possibilities. Similarly there is a trade-off between limiting access to a pre-defined list of authorised courses – potentially difficult to navigate – and encouraging ILA use. France recently dropped such lists in the interest of simplicity and efficiency as the list created bottlenecks. But constraints in the use of ILAs remain in many countries: training must be in high demand occupations in the United States ITA; it must fall within one of the 13 approved curriculum areas in Scotland; it must be in areas of training priority in Portugal; or simply labour market oriented in the Flanders.

Generosity is another key determinant of ILAs use. Some ILA schemes provide relatively limited amounts of financial support (GBP 200 in Scotland, EUR 175 for employed persons in Portugal, EUR 250 in Flanders) thus allowing mostly short-duration training. By contrast, the narrowly targeted United States ITA are more generous, providing up to USD 5 000 for jobseekers and USD 10 000 for displaced workers. In France, the CPF entitlement was expressed in hours until December 2018. This changed to a monetary endowment as of January 2019 to increase transparency. Since then, EUR 15 are credited for each hour of work, up to EUR 500 per year and with a ceiling of EUR 5 000. For the low qualified, the maximum amount is capped at EUR 800 per year of work, up to a ceiling of EUR 8 000. Until 2018, these credits were often complemented by additional funding from the training funds, the public employment service or the regions, especially in the case of jobseekers.

ILAs raise specific issues in terms of training quality, as public entities no longer have a contractual relationship with the training providers that would allow them to put incentives for quality/performance in place. The failure of the ILA scheme in the United Kingdom in the early 2000s provides an example of the importance to regulate training providers. This is dealt with by establishing lists of recognised training organisations (e.g. in Flanders, Germany, Scotland, Upper Austria,) or training programmes (e.g. France, US ITA). The French *CPF* reform has introduced the obligation for providers to report predefined performance criteria – the so-called data-docks, as well as the obligation to choose among certified training.

Source: OECD (forthcoming), Individual Learning Accounts: Panacea or Pandora's box?

The extent to which ILAs cover under-represented groups differs significantly across countries (OECD, forthcoming[28]). SkillsFuture Credits in Singapore and the *Chèque annuel de formation* in the Geneva Canton are almost universal as they cover all adults above a certain age. However, most schemes limit eligibility to active individuals, with some focusing exclusively on jobseekers or employees, while others combine different employment status (Table 6.2). The French scheme covers all active persons. The self-employed are less likely to be covered than employees, limiting the role that ILAs could play for own-account and platform workers.

Besides employment status, ILA schemes sometimes restrict eligibility according to income or skill level in order to target under-represented groups. For example, only low-income individuals are eligible to the *Bildungsprämie* in Germany, the ITA in Scotland and the ITA in the United States. The Flemish scheme has been restricted to low- and medium skill workers since 2015 as was the Scottish scheme until recently and the Austrian *Bildungskonto* at various times since its inception.

Other ways of targeting priority groups are through modulating the amount of support provided. In France for example, employees with no qualifications and early school leavers benefit from higher rights, as do, in the Austrian *Bildungskonto*, women returning from child-related career breaks, low-income employees above 50 years of age, individuals with only compulsory education level and no vocational credential, and immigrants studying German.

These targeting mechanisms are key as there is evidence that, as in other types of training schemes, low-skilled workers participate less than the high-skilled where access is not restricted to them. This bias partly reflects the difficulty of solving the under-representation issue through an instrument based on the ability of participants to be autonomous and navigate complex training access rules. It also points to the importance of providing quality information/counselling mechanisms. However, restricting access to some groups at the same time reduces the transferability property of the schemes.

Table 6.2. Individual Learning Accounts coverage

| | Employees | Self-employed | Unemployed | Inactive |
|---|---|---|---|---|
| ITA United States[1] | | | ● | |
| Opleidingscheques Flanders | ● | | | |
| Bildungsprämie Germany | ● | | | |
| Cheque formacão Portugal | ● | | ● | |
| Bildungskonto Upper Austria | ● | ● | ● | |
| CPF France | ● | ● | ● | |
| ITA Scotland | ● | ● | ● | |
| Chèque annuel de formation Geneva[2] | ● | ● | ● | |
| SkillsFuture Credit Singapore | ● | ● | ● | ● |

1. The US ITA scheme also covers displaced workers;
2. The required professional usefulness de facto restrains access from inactive persons.
Source: OECD (forthcoming[28]), Individual Learning Accounts: Panacea or Pandora's box?

Irrespective of the potential to serve under-represented groups, actual participation in ILAs remains modest in most cases (OECD, forthcoming[28]). In France and Singapore, the two recently implemented real ILA schemes with rather large potential coverage, about 1.7% and 4.2% of the labour force respectively participated in the scheme in 2016 and 2017, partly reflecting their very recent implementation. In Upper Austria, about 2% of the labour force got training financing from the *Bildungskonto* in 2017, and participation to the Scottish ITA declined from a maximum of 2% of the labour force in 2010-11 to 0.7% in 2017-18. In the United States, participants to the ITA represented 1.2% and 0.6% of the unemployed in the states of Michigan and Washington respectively. The former Lifelong Learning Accounts in the United States concerned only a few hundred workers in total. For the time being, existing schemes are far too modest in scale to be able, on their own, to increase training participation overall, even less so to reduce the gap between high-skilled, full-time permanent employees and the rest, at least in the absence of adequate counselling. The French scheme is promising because of its large potential coverage and generosity. In addition, the recent changes aiming to make it more accessible and improve take up. Nevertheless, it is too early to draw conclusions on its effectiveness.

## 6.5. Building adequate financing, governance, and quality assessment mechanisms

Increasing the coverage and inclusiveness of adult learning systems to meet the increasing needs of changing labour markets requires a significant increase in financial resources, a good governance structure and the provision of high-quality training. This section explores policy options to: (i) ensure that training is of good quality and is aligned to current and future labour market needs; (ii) build financing mechanisms that are adequate and equitable; and (iii) set governance arrangements that make different parts of adult learning systems work well together. It provides a short summary of recent OECD work on the functioning, effectiveness and resilience of adult learning systems across countries (Box 6.1).

### 6.5.1. Quality of training and alignment to current and future skills needs

Despite the crucial role that adult learning stands to play in maintaining workers employability, there is often a disconnect between the content of training and labour market needs. For example, in Italy a sizeable part of the training provided by Training Funds concerns compulsory occupational health and safety, while very little is focussed on developing digital skills (OECD, 2019[50]). In France, the top type of training undertaken by users of the Individual Learning Account is foreign languages. Examples of this kind could be provided for many other OECD countries.[42]

To improve alignment and usefulness of training, firms and policy makers need, in the first place, to understand what skills are needed, now and in the future. Skills assessment and anticipation (SAA) exercises are conducted on a regular basis across many OECD countries – typically by ministries, regions, social partners, or independent research bodies – with the objective to produce information on current and future skills needs.

SAA information typically feeds into a number of policy areas (employment, migration, education) (OECD, 2016[84]). In adult learning, SAA information are used by policy makers in several OECD countries to inform adult learning strategies and/or adult learning programmes, for example to design courses for job seekers delivered through the PES.

SAA exercises are also being used by policy makers to steer individuals and firms' decisions to develop in-demand skills. For instance, the availability of financial incentives (e.g. tax exceptions, subsidies) can be limited to certain training programmes that help fill existing skills gaps in the labour market (OECD, 2017[31]).

Similarly, policy makers sometimes use SAA information to adjust the generosity of financial incentives in line with skills shortages, i.e. granting more generous financial incentives when training develops in-demand skills.

A softer way of steering individuals and employers towards the development of in-demand skills is by ensuring that SAA information reaches prospective learners, in a view to help them make informed skills decisions. For this purpose, SAA information can be made widely accessible for example via career guidance websites, information sessions, and/or public awareness campaigns. One example of career guidance website is MySkills in Australia – which allows adults to download careers information sheets covering a range of manufacturing sectors.

On top of identifying current and future skills needs, and ensuring that training reflects those identified needs, OECD countries also need to assess the effectiveness of training ex-post. In this respect, impact evaluation can help policy makers understand what adult learning programmes work and for whom, which is crucial especially in the context of tight budgets.[43]

Despite its importance, the use of impact evaluations remains rare in adult learning (OECD, 2019[1]). Many adult learning programmes still go unevaluated in many OECD countries, and their impact remains unknown. Even adult learning schemes that are widely used across the OECD – e.g. training levies – lack robust evidence on their effectiveness (Müller and Behringer, 2012[85]).

That being said, some OECD countries are building a strong impact evaluation culture. In Germany, for example, the implementation of the 2003-2005 reforms to active and passive labour market policies was explicitly tied to an evaluation mandate. In Australia, the Try, Test and Learn Fund – set up in 2016 for trialling new approaches through a range of projects and programmes (including training programmes) that aim to moving move at-risk income support recipients onto a pathway towards employment – uses a range of impact evaluation methods to test effectiveness and learn from results. In the UK, the first phase of the National Retraining Scheme (NRS) – which aims to give every worker the opportunity to upskill or retrain for the new digital technologies – includes a phased series of interventions which will build on the evidence base on what works. The European Social Fund made it compulsory in the 2014-2020 programming period to assess, through impact evaluation, to what extent the objectives have been achieved, including on adult learning activities (European Commission, 2015[86]). In France, the Skills Investment Plan – which aims at training 1 million low-killed job seekers and 1 million young people – includes an experimentation and impact evaluation strategy steered by a scientific committee. In fact, it is of paramount importance that the evaluation strategy is conceived together with the measures themselves in order to guarantee rigorous assessment.

To guarantee that training is of good quality, many countries have put in place accreditation and certification mechanisms of training providers. These mechanisms are essential to ensure that training providers and programmes comply with minimum quality requirements, and can help individuals, employers and institutions make informed choices about training investments (OECD, 2019[1]).

### 6.5.2. Financing

Adult learning systems need adequate and sustainable financing to function well. While ensuring adequate funding for adult learning is a key policy challenge today, arguably it will become even more pressing in the future. As the demand for adult learning is likely to increase in the context of the mega-trends, the financial resources devoted to adult learning programmes will need to be increased. Indeed, the changes necessary to scale up existing adult learning systems, broaden coverage and increase quality will indeed require significant financial resources.

Establishing who should pay for adult learning is not straightforward, however. There needs to be an equitable sharing of the financing of adult learning in line with ability to pay and the benefits that accrue to individuals, firms and society. This requires a 'healthy mix' of co-financing by government, employers and individuals.

Within the context of tight public budgets, in the future there is an urgent need to engage employers and individuals further in sharing the burden of adult learning financing. Governments across the OECD use a range of financial incentives – e.g. tax incentives, subsidies – to encourage firms and workers to contribute to adult learning financing, and reduce under-investments (OECD, 2019[1]). Moreover, social partners are also involved in the financing of adult learning programmes in many OECD countries (OECD, 2019[4]), which can help further share the burden of adult learning spending among firms and workers. For example, in several OECD and developing countries – e.g. Italy, South Africa – social partners are involved in the management of training funds, associations which aim to finance workers' training using resources collected through a levy imposed on employers (OECD, 2019[50]).

### 6.5.3. Governance

There is only so much that governments can do in enhancing access to adult learning for vulnerable groups, as adult learning is a shared responsibility between the government, firms and adults themselves. Indeed, training programmes designed for adults at greater risk of being left behind are often under the responsibility of different actors (e.g. different ministries, PES, social partners, stakeholders). For example, social partners play a very important role in in adult learning financing; in conducting Skills Assessment and Anticipation (SAA) exercises; and in influencing adult learning provision through sectoral collective bargaining and tripartite agreements – see Chapter 5 and OECD (2019[4]).

In this complex context, building mechanisms for cooperation between the government and different stakeholders – e.g. social partners, training providers, civil society, NGOs – can help governments align adult learning programmes to local needs, facilitate the sharing and replication of good practices, and improve training quality. Indeed, because of their proximity to learners, these stakeholders are well placed to understand the skills and training needs of adults.

Some interesting new governance initiatives are emerging specifically in the context of the future of work. For example, in Canada, the Budget 2018 established Future Skills Councils – formed by practitioners and experts from the private, labour, education and training sector, academics and NGOs – to provide advice to the Minister of Employment, Workforce Development and Labour on skills development and training priorities for the future of work. Similarly, several OECD countries have put in place ad hoc strategies to improve basic digital skills of the population. To cite a few examples, this is the case for the Digital literacy strategy 2015-2020 in the Czech Republic, the *InCode 2030* strategy in Portugal, and the National Digital Strategy 2016-2021 in Greece. Also, most future of work strategies include an adult learning component. These broader strategies typically look at how adult learning systems need to evolve in the context of a changing world of work. One example is the German Re-imagining Work White Paper published in 2017, which provides a wide societal reflection on the future of work in Germany including on topics related to adult learning.

Finally, good coordination efforts are important not only within the adult learning system, but also between adult learning and other policy areas. In fact, adult learning policies are deeply anchored in a variety of policy fields – e.g. welfare, industrial policy – which can influence and reinforce each other. To give few examples, family policies that expand access to affordable early childhood education and care (ECEC) can free up time for parents to take up adult learning opportunities. Likewise, industrial policy deeply relies on adult learning and human capital development strategies to achieve its goals.

In this context, strengthening horizontal coordination between different ministries, – for example by establishing inter-sectoral bodies – could help ensure that policies designed by different ministries are mutually reinforcing. Inter-sectoral bodies on adult learning exist in several OECD countries (OECD, 2019[1]), and sometimes they focus on topics that are specifically relevant in the context of the future of work. For example, Japan established the Council for Designing 100-Year Life Society in 2017, with the aim of bringing together different stakeholders to discuss the policy challenges associated with population ageing, including workers' continuous up-skilling opportunities.

## 6.6. Concluding remarks

The future of work will bring about substantial changes in skill requirements, and better access to adult learning opportunities will be crucial for workers to benefit from these changes. Yet many adults today do not participate in training. Participation is especially low amongst those most in need of upskilling and reskilling and among the rising number of workers in non-standard employment arrangements. Moreover, training programmes available are not always relevant and useful, so there is a need to improve training quality and make adult learning systems more aligned to changing skills needs.

Adjustments at the margins of existing adult learning systems are unlikely to be sufficient. In view of the scope and the speed of the changes taking place, a significant overhaul of adult learning policies is needed to make adult learning systems future-ready for all.

Several policy options exist to start going in this direction (Box 6.15). Because each policy should not be taken in isolation, countries should develop comprehensive adult learning strategies, which not only aim to make adult learning systems more inclusive with regards to groups at highest risk of being left behind, but also include measures to align training content more closely with changing skill needs and to improve its quality. An adult learning strategy should be built on good governance and financing structures involving all relevant stakeholders, and embed adult learning within a broader framework of policies – e.g. labour market regulation, social policy, collective bargaining – to help make the future of work more rewarding and inclusive.

---

### Box 6.15. Policy directions

A comprehensive adult learning strategy is needed to face the challenges of a changing world of work and to ensure that all workers, particularly the most vulnerable, have adequate opportunities for retraining throughout their careers. As part of this strategy, countries should consider the following policy directions:

- Foster a mind-set for learning among both firms and individuals. This could be done by strengthening career guidance for all adults; putting in place public information campaigns to raise awareness of the benefits of learning; and ensuring that wages reflect more closely the productivity gains resulting from training participation.

- Lower barriers to training by:
  - o Tackling time constraints through modular training options, training delivered outside of working hours or online courses, as well as by providing workers with education and training leave.
  - o Lowering the cost of training by providing financial incentives for the most vulnerable groups in the labour market.
  - o Reducing entry barriers to training courses for workers with low qualifications by strengthening the recognition of skills acquired through experience.

- Encourage employers to train groups at risk. This could be achieved by lowering the cost to employers of training at-risk workers, for example by means of targeted financial incentives.

- Target adult learning policies such as financial subsidies, and career guidance services on the groups that need them most, including non-standard workers.

- Tackle unequal access to training based on employment status. Equal rights clauses have been introduced in most countries to ensure access to training for employees in some non-standard contracts, such as part-time, fixed-term, and temporary agency workers. In practice, however, these workers may not acquire rights to training, which often accrue with job tenure and depend on the numbers of hours worked. Moreover, self-employed workers are still very rarely covered by training rights legislation.

- Make training rights portable between employment statuses. Individual learning accounts have been proposed and implemented in a few countries as one way for workers to acquire and accumulate training rights irrespective of their employer or whether they change jobs or employment status. However, if vulnerable workers are to benefit fully, such schemes need to be complemented by more personal, face-to-face support delivered by specialised career guidance officers and informed by quality information on labour market needs.

- Ensure that training is of good quality and aligned to labour market needs through: the collection and use of high-quality information on skill needs; accreditation and certification of training providers; and a strong culture of evaluation of the effectiveness of policies and programmes.

- Strengthen the governance of adult learning systems, involving all relevant stakeholders, to ensure coherence and co-ordination of adult learning policies. Adult learning is a shared responsibility that calls for the active involvement of all stakeholders, including all levels of government, the social partners, training providers and adults themselves.

- Share the financial burden of scaling up adult learning systems. Significant financial resources will be required to scale up existing adult learning systems, broaden coverage and increase training quality. This calls for a healthy mix of co-financing by government, employers and individuals that takes account of ability to pay and the benefits obtained.

## References

Acemoglu, D. and D. Autor (2010), *Skills, Tasks and Technologies: Implications for Employment and Earnings*, National Bureau of Economic Research, Cambridge, MA, http://dx.doi.org/10.3386/w16082. [9]

Allinckx, I. and D. Monico (2016), *Vocational Education and Training in Europe: Belgium*, CEDEFOP, https://www.refernet.de/dokumente/pdf/2016_CR_BE.pdf. [60]

Autor, D. (2001), "Why do temporary help firms provide free general skills training", *The Quarterly Journal of Economics*, https://economics.mit.edu/files/590. [87]

Backes-Gellner, U., Y. Oswald and S. N. Tuor (2011), *Part-time work and employer-provided training: boon to women and bane to men?*, Leading House Working Paper No. 58, http://repec.business.uzh.ch/RePEc/iso/leadinghouse/0058_lhwpaper.pdf. [73]

Becker, S., K. Ekholm and M. Muendler (2013), "Offshoring and the onshore composition of tasks and skills", *Journal of International Economics*, Vol. 90/1, pp. 91-106, http://dx.doi.org/10.1016/j.jinteco.2012.10.005. [11]

Bekker, S. and M. Posthumus (2010), *Self-employment in the Netherlands*, European Employment Observatory Review, 2010(July), 1-7. [51]

Bologna, S. (2016), *Le mouvement des freelancers: origines, caractéristiques, et développement*, SMart, https://smartbe.be/fr/comprendre/publications/education-permanente/le-mouvement-des-freelances-origines-caracteristiques-et-developpement/. [54]

Broughton, A. et al. (2018), *The experiences of individuals in the gig economy*, UK Department for Business, Energy and Industrial Strategy, https://assets.publishing.service.gov.uk/government/uploads/system/uploads/attachment_data/file/679987/171107_The_experiences_of_those_in_the_gig_economy.pdf. [67]

Busby, C. and R. Muthukumaran (2016), *Precarious Positions: Policy Options to Mitigate Risks in Non-standard Employment*, C.D. Howe Institute, https://www.cdhowe.org/sites/default/files/attachments/research_papers/mixed/Commentary%20462_0.pdf. [41]

Cabrales, A., J. Dolado and R. Mora (2014), *Dual Labour Markets and (Lack of) On-the-Job Training: PIAAC Evidence from Spain and Other EU Countries*, IZA Discussion Paper No. 8649, http://citeseerx.ist.psu.edu/viewdoc/download?doi=10.1.1.652.4924&rep=rep1&type=pdf. [44]

Cahuc, P., S. Carcillo and A. Minea (forthcoming), "The Difficult School-To-Work Transition of High School Dropouts: Evidence from a Field Experiment", *Journal of Human Resources*. [30]

Carpentieri, J. et al. (2018), *Goal Guidance and Orientation for Adult Learners: Final cross-country evaluation report*, UCL Institute, https://adultguidance.eu/images/Reports/GOAL_final_cross-country_evaluation_report.pdf. [24]

Casano, L. et al. (2018), *Il futuro delle professioni nella Economia 4.0 tra (nuove) regole e rappresentanza*, Adapt University Press, https://moodle.adaptland.it/pluginfile.php/33938/mod_resource/content/0/2018_confcommercio_futuro_delle_professioni.pdf. [59]

CIPD (2017), *To gig or not to gig? Stories from the modern economy*, CIPD, http://To gig or not to gig? Stories from the modern economy.  [64]

Dauth, C. (2017), "Weiterbildung Geringqualifizierter und beschäftigter älterer Arbeitnehmer in Unternehmen (WeGebAU)", in Möller, J. and U. Walwei (eds.), *Arbeitsmarkt kompakt*, Institut für Arbeitsmarkt- und Berufsforschung der Bundesagentur für Arbeit (IAB)/ Bertelsmann Verlag , Nürnberg/ Bielefeld, http://dx.doi.org/10.3278/300939w.  [81]

De Grip, A. (2012), *The effects of training on own and co-worker productivity: evidence from a field experience*, The Economic Journal 122:560 (2012): 376–399, http://ftp.iza.org/dp5976.pdf.  [47]

De Stefano, V. (2016), *The rise of the «just-in-time workforce»:On-demand work, crowdwork and labour protection in the «gig-economy»*, International Labour Organization, https://www.ilo.org/wcmsp5/groups/public/---ed_protect/---protrav/---travail/documents/publication/wcms_443267.pdf.  [70]

Ebisui, M. (2012), *Non-standard workers: Good practices of social dialogue and collective bargaining*, Working Paper No. 36, International Labour Organization, http://www.oit.org/wcmsp5/groups/public/---ed_dialogue/---dialogue/documents/publication/wcms_179448.pdf.  [40]

Ehlert, C. (2012), *Temporary Work as an Active Labor Market Policy: Evaluating an Innovative Activation Program for Disadvantaged Youths*, IZA Discussion Paper No. 6670, 2012, http://ftp.iza.org/dp6670.pdf.  [46]

Estonian Unemployment Insurance Fund (2019), *Work and study*, https://www.tootukassa.ee/eng/content/work-and-study.  [33]

Eurofound (2018), *Job security councils*, https://www.eurofound.europa.eu/observatories/emcc/erm/support-instrument/job-security-councils.  [43]

Eurofound (2018), *Joint purchase training*, https://www.eurofound.europa.eu/observatories/emcc/erm/support-instrument/joint-purchase-training.  [35]

Eurofound (2017), *Exploring self-employment in the European Union, Publications Office of the European Union*, Eurofound, https://www.eurofound.europa.eu/sites/default/files/ef_publication/field_ef_document/ef1718en.pdf.  [57]

European Commission (2019), *Sweden - For students*, https://ec.europa.eu/social/main.jsp?catId=1130&intPageId=4806&langId=en.  [29]

European Commission (2018), *Employment and Social Developments in Europe 2018*, European Commission, https://ec.europa.eu/social/main.jsp?catId=738&langId=en&pubId=8110&furtherPubs=yes.  [14]

European Commission (2015), *Monitoring and Evaluation of European Cohesion Policy (European Social Fund) - Guidance document*, European Commission, https://www.portugal2020.pt/Portal2020/Media/Default/Docs/AVALIACAO/4-ESF_ME_Guidance_Jun2015.pdf (accessed on 23 July 2018).  [86]

European Commission (2010), *Self-Employment in Europe*, European Commission. [55]

European Commission/EACEA/Eurydice (2015), *Adult Education and Training in Europe: Widening Access to Learning Opportunities. Eurydice Report*, Publications Office of the European Union, Luxembourg, http://www.erasmusplus.sk/uploads/publikacie/2015_AEducation_LOAccess_Eurydice_Comp arative_Report_en.pdf (accessed on 9 July 2018). [21]

European Parliament (2016), *The situation of collaborative workers in the collaborative economy*, European Parliament, http://www.europarl.europa.eu/RegData/etudes/IDAN/2016/587316/IPOL_IDA(2016)587316_ EN.pdf. [63]

EUROSTAT (2019), *CVTS Database - Eurostat*, https://ec.europa.eu/eurostat/web/education- and-training/data/database (accessed on 17 January 2019). [19]

Fagan, C. et al. (2014), *In search of good quality part-time employment*, İnternational Labor Organization, https://www.ilo.org/wcmsp5/groups/public/@ed_protect/@protrav/@travail/documents/publica tion/wcms_237781.pdf. [76]

Fialho, P., G. Quintini and M. Vandeweyer (forthcoming), "Returns to different forms of job- related training: Factoring in informal learning", *OECD Social Employment and Migration working papers*, OECD Publishing, Paris. [17]

Finn, D. (2016), *The Organisation and Regulation of the Public Employment Service and of Private Employment and Temporary Work Agencies. The Experience of Selected European Countries – the Netherlands, Denmark, Germany and the United Kingdom*, Learning and Work Institute, https://researchportal.port.ac.uk/portal/files/4005870/PES_PE_TWA_in_4_European_Countri es_L_W_Report_DF_May2016.pdf. [38]

Fouarge, D., T. Schils and A. de Grip (2013), "Why do low-educated workers invest less in further training?", *Applied Economics*, Vol. 45/18, pp. 2587-2601, http://dx.doi.org/10.1080/00036846.2012.671926. [26]

France Stratégie (2018), *Favoriser le développement professionnel des travailleurs des plateformes numérique*, France Stratégie, https://leplusimportant.org/2018/02/08/favoriser-le- developpement-professionnel-des-travailleurs-des-plateformes-numeriques/. [65]

Frey, C. and M. Osborne (2017), "The future of employment: How susceptible are jobs to computerisation?", *Technological Forecasting and Social Change*, http://dx.doi.org/10.1016/j.techfore.2016.08.019. [6]

German Federal Ministry of Labour and Social Affairs (2017), *Re-imagining Work White Paper White Paper: Work 4.0*, German Federal Ministry of Labour and Social Affairs, https://www.bmas.de/SharedDocs/Downloads/EN/PDF-Publikationen/a883-white- paper.pdf?__blob=publicationFile&v=3. [79]

Hara, H. (2014), "The impact of firm-provided training on productivity, wages, and transition to regular employment for workers in flexible arrangements", *J. Japanese Int. Economies 34 (2014) 336–359*, http://dx.doi.org/10.1016/j.jjie.2014.10.002. [72]

HR Tresury (2018), *Taxation of self-funded work-related training: Consultation on the extension of tax relief for training by employees and the self-employed*, HR Tresury, https://assets.publishing.service.gov.uk/government/uploads/system/uploads/attachment_data/file/689227/PU2152__Consultation_on_self-funded_training_web.pdf. [58]

ICLG (2018), *Employment & Labour Laws and Regulations 2018*, The International Comparative Legal Guide. [74]

IDEAconsult (2015), *How temporary agency work compares with other forms of work*, IDEAconsult, https://www.weceurope.org/fileadmin/templates/eurociett/docs/Social_dialogue/joint_project_2013/Final_report_IDEA_Consult__How_temporary_agency_work_compares_with_other_forms_of_work_.pdf. [39]

ILO (2016), *Non-standard employment around the world*, International Labour Organization, https://www.ilo.org/wcmsp5/groups/public/---dgreports/---dcomm/---publ/documents/publication/wcms_534326.pdf. [77]

Jansen, G. (2017), *Solo self-employment and membership of interest organizations in the Netherlands: Economic, social, and political determinants*, Economic and Industrial Democracy 1–28, https://doi.org/10.1177/0143831X17723712. [56]

Kässi, O. and V. Lehdonvirta (2019), "Do digital skill certificates help new workers enter the market?: Evidence from an online labour platform", *OECD Social, Employment and Migration Working Papers*, No. 225, OECD Publishing, Paris, https://dx.doi.org/10.1787/3388385e-en. [69]

Lejeune, V. (2017), *La formation professionnelle pour les freelances : un combat à mener ?*, Service Formation - SMart, https://smartbe.be/wp-content/uploads/2017/12/15-17-formations_freelance.pdf. [53]

Luxembourg Government (2019), *Financial aid for in-company continuing vocational training*, https://guichet.public.lu/en/entreprises/financement-aides/aides-emploi-recrutement-formation/formation-professionnelle-continue/fpc-entreprise.html. [82]

Luxembourg Government (2019), *Skills Bridge*, https://www.skillsbridge.lu/. [32]

Martin, J. (2018), "Skills for the 21st century: Findings and policy lessons from the OECD survey of adult skills", *OECD Education Working Paper*, Vol. 166, http://www.oecd.org/officialdocuments/publicdisplaydocumentpdf/?cote=EDU/WKP(2018)2&docLanguage=En (accessed on 14 June 2018). [15]

Mathou, C. (2016), *2016 update to the European inventory on validation of non-formal and informal learning,Country report France*, Publication Office of the European union, Luxembourg, https://www.legifrance.gouv.fr/affichTexte.do?cidTexte=JORFTEXT000028683576 (accessed on 16 October 2018). [25]

Müller, N. and F. Behringer (2012), "Subsidies and Levies as Policy Instruments to Encourage Employer-Provided Training", *OECD Education Working Papers*, No. 80, OECD Publishing, Paris, http://dx.doi.org/10.1787/5k97b083v1vb-en. [85]

Nedelkoska, L. and G. Quintini (2018), *Automation, skills use and training*, OECD Publishing, Paris, https://dx.doi.org/10.1787/2e2f4eea-en. [7]

OECD (2019), *Adult Learning in Italy: What Role for Training Funds ?*, Getting Skills Right, OECD Publishing, Paris, https://dx.doi.org/10.1787/9789264311978-en. [50]

OECD (2019), *Getting Skills Right: Creating responsive adult learning systems*, OECD, Paris, http://www.oecd.org/els/emp/adult-learning-systems-2019.pdf. [3]

OECD (2019), *Getting Skills Right: Engaging low-skilled adults in learning*, OECD, Paris, http://www.oecd.org/employment/emp/engaging-low-skilled-adults-2019.pdf. [5]

OECD (2019), *Getting Skills Right: Future-Ready Adult Learning Systems*, Getting Skills Right, OECD Publishing, Paris, https://dx.doi.org/10.1787/9789264311756-en. [1]

OECD (2019), *Getting Skills Right: Making adult learning work in social partnership*, OECD, Paris, http://www.oecd.org/employment/emp/adult-learning-work-in-social-partnership-2019.pdf. [4]

OECD (2019), *OECD Skills Outlook 2019: Thriving in a Digital World*, OECD Publishing, Paris, https://dx.doi.org/10.1787/df80bc12-en. [13]

OECD (2019), *OECD Skills Strategy Flanders: Assessment and Recommendations*, OECD Skills Studies, OECD Publishing, Paris, https://dx.doi.org/10.1787/9789264309791-en. [27]

OECD (2019), *Policy Responses to New Forms of Work*, OECD Publishing, Paris, https://dx.doi.org/10.1787/0763f1b7-en. [61]

OECD (2019), *Priorities for Adult Learning Dashboard*, http://www.oecd.org/employment/skills-and-work/adult-learning/dashboard.htm. [2]

OECD (2018), *Good Jobs for All in a Changing World of Work: The OECD Jobs Strategy*, OECD Publishing, Paris, https://dx.doi.org/10.1787/9789264308817-en. [68]

OECD (2018), *Job Creation and Local Economic Development 2018: Preparing for the Future of Work*, OECD Publishing, Paris, https://dx.doi.org/10.1787/9789264305342-en. [20]

OECD (2018), *OECD Employment Outlook 2018*, OECD Publishing, Paris, https://dx.doi.org/10.1787/empl_outlook-2018-en. [34]

OECD (2018), *The Future of Social Protection: What Works for Non-standard Workers?*, OECD Publishing, Paris, https://dx.doi.org/10.1787/9789264306943-en. [42]

OECD (2018), *Working Better with Age: Korea*, Ageing and Employment Policies, OECD Publishing, Paris, https://dx.doi.org/10.1787/9789264208261-en. [80]

OECD (2017), *Employment and Skills Strategies in Slovenia*, OECD Reviews on Local Job Creation, OECD Publishing, Paris, https://dx.doi.org/10.1787/9789264278929-en. [83]

OECD (2017), *Financial Incentives for Steering Education and Training*, Getting Skills Right, OECD Publishing, Paris, https://dx.doi.org/10.1787/9789264272415-en. [31]

OECD (2017), *Getting Skills Right: Skills for Jobs Indicators*, Getting Skills Right, OECD Publishing, Paris, https://dx.doi.org/10.1787/9789264277878-en. [12]

OECD (2017), *OECD Skills Outlook 2017: Skills and Global Value Chains*, OECD Publishing, Paris, https://dx.doi.org/10.1787/9789264273351-en. [10]

OECD (2017), *Preventing Ageing Unequally*, OECD Publishing, Paris, http://dx.doi.org/10.1787/9789264279087-en. [16]

OECD (2016), *Back to Work: Finland: Improving the Re-employment Prospects of Displaced Workers*, Back to Work, OECD Publishing, Paris, https://dx.doi.org/10.1787/9789264264717-en. [36]

OECD (2016), *Getting Skills Right: Assessing and Anticipating Changing Skill Needs*, Getting Skills Right, OECD Publishing, Paris, https://dx.doi.org/10.1787/9789264252073-en. [84]

OECD (2016), "New Forms of Work in the Digital Economy", *OECD Digital Economy Papers*, No. 260, OECD Publishing, Paris, https://dx.doi.org/10.1787/5jlwnklt820x-en. [66]

OECD (2016), *OECD Employment Outlook 2016*, OECD Publishing, Paris, https://dx.doi.org/10.1787/empl_outlook-2016-en. [8]

OECD (2015), *Back to Work: Canada: Improving the Re-employment Prospects of Displaced Workers*, Back to Work, OECD Publishing, Paris, https://dx.doi.org/10.1787/9789264233454-en. [37]

OECD (2014), *Employment and Skills Strategies in Korea*, OECD Reviews on Local Job Creation, OECD Publishing, Paris, https://dx.doi.org/10.1787/9789264216563-en. [62]

OECD (2014), "Non-regular employment, job security and the labour market divide", in *OECD Employment Outlook 2014*, OECD Publishing, Paris, https://dx.doi.org/10.1787/empl_outlook-2014-7-en. [18]

OECD (2010), *OECD Employment Outlook 2010*, OECD Publishing, Paris, https://doi.org/10.1787/empl_outlook-2010-en. [71]

OECD (forthcoming), *Individual Learning Accounts: Panacea or Pandora's box?*. [28]

Pedersini, R. and D. Coletto (2010), *Self-employed workers: industrial relations and working conditions*, European Foundation for the Improvement of Living and Working Conditions, https://www.eurofound.europa.eu/publications/report/2009/self-employed-workers-industrial-relations-and-working-conditions. [52]

Rathgeb, P. (2016), *Strong governments, precarious workers : labour market policy-making in the era of liberalisation*, European University Institute. [78]

Spermann, A. (2016), "How can temporary work agencies provide more training?", *IZA World of Labor*, http://dx.doi.org/10.15185/izawol.251. [45]

Stuart, M. et al. (2013), *Union Learning Impact Report*, Centre for Employment Relations Innovation and Change, University of Leeds, https://www.unionlearn.org.uk/sites/default/files/publication/Leeds%20Union%20Learning%20Impact%20Analysis%20June%202013.pdf (accessed on 3 October 2018). [23]

Stuart, M. et al. (2016), *Evaluation of the Union Learning Fund Rounds 15-16 and Support Role of Unionlearn*, University of Leeds, https://www.unionlearn.org.uk/sites/default/files/publication/ULF%20Eval%201516%20FINAL%20REPORT.pdf (accessed on 3 October 2018). [22]

UCM (2017), *Congé éducation payé*, https://www.ucm.be. [75]

288 |

Voss, E. et al. (2013), *Temporary Agency Work and Transitions in the Labour Market*, WMP [48]
    consult, http://www.wilke-maack.de/wmp_publications/the-role-of-temporary-agency-work-and-labour-market-transitions-in-europe/.

WEC (2016), *The Future of Work: white paper from the employment industry*, World Employment [49]
    Confederation, https://www.weceurope.org/uploads/media/WEC-Europe_The_Future_of_Work_-_What_role_for_the_employment_industry.pdf.

## Notes

[1] Low-skilled adults refer to adults who score at level 1 or below on the PIAAC literacy scale. When discussing policy options, the low-skilled refer to adults with low qualifications.

[2] This report focuses on adult learning that is job-related, i.e. adult education and training that is expected to have some effect on performance and productivity at work. Job-related adult learning subsumes: 1) formal education and training, which leads to a formal qualification; 2) non-formal education and training that doesn't necessarily lead to formal qualifications, such as structured on-the-job training, open and distance education, courses and private lessons, seminars and workshops. All types of training are considered regardless of training providers and beneficiaries, e.g. it includes training provided to the unemployed, in the context of active labour market programmes, or training provided to workers by firms.

[3] Informal learning is another important way through which adults can gain new skills. According to PIAAC data, across the OECD on average, 63% of workers participate in informal job-related adult learning at least once per week (Fialho, Quintini and Vandeweyer, forthcoming[17]). While important, informal learning goes beyond the scope of this chapter.

[4] While averages at the occupational level are a useful summary measure, there remains significant variation within occupations.

[5] Nedelkoska and Quintini (2018[7]) carry out a shift-share analysis of the difference in the risk of automation across countries and find that occupational composition and difference in job tasks account for about the same share. The authors also provide country-specific evidence of changes within and between occupations. Exploiting panel data for Germany and the United Kingdom, they show how jobs have become more intensive in less automatable tasks. Bottleneck tasks such as analytical and social skills have become more common within occupations but the employment share of occupations that already perform those tasks intensively has also increased. On the other hand, in both countries, the decline in tasks involving physical strength has primarily happened through the reduction in the number of occupations that were intensive in these tasks.

[6] As measured in the OECD Skills for Jobs database (https://www.oecdskillsforjobsdatabase.org/).

[7] More generally, non-standard employment refers to all types of employment that are not full-time, open-ended, dependent employment (see Chapters 2 and 4).

[8] For statistical purposes, in this chapter the term "displaced worker" refers only to people that have been dismissed for economic reasons and are still unemployed, while more frequently in the literature this term is used for all those losing their job due to economic change, independently of being still unemployed or not – see OECD (2018[34]).

[9] Nevertheless, caution is still required due to possible unobserved characteristics being simultaneously correlated with observable factors and training.

[10] Running the analysis by country broadly confirms the pooled-sample results regarding the difference in training participation by contract type. Temporary workers – workers with fixed-term contracts and/or temporary agency contracts – receive significantly less training than their counterparts on indefinite contracts do in the Czech Republic, Estonia, the Netherlands, Northern Ireland and Norway. On the other

hand, they receive more training, and the difference is statistically significant, in Australia, Belgium, Israel, Poland, Slovenia and the United States.

[11] Organised training that does not lead to a certificate, often consisting of job-specific training provided through employers.

[12] Organised training that leads to a certificate, often consisting of general courses provided within the education system.

[13] I.e. training that is paid for or organised by the employer.

[14] Information on the characteristics of individuals who participate in training is not available in CVTS.

[15] Each group faces specific challenges, although heterogeneity exists even within the same group as it may include individuals in very different employment situations.

[16] OECD (2019[5]) outlines seven practical action points for stakeholders involved in adult learning policies for low-skilled adults.

[17] *Modelo Educación para la Vida y el Trabajo.*

[18] This lack of a return for the individual needs to be balanced by the social return, which may be higher because of greater job retention and fewer/shorter spells on out-of-work support.

[19] The risk of automation associated with each individual job is computed based on the methodology developed in Nedelkoska and Quintini (2018[7]). Workers in jobs a high risk of automation overlap to a large extent with low-skilled workers in low-paid jobs. But the overlap is not exact. Some low-skilled jobs – particularly those involving caring and assisting others – are not likely to be automated any time soon. On the other hand, some middle-skilled job have a significant routine component and could be subject to automation. As a result, while many of the policies put in place for the low-skilled would apply to workers in jobs at high-risk of automation, additional measures for this latter group may be needed.

[20] *Contrat de sécurisation professionnelle*, frequently abbreviated as CSP.

[21] The interpretation of temporary work status is complicated in the United States due to the broad application of the "employment at will" principle by which any employment relationship can be terminated at any point in time at the will of the employer or the employee.

[22] Article 6, para.2 of P.D. 81/2003 (A' 77)

[23] Temporary agency workers need to have worked for 1 600 hours in the same profession in the previous 18 months; and 600 hours of work have to be done in the temporary work agency at the moment of the request. The request has to be done 12 months before the beginning of the leave.

[24] *Accord pour la non-discrimination, l'égalité et la diversité dans le cadre des activités de mise à l'emploi des entreprises de travail temporaire.*

[25] TWAs provide training to their workers for different reasons. Autor (2001[87]) shows that in the United States, TWAs use training to induce self-selection and perform screening of worker ability.

[26] www.form-and-go.it.

[27] This group may not be particularly vulnerable per se, as some may be professionals who do not need particular support, or who could get the required training if needed.

[28] Or towards the self-employed more generally.

[29] OECD/EC questionnaire on "Policy Responses to New Forms of Work".

[30] The amount is based on the incomes of the previous tax year and capped at 4 times the social minimum wage for unskilled workers i.e. gross amount of EUR 7 691.84 per month as from 1 August 2016.

[31] As well as employees and entrepreneurs.

[32] *Finanzielle Unterstützung von beruflichen Aus- und Weiterbildungen.*

[33] OECD/EC questionnaire on "Policy Responses to New Forms of Work".

[34] OECD/EC questionnaire on "Policy Responses to New Forms of Work". See also: https://springboardcourses.ie/blog/whats-new-to-springboard-this-year.

[35] *Fachkräftestipendium.*

[36] OECD/EC questionnaire on "Policy Responses to New Forms of Work".

[37] The remaining 20% of gig economy workers report that nothing would stop them from developing new skills in the future.

[38] Babbel and Duolingo offer online courses to learn foreign languages.

[39] Although the effect was larger for men than for women.

[40] Due to small sample sizes, the information on barriers to train is only available for a few countries.

[41] Extended Employment Insurance and Training Incentive – EEITI.

[42] OECD (2019[3]) outlines seven practical action points for stakeholders involved in adult learning policies to enhance the alignment of training to labour market needs.

[43] It has to be acknowledged that it takes time to carry out impact evaluation analysis. Therefore, there may be a long elapse of time between policy implementation and adjustment of training programmes in line with the results of impact evaluation analysis.

# 7 Left on your own? Social protection when labour markets are in flux

This chapter assesses challenges for social protection policies in a changing world of work and presents evidence of support gaps in public policies affecting different types of workers. Key policy challenges include a greater need for support resulting from greater employment instability or lower earnings among some groups; a reduced accessibility or adequacy of social protection measures that were designed around stable forms of dependent employment; and sustainability challenges, e.g. due to opportunities for avoiding participation in risk-sharing provisions. Accessing adequate support can be especially difficult for workers in less secure forms of employment. But support gaps are small in some countries that adopt fairly different social protection strategies, suggesting that accessible support can be achieved with different blends of social insurance and means-tested assistance. The chapter discusses alternative reform avenues and illustrates country approaches to prepare income support and reintegration measures for the future of work.

The statistical data for Israel are supplied by and under the responsibility of the relevant Israeli authorities. The use of such data by the OECD is without prejudice to the status of the Golan Heights, East Jerusalem and Israeli settlements in the West Bank under the terms of international law.

# In Brief

## Key findings

Social protection systems play a key stabilising role, especially in the current context of heightened uncertainties about the pace and extent of labour market changes. The digital transformation will no doubt create many new opportunities, but will also render a growing number of current workers' tasks redundant and will require substantial restructuring. There is evidence suggesting that these trends are already making job losses and employment changes more frequent for many workers (Chapters 2 and 3), increasing their needs for income and re-employment support. Effective social protection provides a buffer against the individual and social costs of these adjustments and can ensure that those losing their jobs have the time to find good job matches or undertake training if needed. In doing so, it can also counter calls for policy responses that stifle economic dynamism, such as creating barriers to trade or innovation. At the same time, the future world of work presents distinct and sizeable challenges that may undermine the prevention, protection or promotion capacities that have guided the development of present-day social protection systems. This chapter examines the nature and extent of these challenges and discusses reform avenues to tackle them.

The main findings are:

- Future technological and labour market developments are inherently uncertain. But this can be no excuse for delaying reforms that are needed to make social protection future ready. Changing employment and income risks and elevated uncertainty, including about governments' policy responses to labour-market changes, highlight the vital role of social protection in stabilising incomes and managing risks. But they also increase the individual and social costs of ineffective or inaccessible protection.

- Some social protection systems are not well prepared for the faster pace of job reallocation (the destruction and creation of jobs in different firms and industries) that is likely to accompany the adoption of new production technologies. For instance, in a majority of OECD countries, fewer than one third of jobseekers receive unemployment benefits.

- Technological advances make alternative work arrangements a viable option for a growing share of jobs and provide opportunities for organising work through contractual arrangements that may bypass traditional employer-employee relationships. Legal safeguards and social protection provisions that were designed around traditional forms of employment may no longer apply to workers with "non-standard" contracts, or not to the same extent. This not only creates inequitable, and possibly regressive, treatment of workers based on their employment status but also erodes the financial sustainability of social protection provisions.

- Accessing social protection can be especially difficult for workers in less secure forms of employment even though their need for support is often particularly urgent. In some countries, workers engaged in independent work or short-duration or part-time employment are 40-50% less likely to receive any form of income support during an out-of-work spell than standard employees (e.g. Czech Republic, Estonia, Latvia, Portugal and Slovak Republic). Accessibility gaps can be especially large for the self-employed. For non-standard workers who do receive support, the level of benefits that are available during an out-of-work spell are often markedly lower than for standard employees (e.g. Greece, Italy, Slovenia and Spain). Unless access gaps are closed, further increases in non-standard employment will have negative consequences for inclusiveness and equity.

- Pension coverage also tends to be less comprehensive for non-standard workers than for regular employees, exposing them to greater risks of low income and poverty in old age. In many countries, the self-employed can (partially or fully) opt out of pension schemes that are mandatory for dependent employees. In some countries, contributions are entirely voluntary for most self-employed. In others, mandatory contributions are lower for the self-employed than for employees (Austria and Portugal), or feature options that allow the self-employed to reduce their (mandatory) contributions (Poland and Spain). Each of these provisions leads to reduced future pension entitlements.

More volatile career patterns or a growing diversity of employment forms pose specific challenges for social protection provisions that link support entitlements or financing burdens to past or present employment. But future labour markets nonetheless leave room for a range of different social protection strategies.

- Most countries' social protection systems employ a mix of different design principles, such as targeting on current needs (means-tested assistance benefits), conditioning on past employment (earnings-related insurance benefits), or providing flat-rate entitlements (universal and unconditional support).

- In the context of rapid job reallocation and a growth of alternative work arrangements, these provisions translate into specific policy challenges that differ between countries. Central social protection pillars, such as insurance or income-targeted assistance, will remain viable but they will need to adapt to new and changing risks.

- Yet, given countries' specific labour markets and institutions, a pursuit of generic policy prescriptions, such as a universal basic income or an exclusive reliance on last-resort safety nets, may be counter-productive as it can distract attention from positive reform steps that countries can take in the context of existing social protection strategies.

Many countries are actively assessing the challenges that automation and changing working arrangements pose for social support systems. Countries' reform experiences provide valuable pointers to policy options and priorities. Some of the challenges concern "legacy" issues that are not new in the social protection debate. But the prospect of future labour market transformations often makes tackling them much more urgent.

- Key priorities include: i) the correct classification of workers' employment status (Chapter 4); ii) entitlement criteria that respond readily to changes in people's need for support; and iii) making social protection rights portable between sectors or jobs.

- Social protection provisions can themselves contribute to a growth of non-standard employment. For instance, in the Netherlands, the total employment cost for a dependent employee can be 60% higher than for an otherwise similar independent contractor. Different contribution burdens for different workers have existed for a long time in many countries and lower contributions can reflect specific risk patterns and fairness considerations. But when alternative forms of employment, such as contract gig work, micro jobs or casual work become more readily available, large disparities in labour costs between contractual arrangements are more likely to act as powerful drivers of employment and hiring decisions than in the past.

Novel forms of employment are also blurring the distinction between in-work and out-of-work categories. This raises new questions about the scope and ambition of employment-oriented social protection and activation (measures to strengthen people's chances of re-employment and lessen any disincentives to work).

- Comprehensive and tailored employment-support packages can be difficult to access for those in alternative work arrangements, reducing their chances of benefiting from the career opportunities that dynamic labour markets offer. Income support typically serves as the main gateway to labour market reintegration measures, and tackling gaps in income support provisions is therefore key in this context.

- In addition, a careful review of the design and implementation of activation approaches should ensure that active labour market programmes remain well adapted to the needs and circumstances of jobseekers. A growing number of "part-time unemployed" (jobseekers with intermittent or part-time employment, including low-paid independent work) may call for a greater focus on facilitating advancement to good-quality employment, e.g. by shifting resources from work experience programmes or direct job creation towards job search assistance, tailored training and career counselling.

- Policy makers should also review whether existing activation and reintegration measures yield an appropriate balance of demanding and supporting elements that is in line with policy objectives for job quantity and quality. For instance, enforcing job-search responsibilities and other requirements for the part-time unemployed may be a necessary counter-weight to extending benefit rights to these groups.

- Likewise, with broadening options for when and how long to work, removing disincentives that discourage better-paid and more stable work becomes an increasingly pressing priority in the future world of work.

Adapting social protection to the future of work is likely to create additional financing strains at a time when social protection budgets are already under pressure in many countries.

- Keeping funding levels in line with evolving needs for support requires a determined and co-ordinated approach and a policy debate on how new or expanded initiatives will be paid for, and who should pay, especially if evolving production technologies exacerbate a decline in the shares of national income that go to workers.

- Key policy levers for tackling a shortfall of social protection resources include not only a suitable balance of revenues from labour and non-labour tax bases, but also the cost-effective delivery of support, as well as better revenue collection technologies and enforcement. Digital technologies are no panacea for increased efficiency but they can play an important role in these efforts.

- Ensuring that social protection systems remain fiscally sustainable also calls for limiting opportunities for opting out of collective risk-sharing provisions, and for tackling unintended incentives that distort employment, hiring or layoff decisions.

## Introduction

The past 10-15 years have produced a remarkably broad global consensus that well-designed social protection (SP) is essential for inclusive labour markets and growth, and that it must be strengthened in order to meet global development goals (OECD, 2018[1]; OECD, 2018[2]; ILO and World Bank, 2016[3]; United Nations, 2015[4]; European Commission, 2017[5]). But, in addition to longer-standing SP challenges linked to globalisation and population ageing, technological advances and associated changes in the world of work also give rise to concerns that existing SP strategies could be fundamentally compromised in some countries – e.g. World Bank (2018[6]), European Commission (2018[7]) and ILO (2018[8]). This chapter discusses the challenges that changing work patterns and an uncertain future of work pose for SP policies, and for those in need of support. It first presents new evidence on the readiness of existing SP systems to extend support to groups who face labour market risks as a result of digitalisation, automation and new forms of employment. The chapter provides concrete and "people-centred" indicators of the support that SP provides for individuals in specific labour market circumstances. The second part of the chapter reviews options to strengthen the prevention, protection and promotion functions of SP policies in different country contexts.

Automation, technology-assisted divisions of labour and algorithmic workforce management, e.g. through online platforms, have already brought fundamental change to production processes and to the world of work, and they will continue to do so. Eventually, as productivity gains and income growth feed through the economy, the resulting opportunities should be shared more widely. But productivity-enhancing technologies will not immediately and automatically lead to inclusive growth.[1]

The labour-market transformations that are underway add substantial uncertainty to workers' careers and their incomes. Perceptions of income insecurity are driven by uncertainties on several levels, including the likely size of any gains and losses, their timing, and also the pace and direction of policy responses to those changes. Well-designed and accessible SP helps workers and their families succeed in a volatile world. Countries with more effective and employment-oriented SP systems are in a good position to cope with rapid change and to harness the resulting opportunities for shared and inclusive growth. But the labour market changes resulting from automation and new forms of employment also pose significant challenges if SP provisions fail to adapt to the evolving realities of the world of work.

This chapter explores gaps in existing social support provisions and those that may result from ongoing labour market transformations. Section 7.1 provides an overview of the main channels through which an acceleration in the job reallocation process and more varied and fragmented employment patterns may alter the functioning of SP and impact its effectiveness. Section 7.2 presents evidence on SP gaps between standard employees and workers in non-standard forms of employment. It summarises information on the statutory rules regarding SP for non-standard workers and discusses reasons why non-standard workers may not receive support even if statutory rules do not formally exclude them. The section then presents new empirical evidence on the level of support that standard and non-standard workers actually receive in practice. Section 7.3 considers options for how to address SP gaps, and for preventing SP from becoming less adequate in the future. The discussion is structured around illustrations of policy initiatives that countries have considered or implemented.

## 7.1. Prevention, protection, promotion: Social protection and the future of work

SP helps individuals and families to manage risks and provides support to make economic or social disadvantage less concentrated on specific regions or groups, and less damaging for people's longer-term prospects. It also seeks to maintain and improve living standards and to lower the costs associated with job reallocation by pooling labour market risks. From an economy-wide perspective, risk pooling, income-smoothing, redistribution and enabling support foster resilience against systemic uncertainties, including those related to the speed and magnitude of future labour market transformations.

SP can also act as a "backstop" to other policy levers, such as skills policy and labour market regulation (Chapters 4 and 6). While those policies seek to further workers' employability and protect their interests, adapting them takes time. Necessary reforms may therefore lag behind rapidly evolving labour market realities. For instance, low-skilled workers are already the least likely to receive training and, where production processes become more fragmented and job tenure falls, firms' and workers' incentives to invest in firm-specific skills may weaken further. Accessible SP constitutes an additional layer of support when other policy channels are not (yet) effective.

Labour market transformations alter the functioning and the effectiveness of existing SP provisions through several channels. More volatile labour markets with growing under-employment (Chapter 3) and unequally distributed labour market risks produce growing demand for income protection and employment support. The financing of such support relies in large part on contributions or taxes levied on incomes from work, and this resource base can be at risk when labour's share in national income declines or if individual financing burdens are lower for new or growing forms of non-standard work. Unequal financing burdens or SP entitlements, in turn, can shape labour market changes, e.g. by promoting certain types of dependent or independent employment while discouraging others.

In many countries, SP coverage is ill adapted to non-standard forms of employment, with unstable and overlapping jobs (see Chapter 4 for categories and definitions). For instance, own-account self-employed workers often have little or no access to key SP provisions, such as unemployment benefits and related job-search assistance. Those with on-call (including "zero-hours") contracts may have access in principle but they might be effectively barred from out-of-work support due to legal ambiguities of what constitutes an "out-of-work" situation for somebody with no minimum working hours. Those with frequent employment gaps or transitions between activities may not meet relevant employment requirements or, if they do, the timing of support may not correspond to individual needs (Section 7.2).

Reduced de-facto coverage, in turn, compromises the sustainability of SP. Risk sharing through collective protection systems has unique strengths not only in terms of equity objectives but also on efficiency grounds (Chetty and Finkelstein, 2013[9]; Gruber, 1997[10]; Barr, 1989[11]). Key labour market risks, such as unemployment and low earnings, are uninsurable without government intervention, such as mandated membership, price setting or related regulation (Boeri and van Ours, 2013[12]). A shrinking group of SP members or contributors, e.g. as a result of readily available alternative work arrangements that allow bypassing SP provisions, can undermine the foundations of risk pooling. If mandates are partial or weakly enforced, those with comparatively lower risks (the "good risks" in insurance terminology) can minimise their contributions or choose to opt out entirely, implying greater financing burdens or weaker protection for the remaining higher-risk groups (Section 7.2.1). In the absence of regulation or public subsidies this produces further opt-out incentives and, ultimately, a cycle of escalating costs and declining reach of SP (Rothschild and Stiglitz, 1976[13]; Akerlof, 1970[14]).

Countries may operate different mandates in different parts of the SP system, e.g. if the unemployment scheme is optional for some workers while membership in the pension scheme is mandatory. Such differentiation can go against more encompassing concepts of social risk sharing across both individuals and risk types and, in doing so, it may exacerbate selective opt-in/opt-out behaviour. For instance, low-income/unemployment and longevity risks are typically negatively correlated (OECD, 2017[15]). When given the opportunity, higher-income or higher-skilled individuals may opt out of unemployment insurance but may wish to retain membership in a pension system that favours people with long life expectancy. Packaging unemployment, pensions and other SP elements through a unified set of mandates and regulations reduces the scope for "cherry picking", and can help to maintain a more diversified risk pool, making SP attractive for broader sections of the population.

The extent of explicit or implicit redistribution between groups is another key determinant of the protection against earnings risks. Income assistance programmes that are financed through general tax revenues redistribute towards individuals in need without linking entitlements to own contributions. On the other end of the spectrum, individual savings, whether voluntary or mandated, also support consumption smoothing in the event of reduced earnings ability. But in the absence of any redistribution at all, vehicles such as individual savings accounts do not enable risk pooling across groups. They also provide little support to groups who are unwilling or unable to save enough (e.g. because they have care responsibilities or are born into poverty), and they cannot insure against catastrophic events that endanger livelihoods and overwhelm people's own capacities to absorb or reverse a situation of economic need (e.g. a long-term or permanent loss of earnings ability). "Actuarially fair" insurance provisions also do not feature any explicit redistribution, as the present value of expected lifetime contributions equals the present value of expected lifetime benefits. But in practice, actuarially fair risk pooling nevertheless results in redistribution, in the sense that an insured person will typically get out either more or less than they paid in.[2]

The specific policy challenges that arise in evolving labour markets are shaped by the design principles governing existing SP systems (Sections 7.3.1 and 7.3.2). However, regardless of countries' specific SP designs, the provision of adequate SP financing can be expected to move up the policy agenda, especially if existing coverage gaps are to be addressed (Section 7.3.5). Budgetary pressures and evolving perceptions of who benefits from SP, and who pays for it, may alter the political dynamics in the SP debate. In a rapidly evolving labour market, a major continuing challenge will be to ensure broad buy-in and a consensus among most people that they continue to be better off with adequate SP in place (Hills, 2017[16]).

## 7.2. Social protection for alternative forms of employment: What are the gaps?

### 7.2.1. Statutory access

Statutory access varies by employment type and by SP branch. Temporary and part-time workers are in principle covered in the same way as permanent full-time employees in most countries and for most risks, as long as they satisfy minimum employment periods (Figure 7.1), earnings thresholds and other eligibility requirements, such as low family income. Some countries operate exemptions for specific non-standard contractual arrangements, such as casual employment, seasonal work or hybrid categories and some of these are noted below (see Chapter 4 for an overview of different non-standard forms of work). By contrast, statutory access to SP for self-employed workers is very frequently restricted in contributory SP systems (Figure 7.2). Indeed, SP provisions that were mostly set up with a steady employer-employee relationship in mind do not easily accommodate the self-employed:

1.  *Double contribution issue*: Who should be liable for employer contributions in the absence of an employer? In practice, total formal contribution burdens are frequently lower for the self-employed than for dependent employees (Section 7.3.5). Requiring the self-employed to pay the equivalent of both employer and employee contributions brings formal burdens in line with dependent employees. But effective burdens may be higher for the self-employed, especially those with lower earnings, because minimum wages typically do not apply to them or because they may lack the bargaining power to shift any contribution-related costs onto their clients by charging higher prices.[3]

2.  *Fluctuating earnings and avoidance*: The self-employed, along with some atypical employees such as on-call workers or those with zero-hours contracts, are often paid at irregular intervals, either because of time lags between work and payment, or because demand for their services is erratic (ISSA, 2012[17]). This complicates the calculation of contributions (as well as the assessment of entitlements). In particular, self-employed workers may be able to avoid or lower contributions by optimising their contribution base, e.g. through timing their work or earnings, see Section 7.3.3.

3.  *Moral hazard*: Demand or price fluctuations affecting self-employed workers are difficult to distinguish from voluntary idleness and this complicates the provision of unemployment insurance in particular. For instance, there is no employer to confirm a layoff and efforts to re-establish a business operation are more difficult to monitor than the search for dependent employment.[4] Where self-employed individuals can claim unemployment benefits, they typically need to meet relatively stringent requirements to demonstrate that their business is no longer operational.[5]

When self-employed workers do have access to social protection, it is frequently on a voluntary basis. This partly reflects specific risk patterns and fairness considerations, e.g. as entrepreneurs seek to make a profit in return for taking on business risks, may be less risk averse, and therefore may not require insurance to the same extent as employees. However, the same rationale for opt-outs could be invoked more broadly, e.g. for employees who face lower risks or are less risk averse than others. Ultimately, strong reliance on selective or voluntary SP membership widens the scope for gaming social risk-pooling systems, resulting in insurance becoming inefficiently narrow and unaffordable for those who need it. In particular, low-earning individuals may underinsure even when social insurance provisions offer attractive cost-to-risk ratios.[6]

Country experiences with voluntary schemes illustrate that selectivity typically leads to low coverage or a need for significant subsidies to keep risk sharing financially viable (Box 7.1).

## Figure 7.1. Employment requirements for unemployment benefits range from 3 to 24 months

Number of months, 2018

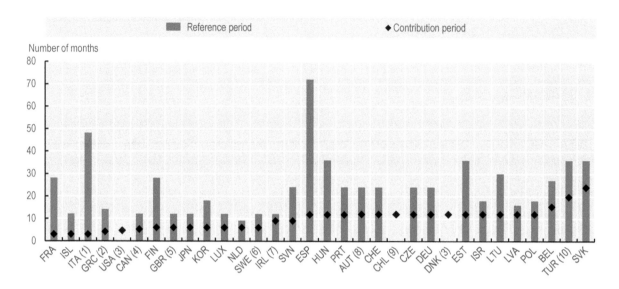

Note: (1) And at least 30 days of employment in the 12 months prior to the start of the unemployment spell; (2) Or 200 days in last two years; (3) Earnings condition also; (4) Assuming 40 hour work week; (5) 6 months in any one of the past two years plus minimum-earnings requirement. (6) Must also have been a member of the insurance fund for at least 12 months; (7) Or 26 weekly contributions in each of the previous two years. Must also have made 104 weekly contributions in whole career; (8) 28 weeks for repeated employment; (9) Must have 12 months of contributions since a previous unemployment spell; (10) Must also have been continuously in work for last 120 days.
Source: OECD tax-benefit model and policy database, www.oecd.org/social/benefits-and-wages.htm.

*StatLink* 🔍📊 http://dx.doi.org/10.1787/888933967224

---

### Box 7.1. Voluntary insurance: Country experiences

Membership in non-mandatory insurance schemes is often organised on an opt-in basis. Not all voluntary schemes are of opt-in type, however. For instance, voluntary pension insurance for marginal employees (mini jobs) in Germany are auto-enrolled since 2013. In all cases, voluntary membership risks adverse selection of members: where insurance premiums are uniform, those with the highest risk have the biggest incentive to join. If the scheme is entirely self-funded, this can lead to a vicious circle of contribution hikes and low-risk members leaving; if the scheme is publicly subsidised, costs can increase (see Section 7.1).

An example of this mechanism is the Canadian Special Benefits for Self-employed Workers (SBSE) scheme, which provides access to maternity and parental benefits, sickness benefits and care benefits for ill family members since 2010. Self-employed workers pay the same contribution as standard employees but they do not pay the part that employers would cover for dependent employees. In the first year of benefit pay-outs, over three quarters of claims were for maternity and parental benefits, two-thirds of opt-ins were women (who represent only 43% of all self-employed workers), and two-thirds were between the ages of 25 and 44 (compared to just one third of all self-employed). Opt-ins also had significantly lower incomes than other self-employed workers. As a result, premiums covered less than one-third of benefit payments (Employment and Social Development Canada, 2016[18]).

In 2007-8, reforms of the voluntary unemployment insurance in Sweden linked employee contributions to unemployment risk and raised average premiums by 300%. Membership in the Unemployment Insurance Funds dropped by around 10 percentage points in the following years. Groups that were particularly likely to exit the system included older workers over the age of 60, who have the lowest unemployment risk of all age-groups, and young workers under the age of 25, who typically have low earnings and short unemployment durations (Kolsrud, 2018[19]).

Self-employed workers in Austria can opt into a short-term sickness benefit programme, and about 8% of eligible self-employed workers do. In 2016, close to half of those who were covered received a benefit. The average benefit duration was 22 days, nearly twice the average sick-leave duration among dependent employees, who are subject to mandatory insurance, highlighting moral hazard risks. In response to the resulting deficits in the programme, the minimum benefit was cut significantly in 2017 (Fink and Nagl, 2018[20]).

Some schemes also offer choice in the level of contributions. For instance, self-employed workers in Latvia and Spain could choose the contribution base (and hence the level of contribution) in the unemployment and occupational injury insurance. Similar to selectivity mechanisms in insurance provisions with voluntary membership, higher-risk individuals can have an incentive to choose higher contributions in order to maximise their entitlements. Yet, if the system is explicitly redistributive, that is if it offers higher replacement rates for low incomes (contributions), there is a clear incentive to make the lowest possible contribution. In both Latvia and Spain, approximately nine out of ten self-employed workers chose to pay the minimum contribution (Arriba and Moreno-Fuentes, 2017[21]; Rajevska, 2017[22]).

*Statutory access for non-standard workers varies by social protection branch*

Unemployment benefits are the least accessible branch of SP for non-standard workers. Eleven of the 28 countries shown in Figure 7.2 (bottom left panel) do no not offer any kind of unemployment protection for self-employed workers. Access is also restricted for some forms of dependent non-standard work, e.g. casual workers in the United States, or para-subordinate workers in Italy (SSA and ISSA, 2017[23]; Raitano, 2018[24]). Extensions of unemployment-benefit coverage for self-employed workers have been legislated or discussed recently in a number of countries, including France and Ireland. Spain made a previously voluntary unemployment insurance scheme for self-employed workers compulsory from early 2019 (see also endnotes 9 and 12).

The rules for accessing incapacity benefits – covering short-term sickness, work accidents and disability – vary across countries and types of non-standard work. In all three of these schemes, statutory access for non-standard dependent employees is mostly similar to standard employees. Exceptions include Australia, where casual workers are not entitled to cash sickness benefits (an employer-provided benefit), the United States, where casual workers do not have access to accidents-at-work insurance, and Italy, where some para-subordinate workers are not covered by short-term sickness insurance. However, only 14 of the 32 countries shown in Figure 7.2 offer similar access to benefits for self-employed workers (top right panel). Statutory access is weakest in the case of accidents at work. Many – although not all – genuine self-employed workers indeed have considerable control over their working environment and, as in the case of unemployment benefits, insurance against work accidents can therefore be prone to moral hazard (see also Chapter 4). But the exclusion of the self-employed does create important SP gaps for those with genuinely risky activities, including for workers who are wrongly classified as independent, or who are in the "grey zone" between self-employment and dependent employment, e.g. those with a de-facto employer.

When contingencies are independent of a specific job, protection for non-standard workers is more easily available. For instance, social assistance or minimum income schemes are typically financed through general tax revenue, and legal entitlement rules are based on need, regardless of past employment type, duration or stability. Family benefits, such as child allowances, are typically universal or means-tested, and statutory access to maternity benefits, which are often contributory, also tends to be similar for workers in standard and non-standard forms of dependent employment. An exception is Italy, where "workers on vouchers" and foreign seasonal workers do not have access to contributory family benefits (Jessoula, Pavolini and Strati, 2017[25]).[7] Maternity benefits often have separate provisions for independent workers (Figure 7.2, top left panel). Yet, in all countries with compulsory maternity coverage for standard employees, self-employed workers can either opt into the main scheme voluntarily, or they have access to a separate benefit that is typically less generous than for dependent employees (lower benefit amounts and/or shorter duration).

Pension rules often differ between the self-employed and dependent employees (Figure 7.2, bottom right panel). In some countries, the self-employed can voluntarily join earnings-related schemes that are mandatory for employees (e.g. Germany and Australia).[8] Chile has sought to incorporate the self-employed into the mandatory pension scheme through auto-enrolment since 2008. Opt-out provisions were retained, however, and the majority of the self-employed have continued to opt out so far. A few countries provide the self-employed with partial pension coverage, reducing both contributions and benefits in the mandatory scheme, or they subsidise pensions of the self-employed through a more favourable benefit formula. For instance, in Denmark, Japan, the Netherlands, and Switzerland contributions for the self-employed are mandatory for the basic pension pillar only. Box 7.2 summarises additional aspects of pension provisions for non-standard workers.

In countries where non-standard forms of work are frequent, statutory restrictions can inhibit effective insurance against major risks for a significant share of the workforce. For example, Greece and Italy, both countries with large shares of self-employed workers, show sizeable gaps in statutory access to sickness, invalidity and accident insurance as well as unemployment insurance for self-employed workers. Yet, statutory restrictions are also common among some countries where self-employment is less common, e.g. in the case of unemployment insurance in Canada, Japan, Norway, and United States. Figure 7.2 therefore does not display any obvious bi-variate correlation between SP provisions for self-employed workers and the incidence of self-employment. The lack of a bivariate link between statutory SP entitlements and the incidence of non-standard work is not surprising as the choice of employment form depends not only on expected benefits but also on many other factors, notably any taxes or mandatory contributions to the financing of SP (see Section 7.3.5).

### 7.2.2. How much protection is available in practice?

Comparisons of legal eligibility rules give an incomplete, and possibly misleading, picture of the support that is available in practice for different labour market groups. The limitations of "systems focussed" comparisons based on statutory access rules are twofold. First, beyond availability, the content and generosity of support will generally differ across types of workers and across countries. Second, statutory access is not the same as actual access:

- Non-standard workers may have characteristics that make it difficult for them to meet entitlement criteria, even when they are the same as for standard workers.
- The implementation of SP rules may differ between groups in practice and the implicit cost of claiming benefits may dissuade eligible people from applying.
- Contributions to some SP elements may be voluntary for some categories of workers, who may opt out of or seek to bypass applicable rules if they perceive future benefits as small relative to the immediate individual cost.

## Figure 7.2. Statutory access for independent workers is often limited

Statutory access to social protection for the self-employed compared to dependent employees ("employees") by social protection branch and incidence of self-employment, 2017

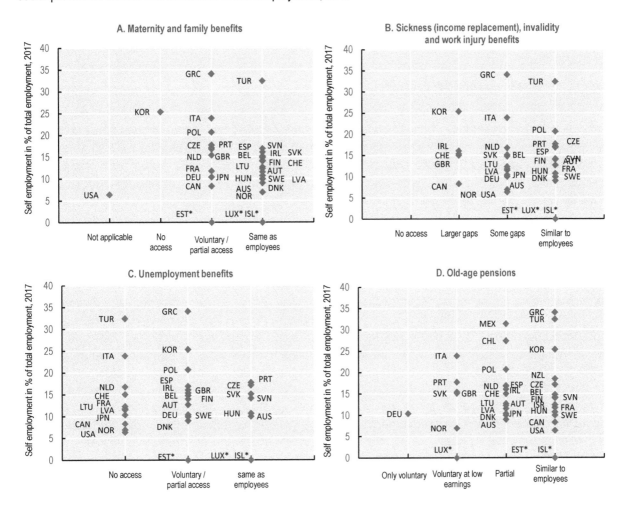

Notes: Gaps between standard dependent employees (full-time open-ended contract) and self-employed workers. "Partial access" to benefits can arise if a) eligibility conditions, benefit amounts or receipt durations are less advantageous for self-employed workers; b) insurance-based and non-contributory benefits co-exist and individuals can access only the latter (e.g. only basic pension and not earnings-related); or c) the self-employed can choose to declare a lower contribution base while dependent employees pay contributions on full earnings (possibly subject to a ceiling). "No access": compulsory for dependent employees but self-employed are excluded. * Data on self-employment incidence is missing/incomplete for Estonia, Iceland and Luxembourg and refers to 2015 for the Slovak Republic and to 2014 for Latvia.

*Maternity and family benefits:* "no access": access to neither maternity benefits nor family allowances, "voluntary/partial access": voluntary or partial access to both schemes, or full access to one, but no access to the other. "Not applicable": schemes do not exist.

*Sickness, invalidity and work injury benefits:* "no access": access to none of these benefits, "larger gaps": less than full access to all of the benefits and no access to at least one; "some gaps": no access to one benefit and at least partial access to the others, or voluntary or partial access to all three benefits; "similar to employee": at least partial or voluntary access to all benefits, and at least full access to one.

*Old-age pensions:* "voluntary at low earnings": coverage is generally similar to employees but opt-out is possible if earnings are below a certain threshold. "Similar to employees": mandatory coverage as for employees but contributions may still differ.

Source: Pensions: OECD (2017[26]), MISSOC (2018[27]), Social Security Administration (2018[28]). Working-age benefits: Australia: Whiteford and Haron (2018[29]), European countries: adapted from Spasova et al. (2017[30]), Canada, Japan, Korea: Information provided by country delegations to the OECD, USA, SSA and ISSA (2012[17]). Share of self-employment: OECD (2018), "Labour Force Statistics: Summary tables" and OECD Employment and Labour Market Statistics (database).

StatLink 🔢 http://dx.doi.org/10.1787/888933967243

Alleviating risks of old-age poverty can be particularly challenging for workers on non-standard contracts with low contribution levels and patchy contribution records. Pension systems in OECD countries have a number of features and characteristics that are relevant for non-standard employees and for the self-employed.

**Contribution breaks and first-tier pensions**

Where pension benefits are linked to contributions (and thus earnings), eligibility rules may require minimum contribution periods. Taking account of mandatory and quasi-mandatory schemes, a 10-year out-of-work spell combined with a late career start reduces pension entitlements by 20% on average across OECD countries (Figure 7.3, Panel A). In some countries with basic public pensions (Ireland, New Zealand, United Kingdom), mandatory pensions are not affected at all, while the penalty exceeds 30% in Mexico, Turkey and Chile.

Policy makers have a number of policy tools at hand to loosen the link between contribution histories and pension entitlements. Contribution periods can be credited for some out-of-work spells, such as unemployment or childcare-related leave, and first-tier pensions can be designed to be independent of work histories.

First-tier pensions are either contributory or non-contributory. Minimum pensions and contribution-based basic pensions are only granted to retirees with contributory records and their level may depend on the total contribution period. By contrast, residence-based basic pensions and guaranteed minimum income (social assistance) provisions for retirees are unrelated to contributions. Pension systems in most OECD countries include either a residence-based basic pension, a minimum pension, or a social assistance benefit alongside earnings-related pension provisions. Across the OECD, the level of income provided by non-contributory pensions is about 35% of median disposable income on average (Figure 7.3, Panel C). Access requirements vary considerably across countries with contributory first tier-pensions, however (Figure 7.3, Panel B). When minimum contribution requirements are relatively stringent, meeting them can be challenging for non-standard workers.

**Old-age pensions for the self-employed**

Figure 7.2 (right bottom panel) shows the extent to which pension scheme membership provisions differ between standard employees and the self-employed (see main text in Section 7.2.1). In addition, total old-age pension contribution rates are frequently lower for the self-employed than for employees, e.g. in Austria (18.5% versus 22.8%), Ireland (self-employed pay the employee part of 4% only), Norway (11.4% versus 22.3%) and, as from 2019, in Portugal (a reduction of roughly one fourth for self-employed). Some countries provide for lower contributions or exemptions for certain categories of self-employed workers, e.g. for some sectors or types of activity (Germany, Italy), during an initial period of business operation (Austria, Finland, France, Norway or Poland), for those combining independent and dependent employment (Belgium, Greece, Slovenia) or below an earnings threshold (Italy, Ireland, Luxembourg, the Slovak Republic and the United Kingdom). As a result, some self-employed might expect lower pension replacement rates than dependent workers with similar earnings, and they face higher risk of relying only on non-contributory benefits.

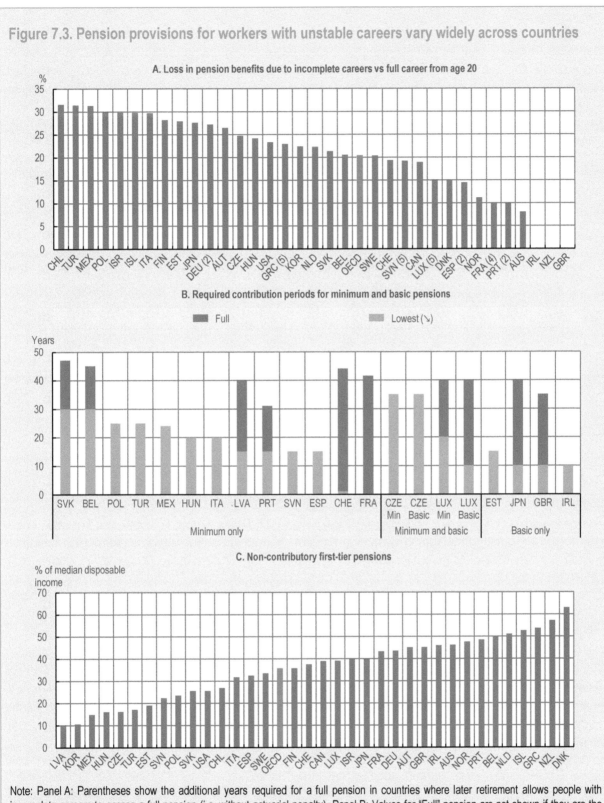

**Figure 7.3. Pension provisions for workers with unstable careers vary widely across countries**

**A. Loss in pension benefits due to incomplete careers vs full career from age 20**

**B. Required contribution periods for minimum and basic pensions**

■ Full    ■ Lowest (↘)

**C. Non-contributory first-tier pensions**

Note: Panel A: Parentheses show the additional years required for a full pension in countries where later retirement allows people with incomplete careers to access a full pension (i.e. without actuarial penalty). Panel B: Values for "Full" pension are not shown if they are the same as for the "Lowest" pension. In the Slovak Republic, there is no upper limit for the minimum pensions as it increases with each additional contribution year. Panel C: Non-contributory pensions include social assistance and residence-based basic pensions.
Sources and definitions: OECD (2017[15]; 2018[31]; 2017[26]).

*StatLink* ⟶ http://dx.doi.org/10.1787/888933967262

An indirect way of lowering contribution burdens is to allow self-employed some flexibility in the contributions base that they declare (Finland, Latvia, Lithuania, Poland and Spain). When the contribution base can be chosen relatively freely, contribution floors are needed to counter avoidance strategies and the potential pension gaps that these create. But, depending on their design, contribution floors either lead to very high effective contribution rates for those with genuinely low earnings, or they exclude those with earnings below the minimum base from earnings-related pensions altogether. Most countries use taxable income as the contribution base for self-employed but some provide additional adjustments. In some countries, clients of the self-employed are required to pay part of the pension contributions that are due for some categories of self-employed workers (Austria, Germany, Italy and Portugal). This solution can be administratively demanding but can be an attractive method for broadening coverage while sharing SP financing costs.

- Access to the *overall* support package is difficult to assess from the rules that govern separate individual SP elements. Depending on countries' policy approaches, support for out-of-work or low-income groups is frequently spread across two or several SP branches. For instance, in-work support or guaranteed minimum income programmes can fill some of the gaps that first-tier out-of-work support leave for workers in independent, unstable, or part-time employment.

- Finally, a focus on relative access gaps between standard and non-standard workers hides country differences in terms of the overall reach of support, and the coverage gaps that may exist for standard workers as well. For instance, on average across countries, two out of three jobseekers did not receive unemployment benefits in 2016, but coverage differed markedly between countries, ranging from under 10% in Italy, Slovak Republic, Poland, Greece and United States to more than 50% in Belgium and Finland (Figure 7.4).

From an inclusiveness perspective, a people-centred policy discussion requires information on the actual support that people receive in different labour market circumstances. This section presents new results on SP gaps that are observed in practice. The approach consists of estimating a statistical model of benefit entitlements controlling for the most important determinants of social benefits. As benefit access and amounts often depend on past events, the analysis relies on longitudinal household data that include information on current and past employment and earnings. The main variable of interest is the value of the *total* benefit package, rather than any individual category of social transfer, reflecting the fact that countries provide support through different channels and programmes. The sample comprises all working-age individuals aged 18-64 who are not retired and not in full-time education. The policy scope comprises the most important social transfers to working-age individuals and their families: unemployment and disability benefits as well as housing, family, in-work and guaranteed minimum income (GMI) transfers. Box 7.3 summarises the main steps of the empirical approach.

The focus on working-age cash benefits is a practical consequence of limitations in the panel data, which contain no systematic information on support that is provided in kind rather than in cash. Moreover, the panels are restricted to a time window of four years or less making the approach unfeasible for retirement benefits (which often depend on contribution histories over much longer periods). However, in the future-of-work debate, reasons other than data quality may motivate a specific interest in working-age support that is provided in cash. Indeed, for those experiencing technology-related unemployment or employment changes, income-support entitlements during working age are likely to be the most immediate concern. In addition, in-kind support, such as housing or active labour market programmes, is often tied to working-age benefits. While the rest of this section therefore focuses on working-age benefits, Box 7.2 above discusses implications of non-standard work patterns for retirement incomes.

Figure 7.4. Only a minority of jobseekers receive unemployment benefits

Coverage among unemployed and discouraged workers, 2016

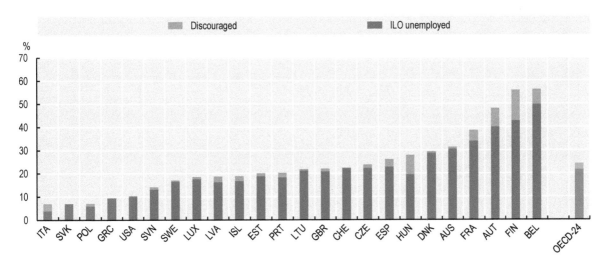

Note: In some countries, unemployment benefits can be received by people who have some work attachment (part-time unemployed) or who are not available for work (labour market inactive). The number of unemployment-benefit recipients can then be much higher than suggested by these coverage rates. See OECD (2018[32]) for detailed results by employment status. The OECD SOCR database provides benefit recipients totals by country (www.oecd.org/social/recipients.htm). "Discouraged" refers to people without employment who are available for work but are not actively looking for a job. "ILO unemployed" (based on the definition of the International Labour Organization) refers to out-of-work individuals who want a job, have actively sought work in the previous four weeks, and can start working within the next fortnight. Those who have made arrangements to take up paid employment or self-employment in the near future are also included in the definition of ILO unemployment. OECD-24 corresponds to the unweighted average of the countries shown. 2015 figures for Australia. LFS data for Sweden do not include benefits that are accessible to jobless individuals who: i) are not in receipt of core unemployment benefits; and ii) satisfy other conditions such as active participation in employment-support measures. ILO: International Labour Organization.
Source: OECD (2018[32]) using Household, Income and Labour Dynamics in Australia (HILDA) for Australia; European Union Labour Force Survey (EU-LFS) for European countries; and Current Population Survey (CPS) for the United States. Some European countries are excluded due to missing information in EU-LFS data.

StatLink ᐃ𝒮🗐 http://dx.doi.org/10.1787/888933967281

Results are intended as shorthand summaries of benefit accessibility and generosity in comparative perspective and for both standard and non-standard workers (see Figure 7.5). The implied access gaps between standard and non-standard forms of work reflect policy provisions that were in force during the income reference period in the data (around 2014) and therefore do not account for policy reforms that were enacted since then, including in some of the countries where the estimated gaps are large.[9] With that qualification in mind, estimated access gaps were largest in Estonia, where non-standard workers were only half as likely as standard workers to receive benefit support following job loss, and more than 60% of out-of-work individuals with past non-standard work are estimated to go without any benefit support during a 12-month out-of-work spell (Panel A). Gaps were also large in Czech Republic, Latvia, Portugal and Slovak Republic. A notable result is that several countries with comparatively good access to out-of-work support for standard employees also provide accessible support to those with past non-standard work (Austria, Belgium, France, Hungary and Luxembourg). Benefit accessibility for those with past continuous full-time work was also high in Iceland, Slovenia, Spain and the United Kingdom, but moderate gaps for non-standard workers existed in these countries (albeit statistically insignificant in the United Kingdom). In Greece and Italy, even standard workers only had a 50% chance of receiving benefits following a job loss.

Figure 7.5. Non-standard workers receive little support in some countries

Overall support package for working-age individuals, 2014-15

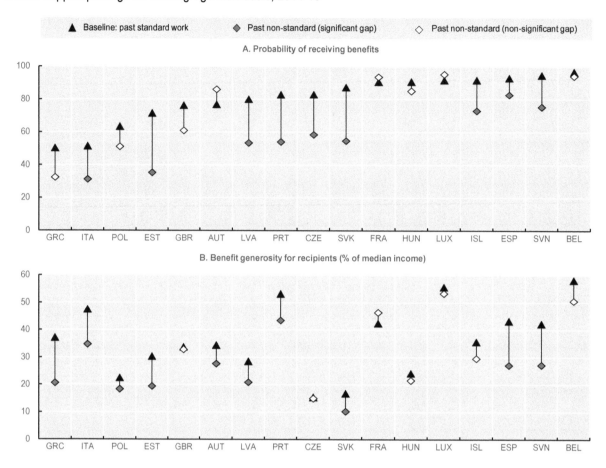

Note: Predicted benefit receipt during an entire year comparing: i) an able-bodied working-age adult who is out of work, had uninterrupted full-time dependent employment with median earnings in the preceding two years, and lives in a two-adult low-income household without children ("baseline: past-standard work", triangle-shaped markers); and ii) an otherwise similar individual whose past work history is "non-standard": mostly in part-time work, mostly self-employed, or interrupted work patterns during the two years preceding the reference year ("past non-standard", light and dark diamond-shaped markers). Additional results for different categories of non-standard work are available for some countries (see main text).

Statistical significance refers to the gaps between baseline and comparator cases (90% confidence interval). Full-time students and retirees are excluded from the sample. Details on data and model specification are summarized in Box 7.3 and presented in further detail in Fernández, Immervoll and Pacifico (forthcoming[33]). The data source, the European Union Statistics on Income and Living Conditions (EU-SILC) covers additional countries but they are excluded here because effective sample sizes were small (e.g. Ireland, Lithuania), because the required micro-data were entirely unavailable (Germany), because key employment-status variables are recorded only for one individual per household (Denmark, Finland, the Netherlands and Sweden), or because of partial or partly conflicting information on income or benefit receipt (Norway). Source: OECD calculations using EU-SILC panel data.

StatLink ᵐˢᵖ http://dx.doi.org/10.1787/888933967300

The predicted average size of the overall benefit package for recipients (Panel B) also varies enormously across countries, ranging from around 20% of national median incomes or less in parts of Central and Eastern Europe (Czech Republic, Slovak Republic, Poland, Hungary) to above 40% in France, Italy, Portugal, Luxembourg and Belgium. Generosity gaps for non-standard workers were largest in Southern Europe (Greece, Italy, Portugal, Spain), as well as in Estonia and Slovenia, exceeding 10% of median household income. As benefit amounts are measured over a year as a whole, these country patterns reflect differences in benefit levels in a given month, as well as in the duration of benefit payments.[10] They also account for the full range of benefits that may be available to the different out-of-work individuals shown, i.e. not only unemployment benefits but also any cash housing or social assistance transfers.

Across countries, there is no obvious link between accessibility and generosity. For example, both the accessibility and generosity scores were high in Belgium and comparatively low in Poland. Benefit access in Italy was comparatively difficult for both standard and non-standard workers, but benefit levels for recipients were fairly high. Hungary shows the opposite pattern, with high implied coverage but low benefit levels. There is also no clear link between overall benefit generosity and the size of the gap between standard and non-standard workers. Generosity gaps were statistically insignificant in some countries with comparatively modest benefit amounts (e.g. close to 15% of median income in the Czech Republic and below 25% of median income in Hungary), but also in others where benefits exceeded 50% of the median (Belgium and Luxembourg).

In five countries both coverage and generosity gaps between standard and non-standard workers were statistically insignificant: Belgium, France, Hungary, Luxembourg and the United Kingdom. These results suggest that effective support for non-standard workers is achievable in the context of quite different social-protection systems and targeting strategies. For instance, out-of-work support in the United Kingdom is flat-rate, comprising an initial insurance benefit for dependent employees with the required contribution record, and means-tested support for active jobseekers with low family incomes and assets. Hungary and Belgium offer earnings-related unemployment protections to both standard and non-standard workers. In Hungary, non-standard workers, including the self-employed, can be entitled to unemployment benefits (Albert, Gáspár and Gal, 2017[34]). In Belgium, non-standard workers are also entitled to unemployment insurance benefits though benefit amounts are much more generous than in Hungary, and benefits for self-employed workers in Belgium account for household needs (De Wispelaere and Pacolet, 2017[35]). In both countries, means-tested support provides further layers of protection for those not entitled to insurance benefits. Recipient numbers of lower-tier social assistance are also substantial in Luxembourg but non-standard workers had (statutory) access to first-tier unemployment benefits as well (Pacolet and Op De Beeck, 2017[36]). In France, a key explanation for the insignificant coverage gaps is the very short qualification period for unemployment benefits (Figure 7.1), paired with a possibility to retain unused benefit entitlements for future out-of-work periods and to cumulate benefit rights across successive out-of-work spells for the (large and growing number) of workers with short-duration employment contracts. France also provides multi-layered income support that benefits workers in other types of non-standard employment (as well as others who may not qualify for first-tier insurance benefits). For instance, self-employed workers in France did not have access to unemployment benefits during the 2014-15 period shown in the results, but income-targeted social assistance and housing benefits do provide additional layers of income security for jobseekers with low household incomes.[11,12]

The empirical results highlight instances where SP gaps between standard and non-standard workers were large. But it is important to note that policy challenges can also arise in countries where the reported gaps are small or insignificant. First, the results refer to someone who remains out of work for an entire year, whose income is in the bottom 10%, and who has worked prior to the reference period. In other words, this is an individual who would qualify as deserving of income support by most standards and the provision of adequate support in such circumstances arguably represents a modest benchmark of effectiveness for SP systems. Support gaps may be significant and widespread for non-standard workers in other situations, for example: for those with some intermittent work during the year; for individuals with a working partner whose earnings lift household income beyond the poorest 10%; for those losing employment as a result of poor health; or for recent parents who take time off work to care for their children.

Second, gaps are calculated on the basis of micro-data that are necessarily backward looking. They therefore reflect recent labour-market realities and employment categories as recorded in these data. The present results therefore do not capture gaps that may exist for newly evolving alternative working arrangements, such as platform work. Updating the estimates at regular intervals, and as data with more granular information on employment categories become available, would allow monitoring SP gaps as the future of work takes shape. Such regular monitoring is desirable and should examine support gaps for a wider set of circumstances than is reported here.

Third, the gaps in Figure 7.5 are calculated taking an average across several types of past non-standard work, including part-time dependent employment, temporary work and self-employment. As shown in Figure 7.2 above, statutory access to many benefits is often especially limited for the self-employed, which suggests that obtaining support could be very difficult for some subcategories of independent workers, even in countries where gaps are insignificant between standard and non-standard workers more broadly. Caution is therefore required in drawing conclusions on specific policy challenges across countries solely based on Figure 7.5. Breakdowns of SP gaps for different types of non-standard work would further enrich policy reform discussions and preliminary results from such a more granular analysis are presented in Figure 7.6. These results disentangle part-time employment, unstable employment and self-employment and are available for six countries where data samples are sufficiently large for a disaggregated analysis: France, Greece, Hungary, Italy, Spain and the United Kingdom.

The estimates indicate that support gaps can indeed vary markedly across different forms of non-standard work but that this need not be the case.[13] In Spain, *part-time workers* were somewhat less likely than standard employees to receive benefits during an out-of-work spell, but the difference was comparatively small (10 percentage points, Panel A). In the other five countries, benefit accessibility gaps between part-time workers and standard employees were statistically insignificant.

In Italy and Spain, those with *interrupted work* histories were less likely to receive out-of-work support than standard employees. But in four of the countries shown, benefit accessibility gaps for workers in unstable employment were statistically insignificant. In some of them, workers can qualify for unemployment insurance benefits after comparatively short periods in work (e.g. three months in France and six months in the United Kingdom, see Figure 7.1). It should be noted, however, that the gaps were calculated assuming the same earnings levels for the different worker categories (see figure notes). They therefore do not reflect accessibility issues that may exist for low-paid workers in particular. For instance, some countries require minimum earnings levels for employment to count towards unemployment insurance entitlements (e.g. approximately 16% of average full-time earnings in the United Kingdom). In these cases, accessing support can be more difficult for individuals with very short working hours or with extended out-of-work periods in-between employment spells.

Accessibility gaps for those with past *self-employment* were sizeable in four of the six countries, with implied coverage rates for out-of-work individuals as low as 10% in Italy and around 25% in Greece, Spain and the United Kingdom. Where unemployment insurance is not open to the self-employed (see Figure 7.2), they will need to rely on lower-tier income support, such as unemployment assistance or guaranteed minimum income benefits. These transfers typically feature strict access requirements, including income and asset tests, and are subject to significant non-takeup, which lowers their effective reach. Assistance benefits also tend to be less generous than insurance transfers. For those self-employed who do receive income support, predicted benefit amounts are therefore frequently lower than for standard employees. Exceptions are the United Kingdom (where flat-rate insurance and assistance benefits pay similar amounts), as well as France (where the generosity gap for the self-employed was bigger than in the United Kingdom, but statistically insignificant).

Benefit accessibility in France and Hungary did not vary substantially across different types of non-standard work: relative to standard employees, accessibility gaps were minor for all three categories (part-time work, self-employment and unstable work). Benefit levels were much lower in Hungary, however, while estimates for France suggest that income support may have been somewhat *more* generous for out-of-work individuals with a recent history of unstable or intermittent employment.

## Figure 7.6. Support gaps can be sizeable for the self-employed

Overall support package for working-age individuals, 2014-15, selected countries

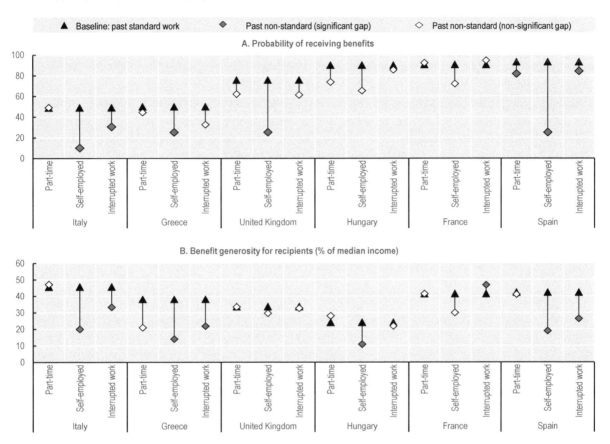

Note: Predicted benefit receipt during an entire year comparing: i) an able-bodied working-age adult who is out of work, had uninterrupted full-time dependent employment with median earnings in the preceding two years, and lives in a two-adult low-income household without children ("baseline: past-standard work", triangle-shaped markers); and ii) an otherwise similar individual whose past work history is "non-standard": mostly in part-time work, mostly self-employed, or interrupted work patterns during the two years preceding the reference year ("past non-standard", light and dark diamond-shaped markers).

Statistical significance refers to the gaps between baseline and comparator cases (90% confidence interval). Full-time students and retirees are excluded from the sample. Details on data and model specification are summarized in Box 7.3 and presented in further detail in Fernández, Immervoll and Pacifico (forthcoming[33]). The data source the European Union Statistics on Income and Living Conditions (EU-SILC) covers additional countries but they are excluded here because effective sample sizes were small (e.g. Ireland, Lithuania), because the required micro-data were entirely unavailable (Germany), because key employment-status variables are recorded only for one individual per household (Denmark, Finland, the Netherlands and Sweden), or because of partial or partly conflicting information on income or benefit receipt (Norway).

Source: OECD calculations using EU-SILC panel data.

*StatLink* 🔗 http://dx.doi.org/10.1787/888933967319

## 7.3. Addressing social protection gaps: Key policy issues

The results presented in the previous section suggest that different SP strategies can be effective at limiting support gaps for workers in non-standard forms of employment. But where gaps do exist, they may become more widespread and reduce the effectiveness of existing SP provisions if ongoing labour market changes lead to a transformation of the standard employer-employee relationship, or to greater labour market churn and heightened employment instability.

Box 7.3. Benefit access and generosity: A statistical model accounting for key policy levers

Box 7.3. Benefit access and generosity: A statistical model accounting for key policy levers

The empirical work proceeds in two steps. A first step estimates the relationship between individual benefit receipt and a large number of key structural drivers of support, including previous and current work status and earnings, current household income, family composition, housing tenure and any health limitations.[14] This type of information is typically available from household panel data. The current analysis uses three-year panels of the European Union Statistics of Income and Living Conditions (EI-SILC), and pools observations from two survey waves (2014 and 2015) to increase sample size.[15] The effective sample sizes range between 3 500 observations in Iceland and 20 600 in Italy. The dependent variable is total social cash benefits received during an entire year. It therefore accounts for both the average generosity of monthly benefit payments and the durations of benefit entitlements (as well as any waiting periods or other possible gaps between benefit entitlement and pay-out). For benefits that are observed at the household rather than the individual level (family benefits, GMI benefits), amounts are allocated to all adult household members on a per-capita basis. Model specifications are consistent across countries and include the following independent variables, along with relevant interactions and higher-order terms: main employment status during the reference year; pre-transfer household income during the reference year; main employment status during the preceding two years; earnings during each of the preceding two years; family situation and number of children; health status; housing tenure and housing costs; education level; gender; and age.

Separate models are estimated for benefit receipt (yes/no indicator variable) and generosity (benefit amounts) using a generalized Hurdle approach, as the process that determines whether a person receive social benefits is not necessarily the same as the process that determines the amount received – see Wooldridge (2010[37]) and Cragg (1971[38]). The first model is a logistic regression for benefit receipt at the individual level. The second model is an exponential regression of benefit amounts (entitlements) estimated only on observations with positive benefits. The use of exponential regressions, rather than a standard log-linear model, sidesteps inference problems that arise with predicting levels for log-transformed dependent variables (Wooldridge, 2010[37]). A second step uses the estimated relationships for inference on the benefit gaps between standard and non-standard workers in concrete circumstances ("vignettes") that are defined in a consistent way across countries. For ease of comparison, benefit amounts are shown as a share of median income in each country. The use of a vignette-based analysis facilitates the communication of complex statistical results in a comparative perspective, and the identification of relevant policy mechanisms underlying the observed gaps. A direct interpretation of the estimated coefficients is complicated by interaction effects, categorical variables and other nonlinear functional forms. Significant interpretation difficulties arise also in nonlinear models such as logistic regression as the raw coefficients are often not of immediate interest. In these cases, "marginal effects" (i.e. statistics computed from model predictions for different values of the control variables) allow summarising the entire vector of estimated parameters into a single value using the same metric as the dependent variable (here the probability of receipt and the benefit amount). Standard errors (computed by means of the Delta method), allow inference on the estimated gaps and their statistical significance.

Benefit "gaps" are calculated relative to a baseline "standard" worker who requires out-of-work support: an out-of-work 40-year old who was previously working full-time without interruptions and median earnings, and who lives in a low-income childless couple and in privately rented accommodation. Relevant characteristics for the comparator vignettes are as described in the notes to Figure 7.5 and Figure 7.6.

Source: Fernández, Immervoll and Pacifico (forthcoming[33]).

There are several reasons why gaps can arise, including:

1. Some economic activities do not give rise to SP entitlements (e.g. self-employment in many jurisdictions and casual or irregular work in some);

2. Past employment duration or social contributions are insufficient to qualify for benefits (e.g. if existing employment or contribution requirements are difficult to meet for those in unstable or marginal employment, see Figure 7.1).

3. Non-standard workers are treated differently during the claiming process (e.g. needs assessments for self-employed workers may be based on assumed rather than actual earnings, or an unemployed person searching for self-employment opportunities may not be considered an active job seeker); and

4. Already acquired entitlements are lost during a change in employment status or job (e.g. following a transition from dependent to self-employment when entitlements differ across employment statuses, or between jobs if they are tied to a specific employment relationship).

This section discusses policy options for addressing these and related gaps. It first discusses key challenges arising in the context of social-insurance systems (Section 7.3.1) and in universal and means-tested systems (Section 7.3.2). The remainder considers technical challenges related to volatile careers and earnings (Section 7.3.3), the role of activation policies in the future world of work (Section 7.3.4) and selected options for ensuring sufficient resources to support a growing role of SP in uncertain labour markets (Section 7.3.5).

### 7.3.1. Challenges in insurance-based social protection

Limited transferability of entitlements between jobs is a problem in earnings-related systems when entitlements differ across contractual arrangements or when they are tied to occupational schemes or to specific employers. Harmonising contributions and entitlements across the entire workforce, possibly accompanied by unified governance and administration structures, would make existing entitlements more portable.

Collecting and combining contributions from different schemes in one account, irrespective of the economic activity, is another – administratively simpler – way of ensuring that built-up entitlements are not lost in labour market transitions. For instance, Austria replaced its severance pay scheme with individual pension accounts in 2003. The previous severance-pay scheme only benefited employees upon lay-off, and therefore hindered labour mobility. In the new system, all dependent employees have pension accounts that receive regular employer contributions, but the account itself is independent of the employer and transferable across jobs. Transitions to self-employment suspend further employer contributions but they do not lead to a loss of entitlements. The measure increased job mobility for workers especially in distressed firms (Kettemann, Kramarz and Zweimüller, 2016[39]).

Entitlements derived from individual accounts can be subsidised explicitly (through credits) or implicitly (through the benefit formula). However, without substantial subsidies, individual accounts are a form of government-mandated saving whose scope and objectives differ from social insurance (see Section 7.1). In particular, "pure" individual accounts do not provide any risk sharing mechanisms and therefore cannot insure against catastrophic risks (such as long-term disability). Depending on how contributions are invested, they may also carry significant financial-market risks. As "pure" individual accounts do not incorporate redistribution, they are typically of less value to marginal or part-time workers.

Similar challenges limit the scope of publicly subsidised non-mandatory individual savings accounts that, in combination with means-tested safety-net benefits, have been suggested as an option for achieving adequate income protection for all, while keeping labour costs down (World Bank, 2018[6]). Disadvantaged and budget-constrained individuals can be unresponsive to savings incentives because of myopia, inertia, or information deficits. Subsidies then mainly divert savings toward subsidised products and crowd out unsubsidised savings. As a result, such programmes may mainly benefit individuals who already save even in the absence of subsidies or additional incentives (Chetty et al., 2014[40]).

One option to improve transferability of SP entitlements while maintaining acceptable replacement-rates for middle-income workers is to differentiate between earnings-related benefits (such as pensions, unemployment and short-term sickness benefits) and benefits that have no relation to earnings (health and long-term care) or where income smoothing is not a primary objective (longer-term unemployment or disability). Making the latter broadly accessible would help to safeguard basic entitlements irrespective of labour market transitions. As complements to these safety nets, earnings-related benefits could then be harmonised across contractual arrangements, to improve transferability (Cahuc, 2018[41]; Levy, 2008[42]).

### 7.3.2. Challenges in universal or means-tested social protection

Evolving labour markets arguably blur lines between traditional employment and different forms of independent work. Moreover, new types of atypical employment make it harder to reliably assess whether someone is working at all and how many hours they are putting into their job or jobs. As a result, tying social-protection entitlements and contributions to people's employment status becomes more difficult. If existing strategies do not provide adequate coverage for all those in need, loosening the link between employment and entitlements could be one option for keeping social protection accessible, for resolving imbalances in SP entitlements across employment types, and for supporting labour market dynamism.

Moving towards greater universality through a form of basic income (BI) is an interesting proposal in this debate that has received considerable attention. No country has introduced a BI as a principal pillar of SP, however, and replacing large parts of existing support systems with a universal payment would be a major change. OECD simulations show that an unconditional payment to everyone at meaningful but fiscally realistic levels would require large tax rises as well as reductions in most current benefits, and would often not be an effective tool for reducing income poverty (OECD, 2017[43]; Browne and Immervoll, 2017[44]). Some disadvantaged groups would lose out when existing benefits are replaced by a BI, illustrating the downsides of SP without any form of targeting at all. In view of the immediate fiscal and distributional consequences of a fully comprehensive BI, reforms towards more universal income support would realistically need to be introduced gradually for specific groups (such as youth) or would need to be restricted in other ways.[16] It would also require a parallel debate on how to finance a more equal sharing of the benefits of economic growth. From a broader economic-policy perspective, a downside of universal support is that, unlike out-of-work or needs-based benefits, it does not act as an automatic stabiliser: since it is paid regardless of income or employment status, spending levels do not go up during a downturn, and they do not fall during an upswing.

Another option is to strengthen needs-based support programmes by transforming some insurance programmes into means-tested assistance, or by expanding existing "safety-net" benefits for people with low incomes and no other resources. For example, Italy introduced a social assistance benefit, the *Reddito di Inclusione* in 2018. This will be replaced with the Citizen's Income in 2019, which provides much higher benefit levels and aims to combine income support with activation measures (Bulman et al., 2019[45]). Such safety nets seek to ensure that those with high poverty risks receive basic support regardless of their past employment history or current work patterns. As tightly targeted schemes are financed from general revenues, their financing does not fall exclusively on workers. Non-wage labour costs can be reduced as a result, attenuating the incentives for automation (World Bank, 2018[6]) and encouraging formal employment (Levy, 2008[42]). Replacing contribution-based with general revenue-financed benefits can also help to align non-wage labour costs across employment forms, and thus ease distortions that arise from an unequal legal treatment of contractual arrangements (see Section 7.3.5).

Minimum-income safety nets are therefore an important element in countries' strategies to alleviate poverty. However, targeted minimum-income schemes can be difficult to access in practice due to costly benefit-claiming processes, e.g. because of negative stigma, considerable information requirements and uncertainty regarding eligibility and entitlements, leading to substantial non-takeup (Bargain, Immervoll and Viitamäki, 2012[46]). They also do not offer significant income smoothing, except during spells with zero or very low (household) income. Unless complemented by benefits that provide significant replacement rates for middle-class workers, they do not provide insurance against major income losses for the majority with incomes well above the poverty line. In particular, out-of-work benefits paid in relation to household needs often do not provide any cash support to job losers in dual (or multiple-) earner households. Since re-employment support is typically tied to benefit receipt, the reach of active labour market programmes would then often exclude these groups as well (Section 7.3.4). A related challenge is that, while public support for safety nets can derive from an expectation that only the poorest require assistance, an exclusive reliance on targeting the poor minimises the majority's stake in social protection and risks making funding less stable and potentially more susceptible to political cycles (Lindert, 2004[47]).

Needs-based provisions also risk crowding-out wages or support that is provided by employers as part of the pay package. In decoupling SP entitlements from jobs, a key policy challenge is therefore to ensure that government-provided transfers reach their intended recipients. The combination of an expanded in-work benefit and the introduction of a statutory minimum wage in the United Kingdom during the late 1990s provides a prominent example of such concerns, and of an approach for ensuring that income-tested in-work transfers benefit low-paid workers rather than their employers.[17] However, an expansion of the number of low-paid independent workers who do not benefit from minimum-wage protection makes wage floors less effective in this respect.

### 7.3.3. Technical issues related to volatile careers and earnings

Despite these challenges, needs-based support will remain an essential complement to universal, insurance-based and employer-provided SP, and a necessary form of fall-back support while other SP pillars are adapted to a future world of work. For both needs-based and contributory systems, labour market changes present a number of very practical issues, however. In particular, the earnings of non-standard workers are typically subject to considerable fluctuations, notably in the case of self-employment. This complicates a reliable and timely assessment of household income and need, but also of the base for social contributions in insurance-based systems.[18] Contribution payments that are not deducted at source but paid infrequently are also more visible and more likely to be perceived as taxes (Hershfield, Shu and Benartzi, 2018[48]).

Improved data transmission and real-time reporting of earnings tends to be costly (National Audit Office, 2018[49]) but can alleviate technical income measurement problems. Yet, a more fundamental question is what constitutes an appropriate payment or assessment frequency and a suitable reference period for assessing incomes and earnings. Payment modalities have implications for the responsiveness of SP systems, but also for the behaviour of claimants and contributors. Short reference periods make SP systems more responsive to people's circumstances but can create incentives for gaming the system by timing incomes so as to maximise benefit entitlements or minimise contributions in a given period. For instance, earnings from self-employment can be shifted across periods, while contribution thresholds and ceilings depress individual contributions and total revenues when earnings are volatile. Longer reference periods sidestep such incentives especially in the case of contribution payments. But they can result in delayed and untimely support that does not match people's current, and possible urgent, need for income or employment assistance. A related issue is that self-employed workers can struggle to fulfil minimum work or contribution requirements for benefit entitlement if there are significant time lags between performing work and receiving payment for it, e.g. if they only receive one payment for an extended period of work.

Volatile earnings may affect a growing number of workers in the future and accommodating earnings fluctuations in SP systems may therefore become more urgent. It is, however, not a new problem but rather a "legacy" issue that countries have been addressing in different ways, illustrating the trade-offs involved:

- The Netherlands provides self-employed workers with interest-free loans to bridge temporary low-income periods and related liquidity problems (de Graaf-Zijl, Scheer and Bolhaar, 2018[50]). Building on such a system, one policy option could be a subsequent conversion of (some part) of such loans into benefits, e.g. once the low-income spell turns out to be persistent.

- Denmark has harmonised unemployment-benefit entitlement rules for different types of dependent and independent workers by tying eligibility to taxable income over a three-year period, irrespective of the contractual arrangement. This also improves access for those who combine dependent and independent work. As an accompanying measure, self-employed workers who have ceased their business and receive benefits must not start a new one for six months. This "job search" period seeks to prevent self-employed from combining benefit receipt with continued independent work (OECD, 2018[51]).

- Claimants of the Universal Credit, including the self-employed, in the United Kingdom are required to report earnings on a monthly basis. For longer-term benefit recipients, any earnings from self-employment are presumed to amount to at least the national minimum wage and reduce entitlements accordingly. This circumvents measurement problems for many self-employed claimants and is intended to avoid subsidising small businesses that are economically unviable, or independent workers who would be better off taking up employment in a regular minimum-wage job. However, while simple, this approach puts the self-employed with genuinely low earnings at a disadvantage (Citizens advice, 2018[52]; Low Incomes Tax Reform Group, 2017[53]). In particular, presuming minimum-wage earnings for a group that does not benefit from wage-floor regulations may exacerbate labour market disadvantages for workers who are faced with a choice between low-paid independent employment or not working at all, or who are actively encouraged by employment service providers to seek and accept independent work in the first place.[19]

- New Zealand has instituted a welfare advisory group to address technical and broader issues related to labour market changes, including a growing availability of self-employment options, and their implications for SP capacity and responsiveness (Ministry of Social Development, 2018[54]).

### 7.3.4. Prevention and promotion: Activation policies in future labour markets

Large shares of workers transition in or out of jobs every year. Prior to the global financial and economic crisis, annual job separations and hires amounted to nearly 15% of total employment on average across the OECD. Job reallocation statistics were similar after the crisis, even if trends differed across countries (Falco, Green and MacDonald, forthcoming[55]) – see also Chapter 3. If accelerating technology adoption quickens the pace of job reallocation, the readiness and ability of workers to move from jobs in declining sectors or firms to expanding ones is likely to become an increasingly crucial determinant of future employment trends.

Changing work patterns and new forms of employment raise new questions about the scope and ambition of activation policies and employment-oriented SP. For instance, compared with out-of-work individuals with past standard employment, jobseekers with a history of self-employment can be less likely to rely on public employment services (PES) for their job search, e.g. if a lack of benefit entitlements means that there is no immediate financial incentive for regular interaction with the PES (Figure 7.7). The data in this figure do not provide information on people's main channels for job search, or on the type of past self-employment (see figure notes), and this may explain why the differences between dependent employees and self-employed are in fact comparatively small in several countries, even in those where unemployment benefits are not typically available for self-employed. For some past self-employed, limited

PES engagement may also reflect the availability of alternative job-search channels or a preference for a type of independent work that the PES is not perceived to facilitate. But limited engagement with the PES, for whatever reason, can become a growing concern when independent forms of work increasingly become substitutes for dependent employment.

**Figure 7.7. In some countries, only a minority of jobseekers are in regular contact with the public employment service**

By past employment status, 2017, in %

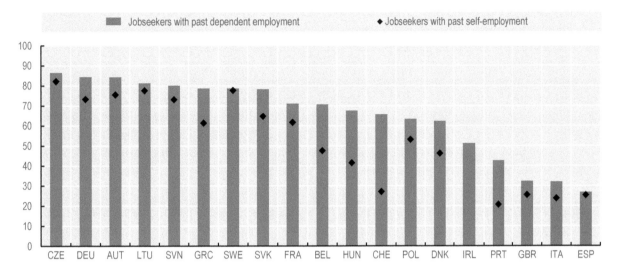

Note: Share of unemployed stating, in the context of questions about individuals' job-search methods, that they "contacted the public employment office to find work during the previous four weeks". Most respondents report more than one job-search method and data do not permit assessing the main one; this can be one reason why differences by previous employment status frequently appear small. Ages 25-64. 2013 data for Germany. Data for Ireland do not include information on past self-employment. Countries with fewer than 30 observations in any category are omitted. Source: OECD calculations using EU Labour Force Survey.

StatLink ᔕᕮᒪ http://dx.doi.org/10.1787/888933967338

*Reintegrating displaced workers*

"Displaced workers" – those facing involuntary job loss for technology-related or other economic reasons – find new jobs much more rapidly in some countries than in others. Whereas nearly 90% are re-employed within a year in Finland and Sweden, that share is only 30% in France and Portugal (OECD, 2018[56]). Providing timely and tailored employment support becomes more challenging when increasing numbers of workers are affected by job displacement, including through automation (see the discussion in Chapters 2 and 3). Some prevention and early intervention measures work best for workers who are laid-off after moderate or longer period of employment with the same employer. Indeed, one important difference between displaced workers and most other unemployed recipients of income and re-employment support is that there is in principle greater scope for proactive measures in the case of the former. Rapid response services, such as PES staff providing counselling or mediation events directly in a work place that will soon close, can jump-start the adjustment process by delivering re-employment services in a timely and targeted manner.

Such early intervention services can be quite effective but, except in the case of large-scale collective redundancies, are not widely used and require a form of social partnership that ensures that employers are actively involved in proactive re-employment measures, as for instance in Sweden (see also

Chapter 5).[20] Where labour markets are characterised by shortening job tenures or a diminished reach of traditional forms of worker representation, engaging employers in prevention and early intervention can become even more challenging. In a future world of work, these measures may become more difficult to access for growing shares of job losers as a result. Broadly available general activation and promotion programmes – for displaced workers and other jobseekers alike – are therefore likely to gain additional importance as central pillars of labour market reintegration strategies.

*Activation of whom and towards what?*

PES may need to adopt more effective outreach strategies to engage with workers who currently have work but may be at elevated risk of unemployment, such as those in unstable forms of work. Even though many countries support some groups of low-paid workers through in-work benefits or wage subsidies, the bulk of existing job-search assistance and related active labour market programmes exclude workers and focus on jobless people receiving out-of-work benefits. With the easier availability of task-based and independent forms of work, and a growing range of options for occasional short-duration or part-time employment, the traditional "in work" / "out of work" dichotomy appears increasingly anachronistic. In fact, in some countries, workers with intermittent employment and/or limited working hours already outnumber key categories of out-of-work individuals, such as those not working for family reasons, those unfit to work, or the longer-term unemployed (Figure 7.8). A strict focus on the jobless denies support from a large number of precarious workers who face barriers to higher-quality employment. It therefore becomes more and more unsatisfactory as basis for targeting activation and re-employment programmes.[21]

Extending access to active labour market support should move in tandem with tackling unintended benefit coverage gaps. For people with intermittent or precarious work this requires a careful review of key qualifying criteria for existing unemployment benefits, such as waiting periods, past employment requirements (see Figure 7.1) and rules regarding the extent and type of work that can be combined with benefit receipt ("part-time unemployment benefit").[22] In many OECD countries, some part-time work is compatible with the receipt of unemployment benefits and some countries offer partial benefits to workers whose working hours are cut.[23] Yet, workers may not always be aware of this possibility (Stettner, Cassidy and Wentworth, 2016[57]). In contributory systems, effective out-of-work support for intermittent workers also requires provisions that allow "unused" entitlements (those that were not used in a given out-of-work spell) to be carried forward to future claim periods. An alternative (and partly functionally equivalent) strategy is the broader integration of out-of-work and in-work support programmes. The United Kingdom's Universal Credit reform is a primary example of such a comprehensive strategy (Browne, Hood and Joyce, 2016[58]; Office for Budget Responsibility, 2018[59]).

The content and delivery of employment-oriented support also need to adapt. First, an evolving target group for active support requires sufficient and reliable resources for employment services and enough qualified frontline staff and caseworkers. User-friendly online services for jobseekers and automated systems that facilitate inter-agency access to relevant data (such as jobseekers' labour market history and programme participation) can speed up initial jobseeker registration and other routine tasks.[24] In general, technology can reduce pressures on operating budgets by creating more time for personal interaction between staff and jobseekers, and it enriches the toolkit for implementing broader activation strategies. For instance, IT-supported systems can support tailored and well-targeted services, e.g. through statistical profiling (OECD, 2018[60]). Yet, highly automated processes also create significant new risks, especially when introduced or used in a context of tight budget envelopes. An aggressive push towards replacing interpersonal contact with digital interfaces can compromise service accessibility and quality, notably for those with limited digital skills or those with complex needs where caseworker discretion is needed. Interventions and programme assignments using new generations of artificial-intelligence based profiling tools and decision support systems may also appear obscure or unfair and, as a result, might reduce their acceptance among some jobseekers, and their readiness for cooperating actively with PES.

Figure 7.8. Unstable work is common, but it may be outside the scope of activation measures

Employment Status over a 12-month period, average across seven countries

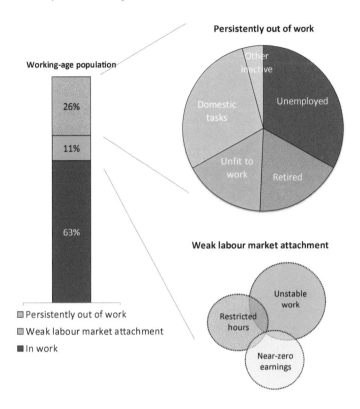

Note: "Weak labour market attachment": working for less than 45% of the potential full-time working hours in the calendar year ("unstable jobs", "restricted hours"), or earning less than one third of the annual full-time statutory minimum wage ("near zero earnings"). Unweighted average across seven countries (Australia, Estonia, Ireland, Italy, Lithuania, Portugal and Spain), for 2014 and for ages 18-64 excluding students and military service.
Source: OECD Faces of Joblessness country studies (www.oecd.org/els/soc/faces-of-joblessness.htm) using EU-SILC for European countries and the Household, Income and Labour Dynamics in Australia (HILDA) survey.

Second, new or growing forms of non-standard work require weighing the intended role and objectives of publicly provided labour market intermediation and employment services. A key issue is to what extent PES should actively connect people to very short-term work engagements ("gigs"), casual work (e.g. on-call employment or "zero hours" contracts) or independent forms of employment. Although the PES' intermediation role can be partly redundant for platform work that is readily accessible online, some PES today already use web scraping technology to consolidate vacancies from a number (sometimes hundreds) of vacancy repositories. For instance, in the Netherlands, more than one third of vacancies that are listed on the PES job portal are sourced from other web resources using such technology. More fundamentally, however, a growing availability of alternative work arrangements raises the question whether employment services can and should prioritise different employment forms when recording openings in their vacancy databases or when offering vacancies to jobseekers. For instance, some Workforce Boards in the United States have held recruitment events for ridesharing services that are offered through online platforms (McKay, Pollack and Fitzpayne, 2018[61]) but such approaches frequently remain experimental and policies and practices differ both across and within countries. Even when active referral to non-traditional work is desired and compatible with PES procedures or guidelines, existing PES funding or reporting mechanisms may discourage it, e.g. if future earnings levels or stability are used for assessing the performance of reintegration measures but PES do not have ready access to information on earnings from self-employment. A growing availability of non-standard work contracts also highlights risks of creating "one-way streets" away from traditional forms of employment, e.g. if jobseekers are encouraged or assisted into self-employment but then have no clear route back to standard employment if they do not succeed in making a living from independent work.

More broadly, governments should review whether existing activation strategies for jobseekers, and those with unstable or low-paid work, strike a suitable balance between encouraging standard and non-standard employment, and are in line with policy objectives regarding job quantity and quality (OECD, 2018[2]). In the context of rights-and-responsibilities frameworks, such a review should for instance encompass the definition and application of "suitable-jobs" criteria, i.e. the type of jobs that benefit claimants must look for and accept in order to avoid benefit sanctions (Immervoll and Knotz, 2018[62]). In particular, integrating jobseekers into any kind of job may not be sufficient for individuals experiencing recurring cycles of precarious work and joblessness. Workers in sectors with significant exposure to automation or restructuring may also require access to employment services that re-assess their employment prospects, provide career guidance and develop coherent re-employment and, when needed, re-skilling strategies (see also Chapter 6).

### Balancing incentives and support

Weak work incentives are rarely the only employment barrier for jobseekers, and often not the main one.[25] But they are central to activation approaches which tie benefit receipt to active job-search and participation in labour market programmes. Importantly, a more fluid labour market with more options for when and how long to work creates more opportunities for acting on positive and negative incentives. This has significant implications for the scope of job-search and other behavioural requirements for benefit claimants, and for the design of tax-benefit systems more generally. First, incentives that favour specific employment forms can become more distortionary and economically damaging than they had been in the past (see Section 7.3.5).

Second, tax-benefit provisions, which create sudden income drops or gains as people vary earnings or working hours, are more likely to affect working time and earnings when choices are no longer constrained to, say, 40, 30 or 20 hours per week – see e.g. Saez (2010[63]). Avoiding excessive marginal effective tax rates (METRs), as caused by very high benefit withdrawal rates or by thresholds for tax liabilities or benefit entitlements, then becomes more desirable. Significant work disincentives, with METRs approaching or exceeding 100%, currently exist in a large number of OECD countries at lower earnings levels (Figure 7.9). With working hours and employment choices becoming more "elastic", there may also be greater policy scope for setting explicit positive incentives towards socially desirable outcomes. This could for instance include tax reductions for inactive spouses taking up work as second earners (Immervoll et al., 2009[64]), or specific tax concessions or benefit bonuses for low-paid workers who move beyond marginal employment and work a certain minimum number of hours.[26]

Third, and perhaps most important, governments should review whether benefit reforms that are intended to tackle benefit coverage gaps create a need to rebalance the demanding and supporting elements of existing rights-and-responsibilities frameworks. Job-search and related activation requirements help in targeting support to genuine jobseekers and restrict opportunities for benefit receipt by others. An emergence of alternative working arrangements, with additional scope for arranging work or earnings patterns in a way that is compatible with benefit receipt, calls for additional efforts to formulate and enforce clear and reasonable responsibilities for benefit recipients. Likewise, extending the scope of job-search responsibilities and provisions for active participation in re-employment measures may be a necessary counter-weight to any extensions of benefit rights to new groups of jobseekers, such as part-time unemployed, those with intermittent employment, or those who entered unemployment after periods of self-employment.

Figure 7.9. Very high marginal effective tax rates can discourage people from working longer hours

Marginal effective tax rate (METR) for part-time workers, 2018

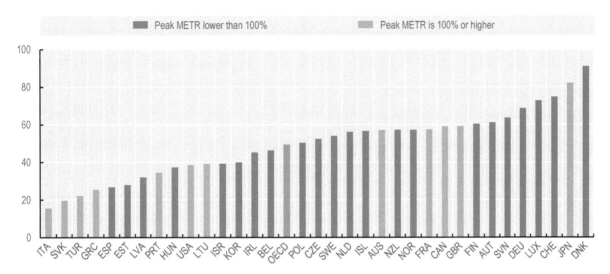

Note: Marginal effective tax rates (METRs) are the share of an earnings increase that is taxed away through higher taxes or reduced benefits. They are shown for an employee earning half the average hourly wage and working between 5 and 40 hours per week. The bars show the overall METR when moving from 5 hours per week to 40 hours per week. "Peak" is the maximum METR when increasing hours in 5-hour steps from 5 hours per week to 40 hours per week. Light-coloured bars indicate countries where peak METRs are at or above 100%, i.e. if there are situations when adding 5 working hours may not lead to higher net income. Calculations are based on four different family types (single, lone parent and dual-earner couple with and without children) and account for income taxes, employee-paid social contributions, and the following social benefits: minimum-income, cash housing, family, in-work benefits.
Source: OECD tax-benefit model TaxBEN (www.oecd.org/social/benefits-and-wages.htm).

StatLink ⫘⫘ http://dx.doi.org/10.1787/888933967357

### 7.3.5. Ensuring that social protection resources match evolving demands

Labour market transformations create new challenges for financing SP systems and can exacerbate existing, longer-standing ones. For a number of reasons, the resources that are needed for the provision of adequate working-age support can be expected to grow as a result. Accelerating labour market turnover in many countries (see Chapter 3), means that a higher share of workers would seek support both at any one point in time and throughout their careers. Closing SP gaps to include non-standard workers and supporting the transition and reintegration of displaced workers in declining industries will require corresponding SP budgets.

At the same time, the resource base for working-age support is being squeezed from several directions. The main funding base of SP systems is at risk of erosion if megatrends combine with rising market power of firms to perpetuate a decline of the labour share in national income – e.g. OECD (2018[32]), Sachs (2018[65]). On the spending side, population ageing puts growing pressures on pension, health and long-term care systems, which absorb increasing shares of available SP resources. Indeed, expenditures on old-age and survivor benefits over the past 25-30 years have grown substantially not only in total but, in spite of pension reforms, also on a per-capita basis. For instance, averaged across OECD countries with longer series of social spending, the spending on old-age and survivor benefits per individual aged 65 and older has grown from 22% of GDP per capita in 1990, to 32% in 2000 and 38% in 2013.[27]

Counteracting a decline in resources for working-age support requires a determined, coordinated and comprehensive approach that will need to include a policy debate on how new or expanded initiatives will be paid for, and who should pay. Key issues in this debate include ensuring that available resources are used efficiently. But it will also require debating options for broadening the tax base and strengthening revenue-collection technologies and enforcement (OECD, 2018[66]). In a context of a future of work with a growing choice of alternative working arrangements, a further challenge is that selective opting-in or opting-out raises sustainability risks in SP systems with voluntary membership (see Sections 7.1 and 7.2.1). This section focuses on two specific financing issues that are closely linked to the design of SP systems: incentives that SP financing provisions can create to encourage non-standard work, and achieving a suitable sharing of SP financing burdens across different employers.

*Tackling financial incentives in favour of non-standard work*

SP entitlements that are financed through an employment relationship represent non-wage labour costs. Where the cost of SP coverage is uneven across employment forms, employers and employees can lower costs by choosing between alternative working arrangements. Although these incentives are only one of many considerations that determine the choice of the most suitable employment form, differences in non-wage labour costs can be large. This is shown in Figure 7.10, which reports gaps in the "total payment wedge", defined as the sum of personal income tax, social security contributions and other compulsory payments as a share of total labour costs, between dependent employees and different types of independent employment. For illustration purposes, results refer to someone with gross earnings equal to the average full-time wage in all cases.

Gaps are large where non-standard workers are excluded from certain parts of SP or if membership is voluntary. In both cases, legally mandated contributions can be significantly lower for non-standard workers as a result. In the Netherlands, the total payment wedge for an employee (51%) is more than twice as high as for an independent contractor (22%), meaning that total employment costs are 60% higher for an employee in this case.[28] Most of the gap in the payment wedge (22 percentage points) is due to employer social security contributions, and a tax deduction for self-employed workers widens this gap further (OECD, 2018[67]).[29] Of the seven OECD countries studied in Milanez and Bratta (2019[68]), the cost difference between hiring a dependent employee and the lowest-cost alternative working arrangement is smallest in Sweden, where independent contractors are included in most public SP programmes, with the exception of the bankruptcy fund (Kolsrud, 2018[19]). While Figure 7.10 focuses on statutory payments, further cost differences between employment forms can stem from employer contributions to SP measures that are part of collective agreements and provide top-up benefits for workers that fall within the scope of these agreements (see Section 7.2.1). De-facto gaps in contribution burdens can also be sizeable if participation in SP provisions is voluntary or allows some type of workers additional flexibility in the contributions they wish to make (Sections 7.1 and 7.2.1).

For workers, non-standard employment is especially attractive if contributions are lower than for standard dependent employment, while benefit entitlements are broadly similar (see Chapter 4). Where possible, both contributions and entitlements should be aligned across employment forms to prevent employers from engaging in regulatory arbitrage in the composition of their workforce. Several countries have taken steps to extend SP coverage to non-standard workers in order to curb a continued growth in their numbers. Austria gradually integrated independent contractors (*freie Dienstnehmer*), a hybrid between self- and dependent employment, into the social insurance system following concerns that employers used this contractual arrangement to avoid or evade social contributions. Since 2008, independent contractors are liable for the same (employer and employee) social security contributions as standard employees. While the number of independent contractors had grown steadily until early 2007, it began to fall after the reform was announced, reaching an all-time low in 2016 (Fink and Nagl, 2018[20]).[30] In Italy, the gradual integration of para-subordinate workers into the general social insurance system since 2012 had similar effects (Raitano, 2018[24]).

# Figure 7.10. Non-wage labour costs vary substantially across contractual arrangements

Total payment wedge by employment form, 2017, in percent

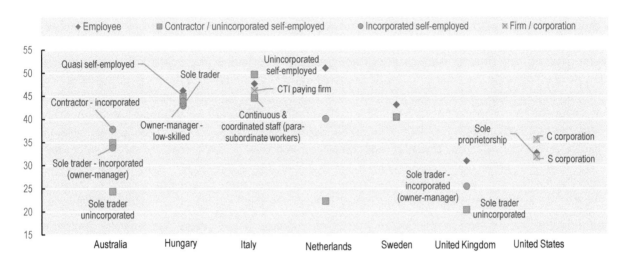

Note: Relevant categories vary by country and country-specific employment forms are noted directly in the figure. The total payment wedge is the sum of income taxes, social contributions and other compulsory payments as a percentage of total labour costs.
Source: Adapted from Milanez and Bratta (2019[68]).

StatLink http://dx.doi.org/10.1787/888933967376

### Balancing financing burdens across employers

A suitable balance of financing burdens between different groups of employers, including in sectors affected by automation-induced job displacement, may require new and innovative models of contribution financing. The financing of out-of-work support with conventional systems of employer contributions frequently does not link the employer costs to their layoff decisions and to the social costs that these layoffs entail. Without such a link, sectors or firms with more stable employment implicitly subsidise those where such layoffs are more frequent. Analogously to risk pooling between workers, this type of redistribution between firms can be desirable as an insurance against unexpected (e.g. cyclical) shocks. But it can lead to optimising behaviour when differences in layoff patterns are systematic or "structural", e.g. if some firms reduce their labour costs by repeatedly hiring and laying off the same workers who can supplement their take-home pay with unemployment-insurance entitlements. In the context of automation, the absence of a link between financing and layoff behaviour creates distortions in favour of accelerated, and possibly excessive, substitution of workers by artificial intelligence or robots in some firms or sectors. Charging unemployment-insurance contributions as a function of layoffs ("experience rating" of unemployment insurance) could counter such distortions, place a greater share of the social cost of displacement at its source and contribute to a level playing field for labour-reliant and automation-intensive production technologies.

The United States is currently the only OECD country that applies experience rating of employer contributions in the context of unemployment insurance (OECD, 2018[32]), although experience rating is somewhat more common in other branches of SP, in particular invalidity pensions and work accidents (OECD, 2010[69]).[31] For unemployment insurance, there is some evidence suggesting that experience rating reduces overall contribution burdens and increases employment.[32] The specifics need to be designed with care, however, e.g. to avoid "cream skimming" (for instance, hiring only workers with low layoff risks to safeguard against rising insurance costs).

## 7.4. Concluding remarks

This chapter has assessed the challenges for social protection (SP) in a future world of work and discussed reform avenues to tackle them. It has presented new estimates of gaps in existing SP provisions, including in employment forms that may become more prevalent as technological and workplace innovations broaden opportunities for alternative work arrangements or increase pressures on workers to accept them. Effective social risk sharing requires broad access to SP provisions and continued buy-in by workers. Unequal SP coverage or financing burdens could inhibit or undermine such a consensus, making protection inaccessible or too costly for those who need it most. Results suggest that reinforcing SP to tackle evolving labour-market risks is feasible in the context of different SP strategies, such as insurance or income-targeted assistance. But it requires determined efforts to adapt benefit provisions and employment support, and to secure an adequate resource base – sometimes by significantly upscaling it – for prevention, protection and promotion measures. One key challenge is to ensure a level playing field by tackling distortionary financial incentives to opt out of SP coverage, circumvent mandatory membership, or "game" the system by timing work or incomes to maximise entitlements or minimise contributions.

Preparing SP for the labour markets of the future requires a pro-active but iterative approach that addresses existing, and sometimes long-standing SP gaps, while adapting policy approaches as labour markets continue to evolve. This chapter presented "snapshots" of gaps in support that is available to broad groups of standard and non-standard workers, using individual-level data for the recent past. Future work should inform the policy reform debate by providing regular updates and by monitoring whether labour-market transformations lead to new gaps in SP provision. For instance, data permitting, such analysis should examine the accessibility and generosity of SP for specific circumstances of non-standard workers, such as employment through online platforms, as well as other forms of independent or dependent work that may emerge in the future.

---

### Box 7.4. Policy directions

Governments should conduct a thorough review of their social protection (SP) systems to examine whether they provide reliable coverage against evolving labour-market and social risks. Most countries mix different SP design principles, such as means-testing or social insurance, and these provisions shape the ways in which rising non-standard work translates into specific SP access barriers. SP provisions themselves can drive trends towards non-standard employment. Where needed, SP provisions should be reinforced to ensure effective income and employment support for workers who are ill-equipped to benefit quickly from the opportunities of technological advances and dynamic labour markets.

Preparing SP for future labour markets requires a pro-active but iterative approach that addresses existing challenges while monitoring and adapting policy approaches as labour markets continue to evolve. Some challenges represent long-standing issues, but they can become more pressing as new technologies provide opportunities for alternative work arrangements. The correct classification of workers' employment status is a pre-requisite for ensuring that they receive protection and support that is appropriate for their circumstances and risks (see Chapter 4).

However, even with well-defined legal categories and suitable enforcement in place, SP provisions can lead to significant support gaps for standard and, in particular, for non-standard workers. In order to ease access barriers to SP policy makers should consider:

- Reviewing SP entitlement criteria, such as employment requirements, waiting periods and rules for combining or alternating benefit receipt with intermittent and other non-standard forms of work;

---

- Enabling workers in independent forms of employment to build up rights to out-of-work support that is already available to standard employees;

- Making SP provisions less rigid by ensuring that built-up entitlements are portable across jobs and forms of employment;

- Maintaining or strengthening risk sharing across all labour market and income groups by tackling financial incentives that reduce the non-wage labour costs associated with non-standard work, such as reduced tax/contribution burdens or voluntary membership;

- Making means tests more responsive to people's needs by shortening the reference periods for needs assessments and by putting appropriate weight on recent or current incomes of all family members;

- Subject to budgetary space, strengthening universal and unconditional forms of support, such as universal child benefits, as complements to existing targeted or insurance-based support measures.

Automation will lead to job displacement for many workers, while novel forms of employment are blurring the distinction between in-work and out-of-work categories. This raises new questions about the scope and ambition of activation and employment-oriented SP. Policy options and priorities include:

- Tackling gaps in income support, which typically serves as the main gateway to labour market reintegration measures. This may require extending support for "part-time unemployed" and other jobseekers with intermittent, low-paid or independent employment;

- Re-assessing the scope of claimants' responsibilities, such as active job search, as a counter-weight to extending benefit rights. Such a review should ensure that the balance between supporting and demanding provisions remains in line with policy objectives regarding job quantity and quality. For instance, governments should consider if and when employment services should actively connect people to potentially precarious forms of work;

- Ensuring that the content of active labour market programmes is well adapted to the needs and circumstances of an evolving client base. A growing share of part-time unemployed may call for shifting resources from work experience programmes or direct job creation towards tailored training and career counselling (see also Chapter 6).

Adapting SP to the future of work will create additional financing pressures at a time when SP budgets are already under pressure in many countries:

- Keeping funding levels in line with evolving needs for support requires a determined and coordinated approach, including cost-effective SP delivery, better revenue-collection technologies and enforcement and a suitable balance of revenues from labour and non-labour tax bases;

- Ensuring that SP systems remain fiscally sustainable also calls for tackling unintended incentives that distort employment or hiring decisions or encourage "gaming" of support systems by workers or employers;

- The rationale for voluntary SP membership should be reassessed in light of labour-market developments. If new and emerging work patterns widen the scope for opting out of SP provisions, such opportunities could compromise the risk-sharing function of SP and erode its resource base;

- Governments should also assess whether existing SP financing mechanisms achieve a fair balance of burdens between different employers, e.g. between those making little use of automation and those substituting large shares of their workforce with robots or artificial intelligence.

## References

Acemoglu, D. and P. Restrepo (2018), "The Race between Man and Machine: Implications of Technology for Growth, Factor Shares, and Employment", *American Economic Review*, Vol. 108/6, pp. 1488-1542, http://dx.doi.org/10.1257/aer.20160696. [80]

Acemoglu, D. and P. Restrepo (2017), *Robots and Jobs: Evidence from Us Labor Markets*, https://papers.ssrn.com/sol3/papers.cfm?abstract_id=2941263 (accessed on 19 November 2018). [81]

Agrawal, A., J. Gans and A. Goldfarb (eds.) (2018), *R&D Structural Transformation, and the Distribution of Income*, University of Chicago Press. [65]

Akerlof, G. (1970), "The Market for "Lemons": Quality Uncertainty and the Market Mechanism", *The Quarterly Journal of Economics*, Vol. 84/3, p. 488, http://dx.doi.org/10.2307/1879431. [14]

Albert, F., K. Gáspár and R. Gal (2017), "ESPN Thematic Report on Access to social protection of people working as self-employed or on non-standard contracts: Hungary", in ESPN (ed.), *ESPN Thematic Report on Access to social protection of people working as self-employed or on non-standard contracts*, European Commission. [34]

Allen, R. (2009), "Engels' pause: Technical change, capital accumulation, and inequality in the british industrial revolution", *Explorations in Economic History*, Vol. 46/4, pp. 418-435, http://dx.doi.org/10.1016/J.EEH.2009.04.004. [79]

Anderson, P. and B. Meyer (2000), "The effects of the unemployment insurance payroll tax on wages, employment, claims and denials", *Journal of Public Economics*, Vol. 78/1-2, pp. 81-106. [78]

Arriba, R. and Moreno-Fuentes (2017), "ESPN Thematic Report on Access to social protection of people working as self-employed or on non-standard contracts Spain", in ESPN (ed.), *Access to social protection of people working as self-employed or on non-standard contracts*, European Commission. [21]

Atkinson, A. (1996), "The Case for a Participation Income", *The Political Quarterly*, Vol. 67/1, pp. 67-70, http://dx.doi.org/10.1111/j.1467-923X.1996.tb01568.x. [77]

Autor, D. (2015), "Why Are There Still So Many Jobs? The History and Future of Workplace Automation", *Journal of Economic Perspectives*, Vol. 29/3, http://dx.doi.org/10.1257/jep.29.3.3. [76]

Bargain, O., H. Immervoll and H. Viitamäki (2012), "No claim, no pain. Measuring the non-take-up of social assistance using register data", *Journal of Economic Inequality*, Vol. 10/3, http://dx.doi.org/10.1007/s10888-010-9158-8. [46]

Barr, N. (1989), "Social Insurance as an Efficiency Device", *Journal of Public Policy*, Vol. 9/01, p. 59, http://dx.doi.org/10.1017/S0143814X00007972. [11]

Boeri, T. and J. van Ours (2013), *The Economics of Imperfect Labor Markets*, Princeton University Press, Princeton, New Jersey. [12]

Bonoli, G. (2017), "ESPN Thematic Report on Access to social protection of people working as self-employed or on non-standard contracts Switzerland", in ESPN (ed.), *Access to social protection of people working as self-employed or on non-standard contracts*, European Commission. [83]

Browne, J., A. Hood and R. Joyce (2016), "The (changing) effects of universal credit", in Emmerson, C., P. Johnson and R. Joyce (eds.), *IFS Green Budget*, Institute for Fiscal Studies, London, https://www.ifs.org.uk/uploads/gb/gb2016/gb2016ch10.pdf (accessed on 8 January 2019). [58]

Browne, J. and H. Immervoll (2017), "Mechanics of replacing benefit systems with a basic income: comparative results from a microsimulation approach", *Journal of Economic Inequality*, http://dx.doi.org/10.1007/s10888-017-9366-6. [44]

Browne, J. et al. (2018), "Faces of Joblessness in Ireland: Anatomy of Employment Barriers", *OECD Social, Employment and Migration Working Papers*, No. 209, OECD Publishing, Paris, https://doi.org/10.1787/40958439-en. [91]

Brynjolfsson, E. and A. McAfee (2014), *The second machine age : work, progress, and prosperity in a time of brilliant technologies*, WW Norton & Company. [82]

Bulman, T. et al. (2019), "Tax-benefit reforms to support inclusiveness, productivity and growth in Italy", No. forthcoming. [45]

Cahuc, P. (2018), "France: Social protection for the self-employed", in *The Future of Social Protection: What Works for Non-standard Workers?*, OECD Publishing, Paris, https://dx.doi.org/10.1787/9789264306943-7-en. [41]

Cahuc, P. (2018), "Wage Insurance, Part-Time Unemployment Insurance and Short-Time Work in the XXI Century", *IZA Discussion Papers*, No. 12045, IZA, http://www.iza.org (accessed on 18 January 2019). [74]

Cahuc, P. and F. Malherbet (2004), "Unemployment compensation finance and labor market rigidity", *Journal of Public Economics*, Vol. 88/3-4, pp. 481-501. [75]

Castell, L. et al. (2019), *Take-up of Social Benefits: Evidence from a Nationwide Experiment in France*, Paris School of Economics, Paris. [73]

Chetty, R. and A. Finkelstein (2013), "Social Insurance: Connecting Theory to Data", in *Handbook of Public Economics*, Elsevier, http://dx.doi.org/10.1016/B978-0-444-53759-1.00003-0. [9]

Chetty, R. et al. (2014), "Active vs. Passive Decisions and Crowd-Out in Retirement Savings Accounts: Evidence from Denmark *", *The Quarterly Journal of Economics*, Vol. 129/3, pp. 1141-1219, http://dx.doi.org/10.1093/qje/qju013. [40]

Citizens advice (2018), *Universal Credit and Modern Employment: non-traditional work.* [52]

Codagnone, C. et al. (2018), *Behavioural Study on the Effects of an Extension of Access to Social Protection for People in All Forms of Employment*, European Commission, http://dx.doi.org/10.2767/180611. [72]

Cragg, J. (1971), "Some Statistical Models for Limited Dependent Variables with Application to the Demand for Durable Goods", *Econometrica*, Vol. 39/5, p. 829, http://dx.doi.org/10.2307/1909582. [38]

de Graaf-Zijl, M., B. Scheer and J. Bolhaar (2018), "Netherlands: non-standard work and social protection", in *The Future of Social Protection: What Works for Non-standard Workers?*, OECD Publishing, Paris, https://dx.doi.org/10.1787/9789264306943-10-en. [50]

De Wispelaere, F. and J. Pacolet (2017), "ESPN Thematic Report on Access to social protection of people working as self-employed or on non-standard contracts: Belgium", in ESPN (ed.), *ESPN Thematic Report on Access to social protection of people working as self-employed or on non-standard contracts*, European Comission. [35]

Düll, N. et al. (2018), "Faces of Joblessness in Portugal: Anatomy of Employment Barriers", *OECD Social, Employment and Migration Working Papers*, No. 210, OECD Publishing, Paris, https://doi.org/10.1787/b0fa55e7-en. [90]

Employment and Social Development Canada (2016), *Evaluation of the Employment Insurance Special Benefits for Self-employed Workers*, http://canada.ca/publicentre-ESDC. [18]

European Commission (2018), *Access and sustainability of social protection in a changing world of work*, Publications Office of the European Union, http://dx.doi.org/10.2767/875456. [7]

European Commission (2017), *Commission Recommendation on the European Pillar of Social Rights*, https://ec.europa.eu/commission/publications/commission-recommendation-establishing-european-pillar-social-rights_en. [5]

Falco, P., A. Green and D. MacDonald (forthcoming), "Are jobs becoming less stable?", *OECD Social, Employment and Migration Working Papers*, OECD Publishing, Paris, http://dx.doi.org/10.1787/1815199X. [55]

Fernández, R. et al. (2018), "Faces of Joblessness in Spain: Anatomy of Employment Barriers", *OECD Social, Employment and Migration Working Papers*, No. 207, OECD Publishing, Paris, https://doi.org/10.1787/6149118d-en. [89]

Fernández, R., H. Immervoll and D. Pacifico (forthcoming), "Beyond repair? Anatomy of income support for standard and non-standard workers in OECD countries", *OECD Social, Employment and Migration Working Papers*, OECD Publishing, Paris, https://doi.org/10.1787/1815199X. [33]

Fink, M. and W. Nagl (2018), "Austria: How social protection rules affect self-employed and independent contractors", in *The Future of Social Protection: What Works for Non-standard Workers?*, OECD Publishing, Paris, https://dx.doi.org/10.1787/9789264306943-6-en. [20]

Ford, M. (2015), *Rise of the Robots: Technology and the Threat of a Jobless Future*, Basic Books, New York. [86]

Graetz, G. and G. Michaels (2015), *Robots at Work*, https://papers.ssrn.com/sol3/papers.cfm?abstract_id=2575781 (accessed on 19 November 2018). [71]

Gruber, J. (1997), "The Consumption Smoothing Benefits of Unemployment Insurance", *American Economic Review*, Vol. 87/1, pp. 192-205, https://www.jstor.org/stable/2950862. [10]

Hershfield, H., S. Shu and S. Benartzi (2018), "Temporal Reframing and Savings: A Field Experiment", *SSRN Electronic Journal*, http://dx.doi.org/10.2139/ssrn.3097468.  [48]

Hills, J. (2017), *Good Times, Bad Times (revised Edition): The Welfare Myth of Them and Us*, Policy Press.  [16]

Hofer, H., R. Hyee and G. Titelbach (forthcoming), "Where did all the independent contractors go?", *IHS Working Paper Series*, IHS, Vienna.  [92]

ILO (2018), *Innovative approaches for ensuring universal social protection for the future of work*, https://www.ilo.org/wcmsp5/groups/public/---dgreports/---cabinet/documents/publication/wcms_618176.pdf.  [8]

ILO and World Bank (2016), *A shared mission for universal social protection. Concept note*, https://www.ilo.org/wcmsp5/groups/public/---dgreports/---dcomm/documents/genericdocument/wcms_378996.pdf.  [3]

Immervoll, H. et al. (2009), "An Evaluation of the Tax-Transfer Treatment of Married Couples in European Countries", *OECD Social, Employment and Migration Working Papers*, No. 76, OECD Publishing, Paris, https://dx.doi.org/10.1787/227200406151.  [64]

Immervoll, H. and C. Knotz (2018), "How demanding are activation requirements for jobseekers", *OECD Social, Employment and Migration Working Papers*, No. 215, OECD Publishing, Paris, https://dx.doi.org/10.1787/2bdfecca-en.  [62]

ISSA (2012), *Handbook on the extention of social security coverage to the self-employed*.  [17]

Jessoula, M., E. Pavolini and F. Strati (2017), "ESPN Thematic Report on Access to social protection of people working as self-employed or on non-standard contracts - Italy", in ESPN (ed.), *Access to social protection for people working on non-standard contracts and as self-employed in Europe*, European Commission.  [25]

Kettemann, A., F. Kramarz and J. Zweimüller (2016), "Beyond Severance Pay: Labor market responses to the introduction of occupational pensions in Austria", *Mimeo, University of Zurich*, http://www.econ.uzh.ch.  [39]

Kolsrud, J. (2018), "Sweden: Voluntary unemployment insurance", in *The Future of Social Protection: What Works for Non-standard Workers?*, OECD Publishing, Paris, https://dx.doi.org/10.1787/9789264306943-11-en.  [19]

Levy, S. (2008), *Good intentions, bad outcomes : social policy, informality, and economic growth in Mexico*, Brookings Institution Press.  [42]

Lindert, P. (2004), *Growing Public*, Cambridge University Press, Cambridge, http://dx.doi.org/10.1017/CBO9780511510717.  [47]

Low Incomes Tax Reform Group (2017), *Self-employed claimants of universal credit-lifting the burdens*, Chartered Institute of Taxation, London, https://www.litrg.org.uk/sites/default/files/Self%20Employment%20report%20FINAL%20for%20release.pdf (accessed on 8 January 2019).  [53]

Masso, M. and I. Kadarik (2017), "ESPN Thematic Report on Access to social protection of people working as self-employed or on non-standard contracts: Estonia", in ESPN (ed.), *ESPN Thematic Report on Access to social protection of people working as self-employed or on non-standard contracts*, European Commission.   [84]

McKay, C., E. Pollack and A. Fitzpayne (2018), *Modernizing unemployment insurance for the changing nature of work*, The Aspen Institute.   [61]

Milanez, A. and B. Bratta (2019), "Taxation and the future of work: How tax systems influence choice of employment form", *OECD Taxation Working Papers*, No. 41, OECD Publishing, Paris, https://dx.doi.org/10.1787/20f7164a-en.   [68]

Ministry of Social Development, N. (2018), *Establishing the welfare expert advisory group*.   [54]

MISSOC (2018), *Mutual Information System on Social Protection*, https://www.missoc.org/missoc-database/self-employed/.   [27]

National Audit Office (2018), *Rolling out Universal Credit*, https://www.nao.org.uk/wp-content/uploads/2018/06/Rolling-out-Universal-Credit.pdf (accessed on 25 January 2019).   [49]

OECD (2018), "Back to work: Lessons from nine country case studies of policies to assist displaced workers", in *OECD Employment Outlook 2018*, OECD Publishing, Paris, https://dx.doi.org/10.1787/empl_outlook-2018-8-en.   [56]

OECD (2018), *Good Jobs for All in a Changing World of Work: The OECD Jobs Strategy*, OECD Publishing, Paris, https://dx.doi.org/10.1787/9789264308817-en.   [2]

OECD (2018), *OECD Economic Surveys: Netherlands 2018*, OECD Publishing, Paris, https://dx.doi.org/10.1787/eco_surveys-nld-2018-en.   [67]

OECD (2018), *OECD Employment Outlook 2018*, OECD Publishing, Paris, https://dx.doi.org/10.1787/empl_outlook-2018-en.   [32]

OECD (2018), *OECD Reviews of Pension Systems: Latvia*, OECD Reviews of Pension Systems, OECD Publishing, Paris, https://dx.doi.org/10.1787/9789264289390-en.   [31]

OECD (2018), *Opportunities for All: A Framework for Policy Action on Inclusive Growth*, OECD Publishing, Paris, https://dx.doi.org/10.1787/9789264301665-en.   [1]

OECD (2018), *Profiling tools for early identification of jobseekers who need extra support*, OECD, Paris, http://www.oecd.org/employment/connecting-people-with-good-jobs.htm (accessed on 11 January 2019).   [60]

OECD (2018), *Tax Challenges Arising from Digitalisation – Interim Report 2018: Inclusive Framework on BEPS*, OECD/G20 Base Erosion and Profit Shifting Project, OECD Publishing, Paris, http://dx.doi.org/10.1787/9789264293083-en.   [66]

OECD (2018), *The Future of Social Protection: What Works for Non-standard Workers?*, OECD Publishing, Paris, https://dx.doi.org/10.1787/9789264306943-en.   [51]

OECD (2017), "Basic Income as a policy option: Can it add up?", *Policy Brief on the Future of Work*, http://www.oecd.org/employment/future-of-work.htm (accessed on 27 November 2017).   [43]

OECD (2017), *Pensions at a Glance 2017: OECD and G20 Indicators.*, OECD Publishing, Paris, http://doi:http://dx.doi.org/10.1787/pension_glance-2017-en.   [26]

OECD (2017), *Preventing Ageing Unequally*, OECD Publishing, Paris, http://dx.doi.org/10.1787/9789264279087-en. [15]

OECD (2014), *Connecting People with Jobs : Activation Policies in the United Kingdom.*, OECD Publishing, https://doi.org/10.1787/9789264217188-en. [85]

OECD (2010), *Sickness, Disability and Work: Breaking the Barriers: A Synthesis of Findings across OECD Countries*, OECD Publishing, Paris, https://dx.doi.org/10.1787/9789264088856-en. [69]

Office for Budget Responsibility (2018), *Welfare trends report*, https://obr.uk/docs/dlm_uploads/WelfareTrends2018cm9562.pdf (accessed on 8 January 2019). [59]

Pacifico, D. et al. (2018), "Faces of Joblessness in Italy: A People-centred perspective on employment barriers and policies", *OECD Social, Employment and Migration Working Papers*, No. 208, OECD Publishing, Paris, https://dx.doi.org/10.1787/e5d510c2-en. [87]

Pacifico, D. et al. (2018), "Faces of Joblessness in Lithuania: A People-centred perspective on employment barriers and policies", *OECD Social, Employment and Migration Working Papers*, No. 205, OECD Publishing, Paris, https://dx.doi.org/10.1787/3657b81e-en. [88]

Pacolet, J. and L. Op De Beeck (2017), "ESPN Thematic Report on Access to social protection of people working as self-employed or on non-standard contracts: Luxembourg", in ESPN (ed.), *ESPN Thematic Report on Access to social protection of people working as self-employed or on non-standard contracts*, European Comission. [36]

Raitano, M. (2018), "Italy: Para-subordinate workers and their social protection", in *The Future of Social Protection: What Works for Non-standard Workers?*, OECD Publishing, Paris, https://dx.doi.org/10.1787/9789264306943-9-en. [24]

Rajevska, F. (2017), "ESPN Thematic Report on Access to social protection of people working as self-employed or on non-standard contracts Latvia", in ESPN (ed.), *Access to social protection of people working as self-employed or on non-standard contracts*, European Commission. [22]

Rothschild, M. and J. Stiglitz (1976), "Equilibrium in Competitive Insurance Markets: An Essay on the Economics of Imperfect Information", *The Quarterly Journal of Economics*, http://dx.doi.org/10.2307/1885326. [13]

Saez, E. (2010), "Do taxpayers bunch at kink points?", *American Economic Journal: Economic Policy*, http://dx.doi.org/10.1257/pol.2.3.180. [63]

Social Security Administration (2018), *Social Security Programs Throughout the World*, https://www.ssa.gov/policy/docs/progdesc/ssptw/. [28]

Spasova, S. et al. (2017), *Access to social protection for people working on non-standard contracts and as self-employed in Europe*, European Commission, Brussels, http://dx.doi.org/10.2767/700791. [30]

SSA and ISSA (2017), "United States of America", in *Social Security Programs Throughout the World: The Americas*, Social Security Administration, https://www.ssa.gov/policy (accessed on 2 December 2018). [23]

Stettner, Cassidy and Wentworth (2016), *A new safety net for an era of unstable earnings*, The Century Foundation, https://tcf.org/content/report/new-safety-net-for-an-era-of-unstable-earnings/. [57]

Tamayo, H. and A. Tumino (2018), "Income protection of atypical workers in the event of unemployment in Europe", *EUROMOD Working Papers*, No. EM18/18, ISER, University of Essex, https://www.euromod.ac.uk/publications/income-protection-atypical-workers-event-unemployment-europe. [70]

United Nations (2015), *Transforming Our World: The 2020 Agenda for Sustainable Development*, https://sustainabledevelopment.un.org/content/documents/21252030%20Agenda%20for%20Sustainable%20Development%20web.pdf (accessed on 4 December 2018). [4]

Whiteford, P. and A. Heron (2018), "Australia: Providing social protection to non-standard workers with tax financing", in *The Future of Social Protection: What Works for Non-standard Workers?*, OECD Publishing, Paris, https://dx.doi.org/10.1787/9789264306943-5-en. [29]

Wooldridge, J. (2010), *Econometric analysis of cross section and panel data*, MIT Press, https://mitpress.mit.edu/books/econometric-analysis-cross-section-and-panel-data. [37]

World Bank (2018), *World Development Report 2019: The Changing Nature of Work*, The World Bank, http://dx.doi.org/10.1596/978-1-4648-1328-3. [6]

**Notes**

[1] See Chapter 2 as well as Graetz and Michaels (2015[71]), Acemoglu and Restrepo (2017[81]; 2018[80]), Brynjolfsson and McAfee (2014[82]), Autor (2015[76]), Ford (2015[86]) and Allen (2009[79]).

[2] Such ex-post redistribution in "actuarially fair" insurance systems is due to a number of reasons. First, risks may not be accurately known or knowable (e.g. if there is no functioning market for insuring certain types of risk, such as unemployment). Second, even if risks were known, they are an ex-ante concept. Those with unemployment spells that are longer or more frequent than suggested by their risk factors will get a better deal out of unemployment insurance, longer-lived individuals will see larger benefits from pensions, etc. Indeed, this type of redistribution from "lucky" people, towards those who are "unlucky" relative to their risk factors is the very point of risk pooling and distinguishes actuarially fair insurance from "pure" savings instruments.

[3] Chapters 4 and 5, as well as OECD (2018[51]).

[4] In addition, earnings levels may fall more readily for self-employed in response to market developments, e.g. because there are no minimum wages and downward wage rigidity does not apply to them. If entitled to unemployment benefits, those with poor earnings prospects may therefore have relatively strong financial incentives to become and remain unemployed.

[5] For instance, claimants of unemployment benefits in Sweden are required to wind down or "freeze" their business and cannot claim benefits again for several years if they once again take up their previous self-employment activity after a benefit spell.

[6] A recent survey of non-standard workers in Europe documented low willingness to pay for social protection (Codagnone et al., 2018[72]).

[7] There is no federal maternity pay scheme in the USA.

[8] Australia further provides tax concessions for small business owners who convert assets into retirement savings.

[9] For instance, Spain took legislative measures to reduce the gaps in out-of-work support and contributions burdens between the self-employed and dependent employees (Royal Decree-Law 28/2018, of 28 December). France has also taken legislative measures to provide access to unemployment benefits for the self-employed (see endnote 12). Italy significantly expanded minimum-income provisions in 2018 and 2019 (see Section 7.3.2) and introduced a number of changes to the unemployment benefit system in 2015 (Pacifico et al., 2018[87]): Minimum contribution requirements are now shorter and maximum benefit durations have been extended. Certain categories of workers who were previously excluded from the unemployment insurance are now covered (e.g. seasonal workers) and some groups of long-term unemployed can rely on a means-tested unemployment assistance programme.

[10] Detailed statutory information on benefit rates and durations is available from the OECD tax-benefit policy database through www.oecd.org/social/benefits-and-wages/.

[11] Although non-takeup remains significant for means-tested benefits in France (Castell et al., 2019[73]), recipient numbers are comparatively high for these assistance benefits. See OECD SOCR database at www.oecd.org/social/recipients.htm.

[12] In summer 2018, the French parliament passed a law that provides for flat-rate unemployment benefits for jobseekers who become unemployed after a period of self-employment with earnings of at least 10 000 euro per year and subject to liquidation of the former business. The benefit, with a duration of 6 months, was scheduled to come into force in January 2019 but implementation has been delayed.

[13] Fernández et al. (forthcoming[33]) extends this approach to other countries.

[14] An alternative approach would be by means of deterministic tax-benefit microsimulation that uses sophisticated computer representations of theoretical entitlements in order to estimate benefit amounts at the individual level, see Tamayo and Tumino (2018[70]) and Browne and Immervoll (2017[44]) for recent multi-country applications. These models typically use cross-sectional data and cannot account for dynamic aspects, such as past work history and employment patterns, that are especially relevant for assessing entitlement gaps between standard and non-standard workers. They also focus on theoretical entitlements and cannot take full account of factors such as stigma, benefit sanctions or voluntary SP opt-ins or opt-outs. Together, these factors can account for differences between theoretical and actual benefit receipt.

[15] The panel component of The European Union Statistics on Income and Living Conditions (EU-SILC) covers four years. But since it is a rotating panel, limiting the time-window of interest to only three years results in bigger samples.

[16] E.g. by tying eligibility to socially useful activities, as in Atkinson's (1996[77]) Participation Income.

[17] For instance, Australia provides for income and asset-tested benefits, as well as SP entitlements, such as sick pay and carer's leave, that are part of the remuneration package of dependent employees (Section 7.2.1). Casual workers, who are employed on an 'as needed basis' are typically entitled to a higher hourly pay rate than equivalent full-time or part-time employees. This usually incorporates a 25 per cent loading instead of entitlements to paid personal/carer's leave, annual leave, notice of termination and redundancy pay under the National Employment Standards. The lack of workplace entitlements contributes to their more frequent receipt of general revenue-financed benefits (Whiteford and Heron, 2018[29]).

[18] Different contribution bases are possible for the self-employed. Where profits are used as the contribution base, self-employed workers can seek to minimise contributions by inflating their costs. Basing contributions on revenues or turnover, by contrast, is technically more straightforward (e.g. for platform-based workers if platforms are obliged to reveal the relevant information). But it may result in excessive contributions for workers performing higher-cost activities. For instance, in France, *micro-entrepreneurs* pay social contributions based on their gross revenue. While contribution rates are lower for those workers in retail or hospitality industries than for workers with more limited costs such as the liberal professions (Cahuc, 2018[41]), they might be excessive if profit margins are low. More generally, self-employed workers draw income from both capital and labour. For those with significant capital income, this could substitute to some extent for social benefits and could reduce the need for publicly provided income smoothing. The distinction between capital and labour income is less meaningful for many self-employed whose capital investments are very limited, e.g. those performing specific tasks on internet platforms.

[19] There have been concerns that the structure of performance-related payments to private providers may incentivise them to encourage or "push" clients towards self-employment (OECD, 2014[85]).

[20] The job security councils operated by social partners in Sweden, demonstrate that early intervention measures can be offered to all displaced workers, including those affected by individual or small-scale layoffs, when employers and unions are constructively engaged.

[21] Their barriers to higher-intensity employment are frequently similar to the employment obstacles faced by the jobless. See *Faces of Joblessness* country studies, available at www.oecd.org/els/soc/faces-of-joblessness.htm.

[22] See Cahuc (2018[74]).

[23] See OECD tax-benefit policy database, www.oecd.org/social/benefits-and-wages.htm.

[24] Recent initiatives in this direction include the Korean WorkNet PES portal, the Digital First strategy in Flanders, Belgium, and the automatic collection and processing of earnings-related information in the context of the United Kingdom's Universal Credit.

[25] Fernández et al. (2018[89]), Browne et al. (2018[91]), Pacifico et al. (2018[87]), Pacifico et al. (Pacifico et al., 2018[88]), Düll et al (2018[90]), Fernández et al. (2018[89]).

[26] The in-work tax credits (Working Credit and Working Family Tax Credit) that existed in the United Kingdom prior to Universal Credit are a primary example of such a policy configuration.

[27] Increasing per-capita spending on pensions is in line with growing employment rates, especially among women, and the resulting growth in the number of people with significant pension entitlements. The average spending figures quoted in the text are for the following 18 countries: Austria, Australia, Chile, Denmark, Finland, France, Germany, Ireland, Italy, Japan, the Netherlands, New Zealand, Norway, Portugal, Spain, Sweden, United Kingdom and United States.

[28] Total employment costs ($T$), gross earnings ($E$) and payment wedge ($PW$) are related as follows: $T = E (1 + PW / (1-PW))$. Payment wedges of 51% and 22% translate into total employment costs of 204% and 128% of gross earnings, respectively.

[29] The contributions gap is due to unemployment and disability insurance, as well as second-pillar pension contributions to which self-employed workers are not entitled (see Section 7.2.1).

[30] The fall in the number of independent contractors was mainly due to a declining inflow, rather than by the dissolution of existing independent contracts. However, the likelihood of being in standard employment within one month of transitioning out of an independent contract increased from 11% before the reform's announcement in 2006 to 13% after the reform's implementation. In addition, the share of workers who transitioned out of the labour force upon exiting an independent contract dropped significantly, in line with the fact that prior to the reform, independent contractors were not covered by unemployment insurance (Hofer, Hyee and Titelbach, forthcoming[92]).

[31] The US system is incomplete in the sense that employers are not charged the full cost of a layoff (Anderson and Meyer, 2000[78]).

[32] For the United States, evaluation results in Anderson and Mayer (2000[78]) point to falling unemployment benefit claims and to positive overall employment effects. See also Cahuc and Malherbet (2004[75]).

# ORGANISATION FOR ECONOMIC CO-OPERATION AND DEVELOPMENT

The OECD is a unique forum where governments work together to address the economic, social and environmental challenges of globalisation. The OECD is also at the forefront of efforts to understand and to help governments respond to new developments and concerns, such as corporate governance, the information economy and the challenges of an ageing population. The Organisation provides a setting where governments can compare policy experiences, seek answers to common problems, identify good practice and work to co-ordinate domestic and international policies.

The OECD member countries are: Australia, Austria, Belgium, Canada, Chile, the Czech Republic, Denmark, Estonia, Finland, France, Germany, Greece, Hungary, Iceland, Ireland, Israel, Italy, Japan, Korea, Latvia, Lithuania, Luxembourg, Mexico, the Netherlands, New Zealand, Norway, Poland, Portugal, the Slovak Republic, Slovenia, Spain, Sweden, Switzerland, Turkey, the United Kingdom and the United States. The European Union takes part in the work of the OECD.

OECD Publishing disseminates widely the results of the Organisation's statistics gathering and research on economic, social and environmental issues, as well as the conventions, guidelines and standards agreed by its members.

OECD PUBLISHING, 2, rue André-Pascal, 75775 PARIS CEDEX 16
ISBN 978-92-64-72715-1 – 2019

9 789264 72715